The electronic publishing business and its market

Pira publishing guide series

The electronic publishing business and its market

Edited by Brian and Margot Blunden

IEPRC/Pira International

© Copyright IEPRC/Pira International 1994

ISBN 1 85802 082 4

Published by
IEPRC/Pira International
Randalls Road
Leatherhead
Surrey
KT22 7RU
UK

Tel: (+44) 0372 376161
Fax: (+44) 0372 377526

This book is in part based upon *Strategic Study on New Opportunities for Publishers in the Information Services Market* © ECSC-EC-EAEC, Brussels–Luxembourg, 1993.

Typeset in the UK by Manton Typesetters,
5–7 Eastfield Road, Louth, Lincolnshire.
Printed in the UK by The Eastern Press Limited,
14 Portman Road, Reading, Berkshire.

Contents

v

Future scenarios for opportunities in EP

Appendices

Preface

Thirteen years ago the International Electronic Publishing Research Centre (IEPRC) was founded in the UK in the House of Lords with sponsorship from the Board of Pira International. The idea was to create a focus for those in publishing and printing to exploit the opportunities likely to arise from electronic publishing (EP). At the time of foundation, IEPRC was greeted with differing reactions. There was a small international community of enlightened publishers who recognized that EP would emerge ultimately and provide business opportunity. Others in publishing regarded EP as a temporary aberration. The response in the printing sector was either one of disinterest or hostility. Thirteen years later the situation is very different.

Today many publishers recognize EP as an important area for strategic development. Probably the most significant lesson learned over the past decade is that of recognizing the length of time and scale of investment required to create market demand in EP. This publication seeks to bring together the accumulated views and experience of practicioners in the business of EP. Editing of contributors' views has been kept to a minimum and the views expressed are those of the named individuals. The editors have contributed the remaining material and sought to bring an element of continuity to the EP business message through the selection of topics. While every effort has been made to check the information and data provided, no responsibility can be taken by the editors or authors for subsequent action based upon the information contained in this publication.

The editors acknowledge gratefully the funding provided by the European Commission (EC) for the strategic study *New Opportunities for Publishers in the Information Services Market*. This study, proposed by IEPRC, was published by the EC in 1993. It was undertaken by Consulting Trust and led by Dr Thomas Laukamm. This book reproduces the majority of the material in that publication by permission of the EC which granted English language nonexclusive publishing rights of that report to Pira International. The editors therefore wish to acknowledge particularly the contribution made to this publication by the material developed in the work of Dr Laukamm.

The publication draws also on a number of other EC sponsored programmes, especially EuroPublishing, TelePublishing and the Training Technology and Telematics Round Table (T3RT) under Delta. The editors wish to acknowledge the material from these programmes and the findings provided by the authors of the many reports used as source material.

In particular the editors wish to thank all authors for their contributions and to express the hope that this publication will provide a useful collection of views and experiences which will aid the successful exploitation of the EP business by publishing and printing organizations. Finally, the editors thank the Chairman and Board of IEPRC for their support and help in this publishing venture.

Brian and Margot Blunden

1

Introduction and EP business overview

Brian Blunden, Pira International, UK

> Today you cannot be a world-class publisher unless you have developed the ability to provide information electronically. Even though only a fraction of documented knowledge has been captured digitally, that trait has become a part of publishers' genetic code, endowing them with enormous flexibility and opportunity; and it will shape succeeding generations of publishers, who will add to our body of knowledge and make information even more valuable to tomorrow's users, through enhanced speed, presentation and availability.

Those were the words of Joseph Dionne, Chief Executive Officer of McGraw-Hill Inc., USA when he gave the keynote address to the delegates of the IEPRC XIIIth Annual Conference in Washington DC on 20 April 1994.

It is this aspiration of the world's leading publishers which has been the driver in the production of this book.

THE EP SECTORS

Electronic publishing (EP) depends for success on market demand. This simple fact has been overlooked on numerous occasions by would-be players in the EP business over the past ten years. Creating market demand is a new experience for most publishers. Many in

---

Brian Blunden, Managing Director of Pira International and Chief Executive Officer of IEPRC, is one of the book's editors.

publishing will dispute this view. They will quote the example of new launches in the magazine or newspaper business and the success of best sellers in the world of fiction. Such a posture is to miss the point. The marketplace for paper-based products is well established. It took some five hundred years to mature. Putting a new brand of product into this well established marketplace and distribution system is what happens when a new magazine, newspaper or fiction volume is launched. The key to success in this process is well managed marketing which embraces promotion, design, production, pricing, distribution and sales. Publishers are expert in this process with paper-based products and as such, they are sophisticated players in the information marketplace. Within their experience publishers are highly competent in marketing and commercial affairs. However, EP presents a whole new set of problems which do not fit the print-on-paper rules which are the primary experience of professional publishers. Nevertheless, the publisher still brings the most useful market and commercial experience to the new information industry marketplace.

At the opposite end to conventional publishing in the information business marketplace there is a pervasive EP activity which is an embedded function of many commercial or industrial sectors, e.g. banking, finance, aerospace, automobiles, travel etc. In these sectors the EP issue is not market demand. The issue here is bottom-line enhancement by more efficient management of information as a functional aspect of a core business. The economics of EP in corporate publishing, as this activity is generically described, is quite different from that of conventional value-added publishing. There are ample case studies which demonstrate the EP embedded function in user sectors and such case studies are included in this publication. The importance of this corporate use of EP to its total development is as a driver of technology solutions. It may also provide new market opportunity to the publisher or printer through the provision of facilities management, though at present this is an unrealized opportunity. The business objectives of EP in corporate publishing are different from conventional publishing. For example, the aerospace manufacturer will gain a cost advantage from use of EP even after high development costs which are well above the consideration of the development department in any publishing house. Thus the corporate publisher is a driver to the development of the EP business as an investor in systems which will often be appropriate for transfer to conventional publishing. The business issue is, who will be motivated to manage the transfer process? This is where strategic thinking is required in the boardrooms of major publishers. Slowly it is beginning to occur. A recent example is the collaboration between Springer-Verlag and AT&T and others in the Red Sage project.

Between the application of EP by conventional publishers and corporate use of EP within a core business there is that sector of the information publishing industry which meets the market requirement for on-demand information that is either volume-dependent or time-dependent. This sector embraces financial information services and the bibliographic database community. The EP issue here has not been one of creating market demand, but instead the enhancement of the functionality of the information service which is the result of technology development — primarily computer hardware and software plus telecoms.

The market demand for business and financial information which is timely and accurate has existed ever since the Western world and Japan developed free-market economies. Thus in financial and banking services over the past 20 years there has been a coincidence of purpose between intrinsic need for timeliness and searchability, with a market demand which is global and players willing to pay a price premium for enhancement in speed and facilitation of information provision. The best examples of this form of EP are Reuters and Dow Jones. An interesting issue here is the relationship between these players and the global business press. The matter is discussed in the scenario chapter of this publication.

The bibliographic EP world has similarities to banking and financial information services, but is largely driven by cost reduction and functionality enhancement through machine searchability. In many product areas it is dependent on the continued budget provision to the academic and research communities for the purchasing of information. The prime driver in this EP market has been, and continues to be, recognition by companies that shared-cost information services are beneficial, and recognition by governments that public funding is needed to support industrial infrastructure. A feature of this EP sector is the lead role of not-for-profit organizations and their dependence on competent database host facilities. The issue of convergence in database hosting and common carrier networks is also discussed in the scenario chapter of this publication.

The foregoing remarks demonstrate that EP is a complex business. It cannot be treated as a cohesive entity. It is further complicated by the tendency of EP gurus and governments in public statements to believe that their perceptions of the EP business — which are often little more than prejudices — represent descriptions of the totality of this EP complex. For any company to command a strategic business posture towards the EP business, it must have an understanding of the EP role in book, periodical and newspaper publishing; in corporate, financial and bibliographic services; in the computer, consumer electronics, TV, cable and telecoms sectors. This understanding needs to be overlaid by a grasp of the issues which link these interests and regulate them in intellectual property rights and cross-media ownership.

The only way to enhance understanding of the EP business and its market is to disaggregate the components for purposes of analysis and then to explore the opportunity for synergy between these components in developing an overall strategy. It is meaningless to make statements about the size of the information industry and its global implications unless such statements are put into a context to which publishers can relate. It is in pursuit of this balance between detailed analysis, pursuit of cross-sectoral synergy and development of a strategic overview that the International Electronic Publishing Research Centre — IEPRC — has sought to make contribution over the past ten years.

EP AND EUROPEAN POLICY IN INFORMATION

Part of the IEPRC contribution has been to stimulate dialogue between the different interests in publishing — books, periodicals, newspapers, corporate, financial and bibliographic services, software and hardware providers — and those concerned with infrastructural development of the communications industry in Europe, namely the European Commission (EC). That dialogue has not been easy. The reasons are understandable. Viewed objectively, European political and business cooperation since 1945 has made spectacular progress, but such progress will continue to face political challenges which require time for mature judgment to develop among politicians. The continued self-interest of the nation-states of Europe will all too often give one-sided perspectives instead of emphasizing common interest in a world where global competition should be recognized as the dominant issue. The need for European vision has never been greater in relation to industrial and economic influence than it is in a shared view of the information industry.

There are issues related to the development of EP in European society at large which must involve national governments. In particular, these issues concern infrastructure and the relationship between information and manufacturing industry. National economies reflect in their success or failure the delicate balance between the vision of elected politicians and the competence of public servants to take that vision and translate it into workable mechanisms which stimulate enterprise, wealth creation and competitiveness. Moulding together in the EC an international public service in Europe is an achievement in itself. In the context of developing the information industry of Europe, and especially the EP business, it is a critical asset which in the past has had some minor downsides. The principal downside relates to a tendency in political circles to have a perception of the EP business somewhat removed from the commercial marketplace. This results in well intentioned support programmes which have not always met the needs of the real players. Because of the requirement for European public servants to have a trans-national and pan-sectoral vision, it is all too easy to treat the EP business — in policy making — as a coherent business entity, which it is not. In the past this tendency to talk in general terms of 'the information industry' has been counter-productive in developing dialogue with the publishing sectors.

However, it would be wrong to overemphasize these transitional characteristics of an evolving Europe as the only impediment to the development of the EP business. An impediment of equal significance is that of stimulating senior publishing management to participate in debate on EP strategic issues and to recognize the need for a new form of creativity in publishing. This requires publishing management to commit to collaboration through alliances, to create a new market, and thus to participate in market demand creation for EP products which will enhance the business and cultural environment of Europe and raise the participation of European enterprises in global information trading.

The result of these postures has been a tendency for the public service in Europe to have a perception of the information industry postulated on the assumption of a single market, in contrast to the practitioners firmly entrenched in a tactical posture based on a view of different publishing sectors as discrete islands of business with little connection between them. This point has been elaborated recently in a study undertaken by Pira International for Comprint 1994.

Preceding the work by Pira International in 1994, a major breakthrough was achieved in 1992/93 when dialogue between IEPRC and DGXIII/E led to the funding by the EC of a study under the title *Strategic Study on New Opportunities for Publishers in the Information Services Market.* The terms of reference for this study were developed by the editors of this publication in consultation with the Board of IEPRC and senior officials of DGXIII/E. The objective for the study was to analyse the real publishing industries of Europe and to reflect their views on the business opportunities in EP and at the same time to provide an overlay of future vision in the context of the global information industry. The consultant selected to lead the study — Dr Thomas Laukamm — was a deliberate choice of an individual familiar with business consultancy, with management experience in the publishing sector, but free from a track record of prejudices on the information industry.

The study and its follow-up action represent a watershed in dialogue enhancement among the EP opinion formers in Europe. The study and report coincided with the White Paper *Growth Competitiveness and Employment* presented by the European Commission. One of the actions of that White Paper was to follow up in 1993 on the chapter of the document headed *Information Society* by the formation of a high-level group of advisers under Dr Martin Bangemann, addressing issues related to the development and interoperability of networks for facilitating the dissemination of information, trans-European basic information services — databanks, electronic mail, interactive video etc. — and new applications in EP.

Further evidence of the positive stimulation provided by the EC-sponsored study was the focus given at the Frankfurt Book Fair in 1993 through EP seminars and meetings for the Heads of Houses in the publishing community. During the same year intensive dialogue took place through IEPRC with the EC on a number of publisher-related inputs to the Fourth Framework Programme. These activities to shape public support programmes to innovation in Europe have been enhanced by linkages with the European Publishers Council and its influence on deregulation in cross-media ownership and the optimization of the protection of intellectual property rights. Further synergy has been gained by links between IEPRC, Pira International and Intergraf through the development of the project *Communication 2000* and collaboration in the exploration of networking EP expertise for the enhancement of skills throughout Europe. All these developments have contributed impetus for electronic publishing in Europe likely to produce a step change in EP business over the next five years. Thus in considering an EP business overview it is appropriate to reassess the conclusions reached in 1993 through the study *New Opportunities for Publishers in the Information Services Market*. What follows is a summary of the study findings which relates them to the current situation of the EP business as viewed by publishers.

NEW OPPORTUNITIES FOR PUBLISHERS IN THE INFORMATION SERVICES MARKET — A REPORT REVISITED

Though by the year 2000 most publications will still be in printed form, traditional print products are being challenged in their leading role in several areas. A contributing factor can be measured by the growth in personal computers (PCs). The penetration of PCs in Europe has reached some 25% in offices (USA 35%) and 15% in homes (USA 20%) and is growing rapidly. Rough estimates show a market potential for electronic publishing* in Europe in the order of magnitude of some ECU12 000 million in the year 2000.

In contrast to this fundamental shift in the user market, many publishers are largely unaware of such changes in the information industry, of new opportunities and threats and the strategic implications of new media. There is at the same time uncertainty about technologies, markets and economics and little vision of the future information industry. Japan is strong in hardware and the USA has additional strength in application software. Europe's strength is in the richness of content for information products.

While this provides European publishers with attractive opportunities for electronic publishing, it is also a threat because their con-

---

*In this study 'electronic publishing' refers to any nonprint media material which can be electronically delivered, sorted and/or manipulated by the user.

tent ownership, mainly based on text, will not be the complete answer for multimedia applications[†]. On the other hand, most global information players in movie and music production are nonEuropean. This is the justification for arguing that European infrastructure must have global players, e.g. very large publishers, and this objective must be part of any EC-supported communications industry strategy.

Since publishing markets are based on languages, electronic publications in the English language find larger markets and give a higher and quicker return on investment. This gives an advantage to publishers based in the USA and the UK and makes the necessary learning phase longer, more costly and riskier for nonEnglish-speaking publishers. This is another example of the need for EC programmes which encourage multinational collaboration in EP prototyping within Europe — a case long advocated by IEPRC. Traditional publishers who do not exploit opportunities in electronic publishing at the right time and with the appropriate strategy to enter the business will lose this business to third parties. The same applies to booksellers and printers: if they do not change their cultures and strategies radically and quickly, they will play a reduced role or none at all in the new information businesses.

Though the USA and Japan appear to be ahead in electronic publishing, in general, publishers in the USA and Japan face the same problems and opportunities as their European counterparts. The differences between USA, Japan and Europe are in their business cultures, competitive environments and the sizes of their home markets.

The greater the multimedia content of the EP product, the less relevant is the ownership of textual content; often the traditional publisher owns only the text. Publishers will have to apply 'single-source multiple-media publishing'[‡], just as the electronics suppliers will have to market multimedia-ready hardware products.

Since different segments of publishing are affected differently by the changing environment, there is no generic strategy for success. Each publisher must find their own way into electronic publishing, but there are some common rules for limiting risks.

[†]'Multimedia' in this context means publishing text, graphics, images, sound, video etc. on one medium.
[‡]'Multiple-media' in this study means publishing on different media such as paper, disk, CD-ROM, online etc.

In *Perspective 2000* (a Japanese forecast study) the traditionally strong position of European publishers with regard to content ownership is expected to be weakened in terms of electronic publishing, due to the fact that multimedia products require content which is not yet available or is substantially controlled by key players other than publishers.

It is suggested that the remaining strength of European publishers will be their established market and customer base. Thus, it should be the primary strategic goal of any traditional publisher in Europe to protect this position and not to give way to third parties offering electronic products to their customers. As, in addition to publishers, other content suppliers will establish themselves as players in the information industry, comarketing and cobranding between traditional publishers and newcomers from outside may become necessary. The strengths of videogame publishers will be significant in this context.

The acceptance of EP will increase as the computer and videogame-literate generation matures and moves into a position of disposable-income purchasing power. Barriers to acceptance of electronic equipment will decline because of more user-friendly technologies and products, available at improving cost/benefit ratios.

As the enabling technologies become available, electronic multimedia publishing will grow and will open new business opportunities which expand the total information market. This technological development will be inextricably interwoven with print-on-paper information products. These changes in technology will enable publishers of paper-based products and printers to enhance their competitiveness providing they have the business management competences and skills so to do. This topic is elaborated in the Pira International report to Comprint 1994 *Communication 2000: Visions and Strategies for Printers and Publishers*.

Growing environmental pressure and legislation directed at paper consumption may force certain segments of print-based publishing to consider switching to EP. There is a perception among consumers, and it is often shared by governments, that EP is intrinsically more environmentally friendly than paper-based communication. The case for this argument is not proven. However, that may not stop legislation antagonistic to paper-based products being implemented because of its political attractiveness. The only solution to this problem in the interests of preserving earth's resources is the further development and use of environmental life cycle analysis (LCA$_{env}$). Collaborative efforts by the publishers of Europe in all branches of publishing — books, magazines and newspapers — should be made at this time to fund the development and application of objective LCA to the publishing process. Such concerted effort by publishers would demonstrate societal responsibility and prove to be good business.

Awareness and willingness among information users to buy and to use EP products will grow owing to the increasing use of enhanced telephony services, TV/VCR, videogames, PCs etc. The willingness to buy EP products will depend on age, perception and the experience of earlier products. Demographic patterns are relevant to market behaviour in this context and the tendency in European countries to an ageing population may slow the demand pattern for EP unless its user-friendliness is enhanced significantly. The consumer's willingness to buy will be strongly influenced by benefits in information content, by entertainment value compared with other entertainment products, or by functional fulfilment such as contribution to distance learning. Ultimately the overriding considerations will be fitness-for-purpose and value-for-money.

Publishers will continue to increase their experience in the technologies which relate to EP. More and more publishers will gain the ability to provide, create and bundle attractive content products and to distribute them to the user at an appropriate price. Market development will be further stimulated by other content suppliers such as travel companies, automotive manufacturers and banks providing services analogous to EP.

In the immediate future the most profitable businesses in EP will be videogames and business-to-business services. This will be supported by the PC as a driver in corporate and office environments. The PC corporate environment will develop rapidly through the use of networking both in-house and with third parties. One example of this business-to-business driver is the development of electronic document interchange (EDI) networks, which then seek to provide opportunity to be carriers for other activities that lead them to the EP market.

Two other driver mechanisms will continue and these are the penetration of the PC or laptop into domestic environments and the introduction of interface devices that enable information providers to exploit the installed base of domestic TV sets. Examples of this development are Philips CD-i products and the Sony Data Discman. It seems likely that the infrastructure in corporate and professional markets will be dominated by computer-based systems and telephony. However, the domestic market for EP products is likely to be based on an infrastructure which is a mixture of TV, computers, videogame and hi-fi equipment, increasingly connected to telephony and cable networks.

Convergence of technologies in computer, television, telephony and video will continue and this will stimulate convergence in the electronics, publishing and networking industries forming the new communication industry. The present pattern of global mergers and strategic alliances will continue across all sectors of the information industry. It is in this context that deregulation of cross-media ownership, advocated by the European Publishers Council, becomes critical to the opportunities for participation in the global marketplace by European players.

The development of the corporate and professional markets for EP multimedia products will justify further investment by the electronics industry, independent of the development of consumer markets. The convergence in technologies and demand in both professional and consumer markets will allow more consumer electronics and computer companies to enter the highly competitive consumer markets. This emphasizes the strategic importance for large European publishers to develop a business policy which takes account of such market intervention.

Initially, for economic reasons, major EP products will be marketed globally. There will be minor EP products serving national markets which will be successful, showing high penetration in vertical markets owing to high added value or wide, but limited, penetration in horizontal markets with lower added value.

The traditional bookshop will be only one among a variety of distribution channels for EP products. Other channels will emerge and will be more successful. Among these will be the use of supermarkets and the techniques of video-shopping applied to EP products. A further development in this distribution challenge could be the use of the 'intelligent kiosk' as a point-of-sale delivery mechanism.

In the immediate future the most serious bottleneck in the development of EP will be the lack of attractive content, mainly due to a shortage of appropriate skills and experience in content producers, whether they be publishers or consumer electronics companies. This situation ought to play into the hands of the traditional publisher, providing they understand the need to invest in, and nurture, a new breed of creativity in the publishing community.

The prototyping initiatives undertaken by IEPRC and Pira International are aimed at providing facilitation to publishers in this critical business area. IEPRC collaboration with the EC aimed at investigating the feasibility of networking European centres of excellence is a further example of collective cooperation to achieve breakthrough in the perceptions of this key development issue, amongst top publishing management.

The consumer electronics industry is likely to achieve company cooperation at both global and national levels. Standardization in hardware and software will be critical to the industry in making EP happen. Some players in the electronics industry will engage in publishing themselves, others will enter into cooperation with publishers without becoming direct competitors. The posture chosen will be a determining factor in the relationship between large publishers and their willingness to develop alliances with consumer electronics companies.

As EP products, especially multimedia EP products, become an accepted part of the media world, product technologies will become less important, while production technologies and economies of scale will gain in importance. As EP matures, the base of competition will become the quality of the content itself, the value added through related services and effective distribution. This suggests that the traditional publisher is in a relatively strong position, providing they have a business strategy to exploit this environment.

EP will evolve from being a technology-driven to a demand-driven business in professional applications, and a supply-driven business in consumer markets. For the next five years EP content development will be in a state of evolution. From this process there will be the slow emergence of a new breed of persons from either the computer programming, games, media or the publishing environment. Successful EP product creators will be in short supply and command high value in the marketplace. In this business, there will continue to be a pattern of small entrepreneurial companies which will struggle to find adequate funding to support their development and to find an adequate base of management skills. Often they will eventually be bought by the larger publishers, by computer companies or consumer electronics companies wishing to diversify. Successful publishers in the new EP business will:

- employ all appropriate media,
- leverage their relations with authors in developing new-content products,
- attract talented authors by developing a reputation for exploiting all appropriate media,
- exploit their backlist for multimedia EP purposes,
- learn to manage the complexity related to the acquisition and trading of rights for components of multimedia EP products,
- bring together and manage the skilled workgroups required for creative multimedia EP projects,
- select or create appropriate distribution channels for multimedia EP products,
- create a brand-image reputation which provides leverage and recognition in the new EP marketplace.

Against this background of rapid changes to the basis of competition favouring nonEuropean players in nearly all aspects of electronic multimedia publishing, support from the EC is necessary to help the European publishing industry develop awareness, skills and critical mass in EP. This becomes even more important strategically in the light of the Japanese and the US Governments' commitments to EP and related hardware industries. The most important recommendations are:

- Support for the European information industry as a whole and the provision of balanced support and funding which encourages collaboration between the electronics and the publishing industries.
- The development of a EC long-term strategic view of electronic publishing.
- The exploitation of EP products and services by European governments.
- The initiation of a network of centres of excellence in EP in Europe which cooperate with the industries concerned — a networked European *Bauhaus* for EP!

THE COMMUNICATIONS MARKET — PUBLISHING AND EP

The communications market embraces all forms of communication associated with the transfer of value. It encompasses the media markets (cinema, broadcast radio and television, cable radio and television, publishing, audio, audio-visual) and other communications means where value is exchanged, e.g. printed products and telecommunications services. Publishing consists of a multitude of heterogeneous activities in terms of products, markets, customers and business environments. Publishing may be defined as a process involving the collection, editing, storage, processing, formatting, distribution and financing of intellectual property. Today the majority of value-adding in publishing comes from paper-based products. The paper-based publishing industry can be divided into:

- *Book publishing:* fiction, nonfiction, education and academic, professional, STM (scientific, technical and medical) etc..
- *Magazine publishing:* consumer, trade and business, hobby and specialist, professional, STM etc..
- *Newspaper publishing:* international general, international business, national, local, free sheet etc..

Although significant cross-ownership exists in publishing — both between conventional publishing products and publishers' ownership of other media — the book, magazine and newspaper sectors each have their own unique characteristic and cross-transfer of experience is limited.

The total market size of the European publishing industry is in the region of ECU70 000 million. The average growth rate of the publishing industry has been approximately 3.8% per year in real terms over the last eight or nine years, with little difference between the various publishing segments. Growth rate in the last two years has been significantly lower at around 2% per year in real terms. Newspapers have suffered more readership erosion of their market than books and magazines. Magazine publishing has been marked by its proliferation in titles in recent years and the development of pan-European titles. Nevertheless, newspapers remain the dominant publishing medium with a share of one-third of the total market. The market share of magazine publishing is approximately 29%, followed by book publishing with approximately 25%. The size of the corporate publishing market is difficult to estimate. The difficulty is caused by problems of definition and the availability of data. The other difficulty in placing a size characteristic on corporate publishing is that much of the activity is internalized in terms of its value. Recently Pira International has sought to develop concepts of communications market mapping in its work for Comprint 1994. Tables 1.1, 1.2 and 1.3 give some size indication of the European publishing and communications market.

There are approximately 60 000 European publishing companies, the majority of these publishers belonging to the book segment. The costs of market entry are traditionally considered as being low in comparison with other industries. However, the increasing fixed costs in most of the publishing segments (e.g. about 80% in paperback

Table 1.1 Publishing industry Europe (EC), estimated market size, 1991 (Million ECU)

Books	Newspapers	Magazines	Corporate	**Total**
18 500	25 000	22 000	10 000	**75 500**
25%	33%	29%	13%	**100%**

Source: SNE, BDB, Business Monitor, Pira International, UNESCO, PEE, Consulting Trust/**Laukamm, T** *Strategic Study on New Opportunities for Publishers in the Information Services Market* EC No 14926 EN (Feb 1993) p B2

Table 1.2 Book market by category, Europe, 1992

Category	Value (Million ECU)	Value (%)	Volume (%)
Fiction	4 000	22	32
Children	2 800	15	18
Education	2 200	12	11
Reference	2 600	14	10
STM	1 700	9	5
Legal	700	4	1
Other	4 500	24	23
Total	**18 500**	**100**	**100**

Source: SNE, BDB, Business Monitor, Pira International, UNESCO, PEE, Consulting Trust/**Laukamm, T** *Strategic Study on New Opportunities for Publishers in the Information Services Market* EC No 14926 EN (Feb 1993) p B2

Table 1.3 Matrices for the communications market in Europe in the early 1990s[1] — All consumption sectors

Final demand	All consumption sectors						
Million ECU	**Media type**						
Type of communication	Printed products	Television and radio	Film and video	Telecoms services	Offline digital media	Music recording	Overall communication type
Transactions	2 066	—	—	350	—	—	2 416
Promotion	52 575.6	18 139.4	568	4 047	**100**	—	75 430
Information	35 700	95 (Eur)	—	**2 407.5** (Eur)	**5 646** (Eur)	—	43 849
Education	4 800	480 (Eur)	280	**752.5** (Eur)	**2 664** (Eur)	—	8 977
Entertainment	35 000	7 437	4 756	**275** (Eur)	**1 230** (Eur)	7 351	56 049
Sum	130 142	26 151	5 604	7 832	9 640	7 351	186 720
Overall media type	**100 997**	**23 850**	**5 210**	**22 437**	**9 640**	**7 351**	**169 485**

Figures in **bold** indicate an expected growth rate in excess of 10% per annum for the rest of the decade
– revenue nonexistent or negligible
Figures may not add up due to rounding
[1] In constructing these matrices, the most reliable figures available have been used. Figures that relate directly to the communication type have been used in the cells and to derive the row totals and the media sum totals. The overall media totals and the overall total are based on official aggregate statistics. It is impossible to tell which of the aggregate figures is the most reliable: it is safest to treat the 'sum' value and the 'overall' value as representing the range.
Source: Communication 2000: Visions and Strategies for Printers and Publishers Intergraf, Brussels, Belgium (May 1994) p 2.7

publishing or 70% in newspaper publishing) as well as growing marketing and distribution costs, requires substantial financial resources. In addition to this, in many publishing segments, e.g. STM, the barriers to market entry are high because of the restricted availability of content and the required expertise. In addition, there are existing competitors with well established customer relations, brand image and distribution channels. With the exception of some protected market niches the degree of competition is usually high in publishing markets. Consumer magazine and newspaper markets demonstrate high intensity of competition.

Profit margins vary from an average of 9% in book publishing to more than 15% in some magazine publishing. The highest profitability is achieved in special-interest niche markets with high entry barriers. The degree of vertical integration varies from segment to segment and has changed over time; however, with the exception of newspaper publishing, the degree of vertical integration is low. The degree of business concentration in most segments of publishing is high and continues to grow. The concentration level varies from country to country, but generally the ten largest publishing companies, and their associated enterprises, control 50–70% of the turnover in most countries. Small and medium size publishers — which are often undercapitalized — are ideal acquisition targets for larger companies since they frequently have strong positions in niche markets and profound expertise in their field of activity. With the exception of a few segments, e.g. STM, the concentration process has tended to be limited to national or language markets. This must be seen in the context of a well developed system of rights selling. More recently the publishing industry has also seen important international mergers and acquisitions by the larger publishing houses. The drivers for mergers and acquisitions are:

- gaining market access,
- achieving access to, and control of, distribution channels,
- exploiting copyright in an international framework or across media to aid the emergence of global publishing concepts,
- looking for economies of scale.

However, there are limits to concentration, and the experience of larger publishers demonstrates the difficulty in realizing synergy between the components of a publishing group. Inevitably there is conflict between financial accountability, which argues in favour of distributed cost centres operating independently within a financial performance framework, and the encouragement of synergy between these entities in a large group. It is not uncommon to find different entities within a publishing group pursuing development activity either unknown or not shared by other components of the same group. At a time when there is technology convergence in the media this is a serious structural weakness within larger publishing houses. It is also at the heart of the problem of how to manage innovation in EP product development.

The network of international publishing houses acquired or built up by a few large media companies limits the growth potential of small and medium-size publishers since international coeditions and coproductions are usually negotiated first within the groups. The recent development of international networks of small and medium-sized publishers — especially in academic and scientific publishing — prove that the benefit of cooperation need not be limited to large publishing houses.

Worldwide there are probably no more than 50 multimedia companies with global activities which will determine the shape of the new EP market. Some of those companies play a major role in publishing — Time Warner, Bertelsmann, News Corporation, Hachette, Paramount Communications, Times Mirror, Thomson Corporation, Gannett, Reed-Elsevier, Reader's Digest, Axel Springer-Verlag, Hearst Corporation, RCS Rizzoli, Mondadori, McGraw-Hill and Pearson — and the importance of this group is growing. The companies categorized in this group are generally:

- of large size,
- generating a turnover of more than ECU200 000 million,
- diversified in terms of media or other entertainment products,
- decentralized,
- composed of a global network of associated companies,
- primarily managed by financial objectives,
- vertically integrated — in production and distribution,
- well equipped with substantial capital resources.

As a rule, the publishing activities of these companies are focused on mass markets, e.g. consumer magazines, fiction books, national newspapers, rather than on special-interest publishing. The publishing business activities of this group have an important strategic function for other media business sectors, e.g. film and television, with regard to the possibility of using content and copyright understanding for other media applications, e.g. television and film. Such business arrangements will become increasingly important with the convergence of media technology.

THE ONLINE INFORMATION SERVICES MARKET

Any attempt to describe the European information marketplace would not be complete without reference to the online segment. This is most reliably reported by the Information Market Observatory (IMO) of the EC. The following material is based on the IMO report of July 1993.

Europe is a world force in online production and distribution. By the end of 1991 35% of all database producers and 30% of online service operators were based within the European Union. According to supply-side indicators for 1990/1 there has been an increase in the numbers of EU databases of 26.3% and database producers of 21.7%. Although these figures, which represent directory entries, need to be interpreted with caution, they nevertheless provide confirmation of trends noted in earlier IMO annual reports. These include the fact that the pattern of database distribution continues to be more highly concentrated in North America than in the EU (2.4 and 2.0 databases per host respectively).

The international marketplace for text and bibliographic online services is dominated by two US vendors: Mead Data Central (MDC) and Dialog. Although EU-based vendors (OR Telematique, Questel, Européenne des Données, GBI and ESA/IRS) occupied five positions out of the top ten world rankings, none came within the range of either of the two US mega-hosts. This tends to support the view that the markets of EU vendors are predominantly national or regional, rather than worldwide.

In 1991 EU-based hosts and information providers generated worldwide sales to the value of ECU300 325 million, an increase of 5.6% over 1990 in absolute terms. Sales of real-time services grew by 4.5%, while online retrospective services increased by only 2.8%. A much stronger pattern of growth was evident in offline sales, notably for magnetic and optical media (which doubled) and document delivery (which trebled). However, revenues from offline sales are still small in relation to total income; the combined income from magnetic and optical media, plus document delivery, was only 5.4% of 1991 total industry value.

The number of people actually able to use CD-ROM titles remains small. Recent estimates suggest that the worldwide installed base of CD-ROM drives at the end of 1991 was around 2.25 million, with 1.44 million in the USA, 0.62 million in Asia and 0.2 million in western Europe. High growth rates are predicted; by the end of 1992, the European installed CD-ROM base was around 600 000 with the largest single national marketplace being the UK (185 000 units). Other leading EU markets include Germany (125 000 units), Italy (85 000), France (50 000) and the Netherlands (25 000). Worldwide revenues for the commercial and in-house CD-ROM sectors have grown from ECU66.5 million (1987) to ECU3200 million (1992). Global revenues from commercial titles and drives were said to amount to ECU2.2 billion in 1992. The long-range impact of the CD-ROM on online markets is likely to be considerable, especially in the academic and library communities where CD-ROM pricing structures can be highly attractive.

EP PRODUCTS AND THE PRINT MEDIUM

With the technology push associated with EP it is easy to assume that print-on-paper publishing is out-dated. This is far from being correct. For many applications of publishing, where large volumes of text or high-resolution images are required, print-based publishing is effective. Simply trying to translate such material into EP format is unlikely to make profits for any publisher. It cannot be repeated too often that user fitness-for-purpose is the first criterion in developing the EP product. The characteristics of EP which give it potential user-advantage are:

- searchability,
- multisensory communication, e.g. visual and audio,
- interactivity,
- rapid updateability,
- high storage capability,

- interconnectivity,
- content manipulation,
- linguistic flexibility, e.g. multilanguage versions of the same product available on demand,
- product personalization,
- on-demand hard copy output.

Success in EP products will be achieved by exploiting its characteristics in unique applications which deliver cost-effective benefit to the user. Emulating successful print publishing products will not succeed. Where high-volume replicative images are what the user needs, print will continue to out-perform EP.

Reading comfort in EP is of particular importance since it is the key to the development of mass markets for electronic displays. Extensive reading of text is an activity for which electronic displays so far have limitations. Changing this situation will require significant technical advances. A full-page-size, high-quality, flat-panel display is a fundamental requirement to make EP devices a success. Many products available today only provide an acceptable quality when the latter is considered with other functional benefits such as searchability or speed of update. Looked at in absolute terms they fall well short of good print quality. Because of this limitation, efforts are made to utilize software to give EP presentation systems advantages that are great enough to overcome their residual quality weakness. Such an approach will satisfy some markets, but will not allow EP to make penetration on any significant scale into consumer publishing. The specification of an acceptable EP reading software device is:

- 'clean' fast page turn to avoid eye strain,
- comfortable browsing capability,
- font size control,
- complete cross-indexing — automatically or semiautomatically,
- incorporation into reading software facilities for handwritten annotation, emphasis and underlining,
- easy interconnection to other EP files,
- user-friendly software to support adjacent processes, e.g. improved file organization.

When comparing print-based publishing with EP, it is too often assumed that prepress technology in printing is static. Prepress technology in printing is itself subject to revolution, much of which is related to convergence with multimedia production. Machine-readable manuscripts from authors and optical reader technology are commonplace in conventional publishing. Standard generalized mark-up language (SGML) has been pioneered in the print publishing sector. Digital artwork reproduction (DAR) is common in several branches of paper-based print production. Electronic data interchange (EDI) is becoming widespread between publishing, printing and paper sectors. Common standards for the transfer of advertising copy between clients, advertising agencies, publishers and printers is growing fast. Desktop publishing (DTP) is widespread in publishing and printing houses and desktop colour manipulation, together with electronic cameras, is leading to new concepts in printing such as stochastic screening. Leading printing houses such as Toppan, Dai Nippon Printing, Donnelley etc. offer advanced facilitation for information management, which permits the publisher to make choices at any time related to the output product, whether it be paper-based or EP. Thus the issue in many respects is not simple replacement of print publishing by EP but the full exploitation of a growing market which offers enhanced choice to the user in communications' products and services. Successful EP in this expanded market will depend on the benefits which the EP product offers to the user and this in turn will depend on creative alliances between publishers, printers and other resource providers and the consumer electronics industry. In Europe this interdependence of several industry sectors to nurture a new market appears to be less well understood than is the case in the USA or Japan. Focusing EC programmes in this area of synergy could do much to generate employment and the regeneration of manufacturing technology in Europe in one of the few markets where expansion is likely over the next decade — namely the communications industry.

The development of a business strategy in a publishing house to determine the optimum balance between paper-based publishing and EP requires support from appropriate methodology. One area of management techniques which can make contribution to this problem is that of supply and value-added chains. Pira International in its work for Comprint 1994 has developed a methodology of value-network analysis applied to a number of publishing and print product areas. By way of illustration Figure 1.1 provides an example of a representative periodical value network showing the current rela-

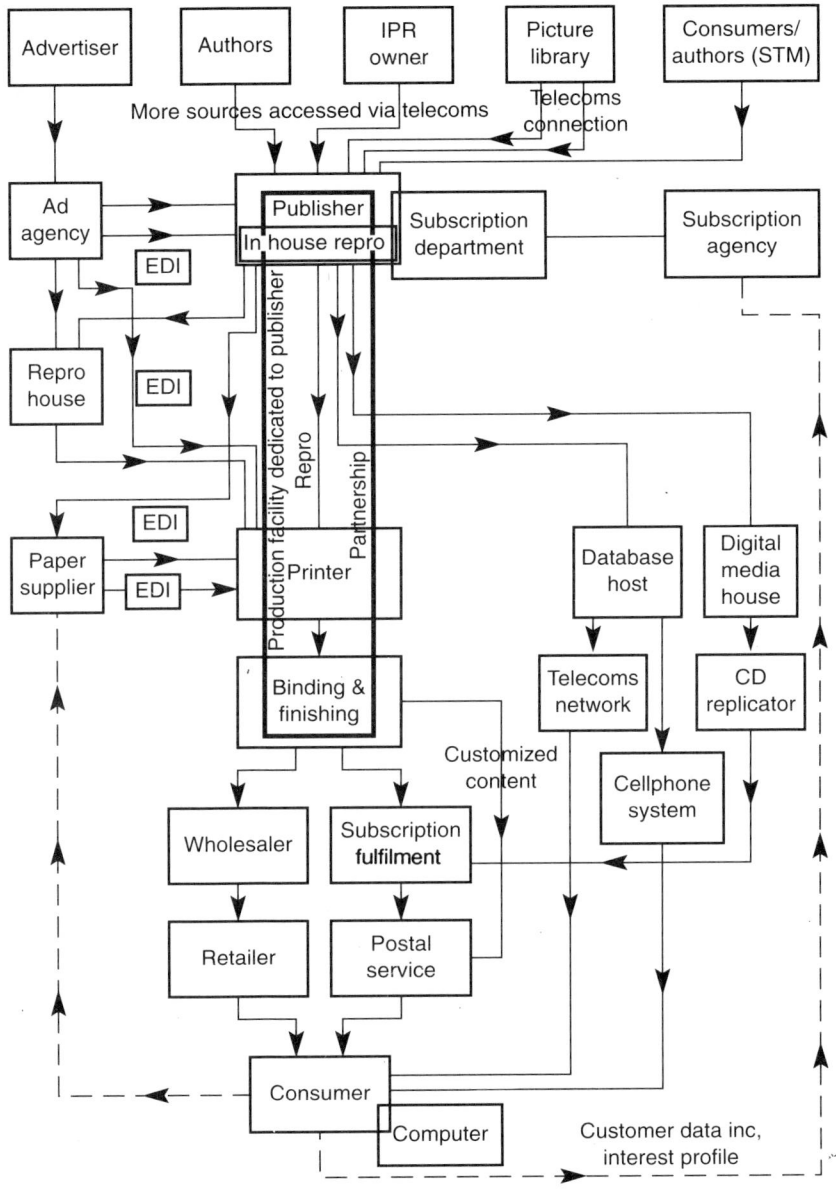

Figure 1.1 Periodical value network (Source: *Communication 2000: Visions and Strategies for Printers and Publishers* Intergraf, Brussels, Belgium (May 1994) p 5.31)

tionships in the value network and those which are likely to occur through the use of new technology including EP[1]. This area of techno-management consultancy will be essential to any publishing house seeking to optimize its posture in relation to paper-based publishing and the development of the EP marketplace.

Any information product may be described in terms of three factors:

- content
- format
- process

Content is the information itself — that which the author or compiler wishes to convey. Content may be categorized in terms of its nature or purpose — as numbers, text, images, sound, music, news, data, advertising or instructions etc.

The format determines the presentation of content. Examples are typography on paper, images on screen, voice from tape or radio etc. At a detailed level, format includes a variety of display features: text in different fonts or sizes; different ways of organizing material; graphics and other images.

The process contains all the steps and technologies required to convert information into a deliverable product, whether provided as a single entity or continuously as a service. The same information content may be presented in different output formats. For the publisher this represents parallel publishing. The essential question for any publisher is how one format may replace another with commercial advantage. The dominant criterion in this choice will be fitness for purpose in relation to the user need.

Overall, publishers feel that new technologies provide business opportunities. Publishers welcome the interest of the EC in the subject of EP for two reasons: they would like more balance between the consumer electronics industries and publishers in the allocation of support programmes; and, as publishers, they are not sure about their future strategic role in electronic publishing — in relation to key players in the USA or Japan and in relation to the balance between content and technology push.

---

[1]Pira has developed the concept of a value network to reflect better the reality in publishing and the rethinking of the value chain concept that is apparent in current strategic planning practice.

Many publishers are sceptical of the more dramatic claims made for EP and consider it simply as another mode of delivery. Some see it as a threat or even as irrelevant to their business. There is continuing uncertainty about technology push, market demand development and economics, as well as the strategic business implications of new media.

The publishing industries continue to feel confident in their business positioning because of their long historical background in publishing skills, content ownership and established relationships with authors, readers and distribution. Few publishers can articulate clearly the degree to which these strengths will be useful for participating in, or defending themselves from, EP developments. As traditional print-based publishing is profitable, many publishers are reluctant to endanger their position by investing in uncertain electronic information products when they can adopt a waiting position or leave this business to third parties and enter the market later by acquisition. There is, however, an increasing awareness that the print-on-paper product is losing its dominant role in some areas. This is currently raising the interest level among publishers in the EP business.

Publishers have difficulty in conceptualizing and creating electronic products. There is a tendency to think in terms of simply transforming content to another medium. There is little evidence of lateral thinking. This reflects the dichotomy in publishing between editorial creativity and the rest of the management functions. Editorial direction is synonymous with creativity in conventional publishing. EP requires a different culture. The new EP culture is more demanding in creativity and needs an intellect able to manage the interplay between content creativity and the exploitation of technology to a greater extent than has ever been needed in print-based publishing. This raises a critical issue of management structure. Laukamm's findings are supported by the research of IEPRC in pinpointing the need for cohesion and continuity at all levels in a publishing enterprise which seeks to enter the EP business market. Failure is often caused by imbalance either with the company's Board of Directors seeing EP as an investment opportunity without proper evaluation or EP enthusiasts in an organization pursuing a project which produces antagonism in the business hierarchy due to a misunderstanding of the investment and timescale requirements for EP product development.

Many players in publishing, electronics and networking have not yet realized the implications of these industries merging or at the very least becoming interdependent. Together they will produce the new information industry, but the balance between collaboration and competition is still being sought. Leading players in the electronics industry have diverse views about their role in electronic publishing, and they do not — with a few notable exceptions — contribute to either the strategic thinking of publishers or the infrastructural development of the new EP business. This is an area where the EC as a pan-European and pan-sectoral agency can play a particularly valuable role in facilitating synergy between organizations that may at a later stage become overtly competitive.

It has been suggested that multimedia communication is a natural human desire through expansion of communication in space and time. Thus, it is postulated that multimedia should not be regarded as a fashion or gimmick of the electronics industry, but instead as an inevitable extension of human lifestyle. At the behavioural level this hypothesis may be valid, pointing to the analogy that man is a multifunctional communicator. If this is so, the analogy must be extended to question how well present multimedia products emulate the sensory and neural systems of the human being. Cursory analysis of this comparison illustrates the crudity of current EP multimedia products and their user interface. The ultimate crudity must be the keyboard as an interface. This indicates a focus area for hardware and software manufacturers with an order of intellectual challenge and investment requirement comparable to the Japanese Fifth Generation Computing Project. However, if one considers developments in speech input, superhighways, standardization of imaging protocols, data compression, touch commands and iconographic language, then the suggestion, that man's natural multimedia behaviour may be emulated in machine form within a decade, is feasible.

There are opportunities for publishers in the EP business but those same opportunities are open to players outside the traditional publishing arena who may be motivated to play a stronger role in demand creation than most traditional publishers. Laukamm in his investigation attempted to quantify the European publishing market segments in 1992 and 2000 and their potential for electronic publishing in the year 2000. He points out that this attempt is only a first approximation but it does give some estimate of the business stakes. His data are reproduced in Table 1.4.

Though it is tempting to express demand for EP products in market figures and profit calculations, the real issues are more strate-

Table 1.4 Market potential — European publishing market segments 1992 and 2000 and their potential for electronic publishing in the year 2000

Segment	Traditional print publishing		Electronic publishing 2000	
	Market 1992 mill ECU	Market 2000 mill ECU	Potential range for electronic publishing %	Market (Average) mill ECU
Books				
Fiction	4 000	6 000	1–10	300
Children	2 800	4 000	15–25	800
Education	2 200	3 300	10–20	500
Reference	2 600	3 800	15–25	750
STM	1 700	2 500	20–30	625
Legal	700	1 000	15–25	175
Other	4 500	6 600	1–10	330
Subtotal	**18 500**	**27 200**	**8–18**	**3.480**
Magazines	22 000	32 500	5–15	3.250
Newspapers	25 000	37 000	5–10	2.775
Corporate	10 000	15 000	10–25	2.625
Total	**75 500**	**111 700**	**6.5–15**	**12.130**

Source: Consulting Trust/**Laukamm, T** *Strategic Study on New Opportunities for Publishers in the Information Services Market* EC No 14926 EN (Feb 1993) pp A13–A14

gic — such as defining the business and the new basis of competition, and the new competitors. This would suggest that market intelligence monitoring, together with continuously updated futures scenarios, is an essential part of a publisher's strategic planning. Publishers, when confronted with a new development, learn fast about the strategic implications of a new business. Publishers are nothing if not entrepreneurial. However, the key issue at this time is whether publishers have available adequate market intelligence and reliable futures-scenario generation? There is little evidence to suggest they do.

One is brought back always to the main issue of EP market identification and creation by publishing, since the potential user of electronically published information products is not able to articulate needs and demand. This situation changes rapidly once an EP product is marketed successfully. It points to the importance of prototyping of EP products by publishers. Unfortunately, publishers have no tradition of managing prototype development, particularly prototyping that requires creative balance between content and technology. It is noticeable that those enterprises which are demonstrating success in prototyping are often those with a background in creative arts such as film making. A good example is the development work undertaken by Time Warner. It is reasonable to conclude that Laukamm is correct in suggesting that market creation will be driven by the two interdependent forces of content provision and technology provision — computer hardware and software, consumer electronics and telecommunications. The finding is also valid that, whereas the content provider — in the form of the publisher — still has difficulties identifying the economic driver to justify business investment in EP, the electronics companies consider EP as an attractive new business for two reasons. These are the stimulation of the electronics business by enhanced demand for hardware and software and the opportunity to generate new income streams by the diversification of electronics companies into the publishing business. This is a persuasive argument for the larger publishers to get on to the learning curve of EP rapidly in order to build business alliances with major players in the consumer electronics sector. It would suggest that publishers entering the EP business must have a strategic plan and treat EP as a separate business mission.

SCALE AND COMPANY SIZE IN EP

The economics of large-scale EP products require a global marketing approach. This raises further issues in Europe of the political attitude towards large companies. There is a tendency in Europe to favour small and medium-size enterprises (SMEs). This favoured status by governments towards SMEs is postulated in the belief that it is such companies which create employment by responding quickly to changes in the economy. Also there is, in some quarters, a belief that large companies are institutionalized and cannot innovate, whereas small companies are more innovative. There is little evidence to support these political suppositions. Like all generalizations they relate only in part to the real world, but the issue bears directly on the development of the EP business. If market making is at the centre of developing the European EP business, then it follows that either large companies must take the lead as patrons of such infrastructure development or there must be a coherent, public, well directed programme to encourage collaboration among SMEs. Clearly, neither stance is manifest in Europe. Worldwide experience suggests there is a minimum critical size for companies to be significant players in market creation in EP. Europe has many publishers of world class, capable of fulfilling this function. US and Japanese experience also indicates that using the supply chain is one of the most effective mechanisms through which to encourage SMEs. However, the supply chain requires within it one or more major players to act as the driver. The conclusion one might reach from considering these issues is that there should be closer cooperation between Europe's leading publishing houses and the government mechanisms for infrastructure development in Europe. Such alliances should spread cross-sectorally to the consumer electronics companies. In turn, this supply-chain structure should be encouraged to create demand which involves SMEs, whether they be publishers, hardware or software suppliers or other suppliers of facilities services to the EP business.

As European publishers are culturally and linguistically national, to create critical mass for European EP products transnational alliances are required and free flow of trade and open communication networks have to be ensured throughout Europe. This is a problem unique to Europe when compared with the principal competitor regions of the USA and Japan. Much progress has been made through dialogue with publishers conducted in the development of the Fourth Framework Programme of the EC, and through the group of prominent advisers set up by Dr Martin Bangemann. Nevertheless, there will be an ongoing need to emphasize the catalytic role of the EC in the development of European EP infrastructure and for the encouragement of synergy through programmes which stimulate collaboration. Above all, these programmes must be based on informed vision and be flexible to take account of rapid changes in technology.

For example, in the work undertaken by Laukamm he sought to elucidate the probable format for the development of EP publishers' products. Since then British Telecom (BT) has announced a massive investment programme aimed at creating 'information superhighways' in the UK, capable of delivering interactive services such as home videos, banking and shopping. The investment is massive, with estimates suggesting that it could exceed £10 billion over the next ten years. It is significant that Dr Alan Rudge, BT's Director of Development, is quoted as saying 'we want to deliver services on-demand, not just provide video'. As well as videos, shopping and banking are cited by Rudge, together with estate agency, travel, holiday and health services and educational programmes. In April 1993 NTT, the Japanese domestic telecoms operator, announced an investment of US$396 million to install fibre-optic communication to all its subscribers by the year 2015. Similarly, in the USA Bell operators intend to extend their fibre networks and Ameritech, which has 12 million customers, has announced plans for a digital video network. A further USA operator, US West covering 14 states, stated in February 1994 that it aims to build a hybrid fibre and coaxial network connecting more than 500 000 customers a year from 1995.

Concurrent with the BT announcement, cable TV companies, mostly backed by American patrons, have been active in the City of London seeking merchant bank and institution support to raise some £6000 million required to build their own superhighway. This development is not simply a case of producing a distribution network for outdated films. The intention is to produce a competitive distribution system to BT offering a variety of communications services from telephony to videoconferencing. This is indicative of the speed of change and willingness of investors to back infrastructure development in European countries in the communications business. The announcements made in the UK suggest that over the next decade there will be an investment in Britain of something in the region of £30 000–40 000 million which will bring about a revolution in communications infrastructure.

Laukamm's findings suggested that at present offline publishing in EP is more attractive to traditional publishers than online publishing. Offline media, such as CD-ROM, CD-i, memory cards and print-on-demand are similar to the traditional print media, insofar as they are not dependent on an adequate national or international network capability. They have the added advantage that users need not be specialists and offline media do not put the reader under time pressure. They allow traditional subscription schemes and leave room for attractive update business. In the short-term these arguments remain valid. However, the developments previously referred to in network infrastructure may come faster than anticipated. This would suggest an even stronger case for publishers getting on to the learning curve with offline EP products so that they are in a position to take advantage of the added benefits of competitive easy-to-use network facilitation when it becomes available in the next five to ten years. Looked at strategically, five years is not a long period for a publisher to develop a serious EP business.

Another aspect of network development bears upon publishers' interests when considering EP — namely distribution channels. There is a widely held view that the traditional distribution channels (mainly bookshops) are unsatisfactory for EP products. A similar view is reported from the USA and Japan. Creativity is needed to find alternative ways of marketing electronic publishing products. In the end, the bookshop will be but one outlet among others. Direct marketing, hardware and software retail shops, bundling with hardware or cobranding with industrial companies will all offer a range of new distribution channels. However, the rapid development of superhighways could be the most significant of all delivery mechanisms. It needs little imagination to perceive the PC or television monitor linked to various modes of information storage and hardcopy output, to configure the concept of radical change in the use of information products both in business and in the home. It is worth noting that Pira International in its technology forecasting has made various predictions concerning the growth of on-demand imaging systems — which could be used in the home. Over the past ten years all the Pira International predictions made have been too conservative. In other words, the development of on-demand imaging systems has outstripped what was considered to be optimistic forecasting.

Comment has been made previously that technologies for producing EP products are available but they do not yet fulfil the needs of publishers. Equally crucial is the application of existing technologies. To be successful, any EP product should not just copy the print product but offer features which go beyond those available from traditional print publisher products. It is worth emphasizing again that EP products demand new talents not normally available in the publishing house. Publishers will have to find this creative talent either outside the industry or by a deliberate plan to provide training in new skills. Laukamm's findings have been confirmed by further experience within IEPRC. The lack of personnel skilled in developing, designing and manufacturing unique EP multimedia products is one of the greatest barriers to successful new media publishing. Also there is a lack of strategic EP skills and vision among top management in many publishing houses. This has become apparent in IEPRC and Pira International consultancy when presenting proposals for collaborative development of prototyping EP products. There is a lack of comprehension at the operating level in those responsible for development, or there is conflict between that functional community and the editorial community, or there is no mechanism for the combined editorial and production staff to conduct dialogue with decision-making management responsible for strategy. This structural defect in some publishing houses is the key difference between the publishing houses successful in exploiting EP market opportunity and those unable to respond.

MARKETING, ECONOMICS AND PRICING

A marketing problem for electronic publishing products is that they are not immediately accessible to the user, in the sense that a book is available for browsing from the shelf. The user requires a reading device with the appropriate search and retrieval software. As it is not generally the content that is the unique selling point (USP) for an EP product, but instead the functionality related to content which provides the USP, the only effective way to communicate the benefits of EP products is by persuading the customer to use them. In the case of EP games this motivation is already established. It has its origins in the social behaviour of a person's desire to participate in competitive games as well as in the more recent stimulation through arcades.

For other products, such as educational material, the motivation is less and depends on synergy with others, such as the various programmes for computers in schools, to create demand. The development of common-access market exposure, such as library use, represents another channel for market development. Retail marketing through 'bundled' sales, in which the product is sold as part of a hardware/software package, has also proved successful. The bundling concept is a means of generating volume sales and has given the CD-ROM business some market momentum.

Another aspect of the EP business is the ongoing sale of updates to existing customers. Users of computer software are familiar with the intense competition between applications such as wordprocessing or spreadsheet software in which the respective programmes go through a continual cycle of enhancement and improvement. This marketing principle is applicable to a wider variety of EP products.

Efforts, such as those made by Philips to develop player devices which have more than one functional facility and can be linked to the installed base of television sets, clearly have a significant contribution to make in developing the marketing infrastructure. Purchasing for purposes of status value should not be underestimated as a market driver. Also, as hardware prices fall, the fashionableness of being involved in information technology will also play its part. However, overall clear patterns of marketing success in EP products have not as yet been established. The practice of Japanese hardware manufacturers in producing products and placing them in the marketplace for evaluative purposes is one of the most useful opinion-forming mechanisms in marketing strategies at this time.

The economics of EP are equally unclear at present. This is hardly surprising, nor is it unusual for the development stage of new products. It has been suggested that if the real price of the Gutenberg Bible were updated to today's values it would be in the region of ECU100 000. Such cost barriers did not stop printing from developing into a highly successful business. The problems associated with cost calculations in EP relate to:

- allocations of origination cost,
- volume demand,
- promotion and distribution costs.

Taking the latter item first, it is not surprising to find that EP product promotion and distribution costs tend to be high. This is because of the need to develop market awareness and the lack of established distribution and sales outlets. The question of price/volume relationship is a similar issue. Until EP products have a mass market demand, it is inevitable that there will be a tendency towards a production price premium. However, this characteristic of EP products tends to diminish quite rapidly if one compares them, like with like, with a sophisticated multicolour print product.

Where an EP product draws heavily on origination that has been used and paid for in a printed product, it is common practice to dismiss this cost component in the evaluation of EP product cost. In the long term this is not possible to sustain as a costing principle, but it is rational in the present state of EP product and market development.

Marketing and cost impinge directly on EP product pricing strategy. Many alternative approaches are at present used to arrive at optimum EP pricing. These include various forms of site licensing, separate charges based on the nature of use, volume discounting, various types of subscriptions and composite pricing through the bundling concept.

Until there are shared precepts of what represents value in EP products, it is unlikely that rational pricing policies can be developed. Pricing uncertainty is one factor hampering the traditional publisher's decision to enter the EP business. The traditional and nontraditional publishers approach EP pricing from different viewpoints. The nontraditional publishers seek to produce a profit from EP products, and the revenue must cover the full cost of the product and contribute profit. On the other hand, traditional publishers may consider EP products as a secondary revenue stream with potential incremental income. As previously suggested, revenue is expected to cover only the added cost and may even be seen as part of an investment in developing market demand. The latter means that the EP version of a product does not have to absorb the fixed cost of the creation which is then entirely borne by the original print version.

It will be argued that this pricing creates a distorted price structure for EP information. This incremental-cost approach has been associated with traditional publishers but it is increasingly common among other participants. Computer timesharing companies have demonstrated a similar pattern of behaviour in relation to online and offline products.

The unique costs associated with EP products also complicate the pricing issue. These extra costs have comparisons in print media which are rarely recognized since they are incorporated into the base price of the printed item and are never seen by the customer. The extra electronic costs are the added computer-processing charges (analogous to warehouse picking and packing) and telecommunications or network operating charges (analogous to postage or freight charge) for online services. These different characteristics require a different approach not only to cost control but also to product pricing. The differences between the two pricing systems, the uncertainty of the resolution of these differences and the resulting potential erosion of corporate earnings create another set of concerns which contribute to the caution of the traditional publisher in entering the EP business.

Publishers are therefore confronted with two choices: protect the print revenue stream by not introducing the EP alternative, or restructure product pricing so that each version contributes appropriately. The former strategy will be effective only in the short term as many publishers have already found. Price restructuring is inevitable.

An important revenue stream for magazine and newspaper publishers is advertising. EP products — especially online — have not proved to offer a suitable platform for advertising so far. By comparison, television has proved to be one of the most powerful media for advertising. Finding a way to exploit advertising revenue streams in EP products is a key issue for their development in the magazine and newspaper sectors. The issue is a complex one that relates to image quality, frequency of update, control of exposure and measurement of effectiveness. In the short term there are no obvious solutions available to the attraction of serious advertising revenue streams into EP products. However, that is not to say that this will fail to be achieved and when it does, it will provide one of the strongest market drivers for magazine and newspaper publishers to enter EP rapidly. The judgment that must be made at this time is whether or not that option will stay open if magazine and newspaper publishers remain relatively ignorant of the EP business.

EP BUSINESS IN THE USA

Data from Frost & Sullivan and Predicast indicate the online information market, the initial EP service, grew from less than US$100 million to about $1000 million between the early 1970s and 1980. Although this growth was dramatic in percentage terms, it still represented a relatively small monetary value. Major economic growth has occurred during the last ten years as another $7000 million has been added to the market. The consumer segment of this business remains small and is represented by about 5% of the present volume.

Prior to 1980 the products, sources and usage were oriented toward government and educational markets. During the 1980s the activity was broadened to include publishers and other information providers who wanted to reach a wider category of users. The number of unduplicated password subscribers for online services increased from almost 300 000 using less than 300 databases in 1975 to nearly two million subscribers using about 3500 databases by 1985. The Internet is a further good example of this growth phenomenon in various forms of online service. It has emerged from the academic and government worlds. The Internet currently has approximately 1.8 million host computers attached to it and is accessed by in excess of 30 million users. Growth in the number of users has been accelerating over the past year and has been particularly strong among commercial users. There are now almost as many commercial users as there are academic users. The services of the Internet are generally free to all users but gaining access to the Internet usually costs modest funding through a subscription and subsequent telecommunications charges. The Internet is of course international in its interconnectivity.

The size of the US EP market is difficult to accurately estimate because different researchers use different definitions for the industry. Knowledge Industry Publications Inc. estimated in 1987 that online revenues accounted for $3.7 million of the $7600 million database market.

The database segment is approximately half of the total business information industry as defined by Vernois, Suhler and Associates. In 1990 online databases were estimated to be about $6500 million or more than one-third of the total business information sector of $23 000 million. Of that total, CD materials accounted for less than $200 million and multimedia materials were too small to measure. It is suggested that the fastest growing market segments are likely to be legal, regulatory, business, scientific and technical.

Link Resources estimated that the volume of commercial electronic information was $175 million in 1979 and increased to $6300 million by 1988. These figures include credit and travel information services.

For comparison, the total US publishing industry, including advertising revenues, is about $55 000 million. EP represents only about 10% of this figure. Of the 50+ large companies that participate in EP nearly all have a strong print publishing base.

In spite of the rapid growth of the online and database segment of EP, it is important to keep that activity in perspective. There are over 90 million households in the USA. More than 95% have TV and radio. In contrast, according to Link Resources, 25% have personal computers. With respect to other electronic equipment, over 80% have VCRs and nearly 50% have answering machines. Almost 75% of those who have access to cable TV subscribe. 40% are aware of services such as Prodigy and CompuServe, but their usage is still low; only a few per cent of the households subscribe. The two million online subscribers represent a small fraction of the potential. In reality, business and education are still the primary users.

CD-ROM's early growth pattern is similar to the online database pattern. The number of available titles has increased from 25 in 1986 to over 700 in 1990. A Dataquest source estimates there are currently 3000 titles. Much of the increase has come either at the expense of online or as a duplicate resource of the online product.

Since the mid-1980s there has been a rush of traditional publishers into the CD-ROM field as the installed base of lower-cost readers grew. There was a convergence of technologies which facilitated the market development. Lower-priced computing capacity and improved CD operating and application technology combined to create a suitable system for the professional information market. As reader prices decline further, they come within reach of the home computer market.

Recent consumer-oriented product development efforts have been extensions of audio CD work. In the late 1980s Sony introduced the Data Discman, a portable CD-ROM player which combined text and graphic display with audio output. This was the most serious effort to date to provide the portability of printed material in an EP unit. Whereas 100 000 Discman units were sold in Japan within two years of its introduction, when it was introduced into the USA in 1991 less success was achieved. Since then Sony has made arrangements with a significant number of publishers to seek to increase the subject matter, and it is anticipated that the market will now grow significantly over the next few years. Most publishers' CD products have added features which differentiate them from their print origins. For example, Grolier and Britannica offer electronic encyclopaedia versions with a related-topic search feature. However, many users consider the current products as rudimentary, albeit interesting, first steps. Today 95% of these products are text-only, but the consensus is that improvements will be made in both design and quality of these EP products during the next few years.

Philips' CD-i technology, which utilizes a TV interface, extends the basic CD system by increasing its interactive capabilities.

The product proliferation caused by the different CD systems, CD sizes and computer operating platforms limits the potential market for any particular published product. This is important in the consumer market. As a result, publishers are forced to create multiple versions of products to ensure adequate market volume. That increases their development costs and decreases the attractiveness of the consumer audience as a secondary market.

With the exception of Dow Jones and a few not-for-profit institutions, the early entrants into the EP business were nontraditional publishers or individuals who left traditional publishing. Data Resources, Chase Econometrics, Wharton and CompuServe are all examples of this phenomenon.

Dow Jones is interesting because it was an exception to the behaviour of most traditional publishers. Unlike its peers, the company was already publishing in more than one medium. It maintained a teletype news service for the financial community in addition to its newspapers. According to company sources, the reporting staff were expected to submit copy for both. During the 1970s the company had begun to build electronic satellite and communications systems which would enable it to produce its newspaper products simultaneously in several plants. Philosophically, if not operationally, the company was concentrating on the information it delivered rather than its physical format. The result was the creation of Dow Jones News Retrieval Service which has grown steadily in success and led to other major EP developments for the company. It is as a result perceived as the role model for business newspaper development into EP.

In the mid-1980s traditional publishers believed CDs had significant advantages over previous electronic media and many began republishing material in that form. Others added CD versions of their electronic materials. International Data Group, through its Emerging Technology Applications Unit, gathers information from throughout the organization to repackage it for the EP market. Ziff Communications' product, ComputerSelect CD-ROM, is repackaged material obtained from several publishers. Publishers of reference material appear to have adopted the CD-ROM media quickly. Industry sources suggest that 20 000 copies of the Compton Multimedia Encyclopaedia CD-ROM have been sold to schools and libraries. Prentice Hall and Houghton Mifflin have dictionary offerings and several others, including Time Warner, have assembled similar reference and historical material for CD publication.

Consumer publishers believe there is an opportunity to successfully produce EP products. Material such Voyager's *Multimedia Beethoven: the Ninth Symphony* extend the audio CD format into that field. The first phase of this effort is well advanced using consumer reference materials. The products include dictionaries, encyclopaedias, desk references, atlases and how-to-do materials. The next phase began about three years ago and focuses on juvenile educational material. Products like Brøderbund's *Where in the World is Carmen Sandiego?* series or Interplay's *Mario Brothers* illustrate this generation. The next foreseeable phase will be children's books where graphic content has significant value. These products are the publishers' efforts to appeal to a different segment of the juvenile market. It is a segment that has historically bought books but has grown up with television, electronic games and computers. Publishers' EP product plans beyond this point will depend on how the home market evolves. None are sufficiently confident about market or technical trends to estimate the course, timing or volume of such products. For many publishers it is a high-risk investment, but one they consider not having any alternative but to make.

Traditional publishers' efforts have been limited mostly to the educational market where school boards have dictated that curricula include EP material. Even in that market the installed base of equipment is relatively small. *Publishers Weekly* estimates that there is one computer for every 22 students in the public school system, or less than a 5% penetration. CD reader penetration is much lower.

Publishers have been conservative in developing materials for a variety of reasons, including lack of familiarity, problems in obtaining rights, cost of royalties, limited market potential and the large investment required. IBM reportedly invested over $10 million in its 280 hour multimedia history product. Based on current multimedia product costs and pricing practices, it will need sales of well over $100 million to recover the full development costs.

It is not possible to quantify the relative influence of traditional and nontraditional publishing in the USA because ownership is complex and the data are limited. In several instances titles that started as nontraditional ventures have been purchased by traditional publishers. Examples are the Ziff Corporation and VNU properties in this category. Knight-Ridder's acquisition of Dialog is another example. Although there are no data summarizing EP title ownership, it appears that well over half of the online and CD-ROM titles on the market are currently owned by traditional publishers.

In contrast to the consumer market, business and industry assign tangible value to information in the USA. They recognize the alternative cost benefits of buying a service rather than developing an in-house facility. They recognize the increased productivity achieved using real-time rather than archival material. They recognize the improved decision accuracy from timely rather than historical information. As a result, industrial and institutional users have been the primary market-force driver of EP in the USA. These users are demanding even better information products and services, better in the sense that they satisfy the combination of end-user needs and expectations more efficiently and economically. Product development efforts are expected to continue in this EP market and demand is expected to grow at a rate more than twice the gross national product (GNP).

There is little evidence in the business community to suggest that EP price influences expenditure or product choice. EP revenues have grown faster during the past decade than any other comparable market. Traditional professional and scientific information also exhibited substantial growth. Slower growth in educational print media is attributed more to changing demographics than to inroads of EP. Interesting information has been developed by the Association of Research Librarians from its large university library membership. Its data suggests that basic changes in behaviour have occurred because of material price increases showing that, in spite of increasing students and faculty populations, the number of serial titles and monographs purchased by university libraries has declined. Yet expenditure level actually increased. The declines have been offset by substantial growth in interlibrary lending and borrowing. The reference driver to sources causing this change was probably EP.

Industry opinion suggests that one of the most significant changes in the next decade will be a further and increasing end-user use of EP. Advances in search and retrieval systems, more user-friendly software including graphical interfaces and improvements in the interactive capabilities of EP products will make them easier and more convenient to the user. One illustration of this phenomenon is the recent introduction of an online electronic clinical journal by the American Association for the Advancement of Science. It is priced to appeal to individual subscribers. Additional articles will be added to the file as peer reviews are completed so that the material is released as soon as it is available. In addition, the product has been designed, insofar as it is possible, so that the reader can access and use the material as if it were a conventional journal. In another project Elsevier Science is reportedly developing an experimental online journal delivery system in cooperation with several universities.

Historically, EP products have found an initial market niche which leads ultimately to their wider success. EP niches are difficult to identify in the consumer market. Several industry leaders, such as Steve Jobs, believe EP must find a major application before its sales will expand. He believes industrial training may be that application. Similarly, Jim Manzi of Lotus thinks that it will have to be a business application, probably one that contributes to improved productivity. Neither foresees a consumer information application large enough to drive a societal change in the need for EP. In a 1991 Fortune article discussing the future of personal computers, both Steve Jobs (founder of Apple and NEXT) and Bill Gates (founder of Microsoft) stressed the likely impact on business. They mentioned improved communications and increased worker productivity. They talked about likely increases in processor and storage capabilities. The principal operating change they anticipated was the growth of EP capability. However, they did not mention publishing as central to this market development. They stressed the office environment and omitted the home. They and other industry leaders stress tangible benefits from EP for the business user but tend to overlook the not intangible entertainment benefits for the consumer. Of course, it is possible that even the great achievers have some limitations on their vision which influence their overall judgment.

Some publishers believe EP products have the potential to expand the consumer audience for certain classes of material by appealing to nonreaders. They believe the addition of sound, motion and interactivity, when added to consumer reference material, children's educational material and children's entertainment materials, will enrich the presentation so that such EP products can compete with TV or electronic games. Also, they believe that EP products based on the well researched and developed inventory of print and related publishers' material will have more diversity than current software-based games. The potential extension of the present print market is a primary driver in current EP programmes coming from traditional publishers in the USA. Several nontraditional publishers, including IBM and Microsoft, have ambitious EP programmes under way, so it is in their interest to encourage the current publishing industry. However, most traditional publishers think that consumer EP will remain a secondary market until there is significant improvement in presentation equipment and content material.

THE EP BUSINESS IN JAPAN

Japanese companies in all sectors seem to be more open to techno-market experiments. Publishers as well as electronics companies apply a more pragmatic approach to new media and let users decide which products succeed, let them gain experience in understanding new technological offerings and then monitor the marketplace reaction. The Sony Walkman and Discman as well as Mavica electronic camera technology are examples of this approach. Whereas European organizations will tend to agonize over the results of market research, the Japanese company produces a prototype and lets the market decide how it will respond.

Japanese society appears also to be more receptive in its use of new technology and this applies equally to electronic publishing. Many kinds of electronic equipment are used by professionals or in the home or as add-on extras in the automotive products business. Retail stores in Japan appear to play a societal role, different from that in Europe and the USA, resembling a forum between high-tech product offerings and the consumer market. In Japanese daily life innovative technology products, particularly electronics, play a greater role and have a higher visibility than in Europe. Japanese hardware companies have been regularly introducing EP products in their home market, and launches of similar products in either the USA or Europe will typically be delayed by up to 12 months.

Japanese society has long demonstrated a profound understanding in the use of consensus relationships. Cooperative programmes and coordinating committees are common within industry sectors, across industry sectors and between the private sector and government. Partners from related industries commonly come together at the precompetitive stage to develop technologies, standards, concepts or products. Once a common platform has been established for activity, competition is no different to that in any other country, but its focus is then on product features and customer benefits as manifested by the competitive ability of the individual company.

It is intrinsic in Japanese thinking to have a perception which is strategic. Decisions are based on hard facts rather than beliefs or visionary missions. Strategic vision is used to give continuity, but real business development and implementation programmes follow step by step, taking into account past experiences and the input of information and data from trial-and-error approaches. Systematic management discipline in terms of market segmentation, market shares, competitive environment analysis and evolution of technologies and customer-related critical success factors feature more prominently in management style than in comparable European management team thinking. Virtually all key players in Japan have a longer view of marketplace development than their counterparts in the USA or Europe.

The instinctive use of consensus to enhance judgment is well demonstrated by the role of MITI — Ministry of International Trade and Industry. It is strongly involved in the process of development across industry and this is also the case in relation to consumer electronics and electronic publishing. A group 'Multimedia 2000' was founded, consisting of members of industries related to consumer electronics and EP and publishing. The Japanese government, as well as major private sector companies, regard EP as of strategic importance and consider it as a business area which will become a global business where content and creativity will be key. The intention is to encourage suppliers of consumer electronics, computers and content material to work together to make EP one of the largest businesses in the next century. All departments of government are asked to cooperate closely to prepare Japanese society and the industrial base for what are thought to be step changes in the communications infrastructure. Only now are the infrastructure processes of government in Europe beginning to come anywhere near this sense of cohesive mission demonstrated in Japan. It would suggest that further impetus is required in Europe, both to make up for lost time and to overcome the natural disinclination towards collaborative activity. Unless a greater sense of collaborative destiny can be generated in Europe, it is unlikely that European content providers, computer companies and consumer electronics businesses will be able to gain any significant role in the global marketplace for EP.

In contrast to Europe and the USA, the leading Japanese printers play a significant role in the emerging EP business. Such printers do not consider themselves as restricted to one medium, but rather see themselves as service providers in data processing, which uses a variety of technologies for the transcription of information into product. Their image is that of high-tech companies which incidentally use some technology called printing. These printers — the best examples of which are Toppan and Dai Nippon Printing — provide advice, consultancy and product development regarding all kinds of media, including optical discs, memory cards, HDTV and of course EP. They play another essential function, which is that of intermediaries between the hardware manufacturers and the conventional publishing industry, with benefit to both. Such printers are also at the centre of prototyping activity for conventional publishers wishing to experiment with EP. Further detailed information on the activities of such companies is provided in another chapter of this publication. It is a strange omission that in no European government support programme, nor so far in the support programmes of the EC, has any effort been made to encourage the development of companies with these characteristics in Europe. For a continent which developed all the modern processes of printing as we know them today, it is ironic that the transformation of these technologies for the communications industry of the 21st century should be so easily overlooked.

It should be noted that the various cooperative programmes in Japan do not exclude competition. Competition is just as severe in the Japanese marketplace as any other. Most of the major Japanese publishers are now handling electronic publications using CD-ROM and IC card in order to utilize their digitized data from traditional print publications. Although the Japanese key players belong to a community which provides a global driving force in EP publishing, it is worth noting that most of them apply step-by-step approaches rather than revolutionary market entries. The combination of a long-term vision and a short-term, low-risk trial-and-error approach is common in the attitude towards the EP market and its development. Sony has played a prominent role in technological facilitation of EP, and this has been complemented by the Japanese Electronic Publishing Association and more recently the International Electronic Book Publishers Committee under the guiding leadership of Kanji Maeda, President of Sanshusha Publishing Company. The collaboration between Sony (and other leading electronics manufacturers), Dai Nippon Printing, Toppan, and publishers in the International Electronic Book Publishers Committee represents a model for emulation in Europe. It is to be hoped that the initiative taken by the EC through the White Paper and the implementation of a high-level advisory group working in conjunction with Dr Martin Bangemann will start to create a focus for strategic thinking in relation to EP in Europe, which is so much needed at this time.

Managing EP technology — prototyping of new EP products

2
Prototyping — the key to electronic publishing product development

Roberto Minio, Brian Blunden and Anne Ankrah,
Pira International, UK

Reference is made many times in this publication to the market demand drivers which lead to EP product development. The EC-sponsored study points particularly to the need for increases in three factors — awareness, ability and willingness — on the part of publishers and users alike, to provide a sound environment for successful growth of EP business: awareness of the potential; ability to handle the technology and manage the changes required; producers' willingness to innovate and, most crucial of all, users' willingness to experiment with novelty and to buy and use new products. In this chapter, we draw on work carried out jointly by publishers, researchers and developers to illustrate how prototyping can contribute to each of these factors. Through demonstration and involvement, awareness is enhanced; the activities of developing and evaluating prototypes expose publishers and suppliers not only to the technologies,

Roberto Minio is Business Manager — Publishing Technology at Pira International and Research Manager at IEPRC (The International Electronic Publishing Research Centre) in Leatherhead, England.

Brian Blunden, Managing Director of Pira International and Chief Executive Officer of IEPRC, is one of the book's editors.

Anne Ankrah is Information Designer at Pira International.

49

techniques and processes but also directly bring to the fore business issues concerning the kinds of products being prototyped; user-centred prototyping is a means of designing products to match what users want or need.

In the business, financial and bibliographic database sectors of EP, product development focuses on information packaging, convenience of delivery and pricing structure. Reuters Business Information (RBI) is the classic model for this type of product development. For something under £500 a month such services will offer anyone with a PC a block of 'free' time to access information from leading newspapers in the UK and the USA. Services such as Reuters will integrate video database facilities into its text base products and will move progressively to offer multimedia services as the demand grows. Other similar information providers, such as FT Profile and MAID, who operate in the same client marketplace, explore continuously combinations of pricing and delivery packages which give them product differentiation. A variation of this group is On Demand Information pioneered by Graham Poulter. His approach is niche marketing of networked services for multimedia delivery. He has focused on the construction industry, offering 'one-stop-shopping' to meet information needs in that sector. The business concept is that of a facilitator-turning-publisher who manages editorially the information needs of a sector and presents solutions through cost-effective delivery and a high level of user convenience. The key to product development in this type of EP business is first to gain critical mass usage in the marketplace — often with a relatively crude product — and then to undertake incremental product development by a mixture of response to demand for increased product sophistication combined with added facilitation through technology development. A natural next stage is the acquisition and control of a critical mass of content in the selected sectors, in order to enhance and stabilize the competitive advantage over other providers to those sectors.

From the viewpoint of the user who needs information, the 'willingness' determining the decision to buy is measurable in terms of cost and benefit (of both the presentation device and the content). This is what sets the book, magazine and newspaper publisher in a development position different from that of the financial, business and bibliographic information provider. It is less easy to identify the needs of users of this publisher community and to specify products to match. The needs are less readily quantifiable and the categories of product that are so well understood in paper publishing (such as the differences between books and magazines) are hardly established at all.

It is among this publisher community where prototyping, as distinct from incremental product development and introduction, has the most to offer in facilitating successful organic entry into the EP product marketplace. In addition to contributing to growth of awareness and progress up the learning curve, the role of prototyping is to enable and test innovation within an approach of prototyping product, piloting products and services with significant groups of users and product introduction. In some cases, as with the kinds of 'need-to-know' business publishing discussed above, even prototyping can be done within the framework of marketed product, or at least involving user groups. Obviously this is particularly useful. Just such an opportunity is being taken by several of the publishing experiments that are currently being undertaken on the Internet and commercial network environments.

What then are the kinds of issues, options or decision points that prototyping can help the publisher to resolve? The overriding issue is the determination of the kind of product that best matches the user's requirements in the tasks that he/she undertakes. A particular aspect of this relates to the selection of platform for delivery of a product. Secondly, prototyping can provide a basis for investigating the feasibility of means of developing product — prototyping the process. The examples from Pira International's projects described below illustrate these two issues.

PLATFORMS AND TOOLS

A measure of real growth in these EP services will be the installed base of presentation devices in business and more particularly in the home. The situation is well summarized by a comment reported in *The Sunday Times* of 27 March 1994 from an interview with Dr Peter Horne, Group Managing Director of Apricot — a British subsidiary of Mitsubishi Electronics. Horne is reported to have said:

> Like hi-fi manufacturers we computer manufacturers are just producing players that play software. The publishers are really the people who will make money. In the long term we will become part of the information business.

Horne predicts that the PC will be the information presentation device, not only in business but also in the home. He is dismissive of the television. This is in marked contrast to the posture of Philips and, to some extent, the Sony position. From the publisher's viewpoint it matters little which presentation technology wins in developing an installed base for EP products, particularly if the publisher's product is manufactured in a way that makes it transparent to presentation demands.

Indeed, the plethora of platforms, some would argue, offers variety in the opportunities for publishers to present product. In other words, the different characteristics of the platforms offer complementary product variety. Consideration of some of the platform attributes will illustrate this point.

The Kodak Photo-CD could be said to be a platform which enables the presentation of electronic coffee table books. There are two interesting aspects to Kodak's Photo-CD which offer exploitation opportunities to the publisher. In the first place it has become a *de facto* standard through the backing it has received from Kodak. Second, Photo-CD has embedded itself into the prepress area of conventional publishing. Thus it is becoming a technology understood by the existing resource suppliers to the publisher — prepress and printers. This is a great advantage when seeking partnerships in product development.

Probably the most significant platform at the present time is the multimedia PC — MPC. The installed base of PCs continues to grow and in future most of them are likely to come with CD-ROM players attached. It is in this direction that Dorling Kindersley with Microsoft have directed their product offerings in their successful development programme. There are also the proprietary platform facilities offered by Sega and Nintendo. As market-makers in global product delivery these two players lead the field and have already made moves to enter publishing. The recent purchase by Pearson, the media combine which controls the *Financial Times* and Thames Television and holds a minority stake in BSkyB, of The Software Toolworks is particularly interesting. The Software Toolworks (TST) is a California-based enterprise and a major supplier to Nintendo and Sega. The recent press quotes by Lord Blakenham, the Pearson Chairman, and Frank Barlow, Pearson's Chief Executive, are revealing. Lord Blakenham is quoted as saying:

The Software Toolworks represents a marvellous opportunity, not only to buy an attractive stake in a market for family entertainment software, but also to bring on board some richly talented people. We still see plenty of exciting opportunities ahead for our main business, in books and newspaper publishing, but as the multimedia markets become a reality, we must grow the television and software capabilities that will be needed in the longer term to make the most of what we have.

In his comment Frank Barlow emphasized the necessity for Pearson to buy proven outside skills in addition to building them in-house in view of the competitiveness and speed of change in the US software industry. This strategy by Pearson recognizes the need for the major publishing house to achieve EP growth, both by organic development and acquisition. The Pearson posture is particularly interesting in view of the spend on interactive video games which in the USA was already in 1992 something in the region of US$5000 million. USA sales of multimedia software for home education in 1993 totalled US$154 million and are likely to reach US$1000 million by the end of the decade. 1994 USA sales of PC-based entertainment amounted to US$430 million and sales are forecast to grow at an annual 30% to 1996. Sales of CD-ROM-based software amounted to US$2600 million in 1992, a rise from US$304 million in 1988. That Pearson plan to invest in The Software Toolworks is indicative of strategic recognition of the importance of 'edutainment' and 'infotainment' software for personal computers and videogames for the future. Although TST was founded only in 1986, the company is prominent in CD-ROM development and publishing as well as being a major supplier of product to Nintendo and Sega. Thus we see here a major media publisher in the form of Pearson demonstrating a strategy of alliance through investment, assisting both the growth of the general PC market and the development of particular market-makers in the adjacent sector of games.

Other significant players in the platform business must include the Apple Powerbook, 3DO, CD-i and the many different offerings of Sony, together with other Japanese players such as JVC and Fujitsu. The challenge for the publisher is to select the appropriate platform, to structure material so that it is made easily compatible with any platform and to decide on the appropriate tools with which to generate or make the products. As an example, Voyager's Expanded Books provide a framework through which to develop an electronic book metaphor. It is a particularly easy route through which to publish if text is appropriately organized.

In this context so-called authoring tools become critical as a means of packaging the assets which a publisher owns or acquires and converting them into multimedia product for electronic publication. The task is to take the creative inspiration in an author's or editor's mind, to provide the tools to convert that inspiration into tangible product and to convey the intended concept to the reader. In a sense the term 'authoring tool' is a misnomer for in this context authoring means the total creative act from inspiration of idea, through the complete process, to product delivery. As yet the development of authoring tools is incomplete. Many of them are at this time 'home-made' or made within the companies that use them. While this piecemeal approach to authoring tools is inevitable at this time, it adds considerably to confusion in the production process. There are of course recognized tools like HyperCard and Microsoft products such as Word, Access and Multimedia Viewer. A further particularly interesting development is that of ScriptX from Kalaeda, a joint Apple/IBM project to produce multimedia tools independent of platform.

There are other tools essential to prototyping and product development in EP, e.g. project management tools. No publisher will succeed in creating complex multimedia products, which are as complicated as substantial pieces of software, without having good project management tools. Database technology is one aspect of the tools required, both for management of this process and for managing the content. If information is well structured many things can be accomplished. Database tools in multimedia production must be able to handle text, still images and video, but also many other kinds of meaningful data that could be part of the product. For example the software tool Mathematica (for 'authors' and 'readers'), which enables the embedding of active mathematical formulae within a document for manipulation and evaluation by a teacher or student or whoever. One can use databases in different ways. One can use them to store information about a document and then apply the database management as a tool to understand those documents or one can put separate pieces of information, or process such information units. Another approach is to put the document actually into the database and a further approach is to make the whole database act as a document which is what is done in using Standard Generalized

Markup Language (SGML) with such products as SGMLDB. In this area of application it must be noted that the technical documentation community in corporate publishing tends to be ahead of conventional publishing in systems development and the use of such database management tools. It is an obvious area for EP technology transfer into conventional publishing.

A further development in database management tools is that of the object-oriented database, and beyond this is the opportunity to have distributed object-oriented databases. The Object Management Group organization is doing work in this area; producing products such as Corba — Common Object Request Broker Architectures. These tools will develop to serve the rapidly changing environment for EP product development from static to continuously delivered networked architecture. Further work in this area is being developed through the project OASIS (Open Assets Storage and Interchange Support) which is a forum for publishers who want to discuss and exchange views on the issues of how to represent information that is licensable and tradable information between databases.

The connection between these issues of product development and authoring or database management tools and prototyping is twofold. The first issue to consider is, does one as a publisher know what the user wants? There really is not much point in structuring assets and holding them in databases unless one relates these issues to what the client user wants. The second point relates to the technical support required for parallel publishing. Most EP development for the publisher takes the form of parallel publishing insofar as it draws on existing content ownership. If the assumption is accepted that a publisher wishes to develop new EP products through prototyping, then an architecture to support data modelling of assets is required which lends itself to fast prototyping at least cost by the staff of a publishing house.

If a publisher has structured information, there are tools that make it easy to produce products in a simple way which can then be used experimentally to assess users' reactions. The Dynatext Electronic Book Browser is one such tool, or set of tools, and it is particularly useful if one is dealing with structured text using SGML. The Sony Electronic Book is another easy way to produce product for market experimentation, particularly if the text has been well structured.

At present there is no well defined prescriptive methodology for the development of new media products. Explorative methodologies, such as rapid prototyping techniques and user-centred design, support the evolution of highly usable state-of-the-art products and the evolution of new markets for these products through exposure to them. Pira International, in collaboration with other leading centres in Europe and supported by the EC, have employed these techniques utilizing technical skills and creativity from many sources to translate the requirements of publishers and users into marketable and market-provoking product categories. The work has investigated a broad spectrum of new media information product categories. What have remained constant are the methods employed successfully to establish and meet publisher and user requirements. A number of projects have been funded under the Research into Advanced Communication in Europe (RACE) programme, aimed at establishing the technology and services which will form trans-European networks of the future. A subset project of RACE is *Europublishing*. The overall objective of *Europublishing* is to improve the publisher's business effectiveness by coupling distributed systems for computer-integrated publishing and publication delivery systems with publishers' marketing, management and decision support systems. Part of this project investigates products and processes associated with knowledge-intensive reference works. One of the Application Pilots of *Europublishing* is aimed at developing a common communications platform for reference-work publishing, which is one of the first areas of publishing to offer a significant potential for new business through the development of electronic and new media products. The concern is to realize a platform for delivery to customers and for use by them of electronic reference works and to demonstrate the applicability of such a platform to diverse publishing products. In addition, the Application Pilot sets out to apply the common tools under development to the production of electronic reference works.

EP PROTOTYPING FOR THE BOOK SECTOR

Two kinds of publishing products addressed by an Application Pilot are Macmillan's *Dictionary of Art* and Disclosure's Financial Information Services. In what follows we describe the work and results from prototype development related to the *Dictionary of Art*.

The goal of the *Europublishing* Application Pilot has been to design, implement and evaluate an EP prototype of the Macmillan *Dictionary of Art* reference work based on selected structured content. To fulfil this goal product prototype categories have guided the experimental activity of interactive design, data visualization techniques, database structuring and mark-up (SGML) and object-network design and development. Three product prototype categories have been worked on:

- art text database,
- hypermedia dictionary of art,
- knowledge of art series.

Prototype description of the Macmillan *Dictionary of Art*

Macmillan's *Dictionary of Art* is a comprehensive, 30-volume reference work due to be published in 1995 on paper. Involving the art history community worldwide, it is one of the largest commercial book publishing projects currently in production anywhere. The impact of this publication will grow through derivative works — translations and conventional and essentially new media products for use by both professionals and the general public. The Application Pilot will develop a digital sampler demonstrating new media derivative products based on the dictionary and it will contribute improvements to the process of publishing the dictionary.

The approach made to prototype development is that of iterative design which results in a constant cycle of design, evaluation and redesign. Within this investigative framework the project programme has demonstrated an important part of prototyping, which is interactivity with the different groups involved in any EP publishing project. In the case of the Macmillan *Dictionary of Art* project these groups have included:

- Macmillan editorial and team members through workshops,
- the editor of the *Dictionary of Art* during project-specific visits,
- art historians and a variety of visiting consultants interested in the project,
- publishers able to contribute their expertise through demonstration and seminar visits,

- new media researchers and developers,
- a broad base of the communications industry and the public through demonstrations at such expositions as SMAU '92 Milano, CeBit '93 Hannover, Frankfurt Book Fair 1993 and MILIA '94 Cannes.

It is clear from past evaluations of prototype development that there is a need to tie user interaction to real data retrieval. While simulated interface interaction has been useful in the past to establish task descriptions and general requirements, we are now in a formative phase of evaluation, assessing ways in which the functionality afforded by the system may be mapped on to the intentions of the user while approaching user tasks. To evaluate both feasibility and usability there is a need to implement a system which can accommodate a vast amount of data, in terms of both database management and complexity management via the user interface.

A prototype should therefore allow users to experience the depth and breadth of the *Dictionary of Art* data, while allowing the designer to evaluate the impact that this type of interaction has on interface design decisions and database structure. This follows earlier findings of research undertaken in the project on the development of a document model, reflecting the interdependency between interface and database design during early specification and supported through object behaviour analysis.

The resulting prototype in this work is a client-server hypermedia system. The article server (in this case supplied by the Unix file system with SGML mark-up) is decoupled from the user interface (in this case the Macintosh operating system and SuperCard) while providing the user with electronic access to all articles on artists in the Macmillan *Dictionary of Art.*

The task analyses and subsequent requirements produced from this work have formed the basis for a model of interaction between art historians and art historical data. This model may be described briefly as follows.

The aim of the art historian is to present a view of history. In order to do this it is necessary to reconstruct history and to categorize phenomena on the basis that certain interrelationships exist. There are two broad ways to view these categories: the relationships either spring from *constant qualities* inherent in all artistic facts, for example time and locations, or from a *process* that is the dynamic development of certain relations, for example 'Munch painted *The Scream* because ...?'. This description ties in with the distinction between concepts and constructs, the former being relatively stable and well defined, the latter dynamic and ill-structured. Art history involves the grouping of phenomena into both concepts and constructs.

Art history is therefore concerned with relationships that can be viewed from a variety of perspectives. One level involves a description in terms of objective information, e.g. date of birth, location of birth, locations of artworks and so on. However, in considering the process by which the artwork has come about the art historian moves away from this 'factual information' into construction and hypothesis formation which involves the analysis and transformation of this objective information. The process of construction varies; these variations are characterized by different strategies.

One way to model the activity of the art historian is to say 'the user is collecting information' as in Marchionini's task model for information retrieval[1]. There is no assumption made as to why users are doing this and consequently no support for the strategies inherent in their search. Under these circumstances the most useful presentation is one of pure facts with no embellishments. This probably accounts for the success of text-based databases.

Another way to model this activity is to create an electronic environment which supports the user's context of wanting information and support his/her intentions, in terms of both well defined art-historical concepts (location, place of birth, dates etc.) *and* his/her endeavours to make sense of ill-structured webs of interrelationships. Information is not a static stand-alone commodity — a brick to be tossed from system to person that would be an 'observer construction' view of information transfer, one which has been prevalent in the design of many computer systems. In contrast, a 'user construction' perspective sees information as clay to be shaped by the perceiver[2]. The traditionally accepted information processing model of cognition has lost popularity in the light of unsuccessful cognitive modelling using computer systems. This is especially the case for 'rich knowledge intensive' domains which are ill-structured and ill-defined. Meaning exists in terms of context and common sense knowledge, both of which to date have proved to be outside the scope of computer models (with the exception of neural networks). If we are unable to model meaning, we must then provide the users with the facility to construct meaning for themselves.

Some types of knowledge organization reflect conceptual relationships more than others (i.e. biological taxonomies and geographical relations). These tend to map readily on to the observer construction perspective of knowledge transfer of factual information. However, beyond this lie issues of organization of information based more on user constructs and user perceptions reflecting user needs. Issues concerning intent, function, appropriateness, source and implication are important here. The static organization of information is not the only issue; a structure is needed for the possible approaches the user will make to the information.

A taxonomy of user styles and problem-solving approaches has begun to be developed in this prototyping project at Pira International. This taxonomy supports interface design decisions throughout iterative prototyping of product categories and complements a more knowledge-based approach to information modelling.

The goal of this work has been to create an environment to support the analysis and transformation of information. What follows describes the interface objects, along with a brief rationale for their inclusion. It is believed that this configuration manages the complexity of the problem space, that is the number of artists' entries available for viewing, and the variety of ways in which the user may wish to view them.

Prototype interface objects and why they are included

In the Application Pilot worked on at Pira International the user interacts via a single screen display. This display is divided in two. The manipulation of data is performed on the right and the result of this manipulation is presented on the left. The user's first action is to select a source of material. In this case he/she chooses the *Dictionary of Art* data. The next action is to filter this source material through a filter of his/her choice. In this case he/she might choose the 'Artists' filter.

The selected artist becomes the focus of all system operations and may be viewed in several ways, one of which is 'summaries'. When this view is selected, the layout on the right hand side of the screen is updated in terms of the summary text located at the start of each article, as well as the outline of subtopics provided for longer articles. The user may click at a specific subtopic such as 'The Blue Period' and go there in the text of the full article. Users may switch between views. If the user wishes to delete the list of artists he/she has made, he/she is now able to begin again with a clean slate. Alternatively he/she could have saved this list as a collection which is time-stamped and ready for viewing at a later date.

This scenario looks at a small part of the functionality available to the user, and a more extensive account is provided in the project report. We will consider now the interface components and their properties:

- *Composite objects:* Composite objects are representations of generic categories which may be transformed into specific instances. There are four categories each represented by one *composite object.*

- *Sources:* These are sources of material available over the network. In this Application Pilot the two available sources are the *Dictionary of Art* and images on Photo-CD (among others Jan van Eyck's painting 'The Arnolfini Wedding') .

- *Filters:* Composite objects may be passed through *filters*, which are themselves *composite objects.* This single interaction mechanism provides the user with a wealth of possibilities in terms of data transformation. *Filters* may reflect the expected hit rates of a transformation making the trade-off between recall ratios and precision ratios explicit to the user. When the user drags an object over a *filter*, an animation begins whereby the data is 'filtered in and then out' of the *filter.* This is to add credence to the metaphor and to give the user a feel for the active transformation he/she is performing on the way he/she is viewing the source data. In this prototype the following *filters* were made available: categories from the *Dictionary of Art*, with the addition of 'Works of Art' and 'New Media Products'. The active *filter* for this prototype was 'Artists':

  ○ Artists,
  ○ Art Works,
  ○ Styles and Movements,
  ○ New Media Products,
  ○ Materials, Techniques and Conservation,
  ○ Theory, Practice and Study,
  ○ Countries and Civilizations,
  ○ Sites and Cities,

○   Forms of Art and Subject Matter,
○   Architecture,
○   Decorative Arts,
○   Bibliographical Material.

● *Artists:* This object is initially a placeholder called 'New Object'. The New Object is classified by the user when they pass the *source Dictionary of Art* through the *filter* 'Artists'. Instances of artists may be added by selecting artists' names in the resulting artists' list extracted from the *Dictionary*. The artists' list is one of the *views* available to the user and is presented on the left hand side of the screen. New additions to the object added in this way automatically appear in the pop-up menu available from the history (of artists selected) option at the base of the object. This menu list is time stamped with the date and time of the *composite object's* creation and the last name to be added is presented in the object description, which is currently visible at the top of the object. That is to say, the object becomes a representation of the last selected artist either from the *Dictionary's* list of artists or from the menu itself. *Artists instances* may in the future be transformed via *filters* and these are presented to the user via the selection of *views*. The *artists* object may be deleted by putting it into the bin, after which the user is returned to the original placeholder 'New Object'.

● *Collections:* Users may wish to keep permanent copies of *composite objects* such as 'artists' with a particular selection of artists. This may be done by dragging the object to the *collections object,* which may be named appropriately for future reference. It is envisaged that collections may be viewed in a workspace other than that outlined in this prototype. This would support users' individualized strategies in analysing and synthesizing the information that he/she has browsed and collected. This workspace will not have the same constraints in terms of design decisions taken to reduce complexity, i.e. number of windows open at one time. Here the user would be more in charge of his/her own data management on the basis he/she has already filtered the data to a manageable degree prior to moving to his/her workspace.

● *Views: Views* represent the range of perspectives a user may choose from which to view the object of their attention (for example the representation of Picasso). *Views* are different to the *filters* already described in so much as they are switched between more frequently; they provide qualification of the operations supported by *filtering* and as such remain under separate control. *Sources* have associated *views*, which are the most appropriate for their particular properties. The *Dictionary of Art* as *source* has five *views*.

- *List:* There is a scrolling list of artists in the *Dictionary of Art*. The user can view chunks of this list alphabetically. This aids access to the vast number of names in the list. When a name on the list is selected that artist automatically becomes the focus of all other operations.

- *Summary:* The introductory text is found at the beginning of each article, along with the contents list for the article. This is particularly useful for longer articles such as Picasso, and it gives a good overview of how the article has been structured; the user may click on items in the contents list to go to an appropriate point in the article (article view).

- *Bibliography:* This provides the bibliographical information cited at the end of an article.

- *Cross-reference:* A list of explicit cross-references within the body of the article is included.

- *Article:* The whole article is presented. Users are able to select the *view* of their choice via a floating palette (a small window, independent of the main displays which may be positioned as desired). A panning camera is used as a metaphor in order to convey the idea of different perspectives on the same data. Movement from left to right maps on to increasing degrees of document disclosure. Each view is colour coded and the presentation area of the left hand side of the screen is updated in terms of this colour on user selection. It is possible to display a view of an artist's entry by dragging this object on to the presentation area, set at a particular *view*.

- *Find function:* If the activity of the user is differentiated in terms of browsing and searching, the objects mentioned above support a flexible form of browsing with less emphasis on directed search, although the data remain in context. So, for example, while looking for an artist called Robert Adams the user is exposed to other artists near Adams' name and to the fact that there are two Robert Adams represented in the *Dictionary*. An alternative to this approach is to move straight from a blank screen to the chosen artist but keeping information in context is preferable to hiding it from the user. Users can get a feel for the size of the database, and the nature of its coverage, and they can select their choices by pointing at entries they know exist rather than by typing in queries for what may be a negative response. However, to support a more directed type of information retrieval, a 'find function' has been included. Find is restricted to looking for the request in the view currently presented.

- *Size:* The size of an article may be accessed at any time and from any view. The size of the article may affect user action — whether they view an article in full or as a summary, view it now or later. *Composite objects* and *views* are in fact all filters of one sort or another. *Filters* passing through *filters* support the transformation of data in an infinite number of ways depending on the available database structure underneath; they also provide the user with a simple means to define and redefine their problem space, reflecting their active construction of this space by the delimitation of another. This supports a close mapping of intention on to functionality. Because a visible and reversible history of this filtration process is provided, users have the freedom to explore a vast amount of data in a way which is supported by the rapid access characteristic of the electronic medium *and* without fear of being overwhelmed by or lost in the complexity of the system. Many sources of information may be integrated without losing the integrity of the context from which they have come.

Emulated database functionality

In the Application Pilot a collection of software tools were written as part of the process of building the retrieval functionality of the prototype. The base of material on which the tools operate in this Application Pilot comprises over 11 000 computer files and occupies some 66 megabytes of storage. Each file contains a marked-up article destined for the Macmillan *Dictionary of Art.* The number of files represents approximately one-quarter of the articles being prepared. Three-quarters of the articles are biographies of artists.

Various lists of terms were extracted from the texts of all articles, namely:

- article titles,
- artists' names,

- nationalities,
- noles (eg 'mezzotint engraver'),
- titles of works of art.

The retrieval functionality was focused on the artists' list, for which file identifiers were retained so as to provide indexes into the file store.

Structural analysis

Dictionary of Art articles comprise components such as sections, headings, bibliographies and author's signature. Each article is stored in an individual computer file along with items such as figure captions and head references that belong with it, plus some labelling and statistical data that is not destined for publication. Components may have subcomponents nested within them, for example a section may contain a heading, a table of contents, and a sequence of subsections. The order in which components occur is mainly fixed, and many components are optional. These structural components and relations can be recognized by a combination of tags, context and the internal syntax of components. Automatic structural analysis of an article file consists of recognizing its components and their organization and building in computer memory a model of the structure which can be output in a variety of forms.

One application of this has been to process one article file at a time and output a summary of the structure in the form of a table of contents, but without any of the actual content of the article. Repeated items such as paragraphs and bibliography entries are not mentioned one by one, but counted and given as a total for the section in which they occur.

Text extraction

The programs for text extraction and presentation form a set of tools which can be fitted together in many combinations, the output of one becoming the input of the next. Thus the commands embodied in the SuperTalk scripts are typically compound commands involving three or four of these programs linked together by a command.

Once portions of text have been extracted, further processing is needed in order to present them in a readily readable form. For example, one operation is to map specially encoded characters to sensible counterparts where available in the basic ASCII set. This deals with accented characters, hyphens and dashes, arithmetic symbols, different sizes of space etc.

Two further simple presentation processes were provided for specific types of content. The first takes a list of headings and indents it according to the levels of the headings. This allows clear and complete tables of contents to be displayed for longer articles. The second reinstates the initial capital letter in phrases currently marked for small capitals. This allows explicit cross-references occurring in an article to be listed.

A third type of process is needed because text is transferred (with its Unix operating system) from the Sun to the Macintosh and the two systems have different conventions for marking ends of lines. A program carrying out the necessary conversion therefore completes the set of tools related to presentation.

Articles in the *Dictionary of Art* vary greatly in length, from a single paragraph to many pages. It is often therefore helpful to users to be given an estimate of the amount of material available before they actually retrieve all or part of it. Similar estimates will also be useful to support automatic presentation and layout decisions in future. A further program was therefore incorporated in the prototype, which gives the size of an article in terms of the number of lines.

Local communication between Sun and Macintosh

The prototype system at Pira International is a client-server hypermedia system with database emulation. The database functionality (supported by the Unix file system with SGML mark-up) is decoupled from the user interface (in this case the Macintosh operating system and Supercard) while the user is provided with electronic access to all articles on artists in the Macmillan *Dictionary of Art*. Communication between the two is based on the Ethershare software product, which makes the Unix file system of the Sun visible to the Macintosh. It does not, however, provide a facility for command execution on the Sun from the Macintosh. A command server program was therefore written to run on the Sun, using the 'named pipe' facility of Unix, so that arbitrary operations can be carried out. In the prototype the issuing of the commands and the reading back of the results are embodied in SuperTalk scripts and are thus completely transparent to the human user.

Object-network user-interface scenario

In this prototype we concentrated on the end-user interface of the hypermedia *Dictionary of Art* for the art historian. It shows a proto-typical session containing search, comparison and extraction of material, supported by an object network.

We also concentrated more on the searching/browsing functionality than on the consumption of the material (reading text/viewing images) because it is more affected by the enormous amount of material available.

The enhanced structuring of the material in the object net enables the reader to search for any combination of objects, taking into account the relations between objects and their attributes, that express the user hypotheses/constructs described in an exemplar fashion. Although much work still has to be dedicated to the generic tools to build up the object network from the articles, the separation of logical content and graphical presentation enabled us already to produce a graphic design of the interface and a plan of the basic functionality and some metaphors to be employed. From this proto-type we hope to gain insight into how to provide the user with all the search functionality that is possible on the object net.

Considering the characteristics of art historians' activities, the ill-structured open-ended tasks they have to perform (user and task profiles) seem to be the most appropriate solution. To support this search style, as much information as possible about the retrieved objects has to be supplied and their direct comparison had to be supported. The result of every query is therefore displayed graphi-cally in order to show the diverse relations among the retrieved objects vividly and to match the presentation quality of a sophisti-cated print product. Consequently, we planned an incremental graphic retrieval based on graphical browsers instead of, or complementary to, a text-based query language. Thus the reader can interact natu-rally with the presentation of his/her query and proceed in specifying his/her requests during the search.

In our work we have studied the interaction paradigms with a graphical browser supported by an intelligent layout mechanism.

Scenario description

In the browser we show graphical objects that represent the retrieved content — objects of the object net with links to an article, a special element within an article, for example a picture. The reader can either access the actual content through these graphical objects or use them to change the presentation of the current selection by displaying different links/attributes, or he/she can formulate another query that results sometimes in a new browser with different content.

In the following a detailed example of an iterative graphical query is given. Our prototype consists of such examples and proposes basic query operations and their realization as graphical interactions.

Query example

An art historian who wants to know about Picasso's formative period and early influences begins by entering the artist 'Picasso'. Next he/she wants to see all artists who have influenced Picasso. There are two ways to achieve that. First, select the graphical object 'Picasso' which means 'add object with relation to Picasso' and then pick from a dialogue which of the relations should be the criterion for adding. If the range of the relation does not unambiguously determine the type of the objects to be added (as in the case where Picasso can have an 'influenced by' relation not only to persons, but also to works of art, styles etc.), the user has to choose the object type from another dialogue. The second possibility is to drag the 'artists' item from the menu of the object types down into the browser and put it on top of the 'Picasso' object. Thus the user would declare that he/she wants to add artists with a relation to Picasso to the display and only the type of relation would have to be specified through a dialogue.

The browser then generates the information graphically. At this point the user chooses another presentation to see which influences fall into the early periods of Picasso's work. As the objects determine the relational information that can be displayed, the menu of object times can also be used to determine the kind of relations the user is interested in (the aspects of the presentation). Here, the user selects the 'time event' item from the menu of object types and adds it to the aspects of the presentation. From this timeline view the user removes the part that belongs to the later periods of Picasso's work and at the same time adds to the works of art that are mentioned in the articles in the context of influences on Picasso.

Prototype Evaluation

The overall goal of our prototype evaluation work has been to identify specific requirements and this has been accomplished jointly by the developers, users, designers and publishers. We have now moved into a more formative phase of evaluation[3], assessing ways in which the functionality afforded by the system may be mapped on to the intentions of the user while approaching his/her tasks. We have chosen an evaluation technique particularly suited to this type of investigation; this is called Cooperative Evaluation[4]. The following provides an overview of this methodology.

Cooperative Evaluation

Cooperative Evaluation is cited by the UK Department of Trade and Industry in their *Usability Now* handbook of evaluation methods for electronic systems[5]. What makes this method distinctive is the collaboration it facilitates between designers and users when they evaluate the system together. This is not the case if a specialist human-factors expert performs the evaluation or if the evaluator takes on the role of a detached experimenter. This technique is founded on the belief that qualitative data of a specific type can on their own provide comprehensive guidelines for system refinements.

So what type of data is required? The interaction of the user with the system may be conceived as a series of three mappings:

- The user has a set of goals or intentions which must be mapped on to a set of possible actions he/she may take with the system. The user's perception of the system via the system's image will guide this mapping.
- The next mapping is from this set of actions to some set of possible effects on the system.
- The effects on the system must be made visible to the user so that they may be mapped back on to his/her intentions. The user's actions may then be perceived as successful or as a failure.

On the basis of this model of interaction Wright and Monk propose that a full account of the user's interaction must contain *both* the user's behaviour with the system and the intentions of the user when taking these actions. The inclusion of intentional context as well as observed behaviour is a key feature of this evaluation technique.

In Cooperative Evaluation the user works through a set of pre-defined tasks designed to test specific aspects of the system. For this evaluation the tasks selected were to investigate the intentions and behaviour of the user when performing different types of comparisons (a key activity for the art historian). Comparison types were differentiated in terms of the immediacy associated with making a comparison on the basis of the data after the data had been found. Was the comparison immediate or was it delayed? Were these variations in behaviour/intention supported by the system or not?

The procedure followed while applying this technique is outlined below.

Method

- *Recruit users:* A single user was recruited for the evaluation reported here. She was an art historian and computer novice.
- *Prepare tasks:* A summary of the tasks is as follows:

  ○ The user was requested to imagine she was reviewing the *Dictionary of Art*; it is the first time that she has seen it and her overall goal is to gain a representative impression of it. First she was to determine the scope of the *Dictionary* using the system, and to determine whether it covers a wide number of artists.

  ○ She was then to select 10–20 artists she felt would be a good test of the *Dictionary's* coverage and treatment of artists. She was required to determine the length of each article and to describe and compare the types of summaries, bibliographies and explicit cross-references each article had.

  ○ She should then select two artists whom she felt were similar in some way and use the articles on them to demonstrate this similarity to the other evaluator.

  ○ Finally she was requested to view the Jan van Eyck article and then to select a 'new media' monograph on the artist's famous painting 'The Arnolfini Wedding'. This brought up the 'The Importance of Detail in Art History' application. She was requested to browse this, paying particular attention to the 'Dictionary of Art' option in the menu. This option brought up an alternative presentation of the Jan van Eyck article, along with a 'guide' through which to access references to the painting in the article.

○ After a break the user was requested to sum up how this experience had been different to a paper-based search/browse and to assess the usability of the system.

- *Interact and record:* A video recording was made of the session which provided both audio and visual records of the interaction. The interaction between the coevaluators was guided by a question and answer technique involving three activities — first, the user was requested to think aloud, saying what she was trying to do and what she had expected the system to have done. She was also requested to ask for advice at any part of the evaluation, and finally the coevaluator (designer) would ask her questions during the session to find out what she was doing and why she was doing it. The designer took notes throughout the session.
- *Formulate recommendations:* Cooperative evaluation recommends the selective analysis of both verbal and behavioural data. It is suggested that the evaluator focuses on two specific types of evidence for problems at the interface — critical incidents and breakdowns. A critical incident has occurred when the user chooses a suboptimal route through which to fulfil her intentions. An efficient way will have been provided by the designer and the functionality is available through this, however the user fails to use it. Breakdowns are key concepts in understanding how we interact with the world[6]. Normally when we are performing a task we focus our attention on that task and not the tools we are using to complete it . For example, if you are hammering a nail you are aware of hammering. However if you hit your thumb while hammering your attention shifts from the task to the properties of the tool. 'A breakdown can be classified as any instance where the user's comments indicate that the system has become part of their subjective experience'[4]. The evaluation session in the Application Pilot described these two types of data and five measures traditionally associated with usability[7].

Conclusions

Aims and objectives

The overall aim of this prototype was to allow the user to experience the depth and breadth of the Macmillan data, while allowing the designer to evaluate the impact that this type of interaction has on interface design decisions and database structure. More specifically, we have been assessing ways in which the functionality afforded by the system may be mapped on to the intentions of the user as he/she approaches their tasks.

For this evaluation the tasks selected were to investigate the intentions and behaviour of the user when performing different types of comparisons (a key activity for the art historian).

The results of the evaluation have been very positive. The interaction mechanism of *filters*, *views* and *composite objects* was extremely learnable and supported the user's behaviour in terms of browsing articles in the *Dictionary* on artists and comparing them. The evaluation was focused on the tasks at hand as opposed to the system and the occurrence of breakdowns was minimal, relating mostly to the user's newness to a computer environment as opposed to the interaction design.

Although a number of critical incidents were observed during the user evaluation session, these were at the beginning and their absence was indicative of the degree of learnability afforded by the interface. This is backed up by the usability ratings. These ratings also reflect the need to extend this interface in terms of functionality where average scores for utility and effectiveness were related to the restrictions placed upon the user in terms of categories to search and presentations to view.

- *Recommendations for design:* Recommendations may be formulated from either a system perspective or a user-centred perspective (Cooperative Evaluation[4]). The perspective selected will affect the design solution suggested by the evidence. Selecting an appropriate perspective is as important as selecting a solution.

Key concepts

A summary of key concepts identified through this evaluation is as follows:

- *Chunking:* The chunking of text into fixed and manageable portions for screen presentation and navigation is essential.
- *Guides:* This idea supports navigation through the text in a specific context. However, the context in which the article was originally written is always available to the user.
- *Colour management:* Support is required for colour calibration and maintenance of consistency over different delivery systems. This is an important issue for networked multimedia.
- *Object behaviour analysis:* This procedure has supported the development of what is perceived as a single moded environment. Moded environments are characterized by the same user actions performing different functions in different modes (often criticized as poor design). In this prototype different objects perform different functions via the same user action in a single all-inclusive interface mode. This mode allows the user to arrange concepts cognitively via the outcome of his/her actions. A *single interaction mechanism* is supported via interchangeable composite objects i.e. filtering.
- *Reference Work Object:* Many objects of relevance have been identified during our work, for example, works of art and dates of birth. This evaluation has suggested that the most important object of relevance for a user browsing and using the *Dictionary of Art* is in fact the 'reference work' object. This is the context which all other material is made meaningful, i.e. summaries, cross-references and so on. One comment made by the user was that, while the summary view was useful to identify the structure of longer articles (via the generated contents list), the introductory text was not packed with the concentrated information that she had expected. Her expectations were based on smaller dictionaries, whose main purpose is to present this sort of summarized information. Taking this information out of the context of the whole article was not as successful as expected. As a major reference work, the *Dictionary of Art* has certain properties which should be reflected in its presentation.
- *Object-network interface scenario:* Diagrams should make information that is implicitly contained in the data — in our case information about the relations between objects — explicit by making them visible. An explicit graphical statement can be the grouping of elements, their ordering along an axis or their connection by a line etc., and the whole organization of the diagram can be

understood as a series of these statements. If these statements reflect facts in the data correctly, the presentation is meaningful; if these facts are relevant to the user's task, the presentation is useful.

Future plans

Our goal is to apply knowledge gained from this prototype and specification to product design. This will result in a series of product showcases delivered on CD-ROM and CD-ROM XA, as well as a product designed for network delivery.

The next stage of our endeavours will be to extend our distributed framework for communications by using ISDN to support LAN-to-LAN routing. In this way the interface outlined in the prototype may be employed to access the *Dictionary of Art* data from remote sites within the UK, Germany and the Netherlands. Further collaboration between the Gesellschaft für Mathematik und Datenverarbeitung (GMD), Germany, and Pira International is planned to merge object-net technology and interaction design.

EP PROTOTYPING FOR THE NEWSPAPER SECTOR

Another example of prototyping is that of a further RACE project entitled *Telepublishing*. This project has been coordinated by DETECON (Deutsche Telepost Consulting GmbH — a subsidiary of Deutsche Bundespost TELEKOM). This project has been under the leadership of Dr Volker Reible of DETECON GmbH.

Communication is the key to publishing, both for production and for delivery. The *Telepublishing* project sets out to be a demonstrator of digital publishing in Europe. Exploiting the combination of modern telecommunications and information technology, the project, jointly funded by the EC and industry, addresses real requirements of the European printing and publishing sectors. Transnational communications have been used to connect editorial, production and printing sites across Europe, providing the distributed infrastructure for a number of applications.

One pilot application within the *Telepublishing* project has been that of the Individualized Electronic Newspaper (IEN). Before attempting to develop prototype facilitation, this project investigated the existing arrangements for the creation of a local newspaper, the production requirements of the editorial part of a regional newspaper and the communications requirements. The work was reported under the *Telepublishing* project deliverable document[8]. This preliminary work identified the newspaper industry's problems from competition with other media, notably television and radio, and also identified a number of thematic issues which needed to be addressed such as text and image integration, transfer of text, image archives and transporting digital images. Further work on this project has been publicly reported[9]. It has been explained that the Individualized Electronic Newspaper (IEN) application pilot comprises both the overall publication process and the reader's access and use of the IEN. A central objective is to demonstrate that in a broadband environment, the production of individualized and electronic publications is technically feasible, and could also be economically feasible. The IEN is an experimental publication which is composed and individualized on demand for a reader, and then delivered electronically. In contrast to individualized fax delivery of single selected articles, the IEN emphasizes the newspaper's function and image that must be reflected in appropriate layout and presentation. In contrast to teletext-style bulletins, adequate user interfaces can now be built to support acceptable and preferred styles of presentation and interaction for readers. The content of the IEN is automatically selected according to a profile of the reader's particular interests from a continually developing pool of 'up-to-the-minute' articles and features. To exploit fully the possibilities offered by broadband for electronic delivery communications, the reader can receive the IEN both as a printable and as a hypermedia product. For a printable product the reader receives automatically composed page descriptions which can be locally printed on paper with the appearance of a conventional newspaper with respect to appropriate layout and presentation of the individually selected contents, including images of advertisements. A fully integrated hypermedia product can also be accessed on a multimedia computer terminal or notebook. In addition to enhancing articles with high quality images, animations and video, the IEN increases current newspaper functionality. It offers access to background material, to databases of classified advertisements, as well as enabling the publisher to provide extended news and related services.

The Application Pilot

The Application Pilot comprises both the publication process (content acquisition, editing and value-adding, production and delivery) and the publication use. The central objective of the IEN Application Pilot has been to indicate that the production of individualized publications is technically feasible and could also be economically feasible in a broadband environment. To achieve this goal, the Applications Pilot has combined two technologies: structured document manipulation tools and knowledge-based systems.

The main idea has been to store the information in, and related to, a daily newspaper in electronic form as so-called structured documents. The description of the material as structured documents comprises the detailed structure of each constituent as well as attributes describing all aspects of future use, e.g. retrieval, layout, presentation. These structured documents serve as a database for the knowledge-based production tools, which perform the automatic production of the individual newspaper issues.

IEN content acquisition

To enable the reuse of material that is electronically available, IEN editors have access to a number of external sources delivering electronic content. They have the tools to convert and restructure the incoming information according to the requirements of their publishing environment.

IEN editing and value-adding

Creating content and adding value to electronic publications demands qualitatively enhanced support for the tasks of the editors. The Editor's Workbench supports the different tasks to be performed for the creation of structured IEN constituents. This includes text and image editing, translation for the multilingual edition and keeping track of article versions. In addition, the Workbench offers means for the establishment of hypermedia links between individual parts of the newspaper (linking) as well as for the specification of the article descriptors for retrieval and presentation purposes (classifying). Preview components enable editors to visualize the effect of his/her specifications and decisions. The Editor's Workbench is linked to a local database containing images and structured documents on which the editor is working, to external information systems for content acquisition and to the IEN archive. Material ready for publication is stored in the 'Pool' of IEN 'Constituents'.

IEN production and delivery

The Pool of IEN Constituents functions as an interface between contributors and readers. It holds the current news articles, pictures and advertisements, background information for topics discussed in the newspaper, e.g. original material such as complete transcripts of interviews, scientific reports, magazine articles, and reference works. The Pool is realized as a structured document base (SDB) and thus serves the databases of the knowledge-based production tools. The 'Content Composer' uses the Pool to select the content of the individual newspaper issue according to the reader's profile. Depending on the choice of media, either a Print Layout Composer delivers an individual print-out of the newspaper issue, following the publisher's layout style, or a Hypertext Presentation Composer generates a hypermedia IEN for specific systems, e.g. HyperNeWS, according to their different presentation specifications.

IEN front page

The IEN demonstration front page is composed for a reader with an interest in current affairs and a special interest in science. While it is made to look much like a traditional newspaper cover page, its functionality is to provide access to a hypermedia IEN: its different multimedia contents, the background information and the extended services. According to his/her mood and information purpose, the reader can choose to flip pages one by one by clicking the arrows. He/she may reach sections of his/her interest directly or make use of the lexicon look-up by pressing the bullet buttons in the contents bar.

In the Application Pilot of the IEN there is an article on 'Fusion fraud' containing new developments on the topical issue of cold fusion. It provides the reader with different background material. Clicking the buttons on this presentation will reveal a chronicle of events, i.e. a series of published articles dealing with this topic (background); transcript of an interview, which may eventually be shown as a video (interview); a collection of bibliographic references (literature); and a number of controversial contributions acquired directly by electronic mail (Netnews).

The IEN is a prototype which seeks to exploit the potential of customized electronic delivery. In this example a traditional newspaper metaphor has been used to guide the reader's interaction with the application. In some ways this is useful and in some other ways it is misleading as the application can support quite different interactions to those of the conventional paper-based presentation. As already noted, electronic delivery of information supports new ways of interacting with the information. This example shows that by moving away from traditional metaphors this new interaction may be exploited more fully. It will be a trade-off in terms of the users' familiarity with the old presentation and their ability to adapt to the new interactions. Once again, good layout supported by user-centred design and rapid prototyping techniques can bridge the gap between user expectations and system possibilities.

Problems of prototyping development in the newspaper sector

The role of the future newspaper has been discussed by the Pira International project team in its report to Comprint[10]. In that report the observation is made that the traditional role of the newspaper needs to be developed to reflect today's complex societal needs for information. Trading companies, government and public utilities all require local information networks (for collection and distribution of information) and these potential clients budget expenditure for this purpose. The issue is how the newspaper business can gain an increased share of those expenditures by managing information networks locally, nationally and internationally — through the use of technology complementary to that currently used for the print-on-paper product. This raises another issue of EP in the newspaper business and it is the important difference in business characteristics between various newspaper categories. Worldwide, there is a community of prominent business newspapers which probably does not exceed 20 in number. These newspapers are significant as opinion formers and as a channel for exchange of judgment on business and financial issues current in the global business community. Clearly there is a relationship between the role of these newspapers and their opinion-forming influence and that of organizations offering database services to the financial and business community. The business development strategy for this community of newspapers will require quite different prototyping facilitation to the rest of the newspaper industry.

There are also those newspapers which are either national or of wide regional influence, and the content which they own and may utilize through EP for parallel publishing purposes is valuable. These are information-rich communities and they have much in common with the information-rich environment described in this chapter when reporting experimental work in prototyping on the *Dictionary of Art*. However, it is questionable whether either the proprietors or the editorial community in this type of newspaper have yet fully realized the potential of development through prototyping to exploit these information-rich resources.

Another distinct community in the newspaper business spectrum is that of the local newspaper. While it might be argued that newspapers in general are an editorial device for the sales of advertising, this cryptic observation would apply particularly to the local newspaper. The local newspaper is an important societal element in local communities. Unfortunately, such local newspapers are often the least well equipped with in-depth management resources to consider how to develop their business function in the community for the future. They are essentially local players, yet they require a global perspective in terms of the enabling technologies which will be available to them to transform their future business. They represent the classic community in publishing, which must distinguish between being in 'the railway business or the transportation business'. Unfortunately most of the prototyping being undertaken currently in this community assumes them to be in the 'railway' business.

PROTOTYPING IN THE CONSUMER MAGAZINE SECTOR

In 1993 Donald Kummerfeld, President of the Magazine Publishers Association of America, in his speech to the German Magazine Publishers Association, indicated growing international awareness of the opportunities for periodical publishers to develop new media products.

In addition, the recent EC-sponsored study about opportunities for publishers in the European information services market recommended the encouragement of alliances between publishers, hardware and other facilities suppliers such as those concerned with cable delivery and telecoms. The same study identified periodical publishers as a significant community in Europe and a sector in which electronic publishing would probably play an increasing role. As already noted, there is steady growth in presentation platforms for consumers to use electronic publishing products in the home. Concurrent with the growth of the installed base of presentation devices for the home by hardware manufacturers, there is much activity in cross-media ownership which has implications for leading periodical publishers. At the same time two further developments are occurring:

- Television programmes, for example about automotive developments or food or drink, which resemble the characteristics of a consumer magazine.
- Technology convergence which is making the editorial direction of magazine publishing similar to the editorial management in the production of television programme series.

What is needed therefore at this time by periodical publishers, hardware suppliers and suppliers of network delivery systems is a feasibility study — through prototyping to define consumer EP products likely to have appeal in the family environment. It is also necessary to examine the feasibility of periodical publishers producing such material from existing products, but in electronic format, which leads to the consideration of experimentation with 'bundled products' placed in the European market place to assess purchasing reaction by consumers. The term 'bundled product' in this context describes an electronic publishing product delivered as CD-ROM, as CD-i or by cable at regular time intervals, which would have within it material that would appeal to all members of an average family.

At the time of writing IEPRC has initiated, in consultation with the EC, a major prototyping feasibility investigation with consumer magazine publishers to develop this concept. The prototyping feasibility study sets out to gain preliminary understanding of production requirements, means of handling electronic advertising, reaction to pricing structures and assessment of the concept of a regular bundled EP consumer product. The objectives of this prototyping study are to:

- select an experimental bundled product, based on material already available to the participating publishers, for preliminary evaluation when delivered to the home as a consumer product,
- explore the feasibility of producing experimentally a model edition of such an electronic product to be used by the editorial staff of periodical publishing companies,
- evaluate the development needs in editorial tools for publishing companies, hardware manufacturers and cable companies for producing the single edition,
- explore the feasibility of parallel experimentation via physical delivery of CD-i and delivery of the same content material via other means such as cable,
- evaluate the first reaction of a sample of European families to such a product in terms of usability, pricing, enhancement and motivation to buy.

Participation in such collaborative prototyping programmes does not exclude concurrent experimentation by individual companies — the two things are complementary. Participation in prototyping may lead either to continued collaborative work or to individual company product development at a later stage. The central issue of market demand creation is also assisted by this process of prototype development. As the market for new media products from periodical publishers must be created, it requires effort greater than that which can be achieved by any single publisher. Thus there is an argument of unique benefit which may be derived from collaborative prototyping programmes in this sector. In addition, in periodical publishing the professional staff must be given opportunity to move up the learning curve in understanding the many different facets of electronic publishing products. Collaborative prototyping projects are an economic way of doing this; they bring the benefits of knowledge sharing at a precompetitive stage. All experimental development projects contain risk; too often that risk causes the project team to insist on claiming positive results and therefore arguing for continuation of the work. Collaborative projects in new media make it easier for companies or groups within companies to exit from such prototyping experimentation without obligation.

This IEPRC-initiated project will be managed by Pira International and will run under the acronym EP-FAMPUB (Family Publishing). The scope of the kinds of new media consumer electronic products is as vast as the collection of available buzz words e.g. individualized, virtual, networked, hypermedia etc. As a starting point EP-FAMPUB is focused on the notion of the 'bundled' consumer product for the family. The notion of this bundled product is 'to provide something for everyone in the family'. It is assumed that such a broad base of interest will be required to create adequate demand to motivate purchasing for a consumer product of this type. It exploits the ease with which different content can be combined in one electronic product; moreover, it is particularly appropriate as a starting point because it provides a testbed for the reuse of existing content that publishers already own. Thus, in feasibility prototype experimentation with such a bundled product there are two broad areas of investigation required. The first relates to production and internal issues of concern to the magazine publishers. The second set of issues relates to market reaction to such a new type of publishing product. EP-FAMPUB will seek to explore these two areas to the level of elucidating them as issues. Again the parallel can be seen here between the principles involved in researching properly an EP product in consumer magazines and that knowledge which has been derived already from the research undertaken into the Macmillan *Dictionary of Art* and its interfacing structures with the user community. For the successful design and publication of new media products by consumer magazine publishers, many issues need to be understood. For example:

- What are the options for including advertising bedded in electronic products?
- Can existing editorial material be used in electronic products?
- Can the same staff work on both paper-based and electronic products?
- What kind of tools are required?
- Can archive material be reused and sold onwards?
- Can electronic products seek to have their own style and form?
- What standards need to be supported?
- What is the feasibility of producing multi-lingual editions?
- Can CDs contain material only accessible to the user with a special key?

Much of what needs to be known about such issues cannot be gained from market research. Similarly, the crude production of pilot products does not yield adequately reliable information. EP-FAMPUB will give rise to these kinds of issues through a properly structured prototyping feasibility study. Other information — such as obtaining user reaction to electronic products, the relevant effectiveness of electronic advertising, the cost benefit of different production approaches — will require more extensive piloting of products and processes. Such work will be implemented through an extension of a feasibility prototyping study or will be the subject of one or more goal-orientated pilot projects in a second phase, which can be undertaken once the understanding of the issues has been built up both in the project and in the individual companies during the initial research phase.

SOME OBSERVATIONS IN CONCLUSION

A recurring central theme in discussion of the EP business is the need to generate market demand. The challenge to create market demand for products which do not exist is immense. Classic market research has little to contribute in this situation. Conceptualizing new EP products is not only a user problem, it is also a problem for those who wish to produce and deliver them. The learning curve in many publishing houses is severe — not to mention the prejudice which is either antagonistic to diversification into EP or unduly enthusiastic. Under these circumstances the obvious way forward is experimentation with prototype products. Facilitators are required for such experimentation and these are available. However, a word of caution is required, because facilitation to prototyping does not mean simply producing the product the publisher has in the form of a disc or any other EP manifestation. Such an approach is to misunderstand and to undervalue prototyping in an irresponsible way. Participation in prototyping should be seen as a means of developing strategy towards EP, whether it is to build a knowledge base from which to pursue acquisition or to develop organic growth within an existing business. The publishing house which has not developed a philosophy towards prototyping has probably not grasped the principles behind either the challenge or the opportunity which exist in the marketplace through EP for the future.

REFERENCES

1   **Marchionini, G** 'Evaluating hypermedia-based learning' *in* **Jonassen, D H and Mandl, H (Eds.)** *Hypertext/Hypermedia for Learning. Proc. NATO Advanced Research Workshop* Springer, Germany (1990)

2   **Dervin, B** 'Information as a user construct: The relevance of perceived information needs to synthesis and interpretation' *in* **Ward, S A and Reed, L J (Eds.)** *Knowledge Structure and Use: Implications for Synthesis and Interpretation* Temple University Press, PA, USA (1983)

3   **Hewett, T T and Scott, S** 'The use of thinking-out-loud and protocol analysis in development of a process model of interactive database searching' *in* **Bullinger, H J and Shackel, B (Eds.)** *Human-computer Interaction – Interact '87* Amsterdam: North Holland (1987)

4   **Wright, P C and Monk, A F** *Cooperative Evaluation: the York Manual Version 1.0 (Technical Report)* Dept of Psychology, University of York, UK (1991)

5   *A Guide to Usability* The Open University, Milton Keynes, UK (1990)

6   **Winograd, T and Flores, F** *Understanding Computers and Cognition* Addison Wesley, Reading, MA, USA (1987)

7   **Bennet, J L** 'Managing to meet usability requirements: Establishing and meeting software development goals' *in* **Bennett, J, Case, D, Sandelin, J and Smith, M (Eds.)** *Visual Display Terminals* Prentice-Hall, NJ, USA (1984)

8   **Hudetz, W, Rachor, U and Weisbrod, H** *Report Defining the Application Pilots and their IBC Requirements and their Relation to an IBC Telepublishing Scenario* Fraunhofer-Institut für Systemtechnik und Innovationsforschung, Germany (1989)

9   **Weber, A and Neuhold, E J** *Distributed Publishing of Electronic Newspapers and Mailorder Catalogues* GMD, Germany (1991)

10 *Communication 2000: Visions and Strategies for Printers and Publishers* Intergraf, Brussels, Belgium (1994)

EP and the book publisher — case studies

3

EP opportunities for reference-book divisions

Alain Pierrot, Hachette Livre, France

Hachette Livre, the book publishing division of the Matra-Hachette communication group, has been publishing reference titles on CD-ROM since 1989 in cooperation with Grolier in the USA (actually before it was acquired by the company) and Hachette Éducation in France. In 1994, a range of monolingual dictionaries and encyclopaedias is being made available in France (*Axis* from Le Livre de Paris and *Zyzomys* from Hachette Éducation on CD-ROM for DOS, Windows and Macintosh; the *Dictionnaire électronique Hachette* on Sony Data Discman; the *Dictionnaire Hachette Multimedia* on CD-i; a hand-held dictionary with Franklin computers), in Italy (*Enciclopedia Multimediale* on CD-TV and CD-i from Grolier Italy) and in the USA (*New Grolier Multimedia Encyclopedia* on CD-ROM for DOS, Windows and Macintosh).

Each of these consumer titles, providing one takes into account the different successes of the platforms on which they have been implemented, can be considered as a leading title as far as numbers of copies go and this has been so in the years when the market for electronic titles was only beginning to build. An interesting fact is that the impressive growth in 1993/1994 of the American market does not seem to have modified this situation significantly; if one sets apart computer games, it may well be that electronic products

---

Alain Pierrot is Director of Electronic Publishing at Hachette Livre, part of the book and multimedia publishing group within the largest French publishing house, Groupe Hachette, with headquarters in Paris.

merely mean *reference* electronic products for consumers (with the probable addition of educational titles).

Of course, one can argue that it was comparatively easy for 'traditional' publishers to try and make their first experiments with electronic publishing in this domain, because most of the data prepared for printing reference books was already held in digitized format. Nevertheless, this opportunistic view of the situation does not explain the lasting success of reference in electronic publishing and its overrepresentation when one compares the ratios in book publishing. Therefore, one should simply consider that the added value of electronic access to reference text and data has become sufficiently obvious to a significant number of users to provide motives for acquiring hardware and gaining access to the respective titles.

Not only can one handle more data than is humanly manageable on a reasonably sized desk when this set of data is stored on a CD, but also there are functionalities such as full-text search and/or hypertext links that are demonstrably offering new opportunities to every end-user.

For instance, as French people do not commonly use — and indeed are not trained to use — such tools as Roget's thesaurus, finding a term that would aptly phrase a concept was a difficult task, which is now actually well fulfilled through French electronic dictionaries. Moreover this kind of query can be adressed without assuming such a determined and coherent *Weltanschauung* as must be implemented in a thesaurus; the compilation of dictionaries with a linguistic description purpose is obviously more flexible and less systematic than the view of encyclopaedia authors, and querying these linguistic dictionaries with any full-text search functionality usually efficiently yields the answer one could have had difficulty in finding in a traditional thesaurus. This is, in fact, a definitive advantage when one wants to find the right word in a situation. It is also an easily demonstrable feature — and has proved to be a convincing one through dozens of public demonstrations— when one wants to argue why a would-be customer should spend the kind of money electronic media access requires, in spite of the obvious disadvantages of electronic display against print.

This kind of analysis of the 1994 situation is the result of very different experiences and no clear view of the market is yet obtainable from the comparatively short history of new media. It is assumed in this chapter that the coherent range of products from

Hachette Livre has emerged from convergent strategies, the stories of which are worth telling in a few words.

Many factors can and have been involved in the decisions to publish on electronic media. If one takes the example of Hachette's first French title *Zyzomys*, the initial decisive incentive has been the opportunity offered by the market opened by the French Ministry of Education when the decision was taken to place CD-ROM playing equipment in educational institutions. The procedure of the *licence mixte* — an up-front payment from the Ministry in exchange for a reduced price offered to schools — guaranteed a market. Titles to be implemented were then selected through meetings with the different textbook publishers, development companies and representatives from the Ministry.

It was then easy to identify an existing asset that would fit the new media and allow a short time of development to meet the tight schedule constraints. Hachette's experience in computer-aided learning in previous years had shown the difficulty of developing purely educational titles, so the best solution was to elaborate from the newly launched dictionary and get a title that could interest all the equipped institutions.

This was also felt to provide the occasion to obtain for the printed dictionaries the text which would be used in the electronic format and present the image of a modern, challenging product. An external company was selected as the developer and packager of the title: ACT Informatique provided the search engine and user interface and in fact conducted the whole operation with only limited control from the editor.

As data were only available as print, data preparation was handled by the developer. The tapes from the typesetter had to be retro-converted into a more manageable format and new features were added which required additional data. It was decided to include full-text search and manage the inflected forms to offer a fast navigation tool. This was the occasion to acquire new skills, because this kind of data did not need to be gathered and stored for the print product.

Another opportunity to learn about the implications of new media access resulted from the decision to add maps to the product. Hachette had the relevant printed maps that could be scanned and displayed, but when it came to identifying the toponyms on the maps with their counterpart in the dictionary, the limits of pattern matching were soon encountered: different spellings had to be harmonized, homographs to be made less ambiguous and the checking of the links between hot spots became a real, new, time- and money-consuming problem.

It was soon obvious that these problems could not be properly managed by software developers and that editors, with relevant competence concerning the data, had to acquire enough knowledge of the implications of the user interface to be able to carry out final editing and additional data preparation.

This was the time, in 1990, when it was independently decided to manage lexicographical data in-house in order to obtain more flexibility in preparation of printed products. A quick survey of the state of the art showed the interest of reference publishers in SGML techniques. A new conversion of the latest typesetting tapes was conducted and data were retroconverted into a simple SGML format, first to prepare the next release of a text-only, one-volume dictionary.

The investment in equipment was kept to a reasonable amount: a couple of Sun workstations with sufficient storage, linked to a network of Macintoshes and PCs, where editorial work could be handled by four in-house editors. Work was also sent to outside contributors and then merged back into the SGML system. During that process, the marketing department identified that it would be better to use a slightly different word-list and to publish an illustrated dictionary. The choice of simple packages such as Author-Editor from SoftQuad proved its worth by that time: the dictionary department switched easily from the priority to publish the text-only dictionary to the illustrated one and links, captions and formats of the pictures were easily managed so that a merged text could be output, ready for interactive lay-out by one operator at MCP, the French typesetting company, who integrated the pictures and exposed the four colour film on its new LS-210, in April 1991. The whole process had taken less than a year.

The same SGML principles were then applied to the wide-range project of *Axis*, the text, video and CD-ROM encyclopaedia from the door-to-door company Le Livre de Paris.

In the meantime, a new release of *Zyzomys* was published with the new text from the dictionary department and new maps from the illustrated dictionary. Text, inflections and links were then implemented or prepared in-house. The availability of structured data also allowed the quick output of an Electronic Book version for Sony's

Data Discman. As this format moved on and sound features were added, it was decided to take advantage of the new functionality and release a version with pronunciation, which could be incorporated in bundle offers for the French launch of DataDiscman.

Through these different paper and EP ventures the reference departments involved had built on their paper-oriented assets a structured SGML database which linked the text of a range of paper dictionaries to a set of more than 1400 pictures, associated with their captions, with inflection lists that allowed full-text 'smart' links tying inflected words to their headword form, to sound files, to toponym lists and to links to maps that would be prepared for printing as well as for RGB display.

This expertise and — to a much larger extent — that of Grolier Electronic Publishing, consolidated the work conducted by Le Livre de Paris to complete its set of encyclopaedic works and publish the first French multimedia encyclopaedia on CD-ROM in 1993, a task which was completed in 15 months, together with Jouve SI, the typesetting and software company which bought MCP.

Consequently it can be said that the introduction of electronic processing of data, together with EP opportunities, not only created more needs to build new assets (inflection lists, sound files, thesaurus, links), but also that it helped shorten the update cycles and merge the different titles of the range of reference products. However, the main advantage EP techniques and opportunities brought was found in the quality requirements they emphasized. Electronic access to data showed somewhat dramatically many structure and text discrepancies which could be erased more easily throughout the database. It was also easier to store any piece of data linked with an entry, even if in some releases it was not used; for instance etymology and phonetics fields were captured and displayed as an option according to need.

Managing different products lines was also a challenge to the usual print-publishing rhythms. Whereas the printed dictionaries are mainly updated on a yearly basis, with a print run in spring to sell the books in May or June, EP opportunities and schedules are more exacting. Hachette Dictionaries' latest title, produced on CD-i with Philips Interactive Media France, Pathé and the Club d'Investissement Média, had to be produced in less than ten months and integrated more data than had ever been incorporated before. This product — with more than 4000 pictures and pieces of artwork, sound, 35 part-screen videos, interactive maps and 150 slide-shows — in fact extended the skills acquired by Hachette's team in articulating multimedia data through SGML techniques as well as improving the content of the reference edition and offering a reference product where keyboard needs would be minimized. A new advance in integration was made as thesaurus data were used to offer a fast and 'clever' access to individual exceptions.

In conclusion, one could say that EP proved to be a complex process where progress was slow but where opportunities were frequent to build new assets and acquire new skills. In 1994, when the market for reference EP has become quite important in the USA and seems to be becoming economically worth the investment in Europe, positions and expertise acquired during the last five years allow us to see the future as offering new opportunities and new challenges. The price war between encyclopaedic titles in North America and the rhythm of new releases could lead to a profound change in the use of reference titles, from investment to yearly updates. If this cultural evolution does occur, reference publishers will need to be more and more aware of EP techniques and the opportunities they offer.

4

Electronic publishing in the fields of law and taxation

Fons Drabbe, Wolters Kluwer, Netherlands

COMPANY POLICY AT WOLTERS KLUWER NV

Wolters Kluwer Law and Taxation is part of Wolters Kluwer NV, a multinational publishing corporation. Wolters Kluwer's objective is to meet and stimulate, on a commercial basis, the demand which stems from:

- the need for *information*, as well as its management and upgrading,
- the need for *knowledge*, *skills* and *training*.

Wolters Kluwer aspires to occupying strong positions in selected market segments in the fields of information and knowledge in carefully chosen countries. To that end the corporation focuses on a number of core activities, namely, legal publishing, medical publishing, publishing in various scientific subjects, business publishing for profit and nonprofit sectors, educational publishing, professional training and trade publishing for specific target groups in selected markets.

Wolters Kluwer is currently active in Belgium, France, Germany, the UK, Italy, the Netherlands, Norway, Slovakia, Spain, Sweden

---

Fons Drabbe is Managing Director of Wolters Kluwer Law and Taxation in Deventer, the Netherlands, which is part of Wolters Kluwer NV, a multinational publishing corporation.

and the USA. In 1993 Wolters Kluwer's net sales amounted to approximately Dfl2600 million and the number of employees totalled about 8000. Further growth is planned for the coming years.

In view of this modern publishing corporation's objectives, capitalizing on the possibilities offered by computerization and information sciences in the publishing process obviously merits particular attention. In the first place, it involves the implementation of computer applications for the traditional publishing process: *Electronics in publishing*. Examples include new logistics systems, voice-response applications, the development of management information systems, building databases, for instance, for the production of folio publications, marketing applications such as advanced direct marketing systems, printing-on-demand, modern desktop publishing techniques etc. Besides these applications, however, the major significance of *electronic publishing* (EP) alongside and in combination with folio publications is increasingly and quite distinctively taking shape.

WOLTERS KLUWER NV'S ORGANIZATION: CENTRALIZED/DECENTRALIZED

The Wolters Kluwer corporation is a delegated, decentralized organization. Responsibility for the development of electronic publications, therefore, lies with the various countries and publishing firms. It is here, at this level, that management must decide whether there are EP opportunities in the product/market combinations concerned. During the past few years, however, a policy is beginning to crystallize whereby, within the Wolters Kluwer organization and internationally, study groups exchange EP experiences, enter into joint research projects and define common strategies.

A few examples of such joint efforts include:

● Publishers in various countries jointly investigated which retrieval software for CD-ROM products currently serves the professional market best. *Dataware* was selected. It was collectively decided to implement this software. An international study group regularly compares experiences and conveys this feedback and the consequent specifications to the software developer. This know-how accumulated from market experiences in several countries allows *Dataware* to continue to develop this software, while Wolters

Kluwer customers have software at their disposal that is improved upon continuously.

- A Wolters Kluwer EP conference is organized annually. During such conferences — the last one took place in Brussels and the next is scheduled to be held in Berlin in 1994 — publishers share their experiences. These practical experiences, and not the technical aspects, form the focal point at these conferences: Which market niches can succeed? How does one deal with a customer's specific network requirements? Which marketing techniques are applied? How are the operations developing? At which prices/rates?

Besides the examples mentioned above, other study groups within Wolters Kluwer research areas such as printing-on-demand, thesaurus development, information storage for independent media, multimedia applications etc.

Following the description of centralized activities at Wolters Kluwer, attention will now focus on actual and practical applications of EP in various publishing companies. Presenting a comprehensive overview of all the applications within the corporation would be extreme. Hence, a selection of brief synopses of a few applications will be presented and, subsequently, a more detailed case study of EP in one of the publishing groups: Wolters Kluwer Law and Taxation.

EXAMPLES OF ELECTRONIC PUBLISHING AT WOLTERS KLUWER

Teleroute

Teleroute is the electronic international transport transaction system of the Wolters Kluwer publishing corporation. It is online in 11 European countries; 20 000 users accounted for four million consulation hours in 1993. *Teleroute* consists mainly of an offer and demand system for international road freight and vehicles. Through a videotex terminal or PC, information regarding available freight and vehicles throughout Europe can be retrieved. Traditionally, European transport company planners spent hours on the telephone to locate freight, return freight or an empty vehicle. Today — with a subcription to *Teleroute* — a transport company simply addresses a terminal or PC, enters the central database and is provided with approximately 8000 new international offers daily.

All information is centrally stored in a computer centre in the north of France. In all countries, access is made available by the national PTTs via the subscriber's own leased lines. Throughout all the relevant countries, information is received in the different national languages and protocols within two seconds. The information provided is 'up-to-the-second' 24 hours a day. All offers pertaining to the previous day are removed automatically each night. *Teleroute* is used by 20 000 transport companies who, collectively, account for more than 100 000 connections daily. Each day the system presents 8000 international and 12 000 national freight offers.

CD-Rom

Within the Wolters Kluwer corporation publishing on *CD-ROM* is booming. Fourteen Wolters Kluwer publishing companies in seven different countries market CD-ROM products. More than 40 separate publications have already been launched; 30 of these CD-ROMs relate to information needs in legal and fiscal markets. The number of subscribers is growing steadily. An inventory in the spring of 1993 revealed that the total number of subscriptions to CD-ROM products at Wolters Kluwer publishing companies amounted to approximately 16 000. The CD-ROM development and market penetration varies greatly in the different countries. Remarkable is the strong position CD-ROM holds in Italy, but its growth in the Netherlands is also significant. Almost all CD-ROM publications are updated several times a year, although four updates annually is most common.

Other electronic media

In addition to the spectacular developments of the European Transport database *Teleroute* and the strongly growing interest in the CD-ROM medium, Wolters Kluwer is also actively engaged in electronic media in many other fields: CD-i, for instance, floppy disks for PC use, document delivery systems, databanks and database publishing, intelligent software etc. The scope of this article, however, deters further elaboration.

WOLTERS KLUWER LAW AND TAXATION

The publishing group Wolters Kluwer Law and Taxation provides legal and fiscal information, mainly in the Dutch language for the Dutch market. However, in view of the increasing importance of international law, the expanding consequence of the European Union and the progression of the English language in international communication, Wolters Kluwer Law and Taxation has, over the past few years, also been actively involved in the English-language publishing company, Kluwer Law and Taxation. The Wolters Kluwer Law and Taxation publishers focus primarily on professional users. Several activities, however, are aimed at the consumer market. Publications for the educational sector are becoming increasingly important.

Significant are the many law books, some of which are published in loose-leaf form in order to guarantee topicality. Furthermore, judgments made by various courts of justice are published. The Wolters Kluwer Law and Taxation publishing companies also produce numerous legal and fiscal journals, newsletters, yearbooks, textbooks and other scientific or professional publications for attorneys, notaries, accountants, tax consultants, government, the judicial branches and the business community. Seminars and courses geared to legal and fiscal fields are also organized. The role played by EP, online services and CD-ROM products, as well as software, is rapidly becoming more important.

The publishing group, Wolters Kluwer Law and Taxation, consists of eight business units: the Dutch-language publishing companies Kluwer Juridisch (Legal), Kluwer Fiscaal (Fiscal), Kluwer Sociaal (Social), Tjeenk Willink and Gouda Quint; the English-language publishing company Kluwer Law and Taxation; the training company Kluwer Opleidingen (Training) and the EP company Kluwer Datalex. These eight publishing companies are supported by centralized services in areas such as marketing and sales, distribution (Libresso), production, administration, computerization and human resources.

EP at Wolters Kluwer Law and Taxation

Early in the 1970s, developments in the field of electronics inspired Kluwer to create new methods which could assist members of the legal community in carrying out their profession. The issue was, indeed, quite simple: How could the legal profession be provided rapidly with comprehensive and reliable information, linked to an extensive accessibility? Moreover, that information should also be available at any time and be completely up-to-date. The concept of assembling an electronic legal databank was logical. The initial step involved recording the contents of all the Wolters Kluwer publishing companies' case law publications on magnetic tape and feeding those contents into a database even before the journal editions were published. In 1975 the process of adapting Status software for the first legal database in the Netherlands was started. Sizable parts of the software needed to be reprogrammed. Communication between the user and computer in the Dutch language was a prerequisite. 'User-friendly' was the catch-word.

It took until 1979 for approximately 40 external test-users in the legal profession, judicial branches, government, universities and the business community to acquire access to this experimental database. These test-users were provided with a terminal and access to the databank free of charge. This method enabled Kluwer to develop the Legal Database prototype with immediate feedback from the user market.

This is how the Kluwer database containing substantial quantities of case law, available online through a full-text retrieval system, originated. It was launched on the market in 1980 and fared sluggishly. It was not until 1985 that Wolters Kluwer Law and Taxation considered the pilot project phase to have ended; in the same year, the electronic publishing company *Kluwer Datalex* was established with the commitment to introduce electronic products to the market on a commercial basis. During the years 1985–1989, an all-out attempt was made to position the online legal databases in the market. The results were somewhat disappointing. Unfamiliarity with the medium, the absence of a technical infrastructure at the potential-user end and the fear of online consulting costs (including telephone charges) combined to form almost unscalable obstacles for a real breakthrough of this new tool. The market ultimately opted for the trusted folio products rather than the insecurity of a new electronic medium.

Software products

As the required rapid breakthrough of the online database did not materialize, Kluwer Datalex publishers assiduously sought other product/market opportunities. In view of the fiscal and legal professionals' strong position in the market, the search focused on electronic aids for fiscal and legal practices. The creation of a publisher's list of user software for the fiscal market was started. Under the name KLUBAS, software programmes were developed which could perform fiscal, financial and administrative tasks for accountants, tax consultants, book-keeping and administrative offices. After the successful introduction of the KLUBAS software programmes, thorough research into the legal discipline was a logical next step. This market analysis resulted in the JURA software list for legal computerization, tailored to attorneys' professional practice.

CD-ROM products

The market introduction of the offline medium CD-ROM in 1988 signified a breakthrough in EP at Wolters Kluwer Law and Taxation. The legal database files, together with the contents of old volumes of other professional journals, were used to develop CD-ROM products. The *Legal Library* was embarked upon, rapidly followed by the *Fiscal Library*. Both CD-ROM libraries contain the case law of almost all the major Dutch-language professional journals. Currently four CD-ROM products have appeared in the *Legal Library* and three in the *Fiscal Library*. The number of subscriptions is growing vigorously. The CD-ROM list has meanwhile expanded and includes discs in the field of European legislation ELEX; the ECO disc on environmental legislation; the *Social Library* with case law in the areas of labour laws; and, among others, a European subsidy disc. Subscribers to Wolters Kluwer Law and Taxation's CD-ROM products receive a new, updated version of a relevant disc every four months. If, during the intervening months, a subscriber wishes to consult recent journal editions which have yet to be put on CD-ROM, the *Topical Legal Database* can be accessed online. This database also contains current news items. The search structure of the CD-ROM and the topical online application are identical; this user-friendliness ensures a solid combination of the offline and online media.

The Central Legislation Data File

Wolters Kluwer Law and Taxation is not only involved in case-law products and software development for professional use, but also in rulings and legislation. In 1984 the decision had already been made to create a centralized legislation file. The file was completed in the late 1980s — approximately 140 million characters representing 30 000 pages of text and, in 1989, it was determined that the Central Legislation Data File should be converted into a media-independent source file. After a thorough study of the hardware and software capabilities, after the development of a suitable DTD and the customary acceptance tests, a decision could ultimately be made. The conversion chore was completed by mid-1992. Wolters Kluwer Law and Taxation now has at its disposal SGML-structured, media-independent, electronically stored files containing the entire Dutch legislation, i.e. more than 8 000 laws and regulations. The file is updated daily. Historical data is appended. A sophisticated cross-reference system is currently being perfected for future hyperlink applications.

The Central Legislation Data File's function within Wolters Kluwer Law and Taxation is twofold. In the first place, it is used as a source of production for the various publishing companies' many legislative publications. Loose-leaf law texts, paperback textbooks etc. are produced from this data file in diverse print versions. The data file is also the source for new electronic publications. Toward the end of 1993, 'Law Library Part I — The Dutch Legislation', a new CD-ROM product created from the Central Legislation File, was introduced. This new CD-ROM, in combination with an up-to-date database service, represents one of the more recent draught horses in the list building of a modern law publishing company.

New opportunities are materializing. The Dutch government would like to establish a General Dutch Legislation Database with online as well as offline products. Initially this database would be intended for use within the national government but other applications are obvious. On the basis of the database already developed, Wolters Kluwer Law and Taxation is currently negotiating with the Dutch government. The Central Legislation File also represents a source for the development of new services in the market: document delivery services, subfiles supplied to specialist users on a subscription basis, providing legislation files to larger clients for use with in-house networks, etc.

New source files

Wolters Kluwer Law and Taxation has made a choice. The publishing company would like to have well-structured, media-independent, electronically stored source files. A logical consequence to this strategic choice is that the development of new information files be continued. The so-called 'delegated legislation' will be included in a new *Central Circular File*. Addresses and other factual information inherent to legal and fiscal professional practices will be stored in a *Central Information File*. Special efforts are going into a *Central Case Law Storage* system. A well-functioning prototype of a case law database was completed in 1993. A large number of case-law journals are already being produced by this method. In 1994 this system will undergo further expansion so that at the end of the year, Wolters Kluwer Law and Taxation will have achieved an SGML-structured, media-independent, electronically stored case-law file. Over the years to come, this file will be updated with new jurisprudence and, in major subsectors, previously published case law will be added. A wide range of folio products will be developed from this database and at the same time many new opportunities for electronic storage and use of case law are also becoming manifest.

The Wolters Kluwer Law and Taxation organization: centralized/decentralized

During the pioneering phase, EP at Wolters Kluwer Law and Taxation was Datalex's exclusive territory. In 1992, however, the green light was given to other publishing companies within the publishing group. Electronic products play such a vital role in the future growth of a professional legal publishing company that every company should develop its own specific applications. Publications transcending operating companies are released by Kluwer Datalex, but all other publishing companies at Wolters Kluwer Law and Taxation must address EP from within their own lists and market niches. In many locations the development of electronic publications has been given serious attention since that date. In the meantime, a significant number of folio publications have been integrated with electronic components, particularly in the form of diskettes for PC users. The contents of these diskette products varies from special software for practitioners' purposes to electronic registers and legal and fiscal models. Another area being surveyed is how the advantages of folio and electronic forms can be combined in multimedia products. New parcels of information evolve, composed from loose-leaf publications with newsletters and diskettes as well as CD-ROMs, which can replace existent publications or which in combination with folio editions lead to better information products.

New products

One of the major challenges during the next few years will be to ensure that internal and external source files are structured identically and that linkage between the files can be effected. A linkage between legislation and case law with good connections and references to literature and comments provide opportunities for new electronic products. The first CD-ROM products, in which such linkages have been realized, were produced for specialized subsectors (corporate law, rent law), and will be introduced to the market in 1994.

Wolters Kluwer Law and Taxation is also researching extensively in other areas. In 1993, for instance, the first *knowledge system* was launched. This is a user-friendly system for the calculation of social benefits in the Social Security Act sector. The software package was developed for use in municipal social services departments. It is highly plausible that in the near future an interesting market will evolve in the area of intelligent software systems. Given their specific expertise, legal and fiscal publishing companies could play a substantial role in these new markets. In the *electronic mail* field as well the first pilot project is currently being introduced. With a high degree of frequency clients receive information, rigorously selected by in-house editors and external sources, in their PC through E-mail.

Future developments

Wolters Kluwer Law and Taxation has, over the past few years, become wholly convinced that the growth of electronic products in the legal and fiscal markets will continue. In some cases electronic products will replace traditional folio products sooner than anticipated. The pioneers of the professional market are already expressing clear-cut demands: information should be accessible digitally and its integration in PC networks should be uncomplicated. The headway CD-ROM is making persists and electronic highways will continue to stimulate online applications. The contemporary publishing company in professional markets can look forward to an exciting era. Numerous copyright, market technical, financial and information technological issues will have to be resolved. This is a challenging perspective. As a result of its efforts and investments in EP, a publishing company such as Wolters Kluwer Law and Taxation will be able to maintain its strong position in the marketplace.

5

Electronic publishing for dictionaries — a case study on the Langenscheidt Taschenwörterbuch Englisch

Hans-Werner Scholz, Langenscheidt Verlag, Germany

INTRODUCTION

The purpose of this paper is to give an impression about the development of EP within Langenscheidt KG. Best-selling printed products are generally the basis for our electronic products.

Langenscheidt's strategy regarding software and hand-held products will be outlined on the basis of *Langenscheidts Taschenwörterbuch Englisch*. This bilingual (English–German, German–English) dictionary provided the database for three of our new electronic products, which will be described here. These are our brand-new hand-held electronic dictionary 'alpha 120', the 8 cm CD-ROM of the Electronic Book standard and the software version of the 'PC-Bibliothek'.

Dr Hans-Werner Scholz is Director of Electronic Media at Langenscheidt Verlag in Munich, Germany. This well established publishing house is probably best known worldwide for its language dictionaries.

MARKETING STRATEGIES FOR ELECTRONIC VERSIONS OF THE 'TASCHENWÖRTERBUCH ENGLISCH'

The first printed edition of this dictionary was published in 1884. When people said 'I'll look it up in the Langenscheidt', it was usually this standard work to which the person was referring. In the early 1990s the contents of this book were completely revised and re-shaped. The introduction of new typefaces made the dictionary even clearer and thus easier to read. All English headwords now appear with their phonetic transcription and the complete work includes more than 120 000 headwords and idiomatic expressions and is one of the best-selling products within its product range in the German-speaking market.

This shows that with this dictionary we can meet the demands of several target groups, who use it for studying, in their professional life or for advanced training — at home, in the office or when travelling. Its great popularity gives this title an excellent starting position for the development of electronic versions. The first step in defining the detailed product specifications for the latter is to distinguish the two different ranges of application, one for use during travelling and the second for use at home or in the office.

For the portable version there are two possibilities:

- The implementation on already-existing hardware platforms such as the 8 cm CD-ROM of the Sony Electronic Book Standard and IC/PCMCIA card versions for hand-held computers from PDA (personal digital assistants) and organizer producers.
- The development of a Langenscheidt hand-held with the publisher taking on the role of the hardware manufacturer.

It is obvious that the second variant contains a much higher risk than the first. Therefore the development of such a hand-held is only preferable in an exceptional case.

The best platforms for private or professional use at home or in the office are floppy disk or CD-ROM versions which will run under popular operating systems like MS-DOS, Windows or Apple Macintosh.

Let us now move on to our concept for the electronic versions of the 'Taschenwörterbuch Englisch' for the following platforms:

- Langenscheidt electronic hand-held
- Multi-CD-ROM
- Windows PC

PRODUCTS

alpha 120

In 1983 Langenscheidt published the first electronic dictionary in the German-speaking market. 'Electronics history is being made by a publishing company', was how the specialist press greeted this new product. Six years later Langenscheidt introduced the alpha 40 on to the market — an improved model containing around 40 000 words. In the meantime the electronic dictionary market was expanding strongly and the number of competing publishers kept growing.

To strengthen our market position for the future, the new product had to fulfil certain conditions:

- The design of the new electronic dictionary had to be stylistically convincing and was intended to be the prototype for a completely new and independent product range. This particular task — the development of the design — was entrusted to *frogdesign*, a leading consultant in this area.
- The second important requirement was the database. For the first time *Langenscheidts Taschenwörterbuch Englisch* was implemented completely on an electronic hand-held device. To guarantee the clear arrangement of the words of the printed work on the display screen, four different proportional fonts were created especially for this purpose. The search program also supplies wild-card search and phonetic algorithms. A further option is the integrated user dictionary, where the user can enter the vocabulary which is important for him.
- The third group of product specifications is organizer functions, which the user expects in addition to the dictionary.

The EB standard

Langenscheidt is one of the pioneers of the Sony EB standard in Germany. This standardized system offers the essential retrieval possibilities for the majority of our users. The 8 cm CD-ROM has enough storage capacity for sound, graphics and pictures to be included for most of our dictionaries. For this reason the Langenscheidt Publishing Group has nine titles of this standard on its list, one of which is *Langenscheidts Taschenwörterbuch Englisch (TWE)*.

Up to now these titles can only be used on an Electronic Book Player. However, in Germany only 20 000 of these players have been sold. This is the main reason why the 8 cm CD-ROM has never been a big economic success.

Nevertheless, we still believe in the basic idea of this product, and thus we studied alternatives to make this platform more attractive to the potential user. Together with Sony Germany, the publisher Rheinbaben & Busch and a German software house, we have now opened a new path for this product.

By installing separately sold software, Electronic Books can now be used on the platforms PC Windows, Apple Macintosh and Sony Data Discman. This raises our potential target group from 20 000 to about 400 000 CD-ROM drive users in Germany — and the 20 000 CD-ROM drives currently being sold every month must be added to this figure. The term 'Multi-CD-ROM' originates from combining the 8 cm EBs with a Windows- or Macintosh-based retrieval software.

The Multi-CD-ROM has a wide range of applications. In the office or at home you will profit from the comfortable and functional personal computer with a big screen. You can copy an entry into a text you are writing with a text-processing program and even print it. In addition to that, you have the advantage of the portable Data Discman when you are travelling. We are sure that the Multi-CD-ROM is a trend-setting product. In the near future more and more portable computers (Laptops) will be furnished with 8 cm CD-ROM drives, like the Panasonic Notebook Computer. Therefore, it is obvious that *TWE* will be published in this new standard too. As an additional feature more than 5000 spoken words will be included.

PC-Bibliothek

The third electronic version of *TWE* is a dictionary in the 'PC-Bibliothek' (PC library). To give you a better impression of the idea behind this product, the philosophy of this new product line will be described. Our target was to make the operation of the PC-Bibliothek similar to the use of the printed reference books. One of the essential features of this new product line is that you can choose one or more books with which you want to work on a desk.

A number of special options allow you to define the search mode exactly, e.g. headword search, wild-card search, full-text search, combined search with 'or', 'and' and 'without' and sound-alike search. You can copy an entry into another programme and print it, you can store an entry together with your personal comments and you can store an entry in a subject catalogue that you have defined yourself.

There is the possibility of searching through several books at the same time, depending on how many titles of the PC-Bibliothek you have placed on your virtual desk. You can use these search options only with the electronic version. We hope that this variety of product specifications will be accepted by professional users who are accustomed to working with the standard works of our publishing group.

Twelve titles from Meyer, DUDEN and Langenscheidt have already been launched as floppy disk versions. The titles include an encyclopaedia from Meyer, five monolingual reference books from DUDEN and, of course, the *TWE*. Four new titles will follow later in 1994.

OUTLOOK

The intention of this brief chapter is to show that our company's current EP activities are concentrated on implementing our printed standard works on different electronic platforms. In this phase we have refrained from adding sound and images to our products. We are sure that the features which our electronic products now have to offer are already very attractive.

Future developments in EP will, however, include more and more multimedia options. We certainly know that useful media supplements will make our reference books more attractive. For example, a CD-ROM version of our *TWE* with voice output of the headwords could be a bestseller. However, we decided that our electronic products will include more multimedia features only step by step. In this way we can keep the necessary investments in check, since I am convinced that we will make money with our traditional print products first of all.

6

Selling the *OED on CD-ROM* to individuals and institutions: how to have your cake and eat it too

Andrew Rosenheim, Oxford University Press, UK

At long last, the CD-ROM market offers more opportunities than pitfalls. Reference works in particular are faring well in the market place and it now seems clear that significant portions of publishers' reference revenues will come from electronic product — increasingly CD-ROMs.

The *Oxford English Dictionary (Second Edition)* is famous, authoritative, eccentric, quirky, and (dare I say it?) typically English. In its electronic development it nonetheless represents and embodies many of the issues and most of the problems any reference publisher encounters when publishing on CD-ROM. Arguably, the CD-ROM history of the *OED* provides something of a paradigm of the history of the CD-ROM industry.

It is worth briefly describing the dictionary's print history, for quite unwittingly this accelerated the work's electronic development. Like many landmarks of Victorian origin, the *OED* was the brain-child of a committee, but the work, chiefly, of one man. As early as

Andrew Rosenheim is Director of Electronic Publishing in the Science, Medical & Journals Division of Oxford University Press, one of England's oldest printing and publishing houses. The *Oxford English Dictionary* is the leading English-language reference book.

1857, the Philological Society of England had agreed on the need for a dictionary of English that would systematically record all the words in the language in all their aspects on an historical basis. However, it was only with the appointment of James Murray as editor in 1879 that progress was made, and in 1885 he moved to Oxford and with the support of Oxford University Press devoted himself full-time to the project.

Like most obsessives (and thus like most software developers), Murray was not an accurate forecaster, and he seriously underestimated how long creation of the dictionary would take — his earliest estimates suggested it would be completed in ten years. In fact, it took over 40, and was finished only in 1928 — well after Murray's death in 1915. There is a curious irony that a work that derives its authority from so many people and from institutions — the University, the University Press — had its catalyst and the long-term vision needed to complete it in this one individual.

Two main things characterized this first edition of the *OED* (to which a small supplement was added in 1933): the use of historical evidence (in the form of quotations from hundreds of thousands of sources) to show the full lineage of a word's meanings; and the exhaustiveness of the dictionary's ambition to include every word in the language.

This scope meant, of course, that the dictionary was immediately out of date. After the Second World War, the growth of the English language (the sheer numbers of new words) and the rise of the language's stature as an international language, made it obvious that the original 13 volumes would have to be added to. In 1957 a new editor, Robert Burchfield, was appointed, and a new team installed. This work came out in four large volumes, known as *A Supplement to the OED*, between 1972 and 1986.

The *Supplement* was a necessary extension to the original *OED*, but also something of an awkward one, for it, too, ran A–Z and thus existed in parallel with the earlier volumes. To remain up to date with this authority on the language, you needed to own both sets; equally annoying, to examine any word exhaustively, you needed to find its entry in both sets as well.

The obvious solution was to merge the two dictionaries, and the decision to do this was taken in the early 1980s by OUP. The scale of this venture was daunting, for neither the original dictionary nor the *Supplement* was in any kind of machine-readable form. Keyboarding the material took 18 months and 80 people; proofreading required the services of 50 people for the same period. Although the bulk of many entries could be mechanically merged through the use of some ingenious parsing programs developed by OUP from ideas originated at the University of Waterloo, Canada, an enormous amount of skilled editorial work was still needed to bring the parallel entries of the two dictionaries seamlessly together.

Out of this vast labour came the printed *Second Edition of the Oxford English Dictionary*, published in 20 volumes in 1989. It integrated the original *OED* and its four-volume supplement in one alphabetical sequence; it also included entries for over 5000 new words. It enjoyed one of the most successful promotional campaigns OUP has ever mounted and well over 10 000 sets were sold at the fairly daunting price of £1500. Arguably it was one of the most successful titles ever published by the Press in its 500-year history.

And it was a book. But not for long. Amidst all the fanfare surrounding the book's appearance — these many man-years of labour, these many hundreds of thousands of pounds — one decision made during the project went generally unnoticed, although in retrospect it was the single most important feature of the entire project. This was the prescient, perhaps even unwitting, decision to make sure that when the entries of the two dictionaries were entered they were tagged in detail. The tag set used was extensive and based on SGML: it had some short-term benefits in helping to merge the two sets of material for efficient print publication, but its long-term significance (hidden at the time) was electronic. For the dictionary — this second edition — was now a database; the preparatory process for print publication had quite unintentionally spawned an electronic future.

The initial electronic development was not especially promising. We published a CD-ROM of the old *OED* (the original 12 volumes) in 1987, and this electronic title reflected what I call the publisher's dilemma in publishing CD-ROMs. What is this dilemma? It can be simply put: any unusual intellectual property, any eccentric database in other words, really requires an individual, tailored, and thus bespoke software development to turn it into a distinguished electronic publication. The difficulty, of course, is that such a development can be exorbitantly expensive. If you are publishing the world's largest collection of Norwegian mosquitoes on CD-ROM, then no matter how superior or individual the software development that accompanies it, you are extremely unlikely to recoup your costs. Selling 18 copies instead of four is not going to make a difference to your initial decision about what you can fund in terms of software development. Commonly, therefore, especially in the early days of CD-ROM development, the publisher was forced to buy a generic retrieval package and software interface, adapted at minimal expense (and thus resulting in minimal adaptation) to the requirements of the database, publish the title and hope for the best.

The best all too often turned out to be strictly mediocre, and the resultant mediocrity of most of the early CD-ROM titles proved a very serious impediment to the development of this form of publishing. It also contributed to the larger chicken-and-egg situation that restricted growth in CD-ROM. People were unwilling to purchase drives for their PCs or Macintoshes because so few titles of interest or distinction were available; concomitantly, publishers were reluctant to develop titles because so few drives were in existence.

The first *OED* on CD-ROM reflected the shortcomings. It was published with software that was not developed specifically for it — and which proved manifestly inadequate. The title was a DOS version only built within the 640 k byte RAM limit. It was unable to take advantage of the graphic capability of the Windows environment; in particular, this meant that fonts were strictly limited and special characters had to be represented for the most part by mnemonics. There was no full-text search and you were confined to searching the database by using eight indexes. The software retrieval was slow, for in its very first appearance the text was uncompressed; indeed, the very first version came out catastrophically on two CD-ROMs. In this version of the *Oxford English Dictionary* you could not search for phrases or pronunciation or run any proximity searches. Exact string searching was required, with no distinction between upper and lower case or accented words. The look and feel was, at best, rudimentary and the performance was quite astonishingly slow.

Yet, by the early standards of the CD-ROM world, this awkward trial was a success; worldwide it sold about 1000 copies in the first three years at a list price of £500 (or $950). I remember my astonishment at finding it listed as a 'best-selling' CD-ROM, such was the embryonic state of the market. Its success resulted in a determination at OUP to publish the full second edition on CD-ROM and to fund a bespoke individual development of the title. Of course, wide sale of the printed volumes, and the relative success of the early primitive CD-ROM, gave us the luxury of confidence that we would sell enough copies of a new CD-ROM version to justify the expense of an individual software development.

In planning the second edition on CD-ROM we knew there was a core institutional and philological market we had to reach and had to satisfy. The question was whether there was a wider market as well. We decided there was. I would like to pretend this conclusion was based on sophisticated market research, the result of surveys and polls, but in fact it was based on that time-honoured publishing practice called having a hunch.

This hunch was that there was a growing market of individuals, owners of computers who were literate — the kind who had spent two or three thousand pounds on kit (including a CD-ROM drive) and wanted something to use with it. If you are never supposed to go broke underestimating the intelligence of the buying public, we none-theless thought we might make money by for once respecting that intelligence. We also felt — and we were proved right — that the traditional arts/science divide of the UK was eroding — in particu-lar, scientists, computer professionals, even businesspeople, had an interest in language, an interest in words. Sadly, the converse does not seem true: many humanists remain deeply uninterested in com-puting.

So we decided to build a CD-ROM for the widest market possi-ble, in order to realize that market. Accordingly we tried to build a product that was immediately accessible — where you could at least do something with it without prior knowledge of the title. We also tried to make it as visually powerful as possible and took the then risky (this was three and a half years ago) step of building the first release in Windows so that the more than 700 special characters of the *OED* could be displayed. We tried, too, with this most sombre of reference works, to maximize the 'fun' element of using the prod-ucts; we were thus especially pleased when *Byte* magazine called the product addictive.

We had also, of course, to satisfy the philologists and lexicogra-phers who would use the *OED on CD-ROM* professionally and intensively — the kind of scholar who wanted all the Romanian derived words found in *Ancrene Wisse* but never used by Jane Austen. We did this by building a separate query language. It had to be learned; you had to type in commands; but it was capable of sup-porting the most rigorous and complicated kinds of scholarly investi-gation.

These two tiers of development required careful supervision. We chose an unknown software house in Rotterdam called AND, chiefly because alone among bidders they respected the unique nature of the database and therefore the exacting requirements of the software. But even they needed watching, and if we learned one lesson from the project it was this — you should respect your developer but do not fall in love. From a publisher's point of view even the finest software developers will, if left unsupervised, do something quite peculiar to the data. At OUP we do not have coders in-house, but the outside ones we employ are controlled by OUP software editors who function as title or project managers. Farming out development without having someone in-house to supervise it will certainly keep your costs down, but the resulting products will also keep your revenues down as well. AND, for example, questioned the need for full-text searching on the CD — who would want that they asked? I explained patiently that the first thing reviewers would do is check to see if their surname was in the database. I know this because the name Rosenheim is not.

Having built this two-tier product, we had to sell it — and in two ways. Reaching the query-language types was straightforward. We used mailshots, library mailings, academic conferences where we showed the product; these methods of marketing are like those we use for books. The main difference has been the need to demonstrate the product, for, with an item so highly priced, people are reluctant to buy it sight unseen.

The wider audience we wanted to reach required a wider promotional campaign. We had learned from marketing other reference titles that computer magazines were natural targets for our promotional efforts to reach a wider audience, since increasingly members of the general public — not merely computer fanatics — often buy copies of the *Byte* magazine or *PC World*. We soon discovered, too, that the editors of these magazines and their reviewers were surprisingly welcoming to a product that was a much more text than software application. It was as if they sensed that users of computers are increasingly stuck for information itself to be supplied in electronic form, not merely in the method for manipulating this kind of information. However, we also wanted our presence felt in general newspapers and magazines read by many computer owners who simply do not want to wade through hundreds of pages of advertisements of trade journals and who could not care less about the latest version of DOS and the latest Local Area Network. Here the fame of the material (the *OED*) certainly helped to attract attention, but we also spent a great deal of time spoonfeeding potential reviewers, such as the late Anthony Burgess. We brought him to Oxford, showed him the software, and took him painstakingly step by step through the product. In his resulting review, he called the *OED* a 'metallic beer mat', but he also made it his book of the year. With him and others, the trick was to overcome their inherent distrust of computers and show how easily the information of the *OED* could be used, and how innovative the software really was. In the USA, we also pushed very hard to promote the product in a general way, and here we were lucky to get on the wire services. This had its unfortunate aspect, however, since over 2000 newspapers, from Muskegan, Michigan to College Station, Texas, ran a quotation from me, declaring that at $895 the *OED2 on CD-ROM* 'was not a casual buy'.

This brings me to the price of the product. Traditionally, there have been two tiers of CD-ROM pricing: up to £5000 for specialized databases such as *Medicore Pharmacological Compilations*; conversely, as little as £20 for games or oddball collections such as several thousand public-domain editions of a vast and bewildering array of literature. We wished to establish middle ground and set the price of the CD-ROM at £495 — unusually for software, well below the published price of the printed volumes. Despite this, we were often criticized for the expense of the product and many people asked how we could charge so much when the physical cost of producing a disc is only about £2. This is a common fallacy and one publishers need to rebut vigorously, for it overlooks the entire cost of developing the software for an electronic title. In fact, it is the combination of software development and physical costs of production that should be compared to the physical unit cost of a book and, as a rough rule of thumb, we try to keep our costs in this sense roughly parallel to those in the book trade. Naturally, once the costs of software development have been recovered, margins are extremely high, given the low physical production costs. But few CD-ROM titles have managed to do this so far; and if CD-ROM titles do begin to sell more widely, competition naturally enters, retail prices fall, and accordingly margins become thinner too.

The majority of our sales of the *OED2 on CD-ROM* were direct. This maximized our margins but may have also reduced the volume of sales; this was not so much a deliberate strategy, moreover, but rather recognition of the fact that distribution channels for CD-ROM were at the time of publication (summer 1992) virtually non-existent, at least in the UK. This has changed dramatically, even in the two years since publication, for now there are many full-time CD-ROM distributors and increasingly traditional software dealers are including CD-ROM titles in their lists.

We resisted the temptation to bundle the *OED2* with the drive, or rather were unable to complete such an arrangement successfully since we insisted that the price of the resulting bundle should always be higher than the price of the CD-ROM alone. Since the price of CD-ROM drives lowers every few months (it is possible to purchase one now in the UK for as little as £150), this meant that an arrangement with the drive manufacturers to bundle the two became impractical. In general, we want to keep the price of the *OED2* at a level where it will still attract the keen individual, yet distinguish the *OED2* quite clearly from smaller, more popular reference works (both our own and those of other publishers) that now cost less than £50 in electronic form. With the *OED2* we feel we have a unique compilation, which does not have much, if any, direct competition, and we also know that once the price does come down it is unlikely ever to go back up again. Since we are already at work at OUP on a third edition of the *OED*, provisionally scheduled for publication in the year 2005, we want to preserve the commercial distinctiveness of the title as well as its intellectual singularity. And I think it is now clear to even the most sceptical viewers that future reference works like the *OED* will increasingly be largely electronic.

7

Electronic book publishing on demand — McGraw-Hill's Primis electronic database publishing system: a case study in the development, implementation and management of on-demand publishing

Robert Lynch, McGraw-Hill, USA

INTRODUCTION TO PRIMIS

Primis is a powerful application of information technology that allows teachers to fully customize textbooks and course materials. In its simplest form, Primis allows professors to select instructional material from a large retrievable database, integrating disparate subjects, ideas and types of information. Teachers then arrange the

---

Robert Lynch is Vice-President of McGraw-Hill Inc, based in Hightstown, New Jersey. McGraw-Hill has wide-ranging publishing activities but is probably best known worldwide for its educational book publishing activities. The group's headquarters are in New York.

selections in the manner that best suits their particular class and teaching style.

The system was developed to take advantage of current technologies and to respond to classroom needs. Primis also maintains the traditions of editorial integrity in this new electronic medium. The heart of Primis is a dynamic information database, always changing and always increasing in size and power, designed to meet the individual course needs of teachers and professors at all levels of education. Finally, but perhaps most important of all, it is a system that enables publishers to respond to the increasing demands for individual control and selection of information through new forms of electronic delivery. Primis is able to meet the challenges of demographic and curriculum changes in education. These challenges include the specific needs of older and foreign students, part-time students and distant learners for shorter and different course materials, as well as the increasing demands to integrate social, historical and international trends into a growing number of courses.

It is also important to note what Primis is not: Primis is not vanity publishing or the customized publishing of professor notes and/or course packs. These publications, although filling a much needed void, do not take advantage of current technologies, nor are they fundamentally an editorially driven publishing venture. It is the latter point that usually defines publishers, that is providing added editorial value. Primis is distinguished from other forms of custom and vanity publishing by the following characteristics:

- *Quality:* the Primis textbook is not a photocopy or reorganized package of existing printed materials.
- *Flexibility:* users of Primis can select, arrange and add materials from the Primis database in specific ordering sequence.
- *Integration:* Primis allows for the incorporation of individual teaching resources, course syllabus notes etc. with materials selected from Primis.
- *Timeliness:* Primis is able to provide an up-to-date text by adding journal articles and information on current events.
- *Diversity:* Primis gives the users options to build books to suit students' needs and abilities.
- *Service:* Primis assures text availability and rapid, dependable delivery by eliminating minimum orders, out-of-stock, and out-of-prints.

- *Value:* in a Primis text students pay only for the material that the professors plan to use.
- *Copyright integrity:* Primis ensures the right, through copyright permissions, to use all material in the database.

TECHNOLOGY BEHIND PRIMIS

Currently we are creating an information base in PostScript. For a publisher this is not an inconsequential consideration. Part of the added value that we bring to the reader, to the user of information, is our ability to define and to describe a page in a manner that facilitates its use. Stuart Lynn of Cornell University has spoken of what he calls the *Gutenberg Paradox:* the fact that Gutenberg used what we now refer to as a Gothic font because it closely resembled the written script of copied manuscripts. This is the paradox: the introduction of a new technology often succeeds when it is hidden or not fully recognized. What I have not heard Dr Lynn mention is what I will call the *Gutenberg Paradigm:* that is, for centuries after Gutenberg and the introduction of new fonts by Manutius, German publishers continued to set books — especially scholarly books — in a Gothic font. I mention this only to draw attention to the power of traditions and of the typographically described page. I believe that what can be acknowledged and is supported by my story of Gutenberg and the Gothic font, is that if the reader must read information either for research or because of job requirements, text is satisfactory and often even preferable. If, however, the reader is making discretionary decisions about what, when and how to read, then the look and feel of the word takes on added importance and may — for pedagogical reasons and/or readability — be essential. I will argue that in fact most reading is discretionary, that we as readers actually have the choice to read or not to read.

PostScript enables us to print not only on high-speed electronic printers but also on smaller minute desktop printers. The Primis system operates on a Sun Sparc 4/390 Workstation. The system's sophisticated software allows for the creation and maintenance of a database; creates and manages a custom book order; retrieves from the database the chapters selected; catenates and refolios the pages; creates a new table of contents; adds a title and copyright page; and creates a cover that includes variable information (professor's name, course number, course name, school etc.).

Working closely with McGraw-Hill, R. R. Donnelley has set up a facility in Harrisonburg, Virginia, to receive and manage orders and print, bind and ship custom books directly to our customers. The facility contrasts markedly with traditional manufacturing environments, for it is the first just-in-time facility serving high-volume demand for the publishing industry.

The Primis Administrative System

The administration of Primis is an entirely separate system, made up of multiple databases. The Primis Administrative System provides for entering an order for a custom-published book, editing the order as needed, confirming the order to McGraw-Hill and providing financial information to interface systems. The Primis Administrative System minimum hardware requirements include: 386 PC or compatible, 25 MHz, 640 kbyte memory, 240 Mbyte hard disk drive and file management software, PC-DOS or MS-DOS 3.3. The Primis Administrative System recommended hardware requirements include: Intel 486 microprocessor or compatible, 33 MHz, 8 Mbyte RAM, 240 Mbyte hard disk drive, DOS 5.0 and Microsoft Windows 3.1 or higher. The primary functions of the Primis Administrative System are: the production of PostScript files (vendors and internal production) including composition requirements and limits, proofing and sampling, PostScript fonts, printer requirements and limits, loading files into the Primis database, management of the database and transmission of the database to a manufacturing facility.

The Order Entry System and Dynamic Index

Subsets of the Administrative System are the Order Entry System and Dynamic Index System. These are separate systems that operate within a DOS environment. The primary functions of these systems include: order entry, order processing, order maintenance, order transmission to printing facilities, invoicing, report generation; generation of McGraw-Hill order number; receipt of order and/or PostScript file, scheduled date of printing, confirmation of receipt of local material; storage of local material, referenced by state, school, and professor. The Dynamic Index allows for the creation of an index from preexisting PostScript files. Although a Primis book consists of parts from multiple sources, the indexed item references the exact page of occurrence.

All orders, whether for sale or for complimentary use, must be created using the Primis Administrative System. Orders consisting of book contents, title page contents and the number of books to be printed at the Licensee Site are transmitted to McGraw-Hill via telecommunications. McGraw-Hill will compile the book and send to the licensee a PostScript file of the book ordered. Upon receipt of the PostScript file, the licensee will print, bind, and deliver the books for resale. Regardless of the on-site availability of the PostScript file, all reorders, including the number to be printed, must be entered into the Primis Administrative System.

McGraw-Hill periodically audits the licensee's distributed Administrative Systems via telecommunications. The system reports to McGraw-Hill all Primis items selected and the number of copies printed either as a single item or in combination with other items.

Summary

McGraw-Hill's Primis system applies simple desktop publishing models to complex manufacturing needs in order to produce tens of thousands of books with millions of pages and to fill thousands of orders within weeks of manufacturing time, producing the first publishing just-in-time manufacturing environment.

Because of the technology fundamental to Primis, we are able to add value to traditional teaching and student materials by enabling the customization of that material and providing new, revised, and updated information quickly and at a fair price. This is the most dramatic advance in publishing today, an advance that was implemented at least three years ahead of all predictions. We have changed the publishing arena from a high-volume, economies-of-scale business to one that is able to respond to the demands of individual customers and to give end-users the power to manage and gain effective control over large and formidable information resources.

BENEFIT TO SPECIFIC TARGET AUDIENCE

Primis has four targeted audiences:

- teachers and students from elementary through graduate school,
- authors,
- publishers,
- bookstores.

The primary audience for Primis is the teachers and students in classrooms throughout all of education. Traditional texts and supplements can never completely anticipate the needs of different courses or enable teachers to incorporate easily within their own course materials other sources of information and learning tools: software, video, timely journal articles, databases and reference works. Primis fully addresses these demands by simplifying access to information resources. The principal benefits of Primis are pedagogical and educational. One positive impact on pedagogy is reflected in the ability to incorporate local or regional ideas, trends and policies and place them within a broader scope. Education is also improved, because the resources are current and varied with regard to level, depth of coverage and focus.

Because of Primis, authors are now able to develop more timely and dynamic information resources and to anticipate the use of non-traditional course materials to accompany their own written material. Not limited to a single, linearly structured book, authors can give full reign to their knowledge and creativity, develop various levels of choice for the reader and enable students to manage within an increasingly large and complex information world.

During the last ten years, publishers of educational material have witnessed a significant erosion of their core business. Used textbooks and the photo-duplication of copyrighted properties for student purchase account for an ever-increasing percentage of all sales of educational material. With Primis we have developed a system that reduces the impact of used texts (for they are customized for one class and have no value in the secondary market); and, because of our database, Primis will replace the need for photo-duplicated material. Other benefits of Primis to publishers are no less significant: inventory is eliminated; books never go out of print, nor are they ever out of stock.

Finally, as bookstores struggle to service the needs of their primary customers, the students, we have developed a system that creates a partnership among bookstores, publishers and academics. By establishing a Primis publishing system on campus, not only can McGraw-Hill supply the course needs of professors and students immediately, but bookstores, as information service centres, can play a new role in the development of that material by providing direct access to the available database.

Global benefits

From the beginning, Primis was seen as a powerful system that would deliver information on an international scale and incorporate information developed indigenously from around the world. Because we are creating a retrievable digital base of information, the same electronic content can be transmitted instantaneously around the world either to computer workstations for direct access or to printing facilities for reproduction and dissemination. The use of some form of optical storage is another delivery method only available with electronic information. Entire libraries can now be stored, be resident and be printed locally. Thus, Primis is both an electronic medium and a more traditional print medium. Primis will have a significant positive impact on the availability of educational material throughout the world.

Important, too, are the long-term implications of Primis. One of the great challenges in providing information to a global marketplace is that these markets require significant content changes and adaptations. Traditionally, this has meant that we must incur costs to adapt content and create new books. With Primis, substantial portions of the database can travel internationally unchanged with the rest needing only partial modifications or additions to meet various cultural and economic demands. The process also works in reverse: material intended for a particular country would be retained and become part of a domestic Primis database for use within the USA. International studies are facilitated both here and abroad. As we move into the more dynamic networking of our information resources, meeting the needs of authors and users of McGraw-Hill information will speed development and increase international cooperation. For the first time in publishing history we have the chance to develop works-in-progress that involve a world body of scholars.

We live in an information-rich society and have the opportunity to maintain a leadership role in the intellectual development and delivery of that information. As important perhaps as economic or technical wealth, control, access and management of information will determine the world leaders of the future.

DISTINCTIVE FEATURES THAT DEFINE ELECTRONIC PRODUCTS

Primis is a platform for the editorial development of digital information. This means that all content is digital, that the digital content is the *content of record*, that is, the final product is defined within its digital format and the content is accessible and retrievable by the customer. There are two 'relativity tests', which publishers can perform to confirm the viability of electronic or digital products:

- relative ease in delivering content in multiple electronic formats,
- relative ease within the electronic content in indexing, organizing, searching, browsing, reading, retrieving, updating, user profiling, transferring and transmitting.

The significance of digital information, which forms the basis of Primis, can be summarized as follows:

- It can easily be reused, revised, reformatted and delivered on different platforms to serve multiple customers and markets.
- It allows the customer to choose material from a number of sources and configure it in the sequence desired.
- Intellectual property rights are effectively obtained and managed with rights holders receiving fees and/or royalties for all uses of their information.
- The publisher retains the traditional role of acquiring, developing and distributing quality information products. The publisher's role is not diminished; in fact it is enhanced in that it challenges publishers to think in much broader terms about the markets they serve. A new publishing model is created: editors will develop information resources (database) for multiple markets with separate sales for specific markets. Marketing and sales will be the primary arbiter of customer needs; as a result of this

shift, marketing, sales and editorial interact and cooperate to produce customized information.
- It allows for the distribution of the database for local printing.

LESSONS WE HAVE LEARNED

Strategic alliances

What are some of the key lessons we have learned in the development of Primis and in the transformation of the editorial and marketing processes? One of the earliest key factors in the development of Primis was to form important strategic alliances. These were not always easy; our experiences can be summarized in four lessons we learned for the success of strategic alliances:

- Large corporations with semiautonomous sales and marketing organizations must have them buy into a strategic alliance established by product development or editorial group.
- Senior management must communicate goals (short- and long-term) which may conflict with any strategic alliance.
- Each allied party should independently reassess any agreement made during the initial planning of the relationship to establish realizable expectations.
- Strategic alliances which form early in a new venture must be flexible and changeable as the nature of the business changes.

Finally, one cautionary note: some partnerships are established as a result of prior relationships, which may not be the best basis for a strategic alliance with a new venture or product.

McGraw-Hill will continue building strategic alliances with a number of other companies. At the same time, we are attempting to build what one might term virtual relationships. These can be defined as direct alliances with the customer wherever and whenever possible. In the case of Primis this would include partnering with a university to develop online systems for the access and retrieval of data. The great advantage to such relationships is that they are customer specific; since they are smaller in scope, they tend to reduce costs of development. It is our belief that working closely with our customer base provides reasonable assurance for success.

Product development

Developing digital products requires the awareness and acknowledgment of the importance of the following critical components in order to achieve success:

- The product must have multiple uses for multiple markets (e.g. the information must be easily reformatted and repurposed).
- Inventory management and costs must be reduced.
- Speed of revisions and updating must increase.
- Speed to market must increase by taking advantage of new forms of marketing, e.g. commercial network activity.
- Cost of goods must be lowered.
- Long-term profitability is more likely than short-term gains.

As product development must recognize positive features of digital information, developers must also be aware of the disadvantages we have come to acknowledge in the development of Primis:

- There was duplication of development and production costs.
- The unanticipated uses of the information needed a change in content.
- Costs increased because of a marketing bonanza (costs of entering multiple markets, costs in restructuring pricing models, additional resources needed to manage additional marketing information).
- Costs of technological developments had to be taken into account.
- The reality and perception of cannibalization had to be faced.

Finally, there are four poignant observations about technology when it is a key factor in product development:

- Use the lowest common technological denominator.
- You are not a technologist; do not just follow advice; know the technology.
- Ask the marketplace what it wants from technology.
- Although technology changes rapidly, users of technology do not — especially if the current product meets the customers' needs.

Economic issues behind the development of Primis

Let me now take a closer look at the business or economic issues surrounding Primis. One early issue raised was how far do we integrate Primis into the orderly course of business planning and development of the traditional product line. I wish business decisions could be made without the reality of internal politics, suspicions and limits of resources, because we essentially made no decision. The burden of a fully loaded profit and loss prevented us from standing alone. However, the use of new technologies and the mysteries of database publishing resulted in a profit centre within a profit centre. All of the editing, production and customer service operations were separate, but most of the editorial and all of the sales were integrated into the College Division. Thus, Primis was to take advantage of a large sales organization, but was limited as to what information to develop and into what markets to sell.

Because it did not stand alone, Primis needed more than a market; more than a marketable product; and more than a market-acceptable price in order to achieve a profit. As part of a larger division, Primis required that senior management reallocate resources. Why? Because to succeed, several elements of the long-term strategic plan had to take effect:

- The College Division had to reduce traditional plant costs (the costs of producing texts).
- We needed to implement a plan of distributed printing to reduce the burden of manufacturing costs.
- We had to restructure our marketing and sales organization in order to take advantage of consultative selling and marketing to new markets.

The reduction of costs is only possible if there is a reduction in the overall costs of handling traditional texts. In other words, if the investment is the same in traditional texts and the investment in Primis is additive, then the savings potential is greatly reduced.

The same can be said for distributed printing. Traditional publishing has long been based on large print runs or the economies of scale. Publishers pay for this printing and pass the costs on to the customer. As long as customers have no alternative and/or accept the results of long print runs (as will doubtless be the case for a long time with novels), then there is little benefit to distributed printing. Primis, however, provides the customer with an alternative. The business consequences are an immediate reduction in net cash revenue; the long-term benefit is higher gross margins.

Distributed printing is also closely tied to marketing and sales. Primis will ultimately succeed if customers subscribe to information, even educational information, on a long-term basis; hence we must create a consultative selling infrastructure with a greater emphasis on customer service. This follows the financial services model: low asset base and high usage turnover. The distributed printing model will also be important if we are to succeed, for database publishing is founded on the principle of the sales of our information base into multiple markets. Today, in an inventory-based model, we can tailor our information only to specific high-volume markets. In Primis, we sell customized material into all markets and develop the database with direct input from sales and marketing. This is, in essence, a reversal of the current publishing model in which editors develop product (a bound book) for a specific market and sales representatives sell into that specific market.

Sociological issues

The economic issues behind the development of Primis were not as significant or challenging as the sociological issues. We knew at the outset that we faced several key challenges to our traditional business: how would our customers react and how would we change not only their behaviour but also the behaviour of editors within McGraw-Hill?

What happened when we announced and launched the system was surprising in many ways. In some cases we had quick answers to our questions, for others, however, we are still searching.

Perhaps most striking and immediate was the realization that in creating a database of information we needed to alter our editorial thinking, to consider how information is created for electronic access and use. An author can no longer conceive of a work within an autonomous environment, but must realize that his or her material will be combined with other material, reused and reorganized to meet isolated needs and be constantly revised. Currently, as stated above, editors acquire and develop information for a specific targeted market. This market is clearly identified and limited because the traditional book is limiting. Now, with Primis, editors acquire information that moves into a variety of markets and is used in a dynamic, very flexible way by the end-user — the reader. Another significant change which affects not only authors, but also editors and publishers, is that revisions to our content will be made quickly and delivered in an updated format to the reader.

Finding or creating or promoting acceptance among our internal editorial community continues to be a difficult task. Authors and professors, on the other hand, quickly accepted Primis and were among the easiest to change. The reaction is logical if one allows for the fact that our customers demand content first; content that is current, editorially developed and delivered in a format which is customized to their requirements.

RESULTS

Primis was announced at EDUCOM in October of 1989 and the system became fully operational in February 1990. At the time we launched Primis we had three primary goals:

- to realize a fully operational system for electronically customized texts and course materials,
- to challenge the marketplace with concepts which dramatically altered the way course materials were selected and used, and
- to sell Primis texts to enough schools to ensure its future development.

In just the first year we not only achieved our stated goals but exceeded them to a degree we could not have imagined.

The operational requirements for the Primis system were as complex as standard publishing procedures, but without the benefit of centuries of tradition. We conceptualized and implemented an entirely new editorial and authoring process which reflected requirements of an electronic media; we developed new editing, design and production policies; we established compositors' typesetting guidelines (file specifications); we created an entirely new and self-sufficient order fulfilment and sales information system; we defined and programmed one of the industry's first sales-representative computerized ordering system. Finally, working closely with R. R. Donnelley, we established all the production requirements — printing, binding, shipping, billing — for the first and only just-in-time manufacturing facility in publishing.

The 1990 sales results of Primis were remarkable, especially considering that 80% of all sales decisions are made roughly between March and May. We sold nearly 25 000 individual texts, sent out approximately 8000 single-copy evaluation texts and had adoptions in almost 50 different community colleges and four-year colleges and universities throughout the USA. In achieving this degree of success we touched a nerve in our customers, for they have universally praised our efforts and sought our attention. Success can be measured in the fact that we have attracted new authors and inspired the seasoned; we have jump-started an entire industry and caused endless counter-manoeuvres on the part of our competitors.

Concrete proof of acceptance and success can be seen in Table 7.1.

Table 7.1 The success of Primis

Year	Size of database in pages	Number of institutions of higher education using Primis texts
1990	7 000	30
1991	30 000	150
1992	50 000	400
1993	100 000	1000

The future

The future of Primis focuses on two fronts: continuing development of a database that meets all our customer needs and taking technological advantage of what we have created. For example, with the creation of digital information we have made multimedia a reality, for until there is an underlying platform of consistently captured text-based information, the powerful educational uses of video, sound and computer graphics can never be fully realized. Finally, we are working hard to make McGraw-Hill's information resource — resources editorially developed to meet specific educational demands — available to schools via high-speed networks.

The acceptance by other publishers has proven to be a different story, as there has been little competitive response. This may be good for McGraw-Hill in one sense, for what we felt to be an initial lead of 18 months has turned out to be much longer; but it also raises questions of whether or not we introduced Primis too soon or whether others were too slow to react? One significant result in other publishers' not accepting many of the concepts behind Primis is that they continue to control intellectual property rights. The issues of rights remain central to database publishing and in all likelihood will dominate the publishing landscape of the future.

CONCLUSION

If Primis or any type of electronic publishing or new publishing venture is to work, we must first know our markets, but then go far beyond that basic knowledge in order to understand and deal with inherent social and economic issues. It is up to publishers to find a balance for what is required, what our customers want and, in the case of Primis, how technology can meet their needs. But, more importantly, publishers must find ways to change behaviour and introduce new modes of thinking, to transform authoring and editing processes and to rethink marketing and sales. Publishers have the opportunity to develop new relationships with the end-user, but in order to do so, all businesses must prepare for a more direct connection to the customer. If publishers are to compete in the provision of information, they must quickly react to the demands of the information users and these demands include not only aspects of how the information is written and developed, but also a commitment to a vision which is, for most of the industry, almost impossible to grasp, let alone to materialize.

EP and the magazine and periodicals publisher – case studies

8

Electronic extensions of a magazine

Rolf Wickmann, Gruner + Jahr, Germany

INITIAL SITUATION AND MOTIVATION

Why should a publishing house like Gruner + Jahr, long successful in magazine publishing, and in recent years successful in the newspaper sector as well, concern itself with the question of whether it should also offer its magazine and newspaper readers electronic products? The answer to this question has many facets: complementing the range of media offered; intensifying the dialogue with the reader and thus solidifying the relationship between a publication and its readers; an improvement of the product range; a timely, positive and 'progressive' modernization of the company's market position through new technological forms and, not least of all, the utilization of additional market and business opportunities.

The final point mentioned above is decisive: the electronic media are not seen as a threat, but rather as a constructive challenge for the print media; a challenge which can lead to further developments in the existing titles in the market, in the interest of and for the reader. Over ten years ago, bearing in mind the burgeoning market for private television and the introduction of videotext in Germany, the question of whether we should participate in such cooperative ventures was actively and intensively discussed. At least in the area of

Rolf Wickmann, who has been a Main Board Director of Gruner + Jahr AG & Co for over ten years, is responsible for all magazine publishing activities of the group; his office is at Gruner + Jahr's headquarters in Hamburg.

private television and radio, this question has in the meantime been answered clearly by our participation in RTL and the Premiere pay TV station, which have both become market leaders.

With regard to interactive electronic media, in the face of the dramatic developments which have taken place during the last two years, the question is certainly no longer 'Why?' but 'How?'. Ten years ago, we were the first publishing house to become active in the Videotext Computer Association. At that time, numerous predictions had led us to anticipate the same dynamic market expansion as we had already experienced with private television. For various reasons, however, this expansion did not materialize. Nonetheless, and despite results which continue to be disappointing, we have remained true to our original commitment. Since that time, this commitment has evolved into a kind of breeding ground for further electronic products. The following article will describe the development of a wide range of electronic ancillary products associated with our business magazine *CAPITAL*.

COMPUTER-BASED ACTIVITIES: THE FIRST STEP

By 1985, when the German videotext system and its approximately 40 000 predominantly professional and semiprofessional users signalled a growing, lucrative audience for electronic messages, *CAPITAL* had already begun offering promotional 'Aktionen' (computer-based activities) — activities which one would more likely call today 'pseudo-electronic offers in the form of so-called computer-based activities'. The basic concept behind these computer-supported promotional activities, which continued to be developed over the years and still enjoy a considerable popularity among readers, consists of printing a questionnaire in an issue of the magazine which the reader then completes and sends in to the publishing house. For a fee of DM20 to DM90 the questionnaire is evaluated by computer. The overall goal of such computer-based activities is to give the reader, based on his/her personal situation, in-depth analyses and advice which could never be featured in a magazine in such individualized detail.

An example

Three of the eight services and promotional activities which are currently offered, either temporarily or on a continuing basis, include:

- *The Salary Analysis:* In a three-page questionnaire, the reader provides information on his/her present salary, his/her occupational experience, the business sector and position in which he/she is currently employed etc. Through a comprehensive statistical analysis his/her detailed individual position is evaluated so that he/she can compare his/her salary to those of colleagues from similar age groups and business sectors. Moreover, he/she is given recommendations on how he/she should assess his/her overall situation and possibly even improve it.
- *The Health Insurance Analysis:* The complicated health insurance system in Germany is frankly so unintelligible that it is nearly impossible for an individual to draw up an optimal health insurance protection programme with a reasonable investment of time. The 'Health Insurance Analysis' can help here by providing a ranking of individual insurance companies based on the reader's personal preferences. The ranking is given in a computer-based evaluation program developed exclusively for *CAPITAL*.
- *The Stock Exchange Game:* In this game the reader receives a fictitious sum of DM20 000 or DM30 000, which he/she can speculatively 'invest' for two or three months under actual stock exchange conditions. The editorial staff follow a package of 100 stocks during the duration of the game. Within the rules of the game, the reader can buy and sell these stocks corresponding to actual stock exchange developments. The winner, in other words the reader who attains the highest investment returns from his/her fictitious start capital during the game period, is normally awarded a monetary prize donated by a sponsor.

From the above description, one can see that as early as 1985 there was already a real need among the readers for individualized as well as up-to-the minute information, and this need could only be met through *computer support*. During the following years, these information services were developed by the editorial department based on the results of reader surveys, modern communications technologies and the desire to intensify the relationship between reader and magazine. All of the prerequisites for success were present: sufficient reader interest, willingness to pay money to participate in and receive the results of such promotional activities, as well as the trust implied in giving the editorial staff private information (salary, taxes etc.) — a willingness which is not to be taken for granted in Germany.

In 1984 personal computers started their triumphant march into the German market. It was evident that PCs even at that time, when high costs limited their initial applications to commercial purposes only, would on a medium- to long-term basis also become established in private households and thus become a permanent fixture in the private lives of our readers. The anticipated expansion of a videotext system connected to personal computers seemed to us to be so logical and commercially profitable on a long-term basis that we concentrated our efforts to create an electronic extension of *CAPITAL* magazine on these two basic technologies, and we still utilize these to the present day.

PCS, VIDEOTEXT AND AUDIOTEXT — PATHS TO A MULTIMEDIA WORLD

The development of electronic extensions to a magazine is a difficult and lengthy process. It is not a decision that one makes today and implements tomorrow. The speed of such developments is determined by numerous parameters and external factors, some of which are random in nature.

Even the question of whether the electronic extensions of a magazine can cause a so-called 'substitution effect' leading, for example, to a drop in the paid circulation, has for the present time been clearly refuted for consumer magazines. The situation regarding trade publications is, however, somewhat different. Anyone who has attempted to read a magazine on a computer monitor — high-resolution or not — probably will not be so quick to join the group of incorrigible prophets who point to the dangers of this substitution effect. The contents of a magazine differ from the identical or at least similar electronic offerings in two essential criteria:

● *Consumability:* A magazine can be comfortably read independently of the location and without further equipment — such as computer monitors. The time that one needs to absorb the information contained in a magazine lies considerably under the time that one would need to absorb the same volume of information from an electronic medium.

- *Active information:* Among other things, a magazine is designed to actively inform its readers about situations and developments about which they would normally not inquire.

This knowledge has already been accepted in the publishing sector, not least because the increasing 'electronization' of the publishing industry has produced editors who were formerly never confronted with electronics in their daily work, but are today in a position to appreciate better both the possibilities and the deficiencies of electronic offerings. From the very beginning, however, there were also editors who were already electronic-minded and whose help was instrumental in removing or reducing the many small, as well as major, hurdles that arose while developing such projects.

Our initial considerations were based on the assumption that there was no single topic which enjoyed a higher interest among all *CAPITAL* readers than the subject of taxes, one of the basic editorial components of every issue of the magazine. The German tax laws have always been, and still are, quite complicated, so it was a logical step for us to offer corresponding PC support to enable the reader to prepare his/her own individual tax returns. We enjoyed such an immediate success with this product idea, even though we had carried out virtually no preparatory market research, that we decided to embark on a second phase. The preparations for this step, however, were much more thorough than for its predecessor.

During the development of this new product, we first decided to carry *CAPITAL* magazine's service-oriented aspect over into the new electronic products as well. Our basic assumption was that personal computers would first be found among the *CAPITAL* readers who had already had intensive experience with PCs in their offices and that these persons would also use a PC as a means for solving their private organizational problems.

Available media surveys helped us first select as a primary target group the *CAPITAL* readers with a pronounced interest in the stock exchange, aged 20 to 49, and with above average annual salaries. By combining the addresses of the participants of stock exchange games from earlier years and of a special *CAPITAL* Stock Exchange Newsletter (*CapitalDepesche*), we had an interesting and low-cost marketing instrument for developing a new product that we called *CAPITAL-Börse* (*CAPITAL* 'Stock Exchange'). This new development features an MS-DOS program for chart analysis, a videotext software decoder purchased in a licensed arrangement, and an additional online exchange quotation service for 1000 securities, index values and currency exchange rates.

This was the first electronic stock exchange service ever offered by a German magazine in combination with videotext and a personal computer. The most important characteristics of this product were derived directly from the requirements we had set down earlier:

- simplicity of installation,
- simplicity in using software,
- high motivation on the part of the reader to purchase and use this software because of the considerable time savings he/she can enjoy while following the course of the stock market.

Based on the recognition that the responsibilities for the electronification of magazines should be concentrated in one location in the publishing house — at least during the initial stages — in 1986 we established a subsidiary, Gruner + Jahr Informationssysteme GmbH, which had, and still has, the task of monitoring technological developments in the market and deciding whether these technologies could be applicable for publishing-based products.

We were more than surprised by the success of *CAPITAL-Börse*, because the product and offer of an online data administration was at the time without competition in the market. From the simple realization that readers who regularly follow developments in the stock market could also have a need to have their portfolios managed, we developed a portfolio administration program which we were able to sell successfully with very little marketing expenditure to a target group which was already partially receptive to such a service.

During the course of servicing the readers' needs regarding these products, we became aware of the importance of a competent and speedy service for the purchaser and subscriber. The lack of knowledge among our readers regarding personal computers and MS-DOS operating systems exceeded even our deepest fears. In many instances, the available knowledge was not even sufficient for the reader to carry out on his/her own PC the instructions given to him/her over the telephone. We needed a learning period of around one year to develop the basic concepts for new products and the consequences which arose from these conceptions. In 1989/1990 we therefore decided to define and develop a uniform database, architecture and user interface created specifically for our needs. Every passing day confirms the correctness of this decision. We have named this central database the Datasafe-Concept, and all new products which we developed in the interim have access to this data source. With Datasafe we have created a platform which offers two decisive advantages:

- The simplest installation by the user through an automatic release administration for all Datasafe-compatible programs.
- A uniform user architecture for all areas of private finance, which no other competitor has yet been able to match.

The release administration mentioned above is especially important because we have no means of 'controlling' the thousands upon thousands of PCs, with the thousands upon thousands of various databases which are in use, whose malfunction or destruction could have fatal consequences for the respective user.

We have not concentrated our electronic extensions on the personal computer alone. For example, the Stock Exchange Game mentioned above has been extended to include a videotext application which is enjoying greater popularity from year to year. When we began work on these developments in 1978, around 10% of the players of the Stock Exchange Game participated via videotext. Today some 500 000 connected videotext terminals represent around 30% of all the players who participate. In 1992 we extended the concept of the Stock Exchange Game to include audiotext as well, so that today when we conduct a game it is in fact a multimedia stock-exchange event which can still be played through the 'classic' medium of postcards as well as via videotext and audiotext.

WHERE DO WE GO FROM HERE?

If one divides the possibilities for a magazine participation into multimedia sectors, the current *CAPITAL* programme is as in Table

Table 8.1 Multimedia segments for the consumer market (based on *CAPITAL*)

	Interactive	Pseudo-interactive	Passive
Online	Interactive Videotex Audiotex Mortgage Rates Stock Exchange Game Net Worth Game *CAPITAL-Börse* Chart Service		
Offline	PC Programs	Computer-based activities	Print products
	CAPITAL-Börse *CAPITAL-Depot* *CAPITAL-Trend* *CAPITAL-Access* *CAPITAL-Chart Trainer* *CAPITAL-Vermögen* *CAPITAL-Fonds* *CAPITAL-Steuern* *CAPITAL-Budget* *CAPITAL-Register* *CAPITAL-Darlehen* *CAPITAL-Rendite* *CAPITAL-Traveller*	Stock Exchange Game Health Insurance Salary Analysis Mortgage Rates Net Worth Game Construction Financing Life Insurance	*CAPITAL Issue* *CAPITAL-Depesche* *CAPITAL-Persönlich* *CAPITAL-Vertraulich* Special Issues

8.1, which shows the present, relatively complete coverage of the market along with conceivable future alternatives and possibilities.

The reader of this chapter will understand that we are not at liberty to explain our future planned projects in greater detail at this point. However, we will continue to orient ourselves along several guidelines which can be summarized as follows:

- *Focusing of contents:* People's interests do not change over time, but the way in which they are interested in the happenings of their immediate surroundings do change indeed. A hundred years ago one played chess. For the last ten years one has been able to play chess against a computer, and perhaps in the future one will also be able to play telechess in a virtual-reality world. The fact, however, that chess will still be played is immutable.
- *Consumability:* With the exception of a few freaks, everyone who uses an electronic medium wants to do it as simply and easily as

possible. Just the necessity of having specialized equipment leads to a certain reluctance, which is not found with magazines. For this reason, electronic media products must make using the medium more attractive, because the user has first to overcome smaller or larger anxieties. In other words, a magazine merely printed on a computer monitor makes no sense at all.

- *Economies:* Despite the temptation to achieve everything which is technically achievable, we will never lose sight of the commercial aspects of magazine extensions. These economic considerations depend to a large degree on the respective target group's willingness to participate.

- *Joint marketing:* A magazine's electronic extensions must remain consistent with the magazine's philosophy. An electronic art calendar offered as a by-product of a sports magazine is unthinkable. Such considerations are necessary but are not sufficient in themselves. An electronic product must also live up to the quality standards of the magazine, because the magazine's readers expect nothing less from the title. Especially when communicating with readers who use several electronic magazine extensions, one finds oneself in a multichannel dialogue with the reader. If the reader is dissatisfied with any one of the various electronic products in terms of quality or service, it can lead to disturbances in the other communications channels as well (e.g. the reader cancelling his/her subscription to the magazine). Not only opportunities await electronic extensions of magazines, but risks as well.

As a general rule, new ventures in the multimedia sector should not be solely oriented to what is technically possible, but rather along product-related guidelines as well. In this framework we will continue to work on new electronic magazine extensions — always in close cooperation with the magazines' editorial staffs.

9

The University Licensing Program (TULIP) — a case study in locally networked full text

Karen Hunter, Elsevier Science, Netherlands/USA

STARTING POINT

TULIP started early in 1991. University systems and library leaders at a number of schools had been talking with us to find a way to accelerate the development of systems for the distribution in electronic form of traditional journal information — information presently found only in print. Elsevier Science was looking at the same question from the publisher's side and was looking for experience on which to make strategic developmental and investment decisions, whether in search software, document delivery systems, PostScript or SGML database files or network development. Elsevier had been participating in a research project at Carnegie Mellon and had been approached by several other universities to join in single-site experiments. While these experiments required little investment on Elsevier's part, they were also highly idiosyncratic and unlikely to define a market or to lead to generalizable findings.

Karen Hunter is Vice-President and Assistant to the Chairman of Elsevier Science bv and works from Amsterdam headquarters as well as the main Elsevier Science USA office in New York. Elsevier Science is one of the companies belonging to the Reed–Elsevier publishing group, UK/Netherlands. The Elsevier Science group is the largest publisher of scientific journals and books worldwide.

During a Coalition for Networked Information (CNI) workshop in early March 1991 and a CNI Task Force meeting later that month, several things came together. The workshop confirmed that we were all struggling with the absence of economic models and needed to move from talk to prototypes. As a publisher, how do you risk changing your business when your customer cannot yet define what it needs and you have little idea of potential revenues? How do you as a library or university know what is most desirable from the users' standpoint when there are few databases of primary literature to use as testbeds? At the Task Force meeting we agreed that if ten or 15 universities would commit to the same basic experiment, then a publisher could justify investing in the creation of a major testbed. University participants outlined a project and organized a group of universities on the spot and TULIP, as it came to be known, was planted.

Ultimately, nine universities decided to participate: Carnegie Mellon University, Cornell University, Georgia Institute of Technology, Massachusetts Institute of Technology, University of California (all campuses), University of Michigan, University of Tennessee, University of Washington and Virginia Polytechnic Institute and State University are the initial participants. The program is planned to run through 1995.

TULIP'S OBJECTIVES

TULIP is a cooperative research project testing systems for networked delivery and use of journals. The participants set three objectives at the outset:

- *Technical:* To determine the technical feasibility of networked distribution to and across institutions with varying levels of sophistication in their technical infrastructure. 'Networked distribution' means sending the information both across the national Internet and over campus networks to the desktops of students and faculty. Elsevier will deliver the journal information to participating universities in standard formats. The universities will incorporate the information in local prototype or operational systems. A wide variety of delivery alternatives, search and retrieval systems and print-on-demand options will be compared.

- *Organizational and economic:* To understand, through the implementation of prototypes, alternative costing, pricing, subscription and market models that may be 'viable' in electronic distribution scenarios; comparing such models with existing print-then-distribute models; and understanding the role of campus organizational units under such scenarios. The overall goal is to reduce the unit cost of information delivery and retrieval. 'Viable' means economically and functionally acceptable to all parties.
- *User behaviour:* To study reader usage patterns under different distribution (technical, organizational and economic) situations. Improvement in the functionality of the information, whether as to article structure or retrieval tools, will also be considered. Certain data will be collected uniformly at all sites for analysis in the aggregate and for comparison among different systems.

BASIC PROVISIONS

Elsevier is providing electronic files for 43 Elsevier and Pergamon journals in materials science and engineering. The files consist of:

- TIFF bit-mapped page images (cover-to-cover, including tables of contents), scanned from the printed page at 300 dpi (600 dpi for certain applications), Group IV fax compression.
- Edited and structured ASCII 'heads' for each editorial item, including bibliographic citation and article abstract.
- Unedited OCR-generated ASCII full text for use in searching, but not for display.

In addition, as TULIP journals are available in SGML and PostScript as a by-product of the production process, they will made available to the participating universities in those formats as well.

Each university receives without charge during the project the electronic full text (bit-mapped and ASCII) for those journals to which they subscribe in paper. They also receive the bibliographic information for all 43 journals and have on-demand access on a pay-per-use model to those titles to which they do not subscribe. All but one university mount the subscribed-to full-text files locally on their own file servers. One retrieves all articles over the Internet on-demand from Engineering Information (Ei). Both models are important to test for efficiency and cost-effectiveness.

CHOICE OF JOURNALS

The participating universities have in common strengths in the physical and engineering sciences. In looking within these disciplines for a target area, we wanted a field in which the researchers in general were comfortable with computer applications and had a higher than average installed base of workstations. An obvious choice might have been computer science itself, but we felt these users would be so atypical in their computer facility as to make it hard to generalize results to other disciplines. Materials science provided a field in which there was both a sufficiently large corpus of frequently cited material and interested faculties. It is also a field in which Elsevier has a large core collection of journals without the need to rely on other publishers, something which everyone thought would only further complicate the process.

Other journals from Elsevier Science may be added later, but all participants want to get operations running smoothly first and see whether the whole process is an effective one.

IMPLEMENTATION

In 1992 the universities prepared plans as to how they expect to implement the Program on their campuses. These plans reflected the hoped-for diversity and include single sites, multiple campuses within one institution (where the files will be mounted on one server for all), a cooperative arrangement between two institutions and the possibility of testing regional network distribution to a much larger group of schools. Access tools and distribution systems on campus also include a wide range of alternatives, from high-resolution images sent directly to desktop workstations to DocuTech print-on-demand of individual articles and of locally sold subscriptions. The goal is to provide as much local autonomy as possible, subject to standard terms and conditions which are outlined in licences signed with each site.

Table 9.1 shows the technical highlights of TULIP.

Table 9.1 University technical highlights

University	Storage/retrieval/search engine	User interface/image viewing/printing
Carnegie Mellon	Derived from Mercury project. Storage on Sun SparcStations with magnetic disks. Newton search engine.	Access via bibliographic indexes such as INSPEC and Mercury interface for searching and browsing. Proprietary image viewer. 2000 Unix workstations available for displaying images. TIFF images 'wrapped' in PostScript for printing.
Cornell University	Storage on EPIC jukebox with optical disks. Access/ retrieval of images via index on separate magnetic disk (3.5 Gbyte). Retrieval via CLASS. Basic relational database as search engine.	X-windows interface. Images viewed on the network at 100 dpi. Images printed centrally on a DocuTech machine at 600 dpi.
Georgia Institute of Technology	Storage and retrieval from an IBM RS-6000/970. Storage on magnetic disks. BRS search engine.	User interface adapted from GTEL/BRS search interface. Experimenting with BRS image search. Printing centrally or sent to user's fax.
Massachusetts Institute of Technology	Bibliographic files under Newton search enginer. Image server software developed by the Library 2000 Group.	Use WILLOW 2.3 (from University of Washington) with MIT-developed Z39.50 driver to operate with Newton. Image viewer/ browser undecided.
University of California	DEC storage server 100. Retrieval via TULIP server on existing mainframe. Central storage at Oakland for all campuses. Access via a & i databases on MELVYL.	Access through MELVYL at present. Once article identified, start up of a proprietary X-windows application using remote computing. Viewing of images on computers with X-windows capability. At a minimum, printing at central sites on each campus.

Table 9.1 *continued*

University	Storage/retrieval/search engine	User interface/image viewing/printing
University of Michigan	Current materials stored on magnetic disks, back volumes on CD-ROM jukebox. Retrieval servers are DECstations 5000/200. Proprietary retrieval system.	TULIPView X-windows-based interface, plus standard library system interface. Image viewer integrated in TULIPView, display on X-windows capable terminals. TIFF images 'wrapped' in PostScript for central and local printing.
University of Tennessee	Initially no local image storage. On-demand retrieval of images from Engineering Information. Access to TULIP articles through Online Library Information Service (OLIS) or Gopher client displaying table of contents.	OLIS interface is standard character-based. Gopher client is menu driven. No image viewing in the first year. Images printed when retrieved from Engineering Information.
University of Washington	Images stored as files on hard disk. Bibliographic material stored online in a database on IBM RS-6000. Search engine is BRS Search.	WILLOW (Washington Information Looker-upper Layered Over Windows), an X-windows based search client developed by UW. Image viewing with SwiftView. Printing can be ordered from 'e-mail print server' for printing.

MAKING TULIP WORK ON THE TECHNICAL SIDE

Although Elsevier Science is to a large extent one publishing company, it actually consists of several different publishing houses in a number of different countries. Journals in the field of material science are published in Amsterdam (Netherlands), Lausanne (Switzerland), Oxford (UK) and New York (USA). As a result of historical technological differences and more recent acquisitions, there exists no single production flow mechanism covering all journal titles within the Elsevier

Science organization. The 43 journal titles in TULIP, for instance, are typeset by some 18 different typesetting companies. Every journal title has its own layout, its own size and its own typefaces.

At present, Elsevier Science is consolidating all these different production methods to streamline the output into one electronic format, which then is the basic material to not only produce paper versions of the journals in their most appropriate typeset form, but also to provide 'real' electronic versions of the journals. As an intermediate step however, for TULIP we use the paper version of the journals to produce scanned images as the electronic form of the journals.

Organizing the production of the TULIP journals into a smoothly running operation was a not a trivial task. The production and distribution of TULIP material is done at two sites: the scanning office processes journal material and produces all electronic material, while the distributor, Engineering Information, customizes the files based on subscriptions and transmits them through the Internet to the university libraries.

In the scanning office the following steps take place to create the TULIP data:

- The scanning office receives the journal issues in a special priority subscription arrangement.
- After logging in the journal issue, the spine is cut off and the pages are fed into a double-sided, high-volume image scanner. As the scanner does not take into account differences in size between journals, the full-size page images are electronically trimmed to the real size of the original page. The page-image files are compressed to approximately 8% of their original size for storage.
- The page image files are fed into an Optical Character Recognition (OCR) process, in which blocks of black and white dots are interpreted into characters, words, sentences and paragraphs of text.
- The top part of the resulting OCRed text is checked and spelling mistakes are corrected, to produce bibliographic information. Title, authors, keywords, abstract, etc. are assigned to specific fields. This is followed by a check on completeness and consistency.
- Every two weeks the material is put together into so-called 'full datasets'. These datasets contain all page images of the journal issues, the raw or unedited ASCII full-text and a master index to the page images, which includes the bibliographic data.

On average, the size of a page image file is 1 Mbyte uncompressed, and compressed (CCITT fax group IV) between 70 and 80 kbytes. The raw ASCII is about 4 kbytes per page, and the bibliographic data of an article is around 1.5 kbytes. The length of articles varies quite a bit, ranging from long reviews to short editorials, but the average article is about seven pages long.

A typical dataset would contain some 500 articles, 3500 pages and take up 280 Mbytes of disk space. In 1992 16 datasets were produced, containing 584 journal issues, 15 910 articles on 112 316 pages. In 1993 there were 20 datasets, containing 622 journal issues and 16 325 articles on 120 532 pages. Datasets were bigger than in the normal production scheme for the 1992 and early 1993 material, as there was a backlog at the start of production in early 1993. The total storage space required for the total 1992 and 1993 TULIP material is close to 20 Gbytes.

Datasets are despatched to Engineering Information's Article Express office in Westbury, NY, where a number of functions are handled:

- For each of the TULIP universities a customized dataset is generated from the original master index. A customized dataset includes all the material from journals to which the university subscribes, be it a paper or an electronic subscription.
- Again for each university an FTP script is generated. The Internet facility File Transfer Protocol or FTP is used to move the files from Engineering Information to the universities and the scripts automate sending of the TULIP datasets including checks on delivery of all files.
- Deliveries are done overnight by executing the FTP scripts. The average size of a dataset is between 200 and 300 Mbytes. Transferring these large amounts of data across the Internet takes between three and five hours per site. Engineering Information is linked to the Internet by a T1 data link with speeds of 1.5 Mb/s.
- The datasets are 'put' on a machine and directory designated by the university. In most cases this is a temporary storage facility. From this temporary storage, the files are transferred to the information systems in which TULIP data are kept for use on the campuses, making place for delivery of the next batch.

Engineering Information also runs an article delivery facility of the TULIP titles, so universities can order articles from journal titles for which they do not hold a subscription. This facility is driven by structured electronic mail messages, allowing for, but not requiring, an automated process on the university side. In the first quarter of 1994 we will also establish at Engineering Information a means for universities to 'pull' recent datasets on demand, to make coordination of dataset delivery easier.

MARKET RESEARCH

Using information technology to bring information to the user's desktop in order to improve the accessibility of scientific information is a major goal of TULIP for Elsevier as well as for the participating universities. What we do not know as yet, however, is which combination of elements (technical, organizational and economic) makes for a successful implementation, 'successful' meaning that users like the system and above all actually use it for their research and study. An important part of the TULIP experiment, therefore, is to gather and subsequently analyse information on the user behaviour under different technical, organizational and economic conditions.

Some of the TULIP partners have built-in major statistical usage tracking applications to do detailed behaviour studies in the coming years. In addition to these local research projects, Elsevier is doing qualitative market research using questionnaires, interviews and the like, as well as quantitative research by gathering usage logs from the TULIP partners. The results are combined to produce overall reports. The privacy and anonymity of the user will, of course, be rigorously protected at all levels.

The information from this research will be used to address a whole range of questions. Examples include:

- How are people using information, by selecting on screen and then printing, or do they read on screen as well?
- Which journals and articles are used most (and least)?
- What times do users prefer to access the information?
- Who are the prime users of the TULIP material: faculty, graduate students, library staff?
- The participating universities offer different approaches to TU-

LIP: how does this affect usage behaviour and what can we learn from that?

In order to be able to answer these questions the development of TULIP has to be monitored closely. How is this organized?

First of all, the information behaviour of users 'before TULIP' is being studied at each university (again, anonymously) at the start of their TULIP implementation. This is done by means of a questionnaire that addresses, for instance, the usage of scientific journals, the different methods of obtaining journal articles and which computing and telecommunications facilities are available. This type of research will be repeated at certain intervals during the experiment, hopefully providing more insights into changes in information behaviour. Second, the usage log files that each TULIP partner will send to Elsevier on a monthly basis will give the basic information on the way the TULIP files have been used at each university. Finally, more indepth, qualitative research is planned during the experiment by means of questionnaires, interviews and focus groups in close cooperation with the TULIP partners.

WHAT IS AHEAD

Many of the strategic questions behind TULIP still have to be answered. We have to gather more user data to understand how or if students and faculty use the files over a longer period of availability. Several additional pricing models will be tested during TULIP's last year (1995). The final evaluation of the efficacy of the Internet for the delivery of large journal files and the relative pros and cons of local storage of large datasets must also be made. We are reviewing the software necesssary to distribute and access the journals and enhance their functionality. Finally, as SGML and PostScript files are tested, these alternative formats will add important additional information.

TULIP has proven a rewarding experimental effort for its active participants. It is not a product test but an opportunity to learn in a cooperative environment more about what is possible and what will be most desirable. We appreciate the hard work and determination of our university partners in making TULIP a reality.

EP and the newspaper
publisher — case studies

10

Newspapers and electronic publishing: an overview

Anton Jolkovski and Livia Burkhardt, INES Media Concepts, Germany

INTRODUCTION

INES — the Initiative for Newspaper Electronic Supplements — came into being in mid-1993, after the IFRA Board decided that a separate organization could better help newspapers investigate and analyse the issues involved in electronic publishing. IFRA (INCA-FIEJ Research Association) is the international association for newspaper and media technology. INES does not want to replace the printed newspaper, but rather aims to develop concepts for electronic products and services to augment it. In addition to analysing issues and developing concepts, INES informs its partner newspapers about technological and other developments in electronic publishing that affect them. Partnership in INES is open to all IFRA member newspaper companies, and to date more than 40 have joined. INES has its offices in Darmstadt, Germany, not far from IFRA's headquarters.

INES believes the printed newspaper will continue to perform an important role in society for many years to come. Indeed, it is our declared aim to ensure the future of the printed newspaper. At the same time, we believe the advent of the digital age has resulted in a

Anton Jolkovski and Livia Burkhardt are Project Managers of INES Media Concepts GmbH, a company which was founded by IFRA, the Inca-Fiej Newspapers Research Association, based in Darmstadt.

plethora of electronic publishing opportunities for newspapers. As technology advances, more and more possibilities will open up, but of course those opportunities are not restricted to newspapers. In fact, these days it seems that everybody wants to become a publisher — including software companies and even hardware manufacturers. Many of them will learn the hard way what the day-to-day business of publishing really involves.

The newspaper industry has hundreds of years of experience in publishing. Newspapers have finely honed mechanisms for dealing with the ramifications of the material they publish. They also have huge and well-structured stores of information about current events, cultural affairs, consumer issues, economic matters and leisure activities. In short, they have content and, as the recent spate of business acquisitions demonstrates, content providers are in heavy demand. Billions of dollars are being invested to upgrade the communications infrastructure, and the companies doing the investing want to make sure there will be traffic on those new channels.

Ultimately newspapers are in the information business, the business of gathering, checking and organizing information, and presenting it in a creative and compelling manner through a combination of various forms of type, photographs and graphics. That is the core of the newspaper's activity — not printing and delivering bundles of paper. Paper was simply the only practical substrate available for the distribution of the information, and that is no longer the case. Today the digital communications revolution offers the newspaper a chance to overcome the limitations of printing on newsprint — a process left over from the industrial age.

WHY NEWSPAPERS SHOULD CONSIDER PUBLISHING ELECTRONICALLY

So far, we have mentioned some general reasons for newspapers to enter the electronic publishing field. We will now examine some more concrete motives.

One reason is purely defensive: before too long, newspapers will need to use the advantages of electronics in order to avoid losing their markets for both advertising and editorial content. A major US-based advertising agency has already said it is tentatively planning to stop using newspapers in its ad campaigns by the end of the decade. It claimed that by that time newspapers will be obsolete as an ad medium. The same agency stated it would reconsider its decision if the newspaper industry moved to keep pace with technological advances. The agency indicated that it hoped newspapers would be able to offer interactivity, multimedia and other sophisticated EP techniques in the near future.

As far as the market for editorial information is concerned, some nonnewspaper companies have acted quite aggressively over the past few years. They are increasingly providing news content directly to the consumer — content that newspapers, especially national ones, could readily offer if they chose to do so (to be fair, we should note that some already do — more about that later). News agencies such as Associated Press, Reuters and United Press International are no longer satisfied with selling to customers in the media industry. Rather, they are pushing their way into homes and businesses by supplying news online via computer networks. AP, for instance, offers news and sports information to all subscribers to the CompuServe computer network at no charge beyond the normal CompuServe fees. Bulletins are updated hourly. For an extra charge subscribers can develop an interest profile and receive items matching that profile in a special file. Reuters also offers news via CompuServe and via America Online, a competing computer network. UPI offers news and sports on America Online. Incidentally, the Windows icon for access to news information on America Online is — what else? — a newspaper.

CompuServe subscribers can even purchase software that will automatically dial up the service according to a user-specified schedule, download stories in the desired categories, and funnel the information into an on-screen 'newspaper' that the user has designed ahead of time. The software is called *Journalist*.

Before the online phenomenon is dismissed as a purely American development, it should be noted that CompuServe has a well-established European operation, with access points in many major cities on the Continent and in the UK.

Another reason for newspapers to enter electronic publishing is not defensive but rather positive: to expand their revenue base — at least in the long term — by 'recycling' information they already have in their possession. Making the information available online can be relatively easy, especially since current and in many cases archival data already is in digital form. Editorial computer systems from companies such as Germany's P.Ink and electronic archives from suppliers such as Digital Collections, also of Germany, make it simple for the newspaper to put information on a host computer.

The technical aspect of publishing electronically can be quite straightforward. However, there are many other considerations, such as the legal situation. The main legal question is one of copyright: Does the newspaper own the rights to republish information electronically? Or will it run the risk of legal action by its editorial staff and/or freelance contributors? Such claims have already been filed against newspapers, charging them with violating contract terms by publishing material electronically. Therefore, newspapers would be well advised to investigate their legal situations closely before getting into electronic publishing.

Another consideration is how to present information on the user's computer screen. A newspaper might choose simply to make available the ASCII output of its editorial system or facsimile images of its pages, but will the consumer find that format sufficiently easy to read and attractive to induce him/her to use the service? Probably not, thus some sort of specially designed presentation may be called for. In designing its on-screen presentation, the newspaper could apply some of its long experience in using design elements such as typefaces and column-based make-up. At any rate, the newspaper should investigate the nature of the differences between screen- and paper-based presentation. It also might consider creating a certain degree of visual similarity between the electronic and printed products to reinforce the newspaper's identity.

Ultimately, electronic publishing offers the newspaper an opportunity to provide something extra that the reader finds informative, useful or entertaining — and is thus willing to pay for. That extra value might come in the form of updated reports between the daily editions of the newspaper. After all, the news in the printed newspaper is usually eight to 12 hours old, while information can be distributed electronically within a few seconds or minutes of an event. An electronic service could also provide new and easier ways for the reader to find exactly the bit of current information that he or she is looking for. With a well-designed user interface, that could be done without compromising either the editor's role in determining the most important stories of the day or the 'serendipity' effect — the reader's accidental discovery of something interesting while browsing. Another attraction could be the availability of reference or background information. Because of space limitations the printed newspaper must concentrate on the latest occurrences; however, an electronic product or service may well have the capacity to offer a vast amount of supplementary information on demand.

Perhaps most importantly, some electronic products offer multimedia presentation capabilities — not just text, photos and graphics but sound, animation and possibly full-motion video. That offers the possibility for a truly new medium, with all elements of a news story in their original form, augmenting the newspaper with the power of radio and TV.

TYPES OF ELECTRONIC PRODUCTS OR SERVICES A NEWSPAPER COULD OFFER

Of all ways to distribute information electronically probably the simplest is the floppy disk. That medium should not be dismissed out of hand. It is simple and cheap, and the hardware the reader needs is widely installed and standardized. If only ASCII text is to be stored, a floppy will hold an enormous amount of information. With commonly available compression–decompression software, a floppy can store high-resolution photographs and even animated graphics and sound bites as well as text. Of course, the biggest drawback of a floppy disk is the need to transport it physically from publisher to reader.

So the floppy disk is best suited to less-urgent information, but it still has potential applications for newspapers. *La Libre Belgique*, a Belgian daily newspaper, publishes a floppy disk every Monday containing the previous week's international, national and economic news content of the newspaper. The floppies are mailed to those who subscribe to the service. The subscriber can build up a database of information, on his/her hard disk if desired, for future reference.

The most popular of the offline publication media is the CD-ROM, with the major advantage of vast storage capacity. A single CD-ROM can hold up to two years' worth of daily newspapers, depending on the format and other variables. Such a disc can be searched extremely quickly and efficiently. Those factors make it a good medium for archival information. Nearly a hundred newspapers worldwide are published on CD-ROM. The major drawback of CD-ROMs for newspaper use is the large amount of time and expense involved in preparing, organizing and formatting the information. Updates are not a simple matter, so there tend to be long lapses between them. In addition, although CD-ROM players are growing rapidly in popularity, they are still found in only a small proportion of home or business computer installations. Thus the market for newspaper CD-ROMs is largely restricted to educational and research institutions.

The large storage capacity and efficient searchability of CD-ROMs, on the other hand, make them suitable for multimedia and hybrid presentations. *USA Today* has published a disc containing not only a couple of years' worth of back issues but a dictionary, thesaurus, rudimentary atlas and other reference works to help the reader answer any questions that might arise when reading the articles. There are also some short sound bites on the disc. As one might expect of a product aimed at *USA Today* readers, the presentation is rather flashy but very user-friendly.

As we mentioned earlier, some newspapers are providing news information online, and others plan to do so in the near future. In Europe, quite a few newspapers are working with videotex services such as Minitel in France. Probably the most ambitious services currently in operation, however, are found on the America Online (AOL) computer network. They are Chicago Online, operated by the *Chicago Tribune*, and Mercury Center, operated by the *San Jose Mercury News*, part of the Knight-Ridder newspaper chain. Both are accessible from anywhere in the USA by anyone who has a computer, a modem, an America Online subscription, and the AOL user software. Both are ASCII text services and offer the full editorial text of the same day's newspaper plus other items such as electronic fora on controversial topics, 'chat rooms' where readers can carry on real-time 'conversations' with others via their computer keyboards and classified advertisements with search capabilities. Mercury Center also offers articles that did not appear in the newspaper and additional material related to printed articles. Chicago Online offers a gateway to Ticketron, a concert and sports ticketing service, so readers can order tickets online, paying with their credit cards.

Mercury Center also offers access to back issues of the newspaper for a substantial extra charge. Many other newspapers put the contents of their electronic archives on remote host systems such as Mead Data's NEXIS or Genios, which is based in Germany. Those services are aimed at the professional documentalist, not the consumer. Newspapers generally have found that the consumer market for archival material is not large enough to justify the expense and effort of making that material widely available and easy to use online. However, that may change as consumers become more used to getting the latest news online. Access to current information might well whet their appetite for access to past information.

In addition to offline products such as CD-ROMs and online services, there is a category of newspaper electronic publications that could be called downloaded products. Whereas the subscriber to an online service browses through a remote database and selects stories that interest him/her, with a downloaded product the reader simply gets online, downloads the entire latest issue on to his/her hard disk and goes offline. Perhaps the best-known such product is *News in Motion*, published by a US company called WalkSoft. *News in Motion* is a weekly publication (though it is expected to go daily early this year) which presents stories and photographs purchased from the syndication services of major newspapers and news agencies around the world. Editors at WalkSoft lay out the stories in newspaper style, with columns, headlines, and photos. They also add such multimedia features as animated infographics and cartoons, and sound bites. When complete, the issue is compressed using common software and made available for downloading via a toll-free telephone number. *News in Motion* reader software handles decompression and presentation. Each issue will fit on a single floppy disk and the subscriber can receive it in that form by mail if desired. The subscriber can store all downloaded issues, thus acquiring a sort of private electronic archive which he/she can search on a full-text basis.

We believe the downloaded product concept holds a great deal of promise and we are not alone in our point of view. Major companies — both conventional publishers and others — are developing such news products, primarily for downloading into hand-held devices such as the personal digital assistant (PDA) or personal intelligent communicator (PIC). The reader would connect his/her device to a phone line — perhaps in an airport — and request the latest news update. The device would dial a 'phone number and download the update, which the reader could then browse while on route to his/her next business appointment.

Of course, that delivery system requires the reader to establish a wire-based connection to the telephone network. An alternative is wireless transmission of news updates via an electronic mail system operating on the cellular phone network. The reader can download those updates from virtually anywhere. A California-based company, RadioMail, is already operating such a service for laptop computers — independently of any newspaper, we should note. But the *Washington Post* is developing a similar system, in cooperation with American Personal Communications.

THE NEWSPAPER AS ELECTRONIC PUBLISHER

In this section we will briefly examine the two basic approaches a newspaper publisher could take when getting into electronic publishing. These approaches reflect contrasting philosophies. Most publishers have taken a middle route, somewhere in between these two approaches.

At one end of the scale, if the newspaper has sufficient resources, it can proceed more or less alone, developing its own hardware and software. That route is open only to the largest of newspaper companies. Associated Newspapers, a major UK newspaper group, is following that path. The advantage is that the newspaper can tailor a system to meet its own needs, with a minimum of compromises, and it remains independent of third-party developers. The main disadvantage is the high cost. If a dedicated system is created, with no other uses except for that newspaper's particular electronic service, the newspaper must bear the cost alone. The risk can be rather high.

At the other end of the spectrum would be a newspaper that does no electronic publishing itself but rather arranges to transfer its contents to a company that has an established infrastructure and expertise in the field. In the case of a CD-ROM, that could mean working with an established CD-ROM publisher. With an online service or downloaded product, it might mean using a 'host' network such as America Online or the Internet. This approach may allow the newspaper to keep its level of investment relatively low and to avoid the need to develop a large amount of expertise in new areas. On the other hand, the newspaper loses a certain degree of control over the product or service, and it may have to make other sacrifices to conform to the requirements of the host. The newspaper's service may also be less visible to the reader, less immediately identifiable, if it is one of many services available on a given host. And of course any company that works with the newspaper on any product or service will demand a portion of the revenue in return.

MARKETING FACTORS THE NEWSPAPER SHOULD EXAMINE

Perhaps the most difficult aspect of electronic publishing for newspapers is marketing. For one thing, the usual approach to market research — interviews, studies of people's habits, and so on — is virtually useless when applied to such a new field. For another, this generally is a newspaper's first experience with a product or service that requires something more than a working pair of eyes and the ability to read. To read an electronic product, the reader needs a particular kind of electronic device, be it a personal computer with a modem or CD-ROM drive, a PDA or something else. With that in mind one of the first things the newspaper should ask itself is whether it wants to aim its product or service at an installed base of devices (if so, which ones?), to anticipate the next wave of devices (what will those be?) or to design its own device and market it. Of course, to choose a type of device is, to a large extent, to choose the potential readership. Another question is what telecommunications infrastructure is needed and whether that structure exists and can be used at a reasonable cost.

The nature of the product or service the newspaper offers will depend on the capabilities of the device used to read it. Marketing and technology are inextricably interlinked, making matters no simpler. Also to be considered is whether the newspaper might be able to create a market by adding value to a particular type of device. For instance, if it decided to develop a news-update service for PDAs, it might cooperate with the suppliers of PDAs and software with the aim of having the news-update software bundled with the devices when they are sold. That arrangement would benefit the newspaper, and it would benefit the PDA hardware and software suppliers as well by creating another application for their product.

Perhaps the market for a newspaper's particular electronic publishing effort will be a rather narrow niche one at first, or even always. Perhaps only business customers will be ready to pay for a given product or service. The chance to gain experience through such an effort should not be discounted, however. That experience may prove useful as electronic publishing grows in importance.

CONCLUSION

Among the advantages that electronic media have over paper-based media are speed of transmission and rapid searchability of vast volumes of information. Daily newspapers in general aim to convey large but easily accessible amounts of the most up-to-date information. So it would appear that they could well make use of electronic distribution to their readers. By doing so, they could maintain their competitive position in the information marketplace, as well as offering better service to their readers.

We have shown that there are many different ways a newspaper can enter electronic publishing. Even though the technologies used in electronic publishing are advancing rapidly, making it difficult to decide which product or service is the 'right' one to offer, it is not too early for newspapers to engage in this field. The fact that there are already quite a few — and very different — electronic products and services being offered shows that the era of the 'electronic newspaper' has begun.

An electronic service started today probably will not be aimed at a large market, and it may not even earn money right away. Nevertheless, it will help the newspaper gather experience in an area which in the future will be of crucial importance.

11

Financial newspapers and the use of EP

John Suckling, The Financial Times, UK

It is over a year since Microsoft and Apple announced that they would modify their standard operating systems to allow the incorporation of video, sound and graphics. Already there have been a growing number of software packages making use of such facilities and not all of them are intended for the games market. Penguin, part of the Pearson group of companies, has published the *Viking Opera Guide*, which incorporates all you need to know about opera — the biographies of composers together with lists of their works and plot synopses but, most important of all, the recorded works by some of the world's greatest operatic singers. From the menu-driven system it is possible to select an aria in seconds. Longman is well established in the area of electronic publishing and counts among its titles Keesing's *Record of World Events* for the decade 1983 to 1992, which contains about ten million words. Longman also produces an interactive English dictionary which gives the user definitions in sound and pictures as well as text.

Viewing what is happening in the electronic publishing/multimedia arena, we find that most of the applications are educational or reference sources. There are few applications which deal with current sources such as a daily newspaper. This is not to say that there are not such products available as pilots or for use within conceptual review panels for gauging user reaction. One of the problems that

---

John Suckling is Manager of Product Marketing at the *Financial Times*, London Headquarters.

the pilot and conceptual schemes are trying to address is whether users will be prepared to read articles from a screen. Using various drill-down techniques, it is possible for the user to follow any number of different avenues of information. However, as you move down any particular route, it is further to backtrack. Unlike a printed newspaper, it is impossible to move to another area at a glance, or turn the page. Even assuming that you know what you require, it takes time to load or return to the top index. However, the latest indexing techniques are providing increased flexibility for the user, allowing better navigation around electronic documents.

It is likely that electronic publishing will change the way in which information is presented to the user. Not everybody reads the same parts of the newspaper with the same intensity, people have different interests and different requirements and the opportunity presented by electronic publishing is that information can be presented to the user which suits individual needs and requirements, whether they be personal- or work-oriented. Preprogrammed intelligent software will present a personalized version of the newspaper. Such software will also learn of your changing requirements from additional articles chosen from the electronic database. While it is possible to define the contents of your personalized electronic newspaper, there is a school of thought that suggests that this may not be entirely satisfactory as it could cause items which might be of interest to be missed. It seems likely that the editor's role in compiling a newspaper, be it conventional or electronic, will continue to be an essential one.

The Financial Times Group has been developing its expertise over several years. Its online information service FT PROFILE has an archived history of over 30 million articles since 1982 covering some 3500 different publications. In addition, FT PROFILE pioneered CD-ROM as a means of archive. The entire text of the *Financial Times* from 1990 onwards is available in yearly volumes, and recently the CD-ROM facility was upgraded to provide a seamless link between the CD-ROM and the Online services for those users who need to ensure that they are using the latest available information.

The difficulty of delivering a newspaper electronically is best summed up by the following user comments — 'It is irritating to wait for particular screens to appear. 90% of the time is not spent reading articles but looking for something pertinent to read.' 'It is boring just reading straight text off a screen. Just because something is technologically possible, it does not mean people want to do it.' Despite this, newspapers, magazines and other publications are becoming more electronic and have been for some considerable time moving from typewriters and typesetting to terminals and publishing systems. Nowadays, every stage of the production process uses electronics. As a consequence, the creation of electronic services has become more practical and cost effective, allowing the various publications within the FT Group to be easily incorporated into the Online/CD-ROM services as a means of delivery to end-users.

However, trying to read a newspaper or magazine from a screen is not the same as having it in your hand. The problem of browsing has yet to be successfully solved. The ability of the human eye–brain coordination to scan a page of print, even of a broadsheet newspaper, and home in on a particular item of interest on the page cannot be replicated. It is at this point that the interfaces between the user and the information become very important. They have to be sufficiently sophisticated to allow the user to find the information required directly, while at the same time being intuitive because users will not accept the need to be trained. As stated previously, software already exists that can present users with a predefined set of reading material. This is achieved by asking them to complete a set of questions designed to establish their preferences. A significant part of this initial definition is the keywords to be used to filter the information content. The user is then offered articles, the contents of which meet the initial criteria set. Subsequent choice of articles is then monitored by the intelligent software, which may modify the selection criteria to reflect the type of articles for which the user shows a preference. It is a fact that the *Financial Times* and other publications from within the FT Group are primarily intended to supply comment or information about business events and activities. As a consequence, there may be a view that its use and experience of electronic publishing is not applicable in the broad context. This is not the case. FT PROFILE has a broad spectrum of customers and it is essential to ensure that the user interfaces are usable by everyone. The proliferation of Microsoft Windows has allowed FT PROFILE to develop a Graphical User Interface (GUI) that benefits directly from the structure and sophistication of the operating system software. The ability to use icons, drop-down menus, scroll bars and the same instruction set between applications for specific regularly required functions, for example printing and saving data, has helped considerably in providing intuitive user interfaces.

In addition to providing a Windows interface, FT PROFILE has developed its own interface, InfoPLUS, which enables the user, through a series of menus, to look for specific information without the need to predefine the publication. This brings a new perspective to the field of electronic publishing, because the user can look for specific information without the need to prejudge whether it exists or not.

As yet FT PROFILE does not include any pictures or graphics, but FT Information has been producing for some time the CD-ROM version of *The Economist*, which does contain graphics, so the expertise exists. A problem solved by Adobe, a software company specializing in computer typefaces, but also by others, is that of allowing electronic documents to be exchanged between different computers, particularly where those documents contain graphics. For example, using the Adobe software Acrobat, it is possible to exchange documents containing graphics and maintain the same look and feel as the original. Such software allows the construction of services which combine both text and graphics/pictures. Combining text with graphics will help the acceptance of electronically published information but a question remains as to when there will be a population of PCs with the communications bandwidth and storage capacity to make such services viable.

The *Financial Times* will continue to develop its online service FT PROFILE and its CD-ROM services, both of which will be developed to reflect user requirements. Both these specialist areas will continue to provide input to the development of electronic services within the Group. In addition, there will be other initiatives such as the pilot project Corporate FT.

The Corporate FT project was a design exercise to gather information from within the organization on the issues likely to be encountered in its creation and ongoing production, as well as being used to gather information from its potential user market as to its acceptability. Unlike many other exercises in electronic publishing, it was not an attempt to recreate the newspaper visually in an electronic form. The content was reproduced verbatim and, to enable the user to navigate around the paper, a comprehensive index was created. In addition, an alert facility was included. This allows a user to define specific triggers, such as company name, which if they appear anywhere, specifically alert the user to the occurrence. Operationally the product was built within a Microsoft Windows environment which allowed several articles to be opened at any one time and the user to flip from one to another at will. In addition to the index, the user had an optional search facility which enabled articles meeting the criteria to be identified and displayed. This latter facility is already available as part of the FT PROFILE service, which has the current FT available online at 1.00 a.m. UK time on the day of publication. It was included in this project for completeness. The reaction from the user panels was mixed and reflects the comments earlier in this article as to the problem of reading or browsing via a computer screen. The user interface was well received, particularly as Windows has become the *de facto* standard, and the interface took maximum benefit from the facilities available. This acceptance of Windows reinforced the experience already gained from the introduction of the *freeway* interface on FT PROFILE. In terms of popularity, *freeway* is very clearly accepted by the users as the number of companies using this to access FT Profile has grown by 50% in the last three months.

The experience at the FT suggests that electronic publishing will not occur over night. It will evolve slowly over time as companies review their equipment needs and replace old technology with new equipment capable of using the emerging services. Electronic publishing does not, as yet, bring any added benefit not already available from a combination of online services and CD-ROM, and FT Information is preeminent in both. However, we will continue to explore electronic publishing possibilities.

12

Newspapers on the way to the interactive future

Leif Andersson, Göteborgs-Posten, Sweden

So here we are with a new kind of future in sight: multimedia and interactivity. The phenomenon will surely be given some new names in the future; just think about SuperScreen, SuperPaper or The Button World? All the same, almost anything can be produced in digital form or converted to digital forms, so of course it will affect the ways we receive and consume text, sound and pictures. The convergence of telecommunication, computer and media industries is powerful and dramatic.

What can the realistic time frame be for these prophecies eventually to come true? And what part will newspapers play in this development?

One can be very confident that newspapers will play an important role in electronic publishing, providing services to old and new customers. The reasons for this statement are very simple:

- newspaper operations are the core of the news industry,
- newspapers know how to manage complex information flows into easily understood products, and
- newspapers will not risk losing their local market dominance, whatever the delivery medium.

Leif Andersson is Director of Research & Development at the Göteborgs-Posten Nya AB publishing group. The company is one of Sweden's leading newspaper publishers and has pioneered a number of EP products.

In an attempt to discuss these matters it is helpful to put development into perspective: what is happening today, what is waiting a short way down the road and what if the vast 'interactive future' actually becomes a reality?

ON THE ELECTRONIC ROAD

Newspapers have been striving for the electronic future since the early 1960s when computers entered the composing room. From then until today there is a straight line of continuous increased use of more sophisticated systems to help produce the daily newspaper.

Today newspapers have organized the production of news and advertising around more or less sophisticated databases. These databases form the base for newspaper activities in electronic distribution, electronic publishing if you like. The first steps were taken in the 1970s to solve internal newspaper problems such as replacing the archive clipping files with their modern counterpart, the electronic library. External access is mainly possible through database hosts and complex search structures combined with costs have held back development of a nonprofessional market.

Then in the 1980s came teletex and videotex. The newspaper database content could be used here also. However, the user interface and the equipment revealed the true background of the technology: it was the engineer's solution looking for problems. There was no big user market except in France where a government programme funded the hardware and communication base for the industry.

The beginning of the 1990s saw audiotex services and fax newspapers along the way. Audiotex is working fairly well (even though in market niches with slow growth) as a presentation and exploration tool for well structured information like classified advertising and short news stories. It also offers possibilities of sending messages to the advertiser or the newspaper. Fax papers have found niches for newsletters where content and timeliness are more vital than presentation form. Markets are growing slowly, but they are believed to be very promising.

GET YOUR NEWSPAPER ONLINE

Today we have online newspapers, which replicate the content of printed newspapers to users equipped with personal computers and modems. Here user interfaces are much better and the options for accessing older material are as useful as the possibilities of communicating with editors and reporters via the database and the electronic mail system. The latest developments are devices where newspaper content is supplemented with moving pictures and sound for selected stories — including tools for navigating the extensive story content.

The most interesting current projects are seen in the USA. Database hosts like Prodigy and America Online (and the recently announced eWorld from Apple) work closely with newspapers to develop information structures and user interfaces. The market reached is still limited to pioneer users — but enormous compared to the videotex projects of the 1980s.

BASE FOR THE WORLD NEWS SYSTEM

So far this has been a technical look at newspaper operations. More important is the process which impacts on a newspaper's content and determines what the modern newspaper brings to its market.

Newspapers and their news collection agencies are the basic engines for the news industry all over the world. If in doubt, take your morning newspaper and compare it to the morning radio and television broadcasts. You will find that the newspaper coverage is deeper and more varied and that broadcast news relies on newspapers to a surprisingly high degree.

Over the last 200 years the newspaper industries have developed advanced systems for collection, evaluation, navigation, presentation and dissemination of news and advertising over a 24-hour cycle. Most of the newspaper's content is not known a day in advance, but the completed printed product meets its reader at the news-stand or in the reader's home within 24 hours.

The newspaper is a tool which keeps the reader continually informed about developments around the world and in the local community. It raises matters of concern to citizens, serves as a forum for debate and comment and scrutinizes politicians and authorities. At the same time it is entertaining and a guide to practical things like shopping, living and personal planning.

This service which a newspaper provides is highly valued by the general public, especially as it comes at a relatively low price. In Scandinavian countries for example, it is not uncommon that eight out of ten people read a daily paper. This is a very strong market position for electronic competitors to attack.

NEWSPAPERS' FEARS AND PROSPECTS

Recent decades have seen disturbing changes in newspaper consumption in many countries. Young adults have tended to rely on television and radio for news and advertising. There is also a fear that younger generations, who see computers as natural tools, will find screen presentation a workable substitute for the printed page. At the same time newspaper strategists see electronic publishing in a wider perspective than ways of providing improved and new services to their customers.

Somewhat down the road, say three or four years ahead, already-existing plans suggest we will find that many newspapers have moved a bit further into electronic services, bridging the time gap caused by printing and distribution. The printed newspaper may then abandon printing things like stock-market listings and material which is actually old news at the time the paper reaches the reader.

In online systems readers will, for example, be able to:

- read, search, print and interact with the full electronic version of the printed paper,
- communicate with reporters and editors,
- submit text or advertisements for publication in the paper,
- participate in discussions among readers and reporters,
- download active spreadsheets for solving various problems,
- receive answers to advertisements and other services.

In optical disk systems pioneering readers will regularly read magazine features with video and audio segments, complemented by factual database content, and probably play various games.

Technology here will help newspapers increase circulation areas; readers who earlier had to wait days for mail delivery will be able to get the electronic version even before the first printed copy reaches its readers. Newspapers will also be able to reach readers with visual impairment or other handicaps.

The market for these kinds of services will probably not be very large in four years' time, but is steadily growing. The fastest growing markets will be found in the USA but the spread around Europe could come surprisingly quickly. For a comparison: who four years ago foresaw the incredible growth of Internet traffic?

MARKET DEVELOPMENT IN A LONGER PERSPECTIVE

These first steps are the easiest for the newspapers, because they are based mainly on present developments in newspaper production and electronic mail systems. Papers may take the technology jump and be surprised that the services generate little interest if they are basically an electronic version of printed products. They then must reassess the difficult question of what audiences with screen preferences actually want from interactive media besides entertainment.

The mainstream in media technology research and development appears to be the following:

- digitization of sound, video and still pictures on common technical standards,
- development of digital radio and television production and transmission,
- utilization of cable television with a capacity of more than 500 channels including telephony,
- development of telephony technology to permit single television channel transmission in parallel with digital telephony on household lines,
- development of hand-held devices combining the functions of computers, telephony and radio,
- development of creative and editing tools for multimedia user devices, combining text, sound, video and still pictures, and, of course
- development of multimedia user systems on personal computer platforms, unfortunately so far without common technical standard.

MILLIONS OF NICHES

As technologies converge into interactive multimedia, so will properties like cognitive levels and suggestive impact from various media. Increased competition will force changes both from products to services and towards greater segmentation and flexibility according to customer preferences.

The market for electronic services may be millions of niches, actually down to the individual level. Information providers will be abundant and the users will have the same problem as always: how to manage the complexity? In order to make this mass of information accessible and useful for the general public, someone must provide tools for navigation, packaging and presentation — to transform data and information into something for immediate or later use.

This is exactly what newspapers are doing in the world of print. The creativity which produces the printed paper today will find multimedia and interactivity providing functions of which editors of today only dream. The craftsmanship needed, especially for video and audio production (which exists in the television and entertainment businesses), is now growing in development projects and will later expand into new kinds of newsroom which are now more visions than plans.

What may newspapers do in the advanced interactive electronic media business? Most likely, there will be a number of products including a printed paper with 24-hour updates. Then there will be some windows in the electronic world where urgent news updates and retrospective material can be retrieved.

Besides functions earlier described, the services may provide solutions to questions like:

- What is the current status of fission development — and how can I describe to my daughter how this works?
- I remember a story some weeks ago on the future of the fishing industry — I want that and some related figures or relevant articles sent to my fax machine at work.
- Are there any houses for sale in an area where the employment prospects are good for an architect and a florist a year from now?
- I am really worried about the future of the Sellafield nuclear plant — can I have addresses to Members of Parliament who want to keep it running?

- This new president in Rwanda — who is he and what has he done before? And by the way – what happened there in 1994?
- I need a summary on the debate about the proposed new local land development and a map to illustrate it — all at my home fax.
- What is the current status of my account with all bank services and please can I postpone payment until after my vacation?
- Dad said I can ask you for the e-mail address of a European penpal with an interest in horses. It must be a girl.

The newspapers' factual databases combined with presentation and navigational tools and with powerful display and interaction devices for users will create new market possibilities.

In addition, assembly of multimedia material for various levels of education leaps to mind, as does the recapture of special interest markets which during recent decades have been exploited by magazines.

Besides providing these kinds of services, newspapers will be gateways to other information providers who want to benefit from the newspapers' standing in the local community, e-mail networks and the like.

THE SUPER MARIO NEWS SYSTEM?

The driving force in multimedia and interactivity will be entertainment. Computer games like Sega and Nintendo are developing at amazing speed and in a couple of years time will most likely be more powerful and versatile than almost anyone can understand today. This may very well be the low-cost way in which multimedia and electronic publishing will enter our homes. So when will the first Super Mario newspaper reach its young audience?

Many problems within the electronic publishing industry have yet to be addressed properly. Here are a few:

- Today's copyright system has developed during years when electronic publishing was not even thought of. If large-scale electronic information dissemination is to become a reality, this must be remedied in some way.
- The consumer will be in total control if mass media gives way to user-requested entertainment and information services. This

means that the user will have to pay directly for what he or she uses. What will this shift in cost distribution mean to the advertising industry, media companies and consumers?

- The cost of equipment and transmission must come down dramatically. Certainly, the proposed information superhighways will not be a free ride.
- Existing print media will not give in easily to new competition. The low cost for the services of newspapers will be hard to match for entrepreneurs wishing to exploit a market that will be comparably small for many years.

CONTENT IS KING

Whatever the medium, content is the most important part. Newspaper publishers have a very strong position in the information market and have during the last years reassessed their positions. Hundreds of years of service to the public have made it natural for readers and advertisers to turn to newspapers for quality of many kinds.

The culture of newspapering is about being of a service to the public: to inform, to guide and to help. These needs cannot be fulfilled by any kind of machine. The future will see a growing demand for help and guidance based on qualified reporting, editing and presentation of information in context. Watch this industry for the future!

EP and the corporate publisher — case studies

13
Knowledge: information: publishing?

Liz Sharpe, Abtrust Fund Managers, UK

Publishing information operates within certain constraints: the volume of information to be published, the number of users, where they are and what level of knowledge the publisher needs to have to select, present, or structure the information in the right way — the 'right way' being the way which provides the highest utility to the target audience. These constraints are constant whether the publisher operates in the consumer, corporate or education markets and whether the publishing medium is electronic or paper. Of all, it is the last constraint, that knowledge of the reader, which differentiates a publisher from a printer and which in the past has allowed passion, flair and skill to use the publishing medium as a vehicle to change lives. (A subset of this last, and most important constraint, is the timeliness of the information. Often regarded as the critical difference between paper and electronic documents, timeliness is only one feature of content selection, structuring and presentation. Because of the success of certain applications, such as Reuters, it has been seen as the main benefit of electronic delivery. This is not the case.)

If we consider changing the first three constraints — volume, geographic distribution and number of readers — these could all be handled at the printing level; we can print bigger chunks more

---

Liz Sharpe has been advising Abtrust Fund Managers Ltd in Edinburgh, Scotland for many years. She is a specialist in funding for new media publishing in the UK and the USA as well as for worldwide cooperative EP ventures. Abtrust is a leading venture-capital investment house.

frequently to more people. In an electronic context, this is not electronic publishing, this is electronic printing. This is an important difference which is being lost in a welter of technology jargon and misunderstanding. The difference is also an important financial one. If we look at the financial results of printers and publishers, then generally publishers make higher margins than printers, because they add value to the information.

We can view the spectrum of publishing markets — consumer, education and corporate — as increasing in information complexity as you move through the three. This means that the opportunity to add value increases. The conclusion is that corporate electronic publishing will generally be higher-margin business than consumer or education. This does not mean that corporate reference material presented on a CD-ROM or through an online database will necessarily be a high-margin business, because it is distinctly possible that in neither case will the medium have been used to add value to the information; only to get it to the user in a different way.

Adding value means selecting the relevant information and structuring and presenting it in such a way that it has maximum utility within the context of the user group, among whom there may be dramatically differing needs. Satisfying that diverse group of needs within a structure which is rich enough is the essence of corporate electronic publishing.

It is even possible within the total process of publishing, i.e. collection, collation and dissemination of information, that the electronic medium allows the *collection* of information which would otherwise have been inaccessible. Here the added value has been embedded through a radical change in content. All retail corporate applications, and many kiosk applications, would fall into this category — where one is collecting market information from consumers prior to purchase. A classic example of this approach is a US company, *intouch*, described later.

Electronic publishing is evolutionary, but even today in the corporate world we have the ability to build, and in some instances have built, revolutionary published products. Our tendency at the moment where these products exist is to call them something else — usually we say, that is a database, not a published product. We seem to have difficulty where both the publishing medium and the usage of the content are dramatically changed in retaining continuous understanding of the underlying published content.

I recently asked someone with ten years experience of CD-ROM-based technical documentation systems if a reference book on semi-conductor design rules was a published product. He replied that it was. I then asked if he regarded a semiconductor design software package with those same design rules, embedded such that they are invisible until violated, as a published product — he did not. Although he came from a technical background, his perception of publishing was essentially paper-based, although the content was the same in both cases, the difference in the presentation — and here I do not mean the screen rather than paper, but rather the way the information was used rather than viewed — caused this person to change his definition.

Interestingly had that content — the design rules — appeared on the screen in a similar way to paper, i.e. viewable text to be refer-enced at the specific request of the reader, he would still have viewed the content as published, only this time on electronic media.

If publishing really is the collection, collation and distribution of information, then surely the goal is for it to reach the user in the most efficient form for his or her purpose. In the example above the most efficient way is to embed the rules of design into the design tool such that the look-up becomes automated. This really is a revolutionary step away from, for example, a more flexible look-up of an encyclopaedia or a dictionary on the screen, whatever the audio or video bells and whistles provided as an extra. The semicon-ductor design example is relatively easy to understand compared to the many examples which are growing where the publisher embeds not reference material in the structure, but real knowledge of which users will need to view the information, how their viewpoints will differ and what processes they will apply to the information. The publisher here produces a framework of understanding into which the user pours his/her content.

It is important to remember in a world increasingly inhabited by technology companies seeking the holy grail of the ubiquitous plat-form, interface or retrieval system, that there are a vast number of different requirements for distributing electronic information in dif-ferent forms on different media to different audiences for different purposes. The corporate market currently exists in various forms which demand increasing technical complexity as it moves from the simple electronic printing and distribution of paper-based informa-tion on electronic platforms, through electronic manuals and online documentation systems, then on to interactive electronic technical manuals, eventually finishing at those applications using virtual worlds with VR (Virtual Reality) interfaces. These all exist today. Research chemists can enter the world of the protein molecule and try various alternatives to see how they can manipulate the structure. As we move through this continuum of applications, not only does the technical complexity increase, but the similarities between paper and electronic presentation diminish rapidly, with the result that many cannot grasp the more complex applications as publishing. We all pay lipservice to the convergence of whichever three circles you choose to converge but, when we see a real example of convergence, we call it something else.

In the simple applications it may be more useful to replicate both the content and layout of documents so that the reader does not have to learn a completely new set of procedures or a new interface. However, in moving on to a more complex application, e.g. online software, it is unlikely one would want to match the electronic presentation with the paper version. As with the silicon design application, the documentation in electronic form must be closely coupled with the task and again, as with the retail application, it is also possible to collect information from the user, i.e. to have him or her annotate the documentation for future amendments to the published documentation.

The most technically demanding application in corporate electronic publishing is currently the IETM — Interactive Electronic Technical Manual. The ultimate goal of the IETM is to provide maintenance documentation which will promote the safe and efficient diagnosis and repair of complex systems. While the IETM arose out of the US Department of Defense's interest in weapon systems, the approach is equally applicable for anything from powerplants to oil rigs.

The information for any of these systems may be stored in several separate physical locations, yet it must dynamically reflect the current state of the system. The information presented to the user may arise locally from the equipment itself or from remote information sources. The technician creates for that specific task a dynamic view of the maintenance manual which has been structured to facilitate just this. Where interactivity and currency of information are involved, we seem to be adding a further layer to the old three-stage publishing metaphor (collection, collation, dissemination). The technology allows us to add that fourth level which with paper is impossible.

IETM is part of a larger DoD initiative called CALS — Computer-Aided Acquisition and Logistic Support. Originally CALS applied to the defence procurement and support of a weapons system throughout its lifecycle whether that is five or 50 years. More recently, it has been proposed that the acronym CALS should now stand for Continuous Acquisition and Lifecycle Support. The reason for this has been the strong take up of CALS by nondefence-related commercial concerns.

CALS sets a framework for any long-lifecycle, design-led product. The more interaction required across disparate groups during the lifecycle the more a CALS-like framework is needed for the electronic publishing of information. CALS would be as beneficial to a large construction project as to a new frigate. The information published in this type of application stretches all the normal publishing constraints. The types of information included vary enormously. There are large numbers of individuals viewing the information from entirely different perspectives. The amount of information is vast and it is frequently updated. I have described below a design-led information system, PDM, from Microdynamics as an example which shows just how generic design-led systems are. PDM is a product aimed not at the defence or aerospace industries but the clothing industry.

To date, these design-led publishing applications have resulted in very large electronic publishing contracts for companies like EDS and PRC. Applications like EDMICS, (a major US Navy project to automate and standardize storage, distribution and retrieval of engineering and logistics information), GIS systems or advanced design applications are often excluded from our definition of publishing, yet only they truly represent the full power we now have when we combine technology and content. They represent a new ability to dramatically expand the metaphors by which we represent knowledge, i.e. information, to include knowledge of the position of information within an interactive process. In no other market is it possible to add value in this way. If electronic publishing allows that process to become more efficient, corporate consumers will continue to spend. Compare this situation to the consumer market, where screen-based entertainment as a percentage of disposable income has remained static for the past five years at around 9%. In many instances of the consumer market only the delivery platform changes. It is, however, this familiarity and link with past products published on paper that allows us to accept this market more readily and to focus a disparate amount of resource into it. This is a mistake.

EXAMPLE APPLICATIONS

intouch

intouch designs, manufactures, markets and supports interactive multimedia previewing information and marketing systems. The company's systems publish information that is helpful to consumers in making purchase decisions, while at the same time collecting preference and demographic information for publication to retailers and product and service providers.

intouch's first application, the music i.Station, integrates previewing of albums in retail music stores with the collection of preference and demographic data for use by recorded-music companies and music retailers to market their products. The music i.Station permits customers to preview an album either by using touch screen menus to browse by artist, genre, album/composition or Billboard Chart position, or by scanning a CD or cassette's UPC over the music i.Station's barcode reader. The system currently provides five 30-second representative samples from each of over 32 000 CDs. In addition, it displays album reviews and music videos and offers discount coupons to users. After each album preview, the music i.Station user rates the album on a five-point scale. Consumers access the music i.Station with an i.Card. The i.Card is issued upon completion of a brief registration form that includes demographic questions. Preview behaviour (which albums were sampled) and preference data for each user can be matched with demographic information from the i.Form so that recorded-music companies and music retailers can track user behaviour.

The changes experienced by music consumers and recorded-music companies during the last several years have created related difficulties for music retailers. The proliferation of new artists and genres and the related increase in inventory have limited the ability of music retailers to provide customer assistance in purchase decisions. Inventory management has become more difficult with the greater number of selections. Concurrently, slowing unit-volume growth, increasing cost of inventory, and increased competition have impacted music retailers' financial performance. From 1990 to 1992, the market share of musical recordings sold through retailers declined from approximately 72% to approximately 62%, with mail order and music clubs gaining most of this market share. Moreover, alternative outlets such as department stores and discount stores have further eroded speciality music retailers' market share. *intouch*'s system is a means of addressing these changes and conferring benefits on the recorded music companies, the retailer and the consumer.

The music i.Station provides the opportunity for the recorded-music industry to generate increased sales by permitting consumers to sample products and by facilitating the sale of older 'catalogue' products which typically have higher gross margins. Users' opinions of a particular album and other data captured with geographic and demographic precision allows marketing, advertising and direct mail to be more effectively targeted. Retailers can generate additional sales by building customer traffic, increasing the frequency of visits to the store, increasing the time spent in the store and differentiating a store from its competitors. The customer data collected by the system facilitates a better understanding of consumer preferences and may allow retailers to more effectively manage inventories and maximize sales. The consumer benefits from a vastly increased selection to browse through and preview and has the opportunity to experiment with genres and artists he or she might not otherwise consider. Consumers may additionally be offered discounts and other offers/information tailored to their tastes.

The music industry is just one example of a broader problem. Consumers are overwhelmed by many purchasing decisions. They are confounded by the number and variety of product offerings and frustrated by the difficulty, time and expense in collecting relevant information to make informed purchase decisions. Often marketers further confuse or overwhelm people by trying to influence their decision with advertisements. As the product marketing 'noise' continues to increase, consumers may benefit from decision-making aids to sort through the relevant information and assist in making the 'right' choice. At the same time, retailers and product providers are overwhelmed by the task of understanding continually changing consumer needs, product preferences, purchase behaviour and demographic trends. Retailers and product providers need to collect better consumer information on an ongoing basis so that they can market their products better and design new products better to meet customer needs.

A variety of other consumers, product providers and retailers could benefit from such a system, e.g. video rentals and sales, computer application software, CD-ROM software sales, business marketing, theme park and retail/mall information kiosks, travel agencies and concert ticket sales.

The i.Station was tested in music retail stores in San Diego and St Louis from late 1992 to early 1993. The tests were run in each city with seven machines located in three stores and their results were compared to three control stores in each city. The test showed that i.Station users were more likely to purchase albums; were likely to purchase more albums per trip to the store; spent more money in the store; spent almost twice the amount of time in the store; and were more likely to make unplanned purchases. In addition, i.Station users tended to shop for and buy music more often than nonusers and tended to be more loyal to the music retailer's stores.

Microdynamics — PDM

Microdynamics is a company specializing in design systems for the apparel industry. Their latest product, PDM, publishes design, engineering cost and manufacturing information related to a piece of clothing. The viewers of the information could be remote manufacturing sites or subcontractors to a major retailer. Recent studies indicate that most individuals in the product development cycle are able to spend only 20% of their time actually designing and developing products while 30–35% of their time is consumed by simply looking for needed information. Often the necessary information cannot be found and extensive duplication of effort results.

PDM provides an automated means to control and facilitate the flow of up-to-date information to authorized participants throughout the organization, over the entire product development cycle. All product information is stored within the electronic equivalent of a folder. All of the relevant forms, illustrations, diagrams, images and even voice notes and full colour photographic quality pictures are collected within such an electronic package.

These per-style packages are entered into a filing system by division or product line, and then by season. PDM maintains three separate folders for each style, which correspond to development phases: design or prototype; engineering or costing sample; and production.

In addition, PDM can even maintain multiple versions of product specifications, which may correspond to differences between production at several locations or changes with specific effective dates.

PDM can publish reports. Standard reports permit the client to check on the completion of major milestone events, and list those styles which have fallen behind schedule. Reports can be easily created which filter through the information created and maintained by PDM to locate styles with requested attributes or properties. This facility can be used to find styles that have been recently modified or which use a certain fabric. Reports can be limited to a specific division and/or season or can gather information across all styles.

PDM is already meeting the product data-management needs of a wide variety of clients, including both multinational manufacturers and retailers as well as smaller customers, who are successfully leveraging the benefits of information technology to achieve the market responsiveness previously achieved by only much larger organizations. These customers are now reporting improved designs, fewer development changes, reduced overheads, faster market response, better audit trails, improved communication and far fewer and much less costly mistakes as a direct result of improved product data management and control.

14

Corporate publishing in Bertelsmann: two examples of publishing services

Erhard Engelmann, Bertelsmann, Germany

DEFINITION

The understanding of the term 'corporate publishing' differs from branch to branch and from company to company. Inside Bertelsmann with its four business divisions it is possible to find several meanings of corporate publishing. Here I refer to two of the Bertelsmann companies which have developed specific services for corporate publishing.

In the prepress area of the printing shops Bertelsmann is going to offer services to help their customers handle complex technologies for high-resolution pictures and high-quality print products. A typical criterion for this service is a longer lifetime of the raw material, pictures or structured text data.

On the other hand Bertelsmann distribution services offer a complete service to help manufacturers manage their documentation in a very effective way. The service starts from collecting or capturing the material, such as pictures, text and drawings, and offers the whole palette of operations up to physical distribution to the end-users, including factoring. Typical applications are technical documentation, in-house publications and product description brochures.

Dr Erhard Engelmann is a Director of Bertelsmann Zentrale Informationsverarbeitung GmbH in Gütersloh, part of the Bertelsmann AG group, one of the largest publishing and media conglomerates worldwide.

In both cases Bertelsmann will expand its offers to other media such as electronic delivery on CD-ROM and online databases. The important point of the services offered is to be independent from creating documentation for specific output media or from particular hardware platforms.

PREPRESS-ORIENTED CORPORATE PUBLISHING SERVICE

Increasingly, the current situation of the market requires product-selling catalogues which have a higher benefit for the customer. At the same time, manufacturers have a need to reduce the costs as a result of financial pressure. It is not possible to find a solution which meets both requests; however, a suitable balance between high quality and cost-effective production of catalogues can be achieved by the use of a corporate publishing prepress service.

Process needs

The criteria for choosing a corporate service in prepress can be summarized as follows:

- The raw material is reused several times. As a rule the structure of the print product (e.g. a catalogue) is nearly the same if the material is reused.
- The final product is structured. For unstructured products it is necessary to find a new structure or a new layout every time. Such work gives no chance to automate the process. To do the work, the owner of the material has to be involved.
- More than one representation of the product is needed with the same raw material. Some manufacturers require the possibility of selling the original products to different user groups. This necessitates several representations of the same material. It also may be necessary to use different media, like CD-ROM and paper.
- The final product should offer high standards of picture quality and colour definition to the customer. For high-resolution and/or full-colour pictures it is necessary to use expensive equipment for scanning and reproduction. This is the benefit of a special service.

All these criteria can be combined. Normally the manufacturer has extensive experience in the production of his/her original goods. He/she needs descriptions and advertisement documents to sell his/her products, but publishing is not in the range of his/her knowledge. Some of the bigger companies have installed their own publishing departments; however, the real problem for them is the lack of specific know-how in electronic publishing.

Objective of the service

The idea of a corporate service in prepress is to support companies in all tasks involved in implementing their documentation to a high quality. The target group of companies for this service are manufacturers who, from time to time, need product descriptions or other documents about their products.

The offer includes the use of some very expensive equipment or specialized software packages. This sharing of the equipment is one of the cost-reducing factors. The high resolution scanners are both needed and important. After scanning the pictures have to be improved and adapted to the required output medium. For many customers it is necessary to archive pictures and other material in electronic form for later productions or for reprints. The production of film for offset printers, including the composing of text and high-resolution pictures, again needs expensive devices.

Another factor is time, and by producing quality layout, the experienced staff of a publishing company can produce the required documents in a shorter time frame than the manufacturer himself/herself. An additional benefit is the possibility of doing this task in parallel with production.

The manufacturer can concentrate his/her activities on marketing and delivering the product. Especially from the marketing side ever higher quality of promotional material is requested. Either the publisher can help with his/her experience in layout or he/she can find an appropriate specialist in graphic design or layout, as he/she normally has such experts on contract.

In addition to the above reasons, such a service can help to coordinate the different suppliers of the material for the documents. The service provider knows both specialists and second sources in case of capacity problems on his/her site and he/she knows the right suppliers, too. In this way the service provider can guarantee a fixed delivery time for the document.

Example 1. Sales catalogues

A large user of the corporate service provided by the Bertelsmann printing shop is sales catalogues. A good example is the consumer-oriented catalogue of a trading house. In this catalogue are offered all the things you need in life, shown in full colour illustrations on paper. The catalogue is published twice a year.

Apart from explanations and user instructions at the beginning or at the end, the catalogue presents a long list of articles. Each item in the catalogue is identified by an order number and described with text, price and additional specifications such as colour or size. Normally each article is illustrated by one or more pictures. The article list is changed by less than 10% from one issue to the next, but sometimes the printed pictures for an item, the text or the price are changed in a specific issue.

The work flow in the service is as follows:

1 All material from former issues of the catalogue is stored in a database called 'title database'. Related to the order number of each article, a set of text blocks, pictures, price information and additional specifications are stored. Pictures are archived in a separate server system and have links into the title database. All objects which are related to an article can be called up one at a time. The list of articles contains every item from all former issues. Because of this, the list is divided into a current list and the backlist.

2 If a new issue of the catalogue is to be published, the current list is updated and the related material is reloaded from a tape archive. Now the basic catalogue data is available online.

3 The trading company delivers new text and changed data for prices and so on for older articles or completely new ones electronically. The information comes step by step and can also contain changes to previous entries. The order of the list in the new edition and first proposals for the layout are delivered handwritten on paper. During the layout process the new text can be modified for reasons of space.

4 The new or modified pictures are delivered as they are. This

could be on paper, film negatives or positives, digital video or only as an idea in the shape of a handwritten proposal. The prepress department scans the pictures, puts them on to the server and sets up the index related to the title database. New images will be treated first. All pictures come into the system at two or three resolutions, one for the layout check at screen resolution, one at highest resolution for offset print. For large pictures a medium resolution image can be scanned and stored for a later scaling down procedure or for an electronic proof of a complex layout. The capture of pictures is done throughout the year and not only during the production of a new issue.

5   Soon after starting the production phase a first draft of the new catalogue is made. Once this draft exists, the trading house can access the title database via specific workstation retrieval software. This method enables the trading house to get a good impression of the page layout and responsible persons in the trading house can suggest corrections and changes to the print shop. This may happen over the 'phone or through the integrated mail system. Direct changes are not considered at the moment because the consistency of data requires a single source responsibility.

6   After a few rounds of changes the final draft is ready. At this stage the customer, in this case the trading house, can see a proof of the catalogue. In the very first edition of the catalogue he/she has thoroughly checked the proof. Today it is enough for the contact person at the trading house to check the page layout on his/her screen with the low-resolution pictures provided. He/she believes the print shop, that the quality will be sufficiently good in print later on.

7   If the customer feels that the catalogue is correct, the films for the printers will be produced and printing is started without a separate blueprint. Normally in the catalogue business the print production time is fixed a long time before finishing the documents. The corporate service manager has to arrange that the material is ready just in time. The partner who cannot fulfil his/her duties in time has to pay a penalty depending on the contract.

The first results of the example described above of the 'corporate publishing service' process make both partners very hopeful of reaching the set goals. During the work a new feeling grows about the responsibility for special tasks within the process, and for the process as such. Based on this new feeling both sides nurture new ideas for additional helpful functions to be realized in the future.

The most important results from this case study are the reduction of production time down to two weeks (excluding acquisition of new picture material) and the possibility of controlling the completion time precisely at every stage. Normally there is now only one loop to check the correctness and quality of the output, as opposed to the four to seven loops previously necessary. A big problem for the print shop is storage capacity for all the pictures. Future developments therefore point to the use of optical media.

TECHNICAL DOCUMENTATION-ORIENTED SERVICE

The domain of technical documentation covers all documents which describe all kinds of products, from small parts to composed aggregates, engines, cars, medical substances, food, software or whatever you can imagine. The specific criterion for technical documentation is that the documentation is not the product, but is absolutely necessary to sell the product.

Companies which produce these products or offer services want to improve their products. They invest much money and time in the development of the products. On the other hand, the acceptance of a product also depends on the manuals or instructions to use the product. Unfortunately not only do manufacturers need knowledge about electronic publishing, but the production of the documentation must take place at the same time as the product is being developed. Therefore the manufacturers need help from publishers in the form of corporate services.

The idea of the corporate service came through performing the physical distribution of printed technical and advertisement material to retailers for the car industry. Also, Bertelsmann has extensive experience in structuring documentation for CD-ROM retrieval systems. The decision was therefore made to build a corporate service.

Process description

Bertelsmann has recognized the need for such a service. Based on recent cooperation with various manufacturers in the automotive industry it offers a corporate publishing service which covers the whole process line of document production, including financial and management requirements. This service is not an unchangeable fixed process; it offers a large number of components which can be combined and tailored to a customer's specific order. To have a base of understanding when working with the customer, Bertelsmann has developed a process description model.

The publishing process can be described by the seven-stage model (Figure 14.1). The stages are data capturing, data structuring, data administration, layout, production, distribution and usage. The model is based on three concepts:

- strict separation of structure and layout,
- media-independent storage of objects,
- transparent dataflow controlled by a management system.

The separation of structure and layout is the baseline for future user-oriented administration of the information components or objects. Although today it is not clear what format will be needed tomorrow for different objects, in this way the stored objects can be used again each time, perhaps after only a simple conversion. The handling of text is a good example. If the text is structured in an object-oriented context and SGML is used as a notation, flexibility and independence from an existing data format can be achieved.

Bertelsmann has developed an internal editorial system based on a database with an object-oriented data model and a notation of the

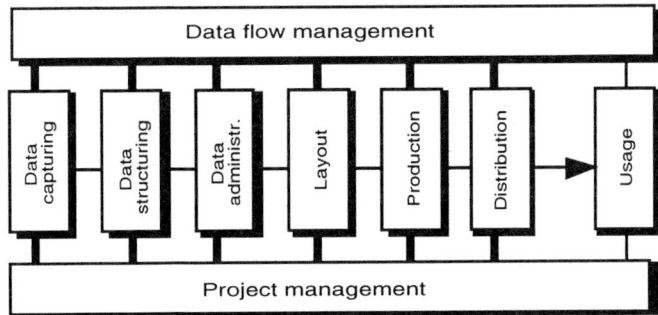

Figure 14.1 Dataflow management — the seven-stage model.

attributes inside the text in an SGML-like format. Additionally, Bertelsmann uses its own data management system for access to CD-ROM, the reason for this merely being better response time and retrieval speed. Today, after several years of work, a vast number of documents have been created based on SGML-structured asset storage. Paper, CD-ROM for Windows PC and a disk for the Sony Data Discman were used as output media.

The concept of media independency is very important. To realize this concept for all kinds of objects like text, pictures and video, it is necessary to use an object management system (OMS). In a large project called DIDOS (Distributed Documenting Services) an OMS was developed. In this project, sponsored by the EC, the spare part catalogue of Grundfos, the largest supplier of heating pumps in the world, was extended from a normal paper version to a multimedia product on a CD-ROM for use with a PC. Based on the OMS, a document management system enables the handling of all necessary data.

An important aspect for the cost efficiency of production is the organization of dataflow. A transparent dataflow guarantees that the administrative systems are available to control the process and bring the documentation just in time to the point-of-sale, together with the product.

Objective of the service

The main objective of the service is to avoid, as far as possible, the need for the manufacturer to spend time and thought on documentation. All the work to document all parts or products should be performed by the service provider.

Typical producers use this service for technical product descriptions, manuals, system documentation for software and hardware or in-house publications. Parts catalogues for professional use are also very typical products. All these types of documents will normally be delivered on paper, but today requests for a CD-ROM or online version are increasing.

Example 2. A complete service for the manufacturer

A big European manufacturer and supplier of electric and electronic parts for cars and other complex engines is one of the first customers

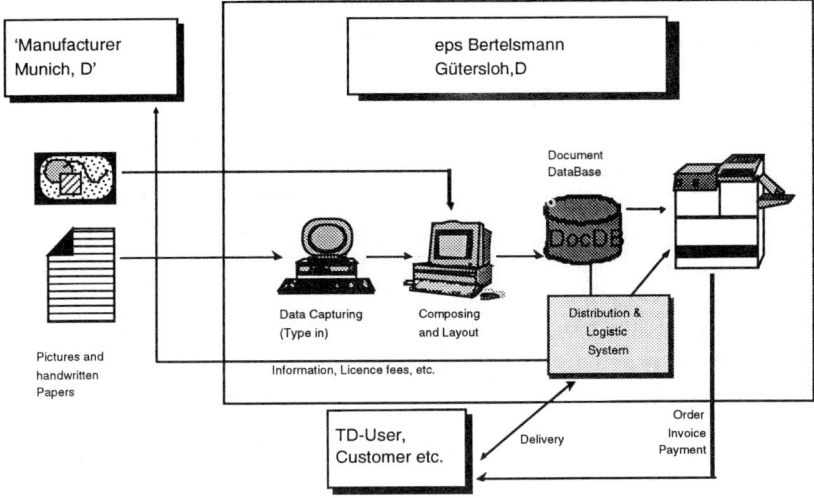

Figure 14.2 Principal dataflow

of the corporate publishing service. The principal dataflow is shown in Figure 14.2.

Bertelsmann is doing all the work across every stage in the seven-stage model. The manufacturer has given full responsibility for quality to Bertelsmann. Based on this idea, the functions are as follows:

- The manufacturer gives all material to Bertelsmann as it is. The material can be handwritten, copied, cut and pasted or come in various different electronic forms. At Bertelsmann the data is typed in or drawn and added to an asset archive. Pictures are scanned or transferred via electronic media into the archive.
- From this archive the documents will be composed on the basis of a handwritten or predefined layout proposal from the manufacturer. Bertelsmann staff work at this stage in constant communication with the manufacturer's employees. Most documents such as data sheets or catalogues are already predefined. Because of this method of creating documents, the whole process is very fast and satisfactory for the customer.
- After producing the page layout for the whole document or parts of it, the pages are printed out and sent to the manufacturer to proofread the content and release or correct the document. The

responsibility for the content has to remain with the manufacturer. Normally, experience shows that not many corrections are needed — usually less than 5%.

- The released documents are stored in the Document Master Page Archive (DMPA) in a final format according to a specific version. All documents are indexed with a few related numbers and keywords for basic retrieval functionality. From the DMPA the documents will be printed out if such a request is received (Print on Demand). CD-ROM production for selected documents is available, too.

- After reproduction of the documents they will be sent directly to the user, normally a repair shop or a parts retailer, together with the invoice. Bertelsmann ships the documents via different channels to the user depending on what the user requests with regard to time and cost constraints. Afterwards all accounting activities will be performed by Bertelsmann.

- For information the manufacturer periodically receives a report about the delivered documents.

This corporate publishing service has been working now for several months. Initial results are very satisfactory for both partners from a functional viewpoint. The constraints to be just in time on the market have also been fulfilled without major problems. The overall calculations of costs and benefits are not complete at present.

CONCLUSION

Corporate publishing services are requested more and more owing to the pressure of time and cost in technical documentation and prepress usage.

The Bertelsmann case studies show that the organization of corporate publishing services works well and provides satisfactory results for the manufacturer as well as for the publisher. A final estimate of revenues and benefits cannot be supplied at present, but all companies expect to receive genuine advantages from these services.

EP and financial services — case study

15

Electronic publishing of financial applications

Michael Pritchett, Extel Financial, UK

THE BUSINESS

Extel Financial, part of Financial Times Group, is acknowledged as an authoritative source of information with its in-depth reporting and information and analyses of business, finance, financial news and the world financial markets. The company's specialist services include real-time global financial news, financial data and company and business information delivered on paper, CD-ROM and online. Extel was founded in 1872 with the laying of the first transatlantic telegraph cable to carry share prices from London to New York. Significantly, the company's biggest revenue earner is still the delivery of share prices and associated information and the company is still achieving technological firsts with new delivery mechanisms for its information. One of these forms the basis for this case study.

RELEVANT HARD-COPY SERVICES

Extel supplies company information ranging from quoted companies' financial results and news announcements to copies of all the circulars it sends to shareholders. Financial results and news an-

---

Michael Pritchett is Product Management Executive with Extel Financial Limited in London. This leading specialist EP financial publisher was recently acquired by the Financial Times newspaper publishing group, in turn owned by Pearson plc.

nouncements are presented in a standard format on the famous 'Extel card', the product for which the company is most widely known. Company circulars include prospectuses for new share issues, takeover documents and any other legal documents that all shareholders receive.

Extel traditionally supplied copies of all of these documents for all quoted companies on microfiche and published directories giving details of professional advisers for takeovers and new issues. However, a document on microfiche is only of use to somebody who knows exactly for what they are looking; it is a directory and can only be indexed on two or three factors.

USER MARKET

Corporate financiers, bankers, lawyers, stockbrokers, accountants and consultants all need access to company announcements. The reasons for this requirement are varied but include researching a company, identifying types of transaction that have succeeded or failed in particular markets and, most importantly, using similar features of historical documents to help construct new ones. In order to make this information available, these professional advisers tended to subscribe to a copy of all the announcements on microfiche, to ensure comprehensive coverage. They would also keep a collection of historical documents they had worked on or come across which provided good examples of a particular feature of a document. This system was time-consuming as it involved filing and could result in duplication of effort within an organization. It was also inefficient: even if a person held a copy of a document, they might not be aware of a significant paragraph on an inside page.

Some organizations achieved much more comprehensive coverage by attempting to obtain copies of all documents for their internal libraries. Internal indexes were sometimes attempted, but the whole operation was labour intensive and could never offer full coverage of all the contents of all the documents; there are about 500 features that can be present in such a document, leading to a huge number of possible combinations.

IDENTIFICATION MARKET

The need for a better system for retrieving this information became apparent to Extel as a result of discussions with customers in early 1991. Extel made a detailed study of the market for company announcements to identify the characteristics which a new product would need and to quantify the market for such a product. This was not an easy exercise. It is not too difficult to research demand for a development of variants of existing products, but customers are much less able to give firm indications about requirements and purchasing intentions for a product of which they have never thought. At an early stage it was hard to get detailed information about requirements, as potential customers were afraid to lose competitive edge or to help a company produce a system that would be available to all. However, given a list of possible features and details of the information held, potential customers would make very useful comments about what would be of most value to them.

VALUE-ADDED CHARACTERISTICS

As a result of this research, Extel came up with the concept of a product that would:

- have the ability to retrieve historical documents,
- enable advisers to consult documents shortly after they had been issued,
- perform full and accurate searches of all documents for specific combinations of features, e.g. a contested takeover in the chemical industry with a certain deal structure.

In order for a service to be of value, it would have to replace other methods of obtaining documents by being updated weekly. Similarly, it would be desirable to avoid the effort previously expended in filing the documents. The ideal method of achieving this would be to supply an image-retrieval system along with a very sophisticated index that could cater for all varieties of document that would be encountered.

The searching mechanism would have the benefit that it would miss nothing and allow a customer the opportunity to build up a picture of how a type of transaction had developed and the variations used. The actual documents could then be referred to as required.

DEVELOPMENT OF THE PRODUCT

In order to provide the features outlined above, Extel investigated the document storage and retrieval technologies available. Although there were many systems that could store document images, there were none that were set up with a searching mechanism enabling the user to build up a description of a document using 500 possible features. The solution came in using a technology called 'Headfast', from Head Software International, to locate summaries of the documents that could be linked to images stored on CD-ROM. However, each CD-ROM will only hold up to about 20 000 sides of A4, and up to 8000 sides are produced each month, so Extel decided to use a six-CD-ROM jukebox.

There is a major difference between this CD-ROM product and the CD-ROM titles which are published generally. In this instance, the CD-ROM is being used as a vehicle to carry very regular updates to a continually growing bank of information. Most titles are published and made available for purchase on a once-off basis until a possible future edition of a title is desirable, in the same way a book is purchased. The emphasis here is on the indexing and timeliness of the documents.

The use of a jukebox ensured that all documents issued could be covered, which meant that customers would not have to maintain their own libraries of paper copies. To achieve this, a CD-ROM would be produced each month which would contain the latest documents in addition to the previous ones. Once the CD was full, it would be retained in the jukebox and a new one would start from scratch. Each week the latest index would be updated on a floppy disk; if an image found in a search had not yet arrived on CD-ROM, it could be made available by other means.

Extel's existing expertise was used to produce a list of the features that a document could have. This was refined through consultation with potential users. The searching facilities were designed so that rather than typing in a word search, a user could use a mouse to select appropriate companies, types of document and features within the document.

BENEFITS TO THE CUSTOMER

'I have been waiting for this service for ten years', said a leading UK stockbroker. The service has allowed users to do something that they have been attempting for some time: to be able to search for examples of a particular type of document and know that the search has been thorough. This means that, when starting a new piece of work, the professional advisers can bring themselves up to date on the details of what their competitors have been doing in the relevant field. They can also discover, often by accident, when their clients have been using somebody else. They can produce new documents more quickly by modifying paragraphs used elsewhere instead of starting from scratch. Above all, they do not have to source and file hundreds of pages a day.

MARKETING

As has been described above, there was a latent demand for this service before it was made available. However, this has been enhanced by adding market data, such as how well a new issue did. Presenting the product as offering a competitive advantage has meant that once one organization in a sector has started to subscribe, others are very keen to investigate. By offering benefits to company librarians as well as to the end-users, the service is championed from a central point within client organizations.

BENEFITS TO EXTEL

The most important benefit of any electronic publishing service which replaces and enhances existing paper-based services is that the revenue stream is protected and enhanced by offering greater added value. Another advantage of the project described here was that it provided a well-defined first step into imaging.

ORGANIZATIONAL ISSUES

As a greater degree of analytical information is provided in the new service, it was necessary to recruit some new staff from outside. In terms of new skills, all the people involved with the product have had to learn to use PCs. The use of image-scanning equipment has required the learning of specific skills. However, the ability to learn to use this type of equipment is becoming more and more common and has not caused any great problems. The shift away from paper products towards PC products has, as a whole, resulted in a tendency to have fewer, highly skilled staff instead of the larger number of staff involved in physical production. Although part of this trend, there was no direct substitution in this particular case.

FUTURE DEVELOPMENTS

The principles which the company has learnt from the first image product clearly have scope for wider application. Within a few years, colour images will be available, updated within a few hours of release. It does seem likely, however, that image technology will still mainly be used to provide a retrieval system for returning documents to paper, as users still like to have something solid that they can carry around.

EP for learning and training
— case study

16

Stimulation of publishers. The new media learning material business: entry strategy options for educational and training publishers

Jürgen Schmidt, Katharina Voss, Ernst Klett Verlag, Germany, Willem Bulthuis, Philips, Netherlands, Roberto Minio, Richard McArthur, Jonathan Wheeler, IEPRC, UK and Bert van Muylwijk, Grant Nelson, VMC, Netherlands

The study report (January 1994) reprinted in this chapter, was compiled by Dr Jürgen Schmidt *et al*, Klett Verlag in collaboration with Willem Bulthuis, Philips Consumer Electronics, Eindhoven, Netherlands; Roberto Minio *et al*, the International Electronic Publishing Research Centre, Leatherhead, UK; and Bert van Muylwijk *et al*, Van Muylwijk Consulting, Eindhoven, Netherlands.

Dr Jürgen Schmidt is a director of Ernst Klett Verlag für Wissen und Bildung GmbH, Stuttgart; he is responsible for business strategy, new media publishing and international projects for the Klett group of companies, Germany's leading educational publishing house.

The STimulation Of Publishers (STOP) study has been undertaken for the European Commission. The project was supported by EC funding under the DELTA scheme, a subset of the EC TELEMATICS programme. Matching funds were provided by a consortium of 25 European publishing companies. Permission granted by the EC to reprint the report in this book is gratefully acknowledged.

INTRODUCTION

There can be no doubt that information technology has irreversibly changed many facets of our world, while at the same time continuing to evolve. On the basis of the latest developments the world of publishing is now at the threshold of fundamental changes in its operations: electronic publishing is no longer a hype word but a reality for many operations.

Education and training is an important socio-economic sector in our society. It deals with educating young people, amongst other things taking responsibility for handing over Europe's cultural heritage to new generations. It deals with training and retraining our workforce and is therefore an important factor in the competitive position of European industry and commerce. It is an important economic factor; everybody receives education and some form of training for which materials are being produced.

This report takes a closer look at the world of publishing for education and training. In particular it analyses the opportunities offered by new media for this market sector and the challenges it is going to meet.

The direct outcome of this report is the observation that many publishers in the training and education sector apparently do not see any urgent need to get into new media products. On the surface this is caused on the one hand by the fact that market sizes and profit margins for traditional book materials are still attractive enough. On the other hand, the technologies involved in new media never seem to reach a 'steady state': development and delivery platforms with their related software 'standards' are constantly evolving. Also, the production of new media products influences and changes the operational aspects of the publishing business: well-known and proven processes and even market definitions suddenly have to be revised and thought through, drawing on the flexibility of management and production units.

However, at the same time in other parts of the world educational and training publishers have already engaged in the opportunities of new media publishing. In Japan and the USA it is a rapidly expanding market. So it is clear that if European education and training publishers want to stay competitive and not lose business, they will have to prepare for entering the new media domain shortly.

This report gives an overview and analysis of the most relevant aspects of new media publishing for education and training in order to provide this industry with information from which it can derive decisions for the near future. Education and training, although disparate markets, are covered together unless otherwise stated explicitly. We begin with a statement of the main options and recommendations resulting from the findings of the study.

Options for actions for educational and training publishers

Have you appointed somebody to read the rest of this report?

- Establish the means to manage innovation within your company.
- Give somebody responsibility for multimedia and electronic publishing.
- Establish a team of key authors who are open for and committed to new media.

If you wait to invest in new media, then *plan* to wait, and prepare.

- Control licensing of exclusive rights to others.
- Set up business mechanisms for parallel publishing.
- Keep the valuable education and training competences in the company by holding on to the right people in the company.
- Implement appropriate budgeting, accounting procedures and calculation schemes.
- Implement DTP (Desktop Publishing) for book publishing.

Take the evolutionary approach!

- Exploit established market positions to launch new media products, e.g. add multimedia products to successful series.
- Do not build large service facilities in-house, buy in services as much as possible.
- Establish a strategy for utilization of new media production services.
- Distinguish between initial and ultimate product and market mix and plan your business start-up accordingly.
- Consider starting with bespoke title development and exploit the

resulting products on the open markets later, but ensure during development that the product will indeed be sufficiently generic.

- Consider the product/market mix where you can create an installed base (instead of waiting for one to appear).

Have you got the value to add?

- Find out whether you have value to add, and where in the chain.
- Maximize your own ownership of rights or set up strategic cooperation.
- Develop a business culture and structure to exploit assets as an essential part of the business.

What do the learners and teachers get out of it, and how do they know?

- Focus on multimedia products with a very concrete added value to teachers and/or learners.

Good products on the market are good for everybody.

- Accept and support the attitude that, at this stage, the market success of good products — even from the competition — is good for everybody.

Technology is not *the* issue, it is just one of the issues.

- Stick to a platform for a while, once you have selected it.
- Do not always go for the most state-of-the-art technology, at least not after the initial trial phase.

Recommendations to the EC

Act jointly with educational and training publishers.

- Investigate with educational publishers where new media are effective for training and education and what the specific added value of such learning material is, and promote this to the education and training society.
- Help publishers identify where installed bases of multimedia sys-

tems exist, especially within European and national government bodies.

- Stimulate the involvement of educational and training publishing in European RTD programmes.

Stimulate business opportunities.

- Take up new media in the EC education and training initiatives, e.g. European schools, knowledge transfer from the R&D framework programmes.
- Do not overencourage the speed-up of technological development.
- Stimulate the innovation in national education systems, through, for example, development of multimedia learning material on European subjects.

Set the appropriate copyright environment.

- Support the needs of industry in assisting with setting legal standards, e.g. following the recommendations of the T3RT report on 'Copyright issues for publishers of multimedia educational and training products'.

Disseminate results.

- Involve publishing and education organizations through a workshop in order to collect feedback and to assure wide dissemination of the report.
- Have a real publication developed on the basis of this study.

THE BUSINESS OF ELECTRONIC PUBLISHING IN EDUCATION AND TRAINING

Definition and scope

All education and training depends on the availability of good-quality learning material. Whether for self-study or classroom teaching, there always is a need for learning material, to be used as preparation, for actual learning, for exercising, or for reference afterwards.

New requirements for learning material are emerging from social, economic, practical, technical or other developments. At the same time, the emergence of suitable, reliable and affordable technologies is enabling the development of new types of learning material.

Electronic or multimedia publishing is where those new requirements and new types of learning material meet. Modern technologies, originating from both professional and entertainment industries, offer new ways of producing and using learning material. These new ways seem closer to the worlds of TV and computers than to the world of printed textbooks. Consequently, it is no surprise that the established education and training publishing industry has not yet embraced the new opportunities fully. It is largely waiting and leaving the initial, often risky, steps to other entrepreneurs, like small start-ups, video companies and large entertainment and game companies.

There are two key disadvantages in this situation. First, it may turn out that the established (print) publishing industry in the end will see no profit from the growth caused by the new media or may even see a substantial part of its market being taken over by other businesses (possibly from outside Europe). Second, the lack of real uptake of new media by the established publishers hampers the large-scale availability of efficient and effective learning material, necessary to develop our youth and to improve our workforce.

Both factors are of great concern to the European Union at large and therefore to the European Commission (EC). The EC, through the DELTA Programme and CCAM funds, has asked the Training Technology and Telematics Round Table* (T3RT) to perform this study to analyse how the situation can be changed, i.e. how European publishers can be stimulated and helped to get into the multimedia market quicker.

Approach

The opportunities for publishers created by new technologies are well analysed by the joint EC/IEPRC† study[1]. While very useful for the European publishing industry in general, that study could not

---

*T3RT: Training Technology & Telematics Round Table, a group of about 25 large European companies all interested in exploiting technology for in-company training, as user or provider.

†IEPRC: International Electronic Publishing Research Centre, an association in which major publishers and the printing industry are represented.

address the specific aspects of the education and training publishers in Europe.

Therefore the present study took up where the EC/IEPRC study stopped and analysed in more detail the strengths, weaknesses, opportunities and threats for the European education and training publishers.[‡] The objective was not to perform quantitative analyses, which would have required considerably more time and resources. Instead, the study has focused on a qualitative determination of the current situation and on the development of concrete recommendations for helping education and training publishers to get into electronic publishing in a profitable way.

The analysis of the current situation took place in the form of a global 'SWOT' analysis by a group of experts in the field and by a series of substantial interviews with key companies in the business. The results of these two input sources were integrated into a loose kind of SWOT overview. This SWOT analysis identifies the key Strengths and Weaknesses (internal factors) of and the main Opportunities for and Threats (external factors) to the established education and training publishers in Europe. Of course, this could only be a coarse cross-section across all European publishers, each of which also have their own specific situation.

The recommendations resulted from in-depth discussion of the outcomes of the SWOT analysis and the interviews. They are aimed at two different target groups. The main set of recommendations is addressed directly at education and training publishers. Another set is addressed to the European Commission.

All recommendations are necessarily of such a nature that there is a need for each company to be carefully assessed individually. Therefore, the main purpose of both the SWOT analysis and the recommendations to publishers is to provide some tools for analysing a specific case and for developing the most appropriate approach to entering the electronic publishing business, to the benefit of those publishers and of all European learners.

[‡]In this study, no clear distinction is made between educational and training publishers, as the borders between those industries are becoming fuzzy, and many publishers are active in both fields.

Product development chains

The core business of educational and training publishers is the development, production and distribution of learning and teaching materials. In general this is usually done at the risk of the publisher, which is developing generic materials for its markets. In the field of training materials publishing, development and production is sometimes done to order ('bespoke titles') from industry by specialized (most smaller) publishers.

In this section the product development phase will be described, stressing the differences between the different sorts of media being developed. In the next section an analysis of the marketing structures of educational and training materials will be given.

Educational print materials

The traditional business of developing print materials (Figure 16.1) is clearly defined and in principle does not pose any problems. Like all product development the phases are planning, preparation, development of the teaching or learning content, production, manufacturing, distribution and finally evaluation. Based on overall market research or knowledge and initial product ideas, decisions taken during the planning stage concern the concrete target group and definition of the content. Authors have to be found and tested, and a detailed concept concerning content and its design (layout) is fundamental for the final product definition during the preparation phase.

The development phase is mainly dependent on the authors' pedagogical work. They work out manuscripts to order and in close cooperation with the editorial department, which has full control over process and content. Rights for pictures and other assets, e.g. reference texts, are bought by the publisher. External graphic artists get orders to draw the graphical elements of the book.

The production process starts with layout, and in cases where DTP is not yet implemented, with typesetting of the manuscripts. External typesetting was one of the most expensive and time-consuming parts of the production process. With the use of DTP this can be dramatically reduced. Preparing the films for printing (reproduction) externally by specialized companies finally leads to printing and book binding. The product can then be distributed and sold, with the help of PR activities.

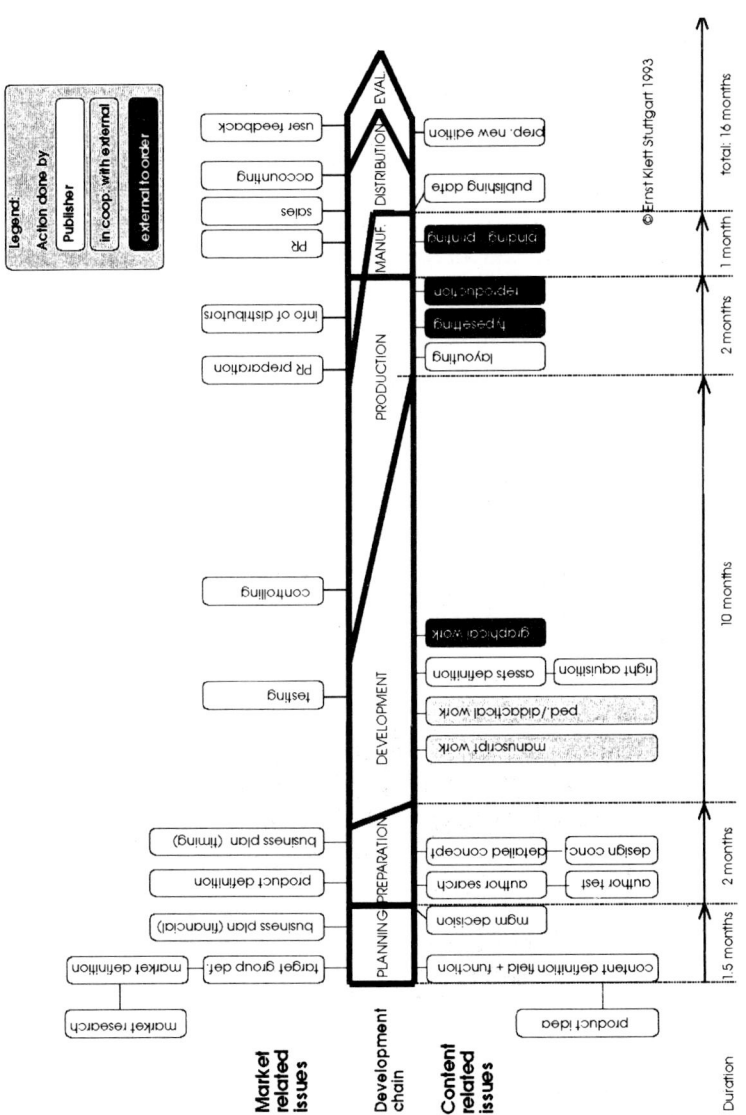

Figure 16.1 Product development chain: educational print materials

As far as the cost structure is concerned, internal and external costs are well known and widely similar. The main internal costs are obviously for the salaries of editors and production people, company infrastructure, overheads and distribution costs. External costs include the acquisition of rights and the technical work in production and manufacturing. While graphic artists are generally paid on a flat rate per item basis, authors normally get royalties after sales have started, and no, or just a small, advance during their manuscript work.

The profit on a product is highly dependent on the number of copies sold, as with higher numbers of copies basically just more paper is needed, while all other costs are more or less fixed. For a typical educational printed product (e.g. 200 pages, four colours,

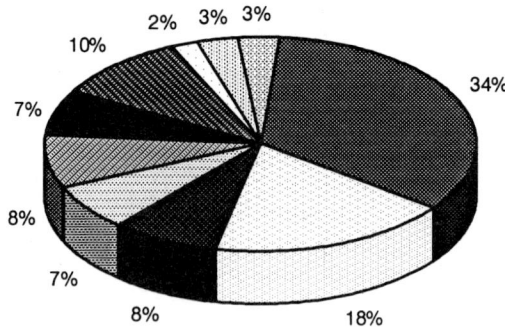

Figure 16.2 The costs of a typical printed publication

high number of graphics and pictures, hardcover, 10 000 copies) the total costs might be divided as shown in Figure 16.2.

Educational audio materials

Audio tapes for education and training have been used for approximately 20 years, and, therefore, there is — as with printed materials development — a well-known development process within publishing companies (Figure 16.3).

Differences compared to the printed materials development chain are, of course, the production handling of voice, sound and music. Recording is usually done in an external studio with a number of freelance speakers, in the presence and under the control of the editor in charge. The technical process of mixing, cutting and masking is then performed by specialized companies. The sales product normally includes a small booklet with educational contents and is packaged by a packaging company.

The cost division of a typical educational audio product (carton package with audio and booklet, audio 80% voice, 10% sound, 10% music; booklet in one colour, 64 pages, 2000 copies) is different for audio tapes and audio CDs as shown in Figure 16.4.

Educational multimedia materials

In contrast to the previously described development chains, educational and training publishers have, as yet, little experience as far as the development process of multimedia products are concerned. On the other hand, one is aware of the fact that as a result of the presentation of a multimedia product on a screen, visual elements play a much bigger role than they do in traditional products. The consequences are clear and are threatening: it is not possible merely to adapt the new tasks into the traditional development processes; there is a need for a whole new working organization that includes new external service providers. Basically this means — at least when starting this business — that publishers fear losing control of the development process. A comparison of the numbers of grey and dark boxes in Figure 16.5 shows this clearly.

In the following some of the most obvious characteristics are described of the development of a 'real' educational multimedia product such as CD-ROM XA or CD-i, where text plays a minor role compared to graphic design, animation and interaction.

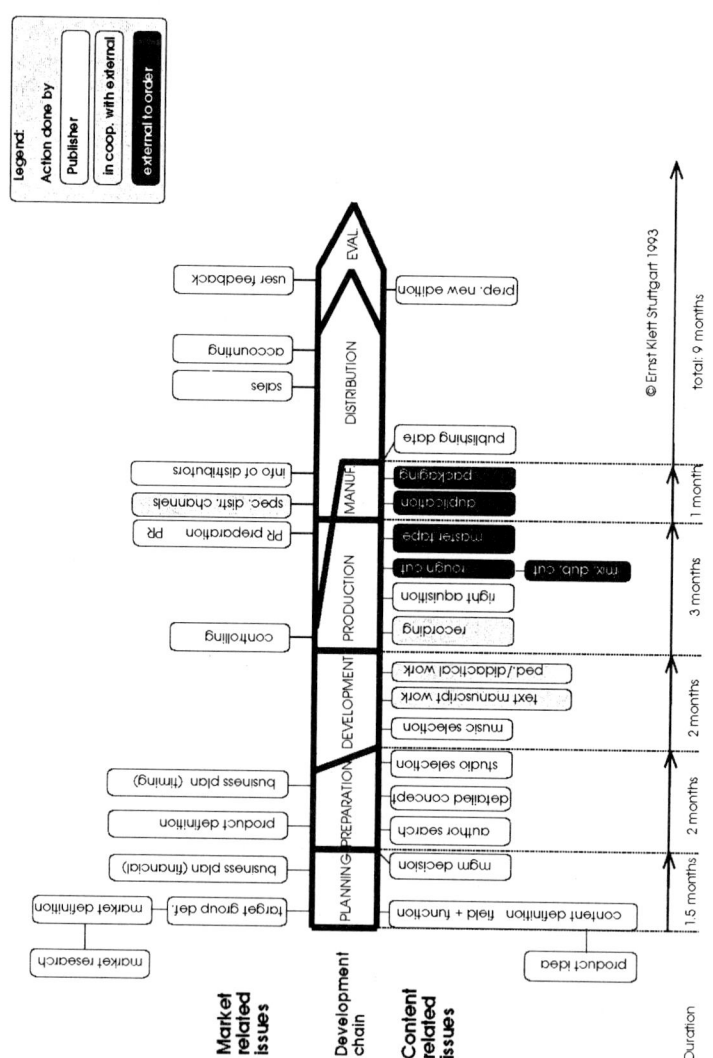

Figure 16.3 Product development chain: educational audio materials (text and sound/music)

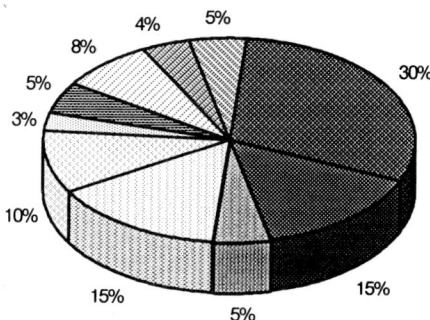

Figure 16.4 The costs of a typical tape/CD publication

While in the traditional process the design concept is of minor importance during the planning phase, this is where the multimedia development process requires the most important considerations concerning the global appearance of the final product, including the screen design, which should lead to the development of a preprototype. Influenced by the potentially very high costs of assets (animated graphic, film, sound), it is necessary to define carefully the assets to be used, mainly by considering what sorts of rights are already possessed and which ones are available in a cost-effective way. To design and produce a multimedia title a development tool, hardware and software, has to be selected — a decision of major

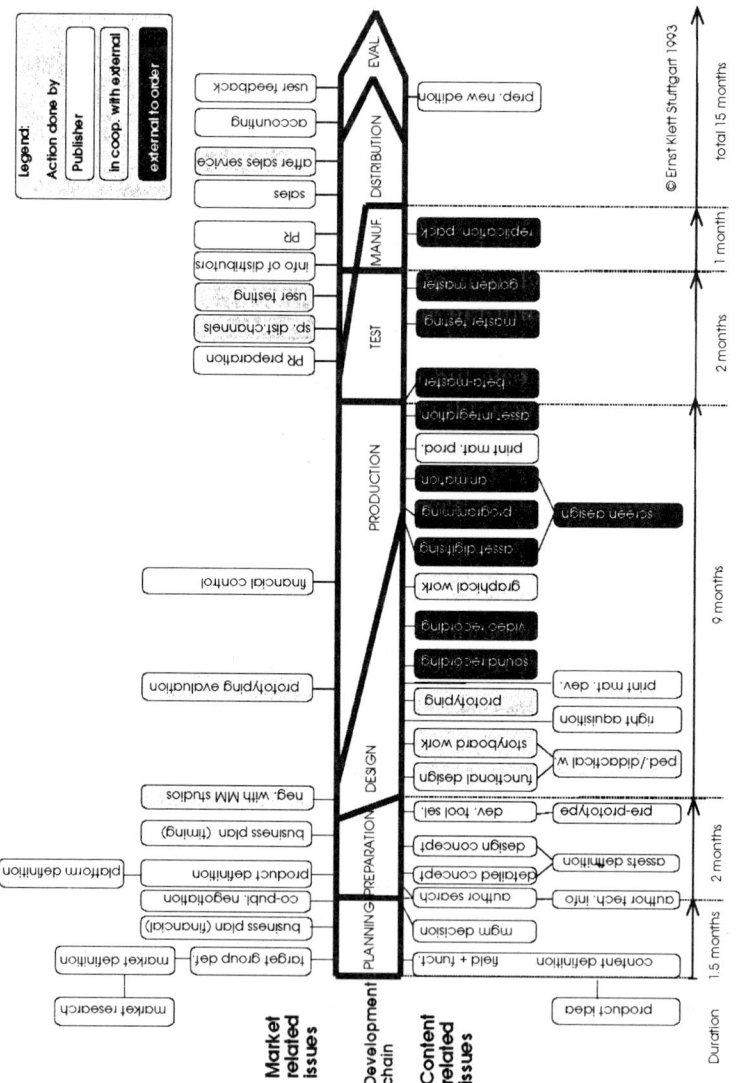

Figure 16.5 Product development chain: educational multimedia

importance for the work to follow, and dependent on the degree of involvement of an external multimedia studio and the sort of work that is done internally or by the authors.

Pedagogical consideration in cooperation with authors leads to the development of the functional design, e.g. concerning the interactivity to be implemented or the hierarchical structure of the different 'screens'. Authors then do not write manuscripts but rather storyboards according to both the functionality and content. All this work has to be prepared and controlled by an in-house editor with related knowledge.

The prototype of the first parts of the storyboard is the first production activity that takes place and this as early as possible. Externally recorded sound and video, as well as graphical elements, have then to be digitized and animated by external specialized companies. The final screen design and the actual programming is done to order by a multimedia studio. After the integration of all assets by the studio a test phase — something totally new for the publishing industry — starts in order to validate the product to a final 'golden' master that then can be duplicated and, together with a printed manual, packaged for distribution.

Besides the organizational aspects of the development process of a multimedia product, one of the most serious and as yet unsolved problems is the acquisition of rights. On the one hand, one needs many more as well as different assets than are necessary in a traditional product. On the other hand, the related industry — photo agencies, music and film agents — and related people like musicians, photographers, graphic artists etc. do not (yet) have any idea about the pricing of assets for educational electronic use. Consequently, prices offered are far too high and initially hinder commercial sensibility on the side of the educational publishers.

As regards the cost structure of the multimedia product development, one must say that experiences so far have been very individual, as existing products do not have any typical structure. Nevertheless, we will try to give an indication on the division of the costs when developing an interactive multimedia CD-ROM title with the following characteristics: 30 screens, 30 background pictures, 10 times 30 second film (bought, not recorded), 100 slides, 30 animated graphics, half an hour spoken voices (newly recorded), 10 minutes music, programming of internal processes, e.g. probability functions, and learner feedback and control mechanisms. Half the rights are considered to be owned already, the rest are being bought for a 'traditional' price. Authors are paid on a flat rate basis, and no royalties. The breakdown is shown in Figure 16.6.

While the relation between internal and external costs for printed materials is 60:40, here this relation is reversed.

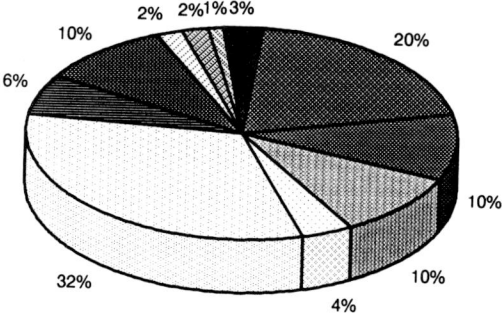

Figure 16.6 The costs of a typical interactive multimedia CD publication

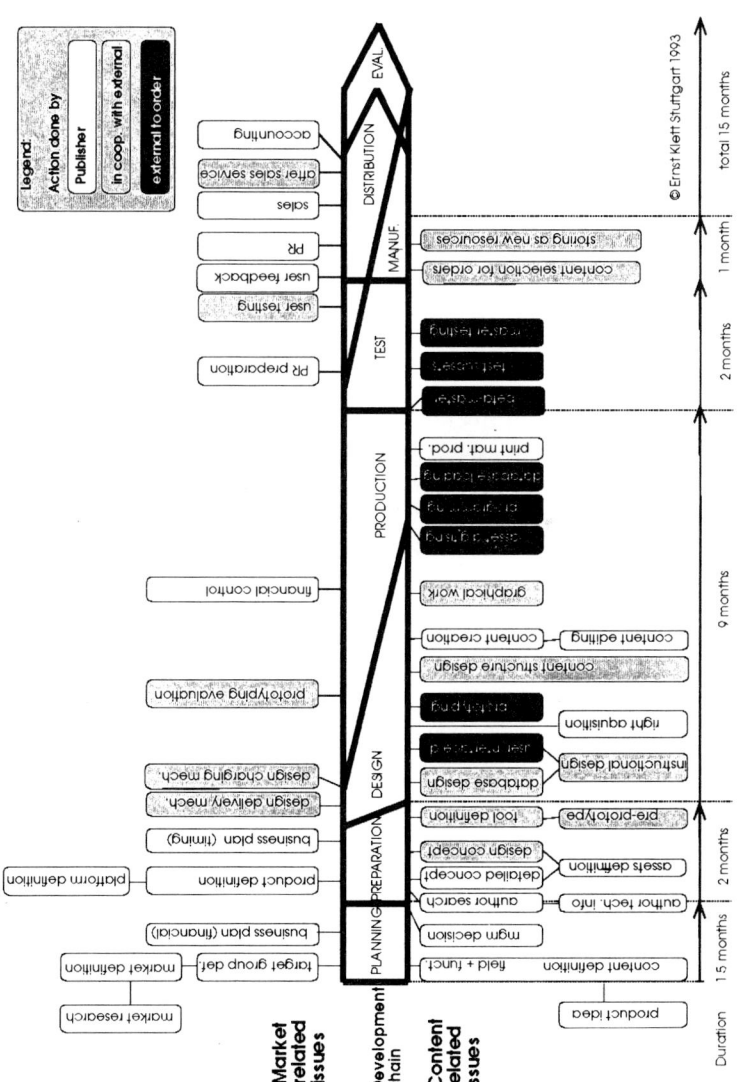

Figure 16.7 Product development chain: educational database

Educational database materials

Database publishing of educational and training material is a future challenge for educational publishers. So far, only noneducational database publishing activities, e.g. in the legal field, are known. Databases might be used for the development of new printed products, or as an online service product for the educational user — trainer or student. In both cases the user interface is the specific aspect which needs to be designed and programmed. Another unique feature is the need of an ongoing feedback from the user to the database. This has to be carefully organized. The development chain is shown in Figure 16.7.

As regards the cost structure it must be said that databases are and will be extremely individual. This is, therefore, hardly the place to go into this further.

MARKETING MODELS IN EDUCATIONAL AND TRAINING PUBLISHING

In order to give an idea of the complexity of the marketing structures in the world of education and training we will describe the currently existing distribution and communication structures. Differences in some European countries will be explained and tendencies regarding the future approach to the markets concerning new electronic types of learning and teaching materials will be discussed.

The markets for educational products

Market definition

In order to select appropriate learning material one must be aware of the specific conditions of the individual learner. From the marketing point of view these conditions define in their combination the different markets for educational products, which have to be of different kinds according to the conditions.

- *Target group definition:* field, function, place. An example is given in Figure 16.8.
- *Needs definition:* from special interest to final exam. For example, an engineer might:

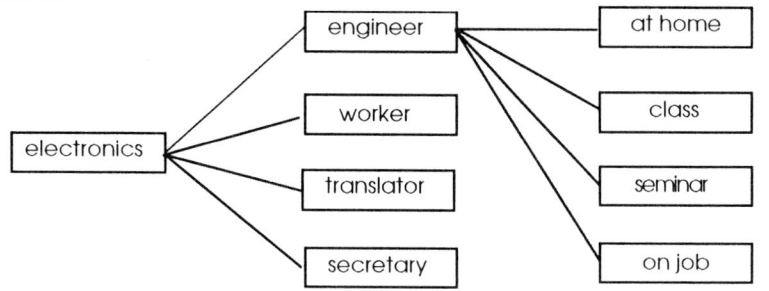

Figure 16.8 An example of a target group definition

- ○ have a private special interest, such as how electronics in a camera works,
- ○ need to use a specific tool for work,
- ○ need to know theoretical background,
- ○ need to pass an exam,
- ○ need management training.

- *Socio-economic definition:* Examples are student, teacher, tourist, computer-freak, ...,conservative, poor, ...
- *Subject definition:* relevance, quality, didactical approach, ..., language, ...
  Examples:

  - ○ relevance: a different sort of information about physical basics is needed by an electronic engineer and, for example, a worker in industry,
  - ○ quality, such as screen resolution for computer graphics, handling of the learning material, mistakes, colourness,
  - ○ didactic approach e.g. compendium versus step-by-step information, conventions of learning and teaching that are different in different countries, traditions in education,
  - ○ language, e.g. French information is of no value to an Irishman.

- *Media definition:* examples: book, CD-ROM, diskette, audiotape, videotape, overhead, transparency, dictionary.

Specific conditions in education and training

Besides the complexity and individualization of the educational markets as described above, there are some more conditions that influence the marketing of educational products.

As in the pharmaceutical industry, where a new medicine has to be approved by the government and the patient has no (or minor) influence on the medicine he/she has to use and to buy — the doctor told him/her — the situation in education and training markets is similar.

- Education and training markets are restricted:

  ○ Learning material, designed for schools or any other institutional body where official exams are held, has to meet the relevant curriculum requirements. If not, it will not be used either by students or by teachers.
  ○ In most European countries learning material for schools has to be approved by official bodies. If the approval is not given, the materials may not be used.

- End-users do not (normally) decide about learning material. Examples are:

  ○ training managers make decisions in companies,
  ○ regional conferences for teachers, parents, financial experts make decisions for schools.

- Trainers and teachers influence decisions by pedagogical means, but do not make purchases (nor pay for them).
- In industry highly specific training needs do not allow the development of generic training materials.
- Individual learners ('self-learners (SL)') are extremely hard to reach. Because of the complexity of the market conditions, generic material does not normally fulfil the requirements of the potential learner; the only exceptions are reference material or foreign language learning courses. On the other hand, very specific SL material does not allow the necessary (expensive) activities for development, distribution and PR.

Distribution and communication channels

General distribution model
There exists a general distribution model in the educational training markets:

$$Providers \rightarrow Distributors \rightarrow Deciders \rightarrow Users$$

Providers are, for example:

- publishers,
- developers like associations, software companies, individuals (e.g. university professors), in-company trainers,
- producers like the IT industry, television.

They all develop and produce the materials according to their own policies. For publishers this is their core business, while for all others publishing of educational material is a sort of side business which either gives added value to their main products or services or — in the case of individuals — is done as a sort of hobby.

Only a few of all of these different educational products made by these providers are sold directly to the user. Instead this is done by distributors, such as:

- booksellers, department stores,
- PC shops,
- mail order companies,
- direct distributors (e.g. door to door, direct sales, ...),
- university copy shops,
- open universities, distance learning institutes,
- the IT industry,
- business associations.

There are dozens of other distribution channels, depending on the sort of educational product. Furthermore, the distribution industry is a very complex structured hierarchical industry. So, for example, in Germany up to three distributing companies (wholesalers) are involved — and earn from the products — before the product itself is on the shelf of a bookseller or a PC shop. And finally the way distribution is handled in different European countries is totally different. This is discussed further below.

Only in the case of SL materials, about which users may decide for themselves (e.g. after they have received information about it from a brochure, a shop or a database) all other sorts of educational material are selected by deciders.

Both in institutional and noninstitutional learning sites, deciders include:

- training managers,
- trainers, teachers, professors,
- conferences in schools, local, regional,
- governmental bodies,
- parents.

Of course, deciders can only decide about materials they know. Deciders are normally not influenced by budgetary restrictions (e.g. training managers in charge of in-house training), so they not only decide about content but also about the financial involvement of the users who have to buy the materials. Users are:

- learners,
- teachers and trainers,
- self-learners.

General communication model

For information, PR and service there exists a general communication model (Figure 16.9). It is in the basic interest of the providers to inform the 'market' adequately about their products. In principle the objectives of this information are: information about the existence of a certain product, including conditions (price etc.), informa-

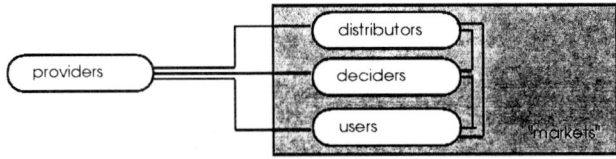

Figure 16.9 The general communication model

tion about the contents and information about how and when to use it. And this information has to be specified according the function of the market player: a distributor needs different information from a decider, etc.

Means of information provision include all sorts of well known PR activities: sales force information, direct mail, advertisements in newspapers and magazines, radio and TV, local and regional exhibitions etc. Future information channels may be databases.

Of course, distributors provide additional PR. As far as retailers (e.g. bookshops, PC shops) are concerned, local PR is normally offered by the providers, e.g. selling aids (posters, presentation kits, window decoration, etc.), on cost price basis.

In the case of regional or national distributors (e.g. direct sale; mail order; door to door etc.), PR is indirectly funded by the providers. The retailer discount is normally (in Germany) between 25% and 45%, but can be up to 80% of the net (without VAT) sales price.

Specific marketing channels

Marketing activities are extremely different according to the specific market conditions and the sort of educational products being promoted. The following examples will show this.

(1) *Textbooks for schools:* The target group for textbooks does not just include students but also teachers, schools, teacher associations and educational ministries.

Schoolbook publishers in Europe are mostly rather big companies compared with other publishers. The once large number of small companies did not survive because of the necessary internal infrastructure needed for the schoolbook business in European countries.

Marketing information is sent by direct mail, for which a continuously upgraded database of all teachers etc. is necessary. Teachers get not only brochures about textbooks but also free copies; 'advisers' visit schools and regional conferences and organize local exhibitions and workshops, where additional teacher versions of the textbooks and other learning materials are offered.

Although schoolbooks are ordered by schools or regional bodies directly from the publisher, the physical distribution of the materials has to be done — in most European countries —

through wholesalers and local bookshops. They just pass the packets on to the purchasing person — and receive (in Germany) about 10% (wholesale) and 25% (shop) of the net price.

(2) *Learning material for self-learners (SL):* SL material is provided by publishers and private or institutional distance-learning institutes that are distributors at the same time. While distance-learning institutes know their customers, the enrolled students, publishers try to sell to the general (= unknown) public.

Basic marketing activities therefore are, on the one hand, to inform the target group (e.g. French tourists who are interested in learning Greek) about the existence of such a product and, on the other hand, to convince distributors to take this product into its basket (e.g. take into stock in a department store).

For provision of information, PR activities in newspapers, magazines, radio, TV etc. are necessary. Local PR in buses, trams might be added. This is all extremely expensive and therefore only practical for products with the chance of a broad market size (like language courses). For PR concerning SL products one calculates about 50% of the turnover, compared with 10% in the case of textbooks, which shows why publishers hesitate to produce and market such materials.

(3) *Generic material for professional training:* Professional training is done in public or private schools, in companies, at seminars or individually. This list directly indicates the problems regarding marketing of training materials: the target groups need to be provided with the respective materials in different ways. Furthermore, as mentioned before, generic material cannot cope with all — mostly very specific — requirements and needs of the learners. So for each profession generic material deals with the basics and provides reference information, but hardly considers its specifics.

In the case of schools, marketing is done as for textbooks. Seminar houses normally use their own materials, perhaps supplemented by some generic products. Individuals are approached by distance-learning institutes or by job- or branch-related local or national organizations through their publications.

Companies are hard to reach by any sort of PR. This has to do with the following circumstances:

- Depending on the size and sort of company in-house training is organized quite differently; big companies may have centralized or decentralized training departments, in middle-sized companies often the personnel department is in charge, while in smaller companies nobody is really involved. As far as manufacturing industry is concerned, production departments often organize their individual — very specific — on-the-job training.
- People in charge of final decisions about training are seldom known. Even in big companies the (perhaps well-known) heads of training departments are mostly administrative people and not involved in choosing training materials. This is done by a few people in charge of the specific training needs.
- Unlike schools people involved in firms often change responsibility or leave the company. This fluctuation makes it especially difficult to bring the right information about training material into firms on a regular basis.
- Finally, firms are used to ordering directly from the providers when buying training material. This is no problem for small specialized providers, but a huge one for publishers that are not willing to ignore the book trade, which is still the main distribution channel for them.

(4) *CBT-material:* There exist a large number of mostly very small providers of CBT (computer-based teaching) materials. They distribute their products mainly by direct mail and they survive because of the relatively high prices of their specialized products.

Real generic CBT for broader use is still rather rare. In the past 15 years most bigger European educational publishers have tried to launch such product lines — and they have all failed.

Nowadays a certain success is achieved with generic CBT that can be used by pupils in addition to textbooks. Distribution channels are the PC shops where students and their parents buy. PR is produced by all providers, mainly in PC magazines and by information sent to teachers, so that they can propose the materials to their students.

National distribution channels

The distribution channels described are, in principle, more or less valid in all European countries, but there are definite differences as far as the following are concerned:

- the organizational structure of distribution industry,
- the financial consequences for the providers,
- the way PR is handled.

Furthermore, in all countries some national ways of distribution exist that are unknown in other countries. In the following we give some examples.

Belgium

Because of the two languages spoken in Belgium, two independent structures of printed-material distribution exist. Training material in French is mostly of French origin and distributed to the book-trade by subsidiaries of French distributors. For the Flemish materials there is a Belgian distribution network. Additionally Dutch providers and distributors sell quite heavily to the Belgian bookshops.

France

The booktrade in France is — compared to other European countries — relatively strongly organized. This is due to the fact that the three huge French publishing groups all have their own distributing companies that provide centrally for the whole country.

Nevertheless only printed materials are sold through the booktrade; there is, like everywhere else in Europe, hesitation about putting other media (like CBT, video, etc.) on to the shelves.

A French speciality is the importance of door-to-door sales. High-priced products (with up to 90% retailer discount) are widely sold to private individuals by specialized companies. Educational products are of course of less importance in this field.

Great Britain

Influenced by the public acceptance of the Open University in Britain, an infrastructure of distance-learning facilities has been developed. Through this channel a large number of private and business organizations sell their and other publishers' products quite successfully.

In the booktrade concentration by countrywide operating chains of bookshops makes it especially hard to launch new products. On the other hand, products that are accepted by these chains potentially sell well.

Germany

The booktrade is extremely conservative in Germany. There has been virtually no chance of selling anything other than books through this channel, but it seems that the awareness of the booktrade concerning modern media products is increasing.

The main place where Germans improve their knowledge is the VHS, the evening classes for adults, organized everywhere in Germany by local bodies. Millions of students enrol in these 'schools' every year. Teachers there are known by the publishers and are informed by direct mail. Students buy the materials in bookshops individually according to the proposals of the teachers.

Italy, Spain and Portugal

In these three countries training and further education traditionally do not play the same role as in other European countries. In the last 20 years, therefore, new forms of distribution of training materials have been developed.

The most obvious speciality is the distribution through newspaper kiosks as *faciculas*, which are training courses for self-study in small pieces, sold regularly every one or two weeks. There are specialized firms that provide these materials to the kiosks. A successful launch of a new product is extremely expensive: nationwide PR on television and in all other public media is necessary.

In these countries private schools are the main providers of training. As these schools are mostly very small and specialized (apart from language schools), it is almost impossible to provide them with the related information and products.

Tendencies in modern media (MM) marketing

Apart from CBT, modern media do not yet play an important role in the educational and training markets in Europe. A number of technology-oriented small firms have been developing some specialized training software, either produced to order or sold for extreme prices. New developments were recently initiated by the EC under the Impact program, where more than 50 consortia are now involved.

As far as marketing is concerned the following tendencies may influence future approaches.

Dependency on hardware

It is obvious that the use — and commercial success — of MM training material is dependent on the related hardware and its existence in the markets. In other words, training material developers are totally dependent on the marketing success of the IT industry, which on the other hand needs the application software for success — the typical chicken-and-egg-problem. Negative experiences with, for example, videodisc, are well known. The IT industry is therefore interested in cooperating with providers in order to market bundled products through their channels.

Internationality

As long as specific modern technology is not available everywhere in the markets, it is — both for the IT industry and publishers — necessary to develop multinational training products. National products will not have a market that is big enough to allow the cost-intensive production. Of course, this imposes a rigid barrier on the number and sort of subject for educational MM materials: the more that cultural traditions in teaching and learning of a subject play a role, the less applications can be developed on an international basis. So far, the main application fields have been language learning materials.

Future distribution channels

The traditional ways to distribute learning materials cannot yet be used for MM products. As explained above, they are either too conservative (e.g. book trade), too specialized (e.g. door-to-door; distance learning institutes) or not applicable (e.g. kiosks). This will improve, provided that offering modern media products becomes commercially beneficial.

Perhaps PC shops may be offering MM materials — but as they are technology-oriented firms, only self-explaining training material can be sold there.

MM training material needs to be explained to potential users so there is a need for new forms of service shops or distance service providers, which will also be able to help in case of application problems. The first examples of such providers have been founded by developing firms. Whether they survive will be dependent on the success of MM technology, the quality of the programs and, of course, acceptance by the users.

In any case, to install a Europe-wide infrastructure of such a kind will take a generation. In the meantime distribution of training material might take place:

- as a bundled product together with the hardware,
- by direct sales activities,
- through video-shops and bookshops, as for video-based products like CD-i,
- and, finally, through training material databases.

MARKET FIGURES

The purpose of this section is not to give an overview of the current market for educational and training multimedia publishing. Such a focused task has never been performed and publicly offered. In fact, such an analysis is suggested in this report as an action worthy of support by the European Union.

What is offered here is a glimpse into many separate reports published over the last five years. It is a useful exercise because it does give a feeling that a market even now exists and that it will certainly continue to grow. What is really missing was well worded even four years ago in the publication SIGCUE (1989)[2]:

> Perhaps the problem most frequently cited by computer-using educators across the globe is the lack of access to current research results and information on the successful education computing practices of other nations.

Publishers also cite a similar concern: no clear picture of successful market or even delivery systems, and no clearly established standards. This is true for individual countries as well as for all of Europe.

Table 16.1 The contrast between school and company markets

Schools	Companies
Conventional in regard to time, objectives, methods and testing	Unconventional: short courses, clearly defined objectives, progressive methods, objective testing
Routine teaching, no immediate challenges	Constant challenges, permanently changing tasks
Success measured by secondary criteria (textbook content, grammars)	Success measured by direct feedback from live communication situations
Large classes (30)	Size determined by objectives (0–20)
Teachers in permanent jobs	Teachers exchangeable
Media use is traditional (books, blackboard)	Multimedia approach

Markets

To begin, we have to remember we are considering two markets. L Reif from Berlitz (which gave 1 441 430 language lessons in 1986 and 2 100 091 in 1990) presented in 1990 the contrast between school and company market (Table 16.1).

Technology

Because this report is constantly referring to multimedia, it is interesting to note that a DELTA BEACON National Survey Report (1993)[3], found that in 220 organizations, the most popular teaching tools were transparencies, video cassettes and computer-based training (both within office-automation software, like word-processors, and dedicated CBT). The least preferred tools were audio cassettes, slides and film. Interactive videodisk and CD-based systems were less preferred but not the least preferred.

Installed base

A lack of installed base is often referred to as a reason not to move into multimedia. However, consider these global and generally published figures:

- By the end of 1994 there will be between five and seven million multimedia personal computers (MPC, Microsoft Windows-based). 80% will be in the USA and most of the rest in Europe. In both continents these are found mostly in homes with educational purposes a primary buying incentive. Probably over 1000 interactive MPC titles will be available in 1994. Educational environments are frequently cited as important buyers.
- Also by the end of 1994 there will be over two million Apple Mac computers with CD-ROM drives capable of multimedia (mostly in the USA). About 750 Apple Mac-compatible multimedia titles will exist. Many titles work on both a Mac and an (M)PC. The new Apple Multimedia Tool specifically supports the simultaneous development of an MPC and MAC version of a title.
- By the end of 1994 there will be one million CD-i players installed worldwide, of which many will be in the home.
- Income from sales of games and player systems like Nintendo and Sega in the USA and Europe is greater than that for box office receipts for movies, being somewhere in the region of ten million dollars. Europe and the USA are almost equally valuable markets. Revenues from hardware and software for the home game market are about equal.
- DataQuest (1989) predicted that in 1993 in Europe there would be 520 000 computers in primary schools, 300 000 computers in universities and, interestingly, 1 250 000 computers owned by faculty, staff and students. On the surface this seems contrary to the commonly held belief that educators shy away from technology.

Finance

The European Union, the USA and Japan all spend about 5.5% of their GDP on education. For example, the UK in 1992 spend $31 000 million on education.

The Optical Publishing Industry Assessment by Infotech (1992)[4] shows that in 1992 eight percent of worldwide CD (not necessarily multimedia) title revenue came from education (including training). This contrasts with 37% for professional, 13% for libraries, 13% for consumer and 29% for corporation. The same report shows that 11% of the CD readers are found in educational environments, 10% in professional environments, 7% in libraries, 52% in consumer and

12% in corporations. Cross-comparing these two sets of figures hints at the effect of the comparatively low prices in the consumer and education markets.

The OPIA Assessment figures for Europe indicate an even larger disparity between market share and revenue: Europe accounts for 35% of the education titles but a very small 5% of the revenue in the same segment! This could reflect Europe still being in the prototyping stage in the electronic education publishing market.

Ovum, in their Multimedia reports of 1992[5] predict that multimedia applications in training will account for 100 million dollars in business by 1995 in the combined USA and European markets. Hardware added brings the figure to over 350 million dollars. This number appears low in light of the fact that three of the largest (mostly technology-based) training providers in only the UK (FutureMedia, Applied Learning and Video Arts) already accounted for well over 45 million dollars in sales in 1992.

In total, the UK spent 4000 million ECUs and France 5000 million ECUs on training. In the UK 70% of this training is paid for by the employer, 10% by the government and 15% by the students (UK Training Statistics, 1993, Government Statistical Office)[6]. European Round Table member companies spend about 2% of their budget on training. The same UK government report gives figures stating that in all of Europe, in a given four-week period, 12% of the European working population received some form of training. The range was from 30% in the UK to 3% in Italy. Most of these people were either advancing their careers or active in initial vocational training.

In summary, general reports indicate an already significant and rapidly growing installed multimedia base of both players and titles. Hundreds of billions of ECUs are spent each year on education and training. What has never been made clear is where these two have met and will meet in the future. Given the size of one market (education and training) and the rapid growth of the other (multimedia), a major joining cannot be too far off. If someone would take on the task of drawing up this one specific picture, perhaps the logic of good investments for publishers would become clear!

AWARENESS FOR THE NEW MEDIA BUSINESS

The results of the interview with 14 educational and training publishers throughout Europe are described below. These interviews took place in October and November 1993.

The list of the publishers interviewed is appended to this chapter as are the interview questions.

The situation of the market (Questions 0.2, 0.3, 0.4, 0.5, 0.9, 0.10)

Most of the interviewees are purely educational publishers. As well as school books, some also publish dictionaries, training materials for adults or specific reference books. All sizes of companies are represented. There are smaller ones (with about 80 employees) and big companies with over 1000 employees. The majority of those interviewed are educational publishers who play an important role in the market. Some are both market leaders and makers. Only one out of all the interviewees was a niche publisher. National educational markets are often targeted by only a small number of publishers. Most of the companies of the interviewees have multimedia products: diskettes, electronic books, CD-ROMs, CD-i's and CDTV. The offers are limited. Educational publishers operate very carefully.

Organization/decision/knowledge (Questions 0.6, 0.7, 0.8)

Half of the interviewees are general managers, while the others are directors of Multimedia Units. On the whole general managers have a good personal, sometimes even professional, knowledge. Only a minority have no specific technical knowledge of multimedia. All directors of Multimedia Units have a professional knowledge. In half of the cases it is the general manager who takes decisions about multimedia production. In other cases, the editors are those responsible. Sometimes the decision is taken in coordination with the multimedia software department and the editors of the related subjects. The board will be kept aware of what is being done and of what is attainable, with IT directors, MM directors or R&D directors acting as the link.

In essence, both possibilities are conceivable: setting up a central unit or involving all editorial personnel.

Responsibilities of a Multimedia Unit can be: assistance to the publishing divisions in new media questions; creation of data resources covering markets, technology and existing and future publishing projects; development of alliances with external producers and distributors in multimedia; provision of financial, legal, production and contractual consultancy; publishing into profitable areas which might otherwise be missed by editorial departments.

The other possibility mentioned is that each editorial department makes its own decisions about multimedia production. The department or person responsible for multimedia/electronic publishing operates as a type of consultancy for these departments.

Development of the market (Questions 1.3, 1.4, 1.5, 1.6, 1.7, 1.8)

The answers on the expected growth were divided into two parts. One half of the interviewees could not give an answer. In their opinion, it would not be possible to obtain a correct figure. The other half expects their business to grow by approximately 4–5%. For the multimedia business, the growth rate will end up at 30–100%. At present multimedia is not a great business, but most of the interviewees were convinced that it would become so in the next 5–10 years. It is important to be in the market now. Those who are not active now will be out of the market when it becomes important. 'You must be ready when the time comes!'

The questions concerning the expected revenues and the number of published titles have been answered very carefully. In the discussion it was mentioned several times how the development of this market is extremely uncertain. Those who indicated figures expected no real growth in the traditional educational market. In multimedia, the situation is totally different. They intend to double or even triple their revenues and numbers of titles.

The number of copies expected to be sold in the traditional educational market will not increase dramatically, like the revenues and the development of these titles. The development of the number of sales of multimedia products will increase to the same extent as the growth of revenues due to multimedia. A current problem, accounting for the very low number of copies sold, are the 'high' prices. The high costs of development, of rights, especially in Europe, and the nowadays still restricted market, makes it necessary to charge high prices. This influences the demand. Figures mentioned for the traditional market amount to several thousands or even millions of copies sold (from 500 000 to 13 million). For multimedia, figures of only 500 to a few thousand were given.

The percentage of multimedia products in education and training materials will not exceed 5% in the coming years. The figures are identical for both the general market and the company business. A variation from area to area could be possible, but the range is still between 0 and 5%.

Statements given concerning the percentage of education and training themes by multimedia products differ between 50 and 70%. Real education or training materials are only a small part of the product offers. Edutainment and infotainment products or reference materials, e.g. dictionaries, account for the main part. Nearly all multimedia products are defined as such. Edutainment is very important in opening the market. In ten years or so pure education and training materials will be available.

Business options (Questions 1.1, 1.11, 1.12, 1.13, 1.14, 1.2, 1.12)

In the future multimedia will play a fundamental role in education and training. Mobility of people, lack of time, the fast technological development process and dynamic changes of business demands are only some arguments in favour of changed habits of learning.

Although multimedia materials are generally very expensive, most of the interviewees feel these new products have a great future. Computer diskettes may be replaced by CD-ROM and CD-i. It is very interesting that, although all of the interviewees see this market as a great opportunity, they themselves act very cautiously.

With multimedia, new product lines can be developed, new markets can be reached (e.g. home learning market for pupils) and new and interesting distribution channels can also be opened to the traditional businesses. When publishers take the first steps into the multimedia market, they try to have high-quality products and be one of the market leaders.

Multimedia products can programme the learning contents according to the user's needs. As a result of the enlarged memory capacities of new media, more contents can be illustrated more clearly. In certain cases, for special learning parts, the user is more motivated and learns more effectively. The target audience can be reached in a more effective way; with multimedia, publishers can offer every learner something of great interest. The knowledge that should be imparted can be apportioned according to the needs of users. In future individualization will be a very important aspect. Multimedia products can be compared to a teacher or trainer: a teacher uses all sorts of media, cassettes, films, written and spoken text etc. Multimedia makes it possible to combine all these different media into one.

Multimedia is also very interesting for educational publishers because of the possible exploitation of their assets: they know their business, their markets, the way educational knowledge must be transferred and they own the contents. The information and computer equipment at schools and institutions will support the development of the multimedia market.

Owing to the restraint on the part of many multimedia publishers there is not a wide variety of materials available. The market is still in an initial stage. The custom of users for applications must be developed. The material support must be improved. Problems arise due to insufficient compatibility of hardware and software, fast technical developments, lack of standards, etc.

In order to reach a large group of customers, it is necessary to offer edutainment products, education combined with entertainment. Because of the entertainment factor, education is usually in the background, so the learning process could be made impossible. The masses can be reached by games, special interest groups by specific knowledge. The cost factor will lose importance with mass production, while specific interest users are willing to pay higher prices.

Multimedia production is initially very expensive. Only large companies are in a position to invest in these developments. Smaller ones have not got the financial background and the necessary resources. There is a risk that the market will only be reached by big companies, and that the smaller ones will not stand a chance. If small companies are also going to enter this market, they will be forced to work with others.

Multimedia is an interesting development and market for educational publishers. Some interviewees mentioned that the format of the CD-ROM could be wrong. CD-ROMs have a very high memory capacity, which might be too big for ordinary educational materials.

It might be useful if educational publishers were to look for further formats.

Multimedia products need electronic editors. The new product has special needs. One problem is the lack of electronic editors who know about the special demands of these media. A possible solution is to train the editors. Some interviewees mentioned that CD-ROMs are a very 'lonely' medium. Publishers must find a way to turn learning with multimedia into a social process.

In order to make them stand out from the traditional products, it is important to add value to multimedia materials. The production of real educational materials with added value is one of the challenges for traditional publishers.

Knowledge of the technical side and the needs of multimedia is crucial for the audiovisual and electronic industry, hardware and software houses, film and TV companies. This could be dangerous for publishers when multimedia newcomers, who have the multimedia knowledge but not the educational background, try to penetrate the market.

The IT industry is a real threat, not only in the sense of having to compete with their products but also in actively buying rights and intending to recruit expertise, e.g. editorial, from traditional publishers. They often offer their employees higher salaries than the traditional publishers do.

It is very difficult for publishers to produce materials for one platform. The speed of technological innovation is extremely high, so they cannot decide which production platform is appropriate. It could be that at the time of market entry, there is already another standard. The absence of dominant standards in the market makes it difficult to produce multimedia products. Product development for all kinds of platforms is not possible. The hardware industry cannot guarantee that products/standards will last a long time, but this could be helpful when publishers make decisions. So far multimedia products generally have a very short product life cycle. Amortization during this time is often impossible.

The opportunities, thanks to multimedia, are double figures of growth in the school market, which is nearly saturated. The formal education sector does not have the resources for major developments. It is important to show the added value of multimedia products to the customers and users. An interesting market for multimedia products is the home and consumer market. Many interviewees believe that the major growth area will be in home-based education: distance learning and supplementary learning.

Some publishers will produce multimedia materials when the company has existing brands or wants to develop brands. They will use book brands in conjunction with multimedia. The image building or branding which arises from multimedia is extremely important. Multimedia is seen in a very positive light by consumers. The effect can be used for other media. The image-building effect can also be used as a challenge to competitors.

Multimedia newcomers to educational and training publishing can represent a threat for the traditional publishers. They have the technical knowledge but not the educational and training know-how; they can exploit all multimedia possibilities. Market shares will be attacked and can lose value. The market will be served by more companies. The media industry tries to seize hold of the education market, and offer a combination of hardware and software as a complete solution. Publishers will be affected by these developments in certain areas of the traditional markets. The hardware and software industry is new competition for publishers. Some interviewees talked about scrambling for access in the home market. Small companies, in particular, are focusing towards very narrow niches.

The fact that more and more newcomers without educational publishing experience are entering this market may damage the image of the traditional publishers.

Rights production (Questions 1.9, 1.10, 1.16)

There are virtually no demands for rights in the education market, so percentages of revenues from rights for multimedia are extremely low. Figures mentioned are between 0 and 1%. There will not be any noticeable changes until 1996.

Most of the educational publishers feel that they do not own durable intellectual property rights (IPR) which can be exploited in the long term. Furthermore, any usage of rights is often made difficult by certain terms of contracts. The majority of the interviewees will use takeover of their own materials in order to derive products from existing materials. The takeover of externally existing materials will only be considered for sound, pictures/movies and illustrations, assets that traditional educational publishers do not have at their disposal. For multimedia production most of them will initially prefer licensing, republishing or the entire development of new materials. There is much uncertainty about the costs when buying rights and the ways and procedures of doing this in the case of nonprint assets.

Entry strategy (Questions 1.15, 2.1, 2.4, 2.5, 2.6, 2.7)

All publishers interviewed will play the role of asset owners in the multimedia business in 1996. They will use materials for multimedia production, but will not sell them to others. None of them will be developers of bespoke materials, i.e. developing for others, as a service to order. They will be title developers as publishers. Their own production is very important; sometimes they are willing to cooperate with third parties, but usually they intend to publish themselves. In the case of a partnership they will deliver/supply the content and the educational/pedagogical knowledge, which the partner will be responsible for technical questions and providing financial assistance. They will distribute themselves. The companies have sales forces for primary and secondary education, for libraries and institutions and for the book trade. They will also distribute for other software developers. They know about the difficulties in reorienting sales forces for multimedia distribution. Some mentioned that they would do packaging, in the sense of putting together multimedia and printed publications.

Most of the publishers interviewed will enter this market very proactively. They will follow a wait and see strategy, especially for nontypical educational products. They want to be very active in academic and educational products and materials in key multimedia areas. Becoming active in the multimedia market means high investments for the majority of publishers, as well as great risks and little knowledge about this new field. To reduce the costs and limit risks, most of the publishers want to form joint ventures. To buy media companies is only one possibility for some publishers. The ones which have enough financial background can do so; the others on the whole can not afford it. Every publisher regards multimedia production as a new operating field. The majority of the interviewees will start with small pilots, so that they can collect experiences that can be brought into further steps. All publishers will prepare assets to be ready for the multimedia market. The production of multimedia materials will sometimes take place in-house or by specialized service companies outside. Publishers take care to build up all possible internal knowledge, and to use outside production only in well-founded cases. They want to prevent any dependence.

Publishers act very carefully in setting up new divisions. Their own multimedia divisions are possible in the future but certainly not at the moment. Some of the interviewees mentioned that a group of editors and technicians are devoted to these matters. If market opportunity arises, some publishers will be in a position to set up spin-off companies. This way is more attainable than others. In case of trouble they can get out much more easily if they are in a company rather than a division. Publishers are very careful when employing specialists. They do not really know how the market will develop and prefer to wait. If necessary they can become active quite quickly. They will hire consultants if they need the special knowledge. In order to be competitive, most of those interviewed planned to train people in time. They want to build up the basic technical knowledge in their company. It is important to think about and create new distribution channels and marketing, adapted to the new media.

The positions of interaction with the industry are very diverse. Some publishers believe that multimedia production cannot be done by just one publisher and that cooperations are necessary. Publishers must stay in close contact with the industrial side. Other publishers think that interaction with industry must be started very carefully. Contacts and cooperations are very difficult, the industry is too indecisive and often only works on short terms. For most publishers, the high standard of their production is endangered by cooperation with certain industrial companies like SEGA or Nintendo. The educational factor of this sort of product remains in the background.

The question of interacting with the technical side has been answered in a similar way. Many of the interviewees stress the necessity of having their own expertise. They prefer an implementation of know-how in their own company by appointing a technical specialist in multimedia and by ensuring that appropriate skills are distributed around the production units. Some are interested in cooperation with the aim of being a service company. The technical side can be useful as consultants.

Most of the educational and training publishers are big enough to publish without interacting with other publishers. Interactions with nontextual asset owners (e.g. sound, movie, etc.) are also possible. None of the interviewees will cooperate with other national publishers. If they consider cooperations, they will only do so with foreign companies. Possible cooperations are those of building up the multimedia image, in commercializing or distribution channels, but never in product development.

The building-up of a 'Multimedia image' can be obtained by really active PR. Speeches and presentations to schools, training institutions and at fairs are necessary. The positive image of traditional educational products should be used for the new media. It is also important to keep the high quality that is usual for traditional products.

The term 'Multimedia' or 'Modern Media' is used in rather general terms and this causes problems. Consumers are irritated, publishers must show them the seriousness of their products.

It is very important to establish support for the new media and to polarize electronic products. It can be useful to unite with industry and support the appearance on the market as one multi-solution.

Information (Questions 3.1, 3.2, 3.3, 3.4, 3.5)

The general conclusion is that the information situation in the typical company is generally fairly good. Authors and customers do not possess sufficient awareness and information about all themes concerning multimedia.

- *Typical company:* The information situation is good, as regards knowledge about the technology, the competition and the market. Deficits exist concerning the skills required and the development process.
- *Authors:* Here the situation is completely different. Authors have, according to the interviewees, some knowledge about technology, but they have practically no knowledge about competition, the market, the skills required and the development process. In general, authors are beginning to inform themselves; some multimedia authors know the market and the required skills well. 'Traditional' authors often stay on 'old' media.
- *Customers:* For customers, the situation is similar to that of the authors. They have little information and awareness about technology and the market. Of course, no information exists about competition, required skills and the development process. The view of customer awareness should be seen in the context that an

important multimedia market is the home market, which has as yet, not been developed. If there is not enough information, publishers will become proactive especially if the short fall exists in their own company. They will also take care of the authors, because these belong to the main assets of nearly every publisher. Publishers are not in the position to improve the situation on the customers' side by themselves. They intend to work together with other publishers or the industry. Changes in the awareness of customers will take a very long time.

The sources publishers mostly use for information are the press, conferences, consultants and experts, other business sectors and technology providers. The interviewees rarely mentioned colleagues or success stories. A success story that was mentioned was the 'Voyager' story. Colleagues are also not informed about multimedia. If there is a lack of information, the affected person often has to get the information from an external source.

Publishers use all sorts of specific information publications. They also get information from conferences, like specific fairs, conferences of IEPRC, Microsoft, Seybold, Digital World or from workshops. Sometimes they are informed by consultants and experts like professors of universities, service companies with competent people, etc. To get more information about the technical side, publishers sometimes have strong contacts with technology providers, the hardware and software industry. In several cases they are also informed by other business sectors like the entertainment industry. Most of the publishers get information from national and international publisher committees or research centres. This information channel is used quite often and is very important for most publishers.

If information gets into companies, it is normally distributed to the editors and product managers concerned with multimedia. Some also distribute the information to all the editors. In many cases the distribution does not run satisfactorily. The information is either not completely available or it sometimes reaches the editors quite late. Most publishers deliver press extracts, reports of conferences and meetings but word of mouth is also used.

External activities (Questions 4.1, 5.1, 6.1, 6.2, 6.3, 6.4)

Activities that have to be carried out to make multimedia a business concern the awareness in the company and the skills. The interviewees take two opposing positions. One group has had positive experiences and in future will do much to stay up to date and to train and inform themselves and a third party. They will pursue and develop their activities. The other has had bad experiences in the past. They will approach these subjects much more carefully.

With regard to the product development chain and the organizational consequences, very few publishers who were interviewed had had any experience. The procedures are mostly unclear, but every publisher wants to take control over the educational framework and to become internally self-sufficient. Publishers sometimes have problems in cooperating with industry and production companies. The same standard, and same starting position (terminology, ideas, demands, etc.), are necessary to make working together easier. In this field much needs to be done.

The most sensible organizational consequences are the creation of a multimedia department or the employment of an expert for each production unit who can act as a type of consulting service. Some publishers are interested in joint ventures. In this way they can reduce risks and costs and expand knowledge. It is also very important to build up support for the new media. A possible solution is to assign one person to this job. He/she will be completely responsible and will be able to support the contact to customers.

In the market there is much that needs to be done. New distribution channels must be found and exploited, traditional retailers often have a negative outlook about selling multimedia products. It is also important to inform customers about these new products; special PR is necessary.

As regards the costs incurred, publishers are not very well informed. They can only estimate the amount. Costs are often considered to be too high so that for some educational and training publishers real investments are not possible. Multimedia products are only on the market for a short time, compared to print materials. If there were more fiscal reliefs, multimedia production would be made easier and the amortization could be within a year or so. Publishers consider the situation in international publishing rights to be most unsatisfactory. Royalties go up to 50% for software. Some publisher organizations are dealing with the copyright problem. The problems associated with intellectual rights and copyright are considerable and need to be solved.

The lack of standards is a problem. The lifetime of technological products is usually very short. The compatibility is not guaranteed. Technology is still user unfriendly.

Too much time is needed for developments. The gap between the beginning of a new product and the market entrance is far too long in relation to the development time of technology.

A great deal must be changed in the market to make multimedia a good business. The awareness of customers and distributors must be developed. Booksellers for example, are not trained to deal with new media. They must learn to present multimedia, to handle the hardware and to teach and inform customers how to handle it. The publisher must also look for other distribution channels. Specific distribution channels are necessary. Some publishers establish new companies.

Another problem is the educational, training and school mindset. Most of the interviewees believe that a new generation of teachers and trainers must grow up if the new media are to become widespread. The real success of multimedia products will only occur in the next generation. Big changes are needed in the education field. Teachers' awareness in particular needs to change. In general children are more used to IT than their teachers. The level of understanding is currently very low. Educationalists are often persuaded that correct learning is only possible with a teacher. Changes in the mindset are necessary.

The technology industry should be careful not to change the standards so quickly and should guarantee a certain constancy and product survival. Hardware must become more effective, faster and with an increased memory capacity. The hardware market must also be improved; the installed base in educational establishments is often disastrous. The industry could put hardware at the disposal of schools, booksellers, etc. Many machines are not suited for use in teaching situations. Publishers should train teachers and trainers how to use multimedia.

Most of the interviewees think that parents are the main actors in making multimedia a business. Parents are the ones who are willing to pay for educational and training materials.

Some publishers are convinced that the commercial use of multimedia will greatly influence educational use. Commercial use should be supported by the public institutions and the politicians. Pushing telecommunications, cable connections, etc. will improve the situation of multimedia in the educational and training field.

The EC should, according to one group of the interviewees, implement standards. Others refuse to have anything to do with this field. The funding of prototypes is another demand of many interviewees. Nobody knows yet what the full potential of the technology is or what such products could do in the educational context. Far more research on these issues is needed. The harmonization of rights and taxes is another important duty that should be solved by the EC. A net of experts and consultants should be institutionalized. Every interested publisher would have the opportunity to get information from these institutions.

SWOT SCENARIOS

In this section the present situation of educational and training publishers is analysed. The strengths and weaknesses (internal factors) and the opportunities and threats (external factors) for the publishing industry are described below. These statements are the results of initial research, many discussions with publishing and modern media experts and the outcome of the interviews.

Market-related factors

- *Traditional products successful:* Traditionally, educational publishers mainly produce print materials, and some audio visuals. The print materials that they market successfully are the core of every publishing activity. There is no actual need to start immediately with electronic publishing.
- *Installed base of (standard) players:* Until now the number of educational publishers involved in the multimedia market has been restricted. The market is still small and fragmented. For publishers standing outside, this market is confusing. No clear structures can be recognized.
- *Price structure:* The price structure, which has not yet been established for multimedia products, represents another threat for the educational publishers. The multimedia market has a wide variety of different prices so it is difficult to make a decision how to

position new multimedia products. Educational publishers cannot offer advice on the established price structure. They have enough problems pricing their own multimedia products. Difficulties also arise as a result of the insufficient knowledge of the price ceiling of customers and users.

- *Value added to existing products:* Existing products increase in value with multimedia products. The product range will be extended. Teachers and self study students can extend paper-based material with multimedia. This provides an opportunity for educational publishers who include multimedia products in their product mix.
- *New customer groups:* With the production of multimedia materials it is possible to increase the number of potential customers. New customer groups will be added to the long-standing customers. There will no cannibalization effect on the print products. Educational publishers have the opportunity to make various self-study products, especially for the home and distance-learning market.
- *Capability to sell complete solutions (including hardware):* Educational publishers do not have the capability and the know-how to sell complete solutions (including hardware) because they are used to being actively involved in marketing to distributors (e.g. bookshops) that are not able and do not want to sell hardware–software packages. Furthermore, smaller publishers lack capacity. Computer and audio-visual companies possess all this know-how and the capacities and therefore have an advantage.
- *Niche markets:* Only a few educational publishers have the experience of developing their products for niche markets. Products have tended to be standardized in order to benefit from the economies of long runs. Print runs are often too large. This represents a main weakness of print publishers. Publishing on demand and electronic media can be the first steps into niche markets, the significance of which will probably increase in the future.
- *New markets through different ways of learning:* An improved quality of learning will open new markets for educational publishers. Interactive multimedia allows for more effective learning material. For home and distance-learning multimedia can be an interesting and effective way of learning. For other learners, such products can widen the range and make it more attractive. Users

will accept such products because of the known educational competence of the publishers. These new possibilities described above are also used by self-study institutes, open universities, correspondence schools etc. The number of competitors for publishers might therefore increase.

- *Marketing channels to education/training institutions:* Traditional distribution channels, adapted to the specifications of the product and to the needs of the user or buyer, already exist. These channels are specifically for educational and training products, as previously described. For multimedia products there do not yet exist tailored distribution channels that can be used by traditional publishers. Therefore there are a range of alternatives. New ones must be created or existing ones have to be adapted. The means of distribution are well known by educational publishers and represent a key strength. Educational publishers know their market very well and therefore hold an advantage over other, noneducational publishers. It must be mentioned that there is also the opportunity for noneducational publishers to break through this traditional segmentation and market their own products, thereby becoming a serious competitor. The possibility to be active in new markets exists not only for noneducational publishers, but also for newcomers.

- *Physical channels for educational or training material — distribution to the learners:* Educational publishers do not only know the distribution channels to education and training places and people, but they also know the channels for educational and training materials. By using well-known channels for traditional materials as well as for multimedia materials they can facilitate the distribution to the market. Existing marketing outlets must be analysed for possibilities of application for multimedia.

- *Distribution channels for electronic media:* Specific distribution channels for electronic media are not used frequently by educational publishers. If they take the opportunity and build round the traditional channels they will be able to reach varying customer groups and thus enlarge the potential market.

- *Distribution channels to home learning market:* Another specification of the distribution of multimedia products is to cater for the special needs and habits of home learners. Home learners are a highly interesting customer group for multimedia products. Dedicated publishers of self-study, hobby and cultural material know this market very well. Problems only exist for publishers who produce materials for other markets and have no experience in that field as yet. The entertainment industry also knows this market very well and can represent a threat for traditional publishers. They have been working on this market for a long time and know customers' needs and habits and the market conditions.

- *Skills to deal with in-house training departments:* Computer training companies possess the skills to deal with the computer departments of customers. This is hard for educational publishers because they have no experience in dealing with this type of customer. Publishers have difficulty gaining access to the channels that the educational hardware suppliers have developed. It is necessary to obtain this access to sell software, CBT-products, for example, to schools. Publishers have not until now had experience in dealing with in-house training departments or with decision-makers in CBT departments. They have been limited to contacts with the educational system.

Business aspects

- *Operational policy, organizational culture:* The organization needed by multimedia rarely coincides with the structure of traditional publishers. In most cases, multimedia production needs much stronger and more complex teamwork. Audio-visual companies are used to these special requirements.
- *Image:* In general, educational publishers have a very solid image in the educational and training world that has been built up by them over a long time. The market is very traditional, so consequently 'exciting' new multimedia products have many barriers to break through.
- *Company size:* Educational publishing companies are sometimes very small, owing to national orientation and specification. They encounter far more difficulties when entering this market. Large investments have far stronger consequences for them than they do for large publishing houses. Larger publishers with educational departments possess more financial possibilities and therefore have advantages in entering this market.
- *Globalization:* Globalization is a strength for some of the very large publishing companies, but a weakness for dedicated educa-

tional publishers, because of their structure, their size and their market. Publishing companies have the opportunity to globalize electronic products first. However, problems arise because other industrial companies, also active in the multimedia market, are already global.

- *Motivation:* Motivation for educational publishers with regard to marketing multimedia products is very different. A great deal of traditional markets are still growing and some are profitable enough, so publishers do not need to change and invest in multimedia. Most computer, audio-visual and entertainment industries need new markets and are therefore very active in this area. If publishers do not recognize this in time, they will miss the chance to develop. They must protect existing markets and perhaps take the chance to reach new markets, which will grow in the future.

- *The role of start-up companies:* The role dedicated to start-up companies is very important for publishers. They can use or buy successful start-ups to enter this market and reduce the risks. It can, however, be difficult to find the right partners.

- *The role of alliances:* Large international publishing companies can establish alliances easily. As a result of their national structure, smaller educational publishers have more problems in establishing alliances. To overcome this weakness, publishers should complement their skills. Computer, electronic, entertainment, broadcasting and communication industries already market across borders or have alliances with strong partners.

Factors related to product development

- *Production costs:* Production costs are a further reason for educational publishers to hesitate about producing multimedia materials. During the learning phase the costs are relatively high because of the lack of experience with the new media. Publishers must generally invest huge sums for developing and producing multimedia materials at the beginning of this new activity. In the next phase, the increasing and maturity phase, it is still uncertain how the costs will develop.

- *Multimedia design expertise:* Most educational publishers find access to multimedia design expertise a great problem. They rarely have a wide experience with software, 'authoring' software etc.

because this does not represent the traditional development and production process. This is to the advantage of production companies or dedicated producers/publishers who specialize in multimedia production.

- *Pilot study experience:* Pilot studies are often very expensive. Many publishers are worried about the high costs and uncertain outcome. Pilots are sometimes managed in isolation without considering all the factors. Some publishers have had bad experiences in the past, so they are now persuaded that pilots are necessary to limit the risks. It must be mentioned that benefit will be lost if there is no transfer of knowledge back to the company.

Copyright aspects

- *Ownership of multimedia assets for products:* Only a few publishers own multimedia assets. Most of the educational and training publishers are text-based. Some exceptions are publishers of language training or science. Dedicated audio-visual companies, which produce linear and interactive videos, already have much experience (e.g. broadcasters) and this gives them advantages over educational publishers. Products suitable for multimedia are necessary. Publishers cannot take every book and produce out of it multimedia materials.
- *Assets suitable for multimedia:* Publishers own textual and pictorial assets can be applied to multimedia products. The assets of educational publishers are suitable for multimedia materials. A problem, however, is that educational publishers do not own all electronic rights and they cannot therefore exploit, owing to contractual restrictions, rights for electronic products. Publishers can store assets in a proper way or make them accessible to others.
- *Backlist exploitation:* The backlist is one of the most crucial forms of capital for educational publishers. The backlist appears as an important source for exploitation for multimedia products. Problems arise from unclear publishing rights concerning electronic media. Publishers have already got the content but need experiences of new media. Exploitation, by packaging print/backlist and multimedia products, can be an important opportunity.
- *Costs for multimedia assets:* Costs and procedures for acquiring the rights of multimedia assets, e.g. film or software, are of a different structure than for the traditional sorts of assets educational

and training publishers are used to dealing with. They do not have this knowledge at present. First modern media experiences have shown that prices are considerably higher than for printed products and a pricing structure has not yet been developed for multimedia.

- *Rights for exploitation in other media:* To be able to use the backlist, it is important already to have the rights for other media. The problem nowadays is that rights are often restricted to print products. Educational publishers may seize their opportunity by exploiting rights used in print for electronic media. They must change contracts or add supplementary agreements, which in any case needs increased involvement (manpower and costs) on the side of the publisher.

- *Ambiguous copyright:* For a majority of educational publishers, the ambiguous copyright for electronic media represents a legal minefield. They do not know how to react correctly without breaking existing laws. Until this problem for educational and other publishers is solved satisfactorily, they will hesitate to turn towards multimedia production. Therefore it is important to harmonize and register copyright issues. It would be helpful to put a catalogue of minimum requirements for agreements at the disposal of educational publishers.

Aspects related to pedagogical issues

- *Pedagogical design skills:* Educational and training publishers are skilled in pedagogical design. Over the years they have learnt about the correct and most effective layout of education materials and about the very important didactic. This knowledge has to be adapted to fit the requirements of the new media and complemented by additional skills.

- *Access to educationalists:* Another strength of educational and training publishers is access to educationalists and to authors. Manuscripts written to order by highly specialized teachers and trainers with professional knowledge on pedagogical issues are one of the most important resources for publishers. There must be a potential for developing scripts which are usable for multimedia.

- *Relations to regulatory bodies:* Relations with regulatory bodies are highly important for educational publishers. Publishers need information about curricula, alterations in schools, etc. They usually cultivate contacts with governments, teachers' associations etc. in order to get their learning materials officially approved for use in schools or state-controlled learning institutions. Traditions of teaching and learning are fixed in curricula, which as a consequence hinder the use of modern media applications in institutional markets. Involving representatives as authors or educational consultants may provide the opportunity to gain access to these institutions.

- *Skilled teachers:* Skilled teachers are very important people for educational publishers. They must use the materials during their lessons and they are the ones who decide which product to use. In most cases, the learners themselves cannot really decide which product to use. In fact, teachers rarely use multimedia products. Perhaps, once trainers and teachers are happy with multimedia, they will use these products as they do now with print materials. Another situation is the home learning group. In general, these learners are not influenced by skilled teachers, but neither are they used to working with electronic media.
- *Understanding user needs:* In general, educational publishers do not have direct contact with the ultimate user. Normally they are in touch with trainers or teachers. Therefore, they do not get feedback from the customers with regard to their needs, but rather feedback from the intermediate players instead. Compared to publishers, self-study institutes and the entertainment industry know far more about the needs of individual customers, and modern media products can be developed accordingly.
- *Ownership of pedagogical methods; subject matter analyses:* Educational publishers own pedagogical methods and subject matter analyses. Consequently, they can reuse these approaches for the electronic version or they can license design or methods. It is sometimes hard to apply pedagogical methods to electronic media. There are differences which must be respected.

Technology-related factors

- *Technical/platform knowledge:* The lack of technical knowledge makes it difficult to deal with platform decisions. This represents another weakness of publishers, except for those publishers who produce games etc.
- *Network infrastructure:* The whole infrastructure of publishers,

distribution organizations, users and buyers, authors etc. is well known for the print sector. The infrastructure of the multimedia sector has not yet been developed. In order to reach the same level as the print sector, much more time and experience is necessary. Furthermore, there is still no cross-border multimedia infrastructure.

Overview: SWOT scenarios and options for actions

Table 16.2 gives an overview on the above-described SWOT scenarios. Under 'Actions' reference is made to the next section *Options for Actions for Educational and Training Publishers*.

OPTIONS FOR ACTIONS FOR EDUCATIONAL AND TRAINING PUBLISHERS

(1) Have you appointed somebody to read the rest of this report?

(1a) Establish the means to manage innovation within your company

Process innovation is well embedded in many publishing companies, as improvement in production processes (e.g. in the form of automation, use of computers) can directly contribute to the bottom line. Product innovation is traditionally occurring only in as far as it concerns the introduction of new products (i.e. new titles or series of titles). However, if products are successful for a long period, e.g. because of stable curricula and limited demand for change from the education system, then the innovation drive is more limited.

The entrance into electronic or multimedia publishing, however, requires a completely new level of innovation. The number of business aspects affected, the implications for all parts of the company, the speed and frequency of innovation steps, and many other factors make this kind of innovation very different from what most publishers have been used too. Particular importance is attached to the fact that it is not a 'one-time' change, but rather the start of an ongoing process of keeping up with market and technological developments.

To cope with this new order of innovation inside existing companies, it is essential to appoint a responsible innovation manager at

Table 16.2 SWOT overview

Market-related factors

	Strengths	Weaknesses	Opportunities	Threats	Actions
Traditional products successful	Successful print products	No need for MM			1(a) 1(b)
Installed base of (standard) players		No market research done/possible	Become one of the first actors	Market still small, fragmented	7(a) 7(b)
Price structure		No clear idea on possible market prices		Not yet established	2(d) 7(a)
Value added to existing products	Existing backlist of educational products	Data not digitized	Add multimedia to existing products		2(e), 5(a) 6(a)
New customer groups	Existing backlist of educational products		Attract new customers by change of target group (e.g. for self-study)		3(a) 3(f) 5(a), 6(a)
Capability to sell complete solutions (including hardware)		No capability; no experience	Cooperate with IT industry	Strength of computer and AV industry	3(a) 3(e) 3(f)
Niche markets		Necessity of large print runs	Specialize by MM product or publishing on-demand	Unusual market approach and calculation schemes	1(c) 2(b) 3(d), 3(e) 5(a)
New markets through improved working quality	Educational competence in the eyes of the users		Offers different way of learning	Competition by self-study institutes, open universities, etc.	3(a) 5(a) 6(a)
Marketing channels to education/training institutions	Key strengths of E+T publishing		Adapt traditional marketing for MM	Opportunity for newcomers to break through traditional segmentation	3(a) 3(e) 6(a)

Physical channels for E+T material distribution to the learners	Key strengths of E+T publishing	Existing distribution channels not yet open for MM			3(a) 3(d)
Distribution channels for electronic media		MM distribution channels not used by E+T publishers	Build up new distribution channels around traditional ones	IT and AV industries create own distribution networks	3(a) 3(d) 3(e)
Distribution channels to home learning market	Strength of dedicated E+T publishing	No experience of 'normal' educational publishing		Strength of entertainment industry (games, edutainment)	3(d) 3(e) 3(f), 6(a)
Skills to deal with in-house training departments		No access for training publishing		Strength of computer training companies	2(a) 3(e)
Business aspects					
Operational policy, organizational culture		Editorial structure does not fit MM development		Strength of AV companies	1(a) 1(b) 4(c)
Image	Solid image of educational competence		Improve image by high-quality educational MM	Educationalists' mindset is high barrier	3(a) 5(a), 6(a)
Company size		When small, problems of financial investments and workforce resources		General publishers are big enough for investments	3(a) 3(b) 3(e)
Globalization	Strengths of few very large educational publishers	No experience of most educational publishers	Start with globalization of MM products	IT and AV industries already global	4(b)
Motivation		No commercial need yet to invest in MM	Protect existing E+T markets with MM	IT, AV and entertainment industries need new markets	3(a)
Role of start-up companies			Buying start-ups to enter MM-markets	IT industry will do this	3(c)

Table 16.2 continued

	Strengths	Weaknesses	Opportunities	Threats	Actions
Role of alliances	Strength of few very large educational publishers	No experience in most educational publishers	Complement skills, product portfolio	Strength of IT and entertainment industries	3(c) 4(b)
Factors related to product development					
Production costs	Very clear for traditional products	Calculation and budgeting schemes restricted to print material		High during learning phase, after that still unclear	2(d)
Multimedia design expertise		No experience, no easy access to	Gain experience by cooperation with specialized companies	Strength of MM production companies, AV industry	1(b) 3(c) 3(b)
Pilot study experience		Pilots often done in isolation	Transfer pilot experience back into company	Repetition of negative experience of the past	3(b) 3(c), 4(c)
Technology-related factors					
Technical/platform knowledge		Lack of knowledge		Strength of IT industry +MM production companies	2(c) 7(a), 7(b)
Network infrastructure	For print material key strength			Not yet developed for MM	1(b) 2(c), 7(b)
Copyright aspects					
Ownership of MM assets for products		Most E+T publishers do not own MM assets		MM assets owned by AV industry	4(b)
Assets suitable for multimedia	Ownership of huge amounts of educational text	Electronic use of assets often restricted	Assets suitable for MM, when stored electronically		2(a) 2(b) 4(a)

Costs		Cost structures in Av industry unknown and different to E+T		Costs for MM rights for E+T high and without structure	4(b)
Backlist exploitation	Existing backlist of educational products	Electronic use of assets often restricted	Major source for MM exploitation		4(a)
Rights for other media		Electronic use of assets often restricted		High involvement for re-negotiation	2(b) 4(c)
Ambiguous copyright		Copyright situation for MM unclear		Legal minefield	4(a), 4(b)
Pedagogical issues					
Pedagogical design skills	Key strength of E+T publishing	But not for MM			1(a), 1(b) 1(c), 2(c)
Access to educationalists	Key strength of E+T publishing	No MM experience on the side of E+T authors			1(c)
Relations to regulatory bodies	Good relations		Involve officials in MM planning	Hindrance because of educational tradition	1(a) 1(b)
Skilled teachers	Access to teachers		Attract teachers by high-quality MM products	Teachers not yet skilled in using MM	1(c) 5(a), 6(a)
User needs understanding		Contact to ultimate learner through teachers, seldom directly	Attract users by high-quaity MM products	Strength of self-study institutes and entertainment industry	5(a) 6(a)
Ownership of pedagogical methods, subject matter analysis	Key strength of E+T publishing	Not directly applicable to MM	Use this approach for MM, or licence		1(b) 1(c) 2(c)

Notes: MM = multimedia; E+T = education and training

senior level. This manager should be made responsible for developing and implementing innovation processes throughout the company, with full support from the company director. Moreover, he/she should assist the overall management in creating an 'innovation culture' throughout the company.

Such an innovation manager should be an 'evangelist', motivating employees and supporting other innovators (often requiring some special budgets). He/she is not necessarily a technical person (and certainly does not have to be the IT manager). Example roles of innovation managers can be found in sectors with traditionally high innovation speeds, such as electronics and computer industries.

(1b) Give somebody responsibility for multimedia and electronic publishing

A wide range of organizational models is possible for introducing multimedia into publishing. They range from giving all production and editorial staff responsibility for developing multimedia products in their particular areas to setting up separate multimedia departments. The first of these extremes leads to a duplication of effort, a lack of coherent publishing policy and methodology and a failure to develop products; the second risks the development of electronic publications at a tangent to company objectives and not utilizing existing resources.

The most effective organizational way of exploiting multimedia opportunities is to appoint a board member or somebody reporting direct to a director with good knowledge of multimedia (existing or new) to carry out the task of liaising with multimedia product champions in all operating units in order to identify opportunities, provide support and training and get multimedia development working within the organization.

(1c) Establish a team of key authors who are open and committed to new media

One of the key strengths of educational and training publishers is their access to authors who are working professionally in the educational environment. These are teachers, trainers, university professors, vocationalists, pedagogical experts etc., all with sound knowledge and experience in both the subject and the didactic (what to teach) and methodological (how to teach it) means.

Traditionally these authors are used to working out manuscripts to the requirements of the publisher, mostly on the basis of a detailed concept that has been worked out by an editor.

So far, most authors have not yet become involved in dealing with modern media developments. As described in the multimedia (MM) product development chain, different work must be performed in order to produce a script of an MM product. The adequate combination of text, sound, pictures and animation and their interactive relation has to be considered, according to the content, the type of learning method and the type of learner.

It is a basic prerequisite for publishers to educate authors to do this job. It would be wrong just to appoint the main author of, for example, a best selling training course to develop a related MM-CD. He/she might be too wedded on traditional pedagogical approaches. A better method would be to select some open-minded and flexible authors and organize a workshop where editors in charge, with the help of an MM expert, could present good examples of (carefully selected) MM products in order to show the (technical) possibilities of designing products. Additionally, there should be a broad and open discussion on where the added value of an MM product is. This discussion will help the editor finally to select such authors who are really open to this new sort of work. The publisher then should invest some money to pay for some first orders — concretely defined and prepared — so that these authors can develop the scripts for a first MM product, even if it has not yet been decided whether this product will really be produced and marketed.

(2) If you wait to invest in new media, then plan to wait and prepare

(2a) Control licensing of exclusive rights to others

In addition to producing and marketing publications, publishers exploit the value of the IPR (Intellectual Property Rights) which they own by licensing to others the use of the content for different markets or other products, such as translations or derivative works. Because of the specific use for which their publications are produced, educational and training publishers rely less on income from secondary licensing than other publishers who may have more reusable assets.

One option for multimedia publishing is to license content to others, and some multimedia developers are indeed keen to obtain publication rights. The superficial advantage of this is that it allows publishers to gain revenue from multimedia development without incurring risk. This advantage is outweighed, however, by the loss of control of content, loss of the opportunities to control development, loss of the opportunities to spin-off additional products, loss of the possibility of learning how to produce multimedia products and a possible poor profile with authors/organizations which wish to see their material exploited in multiple media. Partnerships or alliances, although requiring more work to set up, are preferable to straightforward licensing deals. A restrictive licensing policy will ensure, for example, that, when rights are sold, they are for very specific use in a particular product and particular market. Partnerships can be built up with information owners, developers and other publishers, as well as building on relationships with players in other branches such as broadcasting.

(2b) Set up business mechanisms for parallel publishing

The structure of many publishing houses tends to militate against exploitation of a publication across several media. For example, calculation systems that demand cost recovery and return on investment from the printed version alone tend to rule out projects which are viable if published in parallel but not if costed on the printed version alone. This leads to missed opportunities.

To maximize the opportunities to exploit information and pedagogical material, it is necessary to have the flexibility to cross boundaries between different product types. This demands cooperation and common understanding in marketing, editorial and production and the technical ability to reuse the material.

The basis for the flexibility is to regard content of IPR as assets, to store and manage them in neutral and standard formats so that they can be reused, and to set up structures that will identify in a timely fashion opportunities for parallel exploitation across multiple media. Such structures include the appointment of champions in the appropriate parts of the business, and also require the calculation of value of owned IPR assets and costing of product development in a way that reflects the potential for parallel use.

(2c) Keep the valuable education and training competences in the company by holding on to the right people in the company

Editorial departments of education and training publishers have a precise knowledge about the subject-related pedagogical require-ments and the learning needs of their customers. In addition to this pedagogical competence, editorial department members have the experience and capability to initiate, organize and control the prod-uct development process as well as the marketing-related part, the content-related work, and, as far as traditional media are concerned, the technical production process. In other words, the educational editor can be described as someone (see Figure 16.10) who:

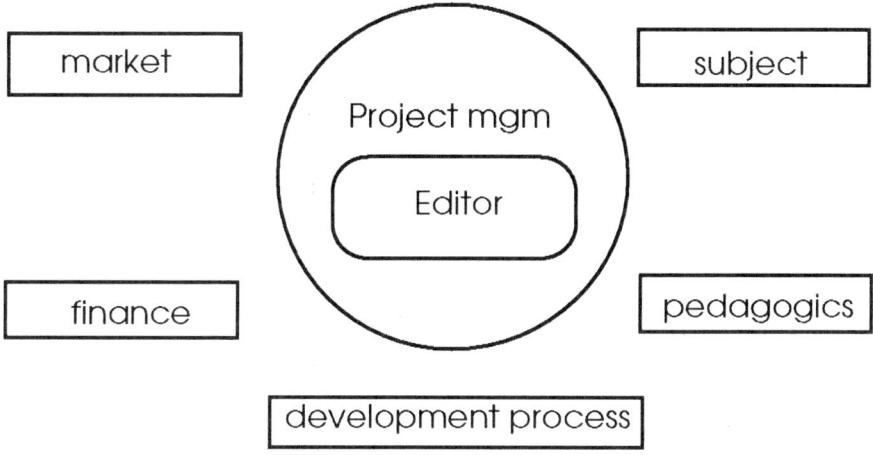

Figure 16.10 The editor and project manager

- is an experienced 'product manager',
- knows the market and the customers,
- is professional in one or more subject areas,
- is deeply acquainted with pedagogical issues, especially with di-dactic and methodological questions,

- knows about financial issues (calculation, budgeting, accounting etc.),
- is highly experienced in organizing and controlling the development process of traditional education and training products.

In order to develop multimedia products, in principle no different qualifications are necessary. The editors, of course, have to learn and gain experience with the different steps within the development process, and understand the consequences influencing the subject, market, pedagogic and finance. In any case it would be wrong to employ an MM specialist as the responsible product manager of electronic product development just because of their preknowledge of (more or less only) the technical parts of the product-development process. The right answer is: to allow and attract conventional but flexible and open-minded editorial staff to learn and/or improve their MM knowledge.

(2d) Implement appropriate budgeting procedures, accounting procedures and calculation schemes

Budgeting, product calculation schemes and accounting procedures are usually based on and focused to the print-materials business. For new media publishing it is necessary to take a closer look at some areas that are not relevant when publishing books. As regards budgeting, one must be aware that there are — besides new sorts of product-development costs, as described above — additional service costs, e.g. for hotline services. Higher costs than in the book business may occur because of the different way of distributing, and, in any case, PR to retailers and the target groups is more costly.

On the revenue side of the budget you should know that in most European countries — in contrast to books — sales prices of nonprinted educational materials are not fixed by law. This may cause trouble when cooperating with the wrong distributors!

Another difference compared with the book business is the governmental VAT regulation for nonbooks, even for educational materials. No VAT or reduced VAT for books is a dream for the electronic-media publishers. Do you know exactly how much VAT you have to ask from your customers? Of course, this influences sales prices and, therefore, calculation schemes. When calculating costs for a new media product you have also to integrate the costs for the added printed manual, exercise material, or other printed matter.

Do not print 5000 copies when you hope to sell only 1000 disks, just because the per copy price is then acceptable. It is much more expensive to throw 3500 away two years later (500 could be used for PR) than accepting a higher per copy price now.

So, our recommendation is not to use the printed-matter schemes when calculating or budgeting new media products, but work out new ones that take care of the different situation in the case of modern media publishing.

(2e) Implement DTP (Desktop publishing) for book publishing

Publishers have got a huge amount of traditionally typeset text material available. This has almost no use for exploitation in modern media products! This is because of the well-known fact that digital data are required. Traditional texts of course could be scanned — but the ratio of mistakes is still 2% to 5%, which means an awful lot of correction work has to be done. Furthermore, printed educational and training materials usually consist of not only text but also tables, pictures and graphic elements that cannot all be scanned to the required quality.

In order to prepare for possible future activities, it is a precondition that all new products, especially the printed ones, should be developed with DTP. Besides the core advantages of DTP — shorter development period and (after the investment period) lower production costs — DTP will automatically produce a bigger and bigger set of digitized data that are prepared for use in new media, too.

(3) Take the evolutionary approach!

(3a) Exploit established market positions to launch new media products, e.g. add multimedia products to successful series

Modern-media products do not play an extraordinary role in terms of the product mix a publisher offers to its customers. It is a basic marketing principle to develop new products for the same target groups which are already well known regarding their demands and the communication and distribution channels to them, instead of looking for new and different target groups for the new products.

This is especially true for such innovative products as new media learning and teaching materials. The positioning of the first new media products should therefore be based on the most successful areas of the traditional business. The advantages are obvious:

- the customers are aware of the competence of the publisher and accept further related products,
- the publisher is already providing this group, by means of PR, with more or less regular information about the programme, so no (or only minor) additional costs will be incurred for communicating the newly published electronic media products,
- the concrete added value that is relevant for the target group can be defined and described because of the knowledge of the needs and demands of the customers.

So, for example, it is sensible for a schoolbook publisher to offer, in addition to a broadly sold textbook programme, either exercises for students or teacher manuals in electronic format. For a training-material publisher it might be advantageous to bundle an existing best-selling training book with a directly related electronic product. As regards the public markets, such as home learners, existing brandnames should be used.

(3b) Do not build large service facilities in-house, buy in services as much as possible

It is not unusual for a publisher to consider starting up in multimedia with a full blown software development group. In the general market (industry at large) it is not unknown for such efforts to die a quiet death, and for that company's directors to swear off multimedia for years to come. Publishers, beware! Software development, many forms of content creation like audio and video, and conversion facilities are not only expensive but require special human resources (skills) not often found (or needed) in a publishing house. This is true even if there already exist large networks, electronic graphic artists and computer layout systems in the publishing house. Many of the tools and skills needed for good interactive multimedia development are not at all required in these situations. Companies who are aware of the costs of the hardware tend to underestimate the cost of obtaining the proper human skills to make good products.

Some may ask 'Then how will we ever develop the experience to enter the multimedia market if all the services are external?' The answer is that experience should and can be obtained, but by investing in those tools and skill developments that complement and enhance current in-house strengths. This would include the areas of interactive authoring, editing, screen layout, asset management (licensing, storage, reselling), packaging and marketing. In regard to the actual programming, a certain level of skill may be desirable, for example in composing 'modules' that are later linked and integrated by the external developer.

External services have several immediate advantages. Such companies are obtaining their skills through projects from a wide range of industry and 'idea' providers. Their current experience in how to make a good interactive multimedia application and what the technical possibilities and trends are is much wider than any publisher could hope to obtain through setting up their own internal services. This is true regardless of whether it is a programming house, an audio/video producer or a specialized multimedia producer who assembles a team for each production.

Another advantage is reflected in an 'economics of scale'. Overall, the rates of external services, although still high, will be less in the immediate future than starting up an entire internal department, since the external services can spread the cost of start-up and continuing capital investment over many more projects. Service groups must also constantly upgrade their facilities in order to reflect the changes in industry and market trends. This kind of updating may not be affordable in-house at a publishing company, resulting in inferior products as time goes on.

The same ability (need) of external services to adapt to industry and market needs (trends) provides a publisher who uses their services with the advantage of flexibility. There is even the flexibility allowed by changing service companies all together. Obviously in times of such rapid change (which, although elsewhere we recommend a slow-down, will never completely stop) and uncertainty (i.e. what platform?) such flexibility is of great importance.

(3c) Establish a strategy for utilization of new media production services

Naturally the previous argument for not (immediately) building up large in-house service facilities raises the need for recommendations for the longer term. Simply depending on various external services on an as-needed basis will not be suitable for developing a fully functioning long-term business. No-one can argue with building up internal experience, even in regard to traditionally nonpublishing skills, if it can be done in a sound business-like manner.

The first step in determining what services should be external is to determine what 'services' would enhance the publisher's current specialities. These specialities include authoring, editing, layout, certain content creation and content management. There are many electronic computing tools that specifically serve both current publishing needs and the need of adding interactivity and mixing media. A strategy based on introducing tools and developing skills in this direction can make sense to directors, managers and staff.

Notice that this strategy for introducing tools does not require a separate new or enhanced service department. Instead, the tools are integrated right into the departments of current lines of business, causing minimum disruption.

Eventually, as markets grow and strategies and trends become clearer, publishers will want to bring many of the more technical (or nontraditional) services in-house. Almost all of these types of services are universally needed or utilized by the output of the different departments in the business. For this reason, these services can best be centralized and provided as a general service to the whole company, similar to the printing division of a publisher. A serious option would be to buy the external service companies previously depended on.

So the general logic of a strategy for utilizing new media services might be as follows: Bring in-house and integrate immediately those tools that match the traditional skills in the traditional lines of business. These tools should, wherever possible, enhance traditional operations and of course support the addition of interactivity. For the immediate future keep external those services that do not support the added-value aspects of publishing (authoring, editing, marketing, etc.) or would be best implemented as 'central' services.

In planning for the future, an early strategy has to include intentions regarding the internalization of the external services. It will be necessary to inform all parties on both sides of activity of the eventual plan. This will allow for solid long-term coordinated growth and an eventual smooth entry of the services into the company infrastructure and culture.

As a final note, good communications, both human and data, with the external services is critical to production. Also important is the external services' understanding of national and cultural peculiarities. These factors must be given consideration when formulating a strategy and choosing services. After a truly careful search it is possible that no suitable external service is available. In this case the publisher should be aware of the opportunity this presents and thought should be given to starting a new external company that serves both the owning publisher and others in the area who must have also run into the same problem. Much more can be learned in this way and the service can, through serving a larger client base, better support the costs of starting up such services.

(3d) Distinguish between initial and ultimate product/market mix and plan your business start-up accordingly

Traditional businesses beginning a new-product-category business tend to focus on their currently most successful traditional markets. This can backfire for three likely reasons: one, these big markets require an unexpectedly large effort to sell both the 'title' and a new way of doing things (i.e. a new delivery platform like CD-i); two, the markets are large enough so as to demand 'consumer' pricing right from the start, resulting in too small a margin; and three, one mistake could sour the company's potentially largest buyer group for years to come.

These three risks go hand in hand with several operational considerations in entering into the multimedia business. Development costs of both the product and the market are relatively high and this demands a good return from sales. There is much to learn in both creating multimedia solutions and in marketing the solutions successfully if a company is to avoid costly mistakes, and the larger the audience, the more learning is required.

In this light the obvious reaction of many publishers is to wait and see what others experience. In order not to be too far behind the competitor who some day is lucky enough to have a big success, the rest of the industry 'dabbles' in various low-cost productions with no real business planning behind the work. But learning is only achieved by real experience and thus success will only come from a serious business effort in the new field.

It becomes clear that the best approach to avoid many risks and at the same time begin the business learning curve of multimedia, is carefully to consider all company current markets and identify smaller markets that may have an installed base (and thus are already educated in electronic publishing) or identify a small market where a new product offers high value and can possibly support significantly higher product costs. At the same time the cost of selling multimedia to this smaller market is lower and the lower complexity of the group reduces the risk of significant mistakes.

The other advantage to this approach is that skill is also developed in recognizing the new market paradigms. In other words it will often be the case that the classic market segments for traditional publications may not be suitable to multimedia. Education is a good example. Class books are designed around a particular grade level and the natural urge is to do the same with the multimedia product. However, it may be more profitable to focus first on 'home education' or on an international market just to reach a significant installed base. In this case the product may be better aimed at learning concepts, as opposed to skills, and thus grade and strict age categories cannot be the basis of the marketing effort.

In any case, as success and confidence grow, the publisher can comfortably, with experience and skills to back them, move into their larger and more complex markets. This entire chain of events, it must be remembered, requires a plan or a strategy right from the start. A wait-and-see attitude could greatly endanger a publisher's leading role in their current markets since start-ups or entry by entirely new but large players (e.g. film industry, game industry) with advanced multimedia marketing experience, could quickly dominate the growing multimedia segment of education and training publishers' traditional business.

(3e) Consider starting with bespoke title development and exploit the resulting products on the open markets later, but assure during development that the product will indeed be sufficiently generic

Entering the electronic publishing market should be done in steps, as illustrated in several of the other recommendations in this report. In parallel with phasing in production capacity and starting with smaller market segments is the idea of phasing in from professional, bespoke (contracted) titles for a particular client to a larger consumer-like base.

The key to this approach is to take a share in the ownership of the early bespoke product with the rights to distribute a more generic version later. These later versions would probably include national versions where cultural and language variations have to be integrated. It is even worth considering taking rights to the 'look and feel' so that a series can be developed from a type of 'template'.

The value of the generic aspects of the early products is where care has to be taken in following this path. For one matter, where content is obviously 'product' oriented (i.e. parts manuals or highly branded content, as in a well-known picture encyclopaedia), the generic value will have to be in the 'look and feel' and the established development process. Be sure then, that these aspects are generic and offer a cost-effective and easy way to produce new titles with new content. At the same time one should keep in mind that all new content can be very costly if not already owned.

The other generic concept is to have a product where the client-specific references can be relatively easily removed, leaving a title with content valuable to a broader market, especially new national versions. An obvious example would be a 'quality management' title. For education this may be a university course or a national school curriculum that, with some dressing up or 'internationalization' makes a nice consumer 'edutainment' product.

As a final note, and perhaps an obvious one, a 'client' may simply be another division of the same company, i.e. School Books Group as a client of the Consumer Reference Group.

(3f) Consider the product/market mix where you can create an installed base (instead of waiting for one to appear)

Education and training publishers are traditionally in the position to market their products (books) to any customer interested in the content at the right price if the marketing channels are available. The only real restriction is the language of the publication, although even that restriction is being reduced.

In the area of electronic publishing, however, it is not sufficient if a customer is interested in the content and willing to pay the price. He/she also has to have the right equipment (according to the right standards) available to play the title. Although some technical developments may reduce the problem of standards, the need to have the equipment still remains. This limits the potential market for a product to that percentage of potential customers who have the correct equipment available, i.e. the installed base.

There are two possible approaches to this problem:

- wait for the installed base (among your potential customers) to be big enough,
- create your own installed base by bundling the required equipment with your titles.

The second approach may not seem feasible, but is becoming more realistic as prices of (consumer-oriented) equipment are getting lower. This approach is especially attractive in cases such as:

- subscriptions to multimedia magazines (e.g. for libraries, schools, professionals),
- bundled deals for complete series of titles,
- highly professional titles (e.g. management training),
- employer-paid employee training (employee learns in his/her own time at home, but gets a free consumer player from his/her employer in return).

Cooperation with hardware manufacturers is another way to distribute new media products to learners. In this case the marketing channels of the computer industry might be used for confronting their customers with a learning product and this could obviously be advantageous for both the publisher and the industry.

(4) Have you got the value to add?

(4a) Find out whether you have value to add, and where in the chain

The roles of educational and training publishers in conventional publishing are rather well established, adding value to the content provided by authors by project initiation or selection, by product and pedagogical concept design and production itself, by marketing to educational and training organizations through established relationships, and by distribution.

While the basic role of publisher can be maintained, the value chain for electronic publications differs and publishers must determine which value-adding tasks they should themselves undertake. Selection of projects for multimedia development is crucial: it clearly does not make sense to invest in areas where the value added gain to you is small, or where you are in too weak a position in the value chain to control or benefit.

An approach to finding out the best projects is:

- to carry out market research to identify the areas where multimedia products are, or are likely to be, in demand,
- to audit one's own company with respect to the value chain; this means identifying internal assets to locate those most suitable for multimedia exploitation (e.g. where you have clear ownership, where assets are in digital form, where the value added potential is good),
- establish access to people, e.g. authors, who can contribute to the development of added value for new media products,
- to match market research to asset audit to develop exploitation plans.

For example, the development of software integrating educational materials with electronic lexica is an example of value-adding in electronic publishing. Whether this is an appropriate area for a publisher will depend on their access to relevant assets (e.g. dictionaries) and to the software development skills required (either themselves or through reliable partnership).

(4b) Maximize your own ownership of rights or set up strategic cooperation

Acquire as many of the (full) rights to assets required in a multimedia product as possible, otherwise your exploitation opportunities will be weakened. Where ownership of particular rights is not possible, or is limited, search for alternative content or fuller rights to the same content; rights owned by different parties for the same content often vary in comprehensiveness.

Where ownership is not desirable for cost/risk reasons, or cannot be bought, consider setting up a cooperation agreement. This may be for a single title or to enable complementary assets to be shared over a range of projects.

(4c) Develop a business culture and structure to exploit assets as an essential part of the business

The current culture of many publishers is built around people; the business is structured around individual products/titles. The value of IPR assets does not appear on the company's accounts — only as the value of published products awaiting sale in the warehouse.

Electronic publishers must know the value of the IPR they own and others (e.g. banks) must also know, so as to treat them as assets of the business.

(5) What do the learners and teachers get out of it, and how do they know?

(5a) Focus on multimedia products with a very concrete added value to teachers and/or learners

Traditional media in the educational and training environment, such as textbooks, workbooks, exercise books, reference books, teacher manuals, audio materials, slide series, videos, training kits, etc., all have their specific methodological value. Teachers, students, self-learners know when and how to use them. This is — so far — not the case with modern-media products. There is hardly any awareness or knowledge about the opportunities for teaching and learning that might be provided by such media. Even more is there still a lack of scientific pedagogical research about didactic and methodological issues.

Consequently the added value of any new media product must be obviously visible to the trainer and/or user. General advantages of electronic media, such as: fast access to specific units, search possibilities, possibility for interrelation of content, etc., or the claim that teaching/learning is faster, more effective or interesting etc., do not suffice.

The concrete added value must be based on the subject-related requirements of the user and his/her work. Examples are:

- For a trainer/teacher who is preparing the next lessons the added value of a new media product may be the possibility to easily select and individually combine exercises and information in order to print and copy them for the students.
- In the classroom realistic presentations of different sorts (e.g. spoken foreign language, photos of foreign places, film on daily life) could be displayed much more easily than by using different tools like a slide projector, video player, etc.
- Individual users/learners may get feedback about more than learning progress, reference information, etc. or may be able to extract, add and change specific information in relation to their specific learning needs.

(6) Good products on the market are good for everybody

(6a) Accept and support the attitude that, at this stage, the market success of good products — even from the competition — is good for everybody

Many publishers fear competition from outside companies like Microsoft and Philips. This concern stems from the fact that these are big companies which have largely committed themselves to a particular technology in which they have a vested interest. Publishers on the other hand are relatively small and have no market incentive to commit themselves to a particular delivery system when there are many to choose from, and thus no incentive to enter the multimedia business. The desire is to wait for a winner, but over time fear builds up as the (big) outsiders continue to invest. Slowly the publisher starts to build up some sort of defensive, rather than offensive, strategy.

Multimedia is still a 'small' market. Many companies, publishers included, would prefer to wait to see which systems and titles prevail. This limits the growth of the market (chicken-and-egg problem). 'Limited growth' is the key word here. Would it not be better for publishers actually to support the sale of competitors' products, even marketing the products themselves, so as to force the market into maturity?

The idea is that all publishers should play their part in the overall industry to promote market acceptance of new media for training and education. If marketing a competitor's product is not practical, then consider actively supporting associations that advance the multimedia industry, such as the CD-i Association, the Optical Publishers Association or the Training Technology and Telematics Round Table (T3RT), advance the formation of European or even national groups focusing on multimedia publishing in education and training.

Supporting the industry and even, indirectly or directly, the competition is a way for publishers to break into the learning curve, help the market find its stride, and thus ultimately give all publishers an attractive business case for aggressively protecting their current markets and sales volumes through the introduction of multimedia publishing to their traditional activities.

(7) Technology is not *the* issue, it is just one of the issues

(7a) Stick to a platform for a while, once you have selected it

Publishers, especially newspaper publishers, are normally very careful about introducing a new format or layout. And if they do, they stick to it for a while before judging the effects. This allows the customers to get used to the format and, more importantly, it allows the publishers to optimize the format and the production process and to recoup the investments in the new format.

In the (still) largely technology-driven multimedia world, there is a tendency to try a new technology platform for just a brief period of time, and, if not directly successful, switch to another. This approach is not only costly (new tools, new skills) but in particular it reduces your competitive edge and brand image. Switching to different target platforms costs not only money, but also time-to-market. Worst of all, it may confuse your customer and reduce their loyalty to the brand.

Therefore, it is often better to stick to a platform for a while, once you have selected it. Even if this is not directly profitable, at least it gives you the chance to build up expertise in designing and marketing multimedia titles. The dedicated technical expertise for other platforms can always be acquired later. However, if you feel you might want to switch to another (or additional) target platform in the future, the following measures might be useful:

- document your title designs carefully, so that they can be implemented on other platforms if necessary,
- capture and store all multimedia assets in the highest quality possible, to optimize the possibility of reusing them later for other target platforms.

(7b) Do not always go for the most state-of-the-art technology, at least not after the initial trial phase

The publishing of education and training material is concerned with its content and structure. It is not a fashion industry. The multimedia world often behaves like a fashion industry, and early adopters (customers) tend to ask for the latest technology. However, this is generally not a wise approach from a business perspective. Using the latest technology often only gives marginal quality improvements, but can imply high additional costs:

- tools for developing titles for the latest technologies are often not yet perfect, affordable or widely available,
- design and development skills dedicated to the latest platforms are typically undeveloped and scarce,
- very new technologies have a limited installed base, and thus an (initial) smaller market and longer pay-back periods.

It is therefore often better to go for a technology which has already been established on the market. In the end, the keys to successful electronic publishing are high-quality educational content, installed player base and good marketing, rather than technical gimmicks.

RECOMMENDATIONS TO THE EC

Act jointly with educational and training publishers

Investigate with educational publishers where new media are effective for training and education and what the specific added value of such learning material is, and promote this to the education and training community

There are many activities initiated by the EC and national bodies on *how* to implement *what* sort of information technology in Europe. The question *why* is seldom touched when education and training is concerned. Of course, there are some very interesting studies made by researchers, mainly in the USA, concerning the effectiveness of multimedia training (in financial terms) or the potentials of modern media in terms of learning speed, knowledge acquirement and 'fun' of learning. But much more has to be done as far as the real value for the learning process and result is concerned in order to convince teachers, trainers, students and, last but not least, the education and training publishers.

Help publishers identify where installed bases of multimedia systems exist, especially within European and national government bodies

Over five million CD-ROM drives have been installed worldwide, attached to only part of the installed base of personal computers, especially DOS and Apple computers. Beyond this there are almost innumerable multimedia-capable communications links and other multimedia systems such as CD-i. In general, this is an attractive market, but simultaneously this reflects the real problem: generality. To attract publishers to act immediately in developing a multimedia business a clear picture, packaged into a single source, of where and how today's multimedia-capable technologies are concentrated, is needed.

To formulate this picture for the entire installed base would obviously be preferred but not a serious recommendation, given both the size of the study target and the existence of numerous relevant commercial reports.

Two foci seem possible for EC initiatives. The first initiative would be an assessment of the current commercial reports concerning the specific categories relevant to training and education, with a focus on the commercial market. It is logical that within the overall categories covered by commercial reports (i.e. industry sectors and/or type of application) that a subanalysis specifically addressing the training and education potential in each of these categories would be valuable. Probably this has not been done because there is no clear market interest in this market segment and there is no market interest because there is no clear picture of the market. Such analyses could be carried out by the report authors in conjunction with several major players representing training and educational publishers.

The second proposed initiative is even more concrete: for the EC and each national government to carry out internal 'audits' of where within their bodies (or funded bodies) these multimedia-capable technologies are concentrated. The idea is not necessarily to analyse the current use of technology, but to provide publishers with a first clear view of clusters within 'government' having market potential and to identify the proper doors to knock on. It would then be up to the publishers to independently carry out their own strategy-focused market research based on these concentrations. With segment views including both 'professional' (i.e. administration offices) and 'public' (i.e. schools, universities), there will clearly be a large number of possibilities of interest to publishers, but only once the picture of installed technologies becomes clear.

Stimulate the involvement of educational and training publishing in European RTD programmes

Involvement has so far been limited: it is particularly important that programmes with an 'education and training' element, such as DELTA, find ways of involving publishers who can both learn and play an effective and realistic market-oriented role in exploiting the work being done by academic institutions.

Stimulate business opportunities

Take up new media in the EC education and training initiatives, e.g. European schools, knowledge transfer from the R&D framework programmes

Such exemplary action, e.g. by introducing training technology into European schools and supporting publication of appropriate titles for them, will demonstrate the potential, promote discussion, stimulate publishers to produce titles, increase awareness and help national educational institutions to develop their own programmes.

In the training area, the dissemination of results of European Research and Development programmes should be improved through the application of electronic publishing.

Do not overencourage the speed-up of technological development

It is clear that publishers in the training and education fields are frustrated by the rapid pace of technological development and thus change. This goes hand-in-hand with their doubts about the ability to predict what installed base to plan on and their concern with producing, via experience, 'user friendly' products. Thus, there is most commonly a 'wait-and-see' attitude. Most current publisher development actions are concerned with keeping up with the competition and establishing a basic level of expertise, and not with a real effort to develop a market.

Standards are one road to easing concerns with rapid technological change, but currently even standards are evolving at a frightening rate, e.g. MPEG-1 $\rightarrow$ MPEG-2; MPC1 $\rightarrow$ MPC2; CD-ROM $\rightarrow$ double speed CD-ROM; CD-i $\rightarrow$ CD-i DV.

It is now apparent that the only way constructively to stimulate real business development in multimedia by more traditional publishers is to advocate the slowdown (even a 'steady-state') of technological developments. Obviously such a simple radical declaration by the EC is unrealistic. What is sensible is to (continue to) encourage, through EC programme criteria, a focus on advancing the use of current, new or at most highly developed experimental ideas (hardware, networks, applications) in EU Programme topic areas within an established framework of available, or soon-to-be-available, modern, mostly distribution-oriented support services (WAN, ISDN broadcasting etc.).

By encouraging this type of 'Action Research' involving the actual 'dealers' in European media and based on generally current technologies, real market-like forces will come into play that encourage the utilization and stabilization of existing technologies and standards. This, in turn, should help develop a stable technology base, which again in turn will support the development of a few 'stable' installed bases on which publishers can confidently base real business planning.

Stimulate the innovation in national education systems, through for example, development of multimedia learning material on European subjects

National education systems in Europe are generally slow innovators. This makes it difficult for educational publishers to justify high investments in new types of (multimedia) learning material. It also slows down the development of competences in the educational publishing industry as well as awareness in the education systems.

Large-scale pilot projects are essential, both to develop these competences and to create an installed base and awareness among school systems. As the initial title development costs are rather high, national pilot projects might create insufficient scales of economy to be really attractive. Overhead costs are likely to be too high. It is therefore recommended establishing pan-European trials, on subjects that require only small national adaptations and do not directly affect national curricula. Topics like the mechanism of the European Union or the European Cultural Heritage might be very appropriate for developing pan-European learning material.

Set the appropriate copyright environment

Support the needs of industry in assisting with setting legal standards, e.g. following the recommendations of the T3RT report on 'Copyright issues for publishers of multimedia educational and training products'

A summary of this report is included in Appendix 16.3. The main conclusions are:

- Copyright issues are highly relevant for the multimedia training material industry, especially in relation to the use of existing assets. Several of those issues are currently unresolved satisfactorily, and are therefore a barrier for the large-scale development and publishing of multimedia training material. It is thus considered highly relevant to keep this area under the attention of the T3RT, and to bring it to the attention of relevant bodies, EC and national ones, whenever appropriate.
- Many of these issues are of generic concern to the overall multimedia publishing industry, and are thus not training-specific. Most of these issues are currently being addressed by governments, organizations, companies, and projects. It is of key importance to keep the training-material developers and the educational publishers abreast of these developments.
- Most of the issues of concern, especially to the education and training world, are related to lack of awareness and expertise. It is therefore considered highly beneficial to provide proper information access, guidance, and possibly training to those involved in development and publishing of multimedia training material.
- One of the specific training-related issues is concerned with the pricing structure for licensing multimedia assets, which is generally not suitable for bespoke and in-house training material. It is highly desirable to enter discussions with relevant bodies and companies to investigate whether special arrangements for such training applications could be realized.
- Publishing education and training material in electronic formats requires different business models and especially different exploitation models, in order to recoup relatively high investments and the difficulty of avoiding illegal copying or use. It is therefore important to support publishers in developing adequate business models, pricing structures and contracts with their customers.

Disseminate results

Involve publishing and education organizations through a workshop in order to collect feedback and to assure wide dissemination of the report

Our research shows that there is wide interest in multimedia among education and training publishers and a need to exchange experiences and learn from each other. Organizations such as IEPRC and STM and programmes such as DELTA and IMPACT should sponsor a workshop to focus this interest around this report.

Have a real publication developed on the basis of this study

Regard this study as an opportunity to stimulate successfully awareness in the educational and training publishing industry. A publication sponsored by the EC and broadly distributed will indicate to publishers that the time is right to be looking at these issues.

REFERENCES

1 **Laukamm, T** *Strategic Study on New Opportunities for Publishers in the Information Services Market* EC No 14926 EN (Feb 1993)

2 *SIGCUE Outlook. Bulletin of the Special Interest Group for Computer Users in Education — International Issue* ACM Press (1989)

3 **Dondi, C and Bellesi, L** *Beacon Market Observatory, National Survey Report 1993* European Commission DELTA project deliverable #4, Brussels (1993)

4 **Schwerin, J B** *The INFOTECH Report: Optical Publishing Industry Assessment* INFOTECH, Woodstock, VT, USA (1992)

5 **Jeffcoate, J and Templeton, A** *Multimedia Strategies for the Business Market* OVUM, London, UK (1992)

6 *Training Statistics* UK Department of Employment, HMSO (1993)

APPENDIX 16.1: INTERVIEW PARTNERS

Overall some 25 European publishing companies contributed to the findings in the STOP study. The following publishers were interviewed using the questionnaire appended as Appendix 16.2 (here only the main interviewee is mentioned).

Grupo Anaya, Madrid, Spain — Dr Marcel Coderch
Axel Andersson Akademie, Hamburg, Germany — Michael Lammersdorf
George Axiotelis and Co. Publishing Ltd, Athens, Greece — Dr Constantine Caretsos
Difusion SL, Barcelona, Spain — Detlev Wagner
Editions la Décourverte, Paris, France — François Gèze
Gentner Verlag, Stuttgart, Germany — Gernot Keuchen
Gyldendal Undervisning, Copenhagen, Denmark — Egon Schmidt
Hachette Education, Paris, France — Claude Bardot
Harper Collins, London, England — Stuart Gill
Heureka-Klett Softwareverlags GmbH, Stuttgart, Germany — Wolf-Dieter Eggert
Longman Group UK Ltd, Harlow, England — Jeff Andrew
NATHAN Editeur, Paris, France — Michel Gudimard
Reed International, Oxford, England — Suzanne Wilson-Higgins
Wolters Kluwer, Maarssen, Netherlands — Dr Joop van Dalen

APPENDIX 16.2: INTERVIEW QUESTIONNAIRE

Ernst Klett Verlag für Wissen und Bildung

EC CCAM-Study
Stimulations of Publishers

Interview-Questionnaire

0. **General questions**
0.1 What is the name of your company?

0.2 What is the traditional business of your company?

0.3 How big is your company?

0.4 What role does your company play in the market?

0.5 Who are your most important competitors?

0.6 What is your function in this company?

0.7 What is your personal knowledge about multimedia in principle?
professional ☐   low ☐
good ☐   none ☐
informed ☐

0.8 Who decides about production of materials/multimedia products in your company?

0.9 Does your company have any multimedia products?
☐ yes, which ones:
☐ no

0.10 Have your competitors had any experience in multimedia-production?
☐ yes, which ones:
☐ don't know
☐ no

1. **Opportunities and threats regarding multimedia production**
1.1 What opportunities do you see for '96 concerning multimedia ?
in general   for your company

1.2 What threats do you see for '96?
in general   for your company

1.3 How much growth do you expect for your business? (from now until '96)
in general
multimedia

1.4 How much revenue (in percent) do you expect (now/'96)?

	in general	multimedia
now		
'96		

1.5 How many titles do you expect to publish (now/'96)?

	in general	multimedia
now		
'96		

1.6   How many copies do you expect to sell (now/'96)?

	in general	multimedia
now		
'96		

1.7   What percentage of education and training materials will be multimedia products? (in general/for your company)
in general   for your company

1.8   What percentage of multimedia products will be education and training materials? (in your company)

1.9   What percentage of the revenues will be from rights sold? (materials)
Now   in 1996

1.10   How much of this will be for multimedia products?
Now   in 1996

1.11   What growth opportunities are open to you, thanks to multimedia?

1.12   How much image building/branding will arise from multimedia production? (for your company)

1.13   Can you foresee any threats from multimedia-newcomers to educational and training publishing?

1.14   How could this affect your company?

1.15   What role will your company play in the multimedia business in 1996?

	yes		some		no
asset owner	1	2	3	4	5
title developer — bespoke (on order)	1	2	3	4	5
title developer — publisher	1	2	3	4	5
distributor	1	2	3	4	5
packager	1	2	3	4	5

1.16   Which materials are used by your company for multimedia materials?
❏   development of new materials   ❏   licensing
❏   takeover of own materials   ❏   combination of those:
❏   takeover of externally existing materials   ❏   others:

2.   Entry strategy
2.1   What is your entry strategy?/How are you preparing for the new age?

	yes				no
wait and see	1	2	3	4	5
joint ventures	1	2	3	4	5
buying media company	1	2	3	4	5
small pilots (with funding from...)	1	2	3	4	5
preparing assets	1	2	3	4	5
outside production	1	2	3	4	5
set up new division	1	2	3	4	5
set up spinoff company (to buy...?)	1	2	3	4	5
employ specialists	1	2	3	4	5
hire consultants	1	2	3	4	5
train people	1	2	3	4	5
set up new distribution channels/marketing	1	2	3	4	5

2.2   How much investment is affected?

2.3   How much ECU do you expect to get back, and when?

2.4   How would you interact with the industry?

2.5   How would you interact with the technical side?

2.6   How would you interact with other publishers (know-how, cooperation ...)?

2.7   How can a 'Multimedia-Image' be built up?

3. Awareness and information

3.1   Is there sufficient awareness and information?

	technology (hard- and software)					competition					market					required skills					development process				
	1	2	3	4	5	1	2	3	4	5	1	2	3	4	5	1	2	3	4	5	1	2	3	4	5
in your company																									
for authors																									
for customers																									

3.2   If there is not enough or no information/awareness, what are you planning to do?

	wait & see				proactive
in your company	1	2	3	4	5
technology					
competition					
market					
required skills					
development process					
for authors	1	2	3	4	5
technology					
competition					
market					
required skills					
development process					
for customers	1	2	3	4	5
technology					
competition					
market					
required skills					
development process					

3.3   What sources do you use for information?

	Yes/No	which one?
press		
conferences		
colleagues		
consultants		
other business sectors		
technology providers		
experts		
success stories		
others		

3.4   Who (how many persons) in your company gets this information and uses these sources?

3.5   How is it distributed in your company?

4. Necessary activities

4.1 What has to be done to make it a business?

	Experiences No	Positive	Negative	Future
Awareness in your company				
Skills				
Product development chain (3 folders)				
Organizational consequences in your company				
take overs — Joint venture in market (by the customer)				
Intern/extern business structure (business chains)/Costs				
Intellectual Publishing Rights				
Technology				
Time input/ resources				

5. Changes in market place

5.1 What has to change in the market place?

Awareness (customers, distributors, booksellers, ...)	
Marketing/Distribution channels (e.g. external training or new channels)	
change educational/school/ training mindset	
Installed base (hardware)	
Technology/Tools	

6. Activities of several bodies

6.1 What could your company do?

6.2 What could the industry do? (hardware)

6.3 What could commerce do?

6.4 What could the EC do?

APPENDIX 16.3

Training Technology and Telematics Round Table (T3RT) — a summary of conclusions of the T3RT Working Group on copyright issues

Working Group Convenor: Roberto Minio, IEPRC
Working Group Members: Jürgen A. Schmidt, Klett KWB; Willem Bulthuis, Philips CE

Introduction

The Working Group analysed the relevance, scope and character of copyright issues in relation to the development and publishing of multimedia training material. This has been done primarily on the basis of discussions with in-house experts and literature analysis.

With so many activities on electronic and multimedia copyrights ongoing in Europe, it is not considered realistic to make any definite statements. Instead the group generated primarily an introduction and first analysis of the subject matter, a summary of ongoing activities by other organizations, and a set of rather concrete conclusions and recommendations.

The Working Group started with the question 'Are there existing answers to copyright issues that arise in preparation, publication and use of multimedia training materials?' The context of the work was as follows.

There is an increasing awareness in the multimedia industry, and among customers in the training area, of the complicated situation around copyright and other IPR (Intellectual Property Rights) issues in regard to developing and exploiting multimedia applications.

Traditionally, copyright is one of the cornerstones of publishing and information trading arrangements. Other rights and obligations — for example concerning translations or collections — rely on agreement about copyright, which thus forms part of a structure that functions in practice.

New technology can appear to threaten the institution of copyright: sometimes this might require adjustment of the application of rules; sometimes the notion of what is subject to copyright might need to be extended.

In addition to agreement about copyright itself, systems are needed for registering and trading rights. Different kinds of associated products — such as music or film — are subject to copyright, but the systems for registering and trading are different to those for paper publications, and different in different European countries.

Copyright for digital publications has been the subject of much discussion touching on the preparation, production, trading and use of such products. Compared to paper, it appears harder to control further reuse of electronic products. With the advent of multimedia and large-capacity storage and delivery systems, the potential for reuse and adaptation of existing material in multiple products has grown, while the cost of new production has not decreased. Electronic products may be traded and reused over networks. The discussions are resulting in new perceptions of information ownership, regulations and changing means of trading different types of electronic information.

Which of these changes are relevant to technology-based training, and how do they apply? Should experiences from the training field be taken into account in the course of these changes to bring about a situation satisfactory to training producers, users, information providers and other involved parties? Are there specific training-related aspects to copyright issues, or are such issues application independent? How can developers and publishers of technology-based training material be supported in coping with the copyright issues?

Work

Observations by the Working Group found that copyright is relevant for developers, publishers, and users of multimedia training material basically for three reasons:

- Each picture, sound etc. used in a training package is owned by somebody and therefore the publisher must pay to sell this picture or sound as part of the package.
- The total training package, including the design and structure, are protected by copyright, which is the basis for the publisher to earn money from selling copies.
- A training package is sold to a user under specific conditions, to protect the rights and interests of the publisher (software packages often are not really sold, but just licensed for use).

Most work focused on the first aspect — rights on raw materials and the final report goes on to discuss: Acquiring rights to use assets, licensing problems, what is copyright, what licences to acquire, current practice and pricing (for text, graphics, photo images, sound, music, video), international aspects (including EC directives), various relevant associations — conferences and workshops; publications; solicitors; legislative and advisory organizations; and projects.

After this global analysis the Working Group identified the main issues of concern and discussed how these issues could be worked out further. The issue areas were legal, pricing, business, awareness and expertise and technical.

Conclusions

The main conclusions from the work performed by the Working Group are summarized below:

(1) Copyright issues are highly relevant for the multimedia training-material industry, especially in relation to the use of existing assets. Several of those issues are currently unresolved satisfactorily, and are therefore a barrier for the large-scale development and publishing of multimedia training material. It is thus considered highly relevant to keep this area under the attention of the T3RT, and to bring it to the attention of relevant bodies, EC and national ones, whenever appropriate.

(2) Many of these issues are of generic concern to the overall multimedia publishing industry and are thus not training-specific. Most of these issues are currently being addressed by governments, organizations, companies, and projects. It is of key importance to keep the training material developers and publishers abreast of these developments.

(3) Most of the issues of especial concern to the training world are related to lack of awareness and expertise. It is therefore considered highly beneficial to provide proper information access, guidance and possibly training to those involved in multimedia training-material development and publishing.

(4) One of the specific training-related issues is concerned with the pricing structure for licensing multimedia assets, which is generally not suitable for bespoke and in-house training material. It is highly desirable to enter discussions with relevant bodies

and companies to investigate whether special arrangements for such training applications could be realized.

(5) Publishing training material in electronic formats requires different business models and especially different exploitation models, in order to recoup relatively high investments and the difficulty of avoiding illegal copying or use. It is therefore important to support training-material publishers in developing adequate business models, pricing structures and contracts with their customers.

Recommendations

Considering the conclusions summarized above, the Working Group recommended the following actions:

(1) Include in general T3RT policy statements the importance of copyright issues for the large-scale market uptake of training technology.

(2) Maintain a discussion platform for copyright issues within the T3RT.

(3) Establish a (formal) cooperation between the T3RT and one or two key information sources for copyright issues. Candidates are a multimedia publishers association, a specialized solicitor, or a specialized EC project.*

(4) Interview a representative set of learning-material developers and publishers, to analyse their specific requirements concerning information, licensing arrangements etc.

(5) Organize the development of an 'information kit' for multimedia training developers and publishers, including a first introduction to multimedia copyright issues and references to relevant literature, organizations and other information sources.†

(6) Develop, together with representative education and training publishers, some appropriate business models for publishing multimedia material, taking into account especially the difficulty of protecting the material from illegal copying or use.

---

*Initial discussions are suggested to be held with, for example, IMPACT, CD-i Association, Simon Olswang, and the OASIS project.
†The action should possibly be undertaken jointly with IMPACT and COMETT. Funding for such an activity might be acquired from DELTA, IMPACT, COMETT, and/or VALUE.

(7) Organize discussions with relevant bodies, especially the Legal Advisory Board of the EC, on the issue of special licence rates for material which is only used in-house.

EP and research/museum documentation —
case studies

17

Commercial and strategic challenges facing the research journal

David Brown, D J B Associates, UK

INTRODUCTION

The international research journal publishing business is estimated at $2500 million. Journals have been the jewel in many large publishers' crowns during the 1970s and early 1980s, when the demand for research literature was at its height. The profitability of the Elsevier Group's operations is to a large degree dependent on the Science Division's activities, with many of their core research journals acting as 'milk cows' for the rest of the company. Other large commercial publishers in Europe have also benefited from the secure revenues which came from publishing journals in the halcyon days of scientific growth in the western world. Learned societies learnt that they could supplement their society funds from expanding their targeted publications to an international audience.

Only now are there concerns that journal publishing may be a liability, and that those publishers who pursued a policy of rapid journal expansion in the past decade may be exposed during the later years of the 1990s to some severe commercial constraints. The concerns are generated by a change in the market behaviour of

David Brown is a consultant to the information industry and Chief Executive of D J B Associates in Kingston-upon-Thames, England. Much of the work referred to here was undertaken on commission for the British Library R&D division.

researchers and librarians; electronic information services are being seen to offer greater appeal than the old-fashioned, slow and increasingly expensive print-on-paper option. There are also concerns that the ability of the existing market structures — the institutional library — is unable to fund the increasing amount of book and journal publications in hard copy, and that this is exacerbated by the inclusion of new electronic media in their collection development programmes.

This chapter explores some of the background to these claims, and looks at what research journal publishers are doing to provide themselves with a future role in the developing electronic information world. The issue is not trivial. Only by achieving a balanced and equitable migration from print to the new information systems being demanded by the emerging generation of researchers will the health of the publishing industry be assured. Not only that, but the efficient process of information dissemination must be continued.

This overview will look at the scholarly journal business. This is defined as those journals serving a specialized research niche, particularly in the natural sciences. The journal functions not only as a medium of information exchange, but more essentially as a vehicle whereby researchers gain international esteem, recognition and in some cases financial reward, for their work. They are ostensibly supply driven, and therein is the crux of the problem.

THE INFORMATION SYSTEM

The twigging phenomenon

There are about 120 000 regular and irregular serials being published as listed in the *Ulrichs Directory*. These have been growing in number during recent years as a result of the demand by researchers active in new scientific disciplines to have their own special information forum. As science 'twigs', the numbers of new journals proliferate. New journals are also launched to cope with the increasing multidisciplinary nature of scientific progress. The number of new journal title launches has been a barometer of the health and energy of international science and technology. So far the barometer has indicated fair weather.

Information studies

In recent years there has been an exception; the sector which 'buys' subscription to such journals has come under increasing strain. The libraries, in academia, in research institutes, in industry, have funds allocated to them that have no relation to the overall growth of scientific effort. The latter is often dictated at national level; libraries on the other hand fight for a share of the local institutional budget, and in the case of the UK have found their share of the total reduced. University libraries obtained nearly 4% of the total campus budget in 1981/82. Ten years later this had fallen to under 3%. Cancellations of journals and resource sharing between libraries of fewer subscriptions became endemic. In the USA the situation was claimed to be even worse, with anecdotal feedback suggesting massive journal cancellation exercises forced on libraries by unrelenting financial officers.

As a result of the concerns about how the university library in the UK can operate under these circumstances, a review was commissioned by the Higher Education Funding Councils and this was chaired by Sir Brian Follett[1]. This report was published in December 1993, with its recommendation to provide more funds to assist the migration of the library into a more electronic mode of operation (with £20 million in additional HEFC funding) seemingly to be broadly accepted. The assumption, if it still exists within the publishing mindset, that libraries are and will remain a cushy market for new printed journals may turn out to be a fallacy.

As part of the Follett Review, the Library and Information Studies Unit (LISU) at Loughborough University conducted a sample of UK university libraries to see what shortfalls existed at libraries both in 1986/7 and 1991/2. The shortfalls in their budget expenditures were as shown in Table 17.1. The growing proportions indicate the inability of libraries in their current form to cope with the ongoing information explosion. Something else may be required for the future, a more electronic-based library for example.

The digital library is, however, a vastly different concept from the library as we know it. A library without walls (and physical publications), a resource centre which researchers use to access remote files and databases of information. It is no longer an institution where books and serials are bought on a regular and regimented basis, a system which publishers have traditionally benefited from. The dig-

Table 17.1 Shortfalls in library budget expenditure

Item	1986/87	1991/92
Textbooks	6%	11%
Research books	13%	18%
Periodicals	11%	15%
CD-ROMs	0%	21%

ital library does require a change in researcher attitudes. It is being promoted extensively in the USA with the National Science Foundation, NASA and NTIA all having their own major projects to promote the digital library concept. The NSF is making available $7. 2 million per annum for four years to create such systems, and NASA has $40 million planned for a digital library of geophysical data.

Evidence on the behaviour of researchers in the UK, and their willingness to adopt electronic information systems, was undertaken by the Royal Society[2]. The coordinator of this project, which involved a mailing to 4400 end-users of research information, was Professor Bryan Coles from Imperial College. Again, the results showed an increasing use of a variety of electronic information systems by end-users and, while the printed journal remained the dominant form of information exchange, this dominance was no longer inviolate.

The British Library itself is also monitoring events in the electronic world through a working party under the chairmanship of Brian Perry. This is helping to formulate policy within the British Library with regard to new media systems and impacts directly on the procedures that should be adopted on legal deposit of nonbook media in general[3].

The above indicate that just within the UK there is a growing concern about the way printed publishing, particularly of research journals, is developing and suggests that these issues need to be addressed as a serious national and international issue. Scientific publications are by their nature international in coverage. However, the publishing industry is not geared up to making a coordinated and concerted action programme that will allow an easy migration from print to digital systems as the market is increasingly dictating.

SUPPLY VERSUS DEMAND FORCES

The crux of the problem is that the forces which create journal articles are out of synchronization with the forces that enable them to be bought. Supply and demand for research information are no longer in balance, and if the truth be told, have not been so for the past decade at least. There have always been rumblings about information oversupply, but the dramatic support given in the USA to the space and defence programme in the 1970s and 1980s has obscured the imbalance in recent decades.

Figure 17.1 shows how the information supply (generated by academic R&D funding in the USA, which has a high correlation with research article output) has exceeded information demand (as illustrated by the sum of the collection development budgets of the largest 100 US research libraries) during the past two decades. The gap is widening all the time.

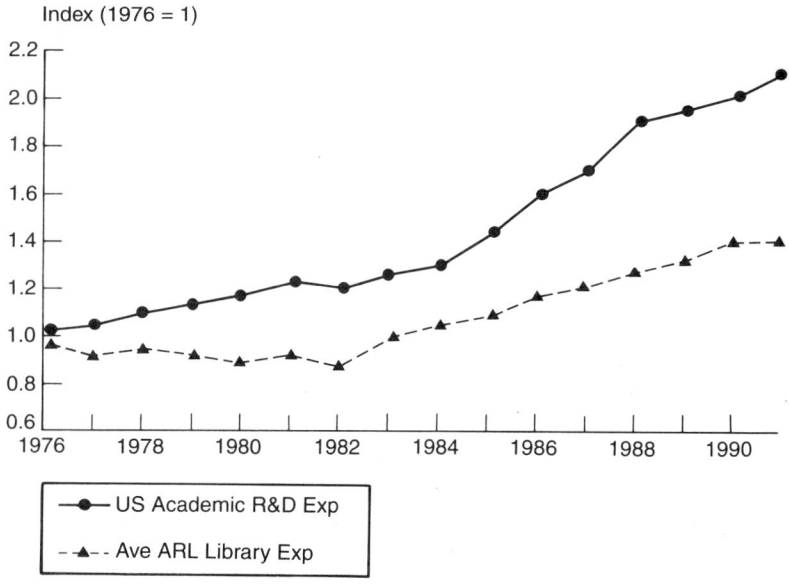

Figure 17.1 US R&D and ARL library expenditure (constant 1982 dollars)

THE SUPPLY FACTORS

As indicated above, the authors of research articles are the culprits. Over 60% of all articles are generated in the university system. This upholds the tradition of the journal as the only acceptable procedure that allows the peer group to evaluate and assess the quality of research work. It takes time for the refereeing process to be completed on an article, but this delay is acceptable to authors if it generates a record of achievement that is supported by the international research community.

Research funds are becoming more difficult to obtain. This is a result of basic natural sciences losing their central role in R&D, with the increasing emphasis on economic exploitation of research results to the benefit of society. Even those basic research projects that are being conducted are increasingly large-scale multinational cooperative projects[4]. This means that there is growing competition for what funding is available, and the basis on which selection is made in allocating such grants is the publication record of the applicant. The higher the impact factor, a measure of citations to a journal, of the publications listed in the application, the greater the chance of winning the scarce research funds. Publications in respected international journals become essential for survival. It is a continuance of the 'publication or perish' syndrome and adds to the amount of information oversupply.

THE DEMAND FACTORS

Demand, on the other hand, is dictated by the ability of research libraries to win a slice of the institutional funds. There has been a growing feeling by the university administrators in particular that the library is an institution within which publications are stored and in many instances — some 50% of holdings — are never consulted from one year to the next. The library does not perform a valuable research service. It is no longer the 'citadel of learning'. Because its funds are cut, its dependency on other research libraries is increased to provide it with backup, to bail it out when articles are demanded which are no longer part of its journal collection. The problems besetting the research library world were described in the Follett Review[1].

The gap between supply and demand would appear to be irreconcilable given the printed formula. Not only is it irreconcilable, but there is also a growing 'frustration factor' that has led to a claim by the library community that publishers are exploiting the situation by overcharging, or 'price gouging'.

NEW REVENUE SOURCES

There have been no new major sources of revenue to compensate for the static central library. A move towards 'convergence' has raised the possibility of the IT and computer departments taking on some of the subscriptions to new information services. In the case of BIDS one-third of the libraries surveyed by Harry East from CCIS showed that funds for the subscription to the BIDS online service were from the IT budgets[5]. There is also a claim that end-users themselves are buying information services — by using credit cards — in such areas as document ordering. However, these remain small and insignificant in the total picture of research funding to support book and journal acquisitions.

THE EXISTING PUBLICATION MARKET

Given this background of a growing supply-versus-demand dichotomy, some of the concerns being addressed by both libraries and publishers can be put into perspective. For the STM (scientific, technical and medical) publishers the restriction in subscription sales is a direct result of a funding structure that allows no flexibility to cope with the ever-increasing flood of research material seeking an outlet in respected journals. There are about 120 000 such serials in publication at present, of which 10 000 represent the core titles. Nevertheless, many of the others still provide a useful, in some cases essential, forum for communication between researchers operating in the outermost 'twigs' of research disciplines. The subscription to such esoteric journals may vary from 400 to 1000 in number. Received wisdom claims that the difficulty in the North American and European research libraries — together responsible for over 70% of all subscription sales — means that there is an annual erosion of between 3–5% per annum. This is confirmed by the latest edition of

Trends in Journal Subscriptions (1994), in which a survey conducted by Priscilla Oakeshott for the Publishers Association showed a 3% decrease in 1992 sales over 1991 for the 809 journals covered[6].

The difficulties which this potentially creates to the bottom-line financial account of publishers have been masked by the price increases which have exceeded annual rates of inflation. However, this process of higher prices leading to even lower subscription sales in future years is leading to an explosive catastrophe. Projections of subscription sales for the bulk of the esoteric journals lead one to the conclusion that within five years many of these journals will be commercially unviable. Even the launch of new titles is not improving the financial lot of publishers. The growth profile of new journal launches has shown a decline over the past few decades, as Figure 17.2 indicates.

If the price spiral is a feature of scholarly journal publishing, is there potential salvation from the reuse of the printed journal articles in other formats? Electronic document delivery (see next sec-

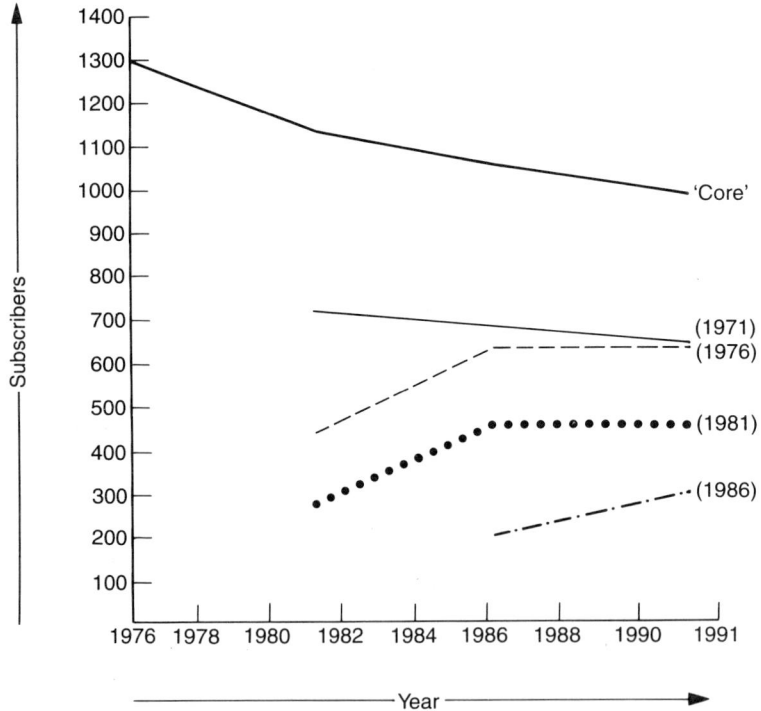

Figure 17.2   Trends in Elsevier journal subscriptions

tion) has often been heralded by the intermediaries — mainly subscription agencies — as a process which could provide new and additional revenues to publishers from a royalty payment for copies made of articles. This process of facilitating article supply over subscriptions is itself dangerous. Many libraries are moving from a holdings strategy to providing access to items, from a 'just in case' collection development procedure to a 'just in time'. The result is that there will be even fewer (underused) journal subscriptions on library shelves and a greater flood of individual article requests satisfied by the many new so-called CAS-IAS services (Current Alerting Service combined with Individual Article Supply).

This new-found revenue source needs to be treated with some circumspection. Within the UK the number of physical loans compared with ILL (inter-library loans) is greatly in favour of the former. The Follett Review found that there were 12 465 097 physical loans (97.1%) and 368 645 interlibrary loans and docdel (document delivery) (2.9%).

It is estimated that the world demand for scholarly articles through interlibrary loan and formal document delivery, i. e. excluding loans, is about 48 million items. Both these processes involve inexpensive delivery of items, and with interlibrary loans it is allegedly (though not in practice) free. In either case the original publisher gets no additional revenues from the use of the printed article. The new electronic document delivery services charge a price which includes the service element of providing a comprehensive database of newly published articles from which to select and a delivery mechanism which can provide a selected article to the researcher within 24 hours (or if held as an electronic image/file, within two hours). These CAS-IAS services also pay a royalty to publishers, usually the rate listed with the national reprographic rights organizations (Copyright Clearance Center in the USA, and the Copyright Licensing Agency in the UK). On average such listed royalty rates amount to $4–5 per article. But the numbers of transactions (requests) remain very small, probably because the total price for an article ordered through such electronic delivery services exceeds $10. Certainly in academia, cost is a vital factor, more so than speed, though in the corporate area this may be less of a constraint. Nevertheless, total numbers using electronic document delivery are less than 1% of the combined ILL/ formal document delivery totals.

Payment for research items by credit card over the networks in support of document orders has been a heralded new departure but is one which is still unproven. One of the leading electronic document delivery services (UnCover) quotes that 30–40% of their article orders are being paid for by credit card. Is this new money, or merely money loaned by the departmental office of a central library? It is still too early to tell, and at present it does not make much difference to publishers.

Other revenues may emerge for those publishers able and willing to sell their header files to CAS-IAS services, abstracting and indexing (A&I) services and directly into the Campus Wide Information Services (CWIS) of large US academic campuses. The returns from this will also not make much of a dent in the growing 'revenue gap' from declining subscription sales. All econometric models that have been put forward in this area (and there are not that many) indicate that the royalty rates to publishers will need to be in the order of $20 per article for publishers to retain a constant revenue income. This is in total conflict with the acceptable price level which end-users will be willing to pay.

SOME LEADING PROJECTS

So the question then becomes whether the new electronic information services are capable of taking over the functionality — and more critically the dimensions of the problems — facing journal publishers. It is suggested that time is running out for the esoteric specialized journal; however, is the time ripe for the new electronic journal to take off? And if so, does the traditional journal publisher have a distinctive role to play in the new scenario?

There is no doubt that there has been remarkable activity in the development of new electronic journals in the USA within the past 12 months. A great deal of attention has been focused on the 'Red Sage' project, an experiment conducted by AT&T, Springer-Verlag and the University of California at San Francisco. This offers individuals on campus access to the images of leading biomedical journals, ranging through the front cover, to contents pages, to individual articles. Searching is through the RightPages software developed in-house by AT&T, but essentially it is a browsing process. TULIP (The University Licensing Program) is a similar project undertaken by Elsevier in the area of material sciences and involves transmitting the images and a dirty ASCII file of 43 journals through the Internet to nine separate campuses in the USA. Each campus has its own search tool. This project will be completed in three years time.

OCLC Inc., through its connection to 17 000 libraries worldwide, has launched its own programme of OCLC Journals Online. Despite a shaky start with its first offering — *The Journal of Online Current Clinical Trials*, which had great difficulty soliciting manuscripts for a project which ostensibly gave no accreditation to the author — two more have recently been launched and a further two are in the pipeline. All run under the Guidon software developed in-house, which also relied on the experiences gained by OCLC in its partnership in the CORE (Chemical Journals Online) at Cornell University.

The *ARL Directory* lists over 40 other electronic journals, most of them in the humanities. Even though more are being announced almost daily, they do not total a great number, and certainly not sufficient to absorb the research material which may become available through the demise of many esoteric printed journals. Also many of these electronic journals — Red Sage, TULIP — are essentially experimental in nature. There is still a long way to go before they are sufficiently robust to serve the international scholarly community.

Some of the other projects which are in an experimental phase include:

- Project MUSE (John Hopkins),
- JANUS (Columbia),
- University of California's 19th Century Literature,
- *New York Journal of Mathematics,*
- *Chicago Journal of Theoretical Computer Science* (MIT),
- *Nuclear Physics Electronic* (Elsevier).

Others are more established, including:

- Gutenberg, Illinois,
- Ginsparg's Preprint service in physics.

The authors within the scholarly community have two main demands from an information service. One is communication; the other is to obtain credits and recognition. So far the funding organizations have given little support to the electronic journals by putting them on a par with the printed journal in terms of recognition for funding purposes. Whilst citation factors (based on number of references to an article or a journal made in any year, and collated by ISI in Philadelphia) remain the sole bibliometric measure used to judge an article's 'real worth', electronic journals will remain a fringe activity in most of the core disciplines. The Follett Review did address this issue by suggesting that consideration should be given in future to publications in electronic journals as having equal weight with printed ones in deciding over fund allocations.

THE NETWORKS

While the above debates carry on, there is a remarkable industry burgeoning on the networks, notably the Internet, which enables researchers to communicate, using e-mail, to deliver large amounts of data, using file transfer protocols (ftp) and to search remote databases for relevant information (Gopher). Within the past few years the numbers of users of these systems have grown to an estimated 20 million worldwide.

Figures are difficult to come by, however, but usages of the software interfaces which allow researchers to scan the universe of files accessible via the Internet have been shown to be escalating. During the past year there has been a 997% growth in the use of the Gopher interface, and the World Wide Web has mushroomed by 341 634%! Nearly two million Internet host services are listed. The rate of such usage can only increase in the next few months as the $100 'Internet in a Box' becomes available to everyone.

These network services have the value of being free at the point of usage. Commercialism is frowned upon. The Internet is essentially a playground for the enthusiast. People communicate in a style and method which is alien to the formal systems operating in the printed publication world. Yet there is a growing overlap. Some of the bulletin boards which have been created in specific subject areas by these enthusiasts (categorized as the Network Nerds in a recent British Library Research presentation by Michael Lesk) are akin to the early letters which were a precursor to scientific journals. Some bulletin boards have elected 'moderators' who perform the functions of an editor. Information is e-mailed to the moderator and he/she, with his/her online referees, decides which items are suitable for 'publication' on the bulletin board over the network. The procedures are uncannily similar, if much faster, than traditional printed publishing, and there is no charge for membership or participation.

This creates a problem for the existing players in journal publishing. How can they participate in this amorphous, uncontrolled information system which has emerged by osmosis from the traditional systems? There are some powerful supporters of the trend to network information systems, not least within the White House, but more specifically within the larger research libraries in the USA. Stung into action by the 'price spiral' of printed journals described above, many leading librarians are staunch advocates in favour of either the learned societies or the library itself taking an increasing role in electronic publishing.

Either way, the problems for publishers mount. Even if they are able to exert some of their influence on the network information systems, how can they earn money from what is perceived as a free public good? Even if purchasable files can be pointed to from a free catalogue of available titles on the Internet, can the price algorithm which would be set recompense publishers for the outlay which they have incurred? There is as yet no answer to these questions, and the amount of experimentation which existing players are indulging in to find answers is lamentably limited.

ELECTRONIC DOCUMENT DELIVERY

It has already been pointed out that electronic document delivery does not bring in the revenues which publishers need to support the subscription revenues. Far from it; it can be claimed (though not proven) that electronic document delivery is a parasite on the mother journal, draining out its life blood with every cancelled subscription it facilitates.

It is interesting that publishers have woken up to the challenges in this area and are establishing consortia to address the problem in a concerted way. ADONIS is perhaps the archetype, but ADONIS only deals with 400–500 biomedical journals, and is largely targeted at the pharmaceutical industry. OASIS (Original Articles in Sciences Information Service) is a new grouping of up to 20 publishers in Europe attempting to establish a role for themselves in document delivery as a prime supplier rather than as an agent for intermediaries (such as A&I and CAS-IAS services). Legal issues prevent too close a dialogue between these publishers, particularly if they are owned by American parent companies where the fear of antitrust legislation is powerful.

The importance of electronic document delivery is however transient in nature. It will flourish and grow in the mid- to late 1990s, as libraries are increasingly forced into the 'access' mode of acquisitions, but will decline as and when the network and electronic journal publishing systems mature and become widely adopted.

Electronic document delivery is also important in that it points the way to 'on-demand' publishing as being the way of the future, rather than packaging a great deal of material within a book or journal, most of which is never consulted. Buying information as and when needed is a logical extension of the changed library management policies. Even though this has a consequence on the amount of material which publishers can charge for and the price per unit at a time when pricing policies are being looked at critically.

STRUCTURE OF THE INDUSTRY

There are some crucial decisions which publishers need to make given the changing market and technologies. How are they coping? Despite the small number of cooperative projects referred to above (Red Sage, ADONIS, OASIS), each publisher is essentially on its own in framing an appropriate reaction. The general feeling is that the ostrich mentality thrives: that it is hoped that the impending events will go away, that the hype being given to electronic publishing will go the same way as the microform challenge in the 1960s.

Trade associations, such as the UK Publishers Association, the American Association of Publishers and the international association of STM publishers, are more focused on the copyright protection issues than on developing a long-term business scenario which will allow an easy and profitable migration from the printed world to the electronic. This is not to denigrate such important legal issues, but with the development of a new economic and ownership model in the USA being considered by the Research Library Network (TRLN) and by the Coalition for Network Information (CNI) among others, the traditional ideas of ownership may be rendered out of date by the new electronic paradigms. There seems to be increasing faculty support for such initiatives and, given that the leading asset which publishers have is their link to authors, this is worrying.

In the meantime, such essential tools as the creation of in-house SGML (Standard Generalized Mark-up Language) Document Type Definitions, a precursor to any electronic information delivery system, is left to the individual publisher. Adobe's Acrobat and similar are being tested by a few enlightened publishers as a competitive advantage rather than by the industry as protective salvation.

One of the main problems the scholarly publishing industry faces in coming to terms with the electronic publishing challenges is its fragmentation. There are thousands of journal publishers worldwide with only a few having the size and resources with which to invest in

Table 17.2 Fragmentation of publishing

	Number of publishers	Number of titles
Worldwide (excluding the UK) Publishers with a turnover in excess of £50 000	51	2 854
Publishers with turnover of less than £50 000 but more than £5000	781	2 996
Publishers with a turnover of less than £5000	11 232	16 057
Total	**12 064**	**21 907**
The UK Publishers with a turnover in excess of £50 000	66	4 232
Publishers with turnover of less than £50 000 but more than £5000	206	1 051
Publishers with a turnover of less than £5000	5 195	7 643
Total	**5 467**	**12 926**

new product development. Elsevier, with 1100 journal titles, Springer (280) and Wiley (250) are exceptions. The typical journal publisher is one with a small stable of four to five titles, run from inexpensive offices, with little overhead, and a one-year budget rather than five-year strategy horizon. Table 17.2 is the structure of journal publishing as seen from one of the leading international subscription agencies (B H Blackwell) in 1993. It would be an impossible task to get these publishers round a table, and even more impossible to get them to agree on a common approach to some generic problems facing the industry.

CONCLUSION AND RECOMMENDATIONS

How many years are there left in printed journal publishing? More to the point, is there a magic pill which will provide solutions to the many problems facing existing research journal publishers?

The existing journal publishers who continue to focus on the printed edition, without investing in future systems (either SGML or in experimental electronic journals) may become the dinosaurs of the information economy. The 1990s show all the signs of a volatile market and it requires a new approach to migrate from the present needs to satisfying anticipated future electronic demands for scholarly information.

Yet the migration path does not appear to be an easy one. There are many directions which it could take. The electronic journal, electronic document delivery and the network environment have been commented on above, but the optical publishing sector may also offer a potential release valve to present-day market tensions. This is particularly the case with books, as explored in-depth in the report by Dr Thomas Laukamm on behalf of the EC[7]. The technical understanding, project management skills and subsequent customer support requirements are totally different from that to which they are accustomed, compared to all the new media technologies' demands.

The key factor is what the market wants. There are precious few investigations as to how researchers will change their habits on information acquisition. The Royal Society conducted a survey of 4000 researchers which came up with an interesting picture of how and why researchers gather their raw data. Similar work has been completed in the past by Almquist in the USA for the Faxon Institute, but, given the severity of the problems which beset the journal publishing system, it is remarkable, and a strong indictment, that so little of the business' total resources have been invested in market research. The dynamics of information acquisition is something which can no longer be left to chance. It is up to publishers to take the challenges of the electronic information business seriously and become professional in their approach to planning for a migration in their product portfolio. Those who do this may make the financially painful transition to publishing into the next millennium. Those who do not face extinction.

ACKNOWLEDGEMENTS

The arguments advanced in this review have been derived from a number of different studies commissioned by the British Library Research and Development Department in the past. Grateful acknowledgement is given to the BL for this support, particularly to Brian Perry and Dr Terry Cannon. However, the BL is not responsible for the way these arguments have been put together; the responsibility for this and the interpretations made lies squarely with DJB Associates.

REFERENCES

1   *Joint Funding Councils' Libraries Review Group: Report* Higher Education Funding Council, UK (1993)
2   *The STM Information System in the UK* The Royal Society, The British Library and The Association of Learned and Professional Society Publishers, UK (1993)
3   'British Library Working Party on electronic publishing' *Serials* Vol 7 No 1 (1994) pp 9–10
4   *World Science Report 1993*, UNESCO Publishing (1993)
5   **East, H and Tilson, Y** *The Liberated Enduser: Developments in Practice and Policy for database Provision to the Academic Community* (1993)
6   **Oakeshott, P** *Trends in Journal Subscriptions 1992* The Publishers Association (1994)

7　**Laukamm, T** *Strategic Study on New Opportunities for Publishers in the Information Services Market* EC No 14926 EN (Feb 1993)

18
Electronic publishing in French national museums

Alain Le Bourvellec and Joël Poix, Réunion des Musées Nationaux, France

France has been experiencing a renewed strong development of its cultural life over the last ten years as indicated by a noticeable growth of regional and government grants for the arts.

The French museums have enjoyed a blossoming of public interest in Paris (Grand Louvre, Musée d'Orsay etc.) and in the provinces (Lyon, Lille, Caen, Grenoble, Saint-Etienne, Strasbourg). At present they are greeting 70 million visitors per year.

During this period the Ministry of Culture has created many databases on museum collections (paintings, drawings, sculptures, antiquities), National Heritage buildings, archaeological sites and libraries. Today four databases are online through Minitel: Joconde (paintings and drawings); Arcade (archives of the works of art bought by the French state in the 19th and 20th centuries); Ethnophoto (collections of photographs belonging to the Musée National d'Arts Populaires, Paris); Mérimée (National Heritage buildings).

These databases did not include images and, mainly for this reason, French museums are planning new developments. For example, the Grand Louvre is seeking to digitize its collection — more than two hundred thousand works of art — with the financial, technical and commercial support of the Réunion des Musées Nationaux and

Alain Le Bourvellec is Director of the Department of Research and Development, and Joël Poix is Head of Audiovisual and Multimedia Publishing at the Réunion des Musées Nationaux in Paris.

the help of private grants. The Musée d'Orsay is involved in a project in which a new database and a communication network with other European museums are being developed. A number of modern art museums have joined Videomuseum to digitize more than a hundred thousand works of art.

The Réunion des Musées Nationaux, as an industrial and commercial public office of the Ministry of Culture, is playing the role of inviting museum visitors, organizing exhibitions and purchasing works of art for the national museums with the income received. The Réunion des Musées Nationaux (RMN) is also the publisher for the French museums. Our editorial policy closely reflects the temporary exhibitions and permanent collections of these museums. The editorial scope of the RMN is confirmed by the more than 160 publications it made available during 1993 with an income of nearly 400 million French francs. These works are designed for the general public and their growing success is due in large part to the magnitude and quality of the temporary exhibitions organized by the RMN.

The publication and distribution of scientific research-based scholarly works complete our public-service mission. These are also showing a strong growth of sales fuelled by our descriptive catalogues of major permanent collections.

An increasing number of both catalogues and original works are being published jointly with companies in France and abroad. In addition, publications for young people are being successfully developed with such series as *Chercheurs d'Art* (Discovering Art) published in cooperation with the cultural department of the Louvre Museum.

The RMN multimedia policy must:

- offer programmes which appeal to specific audiences (general public, young people, educators, scientists),
- adjust to the new technical, legal, financial and marketing constraints inherent in the new technology,
- anticipate and serve the demands of our partners, the French national (and in some case regional) museums and adjust to new methods of disseminating information via information-carrying media and communications networks,
- support the production of multimedia projects based on European culture,

- encourage the emergence of fresh talent in the fields of programming, visual arts, design and scriptwriting among people who are familiar with the new information-carrying media and also have a strong cultural background.

When we consider the levels of investment required and the commercial and marketing constraints involved in distribution, we realize we must concentrate on programmes for which joint production and/or publishing agreements can be concluded in cooperation with partners from France and abroad.

The major guidelines underlying our production strategy for the coming two years are as follows. Most of our multimedia programmes on optical storage media will be produced on CD-ROM for Mac and PC:

- museum art tours,
- great moments of the past,
- young children's collection (art history programmes; discovering painting, sculpture, civilization, famous men and women),
- great historical figures,
- great exhibitions,
- art dictionaries,
- CD-ROM scientific catalogues,
- Photo-CD archives.

We are also aware that electronic publishing is drastically changing the way of designing and printing artbooks. Today it is not only possible to reuse the digitized illustrations of a title in another book or in movies, videos and multimedia but also to manage new methods of knowledge in art. That is the main point.

EP facilitators: telecoms, resource providers, hardware and software suppliers. Telecoms — case studies

19

Broadband — liberating the publishing marketplace

John Cowen, David Greenop, Trevor Johnson, Ian Pearson –
British Telecom, UK

INTRODUCTION

Imagine what it would be like if electricity were provided in the same way as telecommunications? Having just brought a new microwave oven home, you now have to ring up the electricity board and ask for a connection. It must provide 8 amps at 240 volts and 50 Hz AC in two-second bursts every 10 seconds. The electricity company say they can deliver in a few days. Imagine you have to do this for every electrical appliance you buy. It would be a nightmare!

Telecoms must become as easy to access, as easy to use and as much a part of the background as electricity. The infosphere is all about creating this transparency, removing the barriers to information flow, and liberating both the information provider and the user. Figure 19.1 shows how information fits into every area of life, showing similarities between the information cycle and the water cycle. People use information at work and at play, both as a tool and as an end in itself. The publisher's role in gathering, processing and selling information is pivotal. As the figure also shows, those people who do

John Cowen is Media Market Manager for British Telecom and works at BT headquarters in London. David Greenop is Manager of Strategic Network Vision, BT Worldwide Networks. Trevor Johnson is Senior Network Strategist, BT Worldwide Networks. Ian Pearson is Information Technologist-Advanced Applications & Technology, BT Laboratories.

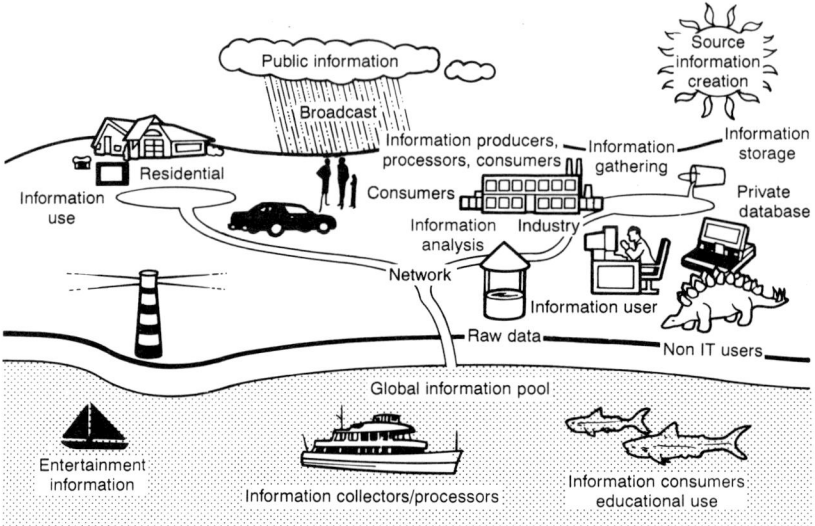

Figure 19.1 The information cycle

not make use of information technology (IT) in some way are rapidly becoming extinct. There will be no Jurassic Park for them either.

This chapter puts a long-term perspective on the development of broadband networks. The broadband market is growing, as the use of information technology increases. The use of IT will increase in three ways: first, a wider range of business activities will benefit from using IT; second, business activities which already benefit from IT developments will increase their use of IT; third, with the growth in home computing, IT has started to penetrate the mass personal market in a significant way.

As we have seen with narrowband ISDN, it is not sufficient for public network operators (PNOs) just to provide a network. They have to demonstrate real benefits to the customers. From the customer's viewpoint these benefits are most likely to arise through the wide availability of suitable end-user applications. PNOs are unlikely to be in a position to provide all of these applications. There will be the need for far greater collaboration between PNOs and other parts of the IT industry. This will result in a clear information chain, as shown in Figure 19.2, with the customer at the centre. As informa-

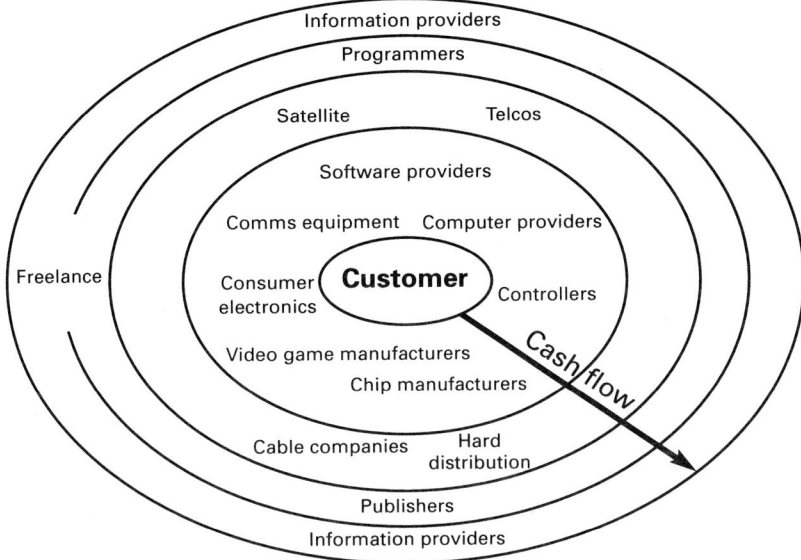

Figure 19.2 The customer and the information chain

tion flows in towards the customer, so revenue flows back to the information provider, with a slice being taken at each layer in between. In this environment the role of the publisher, while still key, is bound to change in response to the dynamics of the supply chain.

A broadband infrastructure is seen as a prerequisite to deliver information applications to the home as well as business. In several countries, cable operators are already providing a widespread distributive broadband infrastructure to deliver entertainment services. Eventually, this infrastructure will probably be upgraded for both-way broadband communications to support a wide range of information applications. This will be driven by the convergence of information, entertainment and communications industries. This is no longer a theory; it is now happening, as illustrated by recent developments in the USA involving the integration between telecommunication operators, cable operators and entertainment programme producers. By the year 2000, it will be impossible to see any clear boundaries between different parts of the IT industry. As we look into the next century, all of us will be making abundant use of processing and

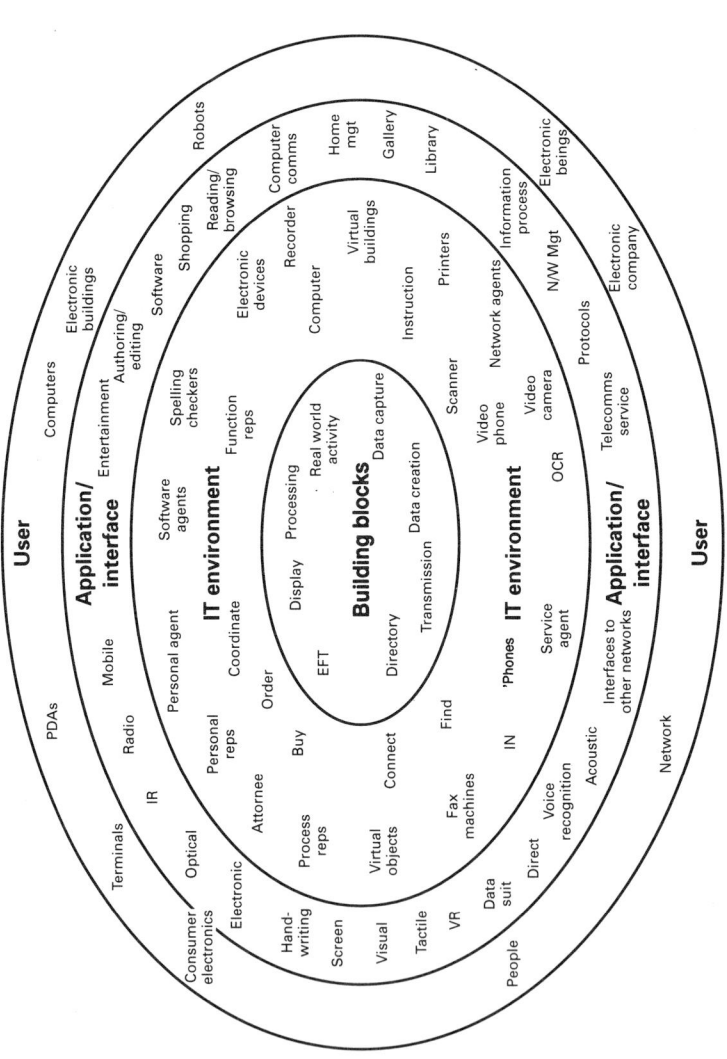

Figure 19.3 The infosphere

communications and we will come to appreciate the added value it brings to the world around us.

THE INFOSPHERE

The term *infosphere* is used to describe this future all-embracing information environment that we shall be living in. The infosphere, Figure 19.3, is an advanced distributed information processing and

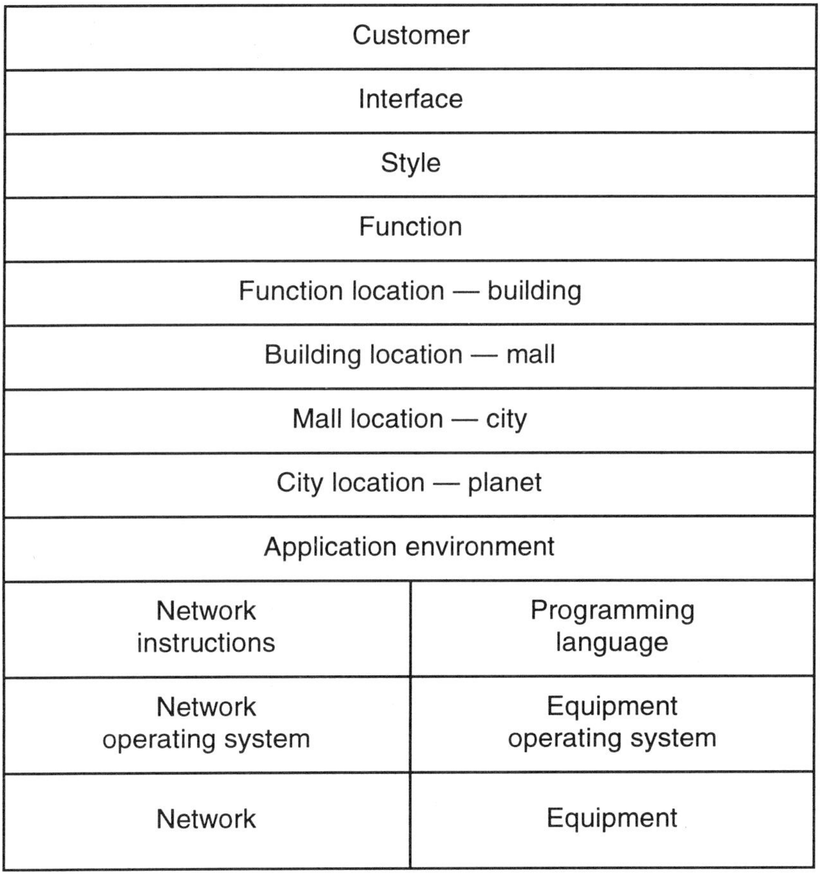

Customer	
Interface	
Style	
Function	
Function location — building	
Building location — mall	
Mall location — city	
City location — planet	
Application environment	
Network instructions	Programming language
Network operating system	Equipment operating system
Network	Equipment

Figure 19.4 A possible architecture for broadband communications

communication environment whose reach extends from the devices people use to access databases and computers situated anywhere on the globe, or beyond. Within the infosphere, the customer can capture, view, process, manipulate or transfer information. Access will be through multimedia interfaces and devices like the new generation of mobile personal computer communicators (PCCs). Intuitive interfaces to sophisticated applications will enable anyone to do anything, anywhere, at any time. These interfaces will follow a layered architecture to allow similar functionality levels to be grouped. A possible architecture is shown in Figure 19.4, and it is clear that there are market opportunities at each layer. The network infrastructure supporting it will have to supply unconstrained bandwidth whether over fixed links or radio.

The layered architecture is best described by example. A customer preferring modern architecture may use a mouse (interface) to browse a modern looking (style) electronic library (Figure 19.5). The library would provide many functions (function layer) such as downloads, all specific to this library (building). The user might find the library in the midst of many other buildings in a common theme (libraries,

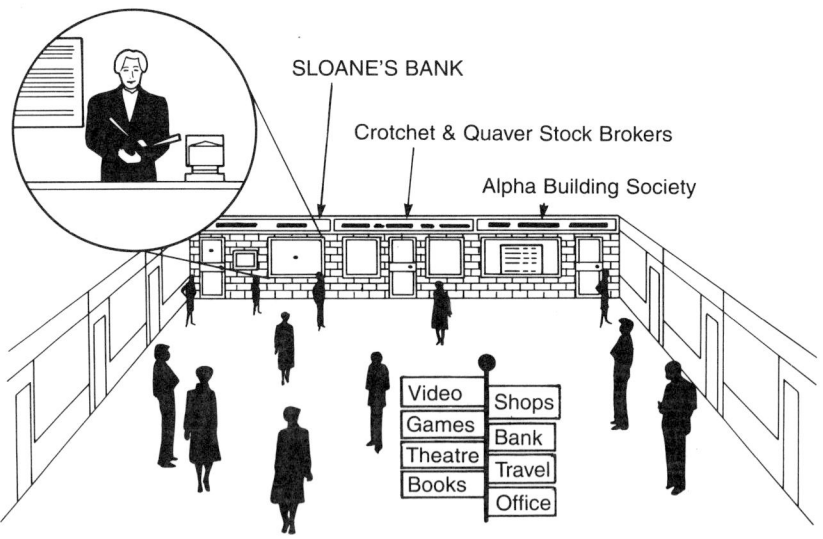

Figure 19.5 The electronic library

book shops, art galleries etc.) (mall layer) and extra functions appropriate to this group may be provided (e.g. subject searches, or appropriate mall decor). There would be many malls with different themes (finance, travel, games etc.), all grouped together by a service provider in a city layer. The planet layer provides an interface to cities available via any service provider (BT, AT&T, Sony, Microsoft etc.). An application environment provides the languages to build these worlds using a combination of computing and network functions. These languages contain network and computing instructions (language), which run over network or equipment operating systems on the network and processing equipment.

THE MARKET

The demand for broadband is increasing for both the business and residential markets. Many households already have access to broadband cable television networks, which are now starting to offer telephony. Businesses want higher-speed data services to transfer information between sites. Major businesses are no longer content with their home markets, but are thinking globally and becoming multinational. Consequently, advanced communications are essential to these companies.

Those industries with widely distributed operations, including conventional publishing, are more and more dependent on telecommunications, reflecting the interdependencies between suppliers and customers. As a result, new telecommunications links and networks are becoming established; perhaps the best example in a publishing context is the rapid emergence in the UK of ISDN as a cost-effective image-file-transfer network for the graphic arts industry. However, for rapid transfer of large volumes of image-rich material, and certainly for multimedia files, much more powerful networks will be required and are made available. A range of actual and potential broadband applications — and their bandwidth implications — is illustrated in Figure 19.6.

Many UK service industries are becoming reliant on telecommunications to provide services, such as databases, directly to their customers. Most of today's tele-services, however, are based on telephony. Publishers and other industries, such as the mail order industry, want to link electronically with their customers, which has

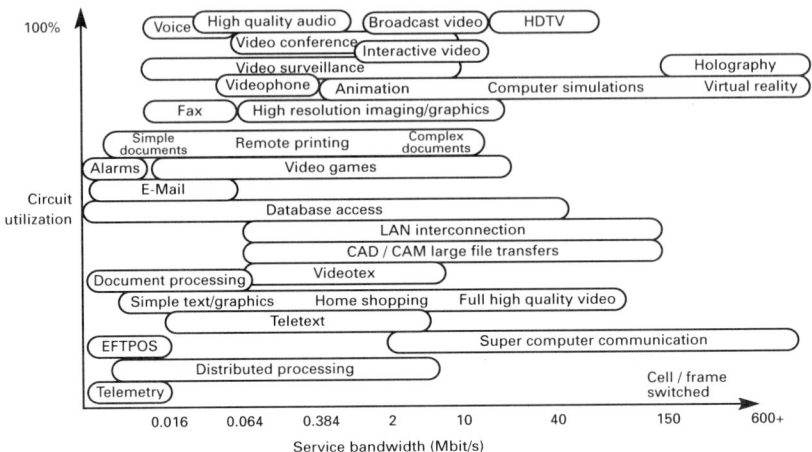

Figure 19.6 The broadband spectrum and its potential applications

obvious benefits. This is a significant trend considering the developments in personal computing.

As business-to-business applications become more commonplace, people will want the same facilities at home as they have at work. For example, they will need to have access to the same computer programs and databases and want to discuss their work with their colleagues 'face to face' over video links. For those with increasing leisure time, new entertainment and educational opportunities will become available. Today people read books and magazines, watch videos, use shopping catalogues, play computer and electronic games, and undertake leisure education or learn new skills, all in the comfort of their home. In the future all of this will be accessed electronically in real time without the need to prebook, providing choice and flexibility. The number and range of services will continue to grow, as users become familiar with the new opportunities provided and make available their own applications over the network.

Marketplaces will change fundamentally as a result of new communications capabilities. Using publishing as an example, we will see increased freelance activity, because individuals are able to access greater processing power to produce higher-quality products. At the same time they will occasionally bypass traditional distribution channels, making their products and services directly accessible to customers. New business opportunities will result for directory providers, who will put customers directly in touch with suppliers, creatively using virtual environments. These directory services will gradually grow in sophistication to incorporate natural interfaces, allowing easier selling and shopping around. Many additional facilities, such as language translation and electronic funds transfer, could be introduced as further revenue-generating enhancements.

As people move away from their families and friends, they will keep in contact using video-conferencing, play games together or order birthday presents from their relative's local shop. Mass-market electronic mail and fax will displace conventional mail and paper administration. Multimedia databases will revolutionize libraries, which may in the short term become places where people can go and access the new information applications. We can expect to see virtual shopping centres which will give customers a greater choice and convenience. Importantly from the ecological point of view, we will see an accelerating displacement of travel by high-quality video communications.

THE ROLE OF ADVERTISING IN THE FUTURE

There is much speculation as to the place of advertising in an all-electronic media environment and its future prospects as a valuable source of income to the publisher. Some commentators argue that advertising will inevitably decline in importance, given the consumer's ability — and, it is expected, probable inclination — to 'zap' any advertisements seen as presenting nothing more than an unwelcome intrusion during an online session.

Some pragmatists argue for a two-tier pricing system, where those users wishing to receive no advertising during an online session can choose to pay a premium over normal rates. While there may be some disagreement on the value of advertising in electronic media, most pundits foresee plentiful opportunities for sponsorship or even for electronic product placement, as is currently the case with some video games.

Advertising on demand?

However, all this is to take perhaps an unduly pessimistic view of the value added potential of advertising that is well executed and accurately targeted. It is not difficult to postulate an electronic media environment where consumers and business users alike would find themselves presented with advertising which matches their interests and needs so closely that they would positively welcome its addition to paid-for programme material. Such a situation would be of immense benefit to both the advertising agencies and their clients: the agency would achieve a far better reach among the target audience and the advertiser would have the means of measuring precisely the access and response rates achieved. Wastage through delivering expensive advertising to the wrong audience would reduce dramatically and the costs saved could be employed in deepening the dialogue with target prospects e.g. a car advertisement could offer the seriously interested enquirer far more detail online, well beyond the capacity of the traditional double-page spread, ranging from an extended video right through to a virtual reality test drive! Advertisers of all types would be presented with the ultimate measure of their agency's success, through monitoring the levels of on-screen ordering — and payment!

The possibilities for estate agencies and holiday companies advertising in an interactive multimedia environment are self-evident. However, this type of advertising would be driven entirely by the user's own personal profile of interests and preferences, and his or her previous information-seeking and purchasing behaviour. Clearly, safeguards would be needed to protect individual privacy and respect changing preferences; advertising in this new environment will work best when the individual feels a sense of control of his or her own personal infosphere.

Opportunities for advertisers and marketers are immense. For the first time it will be possible to obtain lists of consumers showing vast volumes of personal, lifestyle and purchasing data for *each* individual. The relationship between advertiser and audience, between designer, manufacturer, supplier, service agent and individual customer will change dramatically. The potential will soon exist for this relationship to become totally interactive, but the extent of such interactivity in practice will always need to be subject to individual consumer preference and control.

The coming explosion in electronic media channels will bring its own problems for advertising agency media departments, requiring a new kind of relationship with an ever-growing variety of new media owners. Planners will be demanding highly sophisticated decision support systems to ensure that the inevitably more costly multimedia advertisements are delivered only to those individuals who will be most likely to respond.

NETWORK IMPLICATIONS

The impact for telecoms network providers remains to be quantified. However, it is clear that if interactive multimedia advertising becomes successful, there will be yet further heavy demands on the network infrastructure to cope with large volumes of high-bandwidth, instantaneous, image-rich advertising and transactional traffic which will not have existed previously, in *any* form. Such uncertainty argues for a delivery network capable of serving both business and domestic markets with flexibility, and with significant capacity in reserve. Current technological trends imply that such a network must necessarily be provided in optical fibre.

Obviously, the current rate of development in information technology has profound implications for the telecoms network. Figure 19.7 shows how both processing speeds and memory chip capacities are increasing logarithmically, with no sign of slowing down in the foreseeable future. This will have an enormous effect on the intelligence and storage capability of future equipment, in the office and the home. Increased processing, among other effects, allows high-speed data compression, making multimedia applications possible over narrowband networks. This will both stimulate calls on current networks and reduce the amount of traffic per call. In the longer term, owing to the vast number of potential future services, any remaining debate over the need for increased bandwidth will almost certainly tip in favour of the broadband network. Many of these new services and applications will have very different network performance requirements from those currently provided, and the new broadband network must be designed in such a way as to offer a rapid and flexible response to new services and applications.

Multiservice networks, which can handle both high- and low-speed applications, are needed to meet all the customers' requirements. They will handle everything from constant-bit-rate services, like voice and video, to bursty variable-bit-rate services, such as electronic encyclopaedia access. Although compression techniques will reduce bandwidth requirements, gigabyte backbone networks

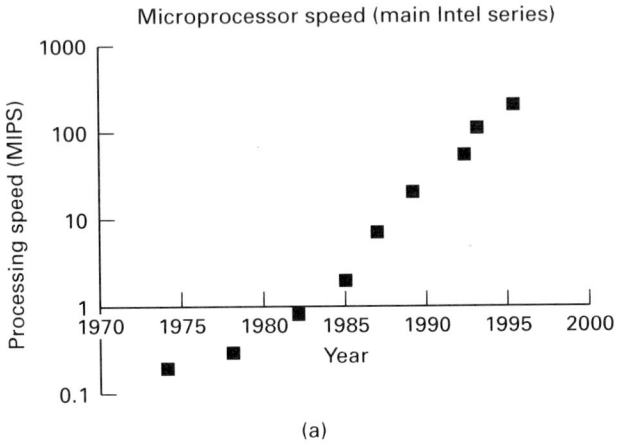

(a)

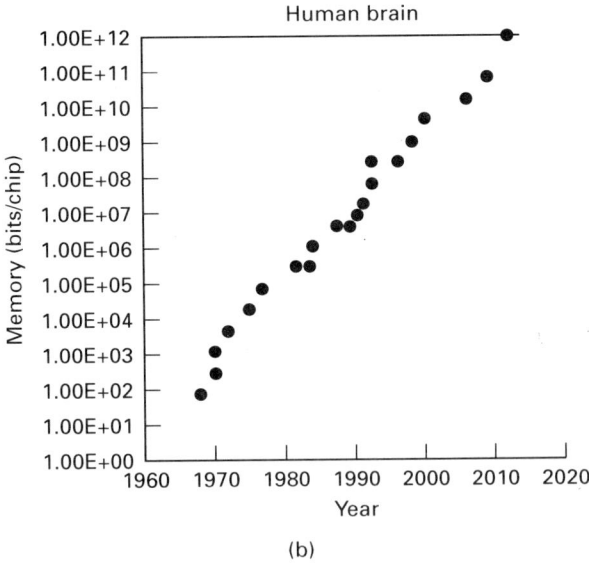

(b)

Figure 19.7 Increases in (a) processing speed and (b) memory

are still needed. The system will be user friendly, with good directory systems and open interface standards to allow inter-working and compatibility between products. Access to the infosphere will be via either fixed links or a short free-space link. We can expect megabit per second free-space links to support portable multimedia terminals, giving users mobility and flexibility. The majority of users will continue to use the fixed network, provided higher-bandwidths are made available. Both office and home will eventually have a fixed optical connection to allow higher-bandwidth delivery of multimedia applications, including video on demand and high-definition TV. Multi-megabit capability will be required for pseudo-independent access of several home appliances. The customer will expect suitable performance criteria, e.g. low delays for applications such as video games and video shopping, and will become accustomed to the new facilities offered via telecommunications.

MOVING FORWARD

New techniques like Synchronous Digital Hierarchy (SDH) and Asynchronous Transfer Mode (ATM) allow voice, data and video traffic to be transported easily over the same network at a variety of speeds. Technologies such as passive optical networks, see Figure 19.8, are maturing rapidly to enable both-way broadband delivery

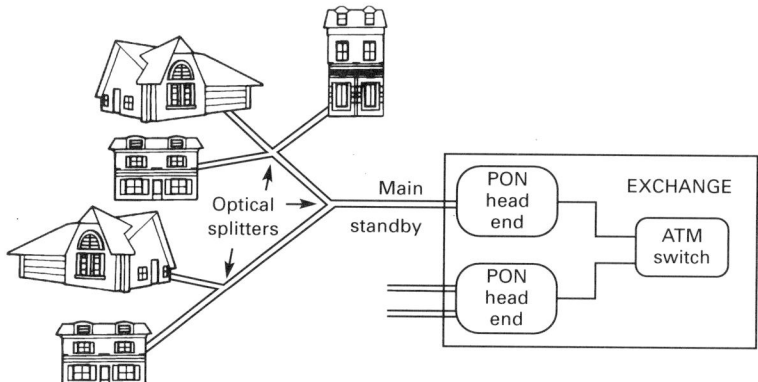

Figure 19.8 New technologies and the customer

capabilities down to the customer. These will be a good platform on which to offer the future services and will work well with the infosphere. Advances in computer programming, such as client/server architecture, encourage distributed computing, while *de facto* industry standards allow data to be transferred between applications. Without these, users would remain constrained despite having a broadband infrastructure.

Many broadband switching trials are taking place or being planned around the world. Most trials are concentrating on cell-based switching technologies such as ATM. Partners in the European Union RACE (Research and Development in Advanced Communications in Europe) programme are developing the technology, user awareness and applications for broadband communications. The partners and users are exploring the development of implementation strategies for integrated broadband communications (IBC) systems, services and applications using advanced communication technologies. Importantly, they are establishing common functional specifications and validation of standards.

A European inter-country ATM pilot is planned for June 1994. The object of this trial is to prove that the various ATM standards are implementable and that different implementations can interwork. At present, 15 public network operators have agreed to participate in the trial. In the UK, BT is following a similar approach to North America by providing both Frame Relay and Switched Multimegabit Data Service (SMDS) to customers. The Frame Relay service provides access speeds of up to 2 Mbit/s as part of BT's Global Network Services (GNS). After a successful trial with the University of London and a successful pilot as part of the SuperJANET contract, BT has now launched an SMDS service, making available high-speed data transmission at sub- 2Mbit/s, 4, 10, 16, and 25Mbits.

LOOKING TO THE FUTURE

Technology is only a component part necessary to make the infosphere a reality. As Figure 19.9 shows, it is necessary for manufacturers to make equipment, network operators to implement it, service providers to provide applications and users to use it. Importantly, there needs to be a philosophy to make it happen. Governments and regulatory bodies are probably the only people who can provide the

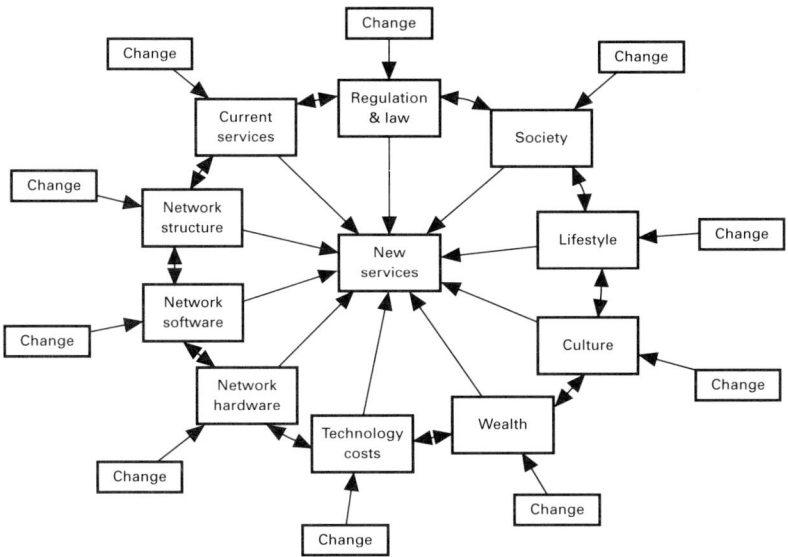

Figure 19.9 New services and new networks

environment to make the information revolution happen. Without this realization broadband is only likely to find a niche market, and its interoperation and integration into a universal environment — the infosphere — will not be achieved. The benefit of the infosphere is that it removes the boundaries between computing and telecommunications, allowing users to think about the task rather than its implementation. As a result the network and all its services will be closer to the user.

The infosphere will gradually grow in sophistication, eventually supporting a wide range of interfaces from simple 'phones to virtual reality and beyond, with the network making up for any lack of terminal intelligence to allow the user the fullest possible access. Service providers such as banks and publishers will build 'virtual buildings' in the environment which the user can then enter at will (Figure 19.10 illustrates the inside of a virtual library, one outlet in the mall of Figure 19.5). People and 'things' may be represented by icons; directories and gateways as doors; products which people buy appear as virtual representations of the real thing. Transactions in this environment could be electronic analogies of the real world.

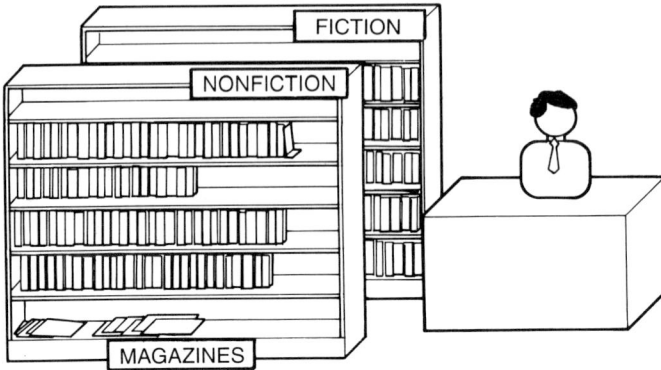

Figure 19.10 Inside the virtual library

Sending a fax may be as simple as picking up the virtual document and handing it to the virtual person. Mimicking the world that the user is already familiar with should help the user adjust to manipulating the electronic world. Although the look and feel of the infosphere may depend strongly on the interface available, the capability will be as full as possible wherever possible.

The infosphere will influence every aspect of our life. Business will benefit as operating costs will fall. Automatic integrated electronic systems will displace manual paper systems, as video displaces travel and as better and easier access to information results from the new environment. Costs due to errors and lost invoices will drop, as will staff costs and those resulting from incompatible computer systems. The individual will benefit. People will be able to remain in touch wherever they are, if they want; not just in touch with people, but with shops, banks, libraries, work, home, in fact anyone or anything connected to the infosphere. Universal interface styles will mean not having to remember complex and archaic alphanumeric sequences. Broadband to the home will have to support low delays for information retrieval, use of different services in every room, with instant access to any of a multitude of services regardless of bandwidth requirements.

It is clear that the shopping-mall-type interface fits well with the layered architecture (which is only one possible approach). There will undoubtedly be competition to provide each of the layers — with software and hardware providers from computing, telecoms and consumer electronics all side by side in this new market. While some layers fall naturally into existing technology areas, the layers between 'interface' and 'application environment' are new territories. Many of the opportunities here will be fair game for electronic publishers.

For the network providers, the infosphere concept will mean new ways of operating. Being just one company among many, with only a subset of the skills needed, will mean alliance with other companies, even competitors. These alliances may sometimes exist for only a short time or for a specific product. It will mean cooperation on many fronts to avoid ruining the potential markets for everyone by incompatible products. It will mean opening access to other service providers and providing the platforms on which they can build their services. Service providers must be free to offer their own look and feel, but they will certainly be under market economic pressure to conform to the general philosophy.

It can be expected that the infosphere will become universal and global, with infosphere intelligence bridging the gaps between regions of differing sophistication, so that services are interpreted appropriately. Only when it is truly global will it achieve its maximum potential by really making the world a smaller place.

It is worth mentioning here that many of the services envisioned for the infosphere exist in embryonic form already on the Internet. Some electronic shopping malls already exist, though their capabilities are still crude, response times are slow for most users and graphic interfaces are just beginning to develop. Network-based electronic publishing of books, music, art and other forms of human expression is developing rapidly. Already tens of millions of users can access these services from anywhere in the world.

PROSPECTS

The information technology areas of telecoms, computing and consumer electronics have been suffering from difficult market conditions for some time. Revenues and profits are showing signs of levelling and even falling in some areas. New markets are desperately needed. We believe that the concept of the infosphere provides the all-embracing framework within which a new marketplace will develop for the mass customization of information services and products.

IT companies are now learning that to compete aggressively and to go in different directions will frustrate their customers and result in a slowly growing market for their products. If, on the other hand, companies cooperate at least on achieving the infosphere, everyone will benefit. There will still be plenty of room for competition as now, but in a rapidly growing market. And, at last, an information and communications environment will have been created in which the electronic publisher will be able to flourish.

CONCLUSION

By widening our vision beyond the traditional view of broadband to encompass all the trends occurring in the computer and entertainment industries, we see an exciting future for telecommunication companies and their customers. There will be market pressure for broadband ubiquity from companies wishing to directly sell to their customer. Individual users will gain doubly, through greater flexibility and efficiency in business and advanced support for leisure activities. As new applications develop, particularly in the leisure industry, broadband and multi-service networks will gain social acceptance and become an indispensable part of our way of life.

The information revolution promised by the infosphere also has a 'dark side'. It may become open to abuse, with the threat of a 'big brother' and an invasion of personal privacy. There is likely to be a growth in services considered socially undesirable, yet policing these types of information movements will be virtually impossible. There are other social implications: already sources of information are being protected and access restricted to those who can afford to pay. Without a clear understanding of the implications of these developments, society in the future will consist of the information rich and poor. As with so much of human technological achievement, it is not the technology itself that is bad, rather the use to which we put it.

The biggest constraint on this vision is the cost; for broadband to take off it must be affordable. For the network operators this will mean some fundamental questioning over the role, purpose and structure of the network. A change in culture by governments, manufacturers, network operators and customers is required for the success of this vision. Partnerships will be the key word, particularly between network operators, consumer electronics manufacturers, software companies and information providers. The technology is available today. What is needed is the will to make the infosphere a reality, and hence to liberate the publishing marketplace.

20

EP applications and telecommunications — projects to stimulate the market and the actors

Volker Reible, DeTeBerkom, Germany

INTRODUCTION

The production process of printing products is characterized by a large number of activities that, in general, run at separate places and on different, dedicated systems. From this arises the requirement of appropriate networking of these systems, since the manufacturing process often has to meet strict deadlines, regardless of whether it is a journal, a magazine or a catalogue which is being processed. By connecting the traditional printing and publishing domain with new information and communications technologies, this field is undergoing far-reaching restructuring. The technical availability of broadband communication on the one hand and on the other hand a marked tendency towards open-systems platforms, i.e. the use of so-called 'general purpose' hardware and software and communication components enables a modification or even a new conception of the procedures. The activities considered cover conventional printing products as well as 'new media' (CD-i, video disc, etc.).

Volker Reible is Head of Telepublishing at DeTeBerkom GmbH in Berlin. This company is associated with Deutsche Telecom, the German national telecommunications operator.

DeTeBerkom is coordinating the following six publishing projects:

- *Telepublishing:* the Individualized Electronic Newspaper as proto-type for personalized information.
- *Bilus:* broadband-based prepress support for layout and repro-duction.
- *Didos:* services for technical documentation.
- *Corgi:* high-speed transfer of gravure printing data.
- *MediaPublishing:* development and application of an author/edi-tor tool for distributed multimedia document production.
- *Europublishing:* distributed editorial and prepress scenarios for reference work and magazine production.

As representative examples, the experiences and results from the Telepublishing and DIDOS projects will be described in detail.

TELEPUBLISHING PROJECT

The Telepublishing project was funded under the RACE programme, a R&D programme initiated by the EC. It is an important pilot and demonstration project for the European publishing and printing in-dustries. Since the printing and publishing industries are preparing their future distributed activities now, transnational communication in the preparation of production phases is even more important than before. For these reasons the question of the cost benefit of commu-nication links for production of multimedia products like magazines or newspapers, books or catalogues is of high interest to them.

Sixteen contractors from five EU countries under the direction of DeTeBerkom were effectively contributing to the Telepublishing project with the realization of two Application Pilots. These pilots were:

- *Application Pilot 1:* Individualized Electronic Newspaper (IEN).
- *Application Pilot 2:* Catalogue Production.

Application Pilot 1: Individualized Electronic Newspaper (IEN)

Introduction
The Individualized Electronic Newspaper (IEN) is a new publishing product, delivered and produced in a distributed environment using advanced information and communication technologies. The application pilot involves both the preparation and the use of the product.

The work in the first project phase was characterized by discussion of product and user scenarios, as well as prototyping the main components for IEN production. The results have been brought together in various reports and resulted in requirement definitions and realizations of system components such as a Structured Document Base (SDB) and an automatically working layout system with integration of visual information for printed IEN issues.

During the last project year the partners have been working on further developments and on the integration of IEN system components, which were also demonstrated when the opportunity arose for interested people inside and outside the RACE community. An example was the demonstration of the hypermedia IEN prototype at the Hypertext '91 conference in San Antonio, Texas, in December 1991. The paper version of the IEN has also been demonstrated on several occasions, e.g. the CeBIT Fair 1992 in Hannover. Responses to these and other demonstrations provided early feedback on the hypermedia and print IEN prototypes.

Final implementations and testing of all IEN components and their subsequent integration into a fully integrated IEN prototype turned out to be a more complex task than expected. The last months were therefore concentrated on the integration of the different components by means of the SDB and the Content Composer for assembling the contents of an IEN issue. Preparatory work for establishing the communication environment was also done.

The IEN Application Pilot was taking full advantage of the generic tools being developed within Telepublishing. In particular man-machine interface (MMI) kernel work, the authoring/editing tools, the tool for multilingual documents (Translator's Workbench) and the implementation of versioning mechanisms were being integrated into the IEN demonstrator.

The overall objectives of the project, the results achieved and the enhancements with respect to the original intentions are described in the following.

General objectives

The IEN is an experimental publication that seeks to exploit the potential of electronic delivery. Based on a profile describing his or her particular interests, a subscriber receives an individually composed newspaper. Depending on network availability, the subscriber's IEN may be delivered at home or at a kiosk. In addition to news items in the form of articles with images, and advertisements, the IEN can also enhance current newspaper functionality, e.g. by including databases of classified advertisements, or by enabling the publisher to offer extended news-related services. To take full advantage of the possibilities presented by electronic delivery, the subscriber may obtain IEN both in print and as a hypermedia product.

Earlier attempts at the electronic publication of news have suffered not only from the limitations of the available technology but also from the lack of additional editorial and compositional work invested in their preparation and production. In contrast to individualized fax delivery of single selected articles, the IEN emphasizes the newspaper's function and its image that must be reflected in appropriate layout and presentation. In contrast to the teletext-style news bulletin approach, adequate user interfaces can now be built nearly at consumer prices to support acceptable styles of presentation and interaction for subscribers. The design of appropriate man-machine interfaces and their demonstration in the pilot is one objective since the acceptability of the IEN for both consumers and those involved in its production, will crucially depend upon the adequacy of the MMIs.

The additional editorial work required to design an individual newspaper conventionally for each of a multitude of profiles is far too expensive. The degree of zoning in today's newspapers already indicates where the limits lie. A central objective of the IEN was to indicate that the production of individualized publications is technically tractable and could be economically feasible in an advanced communication environment. The technical approach was to demonstrate how to overcome the problem by combining two technologies: structured document-manipulation tools with knowledge-based systems.

'Old news is no news': reuse of material is not something one normally associates with newspaper publishing. However, individualized newspaper publication involves a constant simultaneous reuse of content for different profiles. Moreover, in IEN, in addition to reusing the content, multiple products — print or hypermedia — are derived from one and the same collection of material, which is called the Pool of IEN Contents. To provide a basis for this reuse, the design of the IEN — in terms of types of content, desirable layout styles, etc. — must be generic and both the formatted printable product and the browsable hypertext product must be produced automatically. Structured document-manipulation technology and SGML-based systems was one aspect of the approach chosen for the IEN pilot (SGML: Standard Generalized Markup Language is described in ISO Standard 8879). The selection of content for a given profile, on the other hand, and the quality layout of the content for presentation depends on rules of newspaper editing and design, which are best modelled and applied with knowledge-based systems.

A hindrance to the introduction of innovative publications in the marketplace is the diversity of systems available to the end-users. A potential reader will be unlikely to subscribe to the IEN if he or she must buy a particular system to do so, when already in possession of a different, perfectly good, but unsupported, system. To avoid this, the publisher must be able to support a wide range of systems, which means that the cost of supporting each additional printer or hypertext reading system must be incremental and small. An objective of the IEN is therefore to demonstrate how this can be achieved by the consistent use of official or *de facto* standards and by designing the IEN publication system to produce the product in a form that can readily be postprocessed for diverse delivery and customer systems.

The new value-adding functionality offered by the IEN has an impact on the publishing process. This comprises the possibility of a real integrated processing of text, images and advertisements from the creation up to the delivery to the reader. In addition, the publishing of the IEN is a distributed application of the Telepublishing architecture. Therefore, an objective of the IEN application pilot was the investigation of the requirements for future integrated electronic newspaper production with special emphasis on the communication and cooperation aspects.

A specific requirement that was addressed concerned the improvement of currently available man-machine interfaces for joint structure-based document editors.

The general scenario

The Individualized Electronic Newspaper (IEN) offers the reader the possibility of receiving a personalized newspaper issue where the content is automatically selected from a pool of publishable news. The general IEN scenario shows that the individual news items are provided on different endsystems. In the following the different components of the IEN publication environment are described (see Figure 20.1).

The scenario includes the contributor part for the article production as well as the selection of newspaper content according to the reader's information needs and personal preferences, which are specified in a reader's profile. News matching this profile will be retrieved from a database, the Pool of IEN Contents, assembled automatically by the Content Composer and then presented either on paper or on screen according to the reader's choice of media.

To keep the IEN independent of the delivery systems eventually used, the scenario is based on the concept of standardized structured documents. The IEN content is therefore stored in a Structured Document Base (SDB) capable of managing these structures.

On the contributor side of the IEN scenario, an Editor's Workbench integrates the different tasks to be performed for IEN creation. This comprises the definition of the content structure of the document types contained in the publication material (i.e. news articles, including images and advertisements), as well as the editing of text and images, translation for the multilingual edition and keeping track of article versions. In addition, the Editor's Workbench offers means for establishing hypermedia links between individual parts of the newspaper, as well as for adding article descriptors for retrieval and presentation. The Editor's Workbench is linked to a local SDB containing structured documents and images. It handles articles being worked on and is connected to public information systems like news agencies and to the IEN archives.

The Pool of IEN Contents is the central integrating data-storage components within the IEN joint scenario and builds the interfaces to contributors and readers. It contains all the IEN foreground and background material: different article types (such as news stories, in-

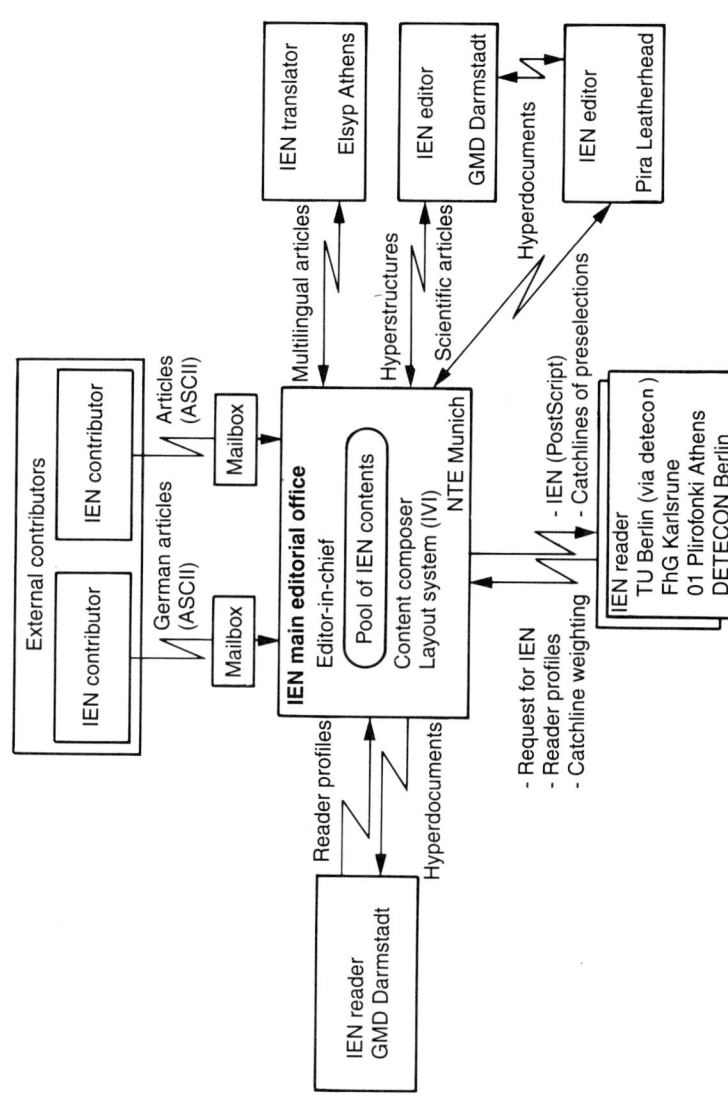

Figure 20.1 Roles and functions in the IEN pilot

depth reports, commentaries, interviews), photographs, advertise-ments, as well as supporting information for topics discussed in the newspaper (e.g. original material, such as complete transcripts of interviews, scientific reports or magazine articles). It also stores reference material to be consulted while reading foreign language articles or articles from the science section, including general lan-guage and sublanguage dictionaries. The SDB has to integrate and store these diverse kinds of data input from the distributed contribu-tors' sites. It also has to deliver the newspaper data to the various delivery systems of the IEN readers.

Depending on the media by which the IEN issue is finally pre-sented, different services for obtaining or accessing the IEN are conceivable. The reader might subscribe in advance to a print ver-sion of their individualized newspaper, or he/she might purchase a newspaper issue printed on demand. Usage of a personal computer at home or in the office might offer the option of daily compilation and print-out of the newspaper according to changing interests; it may also offer interactive browsing of an automatically composed hypermedia issue, or provide direct access to the IEN with its en-hanced services via network connections.

In order to put together the reader's individualized newspaper issue, the Content Composer automatically selects the appropriate IEN articles and pictures out of the Pool of IEN Contents according to his or her initially specified profile. Profile acquisition is done by a component enabling the reader to define his or her personal interest in the different IEN sections, such as national politics, international business, sports etc.

Depending on the customer's choice to read the print or to browse the hypermedia version, either the Layout Composer produces an automatically composed paper issue containing the selected newspa-per material, or the Hypermedia Presentation Composer generates a hypermedia IEN for specific endsystems applying presentation speci-fications to the current newspaper material.

The Pool of IEN Contents provides not only the interface between the newspaper publisher and the reader; it is also directly linked via an archiving module to the IEN archives for outdated articles.

Components of the demonstrator scenario

For the IEN application pilot a demonstrator scenario was to show that the innovative publication concepts developed for this project were technically feasible and efficient.

The central components of the demonstrator are the Pool of IEN Contents, realized as a database managing structured documents, and the Content Composer selecting the newspaper content according to a reader's personal profile. Classes of structured documents are defined using the Standard Generalized Markup Language (SGML).

The Editor's Workbench supports the editing and preparation of content contributions for the Pool of IEN Contents. This requires the functionality of SGML structure editors combined with content structure specification tools.

Articles are not only provided as structured documents, but also come from diverse external sources in different formats. Therefore, a special workplace for converting and/or restructuring imported articles was required, as well as a component for the attribution of links between articles and the classification of articles by descriptors. Preview components enabled the editor to visualize the effect of his or her specifications and decisions. Moreover, the versioning concepts developed for the management of structured documents are applied to the Editor's Workbench, enabling version management of newspaper articles.

The versioning concepts were implemented as an enhancement of the SDB, called the versioned Structured Document Base (vSDB). The vSDB is integrated into the functionality and the user interface of the Editor's Workbench. An task-based man-machine interface for the versioning functions was designed and implemented within the framework of the Editor's Workbench. The man-machine interface covers both aspects of the manual and automatic creation of versions and the navigation through sets of previous states of document parts.

The Translator's Workbench (TWB) is an environment for creating and editing and provides multilingual articles functions to select articles from the Pool of IEN Contents, functions to support their translation in one or more languages, and finally functions to put the translated articles into the Pool of IEN Contents. As the multilingual editing of articles in the IEN scenario will be performed at remote sites, the TWB provides communication functionality for connection to the remote Pool of IEN Contents and for importing/exporting articles from/to it. TWB provides the capability of connecting to remote electronic information services, such as electronic dictionaries, thesauri, libraries, etc. The demonstrator TWB has used information from ECHO databases.

To demonstrate the usage of the IEN, the Layout Composer and the Hypertext Presentation Composer (HPC) were realized within the demonstrator scenario. Both get their input from the Content Composer, which controls access to the Pool of IEN Contents and communication with the reader interfaces. The Layout Composer is directly linked to an IEN Text Formatter that prepares the text for printing according to column width and length specifications and to an IEN PostScript generator for producing the printer format (PostScript is an industry-standard page description language developed by Adobe Systems Inc.).

The HPC also takes input from the Content Composer that provides the content selection for the individual electronic newspaper issue. It automatically generates a hypermedia version for the HyperNeWS hypertext system based on NeWS, Sun's Network extensible Window System.

Special emphasis was put on the investigation and development of the man-machine interfaces (MMIs). This applies to the Editor's Workbench, including user-interface aspects of translation, text import from external sources and versioning, the acquisition of the reader's profile, the access to the print IEN, and the interactive browsing through an IEN along hypertext links.

Achievements

The achievements with respect to the final implementation, testing and integration of the IEN components are described in the following section.

Structured Document Base (SDB)

The SDB, including the Document Application Interface (DAI), which together form a database application offering persistent storage, manipulation, navigation and querying of structured hyperdocuments, was installed in Munich as planned. This is a central component realizing the Pool of IEN Contents. The SDB is implemented in C++ with ObjectWorks 2.4 on a Sun system and was ported from Sybase 4.0 for Sun to Oracle for a DEC MicroVAX Workstation. For this purpose the DAI had to be enhanced in order to be able to discriminate between Oracle and Sybase.

Furthermore, since the Content Composer and Layout Composer were running on a DECstation and Oracle was installed on a VAXstation, a remote database access interface similar to SQL-Net was implemented. It is based on the Unix socket feature (a socket server runs as a demon process on the Oracle side, which can serve multiple individual client processes via TCP/IP between Unix computers connected with Thinwire Ethernet cables) and allows transparent remote access to the Oracle database. A tool box was additionally provided, containing programs at Unix level which facilitate the maintenance of the Pool of IEN Contents (e.g. list name of articles or newspapers currently stored, remove an article or newspaper etc.).

Integration of SDB and Hypermedia Presentation Composer (HPC)

The SDB has been further enhanced to manage special link types and operations to support the HPC. The protocol between the installation of the Pool of IEN Contents and the HPC was designed to be completely based on the exchange of SGML-conformant documents. Based on this protocol, the document type definitions developed for al kinds of contents related to the production of an IEN, such as articles, images and newspaper issues have been extended. The basic cooperation of the HPC with the SDB has been locally tested.

The Editor's Workbench

The IEN editor required support tools for browsing the available content, editing the structured article texts and editing links between articles, as well as the means to classify the IEN constituents (articles which the content composer matches to the reader profile). The editing tools are embedded in the overall IEN Editor's Workbench. The interface for this workbench, based on the 'basket' metaphor common in conventional newspaper editorial systems, was designed and implemented as a prototype in HyperNeWs. Through this interface the editor is able to access articles for editing. The main editing tool is based on the Andrew ToolKit (ATK) editor, whose user interface has been extended to support editing structured documents (e.g. selection of well-structured objects). While editing an article, the editor may preview the IEN network reader's view of the screen/page.

The articles were accessed by the editing tool from the file system. They could also be extracted from the SDB and restored following editing. The final integration step remaining was the full integration of the ATK editor with SDB. The addition to the SDB interface of functionality to inform ATK of updates was accomplished. This allowed the final integration of the versioning and translation MMIs.

The versioning MMI

The implementation and integration of the versioning MMI, the versioned Structured Document Base (vSDB) in C++ on top of the SDB, has been finished. Like the SDB, it has been available via the Internet for all partners since March 1992. The versioning MI has been designed to cover aspects of both the manual and automatic creation of versions, as well as navigating the sets of previous states of parts of documents using a graphical browser.

Translator's Workbench (TWB)

The TWB comprises two modules, the Communication Module and the Translation Module. The communication functionality of the Communication Module has been developed and tested but not integrated under the TWB environment. In particular, articles have been received from GMD Darmstadt by remote login and ftp, the connection to remote databases and other information services has been established and general communication tools have been used. The Translation Module is based on the Structured Document Editor, which itself is based on the X-Windows Andrew Toolkit.

Import Box

The Import Box, realized in Hypercard 1.0, was used for the import of unstructured text documents from external sources like news agencies. After a first testing phase it was decided that it had to be redesigned and enhanced to allow the structuring and classification of any kind of ASCII text. It provided a user interface for the classification staff, capable of reading the text from external sources and displaying it in a WYSIWYG editor window. The user can interactively structure and classify the text according to the document type definition. The corresponding SGML-conformant format is generated automatically and can be imported into the Pool of IEN Contents. Technically, it is generated on a Macintosh, sent via X.25

to a VAXstation and stored into the Oracle database using the Oracle-DAI interface together with the Amsterdam parser system.

Content Composer

One of the central ideas of the individualized newspaper was to realize a knowledge-based Content Composer for the automatic selection of newspaper content from the Pool of IEN Contents according to a specified profile of interest. For the realization of the Content Composer a rule-based approach was followed that enables the intended selection of material to be made from the Pool of IEN Contents. The reader's interest in each section was matched by specific rules for the properties of the available articles. To allow well balanced mixtures of content in an IEN issue, each article has an importance code assigned to it and can have optional paragraphs which do not have to be delivered to each reader interested in the article. In addition, several articles referring to one topic were grouped under specific catchlines, so that the amount of information about a topic can vary depending on the interest of the reader, ranging from just a short message up to a whole group of different types of articles including comments and background information.

The Content Composer served as an interface between various system components. It is started by the Reader MMI and supplied with the reader's specific profile. The connection between the MMI demonstrator for profile specification (Reader MMI, running on a Macintosh) and the Content Composer (running on a DECstation 3100) was realized via X.25. According to the user profile, the Content Composer extracts relevant articles from the Pool of IEN Contents (which was physically stored on a VAXstation in an Oracle RDBMS), via the DAI layer and the remote database access interface. The Content Composer generated output in the form of a number of Unix files: one file containing a series of Prolog statements; files containing pure text, which were the ingredients for the Layout Composer; and one file containing the SGML structure as marked-up content of the newspaper, which was used by the Hypermedia Presentation Composer.

Hypermedia Presentation Composer (HPC)

The introduction of innovative electronic publications to the marketplace has been hindered by the need to support a wide range of end-user systems. Subscribers should be able to access such products using equipment which they already possess, and without being constrained in their future choice of systems. This is only realistic, however, if the cost to the publisher of supporting each additional printer or hypertext reading system is small and incremental. A main achievement of the IEN pilot was to demonstrate how this problem could be overcome, by the consistent use of standards throughout the publication process. This resulted in a product — an IEN issue — which can readily be postprocessed for delivery and presentation by diverse systems. It also resulted in a production process which can be performed over heterogeneous systems. This consistent use of standards has already proven its benefits in the project, for example in the simple exchange protocol between the Pool of IEN Contents and the Hypermedia Presentation Composer.

Establishment of communication links

An ISDN communication link based on the Sun was installed between GMD-IPSI (Germany) and Pira International (UK). ISDN links between NTE as an IEN supplier and IEN readers (FhG-ISI, DETECON) have been installed and tested.

Communication experiments

IEN distributed production process

For the demonstration of the IEN a communication network has to be established which integrates different contributor types and IEN readers. The whole production process, as well as the usage of the IEN, has to be covered to enable a proper evaluation of the demonstrator.

The different types of contributors which were supported were:

- External contributors,
- IEN editors,
- IEN classification staff,
- IEN editor-in-chief,
- IEN layout designer,
- IEN translators.

The production process started with the acquisition, editing, classification and import of IEN articles and associated content into the SDB. The SDB as the central IEN content pool contained all publishable contributions which could be delivered to the readers. It was located at NTE in Munich, which took the role of the IEN Main Editorial Office. Parts of the IEN content were created locally at the site of Local Editorial Offices, while other parts were received from external sources such as news agencies.

Further processing of articles took place at yet another site, e.g. the creation of translated versions of an article. Therefore, two variants of an Editor's Workbench were installed in the IEN demonstrator, one providing version support tools and a Translator's Workbench supporting translations.

The import of articles into the SDB was controlled by the editor-in-chief at the IEN Main Editorial Office, where there was also a Classification Workbench enabling the assignment of keywords to the articles, which are needed by the Content Composer in order to select an article according to the user's interest profile.

When the interactive hypermedia issue was selected, the structured documents were transferred. The HPC located at the reader's site generated a hyperdocument stack from the selected IEN content components according to predefined hyperlinks.

Each of the involved IEN contributors and readers needed a communication line to the Main Editorial Office. The next step was the establishment of an ISDN connection from readers' sites to the IEN main editorial office. The partners having this possibility are FhG-ISI in Karlsruhe, Pira International near London, DETECON Berlin, and the Technische Universität Berlin (via DETECON). For the transmission of plain article text a narrowband communication line was sufficient, because the data volume is rather low (not more than 100 kbyte/day was expected). Furthermore, the transfer of articles to the pool was not time critical, because the preprocessing of articles is the bottleneck in importing text into the SDB and not the data transfer. This would be different if greyscale images were included, when the amount of data would increase drastically. Therefore, it was decided for all communication links with narrowband transfer rates not to include greyscale images in the IEN, instead only vector graphics were used.

The role of the translation office for the multilingual IEN was taken by ELSYP in Athens. ELSYP provided the Translator's Workbench, which is an extension of the Editor's Workbench for the support of translation tasks. The input from ELSYP to the SDB was articles in different languages, which made the IEN into a multilingual product in the last project phase.

GMD-IPSI and Pira International took the roles of local editors. At Pira an Editor's Workbench and an Editor's Local Document Base were installed. At GMD-IPSI the Editor's Workbench included versioning support. GMD also performed the tasks of a layout designer, defining the rules applied by the HPC. In the role of a local editorial office, GMD also provided content for the science section of the hypermedia IEN into the Pool of IEN Contents. For direct change of data between GMD-IPSI and Pira, an ISDN communication link has been established.

THE DIDOS PROJECT

The RACE project R2037 DIDOS (Distributed Documenting Services) has as its main objective to describe, realize, test and evaluate a services environment for distributed documentation. The specific application domain is the technical documentation sector, an increasingly important domain for all service and product delivering companies in the European Union.

The main objective of the DIDOS project is to demonstrate the Service Center Concept (a framework of standards, services, products, agreements, business models, networks and applications) as a useful and beneficial strategy for the technical documentation service sector.

Strategy

The project's approach is illustrated in Figure 20.2. The initial steps were to describe and to cluster the Technical Documentation application sector and to describe the Service Center concept as a framework. Three Application Pilots were established, in order to realize and demonstrate selected aspects and tasks of using Technical Documentation services in a distributed wide area network environment.

Results and experience gained both from the specification, as well as from the realization and tests, will be incorporated into a DIDOS Reference Platform and will be used to produce recommendations to those influencing the relevant sectors; these include service providers, service users, PTTs, system vendors and the EC.

A complete technical platform has been specified and realized integrating two layers of services with basic technical systems and protocols. The structure is outlined in Figure 20.3.

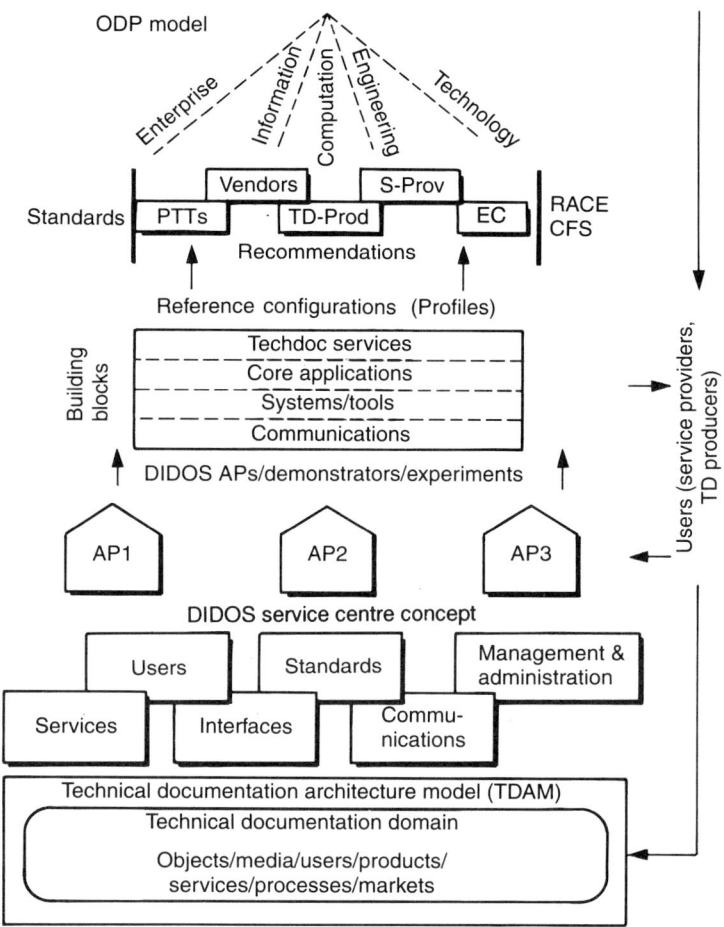

Figure 20.2 The strategic approach of DIDOS

Application Pilot 1

The first Application Pilot is concerned with the composing stages of the technical documentation production process. The key innovative service in this pilot is the Document Application Design (DAD) Service, an innovative technical documentation service, which bundles a range of composing services in a unique way that is enabled by

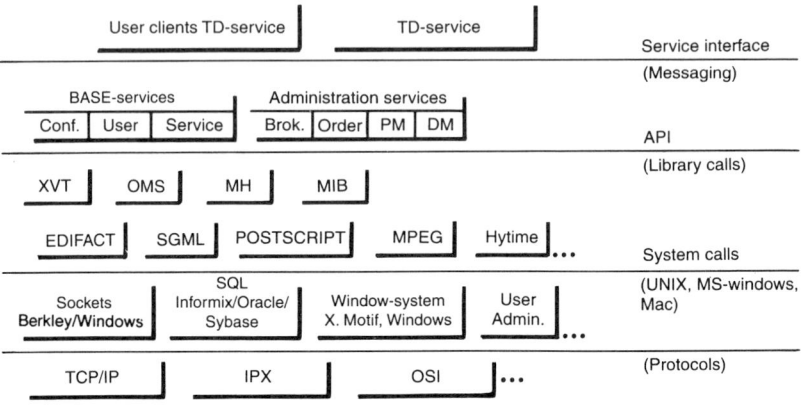

Figure 20.3 The technical platform of DIDOS

the application of the Service Center concept. The DAD Service delivers knowledge and designs solutions of how best to compose technical documentation. This service assists technical documentation producers and service providers to optimize the composing process.

The Service Center Concept provides a mechanism for enabling access to a wide range of specialist services for technical documentation production, including composing services.

Figure 20.4 illustrates how use of the DAD Service acts on the component resources of a document application. The DAD Service manifests itself in different ways according to the particular service that it is offering: consultant, systems designer, prototype developer, information service, typographic designer and trainer are all roles that the DAD Service can play in different circumstances.

The DAD Service that is being realized in this project offers a selection of services whose common theme is that they are all concerned with Standard Generalized Markup Language (SGML). The use of logical structuring techniques is seen to be increasingly important for open interchange and flexible processing of documents in distributed technical documentation production. At the present time SGML is considered to be the most suitable applicable stand-

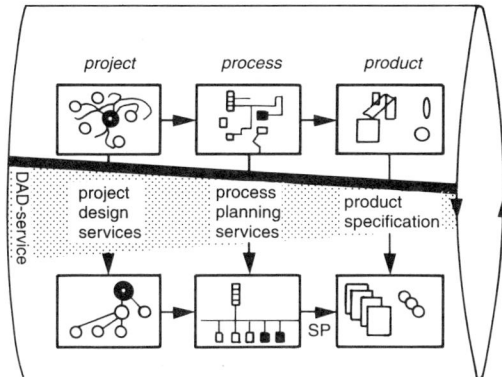

Figure 20.4 Document applications and DAD service

ard. This has impact on a wide range of composing services, so a key task of the DAD Service is to design composing processes that involve the use of SGML.

Services being delivered in Application Pilot 1 include SGML Document Type Definition (DTD) design, layout specification design, SGML tool prototyping, SGML tool testing and evaluation and SGML information service.

Application Pilot 2

Application Pilot 2 is concerned with the application of printing-on-demand and document master page archive services in order to achieve a just-in-time production of technical documentation. Printing-on-demand transactions are flexibly distributed across Integrated Broadband Communications (IBC) networks, to provide any easy and fast access to different print service providers and to employ a large variety of printing technologies including innovative technologies such as Computer-to-Press (CtP). The architecture is illustrated in Figure 20.5.

The expected benefits are:

• Minimization of paper documentation warehouses owing to on-demand printing with low-volume print runs of required documents.
• Physical distribution is avoided when remote printing services

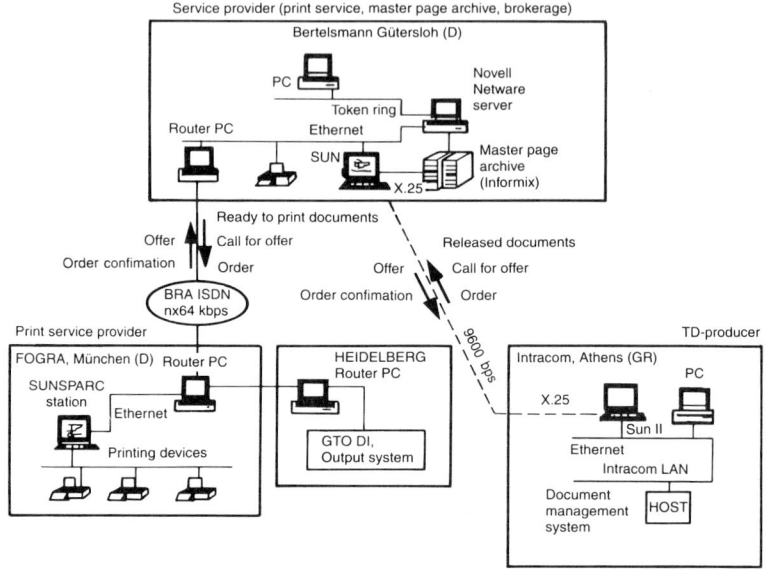

Figure 20.5 Application Pilot 2 scenario

are selected, so that information is distributed electronically and printed regionally, where the customers or end-users are located.

- Using CtP as the currently most advanced printing technique for technical documentation it will be possible to have documentation produced jointly with the product.

- Market transparency and selection opportunities are increased, thus enabling users to make a flexible choice of services in terms of quality, time schedules, providers and other features.

Application Pilot 2 is achieving the mentioned objectives by the realization of different services:

- Building an Electronic Master Page Archive for remote access, where current documents are stored to be available for on-demand printing and for selecting and ordering from different locations.

- Location-independent document selection and ordering access for different customers, including delivery and invoicing.
- Distributed print-on-demand at several locations in Europe (Munich, Gütersloh, London).
- Fast access for CtP printing in Heidelberg (D) provided by several service providers in conjunction with the use of an innovative quality assurance tool for full-colour prints.

Application Pilot 3

Application Pilot 3, illustrated in Figure 20.6, realizes the DIDOS Service Center concept in a distributed environment for production and distribution of technical multimedia documentation:

- It provides a complete range of networked multimedia services in a Service Center configuration.
- It applies the Service Center concept to a multimedia domain by migrating paper documentation services to include multimedia-based documentation.
- It ensures that the services are flexible and can be configured dynamically to actual short-term, long-term and changing production needs.
- It promotes integrated workflow over geographical distance and cultural boundaries by providing quick and easy access to multimedia technology and services. This enables close communication and cooperation between technical documentation producers and multimedia service providers using telecommunication networks.
- The Application Pilot 3 concept is based on existing and emerging open standards and therefore is transferrable to other industrial and business communities requiring interactive multimedia production services.

The Small Object Management System, the facilities for definition of specific object types and the SGML standard are used to establish a high-level specification of exchange formats for technical data, multimedia objects, structures, links and processing instructions. This allows the technical documentation producers internally to produce and maintain most of the information needed in the multimedia documentation. It enables automated updates and configura-

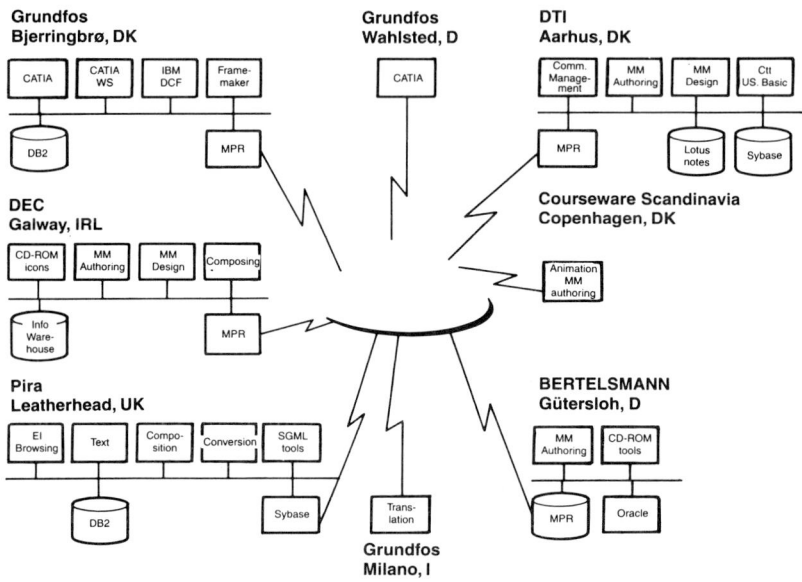

Figure 20.6 Application Pilot 3 scenario

tion of the multimedia technical documentation, which is very important for the technical documentation producer's integration and synchronization of production and documentation.

Evaluation and market exploitation

The project is currently moving forward into the test and evaluation phase. All pilots will be evaluated concerning their technical functionality, their organizational aspects and impacts and concerning their business relevance and potential market exploitation. The project partners are establishing a common evaluation database, where information and results concerning evaluation tasks will be stored.

Groups and discussions have been initiated to prepare a further exploitation of the Service Center concept and to initiate business uptake plans for the period after the project's completion.

CONCLUSION

The application projects cannot be considered as isolated from each other. In particular, the widespread relations and influences of other domains and technologies enable realistic projects to be conducted. The results and procedures can be transferred immediately for commercial exploitation in the publishing sector.

The role of communications will be extended in the near future. The availability of in-house and wide-area ATM infrastructures will inspire new concepts, and lead to modified processes in the printing and publishing sector (Figure 20.7).

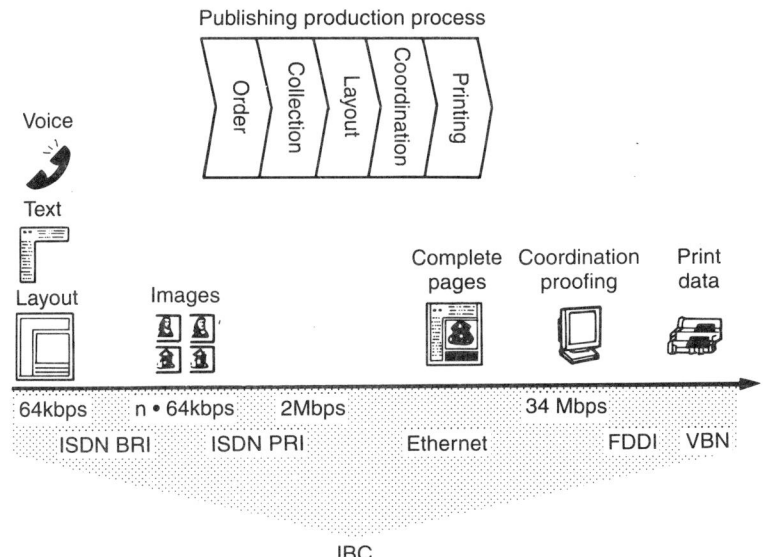

Figure 20.7 Communication requirements in LAN and WAN environments

21

Forces shaping the electronic publishing industry of the 1990s

Donald T Hawkins, Frank J Smith, Bruce C Dietlein,
Eugene J Joseph and Robert D Rindfuss, AT&T Bell, USA

The amount of information available in electronic form has grown rapidly in recent years. As shown in Figure 21.1, there are now more than 5000 online databases commercially available[1]; over the last five years, the average annual growth rate is approximately 10%. These figures do not include electronic information services primarily marketed to consumers, commonly known as videotex (a term that appears to be heading toward extinction)[2]. One of the largest new exhibits opening during the last decade at the Smithsonian Institution in Washington, DC has information technology as its theme. We are truly in a time when technological literacy is growing and when the benefits of the Information Age are being reaped by many.

Dr Donald T Hawkins is a Distinguished Member of Technical Staff at AT&T Bell Laboratories, USA in Somerset, New Jersey. Frank J Smith is Manager, Implementation Engineering at AT&T Network Service Division. Bruce C Dietlein is General Manager of new business development at AT&T Consumer Services. Eugene J Joseph is a member of technical staff at AT&T Bell Laboratories. Robert D Rindfuss is a supervisor at AT&T Bell Laboratories. The chapter is a reprint from *Electronic Networking* Magazine. The editors are grateful for copyright granted by Meckler. Communications to the authors may be sent to Dr Donald T Hawkins, AT&T, Room 34B03, 55 Corporate Drive, Bridgewater, New Jersey 08807.

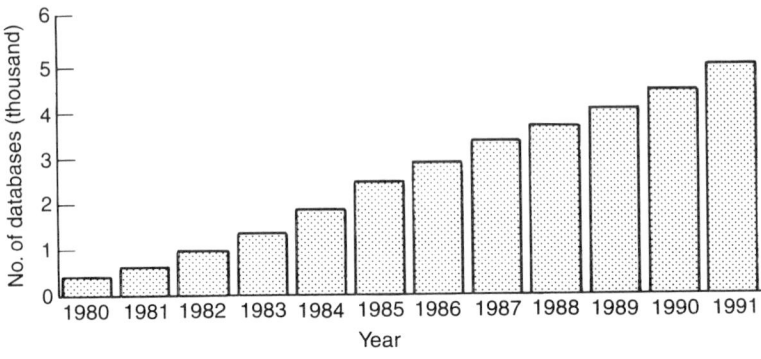

Figure 21.1 Growth of online databases, 1980–1991 (Source: *Directory of Online Databases*, Cuadra/Gale, 1991)

BACKGROUND

Awareness of electronic information is high, especially in the business and professional market sectors, but it has still not significantly penetrated the consumer market. Efforts to do so have not been lacking. In recent years, many new services have been proposed, modelled, prototyped and introduced into this market. Relatively few of them have survived, often bringing disillusionment to their developers, who may view the electronic publishing (EP) industry as complex and difficult to understand. Successful product development depends on a thorough understanding of the forces driving this important industry. This article reports on a study in which seven forces driving the EP industry are identified. Based on these forces, some significant keys to success in this marketplace are derived.

The study began by looking at the traditional publishing industry and some technologies that are prominent and important in the information arena. It soon became clear that, although technology is one of the foremost driving forces in this industry, others are also important; therefore a model of the EP industry portraying these forces was developed. A detailed discussion of each force forms the heart of this article, followed by a summary of the major lessons identified as keys to success in the industry.

This study focuses on the consumer marketplace for electronic information. The approximately 90 million US consumer households represent a largely untapped market for electronic information sources (only about 2% of them access electronic information sources at present)[3]. The worldwide potential market is, of course, much larger. Many of the results and conclusions presented here, however, are not unique to the consumer market; they are equally applicable in the business information market.

DEFINITIONS*

EP means different things to different people. Over the years, the EP umbrella has included services such as online databases, videotex, airline reservations, credit reporting, financial information, newswires, electronic mail, document delivery, electronic journals, and even the distribution of software on the ubiquitous floppy disk (see Figure 21.2). Three of the previous definitions that have been proposed seemed significant to the study; it was recognized that many others exist.

White[4] observed that there are probably as many definitions of EP as there are publishers! He defined EP in terms of the delivery channel and also categorized services according to the channel by which they are delivered. Even as long ago as 1983, Gurnsey[5] felt that 'electronic publishing has been with us for a long time' and that technology was driving the market. He urged caution and predicted that progress would be slower than expected. Gurnsey's definition of EP is bimodal:

- use of electronics — and particularly computers to facilitate the production of a conventional product, and
- use of computers and telecommunications systems to distribute information electronically.

---

*Explanations of abbreviations used in this paper are on page 420.

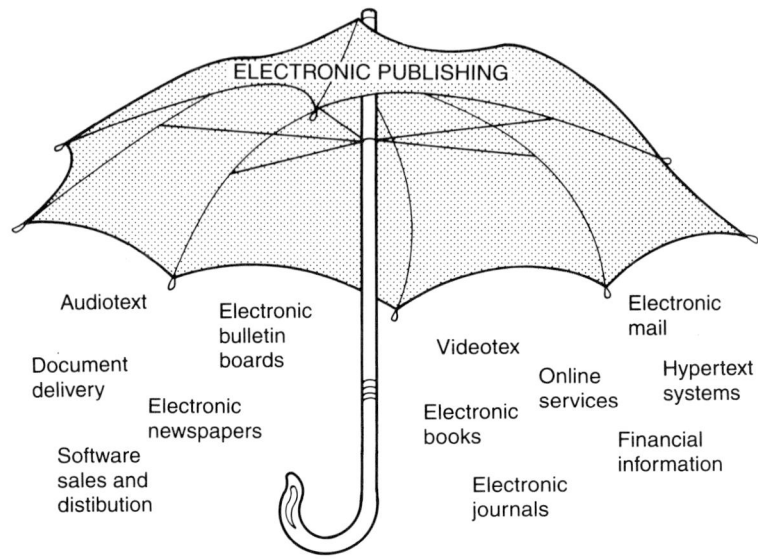

Audiotext

Document delivery

Electronic bulletin boards

Electronic newspapers

Software sales and distibution

Videotex

Electronic books

Electronic journals

Online services

Electronic mail

Hypertext systems

Financial information

Figure 21.2 The electronic publishing umbrella

Finally, Downes[6] proposed that information technology will become synonymous with EP, with the publishing industry being the major player. She predicted that within 15 years, publishers would offer electronic access to most published information in the major disciplines.

Although Gurnsey's definition is specific to the environment of a previous decade, most of today's services are included in it. Both White and Downes emphasize the technological aspects of EP, without including the service or marketplace aspects. It is important to distinguish between electronic publishing and electronic-aided publishing (EAP). The following definitions were used in this study:

- Electronic publishing (EP) is the use of electronic media, computers, or telecommunications systems to deliver information to users in electronic form or from electronic sources.
- Electronic-aided publishing (EAP) is the use of electronic means to produce an information product.

This definition of EP encompasses both the delivery channel and the source of the information, in contrast to the production process. EP is not simply an electronic aid to traditional publishing. For example, most publishers now use electronic systems for editing, layout and so forth, and the spread of inexpensive desktop publishing systems has brought electronic-aided production within the reach of virtually anyone with the requisite hardware and software. The commercial production of newsletters flyers, greeting cards and so forth, although still a large business, has also become a thriving cottage industry. The use of electronic systems simply to produce and distribute a conventional printed product does not by itself constitute EP. True EP, as defined above, includes the information originating from an electronic source or being delivered electronically.

Indexers of articles for online databases do not distinguish between EP, as defined above, and EAP. If one simply inputs the term 'electronic publishing' into an online database, a significant number of the items retrieved will deal with desktop publishing and will have little or nothing to do with electronic information delivery. To illustrate this point, an online search of two well-known and widely used databases, INSPEC and the Computer Database, was done on the DIALOG system using its OneSearch and duplicate elimination features. For each year, the number of references containing the term 'electronic publishing' in either the title or descriptor (keyword) fields was determined. Then, the number of those also containing the term 'desktop publishing' was determined. From 1983 to the present, of the 3139 unique papers indexed by these two databases, 606 (19.3%) of the items indexed under 'electronic publishing' are also indexed under 'desktop publishing'.

An easy distinction between EP and EAP can be made by considering the roots of each. EP, although it uses electronic media to deliver information, has its roots in the publishing industry (the computing, telecommunications and software industries also have had major effects on the EP industry). EAP, on the other hand, sprang from the computer and software industries and is the application of those technologies to the production aspects of the publishing industry. Downes recognizes this important point; although she equates information technology with EP, she states that the publishing industry is one of its major users.

INFORMATION FLOWS BETWEEN PUBLISHERS AND USERS

A knowledge of how information flows from its creators to its users helped us to understand the boundaries of EP and define its markets. We updated and adapted the 'information chain' model of information flows originally proposed by Aitchison[7] for this view of EP, as shown in Figure 21.3. There are many steps and many players involved. In the simplest case, there are only two people in the information chain — the author and the user. The author gives the information to the user, and the user returns feedback or a request for additional information. Although this case can hardly be called publishing, it is relevant because the ultimate business of publishing is essentially that of moving information from its creator (the author) to the user.

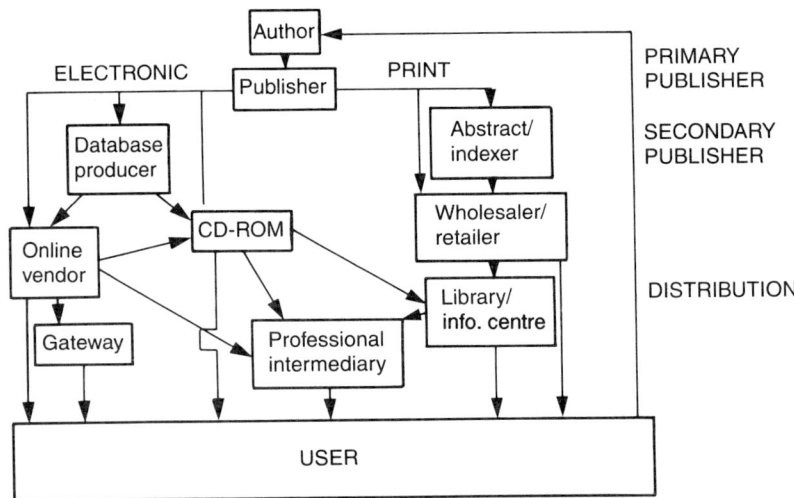

Figure 21.3 The information flow chain

The publishing process begins when an author creates a manuscript and delivers it to the publisher. From there, the left side of Figure 21.3 represents the EP process, and the right side represents the conventional print publishing process. Proceeding down the figure, the primary publisher is shown at the top, followed by the secondary publisher and distributor infrastructures. At the bottom is the user. The chain is completed by a feedback loop from the user to the author (which may not be exercised in many cases, such as books and magazines).

The right side of Figure 21.3 shows the conventional materials supply process from the manufacturer (author) and his or her agent (publisher) through the wholesale and retail distribution chains to the consumer. The distribution may proceed in one or two steps (in the case of wholesale booksellers and retail bookstores, for example) from publisher to user, or there may be several intermediate steps. Note the prominent part that libraries and professional information specialists (intermediaries) play in this distribution chain.

The electronic information distribution chain, shown on the left side of Figure 21.3, is considerably more complex than the print supply chain. The picture is muddied because several of the players have moved into multiple functions. Examples can be found of publishers also performing the function of database producers, database producers being online vendors, and both of these being CD-ROM producers. It is not inconceivable that the user could interact with the original publisher without realizing it, if that publisher is the database producer and the online vendor. Consider the case of Chemical Abstracts Service (CAS), for example. It publishes the printed Chemical Abstracts (CA), from which is derived the online database of the same name. CA is available online through several vendors, but it is also made available by CAS directly through its STN international service. The publisher is therefore both a supplier to and a competitor with other online vendors. If the user accesses the STN system directly and not through a professional intermediary, he or she is obtaining information directly from its publisher. This scenario has interesting market implications. The publisher is able to control the entire distribution chain and may even offer special features or portions of the information exclusively — a fact which has not been lost on competitors and has been the subject of litigation between Dialog Information Services and CAS[8].

Note the central place that CD-ROM has in the information chain and the links it has with virtually all of the other players on the electronic side. CD-ROM is in a pivotal position and is clearly a major force in the industry. (Except for CD-ROM, the components of the information chain are broad services or operations, not technologies. CD-ROM as a discrete technology is included here because of the major role that it plays.)

Besides segmenting the information industry along the traditional lines of print or electronic delivery, Figure 21.3 also distinguishes between publishing and online services. The lower left portion of the figure, containing online vendors, gateways, and (to some extent) professional intermediaries and CD-ROM, is the online information industry; the rest can be considered to be the publishing industry.

BACKGROUND STUDIES

White[4] defined EP in terms of the delivery channel, concentrating on the technologies used. Since then, technology has, of course, made significant advances. Table 21.1 lists major technologies used in both EP and EAP. Those used in EP are discussed later, as relevant parts of the model of the forces driving the industry. To illustrate the distinction between EP and EAP, the EAP technologies listed in the table are briefly discussed below. Subsequent sections describe previous market research and the traditional print publishing industry.

Table 21.1 Publishing and related technologies

Electronic publishing	Electronic-aided publishing
Online information	Desktop publishing
Databases	Phototypesetting
CD-ROM	Laser printing
Gateways	Colour separation and printing
Audiotext	Selective binding
Fax	
Telecommunications	
Packet-switched networks	
Local area networks	
ISDN	
Optical fibre	

Many publishers claim to be using EP when they use computer technology to help them produce a conventional product. They focus on technology to lower costs, shorten the time to press, and improve the quality of the product. Usually, however, the end product is indistinguishable in content, appearance, and delivery channel from a conventionally produced product.

EAP technologies

Desktop publishing

EAP technologies include desktop publishing, computer photo-typesetting and laser printing. Technological advances in microprocessor power and software sophistication have made possible the desktop publishing (DTP) revolution. DTP refers to the use of microcomputer systems to perform the copy-editing, layout and graphics design stages of publishing. Previously the province of large publishers, DTP has become available to the masses with the development of easily used, inexpensive software for personal computers (PCs). Work that formerly required a bevy of editors, graphics artists, layout editors and typesetters, using building full of expensive equipment, can now be performed by a single person using a PC costing $10 000 or less. In fact, DTP has spawned a sizeable cottage industry of entrepreneurs producing newsletters or providing typesetting services to others from their homes.

DTP is revolutionary in its ability to permit high-end professional publishing with extremely low investment and labour costs. DTP is categorized as an EAP technology, not an EP technology, because it is primarily a production aid for a conventionally distributed product.

Computer phototypesetting

The move away from manual typesetting to computer phototypesetting in the 1960s was one of the major developments that spawned today's online information industry. Database producers realized the value of their phototypesetting tapes and, rather than discarding or simply archiving them, used them to build databases for online use. Today, manual typesetting has become virtually obsolete and computer phototypesetting is the norm. Computer phototypesetting is related to EP because it underlies the production of many bibliographic databases, but it belongs in the realm of EAP because it is strictly a production technology.

Laser printing

One of the most significant developments for small-scale publishing has been the laser printer. It, combined with PCs and sophisticated DTP software, has made publishing by individuals and small organizations possible. The greatest benefit of laser printers over other personal printers is the quality of the output. Using resolutions of 300 dots per inch (dpi) and higher, laser printers are capable of rendering typographic fonts with a quality only slightly below phototypesetting, but at far less cost. (Enhancement technology has increased resolutions to as much as 600 dpi, even as costs for these enhanced printers have dropped.) Laser printers also permit extremely short delivery times, making them practical for publishing up-to-the-minute information.

Significantly, the high-speed laser printer makes it practical to print documents on demand. In applications where large volumes of reference information must be available, but documents are actually needed only occasionally, it is more efficient to scan those documents and store them in a large database rather than on paper. When a hard copy is requested, the document can be printed directly by a high-speed laser printer. In a similar application, on-demand printing with laser printers makes it possible to produce personalized or customized documents in which the content of each copy is unique in some way.

PREVIOUS MARKET STUDIES

The electronic publishing industry is the subject of several ongoing market research projects and studies. Of particular note in the present context are those by LINK Resources Inc. and Veronis, Suhler & Associates (VS&A). LINK's latest data[9] shows the annual North American electronic information industry revenues at $9500 million in 1990, predicted to grow to $15 600 million by 1994 — a compound annual growth rate of 10.5%. LINK takes a broad view of what constitutes 'electronic information', including credit reporting, airline reservation systems, financial information systems and legal systems in its definition, along with more traditional information services. All the top revenue-producing services listed by LINK are in the business arena; the consumer marketplace for electronic information accounts for only about $320 million[10], less than 4% of the total market of $9500 million. According to LINK, the major users of electronic information today are credit managers and travel agents, but by 1994 financial information systems are expected to grow and become the most heavily used.

VS&A annually publishes a survey and forecast of the publishing business[11]. We drew heavily on their data in our study of the $98 000 million traditional publishing industry.

OVERVIEW OF THE TRADITIONAL PUBLISHING INDUSTRY

Since EP, according to our definition, has a major portion of its roots in the traditional (print) publishing industry, our study began by reviewing the traditional publishing industry. We had expected that background information would be available in such standard sources as textbooks, and so forth, but we were surprised to find an apparent dearth of such general material; most of the information appears in journals and similar specialized media.

The publishing industry can be segmented according to the product it produces; we have chosen this approach (which is also followed by VS&A in their market research reports), as follows:

- newspapers
- magazines
- books
- directories
- newsletters

A substantial amount of literature on the newspaper, magazine and book segments is available; much less is available on the others. Although a detailed discussion of this industry is outside the scope of this article, a brief summary of each of the above segments, along with our major conclusions, especially in the context of their use of EP technologies, is presented below.

Publishing industry general characteristics

For many years, the publishing industry was dominated by small family-run businesses and the common industry practice was to subcontract out many of the production operations. Recently, however, publishing has come to the attention of large conglomerates which have begun to acquire and consolidate individual publishing companies. Sweeping change has come to the publishing industry;

there were over 400 mergers and acquisitions in the last decade. Among the many changes taking place in publishing has been growth in the use of electronic technology. Large conglomerates have the resources to invest in expensive technological equipment and processes; the publishing industry has begun to use modern technology. Most publishers' concept of EP, however, really translates to EAP. Most of them use electronic systems to produce, format, and lay out their products, but distribution still follows the traditional chain shown on the right side of Figure 21.3.

Figure 21.4 shows VS&A's analysis of 1990 sales for this $98 000 million a year industry, by segment. Newspapers dominate heavily. The annual growth rate averages about 9%; operating margins are about 12–14% for all segments except newspapers which enjoy a 20% margin.

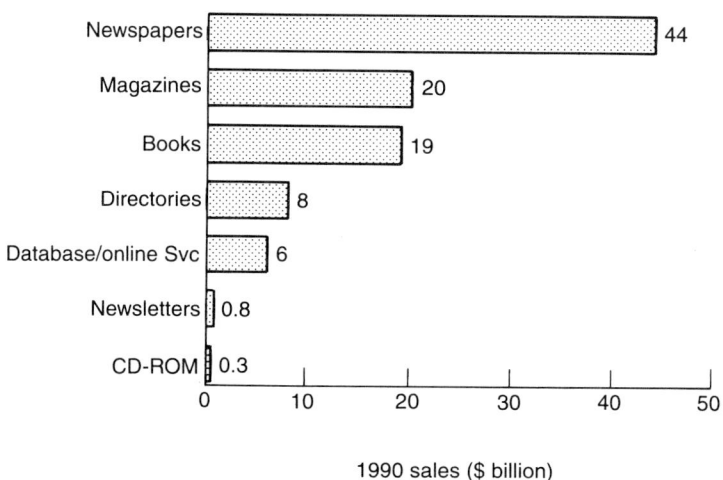

1990 sales ($ billion)

Figure 21.4 Publishing industry sales, 1990 (Source: Veronis, Suhler & Associates)

Newspapers

With 1990 annual sales of about $44 000 million, newspapers dominate the publishing business. Although content production (editorial etc.) represents 32% of a newspaper's costs, advertising (retail, classified, and national) brings in 81% of the revenues. The most significant problem faced by newspapers is a loss of readership, particularly in the 20 to 29 year age group. Many newspapers are turning to technologies such as colour and graphics (*USA Today* is a prominent example) to make the paper more attractive to the 'TV generation'. Audio information technology (audiotext) is also being used to enhance the newspaper product, both for voice-mail responses to advertisements and as a supplementary information source.

Newspaper publishers do not see EP as a replacement for the traditional paper, but they see it as a way to update the paper's image. Most newspapers are using EAP, not EP, to improve their production processes. One of their greatest fears is that EP will cause their highly profitable classified advertising business to decline (classified ads generate half of the profit of a typical large metropolitan daily newspaper).

Magazines

The magazine publisher's major customer is the advertiser, not the reader. Advertisers are becoming increasingly more selective about where they spend their advertising dollars and more demanding of magazine publishers. The technologies of selective binding, in which the content of the magazine can be varied according to subscriber demographics, and ink-jet printing, in which personalized messages can be printed on the magazine, are widely used to customize magazines for individual readers. These primarily EAP technologies were developed in response to publishers' needs for better control over the content of their publications, the desire for more customized and personalized content and concurrent demands by advertisers for closer targeting of their advertisements (thus achieving better control over their expenditures).

Selective binding technology is used to custom-construct magazines and similar publications in real time as part of the production process, varying the content according to reader demographics and interests. The publication is produced in small sections (called 'signatures') which are then assembled under the control of demographic data on the publisher's subscription list. Although both editorial content and advertising can be varied, it is more usual to keep editorial content constant for all subscribers of a publication and customize some of the advertising. Perhaps the ultimate example of selective binding is that of *Farm Journal*, which once produced an issue with over 12 000 separate versions and has created entirely new publications by the judicious and regular use of its sophisticated mailing list and extensive demographic data[12]. A major hindrance to selective binding is cost; the technology is sophisticated and expensive to use. *Time*, *Business Week* and *Popular Science* are examples of well-known publications using selective binding technology.

The ubiquitous personally addressed messages on magazines and catalogues are produced by ink-jet technology. New systems allowing messages to be printed horizontally instead of vertically and inside the publications instead of only on the covers have recently come into vogue. Although most ink-jet messages are used for brief advertising messages, *Time* took the concept a step further with its 26 November 1990 issue. Each individual copy was not only addressed to the subscriber, but the subscriber's name was incorporated into the cover design using ink-jet printing.

The magazine industry is one of the most dynamic areas of publishing, with a large turnover of titles. New magazines appear and disappear with great regularity; over 200 changed hands in 1988. Because of the insistence on targeting by advertisers who want to get the most for their advertising expenditures, magazine publishing is also very fragmented, with thousands of niche markets. There is a magazine for nearly any subject, hobby or industry that one can think of, resulting in a significant market share loss for general interest magazines such as *Life*. Two recent trends are causing concern to magazine publishers:

- Postal and paper costs continue to rise. Reductions in fulfilment and editorial costs have not been enough to counter large increases in postal rates (up 75% since 1988)[13] and paper costs. (According to the Bureau of Labor Statistics, the wholesale price index for paper is growing at about 5% a year.)
- Advertising revenues have dropped significantly, as much as 20% at some magazines[14]. The decline is especially pronounced in automobile, retailing, and tobacco advertising.

To meet revenue declines and rising costs, magazine publishers are seeking out new sources of income; foreign editions and subscription list rentals are popular. Other technologies are also being used to help cut costs. Besides selective binding and ink-jet printing, polywrapping (wrapping several magazines in a plastic bag for mailing) and comailing (including other materials such as advertisements in the bag along with the magazine) have been used successfully by some publishers.

Books

Although book publishing is generally financially healthy, it is beset with some major problems[15]. Not the least is the short shelf life of books; approximately 53 000 new titles appear every year in the USA. With such a flood of new material appearing, only a few books can be financially successful. Book publishers operate with margins of around 14%; manufacturing, marketing and author royalties are the major cost components.

Ever since the creation of textual databases and the software to manage them, visionaries have dreamed of making books available electronically. Now their dreams are becoming reality; there is currently a hotbed of exciting development activity in electronic books and a few commercial products have already appeared on the market. Reviews of technological developments[16] and commercial products[17] relating to electronic books have recently appeared. A major development is Standard Generalized Markup Language (SGML), which provides would-be producers of electronic books with a standard format that can be processed by a wide variety of software. The initial applications of SGML were in the production of articles in professional journals; it is interesting that SGML is now finding commercial uses.

One of the earliest efforts to develop electronic books was Project Gutenberg. Begun as an experiment on mainframe computers at the University of Illinois, Project Gutenberg has moved to PCs. It is staffed by volunteers who collect works already in electronic form or enter the text of books into an electronic database which is made available on the Internet. Several dozen books, including some classic works, the Bible and reference materials, are available. The goal of Project Gutenberg's creators is to make 10 000 texts available for free distribution by the year 2000[18].

Electronic books are currently distributed on traditional media such as floppy disks and, more recently, on CD-ROMs. Sony's two-pound Discman player uses a special 3.15-inch CD-ROM which can store the equivalent of 100 000 pages of text. A few dozen titles are available, and Sony is working with publishers to increase that number. Sony is also working on a player that can accommodate full sized CD-ROMs containing either text or audio[19]. Several companies produce books on disc that can be read on a standard or a laptop PC. Even a laptop is significantly heavier than a Discman, and many PC screens are not suitable for long sessions of reading because they cause eyestrain — factors which will probably limit the market for PC-based books.

Prototypes of electronic books stored on 'smart cards' (plastic cards the size of a credit card with magnetic storage media) have been produced. These are designed to be read on a lightweight unit with an ergonomically pleasing plasma display screen. Proponents of this type of unit envision 'bookstores' which would sell the cards to readers and 'downloading stations' similar to automated teller machines that would allow users to copy the contents of a book to their smart card (for a fee, of course) and read it at their convenience[20]. Books on smart cards are lightweight and compact and can easily be carried from place to place.

Directories

The Regional Bell Operating Companies (RBOCs) and GTE are the major players in *Yellow Pages* directory publishing. Some RBOCs even own captive directory printing presses so that they can control the production process. RBOC directory revenues have grown steadily at 7% a year and currently exceed $8000 million. Directory publishing has been stimulated primarily by population growth and the consequent growth of businesses which must place ads in the *Yellow Pages* to gain visibility.

Since the 1984 restructuring of the US telecommunications industry and the divestiture of the RBOCs by AT&T, independent directory publishers have appeared in the marketplace, causing considerable churn as they enter and depart. Some RBOCs have also entered the territories of others with their directories. Although some of the independent publishers are profitable, others have gone out of business because of a reluctance by consumers to use more than one directory, as well as a reluctance by advertisers to spend money on advertising in the smaller independent directories.

The subscription directory industry, a small part of directory publishing, is spread among many publishers. Subscription directories are primarily sold to libraries and businesses; one of the more well known is the *Thomas Register*, which has an annual circulation of about 10 000.

Production and distribution are the major cost components in directory publishing; operating margins are about 12%. Much advanced EAP technology has been applied to directory production, especially by the market leader, R. R. Donnelley (which prints about one-third of the directories in the USA). As with other segments of publishing, the directory business is becoming more targeted as advertisers become more demanding.

Audiotext-based information delivery platforms are becoming more popular among directory publishers. Known as 'Talking Yellow Pages', they offer a variety of information categories including sports, weather, horoscopes, games and medical information. Revenues are generated by enlisting sponsors of various information segments (i.e. a drugstore might sponsor medical information announcements); however, most Talking Yellow Pages implementations have yet to prove profitable. Recent developments suggest that service providers are implementing fax options as an additional delivery medium. As with newspapers, fax delivery is used to distinguish the product from traditional directories, not to make a profit.

Newsletters
Newsletters are usually highly specialized, catering to small market niches. Some of them, however, enjoy high circulations in areas such as consumer finance and healthcare. The total number of newsletters published is not known, but some directories list more than 10 000 of them[21]. PCs and DTP software have brought publishing within easy reach of the consumer; many newsletters are produced and distributed by a single entrepreneur performing all the functions of a publisher (major publishers account for only 20% of the newsletter market). Costs are therefore kept low, and with high subscription prices, profits can be substantial. Information in some niche areas may be unavailable except through newsletters, and newsletters can deliver extremely current and timely information; for these reasons, prices tend to be higher than for other media. Newsletters also tend to be highly focused with much detail; their principal interest is pleasing their subscribers and customizing the information they present to meet their readers' needs. They are almost exclusively supported by circulation revenues and rarely carry much advertising because the readers expect 'pure' information. Newsletters are also valued for their sensitivity, timeliness, point of view and direct connection to experts in the field. Newsletter subscription prices tend to be high; revenues from them may therefore be substantial even if the number of subscribers is low.

Acquiring subscribers can be difficult for a newsletter publisher because most newsletters are not widely advertised and hence are relatively unknown. Almost by definition, a newsletter targets a small and very select audience. Many publishers, operating on shoestring budgets, do not have the resources needed to embark on an aggressive promotional campaign to recruit subscribers. And, because of the highly focused nature of newsletters, they are unlikely to appear on the shelves of news-stands or bookstores. Owing to their fragmentation and specialization, and also to the merging of the computer and telecommunications industries, newsletters are ripe for the application of EP technology, particularly in the area of widespread, low-cost electronic delivery.

Publishing industry conclusions

The following are general conclusions on the traditional publishing industry:

- The publishing industry is conservative, with mature and entrenched markets.
- Product evolution has been slow, and the industry is slow to change. To combat this trend, many publishing companies began to diversify into other areas. These efforts generally have not been successful, and many organizations in the traditional publishing industry are currently retrenching.
- New technologies are mainly used to enhance well-established products, not to move in new directions. Many publishers are using EAP technologies, even though they claim to be using EP.
- New activities tend to be experimental.
- Publishing is a low-margin business.

CONVERGENCE OF THE TELECOMMUNICATIONS AND EP INDUSTRIES

In common with many of today's industries, telecommunications has had a significant impact on EP and continues to play an integral role in it. Telecommunications is one of the major channels by which information is delivered to users. An early example was the development of public packet-switched networks in the early 1970s, which played a major role in spurring the rapid growth of commercial online information systems. Computers, telecommunications networks and online information technology are becoming pervasive in the publishing industry.

Within the last five years, major events in the telecommunications industry have profoundly impacted both consumer and business marketplaces. Some overlap has already occurred; we can expect this process to continue and perhaps even accelerate. A substantial overlapping of publishing and telecommunications is expected in the next five years as electronic means of information dissemination become more developed. Even today, networks such as BITNET or the Internet are not only used for widespread scholarly communications[22], but they have also fostered simple and rapid worldwide information interchange on both the formal and informal level. Electronic journals with no printed counterparts are springing up[23]; they may bring about large changes in publishing.

As fibre-optic cables proliferate, with a corresponding increase in bandwidth, new electronic information and entertainment services will become available to consumers, and publishers will be forced to change their marketing and distribution strategies to incorporate this technology and meet users' expectations. Networks will become increasingly available to all types of users and will become an ordinary fact of life like electricity. The September 1991 issue of *Scientific American* contains a series of articles presenting a fascinating view of information networks. Even now, consumers depend increasingly on electronic communications for timely and accurate information to support day-to-day business and personal decisions[24]. Unfortunately, we do not yet have a national information network like the electric power grid; there are no 'information outlets' in buildings similar to electric power outlets[25]. Intelligent networks, satellite transmission, integrated services digital network (ISDN) and fibre-optics are important telecommunications technologies that are intertwining EP with the publishing industry.

Recent US legal and regulatory events have also done much to bring EP close to the telecommunications industry. With the approval of the Department of Justice and Judge Harold Greene, the RBOCs have experimented with information gateways. Although many of these services have been terminated, a few still continue. Judge Greene's 25 July 1991 decision allowing the RBOCs to enter the EP industry is certain to have a major effect; exactly what form future services may take remains open to speculation. RBOC gateways are significant because they represent an early attempt to reach the consumer marketplace with electronic information. Even though many of these gateways have failed, the lessons learned will be valuable in the development of similar services in the future.

FORCES SHAPING THE ELECTRONIC INFORMATION MARKETPLACE

This section describes the model of the forces shaping EP. Like most other industries, EP has a variety of forces acting on it and reacts to them in a variety of ways. The field of electronic information has gone through periods of conception, initial development, and rapid growth, arriving at a more mature period in which it has become an industry in its own right. As Figure 21.3 shows, the EP industry has its own infrastructure with raw material suppliers, manufacturers, wholesalers, retailers and consumers.

Based on the above discussion, one might surmise that the EP industry is primarily driven by technology. While technology is a powerful force (perhaps the most powerful) in this industry, and indeed in many others, it is important to stress that technology is by no means the only driving force in the EP industry. To receive a complete picture, one must consider all the forces involved.

Gantz[26] developed a model of the telecommunications networking industry; we have used his framework for our model of the EP industry and have identified seven forces affecting the EP industry: technology, economics, demographics, social trends, government policies, applications growth, and industry trends (see Figure 21.5). This section discusses major trends and events for each force in a 'cause-and-effect' scenario.

Technology

Of the seven major forces shaping the EP industry of the 1990s, technology has the most far-reaching effects. New information technologies continue to appear, and many of them significantly change the direction in which the electronic information industry is moving[27]. Major trends in the technology area that apply to EP are discussed below.

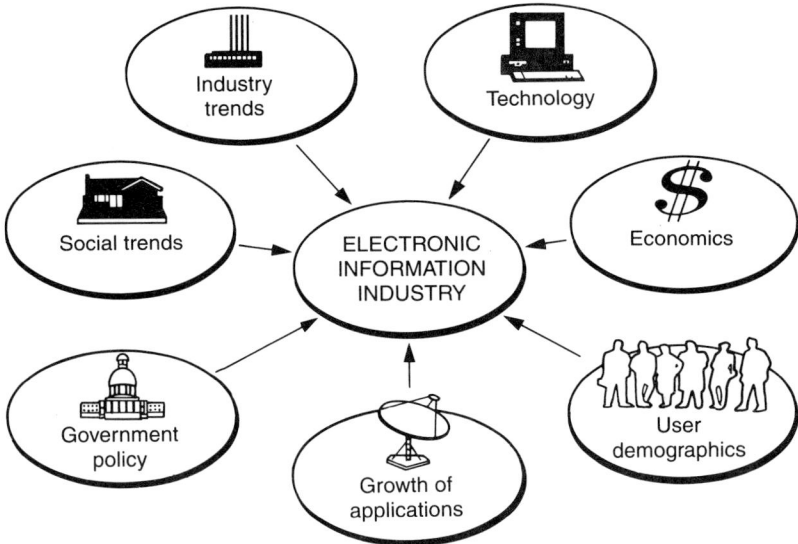

Figure 21.5 Forces shaping the electronic information industry

Online information retrieval systems

Online information includes the well-known commercial systems that sprung up during the 1970s, such as the DIALOG and BRS systems, and also the consumer-oriented videotex systems such as the CompuServeSM, GEnie, and Prodigy services. All these systems share the common characteristic that their access mode is dial-up (usually through a packet-switched network), so the user must have a PC or terminal to do a search and receive the desired information. A recent significant development is the emergence of 'local online' systems, where organizations mount databases locally on their own mainframe and allow access to the information by a closed group of users (employees, for example). Such systems have the advantages of flat-rate pricing known in advance (and therefore simpler budgeting), easily controlled access and the ability to merge local information (such as library holdings) with information from the commercial online databases. For example, the AT&T Library Network makes several databases available for local online access through its LINUS system[28]. These systems have been quite successful in broadening the audience for electronic information. Unless consumers have access to a major library, however, there is little likelihood that they will be exposed to local online systems. A large body of literature on online retrieval is available; for references to further readings, consult the comprehensive bibliography by Hawkins[29].

Optical storage media

Because of their high storage densities (550 megabytes on a single CD-ROM), optical storage media have made large databases of information readily available to consumers. Many databases currently available online are also distributed on CD-ROM. Although the market for CD-ROM databases is still small, with few titles selling more than 1000 copies[30], the CD-ROM industry is becoming one of the most rapidly growing areas of the information scene. CD-ROMs are the data analogues of the extremely popular audio compact discs. There are now well over 1000 titles available[31], and the CD-ROM information industry now has its own journals (*CD-ROM Professional, CD-ROM Librarian* and others). In 1990, the annual Online conference changed its name to the Online/CD-ROM conference, reflecting the growing importance of this area of the electronic information industry. One of the latest developments in the CD-ROM area is the development of networks and 'jukeboxes,' allowing several workstations to be networked to a collection of databases on CD-ROM.

Because entertainment plays such an important role with consumers, technologies allowing user interaction, such as compact disc-interactive (CD-i), will become important. Encyclopaedia publishers are beginning to produce their products on CD-ROM. Some of them, Compton's for example, have incorporated graphics and sound to produce a multimedia product for the mass market[32]. As PC manufacturers begin to bundle CD-ROM drives with their equipment, this market can look forward to a significant expansion. CD-ROM may well be the vehicle by which consumers gain entrance to the world of databases that has long been the familiar domain of the information professional. Many public libraries have installed Information Access Company's Info-Trac system, which stores its information on a CD-ROM. Many Info-Trac workstations keep the CD-ROM hardware in a locked cabinet; consumers may therefore be using databases on optical media without realizing it.

Gateways

In the 1980s, interfaces to aid users in connecting to commercial online retrieval systems were developed. These 'gateways' helped novice users to access systems by performing the functions of selecting a network, establishing the connection, and entering the user's password[33]. They did not perform searches; the user was on his or her own to interact with the system using its commands once the connection was established.

Gateways enjoyed a considerable popularity in the late 1980s. The RBOCs entered the business, and some of them still offer gateway services to users (see the discussion of new telecommunications services below). Telebase Systems' EasyNet service continues to provide access to about 12 information services (collectively mounting about 1000 databases) through a single access point and has taken the significant step of developing a common command language based on the NISO (National Information Standards Organization) standard. The gateway business seems to have fallen into the doldrums, however, and several of the RBOCs have discontinued their gateway services. EasyNet continues to be profitable; and with the acquisition of the EasyLink electronic mail service by AT&T, the EasyNet service may assume a new importance[34]. Hawkins, Levy, and Montgomery[35] proposed the concept of a 'knowledge gateway' and discussed the technologies that would be required to build it. Little progress toward a knowledge gateway appears to have been made since their paper was published, although it is interesting to note that many of the technologies they identified are the same ones discussed here.

Videotex

Videotex services are commonly defined as those offered directly to the consumer market. Many videotex systems place an emphasis on entertainment (games), communication services (chat, messaging, etc.), and home shopping, but they also include information services such as bulletin boards, news, weather and the like[2]. Although some videotex systems still present information to the user as ASCII text scrolling across the screen, a growing number of them now use the North American Presentation Level Protocol Syntax (NAPLPS) to take advantage of flexibility in fonts, colours, and graphical interfaces. Videotex received a bad name in the information world because of several widely publicized system failures in the early 1980s, and it may be for this reason that the term is being replaced by 'interactive services' or 'consumer online services'[36]. The reasons for these failures apply to any EP system, and include:

- An overreliance on the 'newspaper model' of information, where the information system concentrates on news and news-related items such as sports scores, stock prices and so forth. Such systems had difficulty succeeding because of well entrenched competition from newspapers themselves, which offer the same information free or very cheaply.
- A requirement to use expensive dedicated Consumer Premises Equipment (CPE). Especially with unproven services, consumers will not purchase such equipment. Systems must be flexible and able to deliver their output to a variety of CPE.
- Systems must be entertaining and fun to use. A simple ASCII news service does not provide the consumer with much entertainment. Many disposable dollars are used for entertainment; videotex systems must recognize this.
- Early videotex systems simultaneously tied up two important communication pathways into the home: the television and the telephone. Multiple activities were impaired (for example, when someone was using the telephone, other family members could not use the videotex system).
- Unless users are highly motivated, systems with a complicated interface are not likely to be used. Videotex requires the user's undivided attention and concentration and cannot be used in a passive mode when doing something else at the same time. The user must make a conscious decision to access the system, enter commands and respond to its queries.

Today's videotex systems have progressed beyond those of the 1980s, and it appears that some of the lessons of the early failures have been learned. Graphical interfaces, entertainment services, advertiser-supported information systems (such as the Prodigy service), and directory information all exist and are competing for a share of the market, which was estimated by LINK Resources to be $320 million in 1990, growing to $884 million by 1995[10]. However, profits continue to be elusive in the videotex industry, even for organizations such as Prodigy Services Co., which has strong financial backing from its venture partners, and one industry source reported that the mood at the 1991 meeting of the Videotex Industry Association (VIA) was 'depressing'[37].

The well-known French Minitel system is one of the industry's major success stories. Minitel survives because of heavy government subsidies and the trigger application of telephone directory listings. US systems include US Videotel, CompuServe, Prodigy, and GEnie. Of these, CompuServe and GEnie are the healthiest financially; CompuServe offers extensive forums and bulletin boards as well as downloadable software, and GEnie offers entertainment. The prominence of bulletin boards and real-time 'chat' services in videotex systems is interesting; it shows that even in an age of impersonal electronic information, humans have a societal need to contact and communicate with others.

Artificial intelligence/expert systems

Even though progress in artificial intelligence (AI) and expert systems has not been as rapid as first hoped, AI will play an important role in EP in the future. As systems become more complex and the volume of information with which they must deal grows, more and more decision-making must be shifted from the user to the system. Users are not able to deal with complicated interfaces, lengthy menus and so forth. To keep information access simple and attractive (and thus ensure that systems will be used), AI must be built into the systems. Early hopes were that AI technology could be incorporated into electronic systems so that they could perform many of the functions carried out by humans; however, growing complexities and rapid dynamic changes in the required knowledge have largely dashed such hopes[38]. Major areas of potential for AI lie in simplifying the user interface, making intelligent decisions so that users are effortlessly guided through the systems, resolving language ambiguities and so on. Extensive work is occurring in a number of research laboratories, particularly in the application of rule-based expert systems to information storage and retrieval problems.

Imaging and OCR

Imaging, a process of converting printed material to electronic form, has become an important and significant technology as scanners and optical character recognition (OCR) software have improved. Much of the information of interest to users is in hard copy form; converting it to machine-readable format would be a daunting task without imaging technology. Advances in photocopying and facsimile transmission have been applied to scanning technology, resulting in the widespread availability of high-speed stand-alone scanners. Documents are now routinely scanned and converted to bit-mapped images, allowing much closer control and tracking procedures. In environments in which scanning is routinely used, throughput has increased and errors have decreased.

Scanning produces only bit-mapped images; the process can be likened to taking an 'electronic photograph' of a document[39]. If one wishes to search the content of the scanned material, it must be converted to ASCII text — the function of OCR software. Today's OCR software has advanced considerably since the early days of large expensive dedicated hardware; software running on a single PC is now available. Of critical importance is the error rate. Rates of 1% to 2% may appear low, but in large volumes of material such levels are not acceptable — much manual labour may need to be expended to correct errors, even with a 1% error rate. Imaging and OCR technologies will have a major impact on the EP world, especially when OCR error rates are decreased further.

Text management

The growth of imaging technology has led to a corresponding growth of systems to interface with imaging systems and process the output of the OCR process. As more documents are converted to electronic form using imaging and OCR systems, the problem of how to search the resulting text has become more pressing. Locke[40] has called this problem 'the dark side of document image processing'. The text management systems now appearing on the market are specifically designed to handle large volumes of text. Many of them use AI-like techniques, such as concept retrieval, that are far advanced from the traditional Boolean retrieval[41]. The effect of text management systems on the EP industry will be important and widespread as these systems become more sophisticated and as imaging and OCR systems become commonplace.

New telecommunications services

As noted above, the publishing and telecommunications industries are merging. Telecommunications represents a major channel by which information is delivered to users. Indeed, the development of public packet-switched networks was one of the major events responsible for the rapid growth of commercial online retrieval systems. When communications became reliable and costs fell, user resistance disappeared. Advances in telecommunications such as ISDN, satellite communications and higher bandwidth are expected to stimulate new information and entertainment services to consumers' homes. Several RBOCs are proposing to bring fibre-optic cables to homes in their metropolitan areas and provide capability for these advanced services[42]. Networking has an especially significant impact; movement of information over electronic networks has become commonplace and can probably be expected to become ubiquitous within the next decade. Even if they do not access electronic information directly themselves, consumers depend on it to support day-to-day business and personal decisions (for example, in making travel arrangements or arranging credit).

Cellular communications equipment has recently been developed for laptop computers, so information retrieval services can be accessed from anywhere. Some independent information brokers are beginning to incorporate cellular technology into their equipment and are able to perform online searches directly from a client's site or from hotel conference rooms with the assurance that access will be possible even if external telephone lines are not[43].

Multimedia

New ways of communicating are becoming available with the development of multimedia technology such as CD-i, digital video interactive (DVI), CD-ROM Extended Architecture (CD-ROM XA) and interactive television. Multimedia refers to the ability of information producers to combine several technologies (text, still frame and full motion video) in order to offer systems in which the user can interact with the information being delivered. Such systems are not widely distributed yet, but they show immense potential, especially in the areas of entertainment and education. A major limiting factor is the absence of a universal standard. Today's CD-ROMs follow the 'High Sierra' standard, which limits their capabilities to text and data. For multimedia systems to become widespread, the standards hurdle is a major one that must be overcome.

Turnkey EP platforms

Completely operational voice information systems have appeared on the market. Users need not know anything about the technology or how to assemble or integrate such systems. Newspapers and other information providers, for example, are now able to purchase such a system, provide the telephone access lines and offer information services to the users. Purchasers of these turnkey systems can offer their own content, or they can receive standard or customized content from the system vendor.

Advances in Consumer Premises Equipment (CPE)

With the increasing sophistication of PCs, the 'electronic appliance' in the consumer's home is coming closer to reality. PCs will become multipurpose devices used to control all the electronics in the home, including the television, video-cassette recorder and environmental devices such as the heating and security systems. Television and similar video technologies are merging with computers. The current debate is whether the intelligence should reside in the TV set or the computer. Several years will elapse, however, before complete integration is achieved. Today's PCs do not blend well into consumer lifestyles because they are too user-hostile. They are cumbersome and difficult to learn how to use and require too much structured thinking by users. Many of the applications for today's PCs are still highly text-based and are not sufficiently visual, and many of them require proficiency in using a keyboard (although this is changing with the widespread penetration of graphical user interfaces such as the Microsoft Windows system). As AI, natural language and advanced ergonomic designs are incorporated into PCs, we can expect them to find uses in the home far beyond those of today.

These technological developments will continue to have a major impact on the EP industry. Other trends, however, also need to be examined in order to gain a complete picture of the probable direction of EP.

Economics

It is trite to say that economic trends are important. Cost increases affect every sector of the economy and seemingly insignificant or localized events can have far-reaching and major effects. The most significant cost component in publishing (and in many other industries) is labour. Labour costs continue to escalate. Everyone is familiar with efforts to mechanize or automate operations to reduce costs. The publishing business is especially sensitive to costs of paper,

printing and mailing. EP has become increasingly attractive to publishers as they search for ways to disseminate their products more
cost-effectively.

In the EAP area, publishers have been successful in lowering costs
by taking advantage of new technological developments. Rising postage costs have led to electronic presorting. (The US Postal Service
gives substantial discounts if mail is delivered to them already sorted
and ready to enter their distribution system.) Distributed printing is
also under investigation, especially by magazine publishers. If a publisher can electronically transmit material to a local site and print it
close to the customer (as *USA Today* does), not only will costs be
lower, but the information will reach the user more quickly. Service
and quality will thus be enhanced, leading to increased customer
satisfaction.

Slowdowns and a recessionary economic climate have substantially reduced consumer advertising budgets. Advertisers are becoming increasingly demanding of publishers, insisting on close tracking
of subscribers so that they receive maximum return for their advertising expenditures. Electronic information systems are easily able to
keep track of their users and compile statistics to satisfy such demands; Prodigy is one example of an electronic information system
that is heavily supported by advertising.

The economics of EP are not as well understood as those of EAP.
Issues such as costs for electronic database production, migration of
revenues from print to electronic information products, charging for
downloading and reuse of information, and pricing algorithms have
all been prominent at various times in the past decade. Information
producers and system providers continue to wrestle with pricing
issues in their efforts to become (or remain) profitable, and in doing
so, they have created many awkward pricing algorithms which are
confusing to users[44]. Early electronic information systems followed
the model of time-sharing service bureaus in setting their prices,
basing them on connect-times; some major vendors continue to use
connect-time pricing. Others have experimented with flat-rate pricing or have attempted to reduce their dependence on connect-time
pricing; these are encouraging developments. Simple and easily understood pricing is critical in ensuring the widespread use of EP
systems, particularly those designed for consumers.

Demographics

Changing demographic patterns have affected both the type of information of interest to consumers and the delivery channels. The pace of life generally has quickened, making traditional manual methods of obtaining information less used and spurring the move toward electronic delivery. Major trends in this area are the following.

Ageing of America

Figure 21.6 shows the current US population by age group, and Figure 21.7 shows that the median age of the population has been steadily rising over the past two decades. This trend will continue as the 'baby boomer' generation reaches middle age. The baby boomers (usually defined as those born between 1946 and 1964) now comprise 25% of the population, and this percentage is expected to grow to 30% by the year 2000. Senior citizens (over age 65) make up 12% of the population. These trends have changed consumers' informa-

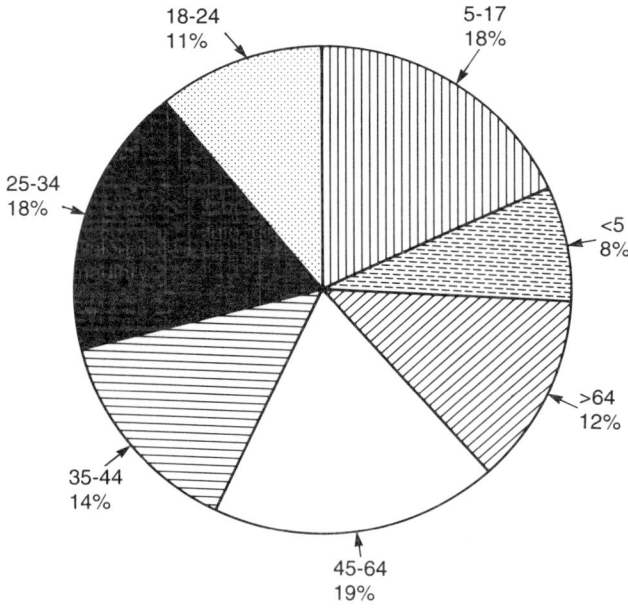

Figure 21.6 US population distribution by age (1990 Census Data) (Source: US Census Bureau, 'USA Statistics In Brief', 1991)

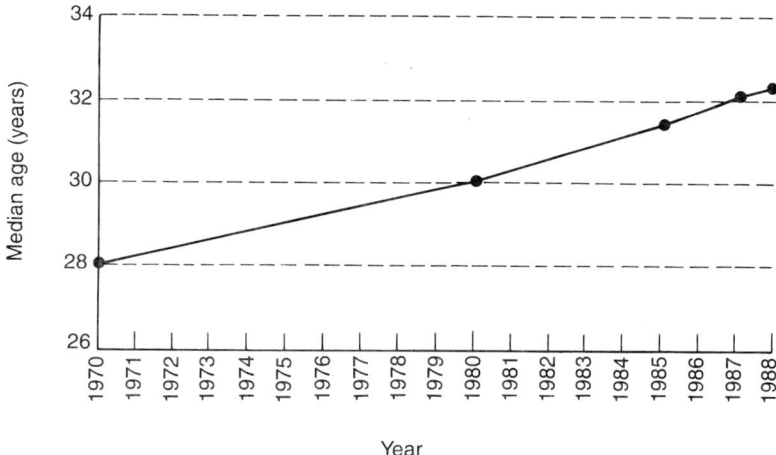

Figure 21.7 Median age of US population (1990 Census Data) (Source: US Census Bureau, 'USA Statistics in Brief', 1991)

tion needs and have made time-saving services and products extremely popular.[45] Niche products, providing detailed and specialized information on a single topic can be expected to become popular; the subjects of health, nutrition, travel, insurance, financial planning and continuing education are of interest to an older more affluent population. With smaller families and incomes from two careers, the baby boomers will have different information needs than previous generations[46].

Increased pressure on baby boomers

Busy two career families do not have time for time-consuming searches to find the information they want. If it cannot be obtained quickly, they will probably do without it. Demand for information delivered electronically through EP systems will therefore increase, because electronic systems offer rapid access to categorized or indexed information. Besides dealing with the pressures of two careers and growing families, many baby boomers are also part of the 'sandwich generation', needing to care not only for young children but also for ageing parents. Time is one of their scarcest resources — another force that will drive the development of electronic information systems.

Emergence of 'power teens'

As the children of the baby-boomer generation grow, they will also become a significant market force. Even now, children, the four to 12 year-old generation commands substantial purchasing power by influencing parental spending — as much as $75 000 million per year (approximately 2% of the US economy)[47]. Teenagers (age 13–19) are technologically aware, and they are smart consumers. Although much of their spending is on recreational products such as video games, kids and teenagers are at the age when they are beginning to make product choices, including information services, which may well remain with them for a lifetime. Marketers have begun to realize that they must not ignore this generation — the consumers of tomorrow who are comfortable and knowledgeable with computers and not reluctant to use electronic information if it is available. With the US birth rate at its highest since 1964, the EP industry must recognize that the kids and teenage markets are substantial ones for its services.

Ethnic and cultural diversity

The USA is increasingly becoming an ethnically diverse and a multi-lingual society. According to 1990 US census data, in some major urban areas, well over 25% of the residents speak a language other than English in their homes, and the number of foreign born residents (about 20 million) is at an all-time high[48]. Today's immigrants are well educated, have strong cultural and family ties to their homelands and want to keep in close touch with them[49]. Electronic information services in nonEnglish languages, not yet widely available, have a good potential for success and should grow in popularity and market share.

Social trends

Closely related to both demographic and economic forces shaping the EP industry are some important social trends.

Telecommuting and home businesses

People are moving away from urban environments into more rural settings in the belief that life has a better quality, costs are lower and real estate is cheaper. One result of this trend is that journeys to the place of work have lengthened significantly. In an effort to lessen or even eliminate lengthy journeys, many organizations are experimenting with telecommuting — employees working from home using a PC and electronic communications such as electronic mail — for one or two days a week. Telecommuters and home business entrepreneurs use electronic communications extensively. They need access to the same resources they may have when they are in their offices, such as corporate libraries, databases, electronic mail networks and so on. Such workers will invariably be heavy users of electronic information and will be a significant driving force for the EP industry.

Convenience and simplification

We have already discussed the increasing time pressures on major segments of society. Consumers are not willing to devote major portions of their time to learning about and using complex products. 'One-stop shopping' and prepackaged products are, therefore, finding a significant success in the marketplace; this applies to information services as well. Using EP, information providers can customize their products and make them more convenient to use. Forward-looking information companies will make full use of the capabilities of EP to produce products that are simple, convenient and easy to use.

Increased focus on home and family

Fundamental changes are occurring in consumers' lifestyles. The baby boomers are maturing and entering their peak child-rearing years and, although pursuing very active lives, are placing an increasing emphasis on their homes and families. 'Cocooning', a new term coined to describe these trends, has been defined as 'the need to protect oneself from the unpredictable, the stressful, and often hostile, outside environment'[50].

This fact has not been lost on catalogue publishers and direct marketers, who are increasing their activities to appeal to this group of consumers. According to market research firms, the number of consumers shopping by 'phone from home has mushroomed from 57.4 million in 1983 to over 90 million in 1989.

In the information arena, cocooning means that new methods of bringing information into the home should enjoy wide acceptance, and existing electronic pathways into the home — telephone and television — will be increasingly used to deliver information services.

Cocooning can therefore be expected to have a significant effect on the EP industry.

Increased focus on quality of life

We have already mentioned the desire of consumers for a better quality of life and the effect these desires are having on the movement of the population away from the cities. Dispersion of the population does not lessen consumers' information needs; indeed, it increases the need to communicate and remain in touch. EP services will play a major role in fulfilling these needs.

Government policies

Although there are many perspectives on this topic[51], government policies affecting the EP industry tend to be regulative and restrictive and are therefore a limitation on the development of new services. Many government policies in the electronic information area are still unclear or ambiguous because they were formulated before the emergence of EP as a way of producing and transmitting information, and the circumstances governing electronic information are often significantly different than those governing print.

Copyright laws

The copyright laws of many countries (including the USA) were promulgated before electronic methods of producing and transmitting information were as common as they are today. Many questions are still unanswered or untested in the courts[52,53]. Using many electronic systems, information can be copied, altered and transmitted, often virtually without detection. Information producers and other rights holders are concerned that they receive a fair remuneration for their intellectual property. Many information producers have resorted to charging higher fees for copying and reuse simply because they are unable to monitor every instance of it. The uncertainties in copyright law as it pertains to electronic information are a significant limitation to the development of new services based on EP.

Fewer RBOC constraints

The RBOCs are heavily regulated, both by the Federal Communications Commission (FCC) and the Department of Justice (primarily Judge Greene who continues to oversee the Modified Final Judgement divesting the RBOCs from AT&T). The RBOCs are active in lobbying for relief from regulation so that they can enter the information services market and also begin to manufacture equipment. In two significant opinions (US vs Western Electric Co., 673 F. Suppl., p. 525, DDC 1987; and US vs Western Electric Co., 1988–1 Trade Cases, DDC 1988), Judge Greene allowed the RBOCs to enter the gateway business, but as already noted, most of their gateway efforts have not been successful. One of the reasons for the failure of RBOC gateways was cost. The RBOCs were not allowed to serve more than one local transport area from a gateway host, and if they wished to serve other transport areas, duplicate individual hosts had to be established. This requirement greatly increased the costs of providing gateway service and also lowered its efficiency. A recent ruling (US vs Western Electric Co., No. 82-0192, DDC 25 July 1991) has removed many of the restrictions on the RBOCs providing information services, including this one. It is widely felt that the RBOCs will eventually be allowed to enter the electronic information business with few or no restrictions. When that happens, the EP business could experience a significant growth spurt. Competition should then increase because of new and well-positioned entrants into the market.

Legislative restrictions on information delivery

The spread of fax machines, telemarketing activities, audiotext systems and direct mail has also given rise to an increase in restrictions on delivery of information, particularly unsolicited information. In response to the 'junk fax' problem, some state legislatures have passed laws limiting the length of unsolicited messages and even the hours in which they could be sent[54]. Telemarketing activities are limited to certain hours of the day in which sales and market research campaigns may be conducted. These are examples of activities by governmental agencies that have limited the spread of information. There are also a range of other issues related to privacy, intellectual property rights, ownership of government information and so forth, yet to be resolved. As the EP industry grows and matures, it is likely that legislation will be passed curbing its activities in a similar way.

Applications growth

As technology advances, new applications continue to appear. New applications are a significant force in the EP industry because they drive the development of more applications and contribute to a maturing of the industry. This section presents several recent significant applications.

Audiotext

Delivery of information such as news, weather, lottery numbers and sports results by voice has become almost ubiquitous in the USA. Early audiotext systems used voice response units with the speech recorded and stored in analog form on magnetic tape. These nonelectronic systems have now largely disappeared. With the development of digitized voice and text-to-speech technology, electronic management of voice files became possible. Most of today's systems store the speech as digitized voice which is delivered to the user. A few of the more advanced systems incorporate information taken from ASCII files and converted by text-to-speech to voice. Electronic systems manage the voice and ASCII files and synthesize the information into a single unified voice message for delivery. When text-to-speech technology becomes more sophisticated and efficient, large textual databases can be assembled (perhaps from real-time feeds of information such as newswires), processed by text-to-speech systems, and delivered orally, as audiotext, to users. Audiotext is therefore rapidly moving toward becoming a fully-fledged EP delivery channel, and steps in this direction are already evident. Some electronic mail systems, for example, allow their users to access their mailboxes and listen to their mail rather than read it.

Despite its popularity, audiotext has several constraints as an information delivery channel. It cannot be used to deliver large volumes of detailed information or long messages because listeners are unwilling to remain on the line long enough to listen to lengthy messages. (The '3-3-3-rule' — a maximum of three menus, three choices and three minutes — is a popular rule of thumb in constructing audiotext information services.) The information is not accessible or deliverable in a tangible or viewable form that can be easily browsed, scanned or reviewed; the listener must commit it to memory as it is heard or listen to it again. Early audiotext systems were repellent to consumers because the voice one heard had an artificial sound. Significant advances in synthesized voice technology have given today's systems a much more human-like sound than the earlier ones, making them more attractive to consumers.

Fax news

A few newspaper publishers have experimented with fax delivery of headline news; fax subscribers thus get the news well in advance of subscribers to the printed edition. From the publisher's viewpoint, one advantage of fax editions is that the cost of the printing, paper and so forth is borne by the recipient, not the publisher. Fax news services have not been completely successful, and several of them have ceased[55]. The *Hartford Courant* was one of the first to try a fax edition and continues to produce it, and the *Los Angeles Times* sends a news summary by fax to diplomats in Moscow. The *Courant* delivers a synopsis of the following day's headlines, stock market closings and weather to subscribers to its fax service when the following day's paper is prepared for publication.

Newspapers have used fax as a delivery channel to test its acceptance and to differentiate themselves from their competitors in order to reach wider markets. Most fax editions of newspapers have relied on circulation for their revenues and do not include advertising, which could be a reason for their widespread failure. In an interesting counter-example, a small newspaper publisher in Illinois has successfully established a totally advertiser-supported fax edition[56]. The venture is profitable, and monthly revenues are growing.

Videotex interconnectivity

Videotex systems, a way to offer EP services to consumers, are usually stand-alone services; little has been done to interconnect them. In 1990, Bell Canada announced that subscribers to its ALEX service would be able to use the information services on NYNEX's INFO-LOOK system. Unfortunately, the INFO-LOOK system ceased operations, so the connection never occurred. Interconnection of consumer online systems would allow more EP services to be made available to a wider user base. Other similar arrangements are starting to appear; one example is the interconnection of the French Minitel system with the Dutch videotex network.

Interactive games

It has often been observed that games and other forms of entertainment are a trigger application for information services. Users frequently subscribe to a service for its entertainment applications, then move into more serious information services; this was one growth pattern for the French Minitel service[57]. Games provide a significant revenue stream for several of today's videotex services, and even allow geographically separated players (who never meet physically) to compete against each other. Since game usage often leads to demand for other applications, the development of interactive games affects the EP industry.

Information on audio cassettes

The growth of this market is relevant because EP techniques can be used to customize content (by assembling it from a database, for example) before it is placed on an audiotape. Books and other information on cassettes have become popular because they are a passive medium and can be listened to while the user is doing something else simultaneously, such as commuting to work. One producer of books on cassette for executives has estimated that 80% of its subscribers use their cassettes in cars[58], and some popular works have sold over 25 000 copies in cassette form[59]. The majority of cassettes are on business or educational subjects.

Customized textbook publishing

A recent application by McGraw-Hill is a good example of how EP techniques can be applied to a traditional industry. A college professor, for example, working with McGraw-Hill, can custom design a textbook for his or her classes[60]. The professor can select chapters from several existing textbooks as well as articles from professional or trade magazines (all must be published by McGraw-Hill, of course) and the resulting customized book can be produced, bound, and ready for use within 48 hours. An initial pilot project involving law and business textbooks began at the University of Southern California in 1991[61]. This process is possible when all the material is already in electronic form and the time-consuming steps of editing, proofreading and layout have already been done. It is a good example of the application of EP techniques to produce a new product. Similar products are expected to appear in the near future.

Industry trends

The final force driving the EP industry is general industry trends. Many of these have been alluded to already.

Alliances between technology developers and publishers

We have already discussed the convergence of telecommunications technology and the publishing industry. Other technologies show the same trend; for example, telecommunications and computing have become closely intertwined. A major effect of these alliances is that new products and services are developed and introduced more rapidly as synergies and economies of scale are exploited.

Nationwide publishing networks

Besides formal networks such as BITNET or the Internet, other networks exist which can be used by those who wish to take advantage of EP. For example, some quick printing chains now offer public DTP facilities in which a user can compose a document and then have it printed at the print shop. The AlphaGraphics chain has taken this concept one step further[62]. The user can submit the disk containing the prepared document to the operator and have it transmitted electronically to another city for printing there, thus bypassing mail and distribution delays and costs. Individuals are thus beginning to use EAP and EP techniques.

More information sources

As mentioned at the outset of this article, the number of commercially available online databases is growing at about 10% a year. This 'information explosion' shows no sign of abating; as it continues, new electronically published products will continue to appear. With such a proliferation of information available in electronic form, simpler access is needed. Users are having difficulties locating the information they need.

Increasing market segmentation

As information markets become more fragmented and segmented, marketers are becoming increasingly concerned that their advertising expenditures be deployed effectively. We have already noted the growth of selective binding in the publishing industry; similar trends can be expected to surface in other industries.

KEYS TO SUCCESS IN EP

Based on the seven major forces shaping the EP industry discussed above, we derived some principles that we believe must be followed to achieve success in EP. This section discusses those principles, and the following section concludes with some general observations and a few further inferences.

Satisfy the needs and wants of users

The first and most important key to success is that any information service (electronic or not) must satisfy the needs and wants of its users. It may be tempting to plunge into a large-scale development effort using the latest technological advances. It is critical, however, to recognize that not only are there other forces that must be considered, but technology alone will not sell services or make money. If a service does not have the information users want, it will eventually fail. Frequently, out of curiosity, users may try a service once or twice, but no service has ever succeeded based on curiosity alone; repeat usage must occur for profits to accrue. Content is therefore critically important, and anyone involved in planning an EP service must carefully consider what content will be offered.

Develop the product line for success

A product-line approach has high potential for success. Many information services have failed because they were too complex. While it can never be ruled out, it is unlikely that a 'killer' application or service remains to be discovered in EP. Success in EP is more likely to be achieved by developing a series of small products, perhaps targeted at several niche markets, and then integrating them into a unified system.

Adapt to the user's environment

Especially in recessionary times, users are reluctant to invest in specialized and dedicated equipment to access EP information services. Requiring the purchase of such equipment is a sure way to limit the potential market. Flexibility in both input and output (i.e. delivery) channels is more desirable. EP service developers must recognize that not only do users' environments differ, but users do not all think like systems developers. More natural system interfaces will do much to promote the use of electronic information systems.

Keep pricing simple

Simple, flexible and understandable pricing is extremely important. Some EP systems seem to be competing with each other to devise complex pricing schemes. Users are beset by a plethora of pricing components: connect-hours, hit charges, telecommunications charges, character counts, network charges, resource units and so on. A variety of pricing schemes exist: flat-rate, usage-sensitive, time differential, baud rate-sensitive and so forth[44]. Especially for consumers, pricing must be simple and easy to understand. Flat-rate pricing is preferable to usage-sensitive pricing, especially when dealing with an interactive service.

'Me too' products will not work

Especially with a complex product like electronic information, products must be clearly differentiated. A service that mimics one already existing (such as producing a database exactly analogous to one in printed form) will have a difficult time succeeding in today's competitive market. Value must be added to promote brand recognition and ensure usage.

Recognize the trigger application

Entertainment has often been the initial reason why users subscribe to a service; then they move on to other applications. Because EP services may be relatively unknown to consumers and may require a substantial promotional investment if marketed on their own, they may be more likely to succeed if they are positioned as part of a service whose main thrust is entertainment. They will then be readily available when users are ready to explore more serious uses of electronic systems.

THE FUTURE EP INDUSTRY

The model of the seven forces driving the EP industry of the 1990s presents an accurate picture of this important industry. From the forces identified, a list of major factors that should help ensure success for those who are contemplating the development of new electronic information services has been derived. The picture of the EP industry that emerges has much turmoil, confusion, and even fragmentation in it. New applications, services and products appear and disappear with great regularity, and most of them are targeted at limited markets. It has become clear that there is no 'mother lode' in this industry, nor is there a major significant application waiting in the wings that will swamp competing applications and be a runaway success. Entrance into the EP industry requires a significant investment and considerable staying power. Estimates of the investment made by IBM and Sears in the Prodigy service range as high as $1000 million[63]. Most new EP services will begin slowly in niche markets. The successful ones will expand carefully and realistically.

Lest it appear that the above analysis is too pessimistic, we hasten to affirm our optimism for the EP industry. As we proceeded with our study, we became convinced that EP will be a significant, perhaps common, part of consumers' lives by the end of the present decade. EP is becoming a consumer application. User-friendly interfaces to large online systems are being developed, large amounts of information are becoming available on optical storage media, communications networks are undergoing steady development, and increasing emphasis is being placed on information customized to individual consumers' needs. Although the EP industry appears to have little infrastructure, that is precisely the reason why it is exciting and stimulating, both for those involved in it and for its users. We look forward to continuing advances and eagerly anticipate the new developments that are sure to come.

REFERENCES

1   *Directory of Online Databases* Cuadra/Gale, USA (Jan 1991) (updated quarterly)
2   **Hawkins, D T** 'And you thought videotex was dead!' *ONLINE* Vol 14 No 6 (1990) pp 113–115

3   *Residential Telephone User Tracking Study* Yankee Group, USA (1989)

4   **White, M S** 'Management guidelines for profitable electronic publishing' *Proc. International Conference on Electronic Publishing and Commercial Publishing* Online Conferences Ltd, UK (1985) pp 197–213

5   **Gurnsey, J** 'Electronic publishing: A market perspective' *ASLIB Proceedings* Vol 35 No 1 (Oct 1983) pp 389–397

6   **Downes, R N** 'Electronic technology and access to information' *Journal of Library Administration* Vol 12 No 3 (1990) pp 51–61

7   **Aitchison, T M** 'The database producer in the information chain' *Journal of Information Science, Principles and Practice* Vol 14 (1988) pp 319–327

8   **O'Leary, M** 'Dialog and the American Chemical Society play a high stakes game' *ONLINE* Vol 15 No 1 (1991) pp 15–20

9   *North American Electronic Information Industry Five Year Forecast, 1990–1995* LINK Resources, Inc., USA (1992)

10   *United States Consumer Online Services Forecast, 1990–1995* LINK Resources, USA (1991)

11   *Communications Industry Forecast, 1991–1995* Veronis Suhler & Associates, USA (1991)

12   **Hanley, K** 'Getting selective' *Target Marketing* Vol 10 No 6 (1987) pp 30, 34

13   **Brown, D** 'Beating the postal rate blues' *Management Review* Vol 81 No 4 (1992) pp 55–57

14   **Foltz, K** 'Magazine industry bracing for shakeout as ads drop' *The New York Times* (30 Apr 1990) p C1

15   **Boswell, J** *The Awful Truth About Book Publishing* Warner Books, USA (1986)

16   **Reynolds, L R and Derose, S J** 'Electronic books' *BYTE* Vol 17 No 6 (Jun 1992) pp 263–268

17   **Potts, M** 'Plugged-in publishing: New generation of electronic books spawns industry visions of a reading revolution' *Washington Post* (5 Jul 1992) H01

18   **Hart, M S** 'Project Gutenberg: Access to electronic texts' *Database* Vol 13 No 6 (1990) pp 6–9

19   **Rawlinson, N** 'Roll over Gutenberg' *Publishers Weekly* Vol 239 No 27 (15 Jun 1992) pp 50–51

20 **Venant, E** 'Are you ready to curl up with a good computer screen?' *Los Angeles Times* (15 Jan 1992) p E1

21 *Newsletters in Print* (4th Ed.) Gale Research, USA (1989–1990)

22 **Arms, C M** 'Using the national networks: BITNET and the Internet' *ONLINE* Vol 14 No 5 (1990) pp 24–29

23 **Piternick, A B** 'Serials and new technology: The state of the electronic journal' *Canadian Library Journal* Vol 46 No 2 (1989) pp 93–97

24 **Solomon, A H** 'Telecommunications in the 1990s — Evolving technologies (Part I)' *Telecommunications Journal* Vol 57 No 1 (1990) pp 43–46

25 **Hawkins, D T** 'Whither a national information infrastructure?' *ONLINE* Vol 15 No 5 (1991) pp 84–86

26 **Gantz, J** 'The networking industry: Reshaping for the millennium' *Networking Management* Vol 8 No 1 (1990) pp 17–28

27 **Hawkins, D T** 'New information technologies — they just keep coming' *ONLINE* Vol 14 No 1 (1990) pp 93–96

28 **Cherry, L L and Waldstein, R K** 'Electronic access to full document text and images through LINUS' *AT&T Technical Journal* Vol 68 No 4 (1989) pp 72–90

29 **Hawkins, D T** *Online Information Retrieval Bibliography, 1987–1989* Learned Information Inc., USA (1990)

30 **Tenopir, C** 'CD-ROM goes consumer' *Library Journal* Vol 116 No 10 (Jun 1991) pp 109–110

31 *Directory of Portable Databases* Cuadra/Gale, USA (Apr 1991) (updated quarterly)

32 **Steffey, R J** 'Compton's Multimedia Encyclopedia: Bringing multimedia to the masses' *CD-ROM Professional* Vol 4 No 3 (1991) pp 13–20

33 **Hawkins, D T and Levy, L R** 'Front end software for online database searching. Part 1: Definitions, system features, and evaluation' *ONLINE* Vol 9 No 6 (1985) pp 30–37

34 **Sosland, M D** 'This data broker is a real tell-all' *Business Week* (27 Aug 1990) p 82A (Correction: Letters to the Editor *Business Week* (17 Sep 1990) p 7)

35 **Hawkins, D T, Levy, L R, and Montgomery, K L** 'Knowledge gateways: The building blocks' *Information Processing & Management* Vol 24 No 4 (1988) pp 459–468

36 **Hawkins, D T** 'Lessons from the 'Videotex school of hard knocks'' *ONLINE* Vol 15 No 1 (1991) pp 87–89

37 'Videotex — in search of a medium' *Information Industry Bulletin* (27 Jun 1991) p 7

38 **Locke, C** 'Making knowledge pay' *BYTE* Vol 17 No 6 (Jun 1992) pp 245–252

39 **Hawkins, D T** 'Imaging: Another technology for the information world. The basics' *ONLINE* Vol 15 No 6 (1991) pp 103–105

40 **Locke, C** 'The dark side of DIP' *BYTE* Vol 16 No 4 (Apr 1991) pp 193–204

41 **Hawkins, D T** 'Text retrieval technologies for image (and other) databases' *ONLINE* Vol 16 No 1 (1992) pp 92–94

42 **Connelly, J** 'Fiber-to-home systems moving into test stage' *Electronic News* Vol 34 No 1727 (10 Oct 1988) p 22

43 **Bell, S J** 'Online without the line' *ONLINE* Vol 15 No 5 (1991) pp 15–25

44 **Hawkins, D T** 'In search of ideal information pricing' *ONLINE* Vol 13 No 2 (1989) pp 15–30

45 'Those aging boomers' *Business Week.* (20 May 1991) pp 106–112

46 **Waldrop, J** 'The baby boom turns 45' *American Demographics* Vol 14 No 1 (1991) pp 22–27

47 **Newcomb, P** 'Hey dude, let's consume' *Forbes* Vol 145 (11 Jun 1990) pp 126–131

48 **Vobjeda, B** 'America's many tongues: Changing how the nation speaks' *Washington Post* (16 Apr 1992) p A01

49 **Mandel, M J and Farrell, C** 'The immigrants' *Business Week,* (13 Jul 1992) pp 114–122

50 **Rose, M** 'The cocooning of America?' *Direct Marketing* Vol 52 No 2 (1990) pp 55–60

51 **McClure, C R, Hernon, P, and Relyea, H (Eds.)** *U.S. Government Information Policies* Ablex Publishing Corp, USA (1989)

52 **Garrett, J R** 'Text to screen revisited: Copyright in the electronic age' *ONLINE* Vol 15 No 2 (1991) pp 22–24

53 **Oakley, R L** 'Copyright issues for the creators and users of information in the electronic environment' *Electronic Networking: Research Applications and Policy* Vol 1 No 1 (1991, Fall) pp 23–30

54 **Hawkins, D T** 'Information delivery — riding the fax wave' *ONLINE* Vol 14 No 3 (1990) pp 98–101

55 **Hawkins, D T** 'Fax newspapers: Publishing or perishing?' *ONLINE* Vol 16 No 4 (1992) pp 95–97

56 **Jones, A S** 'Small fax newspaper shakes up its press rivals' *The New York Times* (12 Aug 1991) p C8

57 **Tompkins, M** 'A second French revolution' *US News & World Report* (7 May 1990) p 56

58 **Spain, T** 'No time to read? Listen' *D&B Report* (Jan/Feb 1986), p 46–47

59 **McDowell, E** 'Many authors seek to be heard as well as read' *The New York Times* (5 Feb 1990) p D9

60 'Textbooks: Have them your way' *Information Week* (6 August 1990) p 30

61 'USC pilot project will customize college textbooks' *Los Angeles Time* (17 Sep 1990) pp D1, D8

62 **Toth, D** 'Letting the customer create' *Graphic Arts Monthly* Vol 59 (Jan 1987) pp 92–93

63 **Shapiro, E** 'Can Prodigy be all things to 1.5 million PC owners?' *The New York Times* (2 Jun 1991) p 4F

APPENDIX 21.1: LIST OF ABBREVIATIONS

AI	Artificial Intelligence
ASCII	American Standard Code for Information Interchange
BITNET	Because It's Time Network
CA	Chemical Abstracts
CAS	Chemical Abstracts Service
CD-i	Compact Disc — Interactive
CD-ROM	Compact Disc — Read-Only Memory
CD-ROM XA	Compact Disc — Read-Only Memory Extended Architecture
CPE	Consumer Premises Equipment
dpi	dots per inch
DTP	Desktop publishing
DVI	Digital Video Interactive
EAP	Electronic-Aided Publishing
EP	Electronic Publishing
FCC	Federal Communications Commission
ISDN	Integrated Service Digital Network

LINUS	Library Network User Service
NAPLPS	North American Presentation Level Protocol Syntax
NISO	National Information Standards Organization
OCR	Optical Character Recognition
PC	Personal Computer
RBOC	Regional Bell Operating Company
SGML	Standard Generalized Markup Language
TV	Television
VIA	Videotex Industry Association
VS&A	Veronis Suhler & Associates

Resource providers — case studies

22

An overview of multimedia software in Japan

Fumio Takagi, Dai Nippon Printing, Japan

HISTORICAL BACKGROUND OF THE PRINTING COMPANY AND ENTRY INTO THE MULTIMEDIA MARKET

Dai Nippon Printing is a comprehensive printing company with a history of 118 years, having been founded in 1876. Initially, the company dealt with selling a typeface called 'SHUEI-type' and provided letterpress printing services. The SHUEI-type has been one of the most popular Japanese typefaces for many years and is widely accepted even today as a common font on workstations.

Technological development in leading Japanese printing companies progressed alongside the advances in electronics development and these activities can be summarized as electronic publishing. The electronic printing process is seen as one aspect of electronic publishing and a typical example is CTS (Computerized Typesetting System), in which typesetting is performed electronically using computer systems. Despite its rather slow popularization because of the large number of different characters included in Kanji, compared with alphabet-based typesetting, electronic typesetting of Japanese characters has progressed rapidly. In addition, thanks to the remarkable development of functional digital scanners for printing, CEPS

Fumio Takagi is Manager of the Research & Development Department at the headquarters of Dai Nippon Printing Co. Ltd in Tokyo. DNP is the largest printing and new media resourcing house for the publishing industry in Japan.

425

(Colour Electronic Prepress System) was introduced for digital prepress processing including image processing and editing. A fully digital printing process is increasingly the norm.

Another aspect of electronic publishing is the use of electronic media. As background to this trend, various types of digitally stored data are highly suited to manipulation on electronic media. The best way to use electronic media is to utilize the Japanese language information processing technology already acquired in the printing field.

Information distribution by electronic media first started in Japan with the CAPTAIN (Character and Pattern Telephone Access Information Network) system, which is similar to Minitel in France. With the advent of CD-ROM, the use of electronic media for publishing became the mainstream of the printing business.

The printing industry is addressing publishing with electronic media as a new business area and is trying to build a variety of systems to promote this new business. One of these is an integrated media conversion system which we named the 'DNP Unified Publishing System' (see Figure 22.1). The purpose of the system is to cope flexibly with tabular information for various forms of publishing and to manage the databases of digitally stored information, as well as to deal flexibly with the needs of various output formats, including electronic media. At present, the system mainly handles textual information. However, it is planned to include other types of

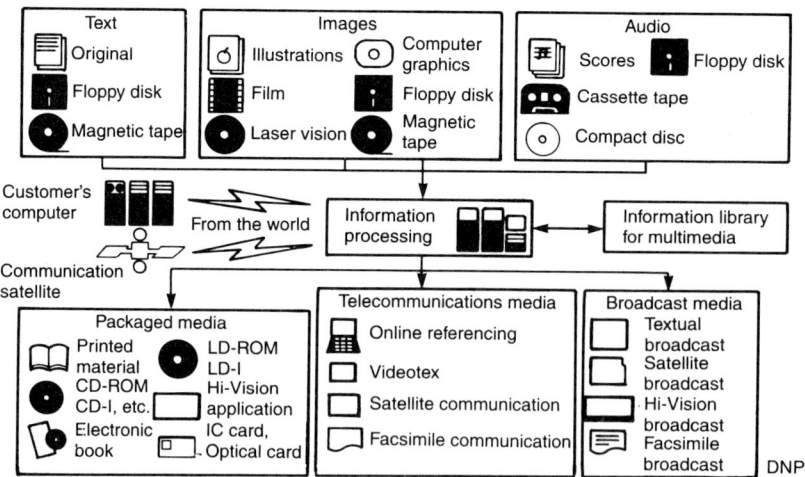

Figure 22.1 The DNP Unified Publishing System

information, such as photographs and other images, in the near future and to build up a system environment facilitating the comprehensive handling of all types of media.

The major publishing format for electronic media today is CD-ROM; the products are made for use with platforms such as personal computers and Sony's Data Discman and so far we have focused on textual information. Since the announcements of CD-i and DVI, however, along with the increasing attention to modern multimedia concepts, it is anticipated that the information communication environment will be significantly improved, so the range of software production is being enlarged to increase business opportunities in this field. The printing industry is expanding from conventional printing to various spheres of business, including image production and information distribution using communications satellites. It is cultivating the new market as the complete designer of information media. Multimedia technology will play the central role in creating new markets for the printing industry.

Production of multimedia software is being carried out by systems having the configuration shown in Figure 22.2, in which the software production process differs according to the individual multimedia platform. However, it is planned to build a system environment which enables comprehensive and efficient software production for a variety of platforms in the future.

SUMMARY OF THE MULTIMEDIA SOFTWARE MARKET

Extent of use of hardware

The popularization of hardware for multimedia in Japan can be represented by the current size of the market for CD-ROM drives. Already about two million video game machines with CD-ROM drives have been sold and this is a fairly large market. The current two major suppliers are NEC Home Electronics with its PC Engine CD-ROM[2] and Sega Enterprises with its MegaDrive. The market size will, however, further expand since Matsushita will begin to deliver 3DO Real, the next generation CD-ROM machine, in the spring of 1994.

Other important factors, as an indicator of the market, are the electronic books supplied by Sony, Matsushita and Sanyo; 300 000

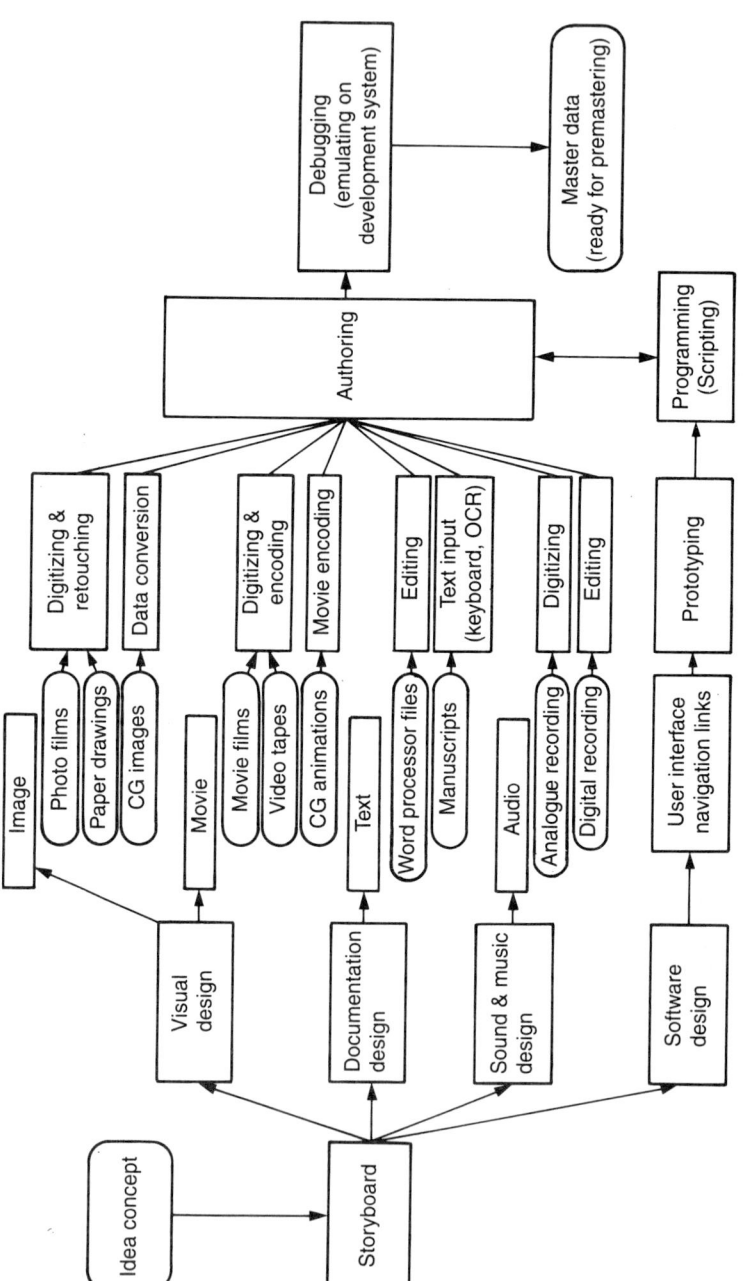

Figure 22.2 Production of multimedia software

units have already been sold. The information delivered started with text and then sound and illustrations were added. It is expected that the range will be expanded to multimedia functions.

The sales of CD-ROM drives for personal computers is steadily increasing and more than 700 000 units are in use today according to one estimate. Hardware growth will closely follow the growth rate of PC CD-ROM software products. It is also a recent trend to supply manuals and user books for general-purpose PCs on CD-ROM, so that a CD-ROM drive is often included as a standard feature.

Other aspects of this market are karaoke machines and car navigation systems. The present karaoke market is dominated by laser disks and CD-G. However, machines designed with CD-i and DVI technology are commercially available now and multimedia applications of karaoke will be promoted. Car navigation systems are installed as a standard feature on new high-end models and electronics manufacturers are supplying the systems as after-sales options.

Software development

Considering the software development situation in Japan, particularly in relation to CD-ROM software, it is estimated that more than 900 titles were produced by the end of 1992. An analysis of Japanese software titles according to the *World CD-ROM Handbook*, issued by Kyodo Keikaku's Publishing Business Division, provides the statistics listed in Table 22.1.

Table 22.1 CD-ROM software titles in Japan

Subject	Number of titles	Percentage
Entertainment/games	423	46.3
Picture book/conversation/language	78	8.5
CAI	31	3.4
Dictionary/encyclopaedia/directory	48	5.3
Audio-visual	36	3.9
Business	51	5.6
Other	246	27.0
Total	**913**	**100.0**

EXAMPLES OF MULTIMEDIA SOFTWARE

Virtual reality system using DVI

A virtual-reality package in the DVI (Digital Video Interactive) format entitled 'Let's go to the Zoo!' was developed to enable mentally and physically handicapped people who are bedridden to roam around in a zoo as a virtual-reality experience by interactive operation on a video screen. Such handicapped people are likely to lose independence and become very negative in attitude or desire, so this software plays an important role in mental therapy and rehabilitation for them.

The system uses DVI motion-picture recording and playback, records stereo images on a CD-ROM, regenerates the pictures on two display screens, with synthesized pictures through half-mirrors. People can have a virtual-reality experience by using synthesized pictures interactively with the aid of polarized glasses, a joystick and a personal computer. The raw elements of the pictures were collected by shooting pictures of animals in the zoo and the program includes 11 kinds of animals which can be seen by selecting one of the settings.

This system was originally developed to provide mental therapy for people who are unable to leave their beds and clinical tests have shown this system to be effective in treating young people suffering from muscular dystrophy. It is hoped that applications in other medical areas can be found. Other virtual-reality technologies such as telepresence and simulation are expected to find uses in this area.

Electronic publishing using HDTV

Hi-Vision is the common name for the High-Definition TV developed by NHK. It has 1125 scanning lines, which is more than double the amount of NTSC systems, a data volume about six times greater in number of pixels and a screen size ratio of 9:16 rather than 3:4 with the current system.

The prime purpose of Hi-Vision is broadcasting. However, because of its high-density recording and display characteristics and the ease of conversion to other versatile media, its application in a wide range of industrial areas such as movies, exhibitions, environmental images, medicine, education, printing and publishing is eagerly anticipated. Its functionality as the means of displaying electronic media is most promising. A wide spectrum of display functions with Hi-Vision enables the consolidation of information of different types, including raw elements of pictures which have been collected as well as other information in the form of text and graphics. The display capabilities of current TV systems such as NTSC, PAL and SECAM are limited because of the screen size ratio of 3:4. Pictures must fit into a very constrained frame size, so close-up shots, as seen in TV pictures, are likely to be common and the picture quality is not attractive in parts of the screen due to poor resolution.

On the other hand, Hi-Vision enables the easy display of various types of information with different data structures by an arrangement of windows on a single screen. Each part has good resolution for viewing. When the display functions are supported by multimedia applications and interactive operations, a more advanced information display/delivery environment will be achieved.

We are now promoting a development program called Hi-Vision Graphics, an electronic publishing form using Hi-Vision technology. The outcome of fully utilizing Hi-Vision capabilities can be seen in the Hi-Vision Gallery System jointly developed by NHK Engineering Service, NHK Enterprise, Ikegami Tsushinki Company, JVC and Dai Nippon Printing.

The Hi-Vision Gallery System, opened in 1989 at Gifu Prefecture Museum, is the world's first picture image gallery which uses the HDTV technology. It features a combination of a programmed gallery system for still pictures and a database for interactive retrieval along with display control functions. The Gifu Prefecture Museum has a complex consisting of a theatre-type gallery with a large 110-inch rear projector, an open-type gallery with a 60-inch projector and a data booth with a 32-inch display which allows users to freely retrieve the database and access the high-definition pictures and graphics.

The production process of Hi-Vision Graphics includes manipulation and modification of image data read in by a scanner, JPEG image compression, combination with text, voice-over and background music and finally recording on a CD-ROM. In the player, the images are decompressed and formatted for presentation and display. The character generator, which provides high-quality fonts for texts suitable for the high-quality display, was also jointly developed by NHK Engineering Service, Ikegami Tsushinki Company and Dai Nippon Printing. The CD-ROM disc format conforms to the still-picture format specification defined by the Hi-Vision Promotion Center.

There are different proposed specifications for high-definition TV, such as HD-MAC in Europe and ATV in the USA. A number of issues for world standardization are pending. Unquestionably, however, the need for high-definition TVs for the home will increase. Along with the wider adoption of HDTV, it is expected that multimedia systems with high-definition displays will be widely accepted by public institutions and also in the personal environment.

Multimedia magazines

Today the market for multimedia publications has not yet been established. However, with the acceleration of hardware development and increased attention to multimedia, there are signs that the trend is toward formation of a market, and more mature achievements are awaited. One program we have produced is the multimedia *Hotdog Press* magazine published by Kodansha. This magazine is designed for enjoying multimedia information on a Macintosh platform as if reading a magazine.

Electronic magazines enable readers easily to access various types of information. However, from a production standpoint, there are a number of issues to be resolved, such as production time and costs, information content, price setting and how to include advertisements. A trial of multimedia advertising is being pioneered by Dentsu, an advertising company. In the process of finally establishing the multimedia publishing market various aspects have to be investigated, such as techniques for including 'infotainment' (information and entertainment).

23

Information management in a new business era

Graham Poulter, On Demand Information, UK

CREATING NEW CLIMATES FOR CHANGE

Most companies today, no matter what business they are in, how technologically sophisticated their product or service or what their national origin, can trace their work systems and organizational structures back to the principles of Adam Smith — the division or specialization of labour and consequent fragmentation of work.

The standard pyramidal structure of most organizations was well suited to a high-growth environment because it was scalable. When a company needed to grow, it simply added workers as required at the bottom of the chart and then filled in the management layers above. A structure ideal for control and planning, it was also made for short training periods, since few tasks were complicated or difficult.

That is how efficiency was once achieved. Today, the reality organizations have to confront is that the old ways simply do not work any more. Suddenly, the world is a different place. In today's environment nothing is constant or predictable — not market growth, customer demand, product lifecycles, the rate of technological change or the nature of competition.

Three forces, separately and in combination, are driving today's company managers deeper into totally unfamiliar territory — *Cus-*

Graham Poulter is Chairman and Chief Executive of On Demand Information plc in Leeds, part of Poulter Communications plc which he founded a few years ago. The group is now becoming a leading UK resourcing organization for electronic publishing.

tomers, Competition and *Change* — not new words, but their characteristics are strikingly different from what they were in the past.

- *Customers:* Since the early 1980s the dominant force in the seller–customer relationship has shifted. Sellers no longer have the upper hand; customers do. They know what they want, when they want it, how they want it and what they will pay. Customers — consumers and corporations alike — demand products and services designed for their unique and particular needs. Customers like these do not need to deal with companies that do not appreciate this startling change in the customer–buyer relationship.
- *Competition:* Niche competitors have changed the face of practically every market. Similar goods sell in different markets on entirely disparate competitive bases: in one market on price, in another on range, somewhere else on quality and others on service before, during and after the sale. With trade barriers falling, no company is protected from overseas competition.

  Just one superior performer raises the competitive threshold for all companies around the world. Adequate is no longer good enough. If a company cannot stand shoulder to shoulder with the world's best in a competitive category, it soon has no place to stand at all.
- *Change:* Customers and competition have changed, but so, too, has the nature of change itself. Change has become both pervasive and persistent. It is normality. Moreover, the pace of change has accelerated. With globalization of the economy, companies face more competitors, each with product and service innovations. Product lifecycles have gone from years to months. The key issue is not only that product and service lifecycles have diminished, but the time available to develop new products and introduce them has also shortened. Today, companies must move fast, or they may not move at all.

Over the last 20 years there have been numerous management 'fads' — management by objectives, diversification, quality circles, zero-based budgeting, 'excellence', intrapreneuring, one-minute managing and many others, all attempting to improve corporate competitive performance, to survive in an ever-changing world.

Every company is replete with rules and practices left over from earlier decades — now they must completely rethink how and why they do what they do. In the late 1990s 'reengineering' the whole business process will be essential to compete successfully in a changing world. Reengineering will be in the 1990s what Strategy was in the 1970s and Quality was for the 1980s.

Reengineering is about innovation. It is about exploiting the latest capabilities of technology to achieve entirely new goals. Breakthrough technology makes feasible activities and actions of which people have not yet dreamed. The challenge most corporations fail to meet is recognizing the business possibilities that lie latent in existing technology.

Meeting the triple challenge

The real power of technology is not that it can make the old processes work better, but that it enables organizations to break old rules and create new ways of working, which makes it critical to companies looking for competitive advantage.

The spectrum of information technologies ranges from shared databases, expert systems, decision support tools, automatic tracking telecommunication networks, to information access and dissemination. It is the latter which On Demand Information Plc has developed extensively and which is now being used in both organizations and the publishing industry to meet the challenge of Customers, Competition and Change.

OLD WAYS SIMPLY DO NOT WORK ANY MORE

Since Gutenberg the principle of producing multiple copies of information, whether it has been produced on paper, film, video and latterly CDs, has prevailed. This method of dissemination was acceptable in a world where the pace of change was slow and organizational structures and costs were not paramount. These methods must be rethought. It is the end of an era.

Today, businesses and institutions generate more information than can ever be used productively — at considerable cost and with little effectiveness. This information is printed, videotaped, recorded, put on a host of readily available media platforms, then distributed by mail or courier. Little or no thought is given to how the recipients will store and retrieve the information when needed. Do you send one copy or ten? Is it out of date by the time they come to use it? Why is it done in this way? Simply because it always has been.

There has to be a better way. One which eliminates these problems yet retains all the communication values of the printed word, colour photographs, movement and sound which is associated with 'old' media platforms. It is these values which aid the process of understanding.

ON DEMAND INFORMATION DOES!

On Demand Information turns convention on its head. Instead of making multiple copies of information (which may be out of date before they are ever distributed) you have just one master copy, which can be accessed by all relevant parties from a single source. This means it can be amended several times per day if necessary, so that no-one ever uses out of date information.

Simply, On Demand Information works like this: digital masters of all information of the traditional media type are held on the On Demand Information central computer. (Think of them as your personal filing cabinets and library systems all in one!) Information remains in its traditional form — pages are typeset, videos move and have sound in the normal way. It is the method of storage and access that is the real breakthrough. With a simple and inexpensive upgrade, existing personal computers can be connected to On Demand Information by an ISDN digital telephone line. You can then call on to the PC screen all the relevant corporate or industry sector information, in seconds, in a quality that is exactly as would be if it had been provided in colour or by watching a videotape.

PUSHING BACK THE FRONTIERS OF TECHNOLOGICAL CAPABILITY

An example of the system's speed and efficiency is illustrated by the fact that six pages of full colour and nine pages of black and white can be loaded on to the PC in just 45 seconds — anywhere in the country and at normal telephone call charge rates. It's fast, it's cheap and it can do much more.

- Once it is loaded on to your PC, you can use or manipulate it any way you want.
- Information can be annotated by digitally recording comments using your own voice. Things can be marked by adding 'note-it' pad comments using a digital 'yellow pen'.
- All information can be stored on your PC's hard disk in your own personal file for access at a future date or forwarding to colleagues.
- If, when you recall information from your personal file, there have been any amendments or updates by the original supplier of the information, these will be automatically updated by the system, so you will never work with information that is out of date.
- Furthermore, if your PC is connected to a colour or black and white laser printer, hard copies can be requested quickly and inexpensively.

On Demand Information is probably the biggest breakthrough in information management and distribution since the creation of the personal computer. Today there is no other system in the world which can provide all these features and benefits.

BREAKTHROUGH TECHNOLOGY

On Demand Information is the result of several years' development from which many unique and patented features have resulted. The system has also incorporated two equally unique subproducts, Video and Search, under exclusive marketing arrangements, which combine to give the total system additional functionality.

It is our policy to continuously evolve the product to meet future needs and with this in mind, many new features are being planned. They will be incorporated in ways which do not make the current product obsolete.

Product features

Graphic images
A powerful feature of On Demand Information is its ability to scan existing colour printed documents or convert DTP-produced files and compress the data extensively. This allows high-speed transmis-

sion anywhere in the country, e.g. 15 pages in 45 seconds, and the ability to reveal them on a PC screen faster than you can turn the pages of a book.

Video

International standards currently compress video material to provide acceptable quality for many applications. In order to provide higher quality images, speed of transmitter and greater capacity to store and playback material, On Demand Information has incorporated a unique video technique which provides a 300:1 compression ratio. This unique system also allows fast compression in real time — so amendments to material can be made quickly — and no additional hardware is required in the user's PC.

Fuzzy Knowledge Search

Finding the important fact or document from the hundreds of thousands of pages of information each industry sector uses and each business produces can often take hours, days or even weeks. Not any more!

Using our 'Fuzzy' Knowledge Search routines, in addition to structured indexes, you simply key in the thought or 'clue' about the subject you want to find. In just five or six seconds you have the exact document on screen, selected from literally hundreds of thousands of pages.

Host computers

The fast, flexible host computer system holds the digital versions of all the colour images and video programmes which would have traditionally been on paper or tape. Designed to interface with the European-wide ISDN network, the computers allow thousands of users to access the same information simultaneously. This unique system will have a series of communication nodes strategically located throughout major cities in the UK to facilitate local call access. Requests for information from PCs to host computers are charged by the national telecommunication companies just like a normal telephone call.

Product functionality

On Demand Information is much more than an information management system, it is a totally interactive personal communications facility. Extensive research into how people with little or no computer experience can use On Demand Information easily has resulted in a number of unique elements which combine to improve efficiency and productivity.

Indexing

The index to any corporate or published product information resides on the individual PC hard disk. This is kept up-to-date by the On Demand Information service support unit automatically — no matter if there are hundreds of thousands of pages or dozens of video and training programmes. Only when the user has quickly identified his or her information needs by 'marking' with the mouse does the system collect the information from the host. This method eliminates the costly 'online' methods associated with text databases.

Fast retrieval of information

Requested information is deposited in the PC's hard disk ready for manipulation. As soon as the first page is downloaded into the PC, the information can be used — the rest of the requested information is loaded in the background. So the maximum delay in starting to work with the information is 15 seconds or less.

Storage and updating

Pages or videos can be stored on the 'personal file' section of the system for regular use. If pages are retrieved from the 'personal file' a few days or weeks later, the system automatically checks with the host to see if any amendments have been made to the information. If they have, then the new pages will be sent to the user's PC. The decision to keep old and new or replace is at the discretion of the user.

Annotations

The system allows the user to add personal notes and comments to any information. Sections of pages can be highlighted with 'yellow marker pen', or 'note-it' stickers can be added. Voice comments can be automatically digitized and linked to the page, which can then be stored in the personal file, or forwarded to a colleague if the user is part of a network.

Confidentiality

Communication and confidential exchange of information with colleagues anywhere in the country is an integral part of the system. One channel of the ISDN2 line is used for voice, the other to exchange images which can be marked by either party.

This feature will be shortly extended to provide a desktop video conferencing facility as an integral part of the confidential exchange of information. All this functionability is operated and charged like a normal telephone call.

User's PC configuration

The On Demand Information system does not use proprietary hardware and therefore will operate on any PC which meets the basic specification. The ideal system for best performance and flexibility is a 386/486 SX 25 MHz terminal with 4 megabytes of RAM, using a 125 megabyte hard disk or link to file server and a 1024 × 768 resolution monitor.

CORPORATE IMPLEMENTATION

Corporate communications in the 21st century — just six years away — will be very different to the traditional 'print and distribution' methods practised for the last few generations. Time has already become a competitive weapon. The success of a new product or idea depends on how quickly staff and customers gain a clear understanding of the proposition. People can do more than just read or watch information — they can actually experience it and interact with it.

One master copy — access for all permitted users

Interactive communication generates positive interest; it enables readers to access and use information the way they want and it compels strong response.

On Demand Information easily makes interactive communication a reality. It operates its host computers on a nationwide basis, into which your information is placed. Just as you would buy time and paper to print your information, now you can buy time on On Demand Information computers. Only staff or nominated customers can gain access to the totally secure 'Closed User Groups' — 24 hours per day, seven days per week.

There is no limit to the number of pages, demonstration videos and training material that can be stored — and hundreds of users anywhere in the country can gain simultaneous access to the same information. The master copy is everyone's copy, whenever they need it. Amendments and updates can be made several times a day if necessary, ensuring staff or customers never use out-of-date information. That last fact alone is destined to save industry a fortune.

Every corporate customer of On Demand Information has a dedicated account manager and team of people to support and administrate the flow of information throughout the customer organization. This service ranges from planning information flow to writing and designing literature, product video or training programmes. It is a system and service designed to improve competitiveness and reduce costs — especially in comparison to the old ways of working and thinking!

TRAINING

Training is an essential and expensive business, which On Demand Information technology and support services are set to revolutionize. Traditional methods are often impractical and disruptive to the smooth running of organizations. Removing people from their normal working environment for a few hours or even days, expecting them to absorb more than 20% on the day and providing reams of support/future reference material is no longer our only option.

Interactive communication — participative, stimulating and memorable

Interactive multimedia distributed to the personal computer via On Demand Information allows the individual to work through a course at his or her own preferred pace, to reach full understanding and competence levels faster than ever.

Interactive multimedia is a low- to medium-cost everyday tool which provides video, text, graphics and pictures in a totally interactive mode. In other words, it can be stopped, started or rewound and can respond to the user in whatever way is best to convey understanding. People grasp things much more quickly compared to the old classroom techniques. It can also deliver an assessment to the student and/or course manager at the end.

Whenever there are alterations in training procedures or product lines, it is quick and easy to amend the one master copy on the On Demand Information central computers. Furthermore, the software allows companies to keep an accurate track of which staff have taken the course, how they performed and who is fully aware of amendments in procedures and products.

To support companies implementing the technology, On Demand Information Production Resources have a wide spectrum of skills needed to produce effective training programmes. These include professional trainers, writers, programmers, graphics and video producers. Alternatively, existing material can be digitized and placed on the system.

CHANGES IN THE WORLD OF PUBLISHING

Just as many corporations have realized that On Demand Information electronic information dissemination methods are more efficient for most types of marketing, merchandising and technical information, so have the traditional publishers of annual directories, standards, technical reports, online text services, newsletters, microfiche services and even some aspects of weekly or monthly trade publications. These services will be more effective if converted to the new media platform.

In partnership with the printed word

This rapid evolution of information dissemination does not, however, herald the demise of the printed word. Daily papers, weekly and monthly trade publications still play a strong social and complementary role in the whole process of business communications. It is these services, which have been inflexible and constantly out-of-date, which will provide added value for customers who adopt the new media.

In this respect On Demand Information publishing division is providing a range of industry-sector services both independently and in conjunction with leading traditional publishers via joint ventures. These meet the needs of those industries which realize that fast, efficient supply of information creates a strong competitive edge in today's markets.

These services are available on low-cost annual subscriptions, and include Construction, Financial and Investor Relations, Sales Promotion, Media, Packaging and Retail. Research has indicated that there are between 80 and 100 market sectors which could benefit from the adoption of the On Demand Information publishing methods. A programme of developments is now being pursued independently and in conjunction with publishing partners to bring these services to market as soon as possible in the UK and the rest of Europe.

THE CREATION OF POWERFUL COMMUNICATIONS

No matter how powerful and innovative the technology, it can be less effective if the quality of the message and how it is presented is not optimized. Why do people recall certain training presentation facts more easily than others? Why do some product features and benefits stick in the mind? It depends on the written and visual techniques used to convey the information.

That is the reason we have created a complementary resource to support the users of On Demand Information. It is a unique digital environment staffed by talented individuals from every discipline in the creative world. Scriptwriters, visualizers, video-producers, sound engineers and all those multidisciplined creative individuals who combine to create powerful messages. Communication with this resource is also state-of-the-art. Approval or amendment of photographs, artwork, training material or business presentations is undertaken on the client's desktop PC — anywhere in the country, in seconds, using the digital highway which is the core of On Demand Information.

In addition to the central facility, On Demand Information has appointed a number of Associate Creative Companies strategically located around the country to provide closer working links. Alternatively, corporations or publishers with in-house resources can be linked directly to the production and digitizing facility in On Demand Information.

We have contributed this chapter to express our stong conviction that electronic publishing is of value and benefit and can also provide profitable business opportunities.

24

Providing EP resources within a publishing group

Michel Bera, Matra-Hachette, France

At very first sight, Matra is more like an engineering company, while Hachette is obviously more in the classical business of editing and publishing; and my colleague from Hachette Livre has clearly already put this all down in his own contribution (see Chapter 3). However, we do have some interesting practical experiences at Matra in the field of multimedia, a term that embraces more than classic EP and such experiences may have come also from other divisions of Matra-Hachette than Hachette Livre; let me mention our expertise on electronic billboarding, a technology that came from declassified military resources in signal processing and can be used in personal broadcasting within interactive television services. At the same time, we gained some insight on customer reactions with the Multipoint experience on French television. Multipoint is an interactive card concept that allows TV addicts to play during game shows or other TV series. The player accumulates winning points that can then be used to buy products from participating companies.

But I would like to concentrate here more on the way I see EP happening in the future. This goes beyond my day-to-day activities within the Matra-Hachette Group.

In my opinion, the EP concept is of a rather limiting nature: after the recent IEPRC conference and study tour, I get the ever stronger impression that different kinds of businesses are mixed under the

---

Dr Michel Bera is Vice-President of Matra-Hachette, Paris. He is responsible for computer policy throughout the group.

same acronyms, which consequently makes strategic marketing increasingly difficult.

The current user becomes more confused each day and just cannot decide whether he/she is supposed to go for the latest Macintosh, a Windows-compatible Taiwanese clone, a Philips CD-i console, or could it be Sega, or rather Nintendo, or perhaps he/she should go for the newest cable subscription, start with an antenna for satellite programmes, look for newer videotext applications, or spend his/her (always smaller) pot of money on home theatre or karaoke technology!

As for software or content, our customer is being offered CD-ROM encyclopaedias, so-called interactive television programming with cable technology, theme parks where lastest virtual reality features manage to warp what is left of his/her mind, and online services to rent cars, fly planes, look for weather forecasts or just chat more or less innocently over the 'phone lines with other online addicts.

Looking for products or services is one part of the task: putting them to work for business or pleasure appears more challenging.

Is multimedia really happening? It appears to me, wherever today's sales people's best lies may stretch, that all hardware configurations fail in running any large line of software: all software drivers are different, all modems just lack manuals, and the combinations of all the different possible GUIs, online protocols, CD-ROM drivers and systems configurations on PCs guarantee an instant headache and, if a rapid cure is not undertaken by a brave customer, profound despair after a while.

Let me tell a personal story: I was looking for sound drivers that add to an IBM Thinkpad multimedia computer in Soundblaster, Roland or Adlib, or even Midi features, so that I could enjoy the latest hottest multimedia game in town, the Day of the Tentacle — a game written by an absolutely unknown company called Lucas Art. Well, that subject just turned off all my usual computer suppliers.

Calling the local sales office that distributes the game in France was of no greater help, for IBM just faintly reminded them of something. On multimedia subjects, of course, calling IBM salespeople or marketing managers was just as bad, for IBM managers could not figure out why a respectable company such as ours would use a multimedia computer to run games software.

I then turned my steps towards the best hackers I had heard of on the Internet: immediately I was overwhelmed by considerable assistance that offered any possible driver; all my hacker friends instantly succeeded in turning my *config.sys* and *autoexec.bat* files into a complete mess, forcing me to completely redesign my PC software (those strange names are supposedly ancient Egyptian lost secret spells, that decide the fate of hundreds of millions of computers on our planet).

I started to scale up my management calls at IBM; those are powers that no grand public person can afford to tap today. At last somebody helped me with a preliminary version of the rare drivers. I can now play the first ten minutes of this best-selling game before bursting into 'out of memory' messages. I am aware of such happenings with Taiwanese clones: to turn on a new game, you need a deep expertise in software configurations.

What is the lesson of this *Three Men in a Boat* type story?

I think that in the fields of EP, and of all the related research that is being done on new products and services, an enormous amount of training is still needed. If we accept the insight — to which I subscribe — that multimedia comes of age as a new tenth art, an art very close to television, movie, photography or comic book, we must seriously consider the way we bring it to the end-user, the *cochon de payant* customer that pays for all this. It will certainly be at least three years before there is enough standardization to provide ease of use in going on the ramp to the electronic highway as a bottomline reality.

In the Legardere Group approach, we feel we have important in-house expertise that has to manifest itself in the near future, when business multimedia products and services achieve two new features: communicability and interactivity.

Interactivity, that is the art of telling a hundred thousand different stories, needs a powerful expertise for scripting. This calls for very sophisticated software engineering technology which no hacker start-up today commands. We believe, however, we can derive it from military, satellite and communication technology. Anyone can understand that in a counter-measure environment, missile guidance software has to react to these hundred thousand scenarios in a very limited amount of time. We understand in the Legardere Group that sound technology, declassified today in home theatre Digital Signal Processing units (DSPs), is the key to the appeal of future products.

We feel also that alliances are sorely needed, when the mother of all standard wars starts in 1995. Such alliances need to be worldwide and must lead to win–win situations. This is the way we intend to go.

To play a strong role in the multimedia world, our group will attract new creativity and bring together editorial and educational expertise, which are available in the Hachette world, and software technology for interactivity, real time and telecommunications, which are in the Matra world. Some fields already produce a profitable bottom line, such as the Grolier encyclopaedia, which has sold more than 1.3 million copies in the USA.

To conclude, we think that less than 20% of the products and services that will be offered to customers in 1997 — a point in time that seems to gather most gurus' focus — exist today or are even in an early project phase or concept stage.

Hardware and software suppliers — case studies

25

CD-i in the professional market

Marijke van Hooren, Philips Interactive Media Systems, Netherlands

INTRODUCTION

CD-i is taking off very well in the professional market. Here are some facts and figures. In the USA alone, more than 750 companies are involved in CD-i, publishers, value-adding resellers and clients, who see CD-i as the ideal delivery system for training, sales and educational applications. A catalogue was published which included more than 250 professional CD-i titles available in the USA at the beginning of 1994. The same number of projects have been completed in Europe.

This article describes in some detail a number of these projects and the reasons why manufacturers have chosen CD-i as a platform.

APPLICATION AREAS

Marketing

In marketing, CD-i is used for in-store marketing (POI/POS), presentations, sales support and market research. An example of a good Point-of-Sale disc is the Yamaha motorbike programme.

Marijke van Hooren is Public Relations Manager of Philips Interactive Media Systems in Eindhoven.

Yamaha

Yamaha wanted to solve a very real problem: with so many different motorbike models and so many different colour schemes, they needed a mountain of promotional literature to address them all. Furthermore, Yamaha seized on the idea of a CD-i POS system because, unlike video, CD-i is fully interactive. Yamaha customers control exactly what they see and hear. CD-i's interactivity not only answers questions, it also asks them as well. Hence, the system prompts customers to other areas of the disc, which include a complete overview of Yamaha's product and brand information, as well as a nationwide dealer list and advice on finance and insurance. In fact, all the information a Yamaha customer could wish to receive.

Yamaha's long-term promotions goal is to secure its identity as a technology innovator with engineering excellence. The association with CD-i's state-of-the-art image is therefore ideal.

Yamaha dealers will also benefit because the system is in effect an additional sales person. CD-i answers questions, points out new purchasing ideas and generally explains to customers why they should buy Yamaha. The sales messages are consistent. The customer gets the story without prejudice or personal opinions; and because CD-i is a machine, it never tires of interacting with Yamaha's customers.

In short, the reasons why Yamaha chose CD-i are:

- It offers a massive amount of promotional material on one disc.
- It provides a new-dimension, additional experience in the showroom.
- It acts like extra sales staff; the system behaves like a sales person.
- It speeds up new product introductions.
- From one central office an entire new promotions activity can be designed and distributed to all dealers nationwide.

Halm International

Halm International, the ink-jet printer manufacturer, uses a CD-i programme for other reasons: it eliminates ordering errors, it is multilingual, and a large amount of information can be stored on one disc.

Even the very best engineered machinery sometimes needs a replacement part. When this happens the user must contact the manufacturer to specify a particular piece — which could be just one among thousands. To complicate matters, the part must be ordered quickly, usually by telephone. And then language barriers can cause misunderstandings and mistakes, especially when the part needs to be described.

Of course, there are service manuals in which the part number can be looked up but these are often not close to hand. They are also difficult to read since they can cover many different machine models. Often, in the rush to get the replacement, the wrong part is specified, causing more delays and ill-feeling for the user.

Halm International has eliminated all those problems with the use of a CD-i programme. 'Our best selling machine has more than 2000 parts, which means CD-i is ideal for our customers. They can zoom into the machine from different angles. Real photos allow them to zoom into the next level of detail. And so on, until they arrive at the single spare part they need — complete with catalogue number' said Rene Laukens, Sales Manager of Halm International.

Communication

In the field of communications, CD-i is used internally and externally. Just one example: Electronic Data Systems produced a presentation disc for the Dow Jones management. And even two annual reports have been published on CD-i.

Training

Caltex programmes has chosen CD-i as their training platform worldwide. One disc replaces six printed manuals and video tapes. The disc is produced monthly.

The Kentucky Fried Chicken programme provides skills training on how to identify chicken pieces, combine them and package them appropriately. The training uses a 'video game'.

A number of generic training titles developed by *Skillmaster*, AMPED and CD-i Training are also available on a wide range of subjects, e.g. language learning, management training etc. For example, Philips choose CD-i for training accountants and business managers on the subject of accountancy. The 'Finance and Accounting for Business Managers' programme interactively explains the practical benefits of finance and accounting in an easy to understand, memorable way. It presents a mix of simulations and business scenarios and asks the user to make decisions affecting the outcome. The results are projected in an instant, to provide immediate feedback.

The user is encouraged to experiment with different business scenarios. This practical, hands-on experience is backed up with advice from a theoretical model on the disc. There is also a quick look-up glossary of the most important terms, and a total of 50 questions posed at different stages of the programme give the user the opportunity to test and enrich his or her knowledge. With this CD-i training disc, Philips intends to save many thousands of dollars each year. Normally, this would be the cost of bringing people from all over the world to a centralized conventional classroom lesson.

Another interesting example is Agfa Gevaert. The main problem faced by Agfa's medical division — and by most multinational organizations — is to train their sales and service staff effectively despite their geographical spread. Before introducing CD-i, sales training involved flying groups of people from all over the world to the Belgian headquarters. Apart from the sheer expense, the effectiveness of training was limited since only small numbers could be accommodated at one time and trainers were having to duplicate their efforts to cover even a fraction of the salesforce.

Language problems, classroom shyness and limited time were also working against efficient and cost-effective training. Since adopting CD-i as an integral part of their training scheme, all of these problems have been overcome. The change began with the introduction of a new X-ray camera by Agfa. Sales and technical staff had to be briefed fully on its functions and, since there was some overlap in the information needed by the two groups, a single CD-i disc was the chosen method. For the price of a postage stamp, all staff are assured of getting exactly the same high level of training, and of doing so in a comfortable environment, at their own pace and in their own language. The disc is currently used in six European countries.

Agfa is enthusiastic about CD-i's effectiveness as a training tool. And as an investment, they have found that returns are realized quite easily. When the disc succeeds in reducing travel costs by 70%, the system becomes profitable. And even if the system is used simply as a way of preparing students before a conventional training course, that 'homework' can reduce the course length dramatically — making better use of trainers' time and cutting down on accommodation expenses.

Reference

One of the most interesting projects is the Elsevier series of 16 interactive discs on anatomy. The first disc contains an enormous number of anatomy photos: 11 000 cross-sections of a human paranasal sinus and an anterior skull base (more commonly known as the nose and surrounding area). And, because each photo is spaced just 20 μm from the previous photo, CD-i can use them in a continuous anatomical build-up sequence, showing video animation. At any time the student can stop the video and study in detail the exact photo he or she needs. He or she can even take a look at the exact same tissue from a different angle: side, front or top.

The 11 000 photo and 700 related images make up the first disc of a complete Paranasal Sinuses and Skull Base CD-i study programme of 16 discs. It will serve as a reference and teaching aid for all physicians, postgraduates and students, as well as an effective, easy and in-depth method for understanding anatomy in general.

Elsevier Science BV knew that medical professionals throughout the world have always wanted to buy pictures such as these, but the expense and bulk of a multi-volume directory was simply too much for most organizations. That is when CD-i came in: on a few discs the entire library could be distributed with ease.

Because there were no litho or print costs, the library is published at a fraction of conventional costs. Distribution is also very economical. The cost savings are shared with the customers, and make the publication affordable to a much wider market. This inevitably results in increased sales.

CONCLUSION

These programmes and the growing catalogue of generic 'off-the-shelf' professional CD-i titles indicate that CD-i is an accepted platform in the professional audio/video communication market.

26

Various publishers' joint ventures with hardware and software suppliers

Charlotte Gutman, CGP, Belgium

The past decade has seen a major upheaval in the suppliers of equipment for printing and publishing. Instead of selling low volumes of bespoke equipment to highly skilled specialist service providers, the industry now sells high-volume, low-cost, easy-to-use equipment to creative users. Designers, publishers and photographers who could never have justified the expense and training requirements of the old equipment, can now exercise fine control and save costs by doing the work for themselves. In the process, many manufacturers have fallen by the wayside, and today's market largely revolves around players that either did not exist or had no involvement in publishing ten years ago.

THE MICRO REVOLUTION

In the early 1980s electronic publishing was dominated by companies such as Atex, SII, Compugraphic, DEC and Burroughs. Computers were already firmly established, but these manufacturers not only wrote their own software, but they often built their own computers too, or at least heavily modified other people's mainframes

Charlotte Gutman is President of CGP in Brussels. This public relations consultancy specializes in assisting prepress, printing and EP companies.

and minis. The size, cost and complexity of these electronic publishing systems mean that only large specialist companies, such as newspapers and directory publishers, could afford them.

The microcomputer revolution changed all that. Initially companies such as Linotype and Typecraft started writing typesetting programs for low-cost standard microcomputers such as the Apple II and the Commodore PET. Then at the start of 1985 the first desktop publishing system was announced: an alliance of the year-old Apple Macintosh, a desktop laser printer called LaserWriter, a page description language from Adobe called PostScript, and an easy to use layout program from Aldus called PageMaker. Linotype's landmark decision to license its high-quality typefaces for use with PostScript, and to build PostScript interpreters for its high quality Linotronic laser imagesetters gave this desktop publishing system credibility in the typesetting market — though it took some typesetters years to accept it.

THE FOURTH WAVE

In 1986 the influential US *Seybold Report on Publishing Systems* predicted the 'Fourth Wave' of publishing systems, where manufacturers would abandon proprietary computers and shift their products to mass-produced 'standard' computers. This quickly proved to be accurate: within three years all the newspaper and document publishing system manufacturers had shifted to either microcomputers or the more powerful 'graphics workstations'. Typesetter manufacturers either abandoned proprietary text and layout terminals altogether or switched to standard products such as PCs, Macintoshes or Sun Microsystems workstations.

In the meantime the Apple desktop publishing system was taking off like a rocket. For the first time an electronic publishing system had appeared which individuals could afford, and it was so easy to use that they could virtually plug in and go. More and more software packages came on to the market, and to support them came the development of low-cost peripherals: scanners and monochrome laser printers for less than $1000, colour printers for less than $5000.

Microsoft introduced Windows for the best selling IBM PC microcomputer in 1985, in an attempt to make it as easy to use as the

Macintosh, and desktop publishing products soon started appearing for this too.

OPPORTUNITIES FOR SMALL DEVELOPERS

One of the key features of Macintosh and Windows is that they allow 'applications' programs to coexist, and to swap files via common formats. So people could run a word processor made by one company, transfer its text to a DTP program from somebody else, and add images from yet another developer.

Suddenly small manufacturers could get into the electronic publishing market without having to either develop their own hardware or write monolithic all-in-one programs. Thus Quark could come from nowhere with a good layout program called XPress and not have to worry about graphics or printing, as users could get them elsewhere. Quark was also one of the first companies to make its products open to third-party developers, who could write 'Xtensions' to add specific features. So a second tier of developers, often self-employed individuals, has sprung up to customize popular programs.

In 1990 Adobe introduced Photoshop, an image handling and retouching program that did for scanning what desktop publishing did for typesetting. Today Photoshop dominates the low end of colour imaging and is even used by many professional repro companies. There is a thriving trade in third-party 'plug-in' special-effects filters and scanner drivers for it.

WORKING WITH THE INSTALLED BASE

Although reading the trade press gives the impression that all new products on the market are based on PostScript, and all files are interchangeable, market conditions are rather different. There is still a huge installed base of proprietary scanners, colour electronic page composition systems and electronic publishing systems in use — they may have been expensive, but they were built to last. Their users are subject to the same market changes as everybody else though and they need to exchange files with other people's proprietary systems, as well as accept clients' PostScript files on disks or via modem. Shira Computers has developed a range of links between apparently incompatible systems.

Data storage and transmission over networks and telecommunications lines is also an increasing headache. Colour images take up much room. Data compression seeks to cut file sizes, and a number of standards have emerged for this, with JPEG currently the most popular. Optibase, an Israeli company, is one of many developers producing specialized hardware and software for data compression.

DIGITAL PRESSES TO CUT COSTS

1993 saw the announcement of the next big stage in electronic publishing, the digital press. These machines cost in the region of $200 000 to $300 000, and are in effect high-volume computer printers, and they look set to revolutionize the economics of colour printing.

KEY COMPANIES

In the next few pages we take a look at some of these key companies in more detail, letting them explain the significance of their product lines and strategies.

Scitex

Scitex brought the world's first colour electronic page composition system (CEPS) to market in the spring of 1979. Its impact was revolutionary: at that time the manual film planning and assembly required for a typical job meant that it could easily take a week or ten days to process through to delivery of plate-ready films. With the advent of the Scitex CEPS, electronically planned final films could be produced within hours instead of days. Scitex remained the sole vendor of such systems for about 18 months until rival manufacturers developed equivalent products.

Initially Scitex provided a universal scanner interface to enable users of *all* scanners to connect to Scitex systems. In 1986 it introduced its own Smart Scanner, the first of a series of high-quality flatbed scanners based on CCD (charge-coupled device) technology.

These were easier to use and took considerably less set-up time than conventional laser-based drum scanners, and they had much of the scanner operator's expertise built-in. The Smart 720 'robotic scanner' (1993) represented a further innovation in quality, speed and productivity, and ease of use. Four cartridges, each preloaded with five cassettes, can be inserted into an automatic loader for unattended operation. The 720 enables automatic recognition of image size, type (positive or negative, transparent or reflective) and orientation (portrait or landscape).

Recognizing the importance of open systems, in 1985 Scitex offered its Handshake protocol as a standard to the industry, facilitating the linkage of hundreds of third-party applications to Scitex systems. Handshake became the *de facto* standard for such file transfers. On the output side, Scitex also developed the Dolev series of internal-drum laser plotters, which give very high accuracy. It scored an industry first with its Logo Controller, which provides direct digital control of the engraving heads of the HelioKlischograph machines for gravure printing. Scitex worked hard on the support and education of customers, maintaining several training centres throughout the US and Europe.

The importance of the growing desktop market was recognized early on: in 1988 Scitex was the first to introduce a system that allowed Macintosh users to send page files into its high-end CEPS systems. This Visionary product was based on an early version of Quark XPress, the layout program which now dominates professional publishing. With its VIP and PS-Bridge products over the next year or so, Scitex was also the first repro manufacturer to offer a direct link from the PostScript world into its systems. Today Scitex claims to have the broadest selection of PostScript compatible products of any vendor; describing these as the hub where high-end, high-quality colour meets the increasingly quality-conscious world of desktop publishing.

In recent years Scitex has worked to expand its range of products to give an *all-digital path*. Its range provides for the completely filmless capture of images (via the Leaf Digital Camera Back); editing on a range of workstations; direct digital high-quality proofing (the Iris high-quality contone ink-jet range or the Kodak Approval halftone digital proofer); on-demand black and white or spot-colour printing (through Scitex Digital Printing's 1000 feet per minute ink-jets). Scitex demonstrated direct computer-to-plate processing as early as 1981 and, when suitable plates became commercially available in 1993, it introduced DoPlate, the industry's first combination imagesetter–platesetter.

Hints for products in the near future include the integration of Iris and Scitex Digital Printing technologies to produce high-resolution, high-speed direct digital colour ink-jet printing. Scitex also says it is investing in other digital printing technologies.

Agfa

Electronic publishing is not a stand-alone issue but a prepress paradigm that evolved from the influx of computer technology during the 1980s. Users have not switched from 'traditional publishing' (whatever that may be) to 'electronic publishing' but their workflows, and many times also their business mission, have gone through a technology-driven transition. In that process, a new publishing environment was gradually established, characterized by a variable mix of electronic and photo-mechanical production tools, distributed prepress activities, and increasing importance of digital data transport.

Agfa closely followed this transition and has adjusted its marketing mix to the changing user requirements. It now says it has products, services and support to cover the variety of workflows that will continue to exist for at least the next decade. Its prepress systems grew out of the typesetting industry rather than colour scanning, so it had no user base of proprietary CEPS systems to worry about. Typesetting took to PostScript before the colour market, so Agfa already had plenty of experience once PostScript's quality was improved to make it viable for colour work.

The adoption of PostScript throughout the publishing and printing industry has created dual user requirements. On one hand, it is being used by a large number of new entrants in colour prepress who are expecting to get standardized turnkey solutions. Simultaneously, that same PostScript imaging model has been embraced by established prepress companies. The latter look for imaging quality and productivity under PostScript that are at least compatible with their existing company standards, which are based on many years of experience in colour prepress.

The company's PostScript product strategy covers both types of user. Its Studio and Arcus desktop colour scanners and its FotoFlow colour-management software allow the new users to get good results despite their lack of experience. Meanwhile its Horizon high-capacity colour flatbed scanner is a best selling model in Europe, finding particular favour with newspapers. At the high-end, Agfa's work to develop high-quality PostScript halftoning techniques, such as Agfa Balanced Screens and CristalRaster, aims to satisfy the highest requirements of quality and performance, as required by established prepress companies wanting to adopt PostScript for top-quality work.

Agfa's photographic know-how also pays off in the design of recording media. In 1990 Agfa's SelectSet high-accuracy internal-drum laser imagesetters were a milestone in PostScript output recording quality. It has built on the success of these with its new SelectSet Avantra imagesetters, intended to be even more accurate than the benchmark colour scanner recorders. Backing these up is Agfa's range of Adobe PostScript RIPs, and a line of prepress production servers.

At the Ipex international printing exhibition in the UK last year, Agfa introduced a digital colour press called Chromapress. This caters for the huge potential market for short-run colour printing with variable page content. Until now this has been an unfulfilled need: conventional printing was uneconomic at short runs, and colour copiers are too slow for anything more than a few tens of copies. This is a very different technology to that used by Indigo (see below). Agfa's Chromapress is a digital four-colour press with a printing engine based on dry-toner electrophotography and using Agfa toners. It is in effect a very fast, web-fed laser printer that can print four colours on both sides of the sheet in one pass.

Chromapress uses Agfa's proprietary RIP technology and interface protocols to provide an efficient front end to keep the work flowing constantly. This RIP development has also been used in the CR-A PostScript interpreter, that can be interfaced with Agfa's XC315 and with other colour copiers that have the capability of being driven as an independent colour printer.

Electronics For Imaging

The publishing market took to the black-and-white aspects of desktop publishing (the text and page-layout parts) like a duck to water. However, for a long time photographic colour remained too difficult to use without extensive training and experience. Electronics for

Imaging (EFI) was set up to bring simple, reliable and accurate colour capabilities to the formerly black-and-white world of desktop publishing.

Its first product was the Fiery Colour Server, which today has 10 000 installations worldwide and is the *de facto* standard for printing PostScript files at high quality through digital colour copiers.

Previously there had been no economical system for short-run colour printing. With the introduction of the first Fiery Colour Server in 1989, you could afford to print presentations, reports and proposals, as well as newsletters, in-house — at substantial savings. Simply connecting Fiery to a PC, Macintosh or Unix network, turns a plain-paper colour copier into an efficient PostScript server, for continuous-tone colour printing of pages containing text, graphics and photographic images. The paper and toner costs of plain paper devices are far cheaper than the special papers and inks needed by many desktop colour printers.

Fiery rapidly found an enthusiastic customer base among print shops, corporate reproduction departments and advertising agencies. Designers, illustrators and advertising agencies connected their PC and Macintosh networks to Fiery, in order to streamline creative and production departments. The Fiery Colour Server rapidly moved into the mainstream. Users found that Fiery produced higher-quality results than desktop colour printers, because of its ability to support continuous tone printing at typical resolutions of 400×400 dpi. The colour and detail resulting from this are far better than the half-tone screening which is the only tone reproduction method open to most desktop colour printers.

Colour management

Since the introduction of colour desktop publishing, the market has expanded to include many novice colour users, who need easier ways to get predictable results when they print in colour. To satisfy this need, Electronics For Imaging introduced the EfiColor management system. EfiColor allows you to ensure consistent colour from the scanner to the computer display, to colour PostScript printing. Thus you can be sure that the colours in the original photograph or graphic are matched as closely as possible by the printed image and the image on the computer monitor. This was what used to require considerable skills from the trade-shop operators. EfiColor uses profiles which alter the colours in the job to take account of the characteristics of individual devices such as scanners or printers. The latest EfiColor Works product allows users to create their own printer profiles.

EFI also pioneered shrink-wrapped applications software that made it easy enough for even novice users to colour-correct scanned photographs and get high-quality printed results. Its Cachet program for the Macintosh allows users to improve poor originals by basing their alterations on visual references rather than complicated controls or calculations.

EFI says that its combination of breakthrough technology and user-friendly colour software has ignited the desktop publishing market, making colour printing available to a huge user base.

Shira Computers Ltd

In the early days of electronic publishing and reproduction, manufacturers developed their own 'proprietary' computers and production equipment. As their use became more widespread throughout the 1980s, users increasingly wanted to be able to exchange work files between companies that might have different manufacturers' systems. They also wanted to be able to buy equipment from more than one vendor, and operate it in an integrated production system.

Shira Computers Ltd, founded in 1987 are based in Kfar Saba, Israel, identified this trend towards open system architecture and easier integration, and so it developed interfacing and input/output solutions for high-end users. Through OEM contracts with major prepress vendors around the world, Shira has created a range of software modules to fill this need.

Today the company has OEM relations with most of the leading manufacturers of prepress systems and devices, including Linotype–Hell, Scitex, Crosfield, Dainippon Screen, Iris, CSI, Kodak and Indigo. With many of these, Shira was the first third party successfully to implement their proprietary system protocols. It is developing new links all the time — the latest are to Dainippon Screen OMEGA-formatted optical disks and Scitex RMX optical disks. More than 500 Shira systems have been installed worldwide.

Shira's current range takes in DDES tape formats, through IT8.4 and IT8.8 online links, to IFEN and TIFF/IT formats. In the *Seybold Report on Publishing Systems* (1 November 1993), Shira was described as one of those companies that 'provide the 'glue' that makes it possible for many of the disparate components of the prepress industry to work together... While Shira may be unsung, it is hardly unrecognized among engineers looking for high-quality conversion of high-resolution graphics files.'

This year the company is releasing a new version of its system that incorporates a PostScript RIP for bridging high-end systems and desktop publishing applications. Shira has also introduced a range of plug-ins to aid productivity and connectivity of work in Adobe Photoshop.

Shira version 3.2 includes the 5D Jaws PostScript level 2 RIP, which provides fast processing for high-resolution proofing and further high-end processing. Once set up, this can process batches of jobs without operator attendance, though its job queues and priorities can be overridden at any time.

Shira's new Photoshop plug-ins — the Link and Open Link — enable desktop publishers to handle large images quickly within Photoshop, and to import CT (contone) images in the native formats of all major CEPS workstations for editing in Photoshop. Afterwards, the Photoshop user can export the file, through Shira, back to a high-end CEPS or send it to desktop layout programs — such as Quark XPress — for further processing and page assembly.

Future plans for the company include developing a true multiplatform Shira system that provides connectivity solutions on the PC, Macintosh, SUN and Silicon Graphics platforms. Shira is also continuing to expand its line of interfaced printers for all segments of the market, high-quality, low-end and wide format, for plate proofing. For example it has recently introduced a proofing module for the Mitsubishi S6600-30 dye-sublimation printer.

Optibase Ltd

Image compression has always been important in the high end of graphic arts, but with the advent of multimedia and desktop products the demand has begun to widen. Images, in particular photographs, take up a huge amount of computer storage space compared to text.

Why compress digital information such as video and images? Practicality. A single second of digital video takes up more than 25 megabytes of memory or disk space. In the race to integrate digital video, images and audio into consumer applications, these large digital files must be manageable using current storage mediums such as hard disks and CD-ROMs.

Optibase Inc, a four-year-old Israeli company based in Herzliya, has developed an extensive range of digital video image and audio compression and expansion products. Many of these concern moving images and video for the burgeoning multimedia market, which combines moving images, text, sound and animations in a form which can be accessed interactively by the end user.

The proliferation of the digital 'information highway' of today and tomorrow depends on compatibility and interconnectivity. For instance, it is the CCITT G3 and G4 standards which allow today's fax machines to communicate, regardless of the manufacturer.

Recognizing the need for advanced digital compression products, Optibase began by developing hardware and software products for image compression and processing. Optibase believes in the International Standards Organisation (ISO) standards: JPEG (Joint Photographic Experts Group) algorithm for digital video and associated audio; Px64 (H.261) algorithm for desktop video conferencing boards; and MPEG (Moving Pictures Experts Group) for compressing moving digital pictures.

The Optibase product line started with OptiTools, a developer's toolkit, and the Image Workshop, an end-user product. They use JPEG compression and are aimed at publishers and multimedia developers who require convenient storage and transmission of still images. Following these products, Optibase released the world's first MPEG video compression and playback products for the PC/AT computer range.

Today, Optibase designs and manufactures a complete line of digital compression, expansion and processing products. It is focusing on providing solutions for the rapidly evolving multimedia and digital video markets. It has an extensive line of digital video, image and audio compression and expansion products including: a family of MPEG playback boards, providing full screen, full motion, digital video and synchronized audio played directly from a CD-ROM, hard disk or network server. The new MPEG Lab Pro is a real-time MPEG encoding system for the compression of digital video and associated audio on a PC/AT. A multifunction Px64 videoconferencing board is in development; as well as a developer's toolkit and boards for building JPEG image applications.

Optibase is providing system integrators and developers with the tools to integrate digital video, images and audio into multimedia applications. These applications include: video kiosks, multimedia databases, presentation and interactive training systems. At present Optibase is working with OEMs in the USA, Europe and Asia to develop videoconferencing and video-on-demand products for use over existing and future telephone and cable networks.

Indigo

With the introduction of Digital Offset Colour, Indigo claims it has given the industry an insight into the future of printing — the ability to output colour publications directly from computer to paper, by-passing film and platemaking.

The first, and so far only, Digital Offset Colour press, the Indigo E-Print 1000, is an A3 sheet-fed machine that prints digitally but uses an offset blanket cylinder to transfer ink to paper. Apart from its ability to print high-quality pages straight from prepress computer data, the E-Print 1000 also allows information to be changed on-the-fly, so every copy can be different. If the digital input data changes, then so does each page, at a rate of 4000 impressions per hour. That is 1000 full-colour A3 sheets, (2000 A4 pages, two-up, single-sided), per hour.

Indigo has spent a decade researching and developing digital printing. It has been granted more than 200 patents for optical, electronic, engineering and chemical innovations.

It is hard to categorize the E-Print 1000. It is not a fast colour copier and it is not a four-colour offset press. It has features and benefits from both but it is essentially a unique machine. The ink system is worthy of special attention. Indigo has developed 'ElectroInk', that behaves as a liquid on the imaging cylinder and blanket cylinder but turns to a solid the instant it hits the paper. The ink is initially imaged on to a dynamic 'plate' cylinder, transferred on to a blanket cylinder and then on to the substrate. There is no residual ink image left on the blanket, as the ink becomes a cohesive film as it touches the paper and in effect peels away from the offset cylinder. A major benefit is that there is no dot gain and, because the ink 'sets' on the paper, a broad range of substrates can be printed, unlike powder toner copiers where the paper choice is very limited. For duplex printing, a holding buffer and refeeding arrangement is used. With each revolution of the

E-Print 1000's imaging drum, a different colour, i.e. CMY and K, or a different image can be printed. This makes the machine very compact since only one set of cylinders is required.

The E-Print will interface with virtually any prepress device via a specially developed Shira universal prepress interface, while in a PostScript environment Indigo offers the Adobe Configurable PostScript Interpreter (CPSI), a Level 2 PostScript RIP running on the Indigo's Sun front end.

What are the applications?

Digital presses allow page data to be received and processed into colour hard-copy very quickly, in short runs and with variable information. The ability to print text or pictures on every copy means that pin-point targeted or personalized marketing can be achieved.

Very short colour runs become viable because the Digital Offset Colour machine is always online, just like a fax machine. Because there are no colour film-separation, plate-making, stripping and make-ready costs, E-Print 1000 can print 50 copies of eight-page A4 brochure just as cost-effectively as 5000 copies — you just pay for the amount of ink and paper consumed.

Indigo's plans

The economic benefits of digital presses are plain to see. Given the level of interest in the market there will no doubt be further developments in Indigo's Digital Offset Colour press technology. The first of the several hundred E-Print 1000 presses already ordered have been installed in Japan and the USA and are being followed by European deliveries during 1994.

MANUFACTURING IN FUTURE

Predicting future directions is always difficult, particularly in an industry that uses the leading edge of computer technology. What seems certain is that the rocketing power of desktop computers will put more and more facilities into the hands of the publisher, while falling output costs and the use of digital presses will allow a wider variety of jobs to be produced, closely tailored to their marketplace.

Manufacturers are in a dilemma though. $1000 scanners and $500 layout programs do not have much profit margin, so they have to sell many of them. However, the market for specialized imaging and printing equipment is always going to be relatively limited compared with, say, a spreadsheet program.

The big manufacturers with lots of staff and enormous R&D budgets may disappear, to be replaced by a cottage industry of plug-in developers, who customize a few big-selling packages, and systems integrators who assemble standard components. Agfa and Scitex are certainly aware of that possibility and are rapidly diversifying; hence both companies' exploration of alternative printing technologies in addition to 'pure' repro.

For the equipment user, the future looks hopeful. The trend towards affordable printing and ever-easier publishing software looks set to continue. In the long term electronic publishing may become a virtually invisible function, with all formatting and printing handled automatically by knowledge-based systems and preset defaults. Some of the creative satisfaction may be lost, but users will always have the option of doing things the good old way. What is certain is that short runs and automation will mean more publishing for less cost.

Publishers are just beginning to explore the potential for putting their products on other media than the printed page. Already there is a growing trend to put information on CD-ROM and distribute it in computer-readable form. Originally this was largely confined to databases of information and collections of back issues of printed text. However, as experience grows, publishers are exploring multimedia: combining moving images, sound and text in an interactive form that lets users choose their own route to access the information.

A related area of development is the publishing of information on 'online' databases which can be accessed over telecommunications lines. Here the publishers will only be selling the pure information: the final printing and perhaps even the formatting will move into the hands of the end-users, who we would call readers.

27

Sony and the Electronic Book

Jun Tanaka, Sony Corporation, Japan

INTRODUCTION

In 1990, Sony Corporation introduced the Electronic Book system in Japan as a consumer-oriented answer to portable high-density storage. Using the 8 cm CD-ROM format and housing it in a protective caddy allowed us to create an image of simple user interactivity, much like a traditional book, and alleviated the fears of those intimidated by computers. Using XA technology, which allows the programming of text, graphics and interleaved sound, we at Sony view the Electronic Book as an entrance into the world of multimedia.

The Electronic Book system is made up of two things, hardware and software, which must work together closely to provide a complete product. The Electronic Book system, like a traditional book, should be usable by 'anyone, anywhere, at anytime'. To do this, we first established a standard: a standardized retrieval system in every Electronic Book player, and a standardized data format in every Electronic Book. This means that any Electronic Book can be played in any Electronic Book player, anywhere in the world. The EBXA logo displayed on the outside of software shows that it complies with this standard.

The Electronic Book itself is an 8 cm CD-ROM. This CD-ROM is stored in a protective caddy to prevent scratching or damage and to enhance its image as a book. Each Electronic Book can contain

Jun Tanaka is Managing Director of the Personal Information Group of Sony Corporation at headquarters in Tokyo.

200 megabytes of information. That equals about 100 000 pages of text, 32 000 graphics or 5.6 hours of digital sound. This means that volumes of paper can be stored on one small disc and taken with you wherever you go. In addition, sound data is perfect for listening to books or learning languages.

ELECTRONIC BOOK COMMITTEE

In order to provide good communication between hardware and software companies, we established an Electronic Book Committee on a country-wide basis. The EBC of Japan meets twice a year and Sony meets with major publishers every month, to hear the input from publishers and work with them to improve our products. This kind of information is a key factor in making this business work.

The Data Discman electronic publishing format is an international format; software from any country can be used on any machine. Establishing a strong format requires close international communication. To facilitate this, representatives from each local EBC formed an International Electronic Book Publishers Committee to discuss the electronic book format, the future direction of electronic publishing and ways in which the hardware and software companies can work to help each other.

SOFTWARE DEVELOPMENT

The next step in the electronic publishing format is the actual making of software. To make Electronic Books, Sony Electronic Publishing Company developed a program which allows companies to easily transfer their data to the EB format. This program, called *SEBAS*, changes SGML data used by the traditional CD-ROM into EB data. Once formatted, our disc-checking program checks to make sure that the disc will work on all EB players, and then it is pressed at one of the disc-pressing facilities all over the world. Based on this program, over 300 software titles have been introduced in eight languages in just three years. There are 103 titles in Japan, and the USA expects to have around a hundred titles by the end of the year. In addition to the countries listed here, discs have been made in Switzerland, the Netherlands and a few other countries.

MARKET-ORIENTED PROGRAMMES

The key to success in this area is the smooth partnership between hardware and software, and Sony has been active in promoting software-oriented marketing to illustrate the merits of the hardware. In Europe there is a campaign underway in Germany, France and Spain to target English-learners. Nicknamed 'English Teacher', this market-oriented project combines the Data Discman Electronic Book player with a series of English-learning software and packages it as a 'teacher' rather than as a piece of hardware with application software. This type of strategy emphasizes the 'user friendliness' of our hardware and makes it easy for the customer to understand what they are buying.

In a similar arena, Sony has developed an Electronic Book player/software package in Japan known as 'Pela Pela' which means 'fluent' in Japanese. This unit is intended for those travelling abroad to have quick access to useful phrases and information. The high-quality XA sound captures the pronunciation of native speakers for easier understanding and learning. This product is being promoted both through traditional retail channels and through travel agencies throughout Japan.

VERTICAL-MARKET PROGRAMS

One of the advantages to this low-cost, portable format is its capacity for high-density storage. This makes the Electronic Book the perfect answer for businesses looking for a low-cost storage device and has been implemented in several businesses with tremendous success. The Police Department in Tokyo has taken advantage of the XA capabilities of the Electronic Book to create software to aid in communication with foreigners in Japan. This disc, which outlines all the rules and regulations of Japanese law and holding facilities, allows Japanese policemen to reference rules in Japanese, which are then translated into one of 12 foreign languages. Because of the compact size of the Electronic Book player, policemen may carry this 'translator' with them as they direct people around the station.

In America, Yellowstone National Park has adopted the Electronic Book format as a storytelling tool. Visitors to the park may rent a 'Tourguide', which tells a story through graphics and sound as visitors travel around the Park. The random access that CD-ROM storage allows means that visitors do not have to follow a preset path, but are free to travel around the Park at their leisure.

NEW HORIZONS

Since its 1990 introduction in the Japanese market and, despite a worldwide economic recession, sales have expanded into 17 countries, and Panasonic, Sanyo and Sharp have all introduced Electronic Book players. Worldwide, an estimated 500 000 Electronic Book players have been sold, with another 300 000 estimated within this fiscal year. The impact the Electronic Book has had, when compared to other multimedia formats, is impressive, and we are proud of the solid progress in the marketplace.

Now that this introductory phase is well under way, we are entering our second stage of development. Until now, we wanted the Electronic Book to be seen as unique and different from other CD-ROM products. Now that we have achieved this, we are ready to bring them closer together, using the EB to promote a unified multimedia platform for all PC platforms. To do this, we will allow the 8 cm CD-ROM to be removed from its caddy for use in licensed CD-ROM hardware. This will allow a user to use his/her Electronic Books on the road in the protective caddy or without the caddy in his/her home computer or CD-ROM-based game player, like the ones made by Sega and JVC.

In opening the caddy, we believe the Electronic Book format will become a standard format for all CD-ROM, an easy-to-use, portable CD-ROM usable in multiple kinds of hardware. Already companies have expressed interest in adapting the EB format to their hardware and we think this unified strategy is the key to the future.

CONCLUSION

What does the future look like for personal information products? For Sony, the Data Discman integrated text, graphics and audio format will remain the centre of the consumer market business. The Data Discman will concentrate on integration with computers, as our new products feature computer connections. Products such as the multimedia CD-ROM Player (MMCD) are targeted at the vertical market and will continue to be used for corporate projects demanding high-density storage with high graphic quality. Other high-end products, such as the CD-i which features full motion video, will also remain in the vertical application area. Because of the growing consumer demand for portable products, I believe the Electronic Book format has a very bright future. The next few years will be very exciting to watch.

The legal environment — case studies

28
Copyright and electronic publishing

Clive Bradley, The Publishers Association, UK

Copyright and electronic publishing are often thought not to mix. Copyright is seen as an old-fashioned concept, reminiscent of Queen Anne, Napoleon and dusty books; electronic publishing is the symbol of a bright new age, offering new, more efficient, lower cost access to information, learning and entertainment. Copyright, they say, stands in the way of such advances, or, as a senior European Commission official put it, 'We must support copyright so long as it doesn't stand in the way of market development'.

That, of course, is to fail to recognize that copyright *is* the market: that what people engaged in writing and publishing valuable materials are engaged in is creating a valuable saleable product, a product that can be put on the market, with a return on the investment of skill and resources in the product, and which, if successful enough, will cause the market to exist and to grow.

The principle of copyright is, indeed, that the creators of valuable written, artistic, graphic and musical works, and of related expressions of such works, such as recordings, performances, audio-visual presentations and, in some jurisdictions, textual and graphical editions, will enjoy a right to exploit that product, as inventors can exploit their original devices through patents, and creators of valuable trading enterprises and brands can protect the origin of their

Clive Bradley is Chief Executive of the British Publishers Association based in London. A lawyer by profession, his particular interest is in copyright issues — now of major concern when related to multimedia publishing.

products through trademarks. It is as modern a concept as the microchip, and it is noteworthy that the great area for conceptual legal thinking of the 1980s and 1990s is intellectual property — copyright and patents and trademarks — just as employment law, the changing relationship between employer and employee, 'master' and 'servant', dominated the 1970s, as collectivization and labour-intensive industry gave way to individual skill and technology-intensive industry.

INTELLECTUAL PROPERTY — A HIGH-PROFILE TOPIC

The capacity, brought about by information technology, to create and disseminate information and ideas in new ways is one of the principal reasons why intellectual property is such a high profile a topic at the moment. From the design and manufacture of superconductors to microchips, to the collation of databases, the need to find effective ways to secure returns for those who make information and ideas and inventions available in attractive, marketable ways that will attract investment has a high economic, commercial and cultural priority.

For new information products and services, copyright stands ready-made and accepted, supported by international conventions adopted throughout most of the world, and a recognized part of the legal system. It establishes international rights to make copies of original written works and, in most advanced jurisdictions, to issue copies of those works to the public — to publish the copies for the first time. They are the rights that enable creators of information products and services (known generally as authors) and those who turn them into marketable products and put them on to the market (publishers) to earn a return to justify their effort, the size of that return being geared, as it should be, to the success and acceptability of the product on the market. Further, international law provides that the products of one country should be protected equally in others and that each country will give the same protection to foreign works as it gives to its own: the so-called principle of national treatment, thus avoiding the complexities and difficulties which would arise if differing levels of protection were applied depending on the country of origin.

THE ARGUMENTS OVER COPYRIGHT

Why then, if copyright is such a satisfactory, internationally accepted system, is there such a controversy? Why, when the European Commission proposes a new directive to harmonize the protection of the intellectual property in software, does all hell break out on the opaque issue of 'interoperability'? Why, when the US courts deny copyright protection to lists of bare facts such as a listing of telephone numbers in the *Feist* case, is this seen as a fundamental challenge to the principle of copyright in original written and published work in electronic form? Why does the European Commission find it necessary to invent a new right, the right against unauthorized extraction for certain factual databases in electronic form? Why, indeed, do many commentators argue that some, significantly different, new form of protection of creative skill and investment in electronic publications will have to be invented — that, as I put it earlier, copyright is seen as being obsolete?

Before attempting to answer these questions, it is worth considering possible alternatives. Clearly, basic requirements must include the identification of an original (i.e. not itself copied) marketable product which can be bought and sold, so enabling earnings to be made, which is not easy given the ephemeral nature and copiability of information products. In a competitive market that return should be related to the success of that product. Also, given that the product will pass in the nature of the market from hand to hand, the ability to protect the marketability of the product must apply to third parties, to the whole world, and not just to the parties to an individual contract.

Indeed, the only alternative to copyright, or something very similar to it, which enables the creators and disseminators of information products to earn a fair reward, would be for these entrepreneurs to be rewarded with a salary, but a salary paid not by the employer, whose own product without copyright would not be protected and so would be incapable of earning a return on investment, but *faute de mieux* by the state, an extraordinary return to socialism in one of the most important and significant growth areas of the economy.

So, again, why is the unacceptability of this and the value of copyright not immediately understood? The reasons, I suggest, are complex, but they include the following:

- New IT-based information products are seen as a brave new world, a marvellous new opportunity (which they are) for information users (all of us) to have easier, cheaper access to information under their own control, not dependent on the use of physical products such as printed materials. Those who argue that this new use of information must be paid for by the user are seen as 'Luddites' standing in the way of advance, not as realists who recognize that any product of value has to be paid for by someone; and the greater the value, the greater the ease of use, the larger the spur to growth, the higher the reward should be. And, if it has to be paid for, surely the actual user should be the payer?

- But, awkwardly, this simple truth comes up against the arguments of consumer economics, that users should not be denied the benefits of getting new products as cheaply as possible, so that, if they can do this by electronic reproduction in the privacy of their own establishments, they should not be denied this facility, even if it involves, well, cheating.

- This problem that unauthorized reproduction is widely regarded as acceptable is exaggerated because, for the first big successful electronic publishers, it has not really mattered. It is an unfortunate accident that the first successful electronically published databases should be in the financial services area, distinguished by the fact that the available information is valueless within minutes of its being published, so that direct online access in real time is the only acceptable product, leaving no room for intermittent piracy or unauthorized reproduction (though networking is changing this situation). Such databases are an unhappy precedent for archival, educational and research databases, which are not time-dependent and which may be published in distributed form such as CD-ROM, CD-i and the like, eminently downloadable and reproducible. This has resulted in the leading entrepreneurs in financial-services publishing downgrading the importance of copyright and its enforceability against anyone who comes into possession of the product, and suggesting that contractual licensing offers all the protection that is needed, to the detriment of the more broadly based electronic information product.

- Copyright has also suffered from an unnecessarily dogmatic view that its purpose is to protect creativity as such, and not the output of writers and publishers which may not be seen as 'creative' in the cultural sense. This has come to the fore in the renewed conflict between the Anglo-Saxon (UK–US–Commonwealth) concept of copyright, which sees it (as described above) as creating a marketable product, and the continental, Napoleonic *droit d'auteur* tradition, that copyright is essentially a cultural concept. With the added problem that the Anglo-Saxon world is to the forefront in new IT-based information products and services, this has resulted in continental copyright experts themselves being reluctant to see copyright extended to new technology-based products.

- The whole debate has additionally become confused with the monopoly/abuse of dominant-position argument, that copyright owners are monopolists, relying on exclusive rights in their products, however competitive these may be between themselves. So antitrust authorities in both the EC and the USA have sought to limit exclusive copyright generally instead of confining their attention to *ad hoc* cases of abuse.

A more rational analysis of the problem is that, far from copyright being unimportant for electronic publications, it is much more important. New information products and services have a number of characteristics:

- They involve a compilation of a critical mass of related but different (in content, presentation and organization) materials.
- They are typically accessed not sequentially, like a book, but in random form as part of a search-and-find procedure.
- Therefore, they are used to obtain access not to the whole, to the mass, but to the actual small, insubstantial parts that come out of that mass.
- Therefore, one might add, they are expensive, as the supplier must provide a lot of well-organized material from which the required bits can be found.
- This process of search, access and finding is the way in which electronic publications are meant to be used. It takes place in the privacy of the office, library, laboratory or classroom, wherever the intended users are. Unlike conventional books therefore, at least before photocopying — itself a form of IT — the act of reproduction cannot readily be controlled.

Because of the different nature of electronic from conventional published materials, the kind of abuse or infringement of copyright is itself different. Infringement takes place less, as piracy has been for books, by reproduction *en masse* for commercial sale than by small-scale, though massive in total extent, unauthorized downloading, reproduction and circulation by the illegal photocopy, by the unauthorized addition of electronic materials to a database, by the circulation of materials through a network, by unauthorized access.

The problems are not then between author and publisher — the forms of licensing for publishing are well understood, even if they are having to undergo change for new media — or between publisher and competing publisher, as for piracy. They are those between publisher and user, the so-called downstream vertical relationship. This is the area in which attention is needed.

Because the user, the consumer of information, can use the information illicitly with consummate, in-built ease and even with a clear conscience, making it difficult for the supplier, the publisher, to know that its work has been infringed, the need is not for weaker copyright protection, riddled through with exceptions such as fair dealing or fair use, or excuses that the illicit access was insubstantial, but for much stronger protection, so that the user knows that illicit access is illegal and subject to penalties. It is necessary that both supplier and user are encouraged to develop systems where a market is created, with the supplier knowing that the market will not be undermined, and the user recognizing that failure to honour the system is a breach of law, unacceptable and subject to penalties.

CURRENT PROPOSALS ARE TOO WEAK

This is the antithesis of what has been happening. The authorities, encouraged by the Luddite cries of users, have been reluctant to help create a workable market in information products: they have turned blind eyes to illegal photocopying, deploying copyright exceptions which excuse much illicit use (the US Copyright Act is weak on multiple copying for classroom use, though college anthologies are being brought under some control); the EC software Directive kow-towed to the 'reverse-engineering' argument, so that copyright protection of software is weakened; worse, the Draft Directive on Legal Protection of Databases fails entirely to comprehend the vital role of the publisher in database publishing, in putting the whole product together in accessible packages, and the way in which databases are created and reused and, catastrophically, seeks to provide two systems of protection for database publishing: a high level when they (the databases, not the content) are 'creative' enough and a low level when neither the database not the contents (for which the author of creative works continues to enjoy individual protection not granted to the publisher) are creative enough — the low level is only available against illicit commercial reproduction, not against the real problem, illicit private access.

THE SOLUTIONS

So what, apart from stronger copyright protection, can be done? For his or her part, the electronic publisher has to recognize that the uses made of his or her products are very different from conventional uses of books. The publisher has to develop licensing and permissions systems available not just to contractual parties but to likely users who are willing to comply with the terms of the licence.

Thus, publishers, and those who like me represent them, are developing forms of blanket collective licences, administered by copyright licensing agencies such as the CLA in the UK for cruder forms of classroom photocopying and elementary uses of electronic resources such as electro-copying. They are introducing more sophisticated, more individual forms of permissions through centralized agencies such as the CCC and the CLA's Copyright Clearance System (CLARCS). They are experimenting with 'site licences'. To achieve better proximity to market conditions, they are entering into licensing arrangements supported by copyright with commercial document supply centres such as UnCover and, if the right extent can be found, with the British Library's Document Supply Centre; they are setting out the terms on which learned materials may be accessed on scientific databases like Adonis.

For users, too, there have to be fundamental changes. 'Consumers' such as teachers, researchers, librarians and information scientists are having to recognize that, when it comes to information, there is no such thing as a free lunch; someone has to pay enough for new media products in a competitive market to permit their availability, and that someone should be as close to the actual use as possible. Thus, the costs of information materials should be as much part of research or classroom budgets as other materials are, and the librarian, in aiding access to such materials, has to recognize that he or she is part of the information chain, buying information from one source and supplying it against payment to another, paying his or her own overheads in the process. All will have to recognize that a workable system depends on having some means of measurement, so that the actual use of materials published can be ascertained, where the more successful or valuable electronic publications are earning the higher rewards. The working of an effective market depends on this.

In time, information technology will contribute its own solutions to allow for uses made of copyrights to produce the necessary returns. Copying resources — whether photocopiers or network terminals — will have their in-built smart card and measurement systems, identifying products accessed and copied by their own in-built identifiers. The technology is already available. No-one regards their telephone bill as an unfair imposition; the information bill will acquire the same familiarity.

However, this requires recognition that the originators and disseminators of information deserve their reward; that they are the crucial part of the copyright cycle, and that copyright deserves and needs strong protection if it is to be workable and if information is not to become a banal socialized resource of striking unoriginality. Copyright is the trading system for works of the mind; it deserves positive support. Indeed, this is vital for a growing information-based economy.

29

The dictionary and the diaries — a look at multimedia licensing practices, 1991 to 1994

Ann Reinke Strong, Springer-Verlag, USA

This chapter was in process when I picked up the *Wall Street Journal* on 23 May 1994 and read about *The Haldeman Diaries* being released virtually simultaneously in book form by G P Putnam & Sons and on CD-ROM by Sony Electronic Publishing Company. The *WSJ* focused on the uniqueness of this venture, stating, 'There has never been anything quite like it in publishing...' It mentioned the content differences (the CD-ROM features all the diaries, 2200 pages of unedited text, plus audio and video while the book has about 1000 pages of edited text) and certain sensitive references excluded from the book but included on the CD-ROM.

While these aspects of the project were certainly important and interesting, I wanted to know whether the CD-ROM was going to be sold through the bookstore channel, the software channels, or both, and if the libraries were apt to purchase one or the other or both. And I was intrigued by the copyright and licensing issues involved in such a venture. Though no-one at Sony could be reached to discuss

Ann Reinke Strong recently joined Springer-Verlag New York as Vice-President for Journals and Electronic Media. Prior to this appointment she was Executive Vice-President of Macmillan New Media (MNM), a division of Macmillan Inc.

the rights issues, I have made the following assumptions about the *Diaries* CD-ROM product.

It appears the rights to publish the book and the CD-ROM were negotiated separately, apparently by Haldeman's agent. There was one author (who was the evangelist for the CD-ROM version), so the rights to the text were a straightforward licensing agreement. The author also contributed his own video (home movies). As for the other content on the CD-ROM, the 700 photos were a mix of licensing, public-domain and author-provided, the newspaper articles and White House logs were public-domain and a 120-page handwritten letter was provided by the author himself, again a straightforward licensing arrangement. There may have been a fee for some of the audio, i.e. commentary, but one has the impression that much of that was also provided by the author.

The software employed is Sony's (proprietary), so there was no additional software licence or royalty to be paid. Also one assumes Sony negotiated the rights to distribute the CD-ROM internationally. Altogether the deal probably consists of one carefully drawn contract with (the late) Haldeman, a smattering of permissions payments for photos and perhaps an audio agreement. Very neat. While the royalty terms cannot have been modest (was there an advance?), the rights for the CD-ROM, taken as a whole, were probably easy to manage and relatively painless. If this is all true, the *Diaries* CD-ROM is a good model to follow.

The rights issues and negotiations surrounding the first multimedia CD-ROM project undertaken by Macmillan New Media (MNM) were difficult and more complex, I believe, not because the product itself was more sophisticated, but because it was produced during the first wave of multimedia products and virtually every rights undertaking was conducted without precedent. The *Macmillan Dictionary for Children*, Multimedia Edition, first released in October 1991, required seven separate agreements, plus several hundred illustration permissions negotiated twice, first for North American rights and subsequently for worldwide rights. The translation of localization rights were additional. Here is a listing of the agreements:

(1) Contract with the Children's Division, Macmillan Publishing Company (advance plus royalty).
(2) Agreement with software provider (royalty).

(3) Agreement with programmer (Work for Hire).

(4) Agreement with audio (originally recorded, Work for Hire).

(5) Agreement with animator for the character 'ZAK' (Work for Hire plus royalties on all representations of 'ZAK').

(6) Agreement with WGBH Design Lab for product design (Work for Hire plus credit).

(7) Agreement with graphic designer for label, package, flyer sheets, advertisements (Work for Hire).

The video planned for the *Dictionary* would have added at least three more agreements: new design work, additional programming and, if the video had been original, not canned, multiple permissions and licensing fees familiar to the TV and movie industry (e.g. location fees), but unknown in the publishing industry, would have been required.

One of the key differences between the *Diaries* and the *Dictionary* is that the development of the electronic edition of the *Dictionary* came many years after the original publication of the book, which occurred when electronic rights were not even a gleam in anyone's eye. The lengthy and cumbersome licensing of illustrative material, for instance, would certainly be avoided today as Macmillan (now Paramount) solicits electronic rights at the beginning of the development of a title.

One expects that the cover design of the Haldeman book was designed from the beginning with the CD-ROM in mind, addressing both the aesthetic and legal issues. Fortunately, the cover art for the print edition of the *Dictionary* had been done as a Work for Hire many years ago and then altered so that there was no permissions trail to follow; but it might have been a sticky problem, as we discovered with other electronic products.

Another difference is that the rights granted MNM by its sister division, the Children's Book Division, were broadly based and included not only MAC and MPC versions of the CD-ROM, but also CD-i rights. In contrast, one expects that Sony has only CD-ROM rights to the Haldeman material, the agent retaining his options for other media such as TV-based technologies. Indeed, the standard Macmillan contract after 1991 retained all electronic rights, and licences were granted more narrowly on a platform-specific basis.

Also, the contract between the Macmillan divisions was exclusive, a type of business arrangement that fell from favour as publishers learned to keep their options open with nonexclusive arrangements. However, this was unfortunate for software developers who, like MNM, believed that the investment required to develop a multimedia product justified the exclusivity of rights.

In part, from the bargaining over exclusive and nonexclusive licences came the more collaborative arrangements such as Random House/Broderbund's 'Living Books' joint venture and the JVI/The Mayo Clinic partnership to produce a series of consumer CD-ROMs on health. (We are seeing and will see far more such collaborations as companies from all sectors of the entertainment, information and communications industries team up for the next wave of TV-based technologies and the much ballyhooed 'Information Highway'.)

One should also mention the Affiliated Label Programs pioneered by Compton's and adopted by several other major players in the industry over the last two years. In such programmes, developers and publishers assign their products to Compton's at (generous) discount terms and Compton's, in turn, market and distribute the products under their imprint. With Compton's critical mass of products, marketing dollars and visibility in the market place, they command the attention of the software, video and book distributors. As a result, they control a significant share of shelf space in the major retail outlets. *De facto*, Compton's have exclusive licences from designated, or all, markets for products in their programmes. (I am interested to know if such a programme, in a modified form, will develop in the STM markets.)

Back to the core business of rights, let me say that, whether one is developing multimedia products for the consumer, library or professional markets, the elements for which rights must be owned or licensed are the same: text, illustrations, figures and tables, photos, audio, video and animation. As the comparison between the *Dictionary* and the *Haldeman Diaries* shows, it is far easier and one expects more cost-effective to develop a CD-ROM and/or multimedia title if it is conceived of as such from the beginning.

If you are mining your backlist assets, and one can certainly understand the business reasons for doing so, you must be prepared to spend money and expertise to solicit the appropriate rights — in some cases rights you thought you had. An electronic rights inventory of your key products, done by a knowledgeable person, should be high on your list and a critical piece of your electronic strategy.

It is essential that you the publisher manage your own rights whether you develop in-house contact with an outside developer, work collaboratively with a developer or simply license your properties. If you choose to develop in-house, the processing of some rights, e.g. performance permissions, can be delegated to a video production house, but ultimately you are liable. I believe it requires that you have a rights manager on your staff, who is familiar enough with video, film, TV, music and photo rights to approve all such transactions in a timely manner and keeps the company out of trouble.

It is worth emphasizing that rights and permissions move on a faster track in the multimedia world. One does not have weeks or even days, sometimes, to approve a request. If you are developing on your own, or with a production company, you often have only hours to make some kinds of decisions.

I suggest, a smart publisher entering into the electronic business of the 1990s should have:

- a worldwide electronic publishing strategy developed collaboratively within the company,
- a multimedia rights inventory of all key titles and assets (e.g. photos, audio),
- an experienced negotiator and computer advocate in charge of electronic rights and permissions (paid well with bonuses),
- a generous rights and permissions budget which he or she is prepared to double,
- a good, electronically savvy, intellectual property lawyer,
- a management team which is enlightened about, and has hands-on experience with, this 'new' technology.

The electronic licensing issues are worth management attention; they are challenging, interesting, and can involve a great deal of money. For instance, I wonder if the *Diaries* will be available on the Internet — officially, I mean... But that is a fascinating subject for another day.

30
Contracting for literary works in digitized format — the Danish experience

Mads Bryde Andersen, University of Copenhagen, Denmark

BACKGROUND

Despite being a small country of only five million citizens, Denmark has no less than three authors' associations. The oldest one, Dansk Forfatterforening (The Danish Writers Association), has traditionally represented all categories of published works, fiction as well as nonfiction, children's literature as well as professional literature. The second, Danske Skønlitterære Forfattere (Danish Fiction Writers) is the youngest; it separated from the Danish Writers Association a couple of years ago upon an insoluble debate over library book royalties. As indicated, it only organizes fiction writers.

The third association is not an independent association but rather a committee. Its name is UBVA which stands for Udvalget til Beskyttelse af Videnskabeligt Arbejde (the Committee for the Protection of Scientific Works). UBVA is a standing committee under Akademikernes Centralorganisation (the Danish Confederation of Professional Associations — in the following referred to as AC). While AC is empowered to negotiate agreements (primarily wages and working conditions) for a broad range of academic confedera-

Professor Dr Mads Bryde Andersen is a Director of the Institute of Legal Science of Copenhagen University. He is a lawyer and leading European expert on new media copyright issues.

tions in Denmark (doctors, dentists, veterinaries, architects, lawyers, academics of the humanities etc.), UBVA is in charge of handling their intellectual property rights (IPRs), i.e. not only copyrights but also patents and others.

It is characteristic of the digital exploitation of scientific works that rightholders have different roles, and indeed roles which may seem difficult to combine. One might claim that this gives rise to conflicts of interest for the people concerned. Others would say that different hats may give a more varied picture of a case and thus also provide the best basis for making the right decisions.

Being the chairman of UBVA, my main purpose in this article is to report on UBVA's experience and achievements in regard to licensing works in digital format. I should add that my role in this context is somewhat dual. Apart from being a writer of works that have been published digitally, I have also served as a publisher's consultant in one major database project (a Danish full-text legal database containing Danish case law). Furthermore, I am a member of the Computer Law Group of the Danish Data Association, a body representing users' interests. When not otherwise indicated, the views expressed in this article are my own — regardless of what hat I might seem to wear.

The present text will only focus on licensing issues in the author/ publisher context. Another major issue with which UBVA has been dealing extensively is the collective administration of digitized works. In that area, the Danish practice should be seen in an international context and space does not allow me to go into that issue too. Interested parties are free to request UBVA's discussion paper on the issue at UBVA, Akademikernes Centralorganisation in Copenhagen.

DIGITAL TECHNOLOGY — DANGER OR PROMISE?

During the last years, UBVA has been faced with a multitude of cases in which AC members have sought guidance when entering contracts for the use of literary works by digital means. The multitude of those cases is due to the variety of IPRs that AC/UBVA represents, not only literary texts (books, articles), editorial adaptation of texts, compilation works, pictures and photos (e.g. in scientific and technical literature) but also graphs and, last but not least, computer programs. Publishers now want to contract for the rights to use those various works with digital technology.

From the *user's perspective* this technology provides promising opportunities. Very few lay-persons feel fear about an effective access to information, particularly when it comes to information on which we depend in our everyday lives. On the contrary, it is a fundamental ideal in our society that information should be disseminated freely in order to benefit as many people as possible. This dissemination is simply the basic condition for the free creation of public opinion, a free market, free consumer choices etc.

But seen from the *rightholder's perspective* this utilization may be problematic. The use of a copyright work in digital format will typically involve its transmission, manipulation and dissemination. If a textbook is being spread to a larger audience by the digital medium with no royalty to the author and at the expense of the royalty-payable paper edition, author scepticism may rise.

The area of scientific publishing in particular shows numerous examples where the new technology is viewed as a threat to rightholders. This is the case when scientific articles or notes are spread via data networks. The reader of a digitally published scientific article has ample opportunity of citing curves and passages to a much greater extent than when reading written text.

At the same time it must be mentioned that the digital technology also makes it possible to *control* such use, e.g. in connection with the continuous numbering of copies combined with encryption techniques. Such technologies can only be applied widely if all users and publishers follow the same standards. Until now, no such standards have been decided.

The fact that digital exploitation of works requires the consent of the rightholder gives him or her a responsibility for the digital development of the publishing industry, at least until we have clear practice on how such contracts shall be made. On one hand, authors and publishers are uneasy about what direction to take. On the other hand, hesitation in handling the rights protected by copyright may hamper an otherwise favourable development. To some extent, we are in the middle of a trench war, where each group of rightholders/ suppliers is on its guard against the steps which other groups of rightholders may take.

MARKET TRENDS IN THE PUBLISHING INDUSTRY

It is usually difficult to predict how a market will develop, but it is particularly difficult to predict the development of markets for information technology. As a result of the rapid development in the relation between price and capacity of computer equipment, digital technology still opens up new possibilities for an efficient and abundant use of information. How this information is actually being used depends on the programs available and how fast these programs will penetrate the market.

We are experiencing an encounter between several types of market segment. First, we have the classical media businesses: the publishing houses, the news producers and the entertainment industry. This segment is characterized by great concentrations, e.g. large-scale publishing businesses, national radio and TV stations and film companies. The situation is somewhat different in the press area, which with very few exceptions (CNN and major international magazines) is typically aiming at locally delimited reader markets with their own specific demands with regard to the contents and appearance of the information.

Another segment is the electronics industry, i.e. the businesses which supply equipment (radio/television equipment, computer equipment, satellite receivers and cable connections). This industry has been characterized by keen competition, carried forward by a great number of not very big suppliers and made possible through a wide use of standards. By applying such standards different sorts of information can be merged into a series of new products (e.g. the so-called multimedia applications). These products will be characterized by a rather comprehensive variety of different elements of works (text, programs, sound, picture etc.) and will thus make significant demands as to precise and adequate copyright licences.

This melting together of different industries has caused some hesitation as to what rates to apply when it comes to distribution discounts etc. In Danish paper-publishing we have trade discounts of approximately 25–35% of the retail price of the book. These rates are much higher in the computer industry. It is not uncommon that the PC dealer obtains discounts of between 35% and 45% and that the rate for the so-called bundled programs, i.e. programs which are sold together with the equipment, is of the order of 55%. If the digital book is moving into a market which is normally demanding computer software etc., one cannot ignore these mechanisms. They will be of importance to the demands which the rightholders can reasonably make on the publishers.

Another important aspect is the question about who will run the digital business. Only a few publishers have tried to define themselves as participants in this new information market. Until they do so, authors may have sound reasons to be cautious in signing away digital rights to publishers. Why give away rights to someone who may not be in a position to put them into use?

NEW ROLES IN THE PUBLISHING INDUSTRY

Why have publishers not been forced to make a move toward the information industry? One important reason may be that publishers have been focusing on one kind of information, namely *text* (illustrations are typically bought separately). Text is the only information type influenced by the paper-publisher and today's publishing involves just a limited extent of editing. The text is almost ready directly from the author's hand.

Publishing texts — and texts alone — may cause some technological indolence on the part of publishers. A paper-publication is based on a well-known technology. The information (text) does not change — neither during the production nor in connection with the utilization. The publisher targets a market which is easily identified around well-known sales outlets (bookshops/book clubs or sales directly from the publisher). The user has no technical problems in getting hold of the information for which he/she is looking. Therefore, the main issue for the paper-publisher is how to make sure his/her product contains the most suitable text for the market.

The picture is distinctively different in digital publishing. A digital book — or an article in a periodical in digital form — can be published with no paper and printing whatsoever. Therefore, digital production takes place in a totally different interaction from paper-publishing. Printing works are no longer involved. Instead a new, important actor appears as the supplier of the program transmitting the text to the user (in the following called the 'display unit').

One of the difficult aspects in digital publishing concerns the software supplier. He/she plays a totally different role in the production of digital books than printing houses do in paper publishing. The quality of the 'display unit' — with regard to actual search facilities, user friendliness and aesthetic appearance — is of vital importance to the success of the digital book and indeed far more important than the binding and paper quality are to the success of a paper-based book. No matter how bad the paper is, the reader can usually find his/her information in the paper-book, but if the display unit of the digital book or the search program in the electronic database is defective or just hard to get at, that book is without value. Simply, the user will not be able to find the information he or she is after.

Apart from the central role of the software house, the software supplier — as opposed to the bookbinder and printer — disposes of a wide range of copyrights. First, he/she will be the owner of the search program itself (the display unit). Second, he/she will typically be the author of the instructions ('manual'), which the user must read to use the program. And in addition, the 'text-engineering' of a digital book may give the software house some rights over the final work.

The publication of periodicals — and the production of articles for periodicals — differs somewhat from the publication of books. The buyer of a book usually knows that it contains the information he/she is looking for, for instance because of good reviews. The size of the book will typically present an actual barrier to whether the user can be bothered to photocopy it. On the other hand, periodicals are ordered on subscription as a rule, because they usually publish certain articles.

The relation between author and periodical publisher reflects another environment compared to book publishing. Many periodicals are established for purely academic reasons in order to disseminate knowledge within a field of knowledge where information would otherwise have difficulties in being channelled appropriately. Such considerations will often influence the economy of the article for a periodical — indeed, from time to time the author may even have to pay to have his/her article printed. Also the editorial decision-making processes in publishing periodicals are typically more distant from the publisher than in book publishing.

A number of these aspects can be handled differently with digital technology. Various alternative methods have been developed of distributing information that is normally printed in periodicals. Many academic fields have their own electronic Bulletin Board Systems (BBS): with the help of PC and a telephone link, users — isolated in time and space — may communicate with each other and exchange experience or research results.

Although the use of such systems constitutes an effective possibility of communicating about well-defined topics, it is subject to a restriction, which is of significant importance to any research career, i.e. that 'publishing' on a BBS does not give merit but may on the contrary cause research results to be 'stolen'. Therefore, BBS communication and other alternative electronic distribution forms will hardly replace publishing of articles in periodicals. However, it is important to be aware of the tendency to use alternative ways of distributing scientific information, since that tendency may have influence on the rightholders' attitude to copyright in periodicals.

DANISH PRACTICE

In spite of a relatively intense publishing activity in the 'digital area', there is still no well-established Danish practice on how to handle digital publishing. In some cases the parties have agreed that their contract should be subject to being renegotiated if a new practice is established at a later stage. In other cases the parties have continued the principles governing a paper-based publication (which seems to have been the case with the publication of certain digital dictionaries). In still other cases, a lump sum has been paid to all contributors according to specific calculation principles. There are also examples to the effect that publishers have paid contributing authors by the hour for their contribution to the preparation of a digital publication.

In December 1991, UBVA concluded an agreement with a major Danish publisher, Gyldendal, regarding the *Great Danish Encyclopaedia*. Through this agreement, UBVA sanctioned a deviation from its prevailing general rules of 29 June 1973 concerning payment by the line for contributions to encyclopaedias. In the first period — where the publisher has extraordinary costs in relation to the planning and editing — 20 per cent should be deducted from the UBVA rates, but higher payment should be due at the end of the period. With an expected edition of 60 000 copies of the *Encyclopaedia*, the authors are to be paid an amount equal to UBVA's general rules.

This rule is expressed in the following provision (cf. point 4.1 of the agreement):

> The articles shall be paid on the basis of the rates laid down in UBVA's rules ...
> From the thus computed payment, one fifth of the fee should be deducted for the

first 20 000 copies. For the next 20 000 copies, there will be no deduction. For copies in addition to this, the computed fee will be increased by one fifth.

UBVA had several reasons for accepting this payment principle — among others the importance of supporting this significant national publication and the possibility of gaining higher royalties if the estimated sale of 60 000 copies was met.

The fundamental step in the encyclopaedia agreement is its principle of *progressive* royalty calculation. Authors usually receive *proportional* royalty as a fixed percentage based on the size of the edition. If we are at all to talk about any tendency in the direction of either progressive or decreasing payment in the case of bigger editions, the tendency is rather in the direction of decreasing principles. It is not uncommon for authors only to receive a small royalty when nonfictional works are published as 'book-club editions'. In this context, the encyclopaedia agreement implies innovation.

The agreement also contains rules about digital publishing of the encyclopaedia. The rules to this effect are found in 3.3:

> 3.3.: The fees earned through the publisher's sale of the right to publish the encyclopaedia in foreign languages — no matter whether it applies to the right to publish it in a printed form *through digital media* or through *other technical methods* — shall be shared in the proportion of 50% to the author and 50% to the publisher.

This provision applies to the sale of the publishing right, i.e. a situation where the publisher (or, in practice, the company Danmarks Nationalleksikon A/S) decides not to proceed with the publication. As for the publisher's own digital publication, the following is laid down in point 3.4:

> 3.4: If the publisher decides to publish the encyclopaedia in another way than the printed form after the publication of the printed edition, the author is entitled to a special fee for this utilization of his work. The size of this fee shall in this case be agreed upon separately between the publisher and UBVA, and the author obliges himself to accept what they agree upon. *In such an agreement, the principles of the present agreement should as far as possible be used.* A possible disagreement about the size of the fee does not affect the publisher's right to publish the encyclopaedia in another way than the printed form. The size of the fee will in such a case be fixed by a committee consisting of three members, cf. ... If the publisher decides only to publish the encyclopaedia in the digital form, the author shall receive a fee for this according to the provisions laid down in point 1, however as a minimum corresponding to a sale of 20 000 copies.

ELEMENTS OF A COPYRIGHT POLICY FOR DIGITAL EXPLOITATION

One may say that rightholders hold the best cards in the bargaining process over digital rights. If the rightholder has not expressly waived his/her rights for the digital use of his/her work, under Danish copyright law he/she can oppose such use. Offhand, this might call for taking a hard line in negotiations with publishers.

If such strategy is chosen, there is a risk that rightholder demands will lead to an obstruction of digital publication. Prohibitive demands may in turn have consequences of a political nature. Copyright law is entirely in the hands of politicians. In countries like Denmark, where copyright is not a constitutional right, the law of copyright has not necessarily come to stay. The only obligation to which the Parliament is subject follows from the conventions which Denmark has ratified and among which the Berne Convention plays the most important role. Copyright was introduced by law and can therefore also be revoked by law.

But even the Berne Convention is not sacred. Although WIPO has traditionally represented a line which is tantamount to a strong protection of the rightholders, other forces are pulling in the opposite direction. Such forces have for instance led to a certain toning down of the protection in regard to computer software. The Council Directive of 12 May 1991 on the legal protection of computer programs introduced a number of modifications to the copyright monopoly. WIPO's convention from 1990 on semiconductor chips can be read as an expression of the same idea about the limitation of intellectual property rights, when vital interests are at stake.

Academic rightholders (i.e. rightholders under AC organizations; see *Background*) are characterized by not being very greedy in their policy. Perhaps because an academic writer typically holds a position where he/she is paid for his/her writing or where he/she depends to a great extent on other works (which to varying extent are copied, borrowed etc.), not all academics feel equally strongly about their own copyright.

In one sense, the scientific writer does not share interests with his/her publisher. This is indeed so in *periodical publishing* where the writer is not paid for his/her contribution. In such publications, the author has an obvious interest in being read (and thus also copied) as much as possible and actually also as cheaply as possible, whereas the publisher has an obvious economic interest in getting as much revenue as possible, irrespective of the degree of real information dissemination which is underlying this.

The classic *publisher's agreement* is structured so that the publisher pays a fixed sum per copy sold. The royalty is proportional and typically it does not change, irrespective of the size of the edition. In certain cases, this scheme is combined with a guarantee payment, and such a guarantee payment can in this case be considered as a principle of decreasing payment. If the contributor to the digital book is to be paid according to these principles, the publisher will demand reduced payment because of the drastic costs incurred in the publication of the first edition.

One may ask whether the time has come for professional writers to consider themselves participants in a commercial experiment through the publication of the digital book. First, the publishing of digital books typically lies outside the publisher's usual capacity. The classical consideration that the publisher is prepared to take risks — and to be able to minimize risks — does not apply as a matter of course when it comes to digital publications. Some might even claim that it is totally outside the publisher's capacity to take on this type of publishing, a thought which is to some extent confirmed by experience in that publishers have entered into joint ventures and cooperation agreements with computer vendors, when they have had to take on this type of publishing.

Second, as already indicated, the academic writer of professional literature — at least within the area covered by the Danish Confederation of Professional Associations — is paid a salary by his/her employer for writing his/her work. If that is the case, the writer may be in a better position to take part in the special business–related risk which a digital publication constitutes.

Rightholders may find it reasonable to take the consequence of this consideration and accept to be partners in a joint venture with publishers and software houses. In such a joint venture, the rights and economic values of the author must be balanced against other rights (e.g. in the display programmes). A joint venture functions by way of openness on budgeting and pricing. If the publisher accepts to work with his/her writer and the software house by way of such openness, new royalty structures may emerge. If both parties agree on sales expectations and cost structures, authors may find it acceptable to receive a smaller royalty rate 'now', in return of having a larger — and surplus-like — royalty when these expectations are fulfilled.

The advantage of adopting this way of thinking primarily lies in the possibility of obtaining an economic balance in the long term. It should also be pointed out that the model is not suitable for the economically sensitive first edition in digital form (which, by the way, will typically be a second edition of the paper publication).

The disadvantage lies in the presumed considerable openness between the involved parties. The publisher must present his/her economic calculations so that the rightholder can get a comprehensive view of the risk he/she is running of never getting paid. Danish publishers have expressed their willingness to do this, but have so far been cautious in putting that willingness into practice, mainly for fear of spending too much practical effort in the process of royalty calculation.

It goes without saying that not all authors have the prerequisites for understanding the details of publisher calculations etc. This may be an argument against having authors participate in joint ventures of that kind. However, such knowledge gaps are not unknown on the labour market. Hardly any members of wage-earner organizations know the details of the union agreement which decides their salary. In this area, we accept a far-reaching delegation from member to organization. So, if the organization is willing to take up the inconvenience, why not so in the copyright field?

PRINCIPLES FOR A UBVA POLICY IN THE FIELD OF DIGITAL COPYING

Based on the foregoing considerations, UBVA has decided that the following principles should be applied in relation to 'secondary' digital utilization of nonfiction works. 'Secondary' in this context is understood as digital publications that follow a paper-based publication of the work, in which the authors will have received 'ordinary' payment for their 'primary' paper-based publications:

- As a point of departure, the rightholder should receive the same royalty rate for the digital publication of a work as for the primary paper-based publication, when the digital publication is aiming at the same target group as the paper-based publication.

- Although no payment has been made for the primary publication in paper form of the rightholder's work, the rightholder should receive a suitable fee, if the secondary publication of the work is directed at a different and much wider target group than presumed for the first publication (e.g. text-TV or popular databases which are marketed in huge editions).

- If the publisher — as a result of uncertain market expectations or special investment needs — does not find himself/herself capable of paying a fee for the digital edition of the rightholder's work, which corresponds to the fee rate for the paper edition, the parties should consider letting the contractual relationship between the rightholder and the publisher be handled as a joint venture, where the author, to a higher degree than in the case of paper publication, takes part in a business venture.

- If the parties choose to proceed according to joint-venture principles, the publisher must present any relevant budget information to the author or his/her organization. The principle of such an agreement may then be that a lower fee is paid (compared with that of the paper edition) for editions which fall below an expected budgetary balance, but in return a much higher fee when they have passed this balance. The rightholder — or the organization — must approve the licensing conditions which must apply to the end-user of his/her digital work.

- If the parties choose to proceed according to joint-venture principles, the agreement between the author and the publisher must be based on a mutual information obligation, and many more decisions than usual in publishing contracts should be presented for the approval of both parties (e.g. decisions regarding the fixing of prices, market segmentation).

- Until the time when — according to the above guidelines — firm well-established practices etc. have been laid down, UBVA is prepared — after a concrete appraisal of the nature of the case — to support the author of each individual digital publication as well as to cover costs in relation to auditing etc. in connection with the commercial decisions that are to be taken.

Creating market demand for EP products — case studies

31

New ways in dissemination of information

Arnoud de Kemp, Springer-Verlag, Germany

THE INVENTION OF PRINTING: A CULTURAL REVOLUTION

It all began in Mainz in 1448, when Johannes Gutenberg invented the process of printing books with the aid of movable types. At that time it was feared that the introduction of the art of printing would mean the end of the written word. Gutenberg himself referred to his invention as 'artificial writing'. It was actually a superfluous invention; there were clerks enough at the time. For this reason he attempted to keep it a secret; it all came out nonetheless and was also copied. It was a comparable situation to that in our own age with hardware and software.

The art of writing was considered the highest art for many centuries, and even when we look back today it is easy to understand why the advocates of the art of writing and those of the art of printing were at loggerheads. For the clerks or scribes in their *scriptoria* (the oldest document delivery services in history), the competition was tolerable at first. However, the number of printing shops increased very rapidly; even as soon as 1480 they produced a total of 8000 titles.

The invention of printing marked the beginning of a great cultural revolution, according to Victor Hugo 'the greatest event in history,

Arnoud de Kemp is Director Corporate Development at Springer-Verlag GmbH in Stuttgart. Springer-Verlag is Germany's leading STM publishing company.

the mother of all revolutions, a complete renewal of the means of human expression'.

In this paper I cite in some detail from the brochure *Milestones in the Development of Techniques of Writing and Printing* by Hanns Karl Scholl, which was published in 1965 to mark the opening of the Department of Writing and Printing Techniques in the Deutsches Museum in Munich.

The advent of the book, followed by periodical publications from 1665 onward, made it possible to impart large amounts of information to a great many people. In fact, the book was the first mass medium. The printed media still remain the most used and, for economic reasons, almost always the best media for storage and dissemination of information. From the information scientist's point of view, the amount and density of information that can be put on paper is considerable.

Books and periodicals, collected and made available as they are in libraries, including personal libraries, are a collective intellectual storehouse for society. They are itemized in inventories and catalogues, and are made available free of charge for consultation or on loan almost anywhere. A book or a periodical is a means to be read or used in the libraries by as many people as possible. These socio-political functions of libraries are very important and are therefore always borne in mind when any matters concerning libraries are considered, including the electronic libraries that seem to be planned everywhere.

One further important advantage of books and journals is that no special equipment — except the reading glasses that age inevitably brings with it — are needed to make use of them. It is impossible to use any other media without recourse to technical equipment.

A number of aspects have to come together to determine when a new revolution will start. The field of information science touches on everything and is developing more and more quickly; this highlights the limitations of the means used hitherto to preserve knowledge and of the current methods of accessing the literature. At the same time, completely new possibilities are opening up for editing, generating, storing and disseminating information.

THE BEGINNING OF THE ELECTRONIC AGE

Electronic data processing has been introduced into administration over the last 15 to 20 years. It may be that there are heads of computer centres who think that automation has made almost anything possible. If so, this is a sign that they have missed the point, because the electronic age is still in its infancy. The digital processing and treatment of texts, illustrations, photos and videos are meanwhile altering everything that goes on in companies and institutions which are concerned with information: these include ancillary suppliers (so-called preprocessing, DTP, typesetters, graphics offices), advertising agencies and marketing departments, publishers, in-house printing shops, picture agencies, photographic laboratories and lithographic printers. Documentation centres, archives and libraries are also affected. And, not least, when primary research results are published, the entire information chain of author → publisher → bookshop → library → reader is affected. Since its introduction by IBM in 1982, the personal computer has become our constant companion, and it is becoming ever more adept in its function as everyone's friendly neighbourhood helper. It has become increasingly easier to operate, and the applications are now almost unlimited. It is estimated that there are around 150 million PCs worldwide, more than 120 million of them running on DOS (Disc Operating System). So far, over 25 million copies of Microsoft Windows have been sold.

As you are no doubt aware, the sum of human knowledge doubles every five years. The complaint that there are too many books is almost as old as the printing press itself. This has come about because everyone who wants to be seen to be playing an active part in science writes and publishes. When new knowledge is published, it is usually only read once. And this single reading involves an enormous input that it is becoming increasingly difficult to justify.

Konrad Adam mentioned (in the *Frankfurter Allgemeine Zeitung*) the case of a British aristocrat who threw his books away after reading them once. His reason: there is no person alive who has time to read a book twice. This flood of information is causing the second great change in society after information science: we can no longer keep track of things. The education system is also overburdened. The progression from book to periodical paper and on to abstract has not contained the flow of information at all. On the contrary, it is now deemed imperative to have the lists of contents available without delay and in machine-readable form.

Information management is facing the difficult challenge of getting the development of major economic problems under control. The German Institute of Economics has calculated that faulty searching techniques cost German enterprises over 20 000 million German marks a year for duplicated work in the research and development sector.

ELECTRONIC PUBLISHING: A CULTURAL DEVELOPMENT?

Since the inception of the first periodical publication in 1665 this form of publication has increased constantly in importance. At present there are between 150 000 and 200 000 science titles. There are no libraries that stock them all; the British Library has the most, with 130 000. At the moment the well-established, frequently cited periodicals have more pages each year. Books, on the other hand, are declining in importance, mainly for economic reasons. Many libraries can buy fewer and fewer books. In our time, electronic publishing seems set for a boom. The new media, information technology, networks, optical discs, the electronic library, and so on — they can solve our problems. Can they not?

As in Gutenberg's time, there are those in favour and those against, initiated and lay persons, technocrats and intellectuals. They say that this duality also applies in the case of librarians and information specialists as opposed to ultimate consumers/users.

Information science offers quicker ways of communicating knowledge, and the problems with the storage stage have been solved as far as technical and economic aspects are concerned, compared with the printing stage. This has led to increasingly bitter competition between these media. The information infrastructure is slewing round to electronic structures. Studies (e.g. by the Fraunhofer Gesellschaft) show that at present 95% of scientific information and documentation is recorded on paper; 4% is stored on microfilm and only 1% in digital form. Forecasts up to 1996 assume 8% optical storage and 2% magnetic storage, a tenfold increase. It should also be pointed out that these figures refer only to volume.

The number of online databases was over 5300 in August 1992 according to Cuadra, while in December 1992 TFPL put the number of titles on CD-ROM at around 3600. The Association of Research Libraries in the USA publishes the *Directory of Electronic Journals, Newsletters and Academic Discussion Lists.* The third edition (April 1993) lists 45 electronic periodicals and 195 newsletters, plus 1152 discussion lists, which means there had been 60% growth in ten months.

The best known electronic periodical is *The Online Journal of Current Clinical Trials,* an experiment launched by AAAS and OCLC. There is interest in this new project, but OCLC complains about the low numbers of electronic subscriptions and about the lack of authors. More titles have recently been announced: *The Online Journal of Knowledge Synthesis for Nursing* and *Electronics Letters Online,* a biweekly publication of the Institution of Electrical Engineers (IEE).

The fields of medicine, physics, chemistry and mathematics will supply most of the electronic publishing for the time being. At a users' meeting of the German Physical Society in Weimar on 9 and 10 December 1992, the many people attending finally established that 'electronic handling of specialist information, and in the long run electronic publishing too will be the cost-cutting and rapid processes of the future for disseminating scientific data'.

The periodical *Science* reported in February 1993 that a bulletin-board project of the American Physical Society involved up to 8000 regular users in 12 months and that physicists were already exchanging 600 preprints by electronic means every month. Goodbye Gutenberg?

The OnLine BookStore is available on the Internet. The first book *The Internet Companion,* (with an introduction by Al Gore) was published, that is to say released, on 17 December 1992 and had 6000 takers within a few weeks.

THE NETWORKS: TEAM COMMUNICATION

This brings me to my next topic: the networks. Apart from telephone conferencing — a facility that is still not used that often — the public, academic and private communication networks do have distinct advantages over the telephone. Instead of only two people being able to talk to each other, such networks make it possible for a large number of persons to communicate. I am not talking here about dialogue with an online host, such as STN or Dialog, but about real communication.

In this connection, three technologies can be differentiated:

- electronic post,
- bulletin-board systems,
- conferences that take place in real time.

The biggest breakthrough came from the academic networks: WIN in Germany, SurfNET in The Netherlands, JANET in England, to name but a few. The costs of academic networks are borne by the universities and access is free of charge to the final user. These networks connect universities and service centres such as PICA, OCLC, the British Library. Data are transmitted at 10 Mbps; some networks have been selected to transmit data at 140 Mbps on a trial basis, as in the case of the SuperJANET project in England. Large bodies of data and also photos can be exchanged in seconds.

DOES THE FUTURE HOLD A 'DATA HIGHWAY'?

The Internet is the network of networks. It is the link that connects the individual networks. The best handbook on the Internet is *The Whole Internet. User's Guide and Catalog* by Ed Krol[1]. Now that commercial organizations are also admitted, use is increasing really fast. While a few years ago use was concentrated on searching in OPACs (Online Public Access Catalogues), more and more files are now available which can be called up with the ftp command.

Some of the well-known retrieval systems are Archie, Gopher and WAIS (Wide Area Information Server). In this connection there is talk of knowledge robots (Knowbots), automatic librarians that flit from source to source and collect and deliver the called-for information.

WWW (World Wide Web) is a hypertext project of CERN. The idea — a very ambitious one — is to build up a worldwide network of hypertext links and webs. Thus it goes much further than Gopher, Archie or WAIS. A search done by way of WWW leads to other documents, by way of gateways to other databases and to other computers with various search languages. HTTP (Hypertext Transfer Protocol) and HTML (Hypertext Markup Language) were developed for this purpose. WWW is based on SGML-type documents (SGML — Standard Generalized Markup Language). The aim is the development of a single standard for multimedia documents (HyTime — Hypermedia Time-Based Structuring Language).

Anyone who goes to the USA will be struck by the increasing frequency of requests for Internet addresses. The body of information available is already so huge that Internet is meanwhile the largest electronic library in the world. The next stage — NREN National Research Educational Network — is in planning and will be a comprehensive Integrated Services Digital Network (ISDN). Precise figures on the numbers of users are lacking. The average numbers I have been able to find are 1.3 million hosts and over 18 million users.

Perhaps you have read the interview with Bill Gates, the founder and proprietor of Microsoft in *Der Spiegel* (issue 20/1993). He is not aiming at an improved television or a PC with a wider colour spectrum; he wants something completely new. His plan is for a 'data highway'. Microsoft has just presented a software product which integrates all the equipment needed in the office.

The separate sectors of computer, print media, photography, film, television, entertainment and telecommunications are growing closer together through technology. In this process we can learn much from office communications, where it has not been the case for some time that people are restricted to words or to the transmission and administration of data.

Photo-CD has been about since September 1992 and it is not intended to be used exclusively as a digital family album. The photographic and computer industries agreed at once on a uniform standard for storage and digitization of colour pictures in photographic quality. Photo-CD is already recognized among the experts as a picture archive and as the master in desktop publishing (DTP). The resolution is about 2200 dpi or 6.3 million pixels or 18 megabytes per picture. In this way every document containing illustrations can be recorded and transported.

Software for processing pictures (PhotoEdge, Shoebox and Renaissance) is now available, so that the gaps between digitized pictures and every other kind of digital data have been bridged. Library networks are now being tuned up to multi-CD networks. The Meridian CD network already has Photo-CD integrated.

ELECTRONIC PUBLISHING

To put it simply, electronic publishing is everything that can be done with digital information in the computer. The material has to be stored in digital form (by inputting, scanning or bitmapping), after which it can be processed further in many different ways (edited, formatted, integrated, structured, etc.). This avoids output media dependence.

The development of SGML made it possible to define document types and to lay down the internal structure for every class of document. This sounds very simple but in reality it is very complicated, and various working groups are investing intensive effort in the implementation of SGML and — wherever necessary — on developing it further. In Germany this is the function of the European Work Group Majour.

Document delivery will become an increasingly more important route for the dissemination of information through digital storage and through high-speed networks. New methods and instruments are in development for current awareness, for improved accessibility and for universal retrievability. The Internet has the part of the highway in all this. What is not so clear is who is in possession of the petrol stations and customs posts or will be operating them. This much is certain: the communication companies and hardware firms are showing more and more interest in EP.

Our most important tasks, and thus the greatest challenges we have to face, are those inherent in the safeguarding of the quality of information and the information services, their authenticity and integrity, and in the development of an infrastructure that will be fair to the greatest possible number of users and have a sound politico-economic basis in the long term.

REFERENCE

1   **Krol, E** *The Whole Internet. User's Guide and Catalog* (2nd edition) O'Reilly and Associates, USA (1994)

32

Electronic publishing: challenge turned into profit

Buddy Naeyaert, Philips Consumer Electronics, Netherlands

INTRODUCTION

CD-i is by now well known as a consumer product and, to a lesser extent, as an interesting cost-effective tool in the professional marketplace. How much effort and time it takes to create such markets is less known. Let me therefore start with an overview of how CD-i started and what we did to make a success of it for the consumer, the creative world (studios) and the publishing world.

Entertainment and information based on CD started at the beginning of the 1980s with CD-Audio, followed in 1985 by CD-ROM, a computer-based format which, by the way, took nine years to grow up. The CD-i base case standard was set in 1988 and has been extended continuously since then. In 1991 we announced Photo-CD and last year we were the first company in the world to introduce Digital Video (full-screen full-motion video) on a five inch compact disc.

The addition of Digital Video completes the system. CD-i now combines audio, still images, digital video, graphics, computer data and text. All this information can easily be accessed when and where you want it. This range of capabilities, combined with the worldwide standardization of the format, make it a very attractive medium for publishers.

Buddy Naeyaert is International Business Development Manager of Philips Consumer Electronics bv at Philips' headquarters in Eindhoven.

CONSUMER PUBLISHERS

Since Philips started with the development of CD-i for the consumer market in 1986, we have been actively looking for partners in the publishing world — first in the USA, where companies like Rand McNally and Time-Life were the pioneers together with Philips Interactive Media of America. In Europe the development started somewhat later with the establishment of Philips Interactive Media Europe, with headquarters in London.

Philips offers publishers several forms of support. They can consult us on how to use CD-i, which studios they could use for their specific project, whether it would be worthwhile to set up their own studio, distribution issues etc. Furthermore, we offer project and technical support during the development and introduction process. Owing to our extensive experience in distributing music software for many years and CD-i software for the last two and a half years, we can offer a worldwide distribution net. And last but not least, a large number of our present titles are copublishing ventures.

At the moment an impressive number of publishers, record companies, Hollywood studios, broadcasters, independent movie producers and audio and video producers have published on CD-i. More than 150 titles are already in the market and Philips expects to add 75 interactive and around 50 Digital Video titles in 1994.

CORPORATE PUBLISHERS

The professional market is even further ahead. In the USA alone, more than 750 companies are involved in CD-i, publishers, value-adding resellers and clients who see CD-i as the ideal delivery system for training, sales and educational applications. Early in 1994 a catalogue was published which included more than 250 professional CD-i titles currently available in the USA. In Europe, the same number of titles have been finalized. How did we start?

We first asked ourselves and our first customers the question: What do users of multimedia actually want from multimedia? Or in other words, what do they desire? And how can those desires be satisfied by the creative multimedia designers and studios? What are the main requirements?

The outcome was: it should be inexpensive, it should be easy to use, it should be flexible, it should be playable via a normal television set or monitor, it should offer more ('added value') than existing media. The added value should be for instance: the programmes are fun to use or, for training and educational projects, the retention of the information is higher.

CD-i was the solution for a number of applications. Let me give you an overview of the various areas. In marketing CD-i is used for in-store marketing (POI/POS), presentations, sales support and market research. Some projects completed in this area are for the Ford Motor Company, Alcon Southwestern Bell, Tissot, Mercedes, BMW and Yamaha.

In the field of communication, CD-i is used internally and externally. Two companies involved are Electronic Data Systems, which made a project for the Dow Jones management, and The Free Record Shop, which published its annual report on CD-i.

A number of generic training titles developed by Skillmaster, AMPED and CD-i Training are available on a wide range of subjects, e.g. language learning and management training. And to name a few company projects, Chrysler, Merck and McDonalds, Caltex and Kentucky Fried Chicken are good examples of in-house training software on CD-i.

Philips recently concluded a deal with AIMS Media (Chatworth, CA) and Pacific Video Resources for the creation of 100 CD-i titles developed for classroom use from the catalogue which won the AIMS Media Award. They will include titles in science, mathematics and social studies.

An interesting development is the integration of information on disc with information in external data banks. CD-Matics, a partner of Philips, developed Tele-CD-i. By means of a simple telephone modem one can access external data banks. This creates a whole new range of applications, e.g. home shopping.

The costs to create a professional CD-i title vary between $20 000 and 100 000.

CREATIVE WORLD

It is not enough, however, to convince your publishing partners that multimedia publishing is the way to future profit. It is even more important to create an environment which allows them to create multimedia products. Without studio or developer support no product can ever be made. An important condition to make a success out of a new system is therefore the availability of authoring tools.

Keywords in the authoring environment are creativity and design on the one hand and production time and costs on the other. The first two challenges are for the entire software industry: which programme to choose, how to choose from the variety of systems or features of these systems.

With respect to the production time and costs, we have put in much effort in creating low-cost tools which are familiar to software developers — Macintosh, Unix and PC-based systems; tools, which furthermore can be used by creative multimedia producers, not only by skilled advanced programmers. This strategy has enabled the faster growth of CD-i titles which are more efficiently and cost-effectively produced.

OptImage, our authoring tool company, is now working on real-time digital video encoding systems for both Macintosh and PC. In addition, OptImage will extend its MediaMogul Authoring tool to allow multimedia producers to create interactive applications for interactive television and video on demand via television set-top decoders. The decoders are expected to be installed in consumer residences for trials beginning during the second quarter of 1994. This gives producers two output avenues: output for broadcast and output to disc for playback on CD-i players.

There is one more important development which I should mention: I^2M (International Interactive Media) has developed Media Playback, a CD-i board that can be plugged into a computer to play CD-i and Digital Video titles. The authoring version of this board will be integrated with OptImage's MediaMogul Authoring system, both for Mac and PC. At the moment, MediaPlayback is currently aimed at expanding CD-i playback to the corporate desktop computer market. One can imagine that this will become a very attractive consumer product.

At present (Spring 1994) more than 250 studios have been set up in all parts of the world.

FUTURE DEVELOPMENTS

Technology does not stand still, however. The future will be in interactive delivery systems, multichannel cable systems, satellite or telephone, but also in packaged media. And it is important that they are compatible.

We recently announced our deal with Bell Atlantic to deliver intelligent interactive terminals ('set top boxes') for digital TV networks, which run over telephone lines. We have opted for MPEG and OS9 in our set top boxes, because we already have a packaged medium — CD-i — available, which can play an important pioneering role towards the networked future.

We realize that there is a long way to go before either the industry or the consumer can benefit from these networks. However, Europe, which is at least two years behind the USA, has to start to tackle issues like costs for infrastructure, copyright problems and the process of bringing together the different industries involved. And we have to set up test sites, where we learn about the demands of the consumers and what they are willing to pay for new services.

In our opinion a cooperation between the technology developers and the owners of intellectual property should be sought, to accelerate the integration of digital techniques into traditional publishing. It would offer the publishing world a new profit carrier for the coming decades and it would offer technology-based companies a broader support for their electronic delivery — or better, publishing platforms like CD-i.

What is Philips doing? Last year we set up the Philips Media group. The aim is clear; we are preparing ourselves for the future. Philips Media brings many of Philips' electronic media and multimedia interests together into one business unit. It comprises seven core businesses: Entertainment Software and Electronic Publishing (CD-i and CD-ROM), Interactive Media Systems and Philips Media Distribution, Cable Television Systems, Programming and Ventures, and Investments.

CONCLUSION

Where are we today? CD-i is the only consumer platform which has been introduced worldwide. The low-cost player can easily be connected to more than a billion colour television sets in the market. The system is easy to use, based on a world standard, every disc plays everywhere and it offers multilingual capabilities.

Worldwide (end of 1993) we have sold 300 000 players and three million discs to consumers. We have been able to bring the price of a CD-i player down to $399. Our broadly based label approach, with approximately 150 titles now available, combined with the attractive price of the hardware, has proven successful.

Worldwide more than 13 000 well informed selected retail outlets are selling CD-i players. A large number of them, in both the USA and Europe, report that CD-i was their fastest selling new home-entertainment product during the last quarter of 1993, outselling competitive systems from five to 18 times. We are confident that we will have around a million players in the market by the end of 1994.

Philips has a long-term commitment to CD-i. We want to offer the consumer a platform that will not become obsolete after a few years. We will continue to enhance the system without losing our backward compatibility. We believe this to be an important strategy, because for developers it is the installed base and not hype that earns them profit, and for the consumer investment protection is important. A number of our developers/publishers are already making profits. To name a few, Capitol Multimedia, Eaglevision, InfoGrames and SPC Vision.

Philips' own publishing activities are not competing with the activities of our partners in the publishing, broadcasting or movie industries. We do not copy existing material but create completely new products. CD-i will not replace present publishing activities, it will offer additional benefits and revenues. It offers the opportunity to enhance printed versions with linear and interactive audio/video programmes. It offers publishers the opportunity to differentiate themselves from the competition.

Estimates on the size of the multimedia market in the 1990s and beyond vary between 400 000 million and some trillions of dollars — a pie which is big enough to offer all of us a substantial piece.

Philips is therefore welcoming all support from the publishing industry and offers support if publishers decide to accept the challenge of publishing on CD-i and change this challenge into profit for all of us.

33

Reinventing publishing in a global electronic mall

Richard Seltzer, DEC Internet, USA

Over the last year, a small change in technology has made an enormous difference in the world of publishing. The Internet, which had been a complex technical communication means for students and researchers, has become a friendly, easy-to-use multimedia environment — a new publishing medium, which has enormous commercial potential.

WHAT IS THE INTERNET?

The Internet is a network of networks. While such services as CompuServe and America Online grow one user at a time, the Internet grows a whole network at a time as entire companies connect. It now has an estimated 22 million users worldwide and is growing at a rate of over 6% — or about a million users — a month (May 1994 figures).

The Internet has no central point of control or governing body. Its anarchic structure derives from the US Department of Defense, which funded its beginnings and wanted a network which could not be knocked out in a nuclear war. Over the last two years, commercial use of the Internet has grown considerably. The US government, which earlier had tried to reserve the pieces of the Internet which it

Richard Seltzer is Director of US Communications, Internet Marketing with Digital Equipment Corporation. He is based in Burlington, Massachusetts.

funded for just education and research, has been backing away, reducing its subsidy, limiting its role, and encouraging commercialization. And commercial Internet providers — independent companies which cooperate through an organization known as the Commercial Internet Exchange (CIX) — have been making it increasingly easy for organizations to connect to the Internet and conduct business there.

Traditionally, these Internet providers charge a low, fixed fee to connect a company's network to the Internet, and there is no incremental charge based on usage. This unmetered pricing scheme encourages ever increasing usage. Once you are connected, it is in your best interest to make the maximum use of this capability.

If you choose to enter this environment, it is important to keep its origins in mind and respect the basic culture. Entering this space is like entering any other culturally foreign environment — like a Western firm going to Japan. Yes, you can do business there; but to succeed, you must understand and respect the culture — the etiquette (called 'netiquette' here) and the expectations of potential customers. Here people often freely share their creative efforts, with no expectation of financial return. One finds a frontier spirit — the people tend to be independent, self-reliant, but ready to lend a hand to a neighbour in need. Surprisingly, new users, even commercial users, often adopt many of the basic tenets of this electronic society with all the passion of the newly converted.

For example, here one does not send unsolicited advertising material. People welcome information that they have asked for, but raise a storm of protest when someone intrudes upon their space uninvited. (This effect is partly cultural and partly economic. Commercial services, such as CompuServe, which cater to the individual rather than to companies, sometimes charge recipients for the mail they receive beyond some minimal level. And no-one likes to pay for advertising they do not want to see.)

WHAT HAS CHANGED?

The Internet has existed for a couple of decades. People exchanged mail and made files — vast libraries of information — available so others could share them. But over the last year, two factors have fuelled enormous growth, and attracted new commercial uses. The

Clinton–Gore administration in Washington has made large amounts of public information, which had been difficult or expensive to find and use, freely available in electronic form on the Internet. And at the same time, a piece of software known as 'Mosaic' has helped transform this information environment and make it readily usable by people with no knowledge of or interest in computers.

Researchers at CERN, the high-energy physics centre in Geneva, had developed the WorldWide Web (WWW) software which made it possible to link information from computers anywhere on the Internet in a hypertext environment. For example, a word in a document on a computer in France could be connected with a document in Australia.

Mosaic, developed in 1993 at the National Center for Supercomputer Applications (NCSA) in Illinois, now lets you use a computer mouse to point-and-click your way freely through that WorldWide Web.

The Web is server software which resides on the computer system which is providing the information. Mosaic is client software which resides in your desktop computer system and lets you browse through the Web. Other Web browsers have been developed, but Mosaic caught on quickly and at this point is the generally accepted standard.

Funded by the US government, NCSA makes Mosaic available for free over the Internet. Anyone who has the technical ability to download it or who can obtain a copy from a friend is welcome to it. (If you wish to include it in products you charge for, however, you need to negotiate with NCSA for a licence.) Versions of Mosaic run on IBM-compatible personal computers, Macintoshes, Unix workstations, VMS workstations, and other desktop systems. The fact that this client software is free can greatly reduce the cost and speed the development of information systems.

With Mosaic and the WorldWide Web, the global book/library of the future is quickly becoming a reality — a realm in which you do not have to go hunting for a work referenced in a footnote, but rather can click and immediately connect to the relevant page, wherever in the world it might be; and from there you can use other hypertext links to follow the train of your thought. In this environment, the electronic book no longer needs to mimic the paper book but can become a new medium of expression. And rather than being limited to the material on a particular CD-ROM, you can access entire libraries quickly and easily.

In addition to text, Mosaic and the WorldWide Web can handle high-resolution, full-colour graphics, sound and even some video (though that is still in a relatively rudimentary form). (*Note*: Your ability to receive the audio and motion video depends on the hardware and software available on your desktop system. The speed of response depends on the machine you are using and the speed of your network connection. Do not expect perfection at this early stage. Audio and large graphics files are downloaded over the network to your local machine before they are presented to you; under the current circumstances, the speed of response is remarkable.)

In addition to the high-tech possibilities, Mosaic can also provide easy access to older information systems, such as videotex and conference files. In other words, in most cases you do not have to reformat your existing files to make them accessible; rather you can use gateways to connect the old world to the new.

WHAT ARE THE OPPORTUNITIES?

Two related and enormous opportunities are opening. Mosaic and the WorldWide Web represent the beginnings of a new mass communication medium. They also create a new environment for conducting business — a global electronic mall. Already NCSA gets over a million queries a day to its listing of 'What is new on the Web'; the growth rate of Web usage is far greater than that of the Internet as a whole. And already a wide array of companies — many of them start-ups — are publishing, advertising and selling directly on the Internet.

WHAT IS UNIQUE ABOUT THIS MARKET-PLACE?

In the Internet today we see not just rapid change, but a rapidly changing frame of reference. You cannot reliably make projections, because business innovations and technological change keep changing the rules of the game. Also, here the culture encourages developers to share with one another, to borrow from one another and to build on one another's work — rather than wasting precious time reinventing what has been done before. This means development happens fast and standards become widely accepted without the need for intervention by industry or government committees. Here small and nimble companies have an enormous advantage — companies which can make decisions and act upon them quickly, which are willing and able to experiment and learn.

How can a publisher make money in this new medium? There is no simple answer to that question. In some ways, the competitive environment on the Internet resembles the early days of the television industry when manufacturers of TV sets provided programming to stimulate sales of sets, and it was unclear what business model, advertising, pay-to-view or some other approach, would predominate. Many of the publishing experiments we see on the Web today are labelled 'under construction'. That is the accepted mode of work here. You do not wait until everything is polished — rather you get online quickly, sample customer response — and keep changing and improving based on demand.

BOOK PUBLISHING STRATEGIES

Today on the Internet we see traditional publishers and bookstores as well as ambitious newcomers experimenting with a wide variety of business strategies. Many see the Internet as a means to promote sales of their traditional products. They make their catalogues and even sample chapters of books available online in the hope of generating mail-order or bookstore sales of printed books, and they are reaching new markets for little cost.

The Fantasy Bookstore in Palo Alto, California put its catalogue on the Web this spring, with the help of Digital Equipment Corporation and offered online ordering of traditional books. This small local operation suddenly began to receive orders from customers in Europe. Apparently, there is usually a delay of a couple of years from the release of a science fiction or fantasy book in the USA to its availability in Europe; and customers there welcomed an opportunity to get those books early.

O'Reilly, well known as a publisher of computer-related books, is experimenting with a multifaceted Internet venture. Their Global Network Navigator includes an online catalogue of their books and also has current Internet-related news articles, an online magazine and paid advertising. Under construction, they have a whole new section devoted to travel with hypertext links to travel-related information at sites all over the Internet. At the heart of their operation is the reference section from their highly popular *Whole Internet Catalog* by Ed Krol. Anyone can access this information for free — the same basic information that is found in the printed book, only here it is constantly updated and in addition it is presented with hypertext links. In other words, if you are interested in chess or sports, you simply have to point-and-click on that word to directly connect to related Internet resources anywhere in the world, without having to concern yourself with addresses. This wealth of free material attracts users, as a well-designed mall attracts shoppers. The Global Network Navigator has become a popular first stop for travellers on the Web.

O'Reilly is not betting on a single business model and is not demanding an immediate return. The company is working creatively within the Internet culture — sharing freely, while preparing to operate a very profitable venture. As patterns of usage and interest emerge, O'Reilly will be in a good position to provide value-added information services for a fee and to attract new advertisers.

Meanwhile other companies are beginning to provide their traditional books in electronic form. They use the Internet and other networks and even direct dial-in service by modem to market their works and also to deliver the finished product as electronic text.

One new venture, the Internet Bookstore in Arlington, Virginia says it plans to offer the complete text of current popular hardcover books in electronic form, at a price which is a large fraction of the hardcover price. Apparently, they have made arrangements with a number of publishers to serve as an electronic distributor. The customer has to pay a membership fee to get a hardware decryption device which fits into a PC. Each text is coded by the Internet Bookstore specifically for each reader, and can only be read by that particular decryption device. This elaborate system protects the publisher's rights to the work, making it difficult if not impossible for the customer to make electronic duplicates; for to accomplish this goal, it creates considerable inconvenience for the customer, and in any case such action runs counter to the spirit of the Internet. One wonders if this method could succeed even with a much lower price.

Currently the *Encyclopaedia Britannica* is being made available over the Internet. As an alternative to a CD-ROM edition, the publishers intend to license online access to their classic reference work to colleges and other institutions. Over the Internet it is possible to limit access to your information to users from a particular computer or a particular domain (a part of the address that indicates the company, organization or college with which the user is affiliated). They are experimenting now to generate demand and assess usage patterns before establishing their price structure for this service.

All would-be commercial ventures on the Internet need to test themselves against the many projects which offer information for free. Regardless of what you may charge for your product in traditional markets, are you providing sufficient added value in your electronic version to warrant the price you charge? This value-adding might be measured in terms of timeliness, ease of use, interesting hypertext links, ability to search a large database, or unique software to enable valuable manipulations and comparisons of text. If you cannot provide such value-adds, then perhaps you should consider lowering your prices significantly, accepting low margins on the expectation of high volume.

In any case, you should be aware that many hundreds of people worldwide are working hard and collaborating to make public domain texts widely available for free in electronic form. Such projects as Gutenberg, wiretap, the Oxford Text Archive and Libellus already offer the full text of hundreds of classic works of literature for free over the Internet – making it possible for professors to assemble their own electronic anthologies, which they can copy themselves for their students at the minimal cost of a blank diskette.

Author and entrepreneur Odd de Presno in Norway uses an interesting strategy to take advantage of the power of free publicity on the Internet and still make a profit. He makes the complete text of his Internet guidebook *The Online World* available for free on the Internet and, for a price, people subscribe to his frequent updates, paying for the added value of timeliness.

MAGAZINE AND JOURNAL STRATEGIES

The Internet poses similar challenges for magazine and journal publishers. Popular magazines such as *Mother Jones* and *Wired* make their back issues available online for free, and may even place the complete text of their current issues online. They see the Internet as a way to market their printed product.

It seems many people use the Internet to sample reading material. They browse and skim. They will read on the screen short items and information which will lose its value quickly as time passes. However, for thoughtful articles and fiction they will seek out a printed edition, once their interest has been aroused by what they sampled electronically.

A new venture called the Electronic Newsstand offers the Internet audience free samples of articles from popular and prestigious magazines. Apparently, the magazines provide not only the articles but also financial backing for the project because of the low cost of generating new subscriptions this way.

Some publishers of scientific and academic journals, such as Elsevier, have been experimenting with delivering electronic editions to libraries for a price. They need to find out the patterns of usage and effects on sales of the printed edition. They need to find the best format and mechanism to protect their rights to the information, while at the same time giving the reader ease of access and use.

There is much opportunity here for collaboration among journal publishers, libraries and abstract publishers to make it easy for a researcher to quickly track down relevant references and retrieve full texts of selected articles online. It might be possible for a journal publisher to make the full plain-text version of current issues available for free, and charge for such value-added services as hypertext links to all references as well as for the ability to do interesting searches in related databases.

By now a number of journals have adopted the practice of publishing preprints of papers free of charge over the Internet — to solicit scholarly comment and also to make time-critical information widely available far faster than is possible with usual printing procedures. In some cases the concept of 'issue' becomes obsolete in the Internet environment, as articles are made available individually, as soon as they are ready.

However, publishers are not at leisure in making such choices. The very professors who traditionally provide them with their content are busy creating their own electronic journals and newsletters and are lobbying to make electronic publication equivalent to print publication in determining academic status and tenure. Already hundreds of periodicals have been created by professors and students around the world and are distributed without restriction and at no cost as plain-text files.

NEWSPAPERS AND NEWS SERVICES

News services have used the Internet and other computer networks for years to deliver news, but it is still a great rarity to see an Internet edition of a daily or weekly newspaper.

The most common news service on the Internet is Clarinet, which provides news feeds that include Associated Press and Reuters to institutions and companies for a fee. Articles are organized as 'newsgroups' by the category of information — so you can go straight to reports about, for instance, commodity markets and not concern yourself with anything else. Public domain search software can also make it easier to find what you want in an ocean of information.

There are interesting opportunities to price such news feeds based on the timeliness of delivery — ranging from instantaneous for the highest price to week-old news for free. In addition, one could offer personalized, targeted summary news feeds for companies with immediate access to detailed back-up information when requested — perhaps using hypertext links over the Web.

The *Palo Alto Weekly* in California is the first example of a printed newspaper made available for free on the WorldWide Web. More are sure to follow — especially in communities where high-technology companies dominate the local economy.

For the next few years, the Internet will probably have little perceptible effect on the circulation of major daily newspapers. The local electronic audience will be just a small percentage of the total audience, and even those with electronic access will continue to buy newspapers anyway. Nevertheless, newspaper publishers can and should move quickly to take advantage of this technology to get incremental revenue, to establish themselves in this new business arena and to gain the experience they will need for long-term success.

For instance, they could post their content each day for free on the Internet. (The material already exists in electronic form and could be readily transferred to a system accessible over the Internet.) Posting daily news online is good promotion/advertising. It is analogous to pasting your pages on a kiosk in a public square or having radio and television quote and talk about your articles. They could use those daily postings (and the related services they could develop) to reach a new and potentially lucrative audience outside their normal circulation area.

The Internet is global. Whatever you post can be read by anyone on the Internet anywhere in the world. Unlike in the business of printed publishing, here added readers add nothing to your production cost. And these added readers (who tend to be educated and technologically informed) could be of interest to your advertisers, and, in the future, might also be willing to pay for value-added information services which you could provide.

Many people outside your circulation area might want to read your material on the Internet. For instance:

- local residents who are travelling for business or pleasure,
- former residents,
- residents who have more than one home or take extended vacations,
- prospective residents,
- tourists interested in coming to your city,
- business travellers planning on coming to your city,
- people with a seasonal or event-oriented interest in local activities (e.g. the World Cup of Palo Alto),
- professional sports enthusiasts (local teams often have fans who live far beyond the range of the local daily).

In addition to the regular content of your newspaper, you could provide directories and background information that would appeal to this new, global electronic audience. For example:

- create a directory of local information of interest to travellers coming to your area,
- add pointers (by hypertext links) to related information that would be of interest to the same set of people,
- on a reciprocal basis, add pointers to Web pages that would be useful and of interest to people from your area who plan to travel,
- select and post by category articles and information from your own paper, and other sources as well, that would be of particular interest to this new audience,
- create a directory of local information tailored to nonresidents with a business/investment interest in your area (if the area is dominated by a particular industry, exploit that by enriching the background material you make available).

Once you have attracted such an audience, usage statistics could provide a basis for paid advertising or for making this a desirable bonus to regular advertisers.

Keep in mind that in this environment you do not force a reader to see an ad by putting it on the same page as the information they want to read. The accepted practice is to give readers the choice and opportunity to connect to advertising material they want to see. For instance, travellers want to know about restaurants, hotels and entertainment; business people want to know about investment opportunities. When the user decides to connect to an ad, the advertiser provides facts and details, rather than marketing hype. There is minimal additional cost involved in making many pages of detailed content available online to those who want it. The interested party does not have to call or write for the details — they are available immediately.

The next natural step is to provide electronic commerce services to your advertisers, perhaps charging by a percentage of the transaction. The order is taken and paid for online.

Only by experimenting will newspaper companies be able to determine what, if any, business models will work for them here, but the risks are great for those who decide to ignore this new arena. Anyone can get into this business, and many will want to, including companies which now advertise with you as well as garage-based start-ups; even companies which operate from a long distance. Companies like Apollo Advertising are already competing for advertising revenue on the Web; and companies like The Internet Shopping Network are learning how to make money using the Internet for home shopping. The window of opportunity is open now, but may not be a year from now.

If newspapers have any intention of being players in this space, they need to:

- stake out a territory,
- learn how to operate in this new environment,
- build a substantial and attractive base of material, establish reciprocal relationships with other information providers and get readers into the habit of visiting their pages.

The advertising gained here will be important, as local connectivity increases and 'narrow-cast' opportunities arise for delivering targeted information and advertising to individuals. This would be the local, retail, in-the-home version of the wholesale, global newsfeeds of today. In an information-explosion environment less is more, and people are willing to pay for that value-added service. (A popular piece of software for reading newsgroups on the Internet today is known as 'nn' = no news. It makes it easier to be selective.)

In this environment, people will probably be willing to pay to receive only the pages or classes of information they want, and to have immediate access to in-depth detail and background information.

As the online audience grows, you can expect your advertisers will create their own Web pages and attractive Internet environments to bring readers directly to them without the need for your go-between service. However, if you provide the most comprehensive, attractive and valuable environment, readers will connect to you first. Then you can provide links to advertisers' pages and charge them on the basis of the number of readers who connect to them through your path. Any advertising-based business depends on attracting an audience. You have to develop the experience and skills necessary to keep your electronic space competitively attractive.

Of course, out-sourcing is an alternative. If you cannot compete in the new electronic environment, you can make deals with others who can, and provide them with your content for a fee. This means you settle for the scraps, and also that you are at risk that your partner will grow strong enough to no longer need you and possibly to expand into your traditional markets. On the other hand, you could take an aggressive stance. A daily newspaper could use its present clout and contacts to establish partnerships with local government and business to establish an attractive, global image/presence for their city on the Internet.

Whatever your long-range plans, you should look closely at the opportunities which are rapidly opening on the Internet, you should assess what of your information can and should be made available for free, and what value-added services you could provide. The opportunities available on the Internet today are intriguing; the growth rate is enormous; and the cost to begin to explore is relatively low. It looks like now is the time to start — to test and learn and try to shape your own future before it is shaped for you.

Those who are already on the Internet might wish to check the examples listed in Table 33.1. Those who would like to learn how to get connected in Europe should contact Tim McMillan at Digital Equipment Corporation, Whiteley Fareham, Hampshire, UK.

Table 33.1 Examples on the Internet

Book publishers

Catalogues of university presses —
gopher://rome.classics.lsa.umich.edu/11Catalogs%20of%20Academic%20Presses

Publisher catalogues — http://jester.usask.ca/~scottp/publish.html

Prentice Hall — gopher://gopher.prenhall.com

Encyclopedia Britannica — http://www.eb.com/eb.htm

Kluwer, Netherlands — ftp://ftp.std.com/ftp/Kluwer/

O'Reilly/Global Network Navigator —
http://nearnet.gnn.com/gnn/meta/internet/mkt/ora/center.html

The Reference Press — http://kaleidoscope.bga.com/RP/top_page.html

Springer-Verlag, Heidelberg — gopher://trick.ntp.springer.de/1

Book stores

List of book stores (worldwide) —
http://www.cis.ohio-state.edu/hypertext/faq/usenet/books/stores/top.html

Future Fantasy Book Store, Palo Alto, CA — http://nsl.pa.dec.com/test/FutureFantasy

Online Bookstore (OBS) — gopher://akasha.tic.com/11/obs

J.F. Lehmanns Facbuchhandlung, Berlin —
http://www.germany.eu.net/shop/jfl/jfl_kat.html

Quantum Books, Cambridge, MA —
gopher://ftp.std.com/11/Book%20Sellers/Quantum%20Books

Electronic books online

Kalevala (Finnish national epic) from Helsinki City Library —
http://www.kaapeli.fi/maailma/kalevala/kalevala.html

Bordeaux and Prague — http://www.cdtl.umn.edu/Bordeaux_and_Prague.html

Carnegie Mellon University (all subjects) —
http://www.cs.cmu.edu:8001/afs/andrew.cmu.edu/acs/library/etexts/namedsubject

English Server (CMU) — http://english-server.hss.cmu.edu/

Gutenberg Project — http://med-amsa.bu.edu/Gutenberg/Welcome.html

Online Book Initiative — gopher://gopher.std.com/11/obi/book

Oxford Text Archive — http://ota.ox.ac.uk/TEI/ota.html

Project Libellus (Latin) — ftp://ftp.u.washington.edu/public/libellus

Table 33.1 *continued*

Runeberg Project (Sweden) — gopher://gopher.lysator.liu.se/11/project-runeberg/txt

Spunk Press (anarchist lit) —
http://www.cwi.nl/cwi/people/Jack.Jansen/spunk/Spunk_Home.html

University of Virginia — http://www.lib.virginia.edu/etext/texts.html

gopher://wiretap.spies.com/11/Books — Wiretap

1993 CIA World Factbook —
http://www.ncsa.uiuc.edu:8001/gopher.uwo.ca/world-factbook93

Big Dummy's Guide to the Internet (Electronic Frontier Foundation) — http://
info.archlab.tuwien.ac.at/doc/bdgtti-1.02_toc.html

Bibliographies online —
http://www.cs.cmu.edu:8001/afs/cs/misc/mosaic/common/omega/Web/
bibliographies.html

Reference works online —
http://www.cs.cmu.edu:8001/afs/cs/misc/mosaic/common/omega/Web/
references.html

Magazines and journals

Boston Review —
http://polisci-mac-2.mit.edu/BostonReview/BostonReview.html

Mother Jones — http://www.mojones.com/motherjones.html

Wired Magazine — http://WWW.ncb.gov.sg/wired/WoWWW.html

Journals (a lengthy hypertext list) —
http://english-server.hss.cmu.edu/Journals.html

Commercial news

Palo Alto Weekly — http://www.service.com/PAW/home.html

Free news

Sports Information Server — http://www.mit.edu:8001/services/sis/sports.html

World Cup USA '94 — http://www.cedar.buffalo.edu/~khoub-s/WC94.html

World Cup in Palo Alto —
http://www.commerce.digital.com/palo-alto/chamber-of-commerce/events/wCup/
home.html

French Language Press Review —
gopher://burrow.cl.msu.edu/11/news/news/general/french_language

Hyperized, value-added news

John Markoff, NY Times article on Internet — http://www.crs4.it/~zip/markoff.html

Cornell, Legal Information Institute — http://www.law.cornell.edu/lii.table.html

Table 33.1 *continued*

Advertising

Apollo Advertising — http://apollo.co.uk

Electric Press — http://www.elpress.com/elpress/overview.html

Oslonett Markedsplassen —
http://www.oslonet.no/html/adv/ON-market.html

Free classified job advertising —
news:misc.jobs.contract
news:misc.jobs.misc
news:misc.jobs.offered
news:misc.jobs.offered.entry
news:misc.jobs.resumes

Electronic commerce

Internet Shopping Network — http://shop.internet.net

CommerceNet — http://www.commerce.net

EP technology and people management

34

Managing and structuring the EP business

Pieter Bolman, Academic Press, USA

INTRODUCTION

Technology has always been and is likely to remain one of the principal, if not *the* principal, motors for change in our society. Many firms have suffered significant losses, and even gone out of business, as a result of technological change that they failed to anticipate. Although from an evolutionary point of view this may be a normal and possibly desirable state of affairs, from the standpoint of people involved, this situation is considerably less comfortable.

It can be successfully argued that since the invention of movable type, publishers have 'suffered' little from technological change; that is, if one considers publishing to be the commercial act (for profit or otherwise) of 'making public', usually in a form that involves print on paper. Of course, there are many ways of making things public, including radio and television broadcasting, and these activities, brought on by technological developments, have had considerable impact on newspaper and magazine publishers. However, they are not usually referred to as 'publishing' and we will leave them outside consideration in this chapter.

Traditionally publishers have connected those who have intellectual properties for sale with those who are willing to pay for it (on

Dr Pieter Bolman is President of Academic Press Inc. in San Diego, California. Academic Press is the second largest Scientific/Technical/Medical publishing house worldwide. (Dr Bolman is currently Chairman of the IEPRC Board of Directors.)

either a need-to-know or a nice-to-know basis). In some cases the creators of intellectual property have a continual relationship with the publishing organization (such as journalists for a newspaper), but most often the 'creator' is an independent agent who makes his/ her information product available for a certain assessment.

As the usual medium for this information product is print-on-paper, and as print-on-paper technology is very well established and ubiquitously available, there is no *a priori* need for the publisher to invest in or own technology. Technology is not therefore his/her strength. The advent of modern, computer-based information technology may change this as its ability to record, organize, manipulate, recover and reproduce information makes it possible to 'package' information in a way that adds considerable value over the traditional ways of 'packaging' in books and journals. As a result, the publisher needs to be thoroughly familiar with the capabilities of this technology.

It is in a sense fortunate that considerable 'subtracted value' is also introduced with the new technology, depending on the end user's specific needs, so that the transition from book to electronic medium is relatively slow in most cases. However, such subtracted values are not necessarily inherent in the technology and have often to do with teething troubles, lack of information infrastructure, user inexperience etc. and, as a result, are likely to be temporary. Another way of describing this phenomenon is by observing that the traditional book and journal forms are remarkably stable media, not least since they are among the least capital-consuming, lowest priced and most user friendly of information packaging formats. They require no special hardware to use (except perhaps spectacles or contact lenses) and the user determines his/her own pace in utilizing them.

WHAT BUSINESS ARE WE IN?

One of the most important requirements facing a firm which hopes to survive technological change is that it must determine in which business it is. This tends to be a much belaboured point nowadays. However, we firmly believe it to be a very pertinent one for reasons that will become clear. Only when a firm knows what its business or added value is, can it determine the impact of technological change. It can then ask whether the business will continue to exist, and whether it might not be better to change to some other business. If a company takes too narrow a view of its business, it could find that the business has been eliminated by some technological change.

A debate of this nature is currently going on in the STM (science, technology and medicine) journals publishing business. There is a not insignificant fraction in the scientific and library communities that believes that with the introduction of workstations on every scientist's desk and the information superhighway being put into place, scientists can freely communicate with each other and, to the extent that peer review is still necessary, that it can be organized at the universities themselves (possibly as an added library function) and that, as a result, expensive (print-on-paper) journals are no longer necessary, thus obviating the need for publishers of these journals. Whatever the merit of the arguments in this specific case, it is clear that some pretty fundamental questions are being asked and that the publisher is not the only one asking them.

There are several ways of looking at a business and its mission and it is clearly not enough to just say that we are in the 'publishing business'. The most abstract way of defining a business is in terms of the performance of a specific function, independent of the process by which that function is currently performed, or by the product by which it is delivered. The story as to how IBM got into the computer business is sufficiently well known not to be repeated here, except that IBM recognized (only just in time and with some luck on its side!) that it was in the business of making and selling machinery for data processing, which was not limited to the punched-card machinery on which it had originally built its business. As is well known, the firm's current problems are a direct result of a belated recognition that machinery for data processing is not necessarily mainframe based and that the market will decide how it will fill its needs in this respect.

By the same token, a publisher is a purveyor of information who performs specific functions for the user, and the nature of these functions determines how technology will impact his or her publishing business. As a consequence, there is no standard way in which a publisher can tackle these problems and 'manage and structure his/her EP business'. However, it would be wrong to suggest that publishers have nothing in common in this regard. In what follows, the above-mentioned STM journals' problem will be taken as an example. The reason for this is not only my familiarity with that kind of publishing, but also the belief that the example is sufficiently complicated for there to be general applicability to other types of publishing. Whether the reader agrees with this remains to be seen, of course.

The 'complication' stems from the need to define the STM journals business in terms of its function, rather than just in terms of the other categories used for defining a business, such as the products delivered, the process utilized, the distribution system applied, the skills needed or the raw materials incorporated.

Many firms can be adequately described in one of these other terms, the criterion for a mission statement being that it is valid regardless of technological innovation and technology used. A publishing company could describe itself as being strictly in the newspaper business (i.e. in terms of its product; many of them do) with the result that it only needs to assess technological change in terms of improving the product or the process of production (e.g. the use of colour, the use of direct text input from journalists — thus bypassing the need to use traditional typesetters, the use of local print facilities and the sending of text files via electronic means etc.). The end result is still a newspaper, as is implied in the chosen mission statement.

A scientific journal as a paper product simultaneously serves a number of functions concurrently, each of which could be (and is) performed separately by different means. Apart from its 'newspaper function' for other scientists, it also serves as an official, authenticated (peer-reviewed) scientific archive which by its standing in the scientific community attracts articles of a certain scope and quality. Such a journal tends to be more important for the scientist as an author (i.e. a research worker who communicates the results of his/her investigations) than for the scientist as a reader: the pecking order of journals (in terms of scientific quality and, hence, prestige) codetermines the author's career advancement and ability to obtain funding for further work. As a reader he or she often becomes aware of work in his/her specific area through other means, such as preprints, conferences, the 'network' etc. and the (paper) journal then serves the function of browsing of serendipitous results that happen to be of interest but were not specifically reported with that interest in mind. The added value therefore is not just in delivering a piece of news that is of interest (the article) but in the accreditation, the quality control, the ranking of research reports according to journal (the 'pecking order'), the browsing, and the archiving (with concomitant bibliographic control). The archive is the official source for

Document Delivery. Nevertheless, none of the 'added value' ingredients is charged for separately. Currently all are included in the subscription price of the physical product that is delivered to the customer periodically. To complicate things further, there is usually a difference between the customer and the end-user. The library buys the journal and the scientist uses it for free — either by publishing in it or by reading it, or both. This latter complication is not without consequence for our structuring the EP business, as we shall see shortly. For now it suffices to conclude that our defining the business that we are in by function, and our desire to remain in that business, means that we not only have to look at the impact of the new technology on our production process, but also on our marketing, distribution and billing arrangements. In other words, there are not many functions in our organization which are not affected by the technology change.

OUR PLACE IN THE INDUSTRY COLUMN

Technology in general is an important determinant not only of a firm's organizational structure but also of the way in which an industry such as the publishing industry, for example, is organized. If a basic technology changes, it is always good to check what kind of impact this is likely to have on the industry as a whole and whether it is likely that our role in the scheme of things is likely to change and/ or whether our technology needs to be adapted in such a way that it remains compatible with the steps in the industry process that follow or precede it.

If one pursues the trail of information from its creation to its ultimate user, then a number of observations can be made.

In the case of the newspaper publisher, we already noted that direct text input from the creator (the journalist) led to a change in roles of one of the players in the industry (in this case an elimination: the typesetter's role became superfluous) and that the technology used by the journalist should be compatible with that of the publisher. As creator and publisher usually belong to the same organization, this compatibility can be assured by organizational hierarchy. Apart from this, standardization in normal text interfaces has progressed to such an extent that it is not really such an issue any more anyway. At the other end of the process we assumed there to be no change: the newspaper is still the end product and can be delivered (and paid for) by using existing 'technology' (i.e. newspaper boys/girls, news agent, mailing services etc).

In the case of the STM journal publisher the situation is more complicated: there are literally thousands of authors, all of whom contribute to several journals belonging to different publishers, who produce scientific files that not only contain normal text, but also mathematical and chemical formulae of great complexity in addition to tables, line drawings, pictures, etc. At the other end of the process, not only should traditional journals still be delivered but it is envisaged that delivery via other media such as CD-ROM and the networks should also take place. The actual detail of such deliveries will depend on the functions that need to be fulfilled. Now that these functions become separable as far as technology is concerned, billing by subscription only becomes questionable. New players enter the industry, network owners and telecommunications companies become the counterparts of the postal authorities. The roles of others change. The library is no longer necessarily the storekeeper of information. The scientist no longer physically needs to go to a library building but can have the information sent via the network. The roles of typesetters and subscription agents will probably be impacted severely. It becomes necessary for the publisher to have his/her technology compatible with both authors and readers, creators as well as users. That, of course, is if the publisher continues to exist.

STRUCTURING THE EP BUSINESS

If this is all true, then the overall EP strategy must be one that involves the other relevant players in the industry. A possible approach is entering into joint experiments with them. When so many functions are impacted simultaneously, it is impossible to predict precisely how and when maximum value is added for the end user, the ultimate market. This seems true both in terms of functionality and in terms of the actual economics of the ultimate 'system'.

There is no alternative to organizing such an EP effort from the top down. The company as a whole is likely to change, new skills will have to be introduced, the traditional functional organizing principles in the company are unlikely to continue to be adequate, and the required zero-based approach can only be led from the managerial cross-over point of these functions: the top of the organization. Moreover, industry players need to be engaged in ongoing discussions and the strategic consequences need to be assessed on a continual basis.

An EP Director is likely to be needed, reporting directly to the CEO of the organization. This person is likely to tread on many a functional toe in the organization, as in our example, the STM journals company. Most, if not all, departments are going to be affected by the change. Clearly, such a person should be very senior and have the trust and continued full support of the CEO if he or she is to succeed. Ideally we are asking for both publishing and technological skills, as well as considerable experience in (project) management.

It should be remembered that generally people with good technology skills are less scarce than those with good publishing skills. By the latter is meant people who know the end-users, their problems and the role the published information plays in solving them. EP is not a technology problem *per se*, it is a publishing problem. The temptation to leave matters to the technical staff should be resisted: 'they should be on tap, not on top'. There is a real danger otherwise that solutions are obtained for which there are no problems.

It is realized that the approach suggested demands a very centralized organization structure. There are at least two reasons for this: the first has to do with the need to oversee all functions that are affected by the change (the 'cross-over point') and the second with the fact that the newly acquired knowledge and skills are not abundant in the organization, at least at this stage; only when sufficient experience has been gained, should decentralization be contemplated.

PRACTICAL MATTERS

We have concluded that the EP director should be a 'sheep with five legs': a senior staff person with a publishing background and both technical and managerial skills. Such persons do exist, but are relatively rare and thus expensive. However, when one realizes that the future of the company may be determined by the ability to adapt to and take charge of technological change, it seems a price worth paying.

The first thing to request from the EP Director is an overall plan. For reasons stated earlier, this plan needs to address the place of the organization in the industry column and assess the impact of technology on the industry as a whole and on the information interfaces of the publisher with other players in particular. These interfaces, and the technological requirements stemming from them, define the boundary conditions within which the organization's EP strategy will have to develop. For example, the author/publisher interface in STM journal publishing is of a many-to-many nature (thousands of authors, hundreds of publishers), and there are a variety of (scientific) text processing systems in use that can deliver a manuscript in machine-readable form (or at least parts of it). As the publisher will still put out a print-on-paper version of the journal and as he/she likes to use the author-prepared file to build up his/her publisher's database from which the typesetter file can be spun off, he/she needs to find a way to manage this interface.

Because so many authors are involved, a standardized language is an obvious way to look for a solution. The publisher needs to assess, therefore, whether he/she needs to be involved in efforts relating to for example, SGML (Standard Generalized Markup Language) and TEX (the latter is software that is used by a great many scientists, mainly mathematicians and physicists, and that has become a *de facto* standard).

As so many publishers (and typesetters) are faced with the same problem, it is only natural that contemplation needs to be given to participate in precompetitive joint efforts in this respect. Compatibility at the other end, the interface with libraries and scientists as readers similarly requires attention. If this interface needs an intermediate, e.g. a network like the Internet, then thought should be given to joining up with companies that have experience in this area. An experiment that is currently taking place is 'Red Sage', in which a number of publishers are involved, together with AT&T Bell Laboratories and the University of California–San Francisco. The aim is to test the technical, business, economic and legal issues surrounding the delivery of scientific journals in a network environment.

These are just two examples of exploring and managing the interface. Each publisher knows his/her own interfaces with 'the outside world' best and should give thought to how it might be impacted and possibly shifted by new technology.

So much for the external organization of EP. Internally, we have assumed (by choosing STM journals publishing as our example), that the main objective of getting involved in EP is that the company wants to stay in its chosen business and that EP is going to change, but not eliminate, that business. We anticipated that most functions in the organization were going to be affected but that the core competencies of the business, the ability to deal with a specified set of informational needs of scientists, were not going to change. This is the reason why we have chosen not to create a separate division. If we had decided to get into the business of satisfying a different set of needs of the same market, we would probably have elected to start a new product division, possibly in addition to what we have described earlier.

PROJECT ORGANIZATION

As we have seen, the EP director has a staff (as opposed to line) function. He or she is a specialist who advises the CEO on one of the strategically most important issues of the day. The fact that this concerns a staff position does not mean that there is no power and/or authority associated with it. Once the EP plan has been formulated and approved, an EP Steering Committee (consisting of senior management) should be set up to oversee the implementation of the plan as whole and of the various part projects that the plan defines.

On this Steering Committee, chaired by the CEO or in his/her absence and with his/her authority the EP director, the individual subprojects are delegated to separate project groups (or task forces), who will be given a clear mission statement and who will report regularly to the Steering Committee. Members of existing departments will be appointed to these groups — depending on the skills and expertise — and for the mission of the project they report to the project leader, who in turn reports to the EP director for the project. An arrangement to this effect should have been made with the project leader's hierarchical boss, clearly specifying the scope of the project and the amount of time that needs to be spent on it. This practice of project management is well documented in the management literature, but it is not necessarily understood everywhere. Examples of subprojects are:

- interface projects such as electronic manuscript submission, SGML, TEX, Internet publishing etc.,
- database related projects, such as structuring the database, manuscript trafficking system, on-demand printing etc.,

- joint (pilot) projects, i.e. with other players,
- marketing projects, such as cataloguing on the network, electronic information exchange with subscription agents, but also user reaction studies etc.

This programme of projects is overseen by the Steering Committee and managed on a day-to-day basis by the EP director. The result of this approach will be that gradually expertise is developed in each department, usually personified in a few people who combine their original skills (such as copy-editing, editorial and marketing etc.) with the newly gained 'electronic' skills. A sort of 'osmosis' should set in that will encourage others to participate. It should be realized, however, that a considerable number of people will resist the changes, either because they lack the skill or aptitude, or because they simply do not want to change. To the extent that old ways continue to be used, they can be accommodated. If they become cynics, they should be removed.

THE IT DEPARTMENT

One final word about the relationship with the IT department. This is an example of an internal interface that can be full of pitfalls if not managed properly. The IT department should be represented on the EP Steering Committee, preferably through its head, if he or she is not part of senior management already. There is a clear overlap in systems used for EP and for Management Information Sytems (MIS). Figure 34.1 depicts this graphically where it concerns the EP production function. It is important to stress that the embryonic EP dog should not be wagged by the usually well-established IT tail. The IT department is a service department that should do precisely that: serve. However, by virtue of the fact that often much money has gone into IT and because of the fact that usually the (not yet amortized) systems have not been purchased with the EP application in mind, there can be considerable friction (or at least inertia) emanating from this department. Once an EP plan has been formulated, a technology plan for the company as a whole should be developed. This technology plan, which becomes a constraint for part of the EP plan, should be written by the head of the IT department with input from both the EP director and the operational functions. It is often

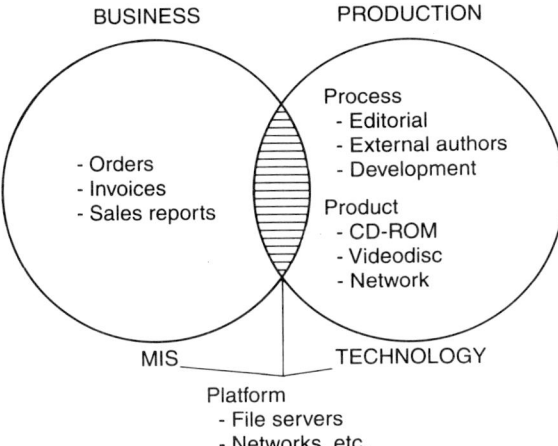

Figure 34.1 The overlap between EP and MIS

worth while to get outside help with this. More and more hardware companies, including DEC and IBM, are setting up consulting services to help 'content providers' with the technological side of EP. It may be worth investigating what they have to offer.

35

The road to electronic publishing is paved with change

Patricia Lauletta, Datapro Information Services, USA

Datapro Information Services Group is a leading provider of information on the global information technology (IT) industry. Our job is to know all there is to know about the products, vendors and technologies that make up the computer and communications industry. Ever since I started working for Datapro in 1988, we knew that it was only a matter of time before our products would need to be delivered electronically.

During the 1970s and 1980s Datapro led the IT looseleaf publishing market with a print product line that included over 40 titles in areas of information technology, such as mainframe and midrange computer hardware and software, local and wide area communications, and vertical market technologies including banking, retail and manufacturing. Each one of these services consists of a master book shipped to the customer at the time of sale. This masterbook is updated monthly by sending the customer supplemental information to be interleaved into their base service. Over 120 Datapro editors worldwide created detailed reports for inclusion in these services using a publishing system called Atex.

Patricia Lauletta is Vice-President of Datapro Information Services Group based at their headquarters in Delran, New Jersey. Datapro offers standard print products, specific handbook products and electronic and news databases covering a wide range of hardware and software and service technologies.

The late 1980s brought significant changes to both the information technology market and to the traditional Datapro customer. Personal computers, which entered the market in the early 1980s, were fast becoming commonplace with our customers. The rate of new-technology introductions had accelerated dramatically resulting in the need for Datapro to deliver information faster. The maintenance of our product became an issue with our customers, as downsizing eliminated many of the clerical and secretarial resources that were once available to file supplements. The looseleaf print format was losing its appeal in the information market. The market was demanding a simpler way to work with Datapro.

Datapro's challenge was to transform the company from one that provided print products to a company that provided information services. Where our customer was once the librarian who used our product for research, our new customer profile included decision makers who would use our product as a resource for making purchasing decisions. As the requirement emerged for custom information, Datapro needed to be less concerned with writing reports to format and more concerned with providing accurate, timely research to fulfil specific customer requirements. The three-month production schedule which had served us well during the 1970s and 1980s had to give way to a more dynamic update methodology which could deliver information 'just-in-time'.

As we moved into the 1990s, it became clear that information was our only product and that Datapro would need to make multiple packaging options available to the market. Datapro also needed to distribute its research information not only in print, but also electronically on CD-ROM and online. It became apparent that to remain competitive, we had to leverage our research across all the packaging options. It was imperative, both from a productivity and employee morale standpoint, that our resources be used appropriately and efficiently.

Leveraging our research meant that the report structure was no longer a viable way for us to store information. This would have to change. Our reports could actually be considered finished puzzles, but we needed access to all the individual pieces that made up that puzzle. To have this type of access meant that each report needed to be broken into the individual pieces or elements; and these elements would have to be stored electronically in such a way that they could be used and reused as required. A publishing system such as Atex, or even BasisPlus, could not give us this flexibility. The concept of a standard relational database system which would store the research in fields or elements was the closest solution on the market. Elements would be stored by product and company. Hundreds of elements would be included in the database to capture all of the pertinent specifications available about the IT industry: descriptive, strategic, and service informative. The elements could then be assembled and reassembled to create the deliverable required.

Another objective of the database project was to integrate all our research into a single repository. Over the years, product developers had built their own information bases for specific product lines. The result was duplicate research efforts, data quality and integrity problems. The single repository database would eliminate this redundant processing. In addition, we wanted to make the research more usable by providing sophisticated search capabilities and by improving our input and extract capabilities. Datapro looked forward to the flexibility to design and deliver new products and services quickly using the elements contained in the database.

An important part of our database strategy was to give our analysts/editors 'off-the-shelf' products for them to use to do their development work. These 'off-the shelf' tools would minimize the implementation training impact. We felt we could continue to benefit from this decision since new staff would require no special text processor skills. Only a basic knowledge of the PC, word processing, and spreadsheet software such as Microsoft's Word for Windows and Excel is required. This strategy has proven to be very successful. The days of putting a new member of staff in a room with an Atex terminal and cassette recorder are long gone. The employees also benefit from having a transferable skill which they can use personally to expand their marketability.

As you might imagine, storing research in reusable elements required considerable changes to the editorial research processes, the allocation of editorial resources, the organization and the mind set within the organization. Prior to the database concept, the editorial processes consisted of assigning an analyst a report title and a deadline. The analyst would complete the report in the proper format and submit it for technical review and copy-edit. Analysts and editors were typically assigned to a specific Datapro product rather than to a technology or a market. The database and its reusable elements meant that the analyst/editor staff would need to be assigned by technology and that experts in certain elements would emerge. For example, some analysts are expert in vendor strategies, while others are expert in products or services. At the end of the day, the work of both analysts needs to be combined to create a standard report or custom deliverable.

Needless to say, this was a tremendous shock to the Datapro corporate culture. Our analysts and editors thoroughly understood the concept of creating a report from beginning to end, but many had a difficult time visualizing their role in creating database elements. The issue of ownership was of extreme importance. Being assigned to a technology, as opposed to a product, caused considerable confusion. Even the off-the-shelf tools were a reason for concern as employees fiercely hugged and held on to those Atex terminals that only months before were their most dreaded enemy. Our road to electronic publishing had indeed hit a pothole.

Today, Datapro's database is in production. All of our analysts/editors have been trained and are using the system. There are close to 30 000 companies, 80 000 products, and two million specifications in the database. Conversion of our total report base is underway.

All of our print products are now delivered on CD-ROM. Our information is available online via Dialog. The database is used to fulfil numerous custom information requests for customers around the world. And yet, we are still at the start of our journey along the road to electronic publishing.

BEFORE YOU 'HIT THE ROAD'

At this point, I would like to share with you some important things to consider before you 'hit the road' to become an electronic publisher.

Make sure your plan has sound project objectives. Know what will constitute project success and the milestones you need to accomplish along the way. Just delivering an electronic product does not constitute success. You will quickly learn that an electronic product developed with an inefficient process is not success and will not get you the productivity gains or added profit margin for which you may have hoped. Learning from the past, leveraging the present, and providing for your future are the keys to the successful implementation of your plan.

You may be asking, 'what can you learn from the past?' The answer is: a great deal. First of all, look around at your staff. The information market is changing to become more flexible; custom delivery of information is the wave of the future. Electronic publishing will keep you competitive in the information content market. Are the people you are bringing into the electronic publishing business aware of that fact? If your answer is no, you need a solid communications plan to get this message across, now, before you start changing processes and introducing new technologies. Electronic publishing will require new technologies. Make sure the benefactors of this technology windfall are ready to handle it. Develop a plan to improve the technology comfort level in your organization.

Keep in mind that some employees are not flexible enough to change, and new employees might be the only answer. Are you ready to deal with the organizational stress of downsizing and process reengineering at the same time? If your answer is no, do not even start this project. Strong communications and management support are required every step of the way to keep employees on board and in touch with new ways of thinking and doing things.

Your business processes will change as a result of your move to electronic publishing. Ultimately you will need to create the ideal business process to be a successful electronic publisher. To create this ideal model, look at your current business practices and then project how they will change as the technology around you changes. Business process reengineering experts would lead you to believe that all your current processes are bad, but that may not be the case. All of the processes should be reviewed, the good ones maintained, necessary ones reengineered, and new processes developed. Process for the sake of process — 'we have always done it that way' — should be removed. At Datapro, we brought together a self-directed employee team to develop that ideal process model. This technique, which is certainly not novel, helped tremendously with employee buy-in as we started to implement some of the new production processes.

Since the major enabler to electronic publishing is technology, it will play a mighty big role in getting you successfully into the electronic business. Most of our organizations have systems currently installed (legacy systems) which cannot be totally ignored. These legacy systems can be useful in your new technology plan, but perhaps in different roles. For example, higher-speed server PCs may be used as editor workstations. In addition to legacy systems, you also have legacy people in place. The skills that you have now in your technology department are not necessarily the skills that you need. The technology staff should be assessed as to their appropriateness for the tasks in front of them.

You will need to find zealots in your organization — those people who really want the company to become an electronic publisher. Use this group as your change agents to bring other people along. There will be some people who doubt that you can change your processes or that these new processes will bring desired results. Sometimes these doubts are founded in fear, but sometimes they are founded in good insight into the company's ethics and founding principles. Listen to these folks, understand their real concerns and deal with it. Do not dismiss these employees as 'tree huggers' stuck in the ways of the past. The tree they are hugging may be the underlying foundation of some things that are right about your organization. If you take time to share your objectives and plans, you can count on these employees to rank among your most loyal. The damaging people in your organization are the cynics. They cannot be convinced and they are not worth the effort. The best place for the cynic is someplace else.

Most organizations have some piece of technology that they do very well. Build on your technology strengths wherever possible. The benefit will be a quicker implementation and a smoother road to your electronic product. Be cautious, however, not to compromise the ultimate goal of your project because you do not understand what technology can offer you. Know what you need technology to accomplish for you and do not compromise on issues such as database structure or development tools. These compromises will keep you from achieving your goal.

Most importantly, your job is to provide for the future. Very often when we plan for the future, we are actually planning for the present. The average application development cycle is 12 to 18 months. The first step in this process is defining system requirements — functions which may not be available for six to 12 months. If you have not taken this development time into your future-planning cycle, you are actually developing requirements for the day the system goes into production, not really the future. Once you have developed your ideal model, make the stretch and project it into the future. Think five years out. Now, you will not ask your IT department to start programming those five-year-out requirements tomorrow, but you want to make sure no technology or process decisions you make today preclude you from getting to your ultimate destination.

It is so easy when you invest in technologies for the future to get caught on the 'bleeding edge'. Stay away from immature tools which can hinder your development cycle and cause unplanned delays as you wait for functions in an upcoming version. Today, technology is turning over rapidly. Some would say much too rapidly. Desktop technologies turn over every six to nine months. It is difficult not to make technology mistakes, but, there are good solutions on the market today, much better tools than when Datapro started on the road to electronic publishing. Through research, find them before you invest.

Stay in the mainstream with your technology decisions. Some of the costliest parts of your move to electronic publishing will be retooling and retraining. Choosing tools for editorial creation that can be self-taught through online tutorial or through standard training programmes will prove less costly in the long run than customized software which will require customized training. Maintenance and upgrade of customized software will also drive up expenses.

REENGINEERING THE EDITORIAL PROCESS

You may not believe it now, but no part of the editorial process will escape change when you become an electronic publisher. Everyday functions like data capture, scheduling, data ownership, archiving, formats, standards, quality control and output functions will need to be reviewed and most likely changed.

The way you capture data changes from being principally an internal, single-source problem to one of multiple sources and multiple feeds. Some of your sources will be electronic — either scanned images, wire services or other outside sources. Data capture from your traditional human sources, internal staff and outside contributors, will also be part of your data capture process. Strict standards and formats for all data captured must be established and maintained. Any deviation from these standards will cause your electronic publishing process to fail.

One of the most challenging changes Datapro faced was moving from a well-defined three-month schedule, where each analyst knew well in advance what their next assignment was, to a dynamic scheduling system. The electronic system schedules Datapro analysts worldwide on the basis of the time required to accomplish each assignment. This worldwide view of assignment protects us from duplicating effort by providing the total view of assignments. In addition, assignments can be changed easily as industry events dictate, eliminating time wasted on assignments whose priorities might have changed during the three-month assignment period of the past. The online scheduling system provides for the scheduling of elements smaller than total reports. Dealing with these smaller elements has been the biggest transition for our analyst/editor team.

And, it is the scheduling of these elements which fuelled the most heated debate over data ownership. Your security software can be used to control things like single write access and multiple read access, but only you can provide the scheme for true data ownership. Regardless of size, you have to establish accountability and responsibility for the smallest element in your information database. These owners must be clearly defined and the proper security added to your system to ensure that this ownership is not violated. It is the data ownership function which ensures the integrity of your database. Without integrity, your database is worthless.

When Datapro was a print publisher, keeping archives of our products was easy. We kept the electronic copy of the Atex files, the blue lines from the printer and, of course, copies of each supplement. An electronic publisher actually has only one of those alternatives available, the electronic files. It is very important to think about archiving data during your database and process design. Traditionally, a database is overwritten with new information and the prior information can be lost forever. Know if you need to keep raw data archives or finished product archives. When to archive is also dependent on what you need to save, as is frequency. And, of course, archives should be properly protected using standard business recovery techniques.

I think every editor-in-chief feels that their editorial team has established standards which they follow religiously. My bet is there are more 'standards' in your organization than you can even imagine. Since our business is built on maintaining a large database of historical information, as well as the most current, our problem was standards that had changed over time. All of this information, regardless of the version of standards to which it adhered, needed to be normalized into a single repository. Not all your information will move into your repository cleanly. Expect to have a conversion effort to move what you need into the database. Be selective and move only what is required to build current and future product. More importantly, standards going forward must be well defined and documented, and everyone must comply. Allowing variation from standards will impact the quality of your electronic product as well as your production cycle. Standard tagging schemes such as SGML are only part of the puzzle. You will also need standards which establish writing styles appropriate for the screen; for example, references to page numbers are out. This strict adherence to standards is counter to the creative instincts of your editorial staff. Establishing the 'standards police' causes conflict but does not necessarily get you the desired result of adherence to standards. Here is where the zealots can really be useful in changing behaviour.

When you find that zealot, see how they feel about formats. Every electronic product has a format. It is a gross oversimplification to think of an electronic product as just information presented on a screen. Your competitive advantage in the electronic market comes from the way your information is represented on the screen and the ease with which you can navigate through it. Formats that are inviting and provide easy access to the most important information are winners. There may be no similarities between your electronic product formats and your print formats. On the other hand, some customers dictate that they be the same. The bottom line is that the format must support the delivery media, be flexible, easily designed and changed.

As a print publisher, all of our quality control functions were at the end of the production cycle, just before the pages went to the printer. In the electronic publishing model, quality control functions have to take place as soon as information is returned to the database. Some online deliverables will be updated in real time. Consequently, the end of the process is when the analyst or editor returns the information to the database, which can be hours, days or weeks before it is needed. The electronic model supports decentralized quality-control rather than a centralized proofing department. Moving the quality-control staff away from paper proofreading is another big cultural change. A paper quality control process for an electronic product is not practical.

Everything we have talked about so far has to do with getting information into the database and handling the information once it is there. However, the problems of output and distribution should not be overlooked. The information industry, in my opinion, will split into two functions: the content providers and the distribution channels. Similarly, the internal organization of an electronic publisher will make the same split. Your analysts/editors will deal with the issues of content. A group of output/delivery specialists will deal with packaging and distribution of your information in various formats. These output/distribution specialists will create output templates for your print output, extract files for your CD-ROM or online deliverables and make sure that content gets to the proper distribution or production process. Multiple output media will require multiple processes.

ROAD HAZARDS

There are many road hazards to watch out for on the road to electronic publishing. Certainly, data conversion can be a considerable problem, especially if you suffer from a lack of standards. Training is a big issue. Your analysts/editors will need a high comfort level with their new technology if you expect a successful electronic implementation. Get them involved in technology decisions early to ensure buy-in. Again, be careful to avoid immature or inappropriate tools. They will drive up your costs, lengthen your development time and prevent you from reaching your objectives.

Never underestimate the role your organizational culture will play in your success. You need the right editorial and technology skills. You need the proper level of organizational preparedness before you can make this move. Techniques like self-directed employee teams can ease the transition. The more buy-in you get up front, the less work you have on the back end to bring the organizational culture along.

THINGS TO REMEMBER

In conclusion, there are a few things to remember on the road to electronic publishing:

- Technology is key to your success. Get involved with your IT department early. Moving to electronic publishing is not a technology project; it is a major business process and organizational cultural change project.

- Organizational changes will be required. Splitting the content development process from the distribution processes, decentralizing the quality control process, streamlining the data entry processes are a few of the areas where organizational changes can occur.
- Expect short-term expenses for long-term gains. The deployment of new technologies and processes is not inexpensive. The return on your investment will be down the road. For now, you should anticipate that expenses will increase.
- Listen to those who defend, counsel those who doubt, but remove the cynics.
- Know when you have succeeded. The quickest way to fail is to not know when you have succeeded. Set expectations for your project, implement your plan in attainable phases and establish quantifiable measures for success.

Information exchange

36

Multimedia and interactivity — fiction, fantasy, or *fait accompli?*

George Sacerdote, Arthur D Little, USA

In recent years, multimedia and interactive information services have been generating significant excitement in the business press. Respected journals such as *Business Week,* the *Financial Times, The Wall Street Journal,* and *The Economist* have written stories on the subject including such breathy lines as 'It is the end of the world as we know it', 'What is arriving in the information highway? Growth', or 'Retailing will never be the same again'. From such headlines one might reasonably conclude that we are on the verge of totally reinventing the information business on a scale that compares to the inventions of the printing press, radio or television.

Curiously, the same journals that are so aggressively touting this revolution are also sounding an equally loud tocsin of caution. The *FT* announces 'Multimedia in handcuffs', and 'Smash-up Delay on the "Information Super-highway"'. *Business Week* writes 'Dial R for Risk' in an article on multimedia, and *The Wall Street Journal* runs a story including the line 'Early attempts show buyers may be leery of Interactivity'.

At the same time, there has been a virtual orgy in the information industry, with companies large and small coupling and decoupling at

---

Dr George Sacerdote is Senior Vice-President of Arthur D Little Inc. at ADL headquarters in Lexington, Massachusetts. He specializes in new media technology, market and strategic issues.

rates reminiscent of pagan fertility rites. Just keeping up a chart of which companies in this industry are merging or joint venturing, or undoing previously announced mergers or JVs requires daily update. Even with such diligence, every time we show a version of Figure 36.1, we learn of yet another major combination or decombination that we have missed.

Just what is going on here? Is there any reality here, or are we just the victims of a colossal case of American promoters hyping something out of all proportion to the true state of affairs? Are we *truly* dealing with the invention of an entire new industry, or are we just dealing with the latest chapter in a long saga? Just what is it that is changing? Is it too early to tell what applications will succeed? What types of companies will become dominant? Is all this interest of importance only in the USA or is it relevant to Europe as well? In the next few pages I will address each of these questions, first from the American viewpoint, and then from the European.

REALITY VERSUS HYPE?

The delivery of content in a variety of interactive formats has indeed become a real business in the USA. For example, the online information industry in the USA has now passed $12 000 million in annual revenues and is rapidly closing in on the book industry's $15 000 million. In 1993 Americans spent more on video games, a quintessentially interactive medium, than they did on movie tickets. The unit volume in electronic encyclopaedias now exceeds that of the printed versions, and as a result traditional industry leaders, such as the *Encyclopaedia Britannica,* are having a hard time sustaining their expensive field sales forces. Services such as CompuServe, America Online and Prodigy now reach millions of users and the growth in their collective subscriber base continues to grow in excess of 20% per annum. Last year, the total volume of merchandise purchased through QVC and Home Shopping Network exceeded $2200 million. The number of users of the Internet has been growing at 15% *per month,* and is now in the many millions of individuals.

As potent as these aggregate statistics are as indicators of the reality of various forms of interactive media, some down-to-earth anecdotes from my personal experience may shed more light on how pervasive these new forms of communications are becoming.

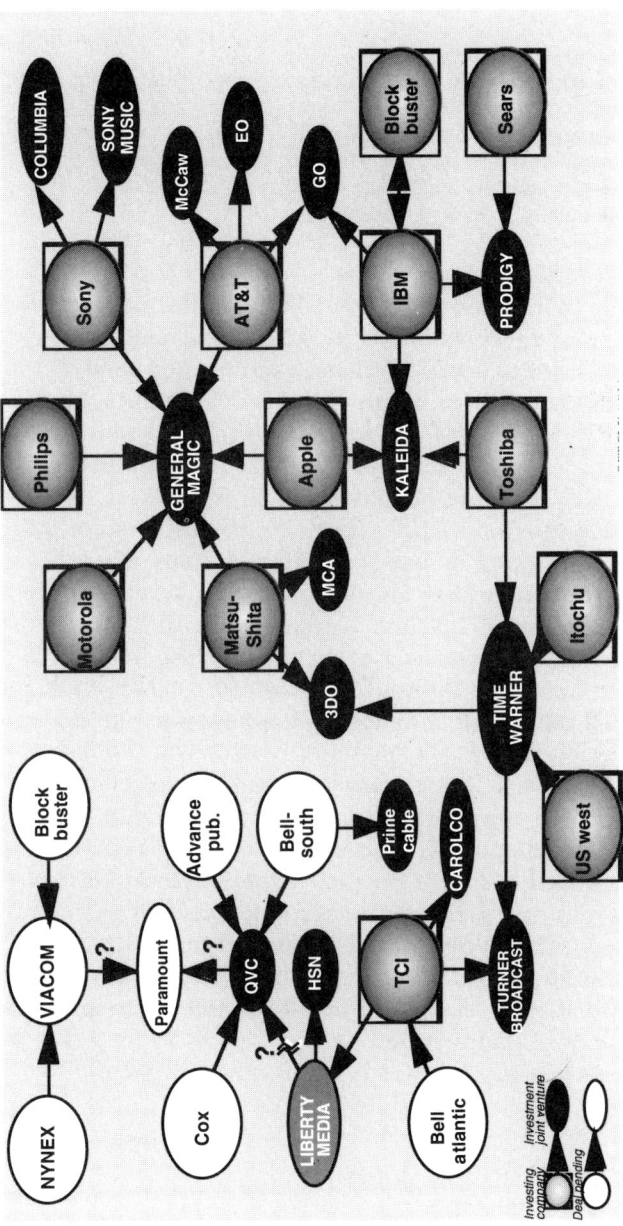

Figure 36.1 The orgy of coupling and decoupling

Two years ago, when I was driving a van-load of 14-year-old boys to a soccer game, I overheard a discussion that went roughly as follows:

'My parents just gave me a subscription to America Online for my birthday.'
'What services do you use on it?'
'I have been logging on to a chat group hosted by my favorite sci-fi author.'
'I prefer CompuServe — they just have a lot more stuff I want.'
'I used the encyclopedia on Prodigy last night to research a history paper; I just didn't have time to go to the library.'

And so on for half an hour.

Less than a month ago, I was talking to the head of one of the US's largest ad agencies. While he was concerned that online shopping might displace some purchasing from traditional channels and therefore render obsolete some of his firm's services, he did not see it as a near-term threat. To prove his point, he asked me if I had ever bought cubic zirconia through QVC. I allowed that I had never watched QVC, let alone bought anything from them. Nonetheless, I had used CompuServe chat groups to obtain product information from vendors as well as user recommendations when I was in the market for a laser printer and again when I wanted to buy a CD-ROM unit for my PC. When I pointed out that these were much more informative channels for my making product decisions than advertising, or heaven forbid, computer store clerks, he began to see the very real threat that interactive shopping poses to his advertising business.

Three weeks ago I met with a school counsellor who advises students on the universities to which they should apply. When I asked how David could gain access to first-hand reports from recent graduates from his school on their experiences at various universities, I was told that there was an active network of past graduates on the Internet. David need merely join in the discussions. When I asked David about this, I learned that he had already found his way to this information channel and had active correspondence with friends at a dozen universities.

So, are we talking reality or hype? You be the judge.

IS THERE ANYTHING NEW HERE?

The remarkable thing is that so much hype is being generated about a family of product evolutions that have been going on for at least a generation. Since the late 1970s Professor Tony Oettinger at Harvard has been mapping the various products and services in the information industry along two dimensions, as illustrated in Figure 36.2. The vertical dimension distinguishes between products and services (e.g. telephone handsets versus providing dial tone), while the horizontal dimension ranges from pure information transport (e.g. telephone service or printing presses), to pure information content (e.g. books, movies or online databases).

Figure 36.2 illustrates how Oettinger's mapping of the information products and services industry might have looked in the early 1980s. Largely companies were content to operate in their own market sectors. Attempts in those days to cross from one sector to another, such as IBM's foray into communications services (Satellite Business Systems and Rolm) or AT&T's entry into the computer industry (remember the 3B2?), generally had unfortunate ends.

In Figures 36.3 and 36.4 we illustrate how this map has been changing since then. Increasingly, companies are hard to categorize according to Oettinger's typology and participate in the industry in multiple ways. Is Apple a computer company or in consumer electronics? Is Dow Jones in newspapers or electronic information services? Is Pearson a newspaper company, a book publisher or an entertainment company?

As part of this evolutionary process we have been exploiting the faster, cheaper computer hardware, the smarter, more powerful software and the increasing amounts of available communications bandwidth to add more and more dimensions to the sensory experiences and broader distribution to content. If we define multimedia as simply the continuation of this process, we see that multimedia has a long history.

At the time of each major step in this evolutionary process, some variant of the new world order was trumpeted about and the incumbent media players indulged in many years of uncertainty. For example, when the first movies with sound were produced, most studios feared the loss of the mystique of the movies and resisted the change aggressively. When RCA launched colour television, it took nearly ten years and significant financial subsidies before broadcasters other

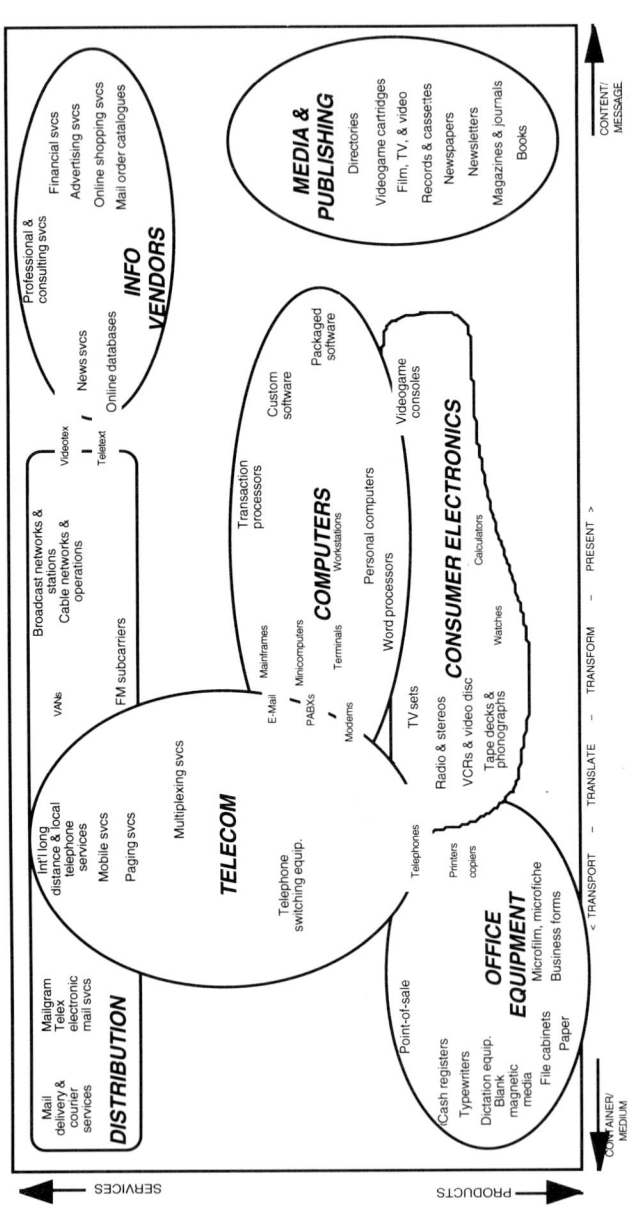

Figure 36.2 Products and services in the information industry. In 1981, separate companies dominated distinct product categories and most of their efforts to cross-segment boundaries failed

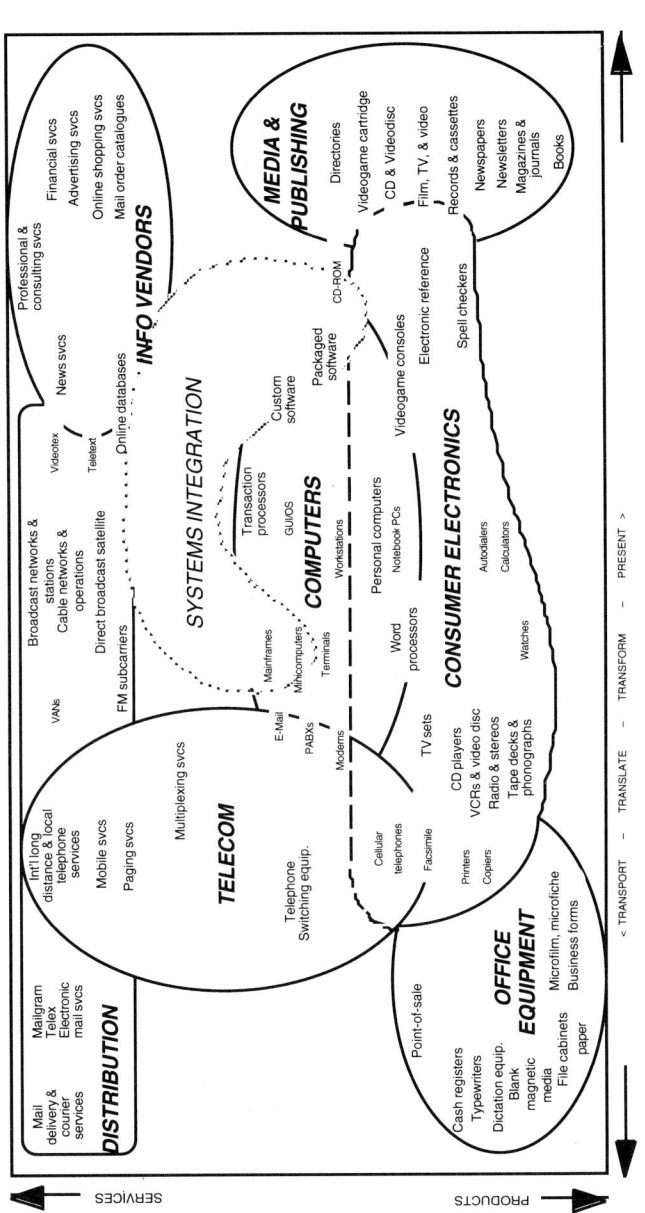

Figure 36.3 Products and services in the information industry. In the 1990s, companies began to cross-segment boundaries, but with distinct divisions

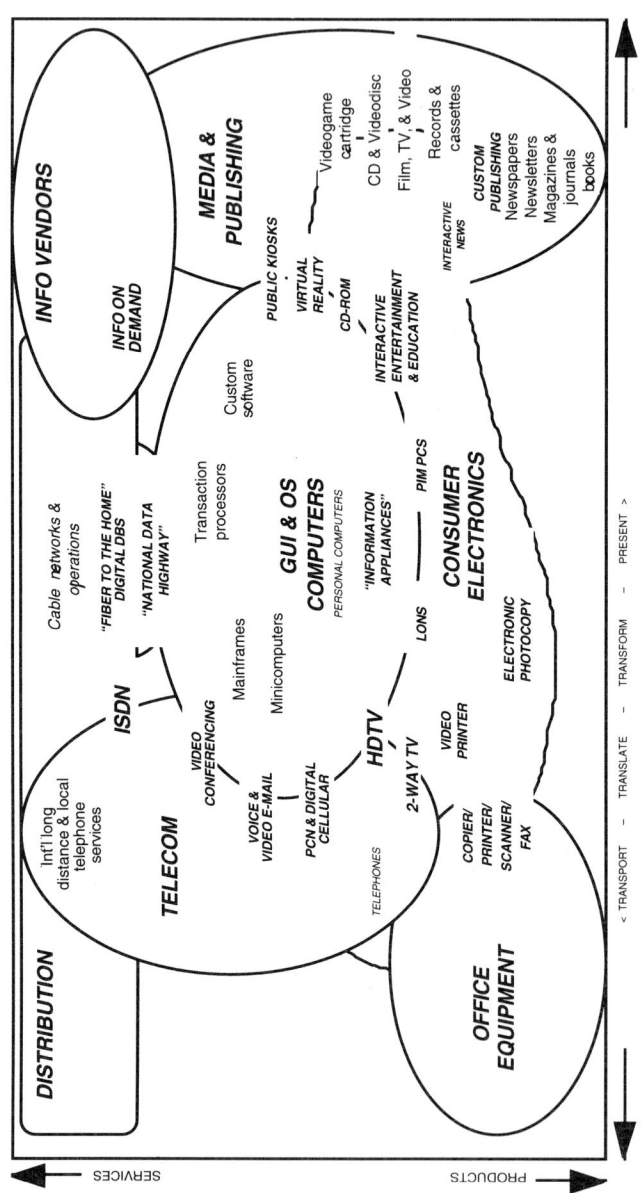

Figure 36.4 Products and services in the information industry. In the next decade, product categories themselves will blur and historical distinctions among companies will follow the same path

than RCA's wholly owned subsidiary NBC would convert to the new process.

Some new multimedia technologies never bore fruit. In the early 1960s two companies launched movies with olfactory components under the names Smell-O-Vision and Aromarama. One of the first such movies was a travelogue about Arabia. First one saw the camel train, and smelled scent of camel... Then one arrived at the Bedouin camp to the scent of roasting goat... Then one entered a tent to the scent of the great unwashed... And so on. Unfortunately, there were technical difficulties: the air-conditioning systems of the time could not change the air in the theatre fast enough, and by the end of the show the room had a mix of smells in it, leaving one with the distinct sense of a garbage dump. Further, the technology added little value as seen (smelled?) from the customer's point of view. Once the novelty wore off, no-one was interested.

More recent multimedia successes include closed-user-group video-conferencing, MTV, home shopping and video games. Recent failures include videotex, interactive video discs and, at least so far, pay-per-view television.

SO... JUST WHAT *IS* NEW HERE?

Lest I leave the impression that absolutely nothing is new here, let me hasten to add that this industry is undergoing significant change, though perhaps not quite at the cataclysmic level suggested by all the hype. First, companies are beginning to change their roles in the value chain; see Figure 36.5. Companies such as Dow Jones that were fully vertically integrated have given up parts of the chain. No longer do they originate all the data on their system. They buy some from others. Further, they have now begun to distribute information through other people's products, notably Sand Point's *Hoover* and Lotus' *Notes*. Other companies have made acquisitions or formed alliances that bring together different parts of the chain. For example, Sega and MGM have recently agreed to jointly develop story lines for simultaneous introduction as films and video games. Sony has acquired several content providers, including a movie studio and a recorded music company. Pearson has just bought Software Toolworks so as to become vertically integrated; now it can produce

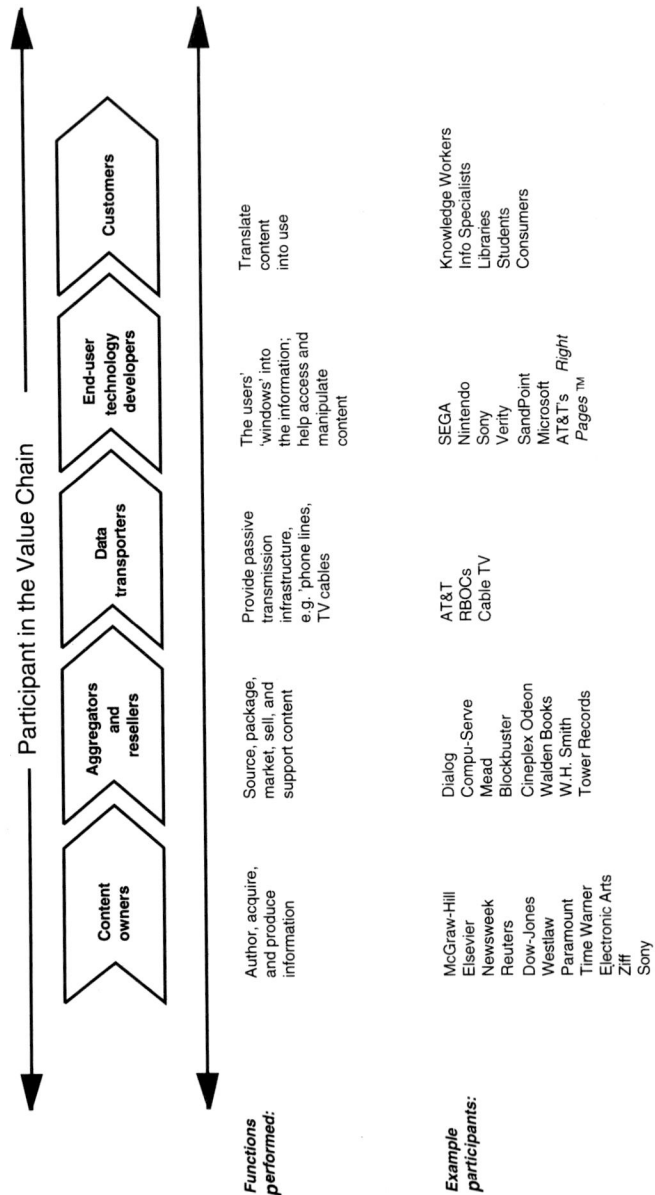

Figure 36.5 The value chain

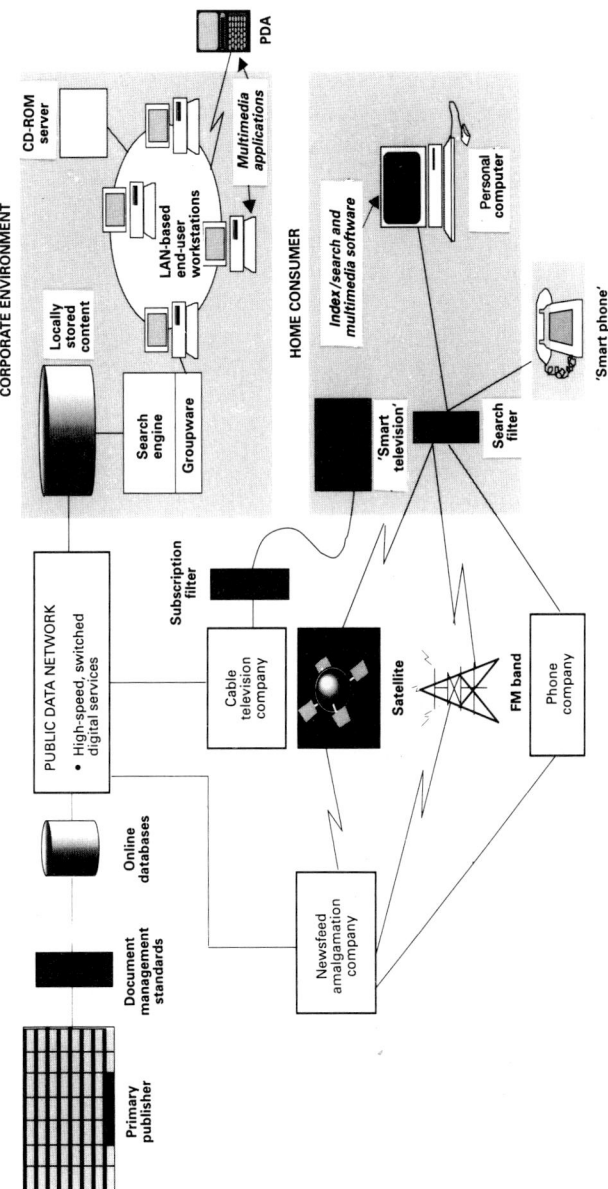

Figure 36.6 Emerging technologies allow content owners to have direct access to information end-users at both home and work

computer games based on children's books owned by one of its publishing imprints.

Another change has been that emerging technologies have made it possible to string together wholly new distribution channels between content owners and their customers, both in the home and in the office. These systems make it possible to deliver *cost-effectively* content from large databases of films, text, videos and music, in a variety of formats, and through a range of end-user devices; see Figure 36.6.

A further change is that the market place is now more receptive to multimedia products than it was two to three years ago. While we seemed stuck for several years in serving the experimenters and early adopters, we in the USA have moved smartly into the early majority phase of the product adoption process. See Figure 36.7. Early majority customers tend to have wholly new buying criteria from early adopters. For example, they are less willing to tolerate almost good enough performance and they are very impatient with systems that are less than transparent to operate. But early majority customers exist in vast numbers, turning the multimedia industry from a specialist cottage industry into one of mainstream America. CD-ROMs are now for sale at K-Mart. Daily newspapers across America now have regular columns devoted to computing. Even the US President is on the Internet (at address President@whitehouse.gov). Closed-user-group videoconferencing is available in a wide variety of companies, and switched videoconferencing among companies awaits only a somewhat greater density of optical fibre to the office. This

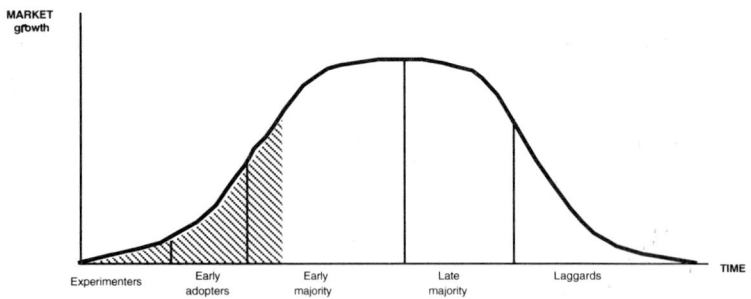

Figure 36.7 In both business and consumer markets, we in the USA are moving from the early adopters to the early majority for many product categories

change is forcing many products to be rethought or superseded, which in turn is leading to a rush of new products to market.

Another change is that both the drivers of the multimedia industry and the likely winner applications are becoming clearer after many years of cloudy crystal balls. As for drivers, many marketers are now reaching the point of understanding how to apply their imagination to the powerful combinations of much more powerful software, much cheaper and faster processors, wider, cheaper bandwidth and vastly improved data compression and signal processing to develop exciting, high-value, content-based products.

WHAT APPLICATIONS WILL SUCCEED?

On the applications side, three distinct categories of applications categories are emerging. First, office applications are already well-established, primarily with online databases, presentation software and videoconferencing that mixes full-motion video with simultaneous access to documents. What we will have going forward will be refinements and natural line extensions of the same. Increasingly, for example, vendors of online databases need to build highly sophisticated front ends on their systems to make them much more readily accessible to casual end-users. And these same vendors, such as Dialog, need to adopt whole new pricing and distribution schemes to reflect the types of value propositions and end-use network systems that are expected by the early majority user.

The second major category is the home/professional. In the USA, we now have some six million knowledge workers working fully or partly at home. We refer here to freelance programmers, graphic designers, solo practitioner consultants, teleworkers and the like. These people have investments of several thousands of dollars in computer and communications equipment. They are competing against others who have access to a variety of professional sources of information, such as corporate libraries, access to database services, or what have you. And they are buying in substantial quantities of professional information of many types from home.

The third category are the consumers. In this category, several applications have already emerged as likely winners. These include:

- *Shopping:* Both via television (e.g. QVC), but also online and via 800 numbers, as we described above.
- *Entertainment:* Including solo and networked video games and movies.
- *Education and training:* Including applications in schools, at home and in the workplace.
- *Personal communications:* Email, and both on-phone and online chat groups have become totally mainstream.
- *Personal finance:* While home banking proved to be a dud, products such as Quicken, Checkfree, and TurboTax have introduced millions to the value of online personal financial management. In turn, online stock brokerage has now become one of the fastest segments of the discount stock brokerage industry.
- *Sex:* Pornography was the breakthrough application for VCRs, and the personals ads have been the killer applications for Minitel online service in France and the 900-line audio services in the USA. At last year's Comdex, the hottest new product by far was the CD-i entitled *Penthouse Photo Shoot*, in which one could fantasize about being a photographer for the magazine of the same name.

WHO WILL DOMINATE THE INDUSTRY?

Financial power in the industry is shifting away from the aggregators and resellers. Traditionally these types of companies have used their dominance of customer relationships to extract favourable terms from the players in different parts of the value chain. Their weakening position is perhaps best exemplified by Blockbuster Video's effort to acquire movie studios.

Data-content owners are gradually raising their demands for royalties for access to their intellectual property. The creators of end-user technology to manage and manipulate the outputs of this industry, companies such as Microsoft and Oracle, are increasingly seizing more of the value creation process. In the last two years we have seen a number of alliances or acquisitions among content owners and end-user technology developers that reinforce this trend. For example, Microsoft acquired a major share of the UK publisher Dorling Kindersley to help establish its interfaces as *de facto* standards in the creation of interactive information products. Pearson in turn has bought Software Toolworks as a vehicle for exploiting more effectively many of its copyrights.

This transition, in which the aggregators become more and more like wholesalers, with wholesaler economics, is not unusual as an industry begins to mature. Some of these middlemen have fought back by seeking to acquire or develop content or end-user systems of their own. For example, Blockbuster, the distributor of videos, has begun to acquire studios and other content-development assets. In addition, Blockbuster has teamed up with IBM to develop new software to make much easier the process of distributing recorded music. Similarly, Dialog has made a minority investment in Individual Inc., a company that has sophisticated software for the selective dissemination of information.

TOWARDS A GENERIC MODEL FOR SUCCESS

In the course of innumerable business strategy assignments for companies in this business, I have distilled five key factors for success in this business.

- *No interactive information service is saleable without content that customers want:* A newspaper without stories and ads is nothing more than a fish wrap. A VCR would be of little use without broadcast programmes to record or movies to watch. A mixed-media presentation with no original ideas would rapidly put its audience to sleep. Anyone who plans to be in some part of this business must either own content, or have very strong relationships with content providers.
- *This industry is mostly one of niche markets, in which the building of customer franchises is paramount:* Increasingly, vendors are finding that delivery of content in various formats to different subsegments of a niche in which they have established dominance is the most economical way to proceed. The model of the movie studio that sells the same content in its original form to cinemas, as videos through the retail channel, as TV programming through the cable and broadcast channels and in the video game format through the game channels is one which is being emulated by many others in this business (see Figure 36.8.). In this way, greatest leverage is obtained from the large cost of developing content

Delivery medium	Consumer					Business Horizontal						Business Vertical								
	Entertainment	Finance	Education	Shopping	Communications	Technology	Marketing sales	Mfg distribution	Financial	H.R.	Data processing	Financial svcs	Government	Aerospace	Chemicals	Defence	Transport	Legal	Telecomm.	Electronics
Newspaper		●																		
Magazine		●																		
Book	●																			
On line or 2-way cable	●	●																		
Broadcast/1 way cable																				
Game machine		●																		
CD or cassette	●																			
Personal computer																				

Figure 36.8 The most successful companies offer solutions in one or more media for very few markets

and establishing franchises for it in the marketplace. The older model, in which the vendor saw himself or herself as an online company, or a magazine company, or a broad-spectrum software company is probably less viable. The worst of all models is the 'measles' model, in which someone decides that somehow this new media market is going to be exciting, and therefore scatters bets all over the market/product table in the hopes of scoring a few winners that will pay for all the failures.

- *The majority of the investments in this business come in the form of intangible assets, rather than capital goods in the traditional sense:* The two predominant asset classes are marketplace assets, such as franchises, subscriber lists and distribution channels, and content assets, such as copyrights, licences, software and know-how. In general, physical assets such as computers and telecommunications equipment account for less than one fourth of the value of companies in this business.

Companies traditionally in the information business are not surprised by this observation, but industrial companies and companies allowed a regulated rate of return on physical plant (such as telephone utilities) often have a hard time understanding this issue. Their internal management systems are not designed to give true pictures of the returns obtained. Information-services subsidiaries of such companies often pay severe penalties because their 'investments' in building franchises and content are difficult to capitalize. Rather, they are taken as direct charges against the profit and loss account, creating all sorts of misunderstandings with parent-company management.

- *One must view new technology through the question of how it can add value as seen through the customers' eyes:* It easy to be mesmerized by some of the exciting technical developments that the technology vendors develop every day. One of the hard parts for product managers is not to be carried away with this excitement. Rather, one must constantly return to the question of how prospective customers will gain utility from the added product features that the technology might make possible. Do these features enable one to meet better the basic needs of prospective buyers, or are they merely cute 'bells and whistles'?

  Product development staff are particularly prone to assuming that they know best what the customer values, without bothering to ask. Conversely, finding out the true wants and needs of the customer is often a formidable problem because we are generally dealing with intangible products (entertainment, information, etc.) that prospective buyers have never seen and do not understand. Consequently, conducting market research in this field is usually best left to experts. These experts have specially developed techniques to enable research subjects to understand the new products and articulate what value it might create.

- *Companies should invest more of their effort in managing large development projects, so that they produce well-defined products on time and on budget, and less in trying to push the technical state-of-the-art:* The industry is littered with the corpses of projects that have gone out of control, and wound up costing two to five times what was planned, and getting to market years late, and often not yielded marketable products. Product development is now typically a large effort involving perhaps dozens to hundreds of people working together for periods of a year or more. As a result, weak project management is almost a guarantee of disaster. Some companies confuse the issue of technical project management with the notion of developing new technology. It is important to remember that the multimedia industry is generally one of applying proven technology in a disciplined way, rather than one of conducting state-of-the-art R&D.

IMPLICATIONS FOR EUROPE

Having now completed my description of the situation in America, where we do indeed have a vibrant market in which numerous products featuring various forms of interactivity are generating tens of billions of dollars annually, let me turn my attention to the European scene.

The European Commission sees a vast gap between the state of the multimedia market in the USA and in Europe, and has concluded that it must do something about the problem. Indeed, there are substantial differences between the state of the development of the USA and European markets for interactive and multimedia services, but the usual 'arm-chair' analyses do not account for this difference. Nor do these analyses suggest how a company wishing to become a participant in the developing European market for such services should proceed.

The EC, for example, sees a need to start a technology 'arms race' with the USA. In its 1993 white paper on the subject, it made such bold statements as 'the development of information and communications technologies ... will have long term effects comparable to the first industrial revolution'. Yet, as we have seen above, multimedia and interactivity are not in the end about pushing the technical state-of-the-art. The EC in the same paper went on to recommend capital investments in communications infrastructure of some 67 000 million ECU over the rest of the decade as a facilitator of creating the state of the art. We saw above that capital assets are not what this business is about. Indeed, the emptiness of the Commission's analysis is perhaps best highlighted by the bold prophecy that they made in the second paragraph of their white paper, 'We are firmly convinced that the European economy has a future'.

Some nay-sayers raise the old challenge of distinctive national markets. For example, they point to differences in language, regulatory environment or media ownership rules among the EC member countries. Is this situation so very different from what obtains in the food, drug, or fashion goods industries? Are there not strong companies in these industries that are able to operate across national boundaries? Why should the information industry be different? Perhaps companies in the information services business should take a lesson in market segmentation from Philips. Philips is able to supply television sets across Europe despite national differences in both the technical standards for broadcasting and in the expectations of how a television should look, feel and operate. Indeed, Philips has been able to use its cleverness in dealing with these national differences to its own competitive advantage versus Japanese manufacturers, whose processes depend on manufacturing economies of scale.

Still others point to national differences in infrastructures as obstacles to building a successful multimedia industry in Europe. For example, they might note that, while some countries such as Belgium, the Netherlands, and Switzerland are almost fully wired for cable TV, other larger countries such as Italy and the UK have less than 10% coverage. 'How', these people might ask 'could we build a cable-based interactive system in Europe under these circumstances?' My response is to remind them of the lessons of medium independence and niche marketing. Italy, for example, compensates for a relatively weak telecommunications infrastructure by having perhaps the greatest penetration of CD-ROM drives in the world. In designing interactive products, one may need a cable version for the Belgian market and a CD-ROM version for Italy. Further, to continue on the Italian example, Bell Atlantic, the US regional telephone company, has just signed a technology licence with the Italian telecommunications giant STET. This agreement provides for Bell Atlantic's video compression technology (to send video over twisted copper pair) to be used in Italy. Hence, an interactive service whose timeliness needs ruled out CD-ROM as a delivery system will be available through the traditional telephone network. One must tailor one's proposed multimedia service to the situation in each regional market.

Another group of nay-sayers will point to Europe's inexplicable slowness in taking up information technology as a third obstacle to development of a European multimedia industry. Indeed, at one level they are correct. For example, fairly uniformly across Europe, PC penetration per hundred population, which runs roughly linearly with prosperity (as measured by GDP per capita), is only at half the level of that obtained in the USA (see Figure 36.9). However, if we were to roll the tape of history backwards five years, we would see that the European penetration today roughly parallels the state of the US market then. Indeed, what is happening is that PC penetration increases not only with prosperity, but also with time as prices fall.

For a marketer planning new products for the European market, this situation is indeed good news. What it says is that, by carefully

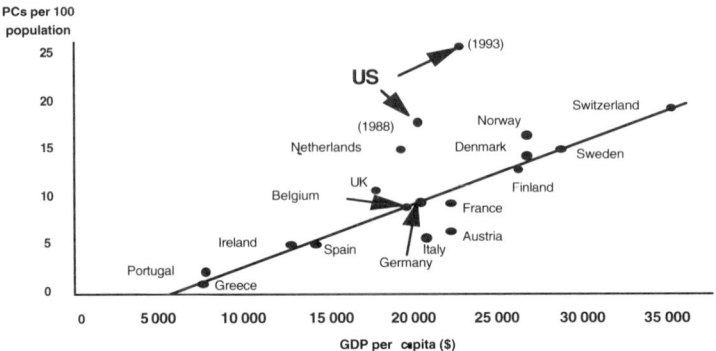

Figure 36.9 Because information technology is penetrating the European markets two to four years more slowly, we can use the USA as a baseline model of how products and markets will evolve in Europe

studying the US market of some five years ago, one can develop some strong models of what types of products are likely to appeal to what types of customers in what time frames. Admittedly, these products will need to be adapted to the needs of local customers, but such adaptation is much easier than having to go through the painful process of developing and testing wholly new product concepts. Further, the clever marketer will see that to make investments in the somewhat more developed US market was a way to learn the lessons of this industry first hand. For this reason, companies such as Pearson, Reuters and Bertelsmann are acquiring toehold companies in America.

I firmly believe that taking a wait-and-see attitude towards the European market is very short-sighted. Those who would wait until the great day in the future when regulations are harmonized, all of the infrastructure is in place, standards are set and intellectual property laws are made uniform will probably discover on that day that the market has passed them by. The cost of catching up will be huge, and perhaps catching up will not be possible.

IN CONCLUSION

The general rules of what companies must do to succeed in this business in both Europe and the USA are quite clear, and are not very different from any other industry. We need to focus on specific opportunities, and not attempt to attack this highly fragmented market broadside. We must focus on our core competencies and make sure that we understand how they add value in customer terms. We must make alliances, acquisitions and buyer-seller relationships with others to cover the complete value chain from product concept to delivery to the end-user. We must of course have excellent products and services. We must time our products correctly in the market. And we have to be prepared to invest in building long-term franchise value for the repeat business that will ensure sustainable profitability once we are established.

The hard part is in resolving the details. Which customer segments to serve? With what products? Delivered in what media? Starting when? Answering these questions correctly will result in great rewards. But, miss on only one and you put much at risk.

Future scenarios for opportunities in EP

37

Scenario elements for the future of the EP business

Brian Blunden, Pira International, UK

It is not possible to be prescriptive in developing a scenario which will fit every publishing company's needs in the EP business as it relates to books, magazines, newspapers, information services and corporate publishing. Drawing an EP scenario for the individual company is just one input to the development of company strategy. It must be particular to the specific needs of that company. What follows in this chapter is a listing of elements in the form of separate scenario statements. These are intended to provide key issues judged to be significant by the editors. The intention is that the reader shall consider these issues, relate them to their own business and thereafter assemble the appropriate elements to be considered when developing a particular EP business strategy. There is no significance in either the extent of detail or ordering of the following elements:

- The world will continue to become an increasingly information-rich environment and we must introduce into our business a systematic means of assessing the opportunity or threat which this new environment will cause.
- Technology does not make an EP business; it is the content and the service provided based on appropriate technology which will make our EP business a successful venture.

Brian Blunden, Managing Director of Pira International and Chief Executive Officer of IEPRC, is one of the book's editors.

- While technology does not make an EP business successful, it is increasingly an intrinsic part of the EP business and it is a major driver for change; we will therefore ensure global monitoring of relevant technological developments in our business.

- We will not wait for global copyright protection or deregulation of cross-media ownership legislation before developing our own business strategy in relation to these two issues; we will be proactive through the appropriate channels of influence to ensure the achievement of the best business environment for publishing within a sympathetic international legal framework.

- We will participate in the EP business and we will have a clearly defined business objective in terms of markets and products; we will start when we have commitment and the appropriate re-sources to sustain that development for a minimum of five years; we have established success criteria to be measured at given time intervals and we have prepared an exit strategy if required.

- We have developed a methodology to compile an inventory of our content publishing assets; we are implementing a review of the value-adding potential from these assets which could be achieved by exploitation through EP.

- We have decided by systematic evaluation of our core business that our business lends itself to development through EP; we need to decide whether to proceed by organic development or acquisition or both.

- Assuming we want to develop into EP through organic growth and acquisition, we must now be sure that we have within our management team the essential skills to make decisions to achieve success in EP; we need to remember what we do not know and what we cannot understand!

- We need to recognize the contribution of our existing customer base; we will undertake research to ascertain their aspirations and frustrations with our existing product and services which could be overcome through EP.

- We must decide whether we wish to be a 'leader' or a 'follower' in the EP business; we recognize that the latter requires critical timing and a learning curve, and the former involves market-making; we are prepared for significant costs and the need for synergistic alliances if we participate in market-making.

- Conventional market research will contribute to our strategy only where a potential market exists; we must therefore participate in prototype development wherever we wish to offer product to a potential market which is not yet developed.

- Innovation management is different from traditional management, in which we as publishers have experience in our routine business; prototyping is an innovative activity; we must be sure we have the skills and resources to manage it.

- Technological convergence and market diversification by non-publishing media companies represent two major drivers in creating the EP business marketplace; we must be sure we understand these drivers, nominate an individual to be responsible for monitoring their impact on our business and have a strategy to relate the impact these drivers will make to our business growth strategy for the future.

- Alliances may be essential to our participation in the EP business; if they are, we must ensure that we bring to any alliance a balanced contribution, a shared business philosophy, a quantified and shared view of benefit and a shared commitment to development which is sustainable by all parties.

- We must decide whether EP is an extension of our business marketplace or a substitution; whichever view is adopted, we must ensure that it permeates our business and changes the management of our content material to give flexibility of action for the future in relation to entry into the EP market.

- As a group of companies where each entity is a cost centre, we must recognize the improbability of synergy in EP between the individual companies; we must recognize that we will either need to 'go it alone', to resolve the issue of synergy or, more likely, to create a separate focus for EP in the holding company.

- We will not allow enthusiasm for EP to denigrate the print-based part of our business, but we recognize the benefits in managing the front-end aspects of our print-based business in a way which enables product transition or development into EP at an appropriate time; we will ensure that an individual is accountable for this technology management.

- Investors worldwide are interested in EP products because this is one of the few growth areas in global markets; we will take steps to protect ourselves from an adverse image among business analysts through apparent inertia towards EP, but we intend to be critical in our judgment of the high market value being placed on new media companies floated; we will make an individual responsible for our image in this particular 'investment virility test'.

- We intend to use the concept of value-added chains and their change, brought about by new technology, to guide our positioning in the EP business.
- We will focus our EP business only on product competitiveness; however we will appoint an individual responsible to assess contributions to our business enterprise from European Union policies and support schemes.
- Our approach to the development of EP will be entirely user-oriented; we will be particularly resistant to technology push.
- We intend to enter the EP business in a small way and with a crude product; our strategy has built into it a timetable for enhanced investment if our initial business objectives are met in financial terms.
- Our entry into the EP business will be highly focused on only one or two products; we will use these products as a learning curve and already have in place a 'new media culture management programme' to socialize EP concepts into our business.
- We intend to use EP products as loss leaders and to underprice our EP products in order to enter the market and enhance the recognition of our image while creating market demand.
- All EP products in our business must be financially self-sufficient with a payback in three years; all content material used from paper-based publishing must bear a realistic transfer charge.
- Our product range depends significantly on advertising income; before we invest in any EP development programme, we will undertake a detailed feasibility study into the possibility of our potential EP products raising advertising revenue.
- Because EP product development will be critical to sustaining our position in the marketplace over the next ten years, we are appointing to the main board a person with experience in cross-media ownership, intellectual property rights and the management of long-term investment programmes in new ventures.
- Although we are very successful in new product launches, we lack the skills of creativity necessary to be successful in multimedia EP publishing; we intend to appoint a senior staff person with this experience in creativity and to require that person to produce within six months a plan describing how we may manage our multimedia creativity needs for the future.

- For us to enter the EP business and simply replicate our print-based products will be a disaster; we must value-add in the EP business; we have set up a methodology to determine how this value-adding will be achieved.

- Our EP products plan for the future will not fit our present channels for product distribution; therefore we are evaluating over the next 12 months a new strategy for the marketing of our EP products, including totally new channels for distribution.

- We have undertaken a comprehensive assessment of the opportunities for EP in our business and utilized recognized external authorities to assist us in this investigation; it is our decision not to enter the EP business over the next two years and thereafter to review this decision.

- We believe interactivity to be a critical characteristic in our EP product range; this conclusion is the result of detailed research into user needs; therefore we will be investing in techniques and products which allow us major development in interactivity.

- Excluding financial and business services, we believe the only EP market which will offer significant turnover and profits over the next five years is that of games; therefore, we intend to enter the marketplace for producing games software for use in arcades, on PCs and in dedicated devices.

- We believe the only area of EP which offers good margins in a growth market is that of facilitation services to sectors which have a high information content in their core business; therefore we will develop a business plan to provide that facilitation, and the focus for our EP business will be corporate publishing.

- EP is essentially an entrepreneurial business with a high level of individual creativity; therefore we intend to fund for the next five years 'an international EP workshop'. This will be for EP publishing what the Xerox Parc centre has been to document delivery.

- We intend to sponsor postgraduate students in centres of excellence around the world in the subject matter of multimedia EP; this sponsorship programme will be used by the production department to assess for the main board an outline strategy for our entry into the EP business.

- We have decided that EP cannot be integrated with our existing business; however it poses a significant threat to our products over the next ten years, and therefore we intend to divert a major portion of our forward investment into acquisition in EP; a mem-

ber of our main board has been made responsible for this diversification programme.

- For the past two years we have studied the developments of EP
  globally and we have concluded that EP will never take more
  than 5% of our marketplace; therefore, we shall not seek to
  develop in this area but instead will enter into alliances with
  suppliers to enhance the quality and reduce the cost of our
  paper-based products.

Appendices

Appendices — data and statistics

Table A1.1 List of top twenty publishers, revenue, 1990 (million ECU)

Time Warner	10 200
Bertelsmann	7 500
News Corporation	7 200
Hachette	4 600
Paramount Communications	3 200
Times Mirror	3 000
Thomson Corporation	2 900
Gannett	2 900
Dun & Bradstreet	2 500
Advances Publications	2 500
Reed International	2 300
Asahi Shimbun	2 200
Reader's Digest	1 900
Axel Springer Verlag	1 800
Hearst Corporation	1 800
RCS Rizzoli	1 700
Mondadori	1 600
McGraw-Hill	1 600
Pearson	1 500

Source: Kagan World Media, Buchreport (No. 13-03/92)/**Laukamm, T** *Strategic Study on New Opportunities for Publishers in the Information Services Market* EC No 14926 EN (Feb 1993) p B15

Table A1.2 Market volume online services, 1989–1990 (million ECU)

Country	1989	1990	Growth rate (%)
UK	2362.7	2638.0	12
France	243.9	287.0	18
Italy	145.8	166.9	15
Germany	23.2	27.1	17
Netherlands	14.5	15.8	9
Spain	7.3	11.6	59
Denmark	4.0	4.7	18
Ireland	3.3	4.0	21
Belgium	0.6	0.9	50
Portugal	0.1	0.2	100
Total	**2805.4**	**3156.2**	**13**

Source: European Information Industry Association/**Laukamm, T** *Strategic Study on New Opportunities for Publishers in the Information Services Market* EC No 14926 EN (Feb 1993) p D3

Table A1.3 CD-ROM titles per product category, 1992 (Sample of 600 titles)

Product category	Percentage
Bibliography	6
Encyclopedias	7
Dictionaries and Language	5
Education (including children)	7
Games	10
STM	16
Business	4
Special Interest (History, Literature, Music, etc.)	13
Software, Graphics, Desktop Publishing	21
Other	11

Source: Consulting Trust, Dataware, Euro-CD, Apple, TFPL Publishing/**Laukamm, T** *Strategic Study on New Opportunities for Publishers in the Information Services Market* EC No 14926 EN (Feb 1993) p D18

Table A1.4 Integrated Circuit (IC) cards, suppliers and their market shares, 1990

In Japan there are mainly two different IC Cards: (1) 'intelligent card'; (2) 'memory card'
(1)   'Intelligent card'

Rank	Supplier	Market size (million ECU)	Market share (%)	Cumulative market share (%)
1	Dai Nippon Insatsu	1.45	41.10	41.10
2	Toppan Insatsu	1.20	33.90	75.00
3	Hitachi Maxwell	0.41	11.60	86.60
4	Matsushita Denki	0.28	8.00	94.60
5	Others	0.19	5.40	100.00
	Total	**3.53**		

This table shows the dominance of the Japanese printers in this business
(2)   'Memory card'

Rank	Supplier	Market size (million ECU)	Market share (%)	Cumulative market share (%)
1	Mitsubishi Ind	9.54	17.00	17.00
2	Hitachi Maxwell	8.42	15.00	32.00
3	Mitsubishi Jushi	7.41	13.20	45.20
4	Fujisoku	7.02	12.50	57.70
5	Toshiba	6.17	11.00	68.70
6	Matsushita Denshi	5.72	10.20	78.90
7	Others	11.85	21.10	100.00
	Total	**56.13**		

Source: **Laukamm, T** *Strategic Study on New Opportunities for Publishers in the Information Services Market* EC No 14926 EN (Feb 1993) p E23

Table A1.5 Penetration of relevant technologies — relevant technical development trends ('faster – better – smaller – cheaper')

1992	2000
Computer power 50 times cheaper than 1982	Portable (CD-ROM-based) information device at 20% of today's computer price
Display 14 inch, 256 colours, 600 ECU	HDTV resolution, thousands of colours, 300 ECU
CD-ROM drives approximately one million worldwide, 300 ECU/unit	60 million drives, half home application (including portables) 100 ECU/unit
Floppy disks store 180 pages of text	2400 pages capacity
High/medium *power consumption*	Low *power consumption*
Telecom modems: 30 pages/minute; voice phone line	120 pages; in addition ISDN
Interaction with user: keyboard, increasingly graphical interface	Keyboard, graphical, touch screen, voice recognition
Documentation: printed manuals	Documentation/help functions on CD-ROM
Databases: text	Text, image, sound databases
Analogue storage dominating	Digital capture, storage, reproduction, distribution
Tape storage media	Disc storage media (DAT only as backup medium)
Storage cost 5 ECU/Mb	0.5 ECU maximum
Scanning images	Digital photography and video processing
Isolated media solutions	Integrated hybrid solutions; hard disk, CD-ROM, online data processing
Archives: paper, microfiche	Optical disks

Source: Information Workstation Group, Consulting Trust/**Laukamm, T** *Strategic Study on New Opportunities for Publishers in the Information Services Market* EC No 14926 EN (Feb 1993) p F5

Table A1.6 Penetration of CD-I

If one relates the potential development of CD-I or equivalent to the past development of CD-Audio sales, conservative projections derived from that approach are:

a) **CD-i type players (million units)**

	1995	2000
USA	1.25	30
Japan	1.00	20
Europe	1.00	20
Total	**3.25**	**70**

b) **CD-i type discs (million units)**

	1995	2000
USA	6.25	150
Japan	5.00	100
Europe	5.00	100
Total	**16.25**	**350**

Source: **Laukamm, T** *Strategic Study on New Opportunities for Publishers in the Information Services Market* EC No 14926 EN (Feb 1993) p F7

Table A1.7 Market for CD-i type products

	1995 million ECU	2000 million ECU
Players	1 600	35 000
Discs.	400	9 000
Total	**2 000**	**44 000**

Source: Tony Feldman, British Library, Philips/**Laukamm, T** *Strategic Study on New Opportunities for Publishers in the Information Services Market* EC No 14926 EN (Feb 1993) p F8

Note: These estimates should be looked at very carefully: The CD-Audio was a relatively simple media replacement in a long established business (music on records), whereas CD-i type products will have to create a completely new demand and market.

Table A1.8 Penetration of Video Games: penetration of households 1992

Japan	45 %
USA	35 %
Europe	15 %

Mobile:	65 %	50 mill units
Console:	35 %	27 mill units

Note: From 1992/93 on CD-ROM will be the main media

Age of users: In Europe 30% of the video games users are older than 18 years, in Japan and USA 45%

Source: Consulting Trust/**Laukamm, T** *Strategic Study on New Opportunities for Publishers in the Information Services Market* EC No 14926 EN (Feb 1993) p F8

Table A1.9 Key factors defining future scenarios in electronic publishing

Constant	Certain	Uncertain
Multimedia communication is human desire	Increasing processing power at decreasing cost	Availability of transparent networking/telecommunication
Expansion in space and time is human desire	Increasing storage capacity	Increasing demand for international publishing products
Acceptance of new technologies higher among younger people	Increasing acceptance of electronic publishing as a computer-literate generation matures	Degree of electronics industry's diversification into publishing
Growing demand for information	Sociodemographic trends – growing ageing population – growing leisure time	Speed of penetration of interactive home applications besides video games
Constant time per day	Growing educational demand	
Acceptance of new technologies based on perceived benefits	Growing environmental awareness (paper consumption)	
	Growing office automation	
	Growing individualization in demand, markets, products	
	Development of information intensive society and economy	
	Convergence of electronics, publishing and networking industries with the information industry	
	Convergence of technologies in computers, TV, telephone	

Source: **Laukamm, T** *Strategic Study on New Opportunities for Publishers in the Information Services Market* EC No 14926 EN (Feb 1993) p H1

Table A1.10 Evaluation of different scenarios

Scenario	Likelihood	Reason
Electronic publishing/ multimedia will not happen or become a business	Very low	• Multimedia is a human desire • Multimedia is a natural evolution • EP is technically available • EP is already happening/business • Multimedia is the integration of already existing media • EP is an add-on, not replacement (but at the expense of some media)
Corporate publishing and professional applications will lead the development of EP	Very high	• Is already a business (e.g. STM) • Clear economics • Clear user needs • Clear user profile • Close relation with text-based products • Niche strategies successful • Demand driven business
Home applications will lead the development of EP	Low	• No clear economics • No clear customer profile • Niche strategy does not apply • Mass-market strategy necessary • Supply-driven business • Only if global application with significant benefits for the user appears • Video games are exceptional
Publishers will gain the same strong position in EP as in print-based publishing	Low	• Their content is only part of multimedia publishing • They have only limited know-how/skills for multimedia products • The traditional editorial experience is a barrier to EP • They are not used to 'publishing on demand' (e.g. for corporate publishing)

Source: **Laukamm, T** *Strategic Study on New Opportunities for Publishers in the Information Services Market* EC No 14926 EN (Feb 1993) p H2

Table A1.11 Offline digital media: description of the sector

The main types of offline digital media are:

Format	Drive	Delivery platform	Developer	Available since
CD-ROM	CD-ROM drive	PC	Philips/Sony	1985
CD-XA	CD-ROM drive	PC	Philips/Sony	1988
Electronic Book	Portable drive	Portable drive or TV	Sony	1990
CDTV	CDTV system CD-ROM drive	TV PC	Commodore	1991
CD-i	CD-i drive	TV	Philips/Sony	1991
VIS	VIS system	TV	Tandy/Micro soft	1992
MMCD	Portable drive	Portable drive or TV	Sony	1992
Mega CD	CD-ROM drive	TV	Sega	1992

Source: Information Market Observatory (1993)

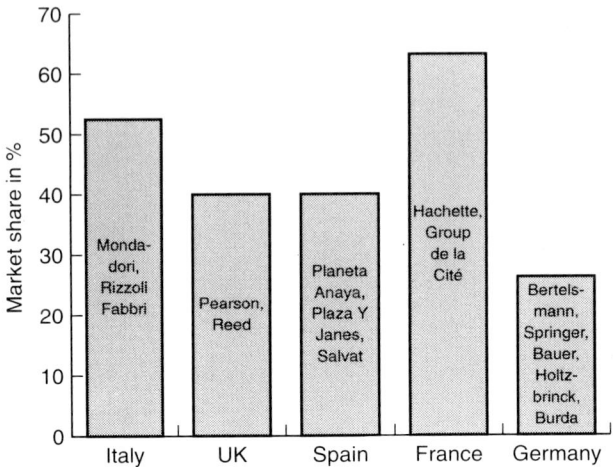

Figure A1.1 Level of concentration in Europe (Source: Consulting Trust/ **Laukamm, T** *Strategic Study on New Opportunities for Publishers in the Information Services Market* EC No 14926 EN (Feb 1993) p B4)

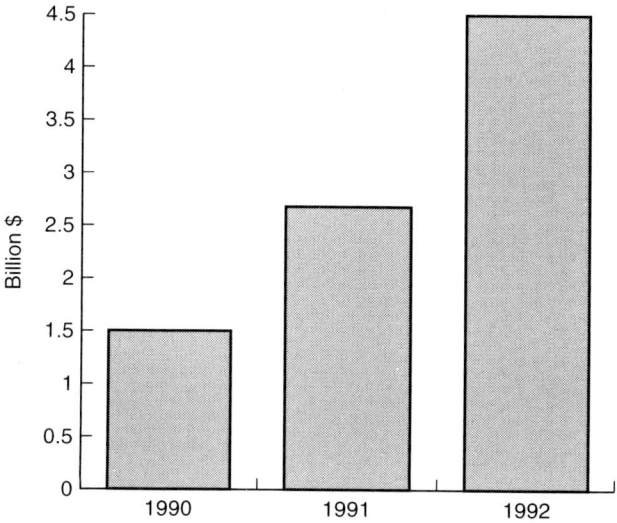

Figure A1.2 CD-ROM sales worldwide (Source: Infotech 1992/**Laukamm, T** *Strategic Study on New Opportunities for Publishers in the Information Services Market* EC No 14926 EN (Feb 1993) p D5)

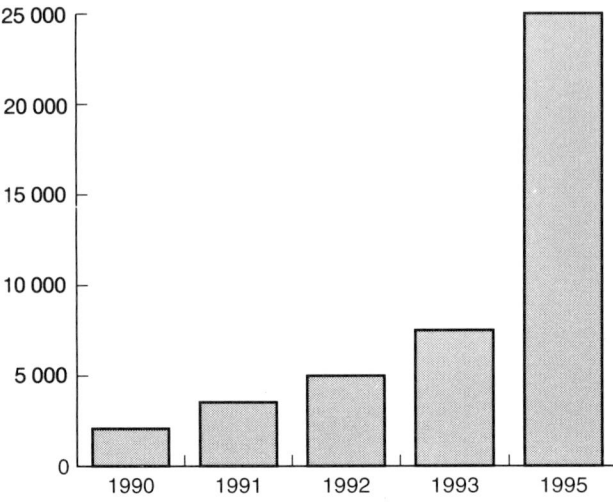

Figure A1.3 CD-ROM titles worldwide (including in-house) (Source: Infotech, Sony, Consulting Trust/**Laukamm, T** *Strategic Study on New Opportunities for Publishers in the Information Services Market* EC No 14926 EN (Feb 1993) p D6)

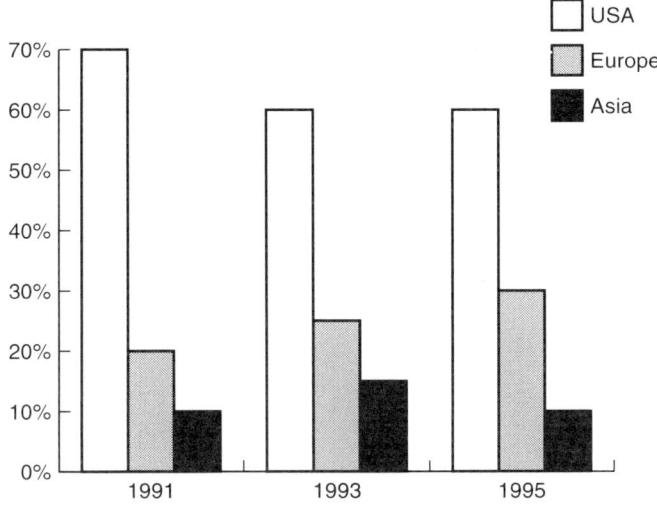

Figure A1.4 CD-ROM titles (Source: Sony, Consulting Trust/**Laukamm, T**
Strategic Study on New Opportunities for Publishers in the Information Services Market
EC No 14926 EN (Feb 1993) p D7)

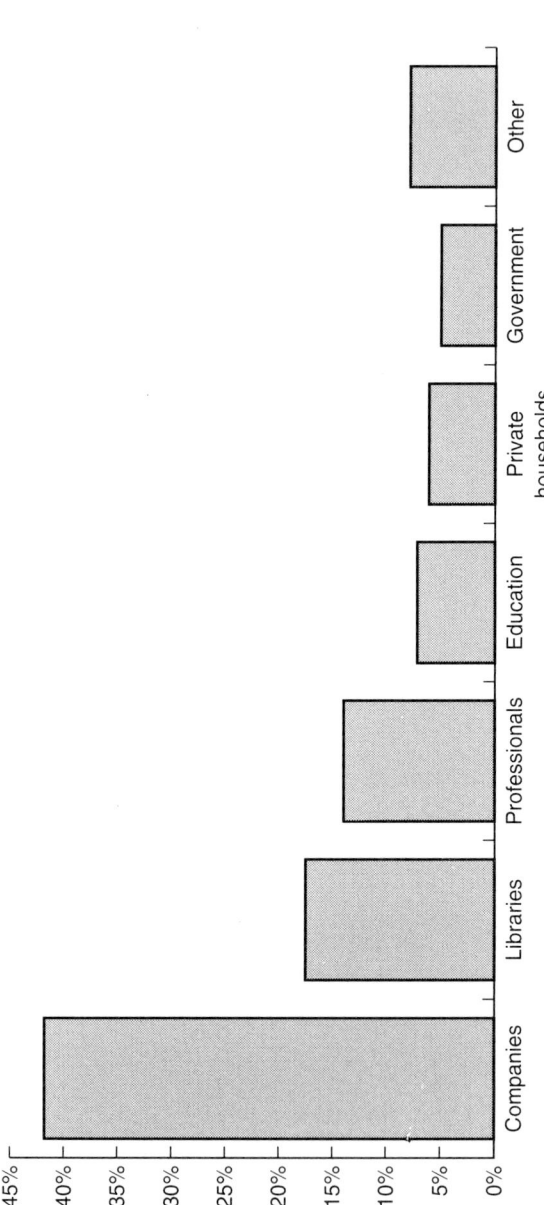

Figure A1.5 Target markets of CD-ROM titles (Source: Infotech 1992/**Laukamm**, T *Strategic Study on New Opportunities for Publishers in the Information Services Market* EC No 14926 EN (Feb 1993) p D8)

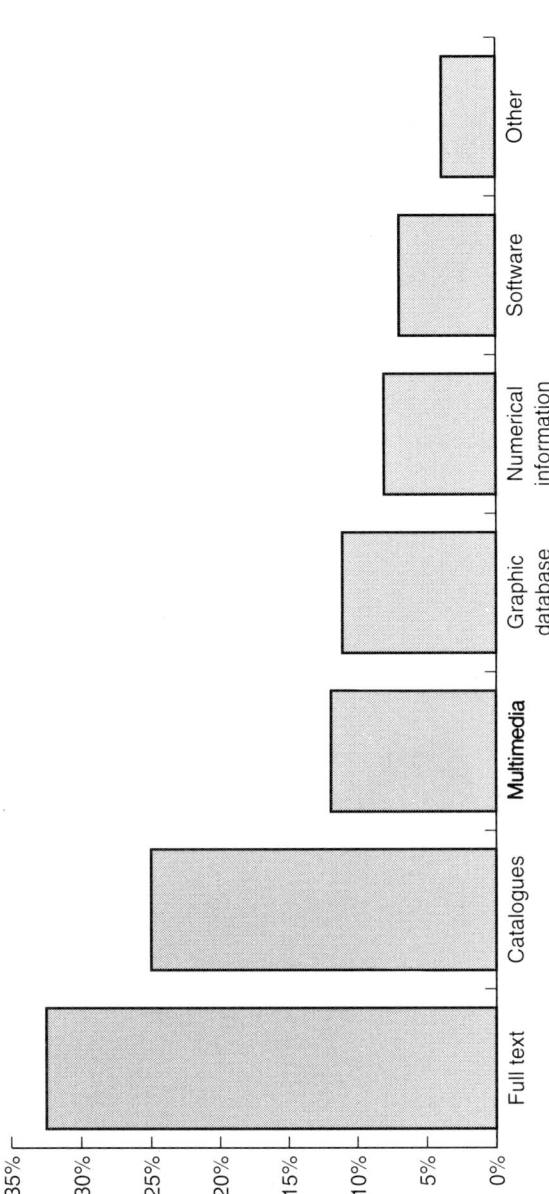

Figure A1.6 Content of CD-ROM (Source: Infotech 1992/**Laukamm,** T *Strategic Study on New Opportunities for Publishers in the Information Services Market* EC No 14926 EN (Feb 1993) p D9)

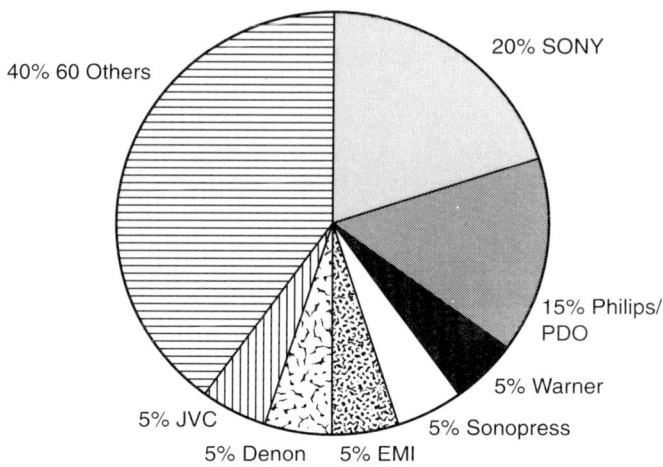

Figure A1.7 The world's key players in Compact Disc manufacturing (Source: Consulting Trust/**Laukamm, T** *Strategic Study on New Opportunities for Publishers in the Information Services Market* EC No 14926 EN (Feb 1993) p D10)

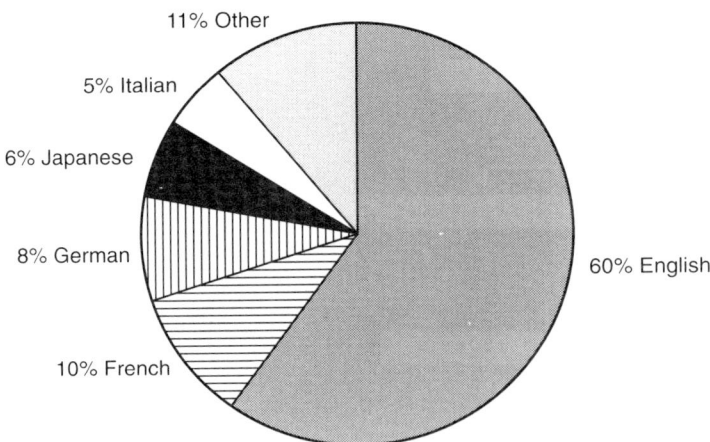

Figure A1.8 Languages of CD-ROM titles, sample of 600 titles, 1992 (Source: Consulting Trust, Dataware, Euro-CD, Apple, TFPL Publishing/**Laukamm, T** *Strategic Study on New Opportunities for Publishers in the Information Services Market* EC No 14926 EN (Feb 1993) p D19)

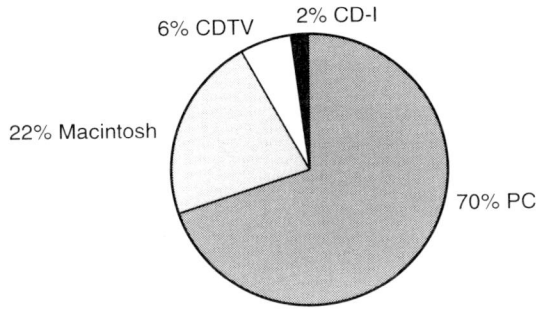

Figure A1.9 Hardware platforms for electronic publishing products (CD-ROM) (Source: Consulting Trust, Optical Publishers Association/**Laukamm, T** *Strategic Study on New Opportunities for Publishers in the Information Services Market* EC No 14926 EN (Feb 1993) p D19)

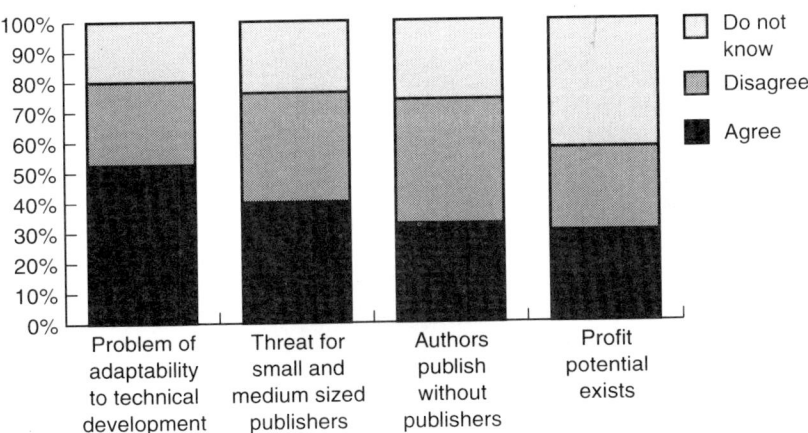

Figure A1.10 Attitudes of publishers towards electronic publishing (Source: **Riehm, U.a.o.,** Elektronisches Publizieren, Heidelberg 1992; Consulting Trust/ **Laukamm, T** *Strategic Study on New Opportunities for Publishers in the Information Services Market* EC No 14926 EN (Feb 1993) p D30)

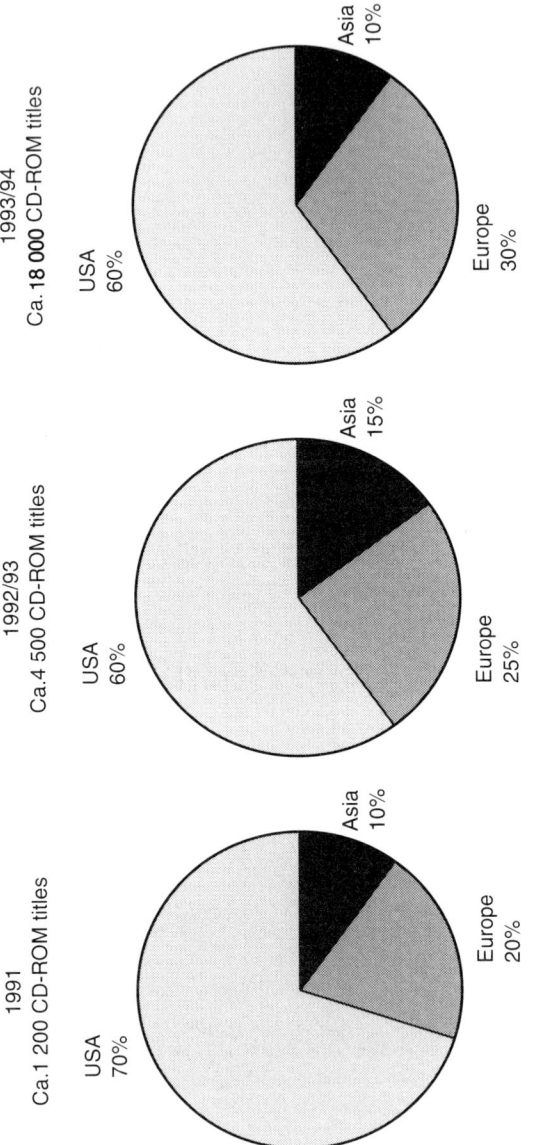

Figure A1.11 CD-ROM titles worldwide, number of titles, 1991–1994 (Source: Sony/**Laukamm, T** *Strategic Study on New Opportunities for Publishers in the Information Services Market* EC No 14926 EN (Feb 1993) p E5)

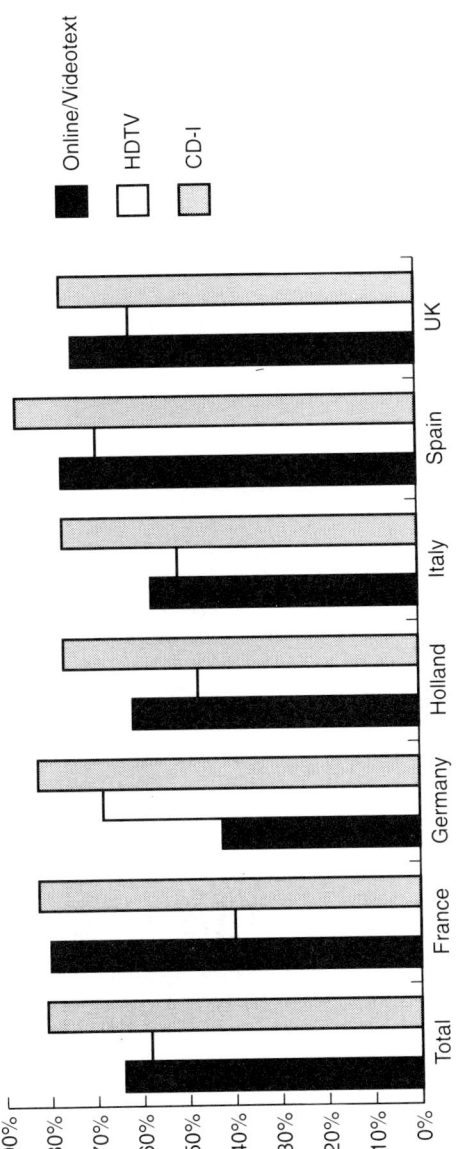

Figure A1.12 Consumer unawareness of media, 1992 (Source: IEPRC, Link, Consulting Trust/**Laukamm, T** *Strategic Study on New Opportunities for Publishers in the Information Services Market* EC No 14926 EN (Feb 1993) p F10)

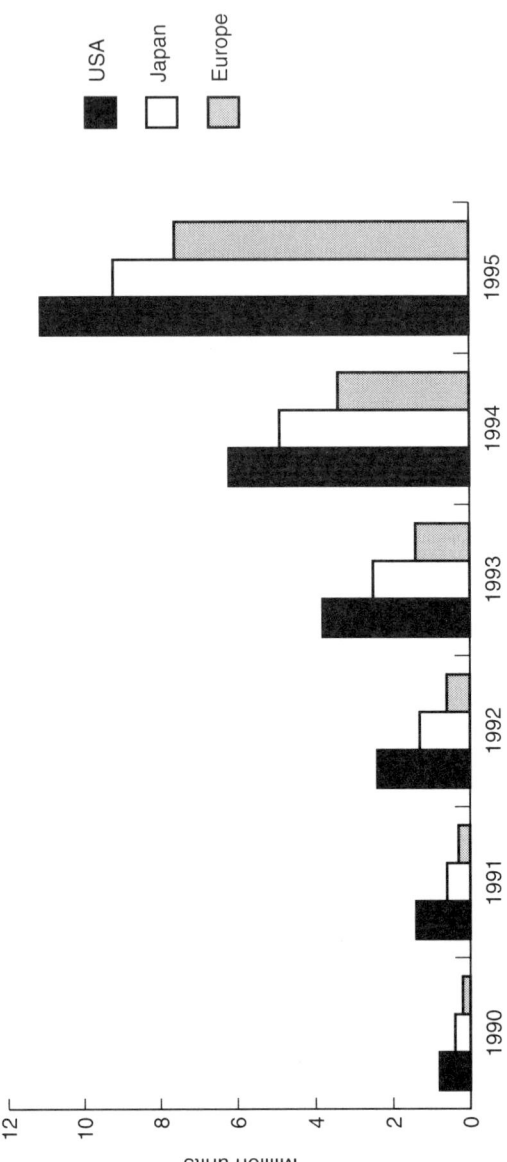

Figure A1.13 Penetration of CD-ROM drives (Source: Consulting Trust, Sonopress/**Laukamm, T** *Strategic Study on New Opportunities for Publishers in the Information Services Market* EC No 14926 EN (Feb 1993) p F11)

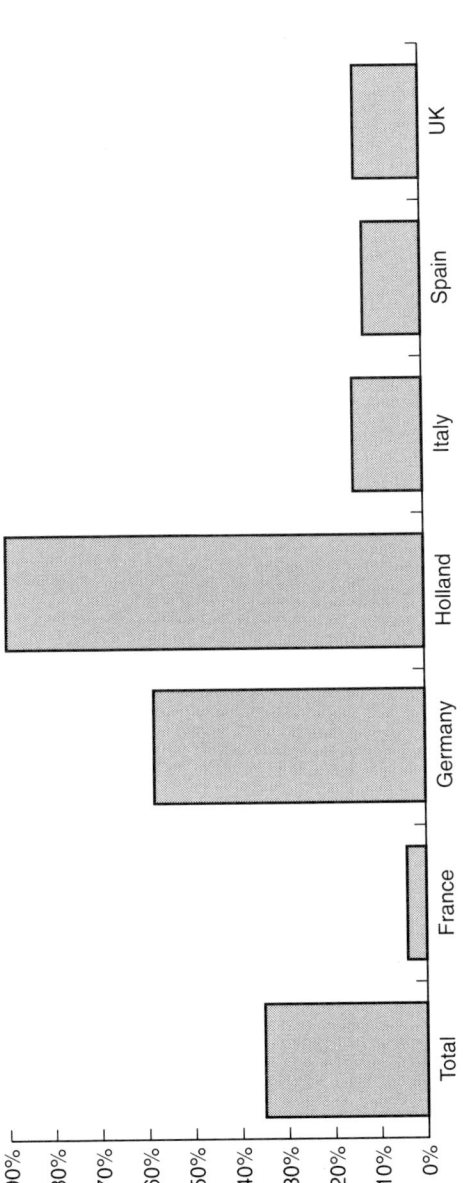

Figure A1.14 Subscription to cable TV, 1992 (consumer households) (Source: *Euromonitor/*Laukamm, T *Strategic Study on New Opportunities for Publishers in the Information Services Market* EC No 14926 EN (Feb 1993) p F12)

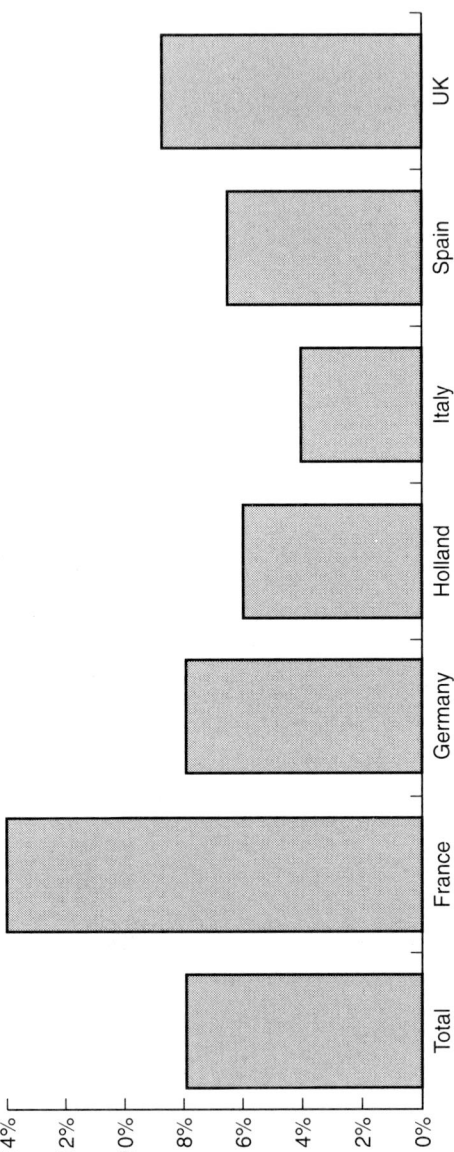

Figure A1.15 Penetration of online information services, 1992 (consumer households) (Source: IEPRC, Link, Consulting Trust/ **Laukamm, T** *Strategic Study on New Opportunities for Publishers in the Information Services Market* EC No 14926 EN (Feb 1993) p F13)

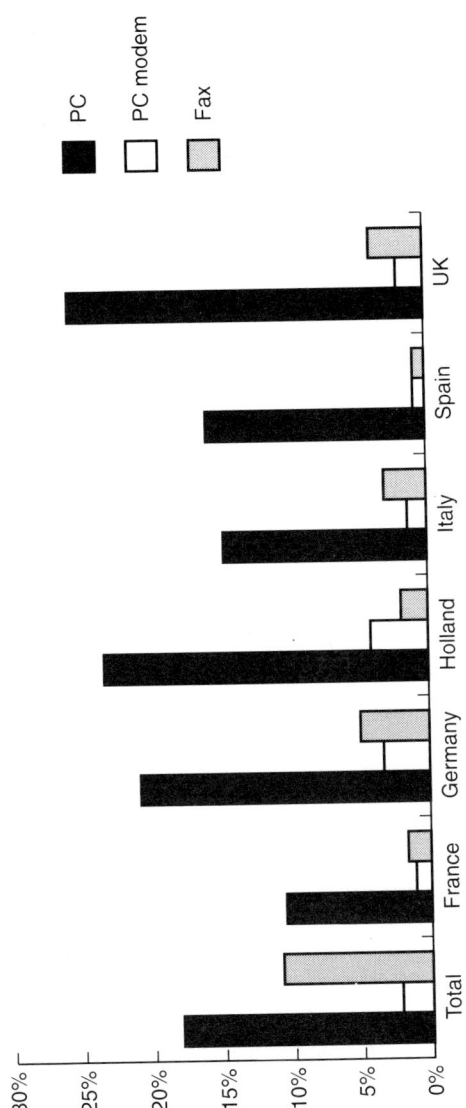

Figure A1.16 Penetration of PC, modem and fax, 1992 (consumer households) (Source: IEPRC, Link, Consulting Trust/**Laukamm, T** *Strategic Study on New Opportunities for Publishers in the Information Services Market* EC No 14926 EN (Feb 1993) p F14)

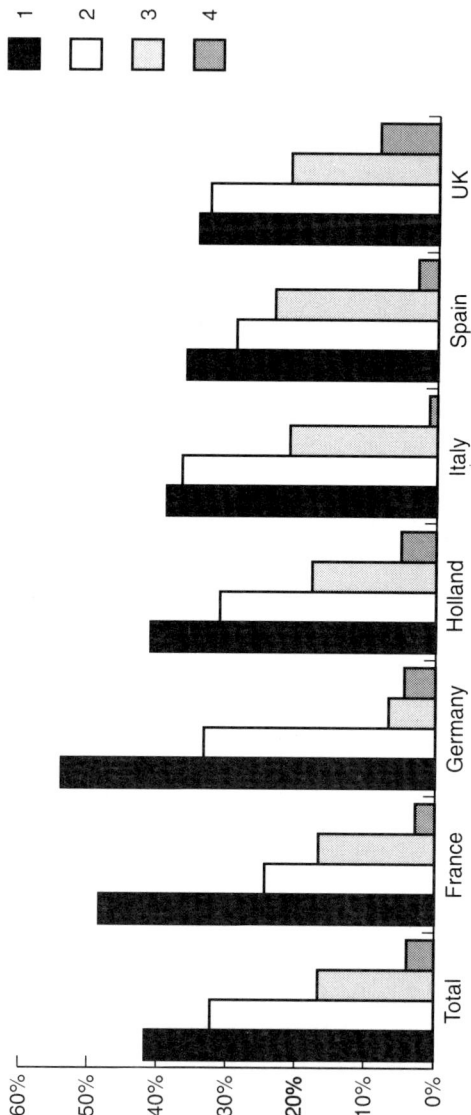

Figure A1.17 Number of household members using the PC (Source: *Euromonitor/***Laukamm, T** *Strategic Study on New Opportunities for Publishers in the Information Services Market* EC No 14926 EN (Feb 1993) p F15)

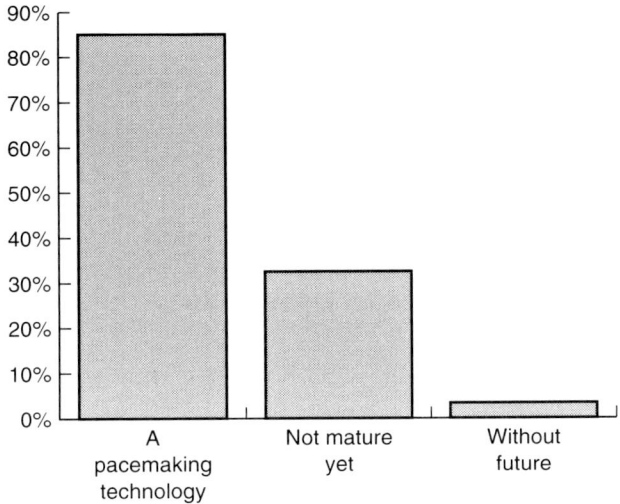

Figure A1.18 In my opinion multimedia is... (Source: DMV Survey Cebit 92, Consulting Trust/**Laukamm, T** *Strategic Study on New Opportunities for Publishers in the Information Services Market* EC No 14926 EN (Feb 1993) p F16)

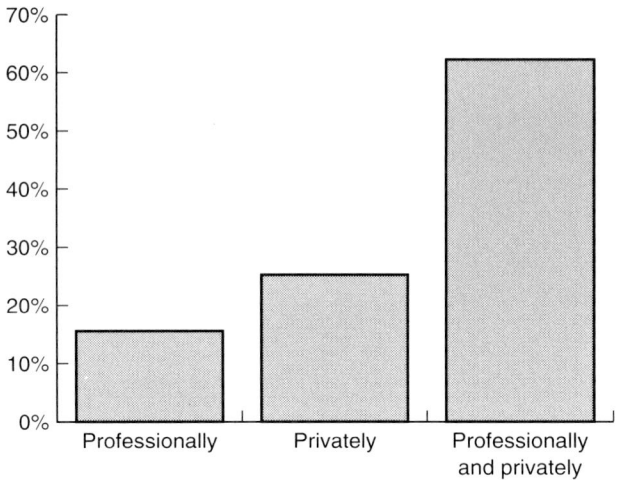

Figure A1.19 I use a computer... (Source: DMV Survey Cebit 92, Consulting Trust **Laukamm, T** *Strategic Study on New Opportunities for Publishers in the Information Services Market* EC No 14926 EN (Feb 1993) p F17)

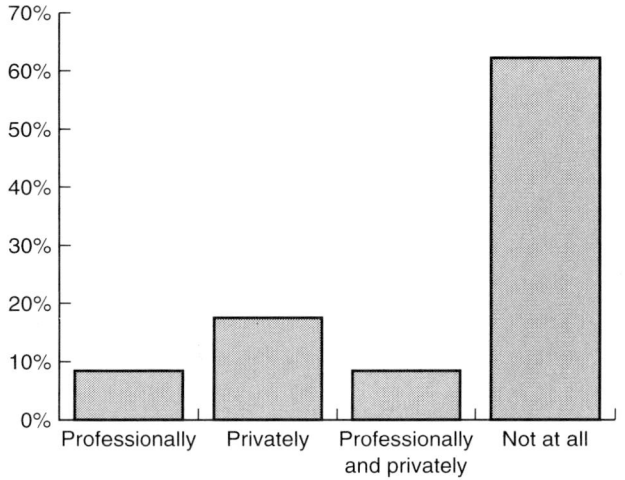

Figure A1.20 I use multimedia... (Source: DMV Survey Cebit 92, Consulting Trust/**Laukamm, T** *Strategic Study on New Opportunities for Publishers in the Information Services Market* EC No 14926 EN (Feb 1993) p F18)

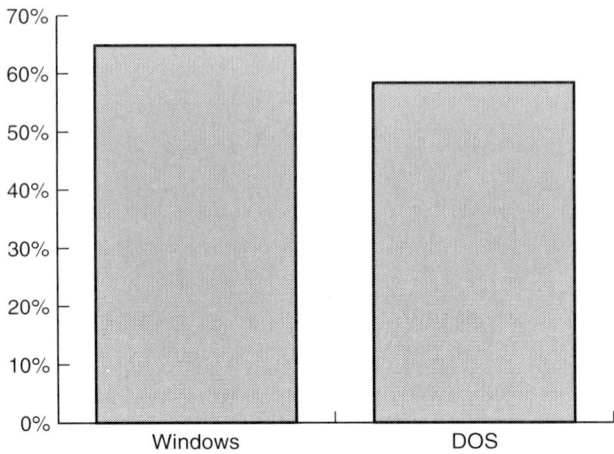

Figure A1.21 Using PC with... (Source: DMV Survey Cebit 92, Consulting Trust/ **Laukamm, T** *Strategic Study on New Opportunities for Publishers in the Information Services Market* EC No 14926 EN (Feb 1993) p F19)

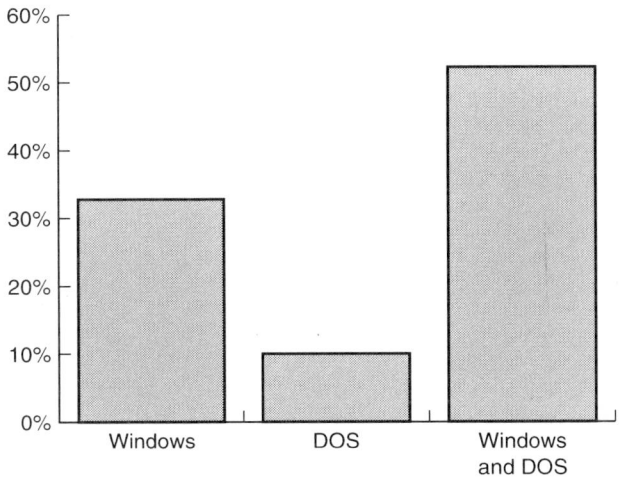

Figure A1.22 I would use multimedia with... (Source: DMV Survey Cebit 92, Consulting Trust/**Laukamm, T** *Strategic Study on New Opportunities for Publishers in the Information Services Market* EC No 14926 EN (Feb 1993) p F20)

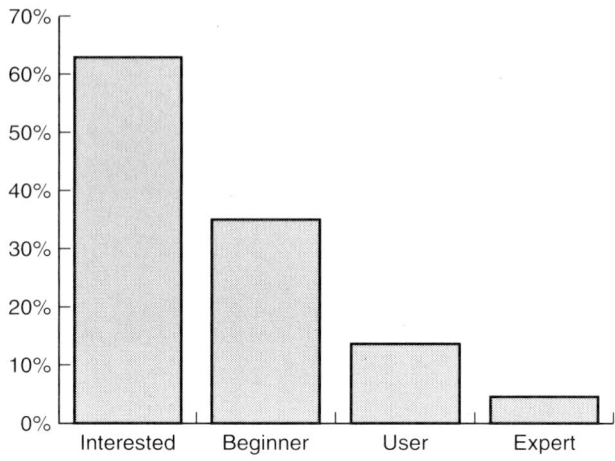

Figure A1.23 Regarding multimedia I rate myself as being... (Source: DMV Survey Cebit 92, Consulting Trust/**Laukamm, T** *Strategic Study on New Opportunities for Publishers in the Information Services Market* EC No 14926 EN (Feb 1993) p F21)

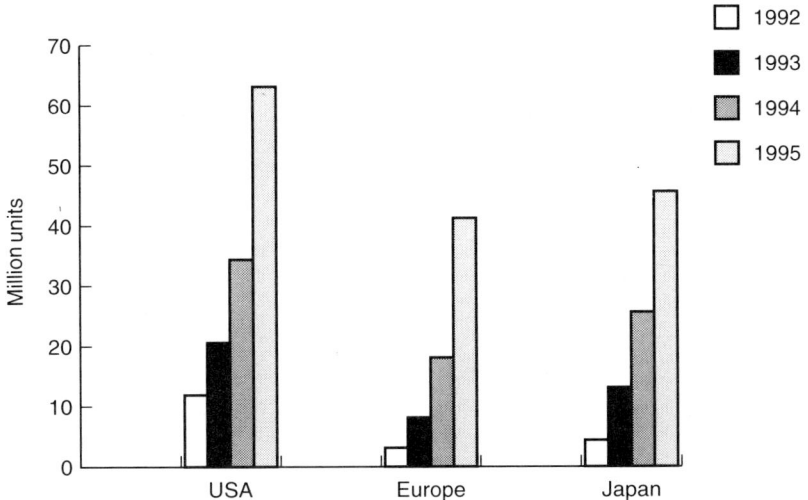

Figure A1.24 CD-ROM demand worldwide, 1992–1995 (Source: Consulting Trust, Sonopress/**Laukamm, T** *Strategic Study on New Opportunities for Publishers in the Information Services Market* EC No 14926 EN (Feb 1993) p G6)

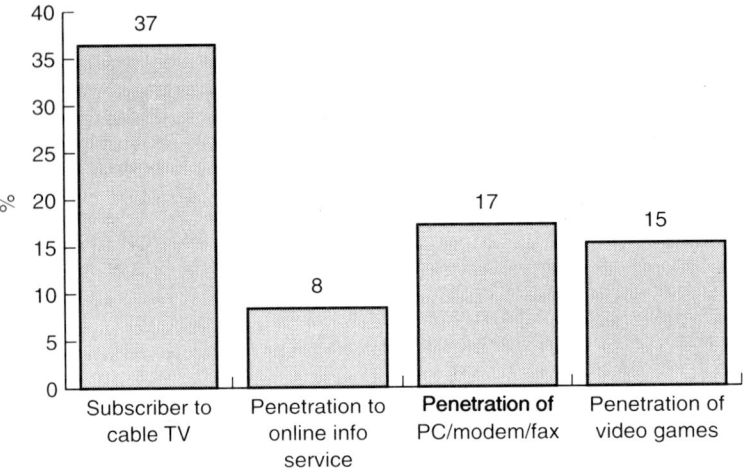

Figure A1.25 Uptake of selected delivery devices in European households, 1992 (Source: **Laukamm, T** *Strategic Study on New Opportunities for Publishers in the Information Services Market* EC No 14926 EN (Feb 1993)